FIELDING TRAVEL GUIDES

# FIELDING'S
# HOLLAND

# Fielding Titles

Fielding's Amazon

Fielding's Australia

Fielding's Bahamas

Fielding's Belgium

Fielding's Bermuda

Fielding's Borneo

Fielding's Brazil

Fielding's Britain

Fielding's Budget Europe

Fielding's Caribbean

Fielding's Europe

Fielding's Far East

Fielding's France

Fielding's Guide to the World's Most Dangerous Places

Fielding's Guide to the World's Great Voyages

Fielding's Guide to Kenya's Best Hotels, Lodges & Homestays

Fielding's Guide to the World's Most Romantic Places

Fielding's Hawaii

Fielding's Holland

Fielding's Italy

Fielding's London Agenda

Fielding's Los Angeles Agenda

Fielding's Malaysia and Singapore

Fielding's Mexico

Fielding's New York Agenda

Fielding's New Zealand

Fielding's Paris Agenda

Fielding's Portugal

Fielding's Scandinavia

Fielding's Seychelles

Fielding's Southeast Asia

Fielding's Spain

Fielding's Vacation Places Rated

Fielding's Vietnam

Fielding's Worldwide Cruises

Fielding's Cruise Insider

# FIELDING'S HOLLAND

## The Most In-Depth and Liveliest Guide to the Culture and Charm of Holland

## H. Constance Hill

Fielding Worldwide, Inc.

308 South Catalina Avenue

Redondo Beach, California 90277 U.S.A.

Fielding's Holland
Published by Fielding Worldwide, Inc.
Text Copyright ©1994 H. Constance Hill
Icons & Illustrations Copyright ©1994 FWI

## FIELDING WORLDWIDE INC.

PUBLISHER AND CEO **Robert Young Pelton**
PUBLISHING DIRECTOR **Paul T. Snapp**
ELECTRONIC PUBLISHING DIRECTOR **Larry E. Hart**
PROJECT DIRECTOR **Tony E. Hulette**
ADMINISTRATIVE COORDINATOR **Beverly Riess**
ACCOUNT SERVICES MANAGER **Christy Harp**

### EDITORS

**Linda Charlton**                    **Kathy Knoles**

### PRODUCTION

**Tina Gentile**                    **Chris Snyder**
**Gini Martin**                    **Craig South**

COVER DESIGNED BY **Digital Artists, Inc.**
COVER PHOTOGRAPHERS — Front Cover **Tony Craddock/Tony Stone Images**
Background Photo, Front Cover **Mike Yamashita/Westlight**
Back Cover **David Hanson/Tony Stone Images**
INSIDE PHOTOS **Netherlands Board of Tourism**

Inquiries should be addressed to: Fielding Worldwide, Inc., 308 South Catalina Ave., Redondo Beach, California 90277 U.S.A., ☎ *(310) 372-4474*, Facsimile *(310) 376-8064*, 8:30 a.m. - 5:30 p.m. Pacific Standard Time.

## ISBN 1-56952-036-4

Library of Congress Catalog Card Number

#94-068349

Printed in the United States of America

# Letter from the Publisher

In 1946, Temple Fielding began the first of what would be a re-markable new series of well-written, highly personalized guidebooks for independent travelers. Temple's opinionated, witty and oft-imitated books have now guided travelers for almost a half-century. More important to some was Fielding's humorous and direct method of steering travelers away from the dull and the insipid. Today, Fielding Travel Guides are still written by experienced travelers for experienced travelers. Our authors carry on Fielding's reputation for creating travel experiences that deliver insight with a sense of discovery and style.

Holland, the gateway to Europe, can be one of the most rewarding and memorable destinations on the continent. Connie Hill's expertise of Holland—its people, its customs and the surrounding region—will take you past the clichés to the untrod corners of this historic and scenic country. Connie's experience as a one-time resident makes her the perfect guide for meandering down quiet back roads and into Holland's hidden corners. Only Connie Hill and Fielding give you the background and the insider tips you'll need to understand the Dutch and their wonderful land. This book is for anyone seeking to discover the real Netherlands.

Today, the concept of independent travel has never been bigger. Our policy of *honesty* and a highly personal point of view has never changed; it just seems that the travel world has caught up with us.

Enjoy your Holland adventure with Connie Hill and Fielding.

R Y P

Robert Young Pelton
Publisher and CEO
Fielding Worldwide, Inc.

# DEDICATION

For my Dutch "family," Gerry, Pieter, Anita, and Marianne Olifiers, whose generosity in friendship has guided me in Holland.


So it is in traveling: A man must carry knowledge with him if he would bring home knowledge.

...Samuel Johnson

# ACKNOWLEDGMENTS

Words can only begin to convey my appreciation to the many people who counseled and encouraged me during the creation of this book. Those who have helped with arrangements for the substantial personal research involved include Barbara Veldkamp of the Netherlands Board of Tourism (NBT) in New York, Willem Schouten of NBT in Holland, and Els Wamsteeker of the VVV Amsterdam. Many provincial and local tourism officials and guides throughout Holland—and in Belgium and Luxembourg—also contributed considerably to my research for this volume, and I thank them for both their aid and interest.

In addition, I am indebted to Helen Goss Thomas for her inspiring example, and to Jean O'Neil for her photograph of the author.

# ABOUT THE AUTHOR

*H. Constance Hill*

H. Constance Hill is a freelance writer whose work has taken her to six continents, of which *the* Continent is a favorite. She has lived in Holland and brings the experience from twenty-five years of travel there and throughout Europe to this book. Her articles appear in a variety of newspapers and periodicals. When not in Holland or on another travel beat, she lives in Boston.

# Fielding Rating Icons

The Fielding Rating Icons are highly personal and awarded to help the besieged traveler choose from among the dizzying array of activities, attractions, hotels, restaurants and sights. The awarding of an icon denotes unusual or exceptional qualities in the relevant category.

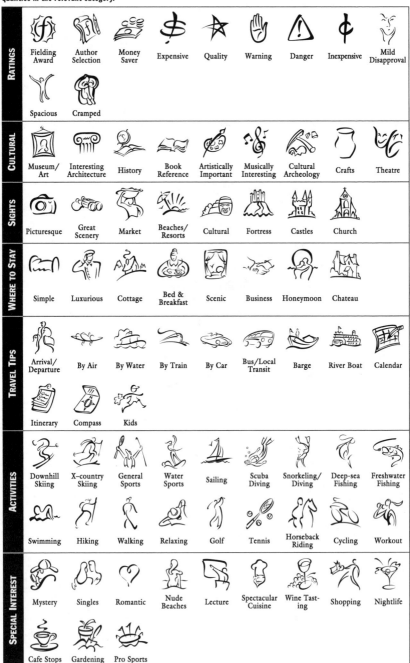

| RATINGS | Fielding Award | Author Selection | Money Saver | Expensive | Quality | Warning | Danger | Inexpensive | Mild Disapproval |
| | Spacious | Cramped | | | | | | | |

| CULTURAL | Museum/ Art | Interesting Architecture | History | Book Reference | Artistically Important | Musically Interesting | Cultural Archeology | Crafts | Theatre |

| SIGHTS | Picturesque | Great Scenery | Market | Beaches/ Resorts | Cultural | Fortress | Castles | Church | |

| WHERE TO STAY | Simple | Luxurious | Cottage | Bed & Breakfast | Scenic | Business | Honeymoon | Chateau | |

| TRAVEL TIPS | Arrival/ Departure | By Air | By Water | By Train | By Car | Bus/Local Transit | Barge | River Boat | Calendar |
| | Itinerary | Compass | Kids | | | | | | |

| ACTIVITIES | Downhill Skiing | X-country Skiing | General Sports | Water Sports | Sailing | Scuba Diving | Snorkeling/ Diving | Deep-sea Fishing | Freshwater Fishing |
| | Swimming | Hiking | Walking | Relaxing | Golf | Tennis | Horseback Riding | Cycling | Workout |

| SPECIAL INTEREST | Mystery | Singles | Romantic | Nude Beaches | Lecture | Spectacular Cuisine | Wine Tasting | Shopping | Nightlife |
| | Cafe Stops | Gardening | Pro Sports | | | | | | |

# TABLE OF CONTENTS

# LIST OF MAPS

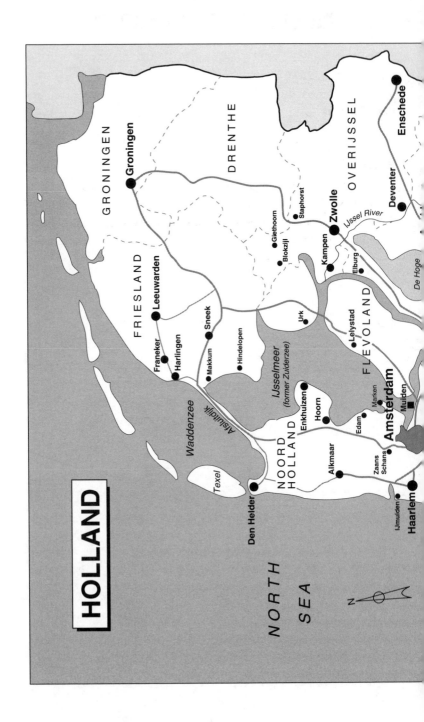

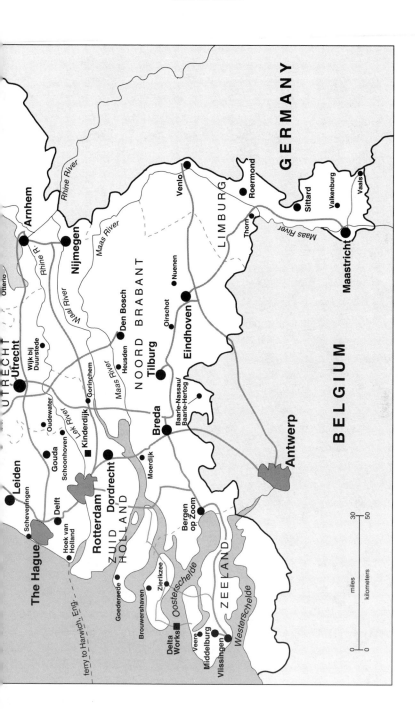

# INTRODUCTION

*Dutch bulbs in bloom carpet the countryside in spring.*

Although counted among the continent's smallest countries, Holland is a significant European constitutional kingdom. In many spheres, in both past and present, the Dutch have exerted an influence within the world well out of proportion to the size of their country. With its flat, barrierless landscape and near continental crossroads location virtually inviting vying European empire builders, Holland has been a contributor to and recipient of European culture for centuries.

Holland thus can hardly be considered off the beaten track. It lies well-placed on the main air, sea, river, rail and highways of the European continent. Yet, somehow, Holland too often is shortchanged in travel guides. Inadequately informed travelers then continue to make short shrift of sights worthy of a much more lingering look. After London, Paris and Rome, Amsterdam is the most visited city in Europe, but even that city's compelling, contrasting appeal of 17th-century charm and contemporary cosmopolitan polish often is seen in short order visits. Hopefully the information presented here will help correct such short-sighted sightseeing.

Undoubtedly, the slightness of its geographic stature—equal to the U.S. states of Massachusetts, Connecticut and Rhode Island combined—has contributed to the fact that Holland is less well-known to overseas visitors than many other European entities. Holland's pint-size portions do, however, offer the advantage of short travel distances. And, due to the particular pattern of its early economic and cultural development, Holland boasts a remarkable array of significant sights conveniently close to one another. The majority of destinations of major interest to travelers are within an hour of each other by train, many much closer.

The small size of Holland has been instrumental in accommodating travelers in another arena. Centuries of seafaring and cross-continental trade led its Dutch-speaking citizens—well aware that few people worldwide spoke their tongue as a first language—to learn other languages in order to reach out to foreign trading partners and travelers. It's a skill the Dutch practice still, and we visitors benefit enormously from it. The Dutch enjoy rather than resent the opportunity to use their English. In Holland, the barrier to knowledge of another culture that foreign language often creates for travelers has been broken down because of the widespread local use of English. Since one of the primary pleasures of travel is meeting and speaking with people locally, we can be grateful to the Dutch for making it possible for us—through *their* command of English—to reach beneath the facade of foreignness to learn about the history and humanity of Holland.

Too many travelers use the small size of Holland as a rationale to "do" its destinations on day trips, which leaves too little time to appreciate the unexpectedly rich rewards that await. Of course, Holland's trains *are* terrific, so it's entirely possible to base yourself in Amsterdam and head out by day to Leiden, Delft and The Hague. However, Holland's capital is the most expensive overnight place to park yourself—not to mention a car—if purse strings are a consideration. Apart from price, if you don't spend a night in a destination that truly warrants being experienced at night as much as by day, you may miss out on what might have been a milestone on your trip. I love Amsterdam and, as much as any traveler, am glad not to move luggage and change hotels too often. But this book will suggest that you do just that occasionally, in order to experience the best in Dutch travel.

In general, the focus of this guide is on the cultural aspects and attractions that make Holland delightfully distinctive within Europe. The purpose of the *star rating of sights* is to help you assess the travel options, and plan and prioritize a trip according to *your* preferred style, tastes and interests. For many "vacation-poor" travelers, getting one's travel *time's worth* is at least as important as getting one's *money's worth*—and I hope this book will enable you to achieve that.

Foremost attention is focused on those Dutch destinations that have delighted travelers over the decades, since places—like works of literature or music—become "classics" for a reason. Facts are rounded out with flavorful details that put the place or attraction in context. Both first-time and repeat travelers to Holland should find coverage enough to enrich their exploration. Driving routes in attractive, interesting areas off the tourist track are included in "On The Road" chapters.

This single volume travel companion provides both background essays ("The Dutch Cultural Legacy" and "The Bulb Field Business") for armchair reading, and comprehensive on-the-road resources for when you're traveling. (See "Transportation" in "Keys to the Dutch Kingdom: Practical Travel Information" for information on getting around Holland.) Food for thought can lead to thoughts of food. (See "Food and Drink", and under "Where to Eat" in individual cities, which also suggests places where you can wet your whistle.) For ideas as to where to rest your head, consult "Where to Stay," star-rated, in several price ranges, under the appropriate city or town. The "Hotel Quick Reference Chart," at the back of the book, provides the most recent prices. Shopping suggestions are noted under individual destinations, but you might want to read "Decorative Arts and Traditional Crafts" for information about buying *Delftware*.

During the decade of Europe's passage from the 20th century into the 21st, we'll be hearing more about such small, stable, self-confident countries as Holland. Not *despite* their size, but *because* of it. In matters politic, so it seems, small is usefully non-threatening: Within the European Union (EU), a small country such as Holland doesn't bruise big-country egos. Small countries are less narrowly nationalistic in their outlook, have fewer areas of ardent interest to defend, and, overall, are more able than some other members to encourage flexibility in the European Union. How contemporary the great Rotterdam-born humanist **Erasmus** (1466-1536) sounds in his 16th-century words: "That you are patriotic will be praised by some and easily forgotten by everyone; but in my opinion, it is wiser to treat men and things as though we held this world the common fatherland of all."

Regardless of a strengthening EU and greater progress towards a single European marketplace, travelers should not fear that there will be a substantial diminishment of the distinctive features that attract them to Holland. Although "Euro-culture" and multinationals seem to thrive in Holland, the unique qualities and values of the country have not disappeared. While it's true that today you may have to seek out the *truly* quaint—women in traditional costumes, men wearing wooden shoes and working windmills—you'll find charming characteristic aspects of Dutch culture all around you.

## STAR-RATED SIGHTS

For readers who find such guidance helpful, the places and attractions included herein have been star-rated. Travelers, most of whom have limited time, and all of whom will face choices as to how to spend the time they do have, may welcome the indications of relative importance consistently applied for the entire country and/or region that this assigning of stars strives to provide, though naturally, you will organize any sightseeing according to your interests. In assigning stars— which has been based on broad considerations outlined below—I have taken into consideration such factors as the general consensus about a sight's significance, which include whether a work or collection of art is regularly mentioned in textbooks or catalogs; long-standing popularity with tourists; and my insight into the comparative interest of the attraction as regards other competing ones in the area. Often, viewpoints and sense-of-place sites, interiors and exteriors, day and night appearances, and events also have been rated. Inevitably, the ratings in this guide cannot help but reflect my interests and tastes. But, however your opinions and mine may differ, I hope the ratings in this guide enable you to have a more enjoyable trip.

★★★ This indicates a must-see sight. It should be a clear-cut first choice for those on a short visit, one worth planning an itinerary specifically to include.

★★ This indicates a significant sight, one that substantially contributes to visitors' impressions of the destination or sense of place.

★ A sight worth consideration as interest and time dictate.

**No stars:** Of sufficient interest to warrant mention.

## *PRICES*

The value of the dollar against the strong Dutch guilder varies, sometimes to the disadvantage of the dollar. And there's inflation to contend with, too. Prices for accommodations are raised periodically: Amsterdam hotels tend to review/raise prices each Nov. 1. Thus, even if you are using this book hot off the press, prices listed in the "Hotel Quick-Reference Table" at the back, and price categories used, may already have changed. As a result, you are cautioned to use the prices quoted as a comparative guide rather than hard fact.

When you wisely select the preselected set course choices of a *prix-fixe*, *tourist menu*, or *dagschotel* (day menu), you may already have lowered the price category of the restaurant you selected, since the restaurant price categories are based on *à la carte* courses. The elimination of a course—servings usually are substantial in Holland—can also make a meal in a given restaurant less expensive than the price category indicated.

### HOTEL PRICE CATEGORIES

Prices are based on a room for two, including private bathroom, VAT, and service. Dutch-style continental breakfast is included at most moderate and lower price hotels, rarely for expensive ones.

**Very Expensive** ----------------------------**Dfl. 450-700**

**Expensive** ------------------------------------- 250-450

**Moderate** -------------------------------------- 150-250

**Inexpensive** --------------------------------- 150 or less

### RESTAURANT PRICE CATEGORIES

The following price categories are based on a three-course dinner for one, without drinks, but inclusive of VAT and service.

**Very Expensive** ----------------------------------**Dfl. 100 or more**

**Expensive**---------------------------------------------- 75-100

**Moderate** -------------------------------------------50-75

**Inexpensive** -------------------------------------50 or less

## *HOTEL RATINGS*

I have used a star rating system to assist you in selecting hotels. The hotel selection in this guide is not meant to be comprehensive, particularly in major cities; rather, it includes properties in a range of prices chosen subjectively for various tangible and intangible factors. Among these are atmosphere, visual appeal and view, furnishings, size of bed and bathrooms, friendliness of the staff, and—as for real estate decisions anywhere—location. An emphasis has been placed on properties which are central or close to districts with sights of interest, convenient to public transportation, and, when available, in scenic settings.

### Deluxe Hotel ★★★★★

A hotel with excellent standards of service and cuisine, and outstanding quality in amenities and atmosphere. The property will have special features, location, or view that raises it above the four-star rating, 24-hour room service, a specialty *à la carte* restaurant as well as a less formal eatery, and often some in-house recreational facilities.

### First-Class Hotel ★★★★

One with superior standards of comfort, cuisine, service and setting. All rooms with private bath and shower, and all accessible by elevator. A wide range of amenities, including restaurant and room service.

### Recommended Hotel ★★★

A hotel that is comfortable, with many amenities, including a breakfast room, bar, and sometimes a restaurant with limited choice menu. Most rooms have private toilet, plus shower and/or bathtub; those without private facilities will have an in-room sink. Some rooms may be accessible by elevator.

### Reasonable Hotel ★★

One with simple standards but considered above the minimum by virtue of some feature that places it above a one-star property. Lobby or other public room used for breakfast service/lounge. Some rooms have private facilities. No elevator.

### Budget Hotel ★

A hotel that meets minimal acceptable standards for plain but decent accommodation. Private facilities unlikely. Breakfast may be available only in one's room due to the lack of a lobby lounge/breakfast room.

## UPDATES

Considerable care has been taken to ensure that the information included in this volume is correct, but change is a constant in the world, even in the small, stable corner of it covered here. While the facts presented are the most up-to-date possible at press time, changes could occur by the time of your visit. Therefore, when travel arrangement particulars are important to you, it's wise to confirm them in order to save yourself inconvenience and expense. Although I cannot be responsible for inaccuracies that result from changes in the travel environment, I will make every effort to keep informed of such developments. Your comments and suggestions for or about the guide are welcome. Write to me c/o Fielding Worldwide, Inc., 308 South Catalina Avenue, Redondo Beach, CA 90277.

# KEYS TO THE DUTCH KINGDOM

*Amsterdam's glass-topped canal boats are close by the VVV tourist office and Centraal Station.*

## PRACTICAL TRAVEL INFORMATION

Holland is exceptionally well organized for travelers, with information offices located virtually anywhere you would want to find one. The great degree to which English is spoken (and written, in brochures and other travel documentation) throughout the country will be reassuring. Nevertheless, even though you can rely on almost always finding someone to answer your questions in English, there

7

may be times when you welcome having the information in this chapter at your fingertips.

## PLANNING YOUR TRIP
### PLANNING AIDS

Holland's tourist offices both overseas and locally are among the best organized and most helpful in the world, and they can provide an enormous selection of tourism literature in English, much of it free. Contact the nearest office for travel information before you go.

In the United States:

**Netherlands Board of Tourism** (NBT), 355 Lexington Ave., 21st. Fl., New York, NY 10017, ☎ *(212) 370-7367, FAX (212) 370-9507;* NBT, 225 N. Michigan Ave., Suite 326, Chicago, IL 60601; ☎ *(312) 819-0300, FAX (312) 819-1740;* NBT, 90 New Montgomery St., Suite 305, San Francisco, CA 94105; ☎ *(415) 543-6772, FAX (415) 495-4925.*

In Canada:

**Netherlands Board of Tourism** 25 Adelaide St. East, Suite 710, Toronto, Ontario, Canada M5C 1Y2, ☎ *(416) 363-1577, FAX (416) 363-1470.*

In the United Kingdom:

**Netherlands Board of Tourism** 25-28 Buckingham Gate, London SW1E 6LD, ☎ *(071) 630-0451, FAX (071) 828-7941.*

### LOCAL TOURIST OFFICES

In Holland, local tourist offices go by the initials VVV, and usually are located in or close to the central railway station or town center (*Centrum*), and are well indicated by prominently displayed signs. There are over 400 local VVVs in Holland, recognized by a triangular VVV emblem; those in larger towns have an additional sign showing an "*i*" (for *Information*) and the word *Nederland*, indicating that you can get information on the whole country and make reservations for lodging—often the only place to book accommodations in private homes—and major entertainment events countrywide. All staff members speak English. The VVV is your source for local and regional maps; public transportation information; walking, driving and bicycle routes; and tourism information in English. Some maps (in Dutch only) are published by the ANWB (Royal Dutch Touring Club), which charges a moderate amount. In general VVVs are open Monday to Friday 9 a.m. to 5 p.m. at a minimum; at Easter, in the Spring (in the bulb district) and in the summer, hours are longer and include weekends.

### DOCUMENTS

A passport is required to enter Holland, but visitors from the U.S., Canada, members of the EC, and most of the British Commonwealth countries do not need a visa for stays up to three months. No immunization certificates are required to enter Holland, and no certificate of vaccination is required by U.S. or Canadian authorities from returning residents.

**U.S. Passports**: Major post offices throughout the country now are able to process passport applications; if your local office doesn't have the forms, it can direct you to the nearest one that does. Federal office buildings also have passport offices. For your initial passport, or if your previous one was issued more than 12 years ago, you need to apply in person (not required for children under 13) with a completed application, proof of U.S. citizenship (a certified copy of birth certificate or naturalization papers), a photo ID, and two recent identical passport photos (full-face, 2" by 2", plain background), and $65 (exact currency, or check or money order made out to Passport Services). If you have a passport not more than 12 years old, you can mail or take it, together with an application and $55 payment, to the nearest passport office. Passports are good for ten years. In an emergency it's possible to get a passport in short order (you can indicate your departure date on the application), but normally you should allow a month and try to avoid the spring rush for summer travel. Your passport is returned by mail. If an applicant is under 18, there are some exceptions to the above; check with the Washington Passport Agency, Dept. of State, 1425 K St., Washington, D.C. 20522; ☎ *(202) 326-6060.*

## HEALTH TIPS

The standard of health care in Holland is among the highest in the world—infant mortality is lower and life expectancy higher than in the U.S. Rest assured that if anything untoward should occur during your travels here, you'll be wonderfully looked after. All Dutch doctors and nurses understand English well, especially since many of their medical courses are taught from English-language textbooks.

**Water**: You can safely drink the water virtually everywhere in Holland. On the rare occasion when this is not the case—such as from a sink in the toilet on a train or one in a rural restaurant—there will be international signage and the word nonpotable (nondrinkable) clearly posted. Bottled water or other liquids usually are available on a train, from a refreshment car or cart. At restaurants, one normally is expected to buy bottled mineral water, but if you've ordered something else to drink and want water too, ask the waiter for a glass of ordinary tap water. It is unlikely to come with ice. Bottled water is available at all grocery stores and many snack stands. It comes as *gaz* or *sin gaz* (carbonated or noncarbonated) varieties.

**Insurance**: Travelers covered by medical insurance are entitled to medical treatment in Holland, so it behooves you to check your policy about coverage abroad and the special procedures to follow for reimbursement. Carry your insurance I.D. with you while traveling, and keep all medical receipts for your insurance company back home. It's an excellent idea to carry photocopies of your insurance policy so that you can hand one over immediately if you require treatment, possibly preventing the need for direct payment. In Holland, the Health Service-Foreign Affairs Department in Utrecht can be contacted during business office hours at ☎ *(030) 618881.* As EC citizens, U.K. citizens carrying a National Health Service certificate are covered for the same medical benefits Dutch citizens have. Your hotel staff should have the names of English-speaking doctors to recommend, and can inform you as to which of the *apotheek* (chemist/ pharmacist) shops that open, in rotation, to cover nights and weekends is on duty.

## SENIOR CITIZENS

Senior citizens who have flexibility of schedule by virtue of being retired are in a position to take advantage of last-minute travel bargain tours and reduced overseas airfares with restrictions they can live with. Some organizations specifically for senior citizens offer discount travel options. The one with the largest membership and, therefore, potentially the most negotiating clout is the **American Association of Retired Persons** (*AARP, 601 E Street N.W., Washington, D.C. 20049*). It is open to all people 50 years and older willing to pay a small membership fee. The **National Council for Senior Citizens** (*925 15th St. N.W., Washington, D.C. 20005*) makes available travel and discount information. Among tour operators that specialize in travel for senior citizens are **Elderhostel Inc.**(*75 Federal Street, Boston, MA 02110* ☎ *(617) 426-8056*), with interesting cultural and educational tours among its offerings, and **Saga International**, *(222 Berkeley Street, Boston, MA 02116* ☎ *(617) 262-2262*), which offers a selection of value-conscious tours worldwide, including Holland, and single destination, extended-stay accommodations for travelers 60 and over.

## STUDENTS

The *Student Travel Catalog* available from the **Council for International Education Exchange** (*CIEE, 205 E. 42nd St., New York, NY 10017*) is a basic source for discount and tour travel information and services for people under 26, students, and teachers. If you qualify for one, make sure to get an **International Student Identity Card**, available from CIEE, before you head for Holland. It opens the door to many discounted rates and fares.

## TRAVEL FOR THE DISABLED

Disabled travelers will find accessible accommodations at tourist attractions, hotels, restaurants, and public transportation in socially conscious Holland. In particular **Mobility International Nederland**, the Dutch member of the international organization (based in London) that arranges individual and group travel programs, can be contacted at *Postbus 165, 6560 AD Groesbeek, Nederland*. The **Netherlands Board of Tourism** produces a brochure (cost Dfl. 1) with general travel information. Also available is a listing of the country's accessible hotel and recreation sites, and rental camper vans with wheelchair-access. There is a special telephone number ☎ *(030) 331252* staffed Monday through Friday, 8 a.m.-4 p.m., through which you can arrange assistance for train travel nationally; call at least one day in advance, by Friday midday for weekends. Amsterdam's Schiphol Airport and its Metro are accessible to wheelchair users with normal arm function. For more travel specifics, a book by Louise Weiss, *Access to the World: A Travel Guide for the Handicapped* (published by Facts on File, ☎ *(212) 683-2244*), contains useful advice and hotel listings. **Mobility International** (*Box 3551, Eugene, OR 97403*) and **Whole Person Tours** (*Box 1084, Bayonne, NJ 07002*) each publishes newsletters and magazines for members, and organizes trips. The **Information Center for Individuals with Disabilities** (*20 Providence St., Boston, MA*, ☎ *(617) 727-5540*) will, for a small fee, provide a list of specialized travel agencies, tour operators, and publications. And the **Travel Information Center** (*Moss Rehabilitation Hospital, Tabor and 12th, Philadelphia, PA 19141*) will send travel information for up to three cities, for a small fee.

## WHEN TO TRAVEL

In Holland, in numbers of travelers, the bulb season (April to late May) rivals July and August as the busiest tourist season. Tourism is especially tied to tulips, which, with early and late blooming varieties, can flower from early April, if the weather is unseasonably warm, to late May, if it's unusually cool. Motorcoach loads of viewers from countries around the world visiting then can make the region feel somewhat tourist trampled. Nevertheless, if you enjoy flowers, the spectacle of the bulb fields in bloom and Keukenhof garden are well worth the crowds. (See separate chapter "The Bulb Field Business.")

On average, April and May are the driest months of the year in Holland. Easter, which may or may not occur during tulip time, is a four-day holiday weekend throughout Europe that results in mass travel movements. Reserve well ahead if your travels are going to span that weekend. Many tourist attractions use Easter as the occasion to open to the public for the tourist season, though some shut again after Easter until early June.

As in much of northern Europe, summer and an eternal hope for sun and warmth keep many Dutch citizens at home for the summer holidays. The daylight hours in summer are dramatically longer than many readers will be used to, due to the high northern latitude of Holland, which is on par with Southern Labrador. The Dutch, living on waterlogged, below-sea-level land, are avid sailors, and many spend the warmer months aboard their craft in the small picturesque harbors of Zeeland or in the historic former Zuiderzee ports around what today is the enclosed IJsselmeer. Should you be heading toward these delightful destinations in summer, particularly mid-July to mid-August, when family travel is in full swing due to school holidays, make sure of guaranteed reservations because hotels in this area are small and limited in number.

Hotels at coastal resorts along the North Sea in Holland, especially those with a beach view, can be expected to be fully booked if the summer weather is inviting. Camping, caravaning, and renting bungalows or apartments all are common ways for Europeans to have affordable family vacations at Holland's coastal and resort areas. Travelers interested in such forms of accommodation should book well ahead, as they would for summer holidays at popular destinations at home.

Most North Americans, however, will be seeking hotel rooms, often in cities and towns. Because business travel is slower in summer, city hotels there may offer bargain prices then, as well as on weekends throughout the year.

In September, there's competition for beds at the best hotels in Amsterdam and other business centers in Holland, due to the post-summer renewal of corporate travel and a new autumn season of trade and professional congresses (conventions). The busiest business months are September and October, and May and June. Away from cities, September can be a lovely and less busy time for travel.

The word for winter in Holland is *dark*. Daylight lasts only from 8 or 8:30 a.m. until 3:30 or 4 p.m. in December and January. But Holland can be at its coziest in winter, with candlelit restaurants and pubs, gala events on the cultural calendar, and a festive celebration of the holiday season.

## SEASONS, CELEBRATIONS AND CEREMONIES

### SPRING

Just before the beginning of Lent, carnival merrymaking takes place in Holland south of Rotterdam"below the moerdijk" (in the part of the Netherlands that has a considerably higher percentage of Roman Catholics than does the more Calvinist Protestant north). **Maastricht**, in the southeast, offers the largest carnival celebration.

The **bulb fields** and glorious 70-acre **Keukenhof** garden (showplace for Holland's local bulb growers) with its millions of tulips and other bulb flowers, burst into bloom from late March until late May. In late April, a **flower parade** with decorated floats winds through the villages of the bulb-growing district.

Holland observes its national holiday on April 30, the **Queen's Birthday**. (It's actually the birthday of former Queen, now Princess, Juliana, but her daughter Queen Beatrix has kept the date for the happy occasion.) There's singing and selling in the streets (thousands take advantage of the one-day, license-free occasion to hold personal "yard sales" in the streets of central Amsterdam.) The May opening of the fresh **asparagus** ("white gold") **season** gives everyone in Holland a gastronomic cause to celebrate. At the end of May, on **Vlaggetjesdag** in Scheveningen, ships are decked in festive flags as the Dutch herring fleet puts out to the North Sea for the start of the herring season. Skippers vie to bring in the first barrel of *groene* (fresh) *haring*, a beloved Dutch treat, which traditionally is delivered to Queen Beatrix.

### SUMMER

Holland's northern latitude brings late-light nights (until 10:30 or 11 p.m. at midsummer) for lingering sightseeing, followed by night-seeing, viewing the marvelously **illuminated building facades**, bridges, towers and other monuments whose architectural details are tastefully highlighted with spotlights, producing scenic (not to mention romantic) settings.

June brings the seasonal start up of **carillon concerts** that continue throughout the summer season. Music of many kinds and other performing arts fill the stages set for the June **Holland Festival**, held mostly in Amsterdam, and the July **North Sea Jazz Festival** in The Hague. In Haarlem, the renowned organ of *St. Bavo's Church* is used for the **International Organists Competition** each July.

## FALL

September returns to the time (during months ending with an "r") for taking mussels from their sea beds, and mouths begin to water. **Fall flowers** are paraded in the area around Holland's Aalsmeer, the world's largest flower auction house, and on colorful floats in September. **Prinsjesdag** is the mid-September annual opening of the Dutch Parliament in The Hague, where Queen Beatrix and royal family members ride in a horse-drawn golden carriage from the "office palace" of Noordeinde to the *Binnenhof.* October's **Delft Old Art and Antique Fair**, one of Europe's most prestigious, offering museum quality art and furnishings, takes place in Delft's *Prinsenhof,* the former palace and site of the assassination (1584) of Prince Willem the Silent of Orange. On **October 3** in 1574 Willem went to **Leiden** to congratulate the town for successfully withstanding a devastating siege by the Spanish, an occasion the city has marked ever since. It was in Leiden that certain English separatists lived (1608-1620) before leaving for the New World aboard the *Mayflower* and founding Plymouth Colony in Massachusetts. A **Thanksgiving Day Service** at Leiden's *St. Pieterskerk*, which these pilgrims attended, is held each year to commemorate the connection.

## WINTER

Winter in Holland brings a cultural glut of goodies: opera, ballet, symphony and dance from fine residential and guest performing arts companies. Late November features the arrival by ship of **Sinterklaas** (St. Nicholas) in Amsterdam. From then until the December 5th evening family celebration, shops, especially bakeries, take on a holiday look with such traditional treats as large pink marzipan pigs and chocolate letters from 2 inches to 12 inches high. Many towns string white lights over streets and along canals. **Sinterklaas** serves as a warm-up for the rest of the Christmas season specialties. The Dutch cheese town celebrates **Gouda By Candlelight**, with the lighting of a Christmas tree and carol singing in its lovely market square, lit only by candles in all the windows of the buildings that surround it; there's carillon playing and an organ concert in Gouda's St. Jan's church. **New Year's** in Holland is observed with masses of fireworks set off at midnight.

One always hopes for skating in winter in Holland, none more than the Dutch. If, a big *if*, the weather gets cold enough, for long enough, the **Elfstedentocht** (11 cities tour) is held. When it's held, beginning well before dawn and lasting until well after dark, hundreds of qualified Dutch competitors and thousands of others undertake a grueling marathon-on-skates across a windswept frozen canal "track" that connects the 11 cities of northern Holland's Friesland province. The event, which was held in both 1985 and in 1986 after a 20-year hiatus due to too-warm weather, is a sort of winter rite of passage for the Dutch, some 90 percent of whom are reckoned to watch at least some of the event on television. (Even members of Parliament take a TV break when winners get close to the finish line.) To the delight of Dutch everywhere, Crown Prince Willem-Alexander completed the *Elfstedentocht* in 1986, with his mother, Queen Beatrix, there to welcome him at the finish line.

## WEATHER

An old joke—that may have originated in England— about having *weather*, rather than a climate, applies equally to Holland. The weather here can, indeed, be remarkably changeable. Holland's weather in the more tourist traveled western half of the country can change astoundingly in a short space of time due to the proximity of the North Sea. However, although at times (most commonly in winter) dreary drizzly windy days can linger, sustained rain for lengthy periods is not the rule. Despite the high northern latitude of Holland, the sea keeps the climate temperate. As a result, extremes of cold and hot are less than in many areas of North America. While you must always be prepared for sudden shifts in the weather, summers can produce superbly warm sunny days, and clear cheerful days appear around the calendar. Countrywide, average daily temperatures range from 50° to 61° Farenheit (10° to 16°C.) in summer and from 35° to 46° Farenheit in winter (2°–8°C.). Year-round, inland temperatures in eastern Holland average about 4° Fahrenheit (2° C.) higher than those on the coast.

| WEATHER IN AMSTERDAM | | | | | | | | | | | |
|------|------|------|------|------|------|------|------|------|------|------|------|
| Jan. | Feb. | Mar. | Apr. | May | June | July | Aug. | Sept. | Oct. | Nov. | Dec. |
| **Lows** | | | | | | | | | | | |
| 31° | 31° | 35° | 39° | 45° | 51° | 54° | 54° | 49° | 43° | 37° | 33° |
| **Highs** | | | | | | | | | | | |
| 41° | 42° | 47° | 54° | 62° | 68° | 70° | 70° | 65° | 57° | 47° | 42° |
| **Days With No Rain** | | | | | | | | | | | |
| 21 | 20 | 20 | 22 | 22 | 21 | 20 | 20 | 20 | 18 | 19 | 18 |

*Average low and high temperatures by month (in Farenheit)*

Locally, temperatures are given exclusively in centigrade (Celsius). The standard conversion formulas are: to turn centigrade into Fahrenheit, multiply by 9, divide by 5, and add 32; to convert Fahrenheit to centigrade, subtract 32, multiply by 5, and divide by 9. (People

who travel a lot always figure a way to make the conversion easier.
One easy way to figure this in your head is to double the Centigrade
reading, subtract 10 % and add 32. Example: The local temperature
is 23°C. 23 X 2=46. 46-5[and rounded up 10%]=41. 41+32=73°F.
To convert the other direction, subtract 32 from the Fahrenheit
reading, add 10% and halve the net. This, in fact, is the same in
mathematical terms as the standard conversion method, but it is easier to accomplish.)

The chart that follows has done the conversion for you. However,
if you don't have it handy and want to know what outside temperature to dress for, another, decidedly unscientific, method will provide you with a quick answer within a degree or so. First, remember
that 16 (C) is equal to its inverted number 61 (F); the same holds
true for 28 (C), which is equal to 82 (F). Using those as baselines,
one Celsius degree is *roughly* equivalent to two Fahrenheit for temperatures in between.

## CONVERSION CHART: CELSIUS(CENTIGRADE)°C/FAHRENHEIT°F

| °C | °F | °C | °F | °C | °F |
|----|------|----|------|-----|------|
| 34 | 93.2 | 19 | 66.2 | 4 | 39.2 |
| 33 | 91.4 | 18 | 64.4 | 3 | 37.4 |
| 32 | 89.6 | 17 | 62.6 | 2 | 35.6 |
| 31 | 87.8 | 16 | 60.8 | 1 | 33.8 |
| 30 | 86.0 | 15 | 59.0 | 0 | 32.0 |
| 29 | 84.2 | 14 | 57.2 | -1 | 30.2 |
| 28 | 82.4 | 13 | 55.4 | -2 | 28.4 |
| 27 | 80.6 | 12 | 53.6 | -3 | 26.6 |
| 26 | 78.8 | 11 | 51.8 | -4 | 24.8 |
| 25 | 77.0 | 10 | 50.0 | -5 | 23.0 |
| 24 | 75.2 | 9 | 48.2 | -6 | 21.2 |
| 23 | 73.4 | 8 | 46.4 | -7 | 19.4 |
| 22 | 71.6 | 7 | 44.6 | -8 | 17.6 |
| 21 | 69.8 | 6 | 42.8 | -9 | 15.8 |
| 20 | 68.0 | 5 | 41.0 | -10 | 14.0 |

## TIME

Holland is in the Central European time zone, which puts it six
hours ahead of North America's Eastern Standard Time (nine hours
ahead of the west coast). Holland is one hour ahead of Great Britain
and Ireland time. Clocks are put ahead one hour for "summer time"
on the last Sunday in March, and back an hour on the last Sunday in
September. Generally, plane, train and ferry schedules reflect these

time changes, but if you are traveling near the date of a time change, it's worth double checking departure times.

**The 24-hour clock:** Since the 24-hour clock often is used to indicate times on transportation schedules and opening hours for museums and restaurants, it's a good idea to understand that time concept. The hours after 12:00 noon continue in numerical order from 1300 through 2400 hours. To translate a time past noon from or to the 24-hour clock, simply add or subtract 12 from the time shown. For example, for a rendezvous at 2000 hours, *subtract* 12 from 20 and you arrive at an arrival time of 8 p.m. If you wish to take a train at 3 p.m., *add* 12 to 3 and then look on the schedule for a 1500 hours departure.

## NATIONAL HOLIDAYS

New Year's Day; Good Friday; Easter Sunday and Monday; Queen's Birthday (April 30); Ascension Day; Whit Sunday and Monday; Christmas; Boxing Day (Dec. 26). In addition to closings on public holidays, it is well to remember that throughout Holland, the Sabbath (Sundays) is observed quite strictly with store closures (except in resort areas, such as Scheveningen). Many Dutch who live near the border slip over into Belgium, where Sunday shopping isn't impaired by such "blue laws."

## *WHAT TO BRING*

In addition to prescription medicines, extra prescription eyeglasses, and copies of actual prescriptions, you know best what personal items are essential to your well-being, at home or away; a small pair of scissors, a sewing kit, double-sided Scotch tape to secure a hem you don't have time to sew, several sizes of safety pins. A lightweight corkscrew is handy if you plan on picnics, either outdoors or in your hotel room when you're too tired to go out for dinner. Clothespins with hanger-shaped tops that fit on a shower curtain rod or other hooks come in handy for personal laundry, for which you should bring a small plastic bottle filled with liquid detergent. A pocket calculator can be useful if you don't like converting the prices of things in your head.

If sound and light are liable to affect your sleep, it's wise to make earplugs and an eyeshade regular travel companions. With earplugs, you can get your beauty sleep while avoiding the wrenching necessity of having to turn down a front hotel room with a fabulous view because of evening and early morning noise from a nearby tram or on-the-hour and half-hour carillon bells, for a quiet but boring room at the back. If you wake with dawn's early light, be aware that it comes as early as 4 a.m. in summer in far-to-the-north Holland. Pack a sleeping mask, however unglamorous it may seem. Once you've worked out how to get a good night's sleep, to make sure you wake up on time, bring a small travel alarm clock (a reassuring backup even if you're staying at hotels with wake-up service).

Then, there's the trusty collapsible umbrella. In Holland, it should be part of your basic wardrobe when you head out each morning, even if there's not a cloud in the sky. Bring one small enough to fit in your purse or carryall, two if there are two of you traveling. Once you've thus insulated yourself from the threat of a little rain, you can take pleasure in dark clouds doing a furious dance in the huge skies above Holland, a sight that often compelled Dutch landscapists to paint.

If you're a shop-till-you-drop sort, pack especially lightly and include in your suitcase an *empty* durable nylon, hand-luggage-size foldable bag for your acquisitions. Should you forget an item or run into weather that runs contrary to the average you're prepared for, never mind: Holland has well-stocked, sophisticated stores where you will find what you need and may even discover a better-designed version of the item you left at home.

## CLOTHES

Experienced wanderers will follow the layered, color-coordinated separates, wash-and-wear wardrobe ideas that enable one to travel lightly, be prepared for a variety of social situations, and look well. In Amsterdam and The Hague, business dress is best for fine restaurants (and top ones in the countryside) and major cultural events; you'll see everything from student casual to evening wear. In the touristic summer season, dress even in cities is somewhat less formal at night, and it can be very casual during the day. A raincoat or rain and windproof jacket is a suggested outer covering any time of year, and a zip-in liner for warmth could prove useful even in summer; wind and dampness can be factors even without rain.

Don't skimp on packing sturdy shoes. You may even consider bringing more than one pair of walking shoes. They could come in handy if the weather turns wet or when those charming cobblestone streets exact their toll on your soles. You'll be able to buy shoes in Holland, but that's hardly the best use of your travel time, and it can be perilous breaking in a new pair during heavy-duty touring. Bring practical evening shoes (low, wide heels and, perhaps, insole cushions); the cobblestones in historic city centers don't disappear with the daylight.

## PACKING AND LUGGAGE

When considering what to pack, it's useful to mentally "walk through" your trip, keeping in mind planned activities and possible temperature variations. Anticipating the likely range of weather conditions is vital. Remember that Holland rarely comes even close to 90°, and instead can be windy and gray during the summer. It's important to include a sweater, windproof jacket and extra turtleneck layer.

In addition to keeping a running list of things you want to take, a good way to remember items that sometimes get overlooked during last-minute packing is to put out an empty suitcase a week or so before departure and, when an item occurs to you, put it in the case then and there.

It's not possible to overemphasize the importance of packing lightly. The flexibility afforded when you free yourself from excess baggage is a major physical and mental lift. My personal packing goal is not to lug around a single item I don't use—except an umbrella. If you're using one city as a base but spending some nights in other places, and will be returning to that city for your flight home, you might consider leaving a bag of items you won't need for the next segment of your trip either as checked luggage at the hotel—for which there usually is no fee, just a tip to the porter—or at a conveniently located train station or airport locker or baggage office.

Amsterdam's *Schiphol Airport* is superbly planned for getting around with luggage carts; there are large elevators, an underground passageway to the airport's connecting train station, and "stepless" escalators that take you and your luggage cart safely up and down. Schiphol is civilized enough to have those lovely free luggage carts, but despite this, when packing for your trip, try to keep in mind that there probably will be occasions when you must be able to manage all of your luggage by yourself. (It's best not to count on finding porters.)

## *TRAVELING IN HOLLAND*
### MONEY

The official monetary units in Holland are Dutch guilders (*gulden*), abbreviated Dfl., sometimes Hfl., or simply fl. (short for *florin*, a former name for the coin of the realm). There are 1, 2.5, and 5 guilder coins. The 100-cent guilder is broken down into 5-cent, 10-cent (*dubbeltje*), and 25-cent (*kwartje*) pieces. The 1-cent piece has been dropped as legal tender; prices are rounded up, or down, to the nearest five cents. Bank notes come in brightly colored 10, 25,

50, 100, 250, and 1000-guilder denominations. The guilder is a consistently strong European currency. At press time, the U.S. dollar was trading at approximately 1.67 guilders.

**Exchange Rate**: Currency exchange rates change daily, so check the financial pages of a newspaper for the most current before you leave. The newspaper figures will be slightly higher than those posted at the *change* desk (or *bureau de change*) at banks in Holland. Traveler's checks usually have a slightly more advantageous exchange rate than currency.

No doubt you know the adage: exchange money *only* at banks. Like much advice that's been around for years, it's basically sound. However, bank service charges—a standard Dfl. 5 (over $3 at current rates) per exchange transaction in Holland—are enough to warrant thinking about *how often* you exchange traveler's checks or cash, as well as *where*. The **GWK** *(De Grenswisselkantoren)*, a nationwide network of Dutch government-regulated currency exchange offices, has locations at airports, major train stations, and border crossing points; most are open evenings and weekends. GWK rates are equivalent to bank rates, but commission charges are slightly higher, though not, in *my* opinion, so much higher that it's worth the inconvenience and waste of time trying to save a few basis points on a transaction. For instance, I like the efficiency of exchanging money at Amsterdam's Schiphol GWK counter, from which I can see the luggage arriving. American Express pays rates somewhat less than banks, but doesn't add a service charge on its traveler's checks. (Of course, they may already have collected 1 percent of the face value when you bought them.)

Unless you get free traveler's checks, as you can from the Automobile Association of America (AAA) if you are a member, you'll be paying coming and going with traveler's checks and you might as well accept the fact. Nevertheless, in terms of their replaceability when lost or stolen (*if* you can supply the check numbers), they're worth it. No matter how many larger traveler's checks you buy, always take plenty in the useful $20 denomination. You will need your passport to exchange traveler's checks.

**Credit Cards**: Credit cards are widely accepted in Holland, although by no means by every hotel, restaurant and shop. Inquire specifically if/which cards are accepted when making reservations at hotels and restaurants. As at home, fewer places take *American Express* than *Visa* (probably the most widely accepted credit card internationally) and *MasterCard*. When you use a credit card abroad, you are charged the exchange rate in effect the day the sale is processed (*not* the day of purchase). Obviously, a lag in transaction processing (which by no means always happens) can work either to the buyer's or the supplier's advantage, depending upon whether your currency is strengthening against the guilder, or falling. Exchange rates from one day to the next rarely change a significant percentage. In my experience, foreign charges have been processed fairly, and using a credit card while traveling abroad certainly can be a considerable convenience. With a major credit card, you can get a cash advance at certain banks in Holland. Check with your card-issuing institution at home for specific details and locations. With a major credit card you can also get cash (in any currency) at Holland's GWK offices. Just in case, you always should travel with the appropriate local telephone numbers and instructions for reporting lost or stolen credit cards.

## WHERE TO STAY

Cleanliness *is* next to godliness in Holland, in every category of hotel and accommodation. Most hotels in Holland have far fewer rooms than North American travelers might expect. Since hotels are smaller, especially in tourist seasons (see "When to Travel"), atmospheric, well-located, reasonably priced properties are liable to be fully booked (although it's always worth inquiring at the last minute, in case of a cancellation or "no-show"). VAT (value-added tax) and service are always included in room rates. Breakfast (some variation on the "continental buffet": breads/rolls, jam, sliced cheese, cold cuts, hard-boiled eggs, fruit, yogurt, cold cereal, and coffee or tea; for an extra charge, you often can order cooked eggs) is usually included in the price at hotels in the three-star and lower category, and occasionally at the four-star category. As elsewhere in Europe these days, the more expensive the hotel, the less likely you are to have breakfast included in the price.

## NETHERLANDS RESERVATION CENTER (NRC)

Established by the Netherlands Board of Tourism and the Dutch hotel industry, this no-fee service enables indivuduals (and travel agents) to get quick, reliable confirmations at some 1700 member hotels in Holland. Concertgebouw and Muziektheatre events in Amsterdam can be booked. Contact NRC by telephone, FAX or mail *(Netherland Reservation Center; P.O. Box 404; 2260 AK Leidschendam; Holland;* ☎ *070-3202500; FAX: 070-3202611).* Private inquiries will be answered by mail.

## WHERE TO EAT

Be aware that if you use the word *restaurant* when inquiring about where to eat, you may be directed to a more formal and, therefore, more expensive dining establishment than you had in mind, since in the local dining lexicon that's what the word "restaurant" implies. In Holland, there's a whole range of lower to mid-range-price dining places—designated as *bistro, cafe, restaurant-cafe, brasserie, petit-restaurant, tearoom, eet cafe, traiteur, snackbar, koffieshop, broodjeswinkel* (sandwich shop), *or pannekoekhuisje* (pancake house)—that might fill the bill and suit your tastes much better.

It may also be useful to know that the term *menu* most often refers to a dining establishment's preselected daily special (a single dish or three-course meal). It's similar to a *prix fixe, table d'hôte, dagschotel,* or *tourist menu.* Tourist menu (in lower case) is not to be confused with the official **Tourist Menu** program, another eating bargain plan, in which some 400 restaurants countrywide offer three courses for the set price of approximately Dfl. 21.50. (NBT can supply a booklet that lists all participating establishments.) If you really do want to see the menu and the whole selection of food available, ask for the *kaart.*

## LANGUAGE

Because English is so widely spoken within Holland, you'll find no easier country in continental Europe to travel in. The citizens of Holland, who have had an outwardly oriented, commercially based economy for centuries, have excelled in mastering other languages, and you'll find their fluency in idiomatic American and English remarkable. From the age of ten until graduation, all Dutch schoolchildren study the language and are influenced by BBC radio and TV from England, as well as American TV programs and films (shown in English, only subtitled in Dutch). This practice is so pervasive that learning English is a near necessity—and fun. That the Dutch enjoy speaking English is obvious; you won't encounter any overtones to the contrary. Only in the remotest regions or among the oldest citizens, will you come across a lack of knowledge of English; even then, there'll be someone nearby who knows it.

## MUSEUMS/MUSEUMKAART

In Holland, museums generally do not close at lunchtime. Most, though not all, Dutch museums close one weekday, with Monday being the most common. If you're planning to do much museum meandering, Holland has a *museumjaarkaart* or museum card (Dfl. 40 adults, Dfl. 15 up to age 18) that provides free entry for a year from purchase date—there is no shorter period pass—at some 375 of Holland's nearly 600 museums, including many of the major ones, which individually may charge Dfl. 7 or more per person. The Museum Card does not waive extra fees charged for special exhibits. The card is available at most museums that accept it and at VVV tourist offices, where you can get publications with information on museums countrywide. The museum card also is sold by NBT in its Chicago and Toronto offices.

## THE HOLLAND WALLET

Also available from the Chicago and Toronto NBT offices—purchase must be made before departure for Holland—is the *Holland Wallet*. The wallet, an actual handcrafted leather one, contains an assortment of items assembled to ease visitors upon arrival in Amsterdam, and save them money. These include two first class train tickets between Schiphol Airport and central Amsterdam; Dfl. 10 in small coins; a phone card worth Dfl. 10; tickets for a canal boat ride and, the Museumboat; admission tickets for the Rijksmuseum, Van Gogh Museum, the Maritime Museum, and the Amsterdam Casino; stamped postcards; and, for when leaving Holland, a Dfl. 10 voucher for duty-free shopping at Schiphol. The Holland Wallet is priced at $79.95 for two adults, $69.95 for one.

## NIGHTSEEING

Some of the most memorable moments during your travels in Holland will be seeing public buildings, churches, castles, and monuments illuminated after dark. After dark may be after 10 p.m. in summer in this northern latitude, but the sights are well worth a late night. The lighted bridges of Amsterdam, romantically reflected in the canals, are scenes you'll not soon forget, nor the many statues, squares, stadhuizen, and steeples that also are artfully floodlit. The summer season, sometimes extending from Easter through September, is when the most monuments are spotlighted, but an increasing number are highlighted year round.

## PERSONAL SECURITY

There is considerably less personal violent crime in Holland than in the United States, but petty pickpockets and car burglars seem part of the worldwide scene these days. Cities have a greater problem with such random occurrences. Amsterdam is an essentially safe and delightful city to walk in, but be particularly watchful around *Centraal Station* and in the neighboring *Zeedijk* (now much gentrified with five-star hotels, but still carrying on as the colorful *Red Light*

*district*). Use bags or purses that close tightly, and carry them close to your body. Keep them in your lap (and/or with straps looped through the arms of chairs at outdoor cafes) in public or congested places, and on public transportation.

A good rule of thumb is: if you won't be needing an item, don't take it out on the street with you. Leave passports (you'll need yours only when checking into a hotel or cashing traveler's checks), extra cash, traveler's checks, airline tickets, rail passes, credit cards and other valuables in a hotel safe deposit box (available at the front desk if there isn't a safe in your room). There's little inconvenience involved in using one, compared to your increased peace of mind. If two of you are traveling together, make it a habit to split your cash, checks, and credit cards between you, thereby minimizing the risk of losing everything in a single incident, whether through forgetfulness or theft. An individual traveling alone should put money and valuables in several places or pockets, never carrying anything in a single purse, wallet, or carryall.

It's important to keep valuable information and photocopies of documents where you can put your hands on them (perhaps at the bottom of your suitcase in a hotel room or, even better, in a safe). The packet should include photocopies of passports (the page spread with your picture is sufficient), instructions of what to do in case of lost credit cards, health insurance procedures, and an accurate list of the numbers of unused traveler's checks. Taking such measures *ahead of time* can save a lot of self-recrimination in the unlikely event that something happens later.

## EMERGENCIES

To contact the police in Amsterdam during an emergency, call ☎ *6222222*. If you need to report a theft or other loss in Holland, go to the nearest police station to file a report, a copy of which will be given to you. If you plan to make a claim back home, your insurance company will want to see a copy of this report as proof of loss.

## EMBASSIES/CONSULATES

**U.S. Embassy**, Lange Voorhout, The Hague; ☎ *070-3624911*

**U.S. Consulate**, Museumplein 19, Amsterdam, ☎ *020-6645661*;

**Canadian Embassy**, Sophialaan 7, The Hague, ☎ *070-3614111*;

**U.K. Consulate**, Koningslaan 44, Amsterdam, ☎ *020-6764343.*

## METRIC WEIGHTS AND MEASURES

Most of the world, including Holland, runs by the metric system (though not the U.S.A., which still steadfastly resists its adoption).

Whether you need to decipher the temperature in Celsius (see the section under "Planning Your Trip: Weather") in order to dress for the day, want to buy 250 grams of Dutch chocolate or to know how high that handsome town hall tower (given in meters in the town's tourist pamphlet), need to fill up the tank of your rental car with liters of petrol, or must know how many kilometers it is to your next destination (see under "Transportation: Car"), you have the means below by which to make sense of metrics—with, perhaps, a little help from a hand calculator.

## CONVERSION CHART: FEET/METERS

| Meters | | Feet | Meters | | Feet |
|---|---|---|---|---|---|
| 0.30 | 1 | 3.28 | 13.72 | 45 | 147.64 |
| 0.61 | 2 | 6.56 | 15.24 | 50 | 164.04 |
| 0.91 | 3 | 9.84 | 18.29 | 60 | 196.85 |
| 1.22 | 4 | 13.12 | 21.34 | 70 | 229.66 |
| 1.52 | 5 | 16.40 | 24.38 | 80 | 262.47 |
| 1.83 | 6 | 19.69 | 27.43 | 90 | 295.28 |
| 2.13 | 7 | 22.97 | 30.48 | 100 | 328.08 |
| 2.44 | 8 | 26.25 | 60.96 | 200 | 656.17 |
| 2.74 | 9 | 29.53 | 91.44 | 300 | 984.25 |
| 3.05 | 10 | 32.81 | 121.92 | 400 | 1312.34 |
| 4.57 | 15 | 49.21 | 152.40 | 500 | 1640.42 |
| 6.10 | 20 | 65.62 | 182.88 | 600 | 1968.51 |
| 7.62 | 25 | 82.02 | 213.36 | 700 | 2296.59 |
| 9.14 | 30 | 98.43 | 243.84 | 800 | 2624.67 |
| 10.67 | 35 | 114.83 | 274.32 | 900 | 2952.76 |
| 12.19 | 40 | 131.23 | 304.80 | 1000 | 3280.84 |

*If you want to convert from feet to meters, read from the center column to the left (1 foot = 0.30 meters). When converting meters to feet, read from the center column to the right (1 meter = 3.28 feet).*

## U.S.A./METRIC CONVERSION

| U.S.A. | Metric |
|---|---|
| 1 ounce | 28.25 grams |
| 100 grams | 3.52 ounces |
| 1 U.S. pound | 0.45 kilogram (kilo) |
| 500 grams | a half kilo (or 1.1 U.S. pounds) |
| 1000 grams | 1 kilo (or 2.2 U.S. pounds) |
| | |
| 1 acre | 0.40 hectare |
| 1 hectare | 2.47 acres |

| U.S.A./METRIC CONVERSION | |
|---|---|
| **U.S.A.** | **Metric** |
| 1 U.S. pint | 0.47 liter |
| 1 U.S. quart | 0.94 liter |
| 1 liter | 2.12 U.S. pints |
| 1 U.S. gallon | 3.78 liters |
| 1 Imperial gallon | 4.54 liters |
| 1 centimeter | 0.39 inch |
| 1 inch | 2.54 centimeters |
| 1 foot | 30.4 centimeters |
| 1 yard | 0.91 meters |

### POSTAL/TELEPHONE/TELEGRAM/FAX

**Post Offices**: Hours in Holland are Monday-Friday 8:30 a.m.-5 p.m., and in some places Saturday 8:30 a.m.-noon.

**Telehouse Amsterdam**: This communications hub, centrally located in the city near Dam Square, is open 24 hours a day for telephone calls, telegrams, money orders and fax services anywhere in the world. An operator dials the call and puts it through to you in an assigned booth; when the call is completed, you pay the exact charge; there's no extra service fee such as hotels add, which can make overseas calls exorbitant.

In Holland, to reach an AT&T USA Direct operator, ☎ *06-0229111*; to reach a Bell operator in Canada or to place a collect or calling card call to Canada, ☎ *06-0229116*. When phoning Holland from North America, ☎ *011 + 31 + city code + local number.* When phoning from North America, delete the first zero from the city code; when phoning long-distance within Holland, *include* the first zero.

**Pay Telephones**: Instructions for using coin-operated telephones are given in several languages, including English. You can make international calls from telephone boxes that display signs with international flags. Dutch pay telephones take 25-cent and one-guilder coins in marked slots. The amount you have remaining shows on a screen; you should drop in more coins during the call when you see the figure nearing zero. Excess coins are returned at the end of a call, but change is not made, so use small coins if calling locally. Rates for calls on all telephones change during the day, and are highest until 1 p.m. on business days, lowest in the evening.

## ELECTRIC CURRENT

Voltage in Holland generally is 220 AC, 50 cycles. If you are bringing small electrical appliances, you'll need a transformer and a variety of adapter plugs in order to ensure a match to varying socket shapes. Personally, I'm for not taking electrical gadgets on travels, primarily because of luggage weight. If you're planning to stay in first class properties, you'll often find a hair dryer in the bathroom, frequently a pants press, perhaps a self-service shoeshine machine in the hall. At many hotels, you can borrow an iron and board or hair dryer by contacting the front desk.

## SMOKING

Nonsmoking North Americans may be unprepared for the *lack* of designated nonsmoking areas in Europe. And cigar smoking still is a tradition in Holland. For years, trains have had nonsmoking cars (in second as well as first class), but progress toward nonsmoking sections in restaurants and nonsmoking rooms in hotels—your best bet is in international chain properties—has been slow. Statistics do show that more citizens in Holland have stopped smoking than in some other European countries.

## PUBLIC TOILETS

The initials W.C. (for water closet) are the most international indication for public facilities, though the term *toilets* is most common. (Don't ask for the "bathroom" unless you want to take a bath; even in hotel rooms with private facilities, the bathtub and/or shower usually is separate from the toilet.) Americans will find public toilets far more available than at home (and almost always clean). Facilities may be free, though it's a good idea to keep handy a couple of *qwarties* (25-cent pieces) for coin-operated toilets. Often there are attendants who make change and keep the place clean. Toilets in Holland are marked *heren* for men, *dames* for women. International signs, with figures in skirts and in pants, often are used.

## TIPPING, VAT

Throughout Holland, VAT (value-added tax) and service are included in hotel and restaurant checks, which will say *inclusief.* However, when service has been good, it is customary to add about 10 percent to restaurant bills, and at cafés to round up the amount by a guilder or so. Tips are included in metered taxi fares, which are relatively expensive in Holland.

A resident of a non-EC country who buys an item with a value over Dfl. 300 is entitled to a VAT refund (17.5 percent in Holland). The procedure is to ask the store *at the time of purchase* for an export certificate (Dutch Form OB90). On leaving Holland with the purchase, have the form endorsed at Dutch customs, and you'll receive the tax refund. If you neglect to get the form at the time of purchase, it's possible to have a Dutch customs official endorse the invoice for the qualifying items, but then you must send the forms back to the store and wait for a refund check.

## NEWS AND NEWSPAPERS

Even certified news junkies will be able to keep up on international events in Holland. In addition to the *International Herald Tribune* (with its American sports scores and standings for the addicted), European-printed editions of *The Wall Street Journal* and *USA Today,* and British dailies such as the *Financial Times, Daily Telegraph,* and *The Times* all are available at major hotels and many news shops in cities and commercial centers. The almost ubiquitous cable T.V.s now available in hotels will, in the western regions of Holland nearer to England, pull in the news on stations from London. CNN International is available at an increasing number of better hotels. Weekly news magazines in English (*The Economist, Time, Newsweek,* Murdoch's *The European*) and plentiful paperbacks are available at airports, major hotels, and in many book stores.

## BUSINESS/SHOPPING HOURS

Basic store and business hours in Holland are 9 a.m.-6 p.m. Monday through Saturday, but many department and other stores are closed on Monday until 1 p.m. Pharmacies (*apotheek* in Holland) are open from 8 a.m. to 5:30 p.m. unless they are designated for longer duty. Small shops, bakeries, and news/tobacco stands, can open as early as 7:30 or 8 a.m. Certain kinds of shops (butchers, bakers, or drugstores/*drogisterij,* which sell toiletries) may close one weekday afternoon. Hours are posted on shop doors. Department stores usually are open from 9 a.m. to 6 p.m.; there is no closing for lunch in Holland. With the exception of certain resort areas, but including cities and large towns from Rotterdam north and even in Amsterdam, most stores are closed tight on Sundays for the Protestant Sabbath. Many stores in Holland are closed Monday until 1 p.m. Late night shopping until 8 or 9 p.m. one weeknight (which varies from town to town) is usual throughout Holland.

## FILM

Airport X-ray machines will become ever more evident in today's screened-for-security travel world. Professional photographers know that, at any setting, X-ray machines can cloud your processed and unprocessed film—low ASA is less sensitive—from its first time through the machine. Effects are cumulative, as with each transfer and connecting flight your carry-on belongings are required to make additional passages through X-ray. I politely ask a member of the security staff (they are not employees of any airline) to hand inspect my rolls of films, and camera if it has film in it; however, he or she is under no obligation and, with security demands tightened, may not have the time nor temperament to do so. If your request for hand inspection is refused, there is virtually nothing you can do about it, hence the wisdom of using a lead-shield pack for both exposed and unexposed rolls of film (although I have heard it said that the X-ray operator then just pushes the setting higher to see through the shield). Film is more expensive in Holland than at home, but if you run out it is readily available at many museums and other shops.

## DUTY-FREE

Amsterdam's Schiphol Airport duty-free shopping is considered among the best in the world. Although it's fair to say that not all purchases can be considered bargains anymore—you'd be wise, if you're considering a major electronic or jewelry purchase, to check prices prior to leaving home so you know what actually constitutes a saving—the extensive selection of shops at Schiphol is, at the very  least, a great convenience for certain souvenirs. Instead of lugging Edam cheeses (which can come to feel as heavy as their cannonball shape implies) with me to the airport, as I once did, I now buy my food purchases of cheese, chocolate, biscuits, etc. at the Schiphol Dutch "deli" after I've checked most of my other luggage. The best duty-free savings will come on Dutch products: savings on Dutch *genever* gin and liqueurs will be more than those on Scotch or sherry, for example. There is a fair selection of flower bulbs approved by the U.S. Department of Agriculture at the airport.

## CUSTOMS

**U.S. residents** are exempt from duty on the first $400 of combined purchases made abroad, as long as they have not made other such claims within 30 days, and as long as the items are for personal use, not resale. Family members may pool their exemptions by filling out a single customs form. Those over 21 may include one liter of alcohol in their exemption. Purchases of documented (keep the papers to show customs officials) antiques (over 100 years old) and original artworks are duty exempt. You may send packages to friends that are clearly marked *Unsolicited Gift of Value Less than $50* (only one package per address) without paying duty on them. If you're following this procedure to avoid duty—packages sent to your home are not allowed as part of your $400 exemption, and separate duty must be paid on them—consider paying the flat 10 percent of value charged for the first $1000 in purchases over your exemption for the security of carrying your items rather than risking damage or loss in the mail.

Certain items are restricted by U.S. law from entry into the U.S. These include articles made with any part of endangered species (The World Wildlife Fund's brochure *Buyer Beware* is available from ☎ *(800) 634-4444* if you're considering designer leathers, furs, etc.). Cuban cigars are not permitted, but the fine Dutch ones are. Food products often cause confusion as to what's allowable into the U.S. Cheeses and vacuum-wrapped smoked fish and other items usually are acceptable, especially coming from such a "clean" agricultural country as Holland. Sealed, boxed, dry items, such as crackers, cookies and cakes are fine. Fruit, vegetables and other plants are never allowed, and most meat is not.

One of the illegal temptations in Holland could be bulbs, bought at Amsterdam's *Floating Flower Market* or elsewhere, that do not carry the inspection certificate of the U.S. Department of Agriculture. If you do arrive at U.S. Customs carrying bulbs that do not have such inspection labels, be sure to specifically declare them and have them hand-inspected by the agricultural expert on duty. Although Holland has high horticultural health standards, the risks associated with unknown insects and diseases coming into a country should prevent anyone from trying to "sneak" uninspected agricultural items through Customs anywhere.

If you take any significant foreign-made articles, such as expensive watches, cameras, binoculars, or designer clothing with you on the trip, it's a good idea to bring the receipts (or other evidence that the items were brought from home) with you for clearing U.S. Customs on return. If you are traveling with prescription drugs, you would be wise to have the prescription with you to avoid possible delays in Customs.

**Canadian citizens** who remain out of the country for at least seven days may receive an exemption on duty for personal goods up to the value of $300 Canadian, but only once a year. Allowances of $100 can be claimed once a calendar quarter after being outside the country 48 hours. Families may not pool their exemptions. The first $300 in excess of the exemption is taxed at a flat 20 percent. Unsolicited gift packages (so marked) with a value of $40 or less can be sent to friends duty free, but you might as well carry all purchases for your-self with you, as they are subject to duty.

## *TRANSPORTATION*
### AIR

Most North Americans will arrive in Europe by air, and Holland of-fers one of the most acclaimed airports in the world for organization and efficiency, **Amsterdam's Schiphol**. National carrier **KLM Royal Dutch Airlines** has the majority of flights in and out of Schiphol (on KLM City-Hopper flights within Europe, trans-Atlantic nonstops, through its partnership with Northwest Airlines, and throughout the globe-spanning KLM system). KLM's U.S. nonstop to Amster-dam gateways are Atlanta, Chicago, Los Angeles, Houston, New York, Orlando, Minneapolis/St. Paul, San Franscisco, Boston, Washington/Dulles, and Detroit. KLM also offers nonstop flights to Amsterdam from the Canadian cities of Toronto, Montreal, Vancou-ver, Halifax and Calgary   ☎ *(800)3.747.747.* Schiphol also offers service and connections on other airlines throughout Europe and worldwide.

Intra-European air service remains an expensive way to travel among European cities, although the anticipated increase in compe-tition among European airlines on European routes as a result of the *Single Europe Act* is expected to reduce rates.

### RAIL

Holland has one of the most dense rail networks in the world. The system is characterized by frequent service (no place served by train in Holland has less than hourly service), integrated schedules, virtu-ally certain on-time arrivals, and international connections that pro-vide efficient rail service from Amsterdam and elsewhere in Holland to all major cities on the continent. The modern all-electric Dutch rail network (**Nederrlandse Spoorwegen** or **NS**), with its bright yel-low carriages, is one of the most efficient, fast, affordable, and easy-to-use systems in the world. Except if you are traveling during busi-ness rush hours and want to avoid the crowds, it's hardly necessary to travel first class (about a 50 percent surcharge), since second class is comfortable and clean. There are smoking and nonsmoking cars in both classes. There are no ticket barriers on the platforms; tickets are checked by on-board conductors. At every station, large schedule boards are located in the main hall, and also at most platforms; find the board with the name of the place you wish to travel to at the top, check the current time, and see when the next train goes. (Schedules use the 24-hour clock.) The schedule will indicate whether the train is **Inter-City** (stopping only at major towns) or a **Stoptrein** (which makes all the local stops listed). The **spoor** column shows the track from which the train departs. Trains invariably leave and arrive on time. The Netherlands Railways operates more than 75 inclusive day trips by train to major attractions throughout the country, mostly between May and September (information at main rail stations).

**Rail Passes:** A number of rail passes are available, all representing considerable savings and flexibility, but it's important to analyze your particular travel plans to see if one meets your needs. Holland is a member of the 23-nation **Eurailpass** network, but Eurail should be purchased only if you plan to make a long-distance sweep of Europe. If you "buy" more territory than you need on a rail pass, you cut into your savings. The **Benelux Tourrail Pass** provides unlimited train travel in Holland, Belgium and Luxembourg for any 5 days (they needn't be consecutive) in a single month. A first class ticket costs $205, second class $137; for those under 26 years of age the price is $102.

For 7 consecutive days of rail travel solely in Holland, there's a **Rail Rover** for Dfl. 152 second class, Dfl. 228 first class. Available only in conjunction with the Rail Rover is the **Public Transport Link Rover** (an additional Dfl. 25), covering the same 7-day period. It's good for unlimited travel on *all* Dutch public buses, trams, and subways. As well as offering potentially substantial savings, these passes make travel wonderfully easy by eliminating the need to stand in line to buy tickets. Holland also offers a 1-day rail pass for Dfl. 63 second class, Dfl. 94.50 first class. **Domino** Holland Passes, sold for three, five, or 10 days of rail travel within Holland during one month, are priced, respectively, at $53 second class/$81 first class; $88/$135; and $159/$243. Available during June, July, and August is a **Summer Tour** pass, valid for 3 days of unlimited travel within a set period of 10 days: second class, one person Dfl. 79, two persons Dfl. 109; first class, one person. Dfl. 104, two persons Dfl. 149.The **Summer Tour** includes unlimited travel on Dutch buses, trams, and Metro for an additional Dfl. 17 for one person, Dfl. 25 for two persons. There also are junior (under age 26), child and family passes at even greater savings. (All prices quoted are for 1994).

Some Dutch rail passes can be purchased in Holland. For those who want to buy passes prior to departure, an order form is available from NBT offices in Chicago and Toronto, as well as a booklet, *Touring Holland By Rail*. The information office of Netherlands Railways in the train station at Schiphol Airport is open from 8 a.m.-8 p.m. Monday through Friday, 9 a.m.-5 p.m. Saturday, Sunday and holidays.

## FERRY

For U.K. citizens and travelers who come to Holland via England, there's the rail-ship overnight crossing between Hoek van Holland (on the North Sea, west of Rotterdam) and Harwich in East Anglia (northeast of London). It's popular since it takes long enough to get a night's sleep; there's also a daytime crossing. The Dutch ports of Vlissingen (Flushing) and Scheveningen (The Hague), and the Belgian ports of Zeebrugge and Ostend offer various crossings of the North Sea and English Channel to and from England's Dover, Hull, and Yarmouth. *Boat trains* to/from London, Amsterdam, and farther afield are scheduled to connect with respective ferry terminals in time for crossings.

Ferries are the least expensive, most adventuresome means of crossing the North Sea, but also the most time consuming. North Americans need to assess whether the experience and/or savings are worth it.

## BICYCLE

Everyone—farmers in *klompen* (wooden shoes), well-suited businessmen and women, and the Queen—rides bicycles in Holland: mothers may have child seats fore and aft; people "walk" their dogs by bike; and shoppers manage a week's worth of groceries on two-wheelers. In many ways, Holland was built around the bicycle. There are some 12 million two-wheelers for a two-legged population of 14 million, and bicycle paths account for as many kilometers as motorways do. An estimated one-third of all transportation in Holland takes place by bike. In a country so geared to bicycles and cyclists, it's great for travelers to know that safe, sturdy, single-gear —more aren't needed since the land's so flat—rental bikes are available everywhere at reasonable prices. Hired bikes cost about Dfl. 8 a day, and must be returned to the original place of hire. You'll probably be asked for a deposit (Dfl. 50-200) and proof of identity (passport or driving license). Some 80 railway stations around Holland have rental bikes and bike parking facilities. Upon presentation of a valid train ticket, you can get a discount on bike hire. In busy travel seasons, it's a good idea to reserve a bike in advance. (For more information, request the 16-page publication *Cycling in Holland.*)

## BUS/TRAM

The key to Holland's urban public transportation is the **National Strip Card** *(Nationale Strippenkaart)*, which is valid on all city buses, trams, and the Metro throughout the country. Each city is divided into transport zones, with standard fares payable according to the number of zones traveled through. Each zone costs one strip, plus a basic charge of one strip. So traveling within one zone (within the *Centrum* in Amsterdam, for example) would cost two strips. Unlimited travel and changes are allowed within each zone until the time—usually an hour from the time you board—stamped on the strip. After folding it to the proper number for your journey, insert the strip in the machine at the rear of tram cars or at the front by the driver on buses. The National Strip Card is available at railway stations, post offices, and GVB *(Amsterdam Municipal Transport)* information and ticket office opposite Amsterdam's *Centraal Station* for Dfl 11 for 15 strips, and Dfl. 32.25 for 45 strips (1994 prices). You can also buy two-, three-, and ten-strip cards at a slightly higher per-strip charge from tram or bus drivers. *Day tickets* for unlimited travel in Amsterdam also are available from tram and bus drivers and in Metro stations. A single day ticket costs Dfl. 12, two days Dfl. 16, three days Dfl. 19.75 (1994 prices).

Holland has a thorough network of national and local buses. There are few places in the country that you cannot reach by bus—which is almost, though not quite, the case with trains. If you are traveling solely by public transportation and off the beaten path, you may well find yourself on a bus in Holland. Local tourist office information and schedules, helpful drivers and friendly fellow passengers, and the lowest transportation cost-per-kilometer all should benefit your bus travel experience.

## CAR

An International Driver's License is *not* necessary in Holland. Your current U.S., Canadian, or U.K. operator's license is sufficient. Driving in Holland is on the right, the same as in North America and other continental European countries. Dutch roads are good to excellent and generally well posted. There are plenty of motorways and highways, though those may not be the best roads for you to follow: the **Royal Dutch Touring Club (ANWB)** puts up six-sided route signs that point to prettier paths, and publishes maps of them. The major rental car companies have offices in cities, but you should book in advance from North America to get the best rates. If you can drive a standard shift—in lieu of an automatic transmission, which is rarer in

Europe—you'll save on the cost of the rental car. Rentals of one week or more may qualify for a special rate: try for unlimited mileage, at a minimum. Remember to ask for all charges up front, including VAT, which adds a hefty 17.5 percent to your rental bill in Holland right off the bat, and insurance. Some companies offer leasing arrangements for a minimum period of three weeks, for which rates are tax- free and include insurance and unlimited mileage. Gasoline (*petrol, benzine*) is pricey, at least twice what it is in the U.S., but driving distances are shorter.

When you rent a car, you won't be required to pass any test of Dutch rules of the road. You'll probably do fine by following the examples of drivers on the road ahead of you, but it's still a good idea to know as much as possible about the procedure . Most important is to be aware of the **priorité à droite:** traffic coming from the right *always* has the right of way, even when you're on the main road and a car is entering from an insignificant side street. Generally, Dutch drivers make a point of claiming their priority, so keep the rule very much in mind. Low beams are required when driving between nightfall and dawn, as well as in bad weather. On certain Dutch dikes (such as the *Afsluitdijk* across the *IJsselmeer*), large signs warn drivers to turn on their lights (**ontsteekt uw lichten**) in broad daylight to counter the unique shimmer of disorienting light reflecting from the flat land and water. Seat belts must be worn by both driver and front seat passenger. There is usually a minimum speed on motorways of 70 km. per hour; maximum speed limit is 120 km. (75 mph). Holland takes a tough stance on drinking and driving. Highway patrols can stop a driver and administer a breathalyzer test on the spot; blood alcohol limits are lower (.08), fines for abuse higher, than in the U.S. Although foreign travelers are treated politely, ignorance of the law will not get you out of a plight. The ANWB in Holland—for roadside assistance, call ☎ *06-0888*—which employs distinctive yellow vehicles, is ready, able, and willing to help distressed drivers on principal roads.

Maps are essential companions for independent travelers, and at no time more so than when one is behind the wheel on unfamiliar roads. As a basic, adequately detailed map for countrywide driving, I recommend the *Shell Grote Autokaart Nederland* (approx. Dfl. 2.95, available from the VVV and bookshops). On the reverse side of this large-scale national map are smaller ones for the four largest cities (Amsterdam, The Hague, Rotterdam and Utrecht) in sufficient detail to get you in and out of town. Signposting on Dutch roads is usually by town name (rather than by route number) in rural areas.

## CONVERSION CHART: KILOMETERS/MILES

| Kilometers | | Miles | Kilometers | | Miles |
|---|---|---|---|---|---|
| 1.6 | 1 | 0.6 | 80.4 | 50 | 31.0 |
| 3.2 | 2 | 1.2 | 88.5 | 55 | 34.1 |
| 4.8 | 3 | 1.8 | 96.5 | 60 | 37.2 |
| 6.4 | 4 | 2.4 | 104.6 | 65 | 40.3 |
| 8.0 | 5 | 3.1 | 112.6 | 70 | 43.5 |
| 9.6 | 6 | 3.7 | 120.7 | 75 | 46.6 |
| 11.2 | 7 | 4.3 | 128.7 | 80 | 49.7 |
| 12.8 | 8 | 4.9 | 136.7 | 85 | 52.8 |
| 14.4 | 9 | 5.5 | 144.8 | 90 | 55.9 |
| 16.0 | 10 | 6.2 | 152.8 | 95 | 59.0 |
| 24.1 | 15 | 9.3 | 160.9 | 100 | 62.1 |
| 32.1 | 20 | 12.4 | 241.4 | 150 | 93.2 |
| 40.2 | 25 | 15.5 | 321.8 | 200 | 124.2 |
| 48.2 | 30 | 18.6 | 482.7 | 300 | 186.4 |
| 56.3 | 35 | 21.7 | 643.7 | 400 | 248.5 |
| 64.3 | 40 | 24.8 | 804.6 | 900 | 310.6 |
| 72.4 | 45 | 27.9 | 1609.3 | 1000 | 621.3 |

*If you want to convert from miles to kilometers, read from the center column to the left (1 mile= 1.6 kilometers). When converting kilometers to miles, read from the center column to the right (1 kilometer=0.6 mile).*

## CONVERSION CHART: LITERS/U.S. GALLONS/IMP. GALLONS

| Liters | U.S. Gallons | Imp. Gallons | Liters | U.S. Gallons | Imp. Gallons |
|---|---|---|---|---|---|
| 1 | 0.26 | 0.22 | 25 | 6.61 | 5.50 |
| 2 | 0.53 | 0.44 | 30 | 7.93 | 6.60 |
| 3 | 0.79 | 0.66 | 35 | 9.25 | 7.70 |
| 4 | 1.06 | 0.88 | 40 | 10.57 | 8.80 |
| 5 | 1.32 | 1.10 | 45 | 11.89 | 9.90 |
| 10 | 2.64 | 2.20 | 50 | 13.21 | 11.00 |
| 15 | 3.96 | 3.30 | 60 | 15.85 | 13.20 |

**Parking**: In cities and many towns in Holland, you will encounter the same problems parking your car as you do at home. Some city hotels offer parking (for a fee), but many can't. Do not be cavalier in

**Danger**

**No entry**

**Closed to all vehicles in both directions**

**End Restriction**

**Speed limit (in kilometers per hour)**

**End of speed limit**

**Parking prohibited or restricted**

**Standing and parking prohibited or restricted**

**Priority over oncoming traffic**

**Oncoming traffic has priority**

**Yield**

**Priority crossing**

**Traffic on roundabouts must give way to traffic entering from the right**

**Motorway**

**Expressway: main road with dual carriageway with two-level intersections**

**Uneven Road**

**Compulsory path for cyclist and riders of mopeds**

**Cycle track, forbidden to mopeds with motor switched on**

**Tourist Information**

**Local Dutch Tourist Office**

In the lexicon of international signage, round mean restrictions or prohibitions, square provides information and triangular warnings.

your observation of parking restrictions, since in cities, especially Amsterdam and The Hague, the so-called "Denver boot" may be used on cars in short order after issuing a parking violation, and your car may be towed as little as 20 minutes thereafter. Recovery fines are steep, not to mention your considerable inconvenience and lost time. (This is a major reason to consider planning a trip without a rental car, or getting one only when exploring and staying in the countryside.) Public parking lots and garages generally are well indicated by signs showing a "**P**."

There are several parking payment methods. The most common for on-street and parking lots is to insert coins in a centrally located meter in the amount indicated for your estimated length of stay; the machine then issues a ticket, stamped with the date and time, which you should display on the dashboard *inside* your car. Sometimes the space where you are parked has a number painted on it that you must punch into the machine in order to get your ticket. If there is a limitation as to how long you can park, it will be indicated (2 hours—*2 uur*). If you park in an unattended garage, you should take a timed ticket from a machine when you enter. Although the machine may not have directions in English, the procedure is fairly straightforward, and a passing person is sure to be able to help. Last, though scarcely least: especially in cities, but a good idea everywhere, do not leave valuables in your vehicle, even in a locked trunk or glove compartment. And *never* leave anything in sight inside your car.

## *MISCELLANEOUS*

### THE ROYAL FAMILY

Holland is a constitutional monarchy, with succession to the throne hereditary in both the female and male lines. The Royal House is *Orange-Nassau*, which has historic links with the Netherlands dating back to the 16th century, and its founder, Willem I, Prince of Orange (1533-84), also known as *Father of the Fatherland*. The present head of state is **H.M. Queen Beatrix**, who was installed on April 30, 1980, after the abdication of her mother, now **Princess Juliana**, (who had succeeded to the throne in 1948 when *her* mother, **Wilhelmina**, abdicated after 50 years on the throne). Beatrix, born in 1938, is married to **Prince Claus**, a German like her father, **Prince Bernhard**. Beatrix and Claus have three sons: **Crown Prince Willem-Alexander** (b. 1967), **Johan Frisco** (b. 1968), and **Constantin** (b. 1969), thus ensuring that Holland eventually will have its first king in four generations. The monarchy is a solidly supported, well-loved institution in Holland. Its informality—somewhat less under Queen Beatrix than when her mother was monarchy—amazes the British (whose monarchy keeps its cachet by keeping at a distance). Beatrix studied at Leiden University (as did her mother) and keeps in touch with her "commoner" roommates from those days. Of the queen's three younger sisters, Princess Margriet and her businessman husband Peter van Vollenhoven are most involved in sharing with Queen Beatrix and Prince Claus the multitude of openings, dedications, and other engagements that make up the royal calendar.

## CULTURAL HINTS

For meetings and greetings in Holland, handshakes are the rule with everyone you meet. There's no separate etiquette for women or men, and it doesn't matter who extends the first hand. A person joining a group already assembled should shake hands with everyone. Handshakes also are repeated all around on departure. If relations with a Dutch acquaintance (man or woman) proceed further, handshakes are replaced with kisses on the cheek. One-time differences in kissing etiquette—one cheek in Holland, both cheeks in France, and three in Belgium—seem to have become standardized into the "European kiss": three kisses on alternating cheeks.

- If there are no empty tables at a café or casual eatery with self-seating, it is acceptable to ask those sitting at a table that has room for you if you may sit down. While it's not suggested you infringe on the others at the table, the situation can lead to pleasant exchanges.

- As in most of Europe, the story above the ground or lobby level is designated the first floor in hotels, offices, and apartment buildings.

- In Europe, calendar dates in events listings, etc., are written day/month/year: April 19, 1995, would be indicated 19/04/95. Since mix-ups in days and months could have serious consequences in matters of hotel reservations or appointments, I find it's best to deal with dates by writing out the name of the month, preceded by the numerical day: 19 April 1995.

- However pragmatic the Dutch approach to societal situations may be, it's a misconception that drugs and prostitution are legal in Holland.

- *Queuing*, the civilized practice of waiting in line until one's turn that's been refined by the British, is not much observed in Holland. For buses, trams, and even in shops, it can be everyone for one's self. But do look around in banks, bakeries, etc.—which sometimes have them in effect just during busy times—for machines from which to take a numbered ticket that places you in line for service.

# THE DUTCH CULTURAL LEGACY:
## ART AND ARCHITECTURE, MUSIC AND THE MUSE

*Rembrandt's "The Jewish Bride" is one of the 17th century Dutch masterpieces at Amsterdam's Rijksmuseum.*

## ART

Dutch artists have contributed substantially to the stores of western art and architecture, and have supplied seminal ideas in many areas of artistic endeavor. In the Netherlands (or Low Countries), geographic location—northern Europe, in contrast to Italy in the south —and the influence of and reaction to ideas introduced by various occupying foreign regimes played a hand in artistic development.

Architectural monuments, under usual circumstances, are bound to the land on which they take form. Thus, save for fire, warfare and urban updating, visitors to Holland in one era and those in the next should be able to see the same visually appealing physical and artistic landmark buildings. Paintings and other smaller fine arts works, on the other hand, are portable, and thus do not remain as dependably on deposit in the countries of their creators.

In the Netherlands, several foreign occupations, as recently as the mid-twentieth century under the Nazis, have greatly affected what art produced there still can be seen there. For example, Dutch painter **Hieronymous Bosch** was a favorite of King Phillip II, the Spanish ruler of the Netherlands (which also included Flanders— what today is Belgium). Philip had much of the mystical artist's work brought to him in Spain, where today it can be seen in Madrid's **Prado Museum**. When the Austrian Hapsburgs oversaw the Netherlands, a large number of early Flemish paintings, and a particularly impressive collection by **Pieter Breugel the Elder**, found their way to Vienna, eventually winding up on the walls of that city's **Kunsthistorisches Museum**.

Although many of the Netherlands' artists have long been recognized as masters of such merit that their works hang in galleries around the world, museums in Holland remain rich in major and representative pieces by its own most renowned artists. Some of the most significant and prolific Dutch painters, among them **Rembrandt, Van Gogh** and **Mondriaan,** are extremely well-represented on their home soil, so much so that certain of the country's museums are virtual places of pilgrimage for their art.

## FLEMISH FOUNDATIONS

The distinctive subjects and styles that we particularly associate with Dutch art from the 15th through the 17th centuries first took form in the late 14th century, in the miniature paintings created to adorn the prayer books/diaries of members of the privileged classes. Those small scenes of seasonal daily life, early *genre* works, if you will, revealed the realism, however naive, that was to become such a differentiating element in the art of northern Europe from that being created in Italy during the same period. The outstanding example is the *Très Riches Heures de Duc dû Berry,* painted between

1410–1416 by **Pol de Limbourg** (today's Limburg provinces in Holland and Belgium) and his two brothers .

The **Master of Flemalle**, today widely thought to be **Robert Campin** (1378/9–1444), the foremost painter of Tournai (then considered part of Flanders), is the creator of *The Merode Altarpiece* (1425–1428). The center panel of that triptych portrays an annunciation scene, and is one of the earliest instances in which viewers can see into a spatial world where everyday reality is represented. The Master of Flemalle did not use an aristocratic or court setting, but a Flemish burgher's house as the setting for the Annunciation, an approach that was a significant departure from the Italian Renaissance aim of representing an ideal world. While some medieval religious symbolism survived in Flemish paintings in Flanders, the desire to depict the world of everyday articles and life framed a whole new sense of **realism**. Gradually, the reverential artistic treatment once reserved solely for religious subjects was applied to all aspects of daily life. Ordinary items thus became "sanctified," and Flemish artists freed from being restricted to religious subjects in order to portray the physical world.

The work of Robert Campin (Master of Flemalle) also marks a divergence between Late Gothic northern European art and Italy's concurrent Early Renaissance in its use of oil in the paint. Previously, medieval panel painters had employed *tempera*, in which finely ground pigments were "tempered," or mixed, with diluted egg yolk. With the substitution of oil for the water-and-egg-yolk mixture, thicker layers of paints were possible. This enhanced artists' ability to render depth, rich velvety hues, and a variety of textures from thin to thick—all of which greatly increased the possibilities for portraying reality. Campin and his contemporaries are called the "fathers of modern painting" not only for their fresh visions of reality, but also for their innovative means of presenting it.

## LATE GOTHIC/NORTHERN RENAISSANCE PERIOD

**Jan van Eyck** (c.1390–1441), long credited with "inventing" oil painting, did indeed add substantial new dimensions to the effects that medium could achieve. He worked in Holland and elsewhere before settling in Flemish Bruges. Among the signed and dated pieces by Jan van Eyck is the famous Ghent Altarpiece, *The Adoration of the Mystical Lamb* (1432), which had been begun by Jan's brother Hubert. The recently restored altarpiece, widely considered the greatest monument of early Flemish painting, has been repositioned in Ghent's St. Bavo church, to aid the viewing of all 20 panels on both sides of the work. A fundamental pursued by Jan van Eyck in his painting was "atmospheric perspective," which actually is more important to our realistic perception of deep space than linear perspective, upon which the Italians placed such high priority.

A third great master of early Flemish painting was, like Campin, from Tournai: **Rogier van der Weyden** (1399–1464), sometimes referred to by the French version of his name *Rogier de la Pasture*. Whereas Jan van Eyck explored the reality made visible by light, shadow and color, Van der Weyden concerned himself more with human feeling. In his portraits, he "interprets" personality, rather than leaving the faces psychologically "neutral." By the time of his death, van der Weyden had had 30 unbroken years of artistic activity in Brussels (where he was the official town painter), and was considered the most influential European painter north of the Alps.

The technically superb works of **Hans Memling** (1435–1494)— many of which are in historic St. Jan's Hospital in Bruges, his adopted home—produced a generation later, are more idealized than Van der Weyden's. And those of **Hugo van der Goes** (1445–1482), who also painted primarily in Bruges, evoke a more emotionally intense response from the viewer.

The oldest known engravings date from about 1430, and show the influence of the major Flemish painters of the period. In the mid-15th century a technical development of surpassing importance in the history of art occured: the appearance of *printed pictures* in books. (The earliest printed books were produced in the Rhineland about 1450—a landmark event that some historians use to mark the passage from the Middle Ages to the modern era.)

Considered second only to the German Martin Schongauer, the first printmaker to gain international fame, is the **Master of the Hausbuch**, who is thought to be Dutch. His prints are intimate and spontaneous, giving the impression of a sketch. The Master of the Hausbuch scratched his designs into a copper plate with a fine steel needle, which permitted fairly free expression in a technique known as *drypoint*. Although the drypoint plates, due to their rather shallow grooves, did not yield many printings, they afforded a wide variety of atmospheric effects. The Master of the Hausbuch was a pioneer in this art form that fellow Dutchman **Rembrandt** would bring to full life a century and a half later in his etchings.

In the 16th century, the Netherlands (Low Countries) experienced the most turbulent times of any European country north of the Alps.

When the **Reformation** began, the Netherlands was a part of the far-flung empire of the Hapsburgs under Charles V (who had been born in the Netherlands), and who also was king of Spain. Protestantism quickly became powerful in the northern Netherlands (today's Holland), and attempts by the Roman Catholic rulers to suppress it led to open revolt. After a bloody struggle, Holland emerged independent and widely Protestant, and the southern Netherlands (roughly corresponding to modern-day Belgium) remained in Catholic-Spanish hands. Amazingly, the political and religious strife of the Reformation, which was particularly intense in both the northern and southern Netherlands between 1550 and 1600, did not have a devastating effect on art in Holland or Flanders.

The Reformation, which began in earnest about 1520, did place painting in northern Europe in crisis. The question arose as to whether painting could, or should, continue at all, since many Protestants objected to images of saints in churches, regarding them as a sign of popish idolatry. As early as 1526, Humanist **Erasmus** of Rotterdam wrote from Switzerland of northern Europe's artistically troubled situation. In a letter commending the German painter Hans Holbein to friends in England, Erasmus wrote: "The arts here are freezing." In fact, only one Protestant region in Europe fully survived the crisis of the Reformation in the art arena: the Netherlands.

During the 16th century, Netherlands' painters struggled—successfully—with two main issues. Even prior to the Reformation, the first had presented itself: how to assimilate the influence of Italian Renaissance art. The second issue, a direct consequence of the Reformation, was the loss in Protestant regions of painters' single best source of income: altar panels (for Roman Catholic Churches). The loss of such traditional commissions led artists to create a repertory of specialized non-religious subject matter to which the Protestant Church could raise no objections. All the secular themes that feature so prominently in Dutch and Flemish painting of the baroque era—*portraits, still life, landscape* and *genre* (scenes of everyday life)—had actually been present earlier, as ancillary elements in the works of the brothers Limbourg and van Eyck, but gradually became better defined between 1500 and 1600. Many artists began to specialize in one particular area.

The idea of specialization in art was not a new one in the Netherlands. **Hieronymus Bosch** (1474–1516), a Dutch artist who was born and worked most of his life in the North Brabant provincial town of 's Hertogenbosch (Den Bosch), filled paintings such as *The Garden of Delights* with fantastic figures and imagery. Clearly, some symbols are suggestive, some in remarkably Freudian form. Original sin seems to loom large, but Bosch's own meanings for his images are mostly unknown to us today. His strange human figures may be almost otherworldly, but there's no question of their connection with the genre tradition that reached rare heights under the genius of **Pieter Bruegel the Elder** (1525–1569). Though Bruegel had traveled to Italy, his paintings of peasant life executed in Antwerp and Brussels were thoroughly Flemish in form and content. Well-educated, a humanist, and patronized by the Hapsburg court, Bruegel chose to paint peasants, with a wealth of wit and anecdote that revealed a degree of observation that was far from simple, and served as an example for genre painters in the Netherlands for generations. Though best known for his specialized attention to peasant scenes, Bruegel's *Return of the Hunters* is one of the first in which landscape is the main subject of a painting.

## BAROQUE PERIOD

In the Roman Catholic southern Netherlands, setting of the *Counter Reformation*, **Pieter Paul Rubens** (1577–1640) was the most collected painter of his time, and the dominant figure in Flemish art during his life and well after. As a trained master painter, Rubens went in 1600 to Rome, birthplace of the baroque style, spending some seven years there. Rubens listened and learned with keen interest in Italy, but does not seemed to have joined any of the artistic "movements"—even though he was certainly influenced by the lighting of Caravaggio's work. While Rubens remained an artist in the Flemish tradition, by absorbing the Italian tradition far more thoroughly than had any previous northern painter, he played a role of unique importance in helping to make the baroque style international. His influence helped to break down the artistic barriers between southern and northern Europe.

Rubens' exuberant, optimistic style, and his skill in making his works seem intensely alive, counteracted the spiritual crisis caused by the explosion of new knowledge of the world (Copernicus' early 16th-century discovery that the earth was *not* the center of the solar system had been an unsettling one for many people). The immediacy and dazzling use of color in Rubens' paintings instilled faith and, emotionally, lifted people out of their ordinary life. Particularly in the 1620s, Rubens used his dynamic style in the design of decorative schemes for churches and palaces. While no similar artistic tradition existed in Holland (where pupils of masters were left free to develop their own individual style), Rubens maintained a robust studio with many pupils and guild-member artists who were well-trained in his style, and who would complete paintings after the master had finished making his mark. The differences in talent between Rubens' work and that of pupils who finished his pieces is most noticeable in paintings originally made as high-placed altar panels—several remain *in situ* in Antwerp—that have been removed to museums.

## 17TH-CENTURY "GOLDEN AGE"

Having achieved *de facto* independence from Spain in 1579, Holland—the seven Protestant northern provinces of the Netherlands—ushered in the 17th century ready to make the most of a period that promised unprecedented prosperity and growth. Dutch 17th-century art is unique not only for its quantity of artists who demonstrated superb craftmanship—besides the acknowledged geniuses, there were many "little masters," a non-perjorative term used only to indicate that these painters are less widely known—but for the realism with which it recorded the face of Holland and its people.

Never before 17th-century Holland had a group of artists looked at the physical world around them with such clarity and set down their observations with such fidelity. Turning away from the religious, mythological and allegorical subjects that had been the themes of the Renaissance (and remained so, to some extent, in Rubens' Flanders), the Dutch portrayed what they saw around them with great artistry but without affectation. It was no coincidence that this new emphasis on realism in art came when and where it did. The age that produced Rembrandt had reason as a guiding principle for its philosophers. One of the foremost was rationalist Rene Descartes ("I think, therefore I am"), who chose to live most of his adult life in Holland (see "The Muse").

The development of certain areas of science paralleled the development of art in Holland. The first important portrait commission that **Rembrandt van Rijn** (1606–1669) received as a trained painter was for the 1632 *Anatomy Lesson of Dr. Tulp* (in the **Mauritshuis** in The Hague). It is an unusual group portrait featuring realistic treatment of a potentially distasteful subject (a human dissection), but its success seems to show that the Dutch were ready to look at the world with realist eyes.

A scientific subject of considerable contemporary interest was optics, and the Dutch were preeminent in the field. The telescope that Galileo adapted for his research had been invented by lens grinders in the Netherlands. Light was of interest to the Dutch artistically as well as scientifically. The light reflected from their flat water-logged land lent a special atmosphere to the increasingly popular landscape paintings. Vermeer flooded his subjects with light, while Rembrandt turned the lamps low for dramatic effect. One of Rembrandt's teachers, Pieter Lastman, who had traveled to Italy and seen what Caravaggio's work conveyed through *chiaroscuro* (the interplay of light and shadow), passed his impressions on to his pupil, who began to use the device with a skill no other artist has since surpassed.

Many Dutch towns, such as Haarlem, Leiden and Delft, had artists' guilds in the 17th century that sought to solicit business for members while controlling competition from outsiders. Amsterdam, however, was an open art market, in which, for the first time in the history of Western art, traditional patronage and guild support were replaced by the interests and tastes of a buying public. The city's expanding prosperous merchant class was the most common source of commissions, but there also was brisk business at artists' own shops, art dealers, and at annual fairs and markets where ordinary citizens could afford to buy paintings. Prices varied, with artists of repute naturally fetching higher prices for their work than more obscure colleagues. The average price for an unsigned picture of a high standard cost about the equivalent of a fisherman's weekly wage. Thus, while art was comparatively expensive, it remained within reach of a large cross-section of the public.

It was a remarkably compact period during which so many outstanding Dutch artists were born—beginning with Frans Hals in 1580. For the following 75 years the world was nearly overwhelmed with the output of artistic works of genius and high talent in Holland. Sales of paintings were supported by a broad segment of society, with members of the general public—whether they could afford to or not—developing a nearly insatiable appetite for investing in pictures. Supply kept up with demand, with literally tens of thousands of paintings of a consistent, astonishingly high standard sold. A Frenchman who taught at the University of Leiden in the 17th century wrote, "There can surely be no other country in the world where there are so many, and such excellent, paintings."

For Dutch artists in the 17th century, it was usual to specialize in subject matter. (Rembrandt is one of the few who did not; although most known for his history paintings and portraits as well as etchings and drawings, he was a world of art in himself). A hierarchy in 17th-century Dutch paintings became established. Artistically, history paintings (mostly produced by Rembrandt), ranked highest, followed in descending order by portraits, genre pieces, landscapes and still lifes.

## PORTRAITS

Portraits were a plentiful source of commissions for artists in the 17th century, since such paintings were popular as a reflection of the prosperous Dutch people's pride in themselves and their achievements. Because the work was there, many artists practiced portraiture in addition to another specialty. Uniquely Dutch were the large-scale **group portraits** of guilds and civic corporations. The most creative artists used imaginative means to make such group configurations more than static records of status, with **Rembrandt's** *The Night Watch* (at the **Rijksmuseum**, Amsterdam) an outstanding example. Rembrandt's self-portraits (40 paintings, 20 drawings, 10 engravings), are an unprecedented legacy of self-examination in Western art. **Frans Hals** of Haarlem (1580–1666), one of the greatest portrait painters of the 17th or any century, considered avantgarde in his day, portrayed subjects from slightly shabby patrons of local inns to aristocratic couples posing for paired full-length engagement mementos to the famous groupings of the *Regents of Haarlem's Old Men's Almshouse* (at the **Frans Hals Museum**, Haarlem). **Vincent van Gogh**, who regarded his own work in portraiture as some of his most promising, admired Hals greatly, and wrote of him, "He tried to achieve the painting of the humanity of an entire republic by the simple means of making portraits."

**Note**: The fashion for large, stiff, starched, accordion-like lace collars evident in many a portrait of the late 16th and early 17th centuries led to a fashion for forks in Amsterdam, since the size and shape of the collars made an extension of the fingers necessary for neat eating.

## GENRE

Genre (scenes from the everyday life of ordinary people) had its roots in earlier Flemish painting, particularly that of Pieter Bruegel the Elder. Into the category, which is almost a trademark of Dutch art, falls a full range of subjects: domestic interiors and taverns, servants and skaters, wenches and willful children. **Jan Vermeer** of Delft produced only 32 small paintings in his lifetime, all finely finished studies of a domestic moment frozen in time. **Jan Steen**, one of the most highly ranked genre painters, supplemented his earnings, and his opportunity to observe people, by running an inn. Delightfully peopled skating scenes were painted by **Hendrick Avercamp** (1585–1634), who specialized in winter scenes. Genre paintings can be anecdotal or reportorial, but often are more complex than they seem, since the situations presented often are meant to also show the moral landscape of everyday living. Just in the realm of genre painters, the early 17th century in Holland produced in rapid succession **Adriaen Brouwer** (born 1605), first of the great genre painters; **Adriaen van Ostade** (1610); **Gerard Terborch** (1617); **Jan Steen** (1626); **Gabriel Metsu** (1629); **Pieter de Hooch** (1629), the most popular genre painter of his day; **Vermeer** (1632); and **Nicolaes Maes** (1634).

## LANDSCAPES

Our English word *landscape* very probably comes from the Dutch *landschap*, an indication that the Dutch virtually can be credited with "inventing" landscape painting, the art of transforming a simple homely scene into a setting of restful beauty. Dutch landscape painters sketched in nature, but composed in their studio. Gradually, they moved the horizon line lower, and let the open compositions create a unified space pervaded by a new sense of shifting light, atmosphere, and weather—the very components of the Dutch landscape that capture photographers' attention today. Landscapes in 17th-century Holland started out as the least popular form of painting, but, by the end of the century, had proven the most popular, and most numerous. **Jan van Goyen** (1596–1656) was among the Dutch landscapists who discovered the beauty of the sky for the first time in the history of art. **Jacob van Ruisdael** (1628?–1682) was Holland's most outstanding landscapist, while **Aert van der Neer** (1603–1677), who sub-specialized in twilight and nocturnal views, **Aelbert Cuyp** (1620–1691), and **Meindert Hobbema** (1638–1709) are others prominent in the period.

## STILL LIFE

Although still life painters supposedly stood on the lowest rung of the 17th-century Dutch art "ladder", still life paintings always were popular with the public. They came into being in the 16th century, carrying the residue of religious symbolism from 15th-century paintings. For all that they could be taken for pure decoration, still lifes, at once the most natural and the most artificial of art work, frequently concealed broader religious and moral ideas of the day. There's great variety in 17th-century still life subject matter, but a common characteristic is carefully arranged, well-recorded objects that almost denote "possession." Still life was a platform for Dutch deftness in realism and technical virtuosity.

**Flower still lifes** were well liked. Individual blossoms always were carefully positioned so that they didn't obscure one another. **Jan Brueghel** (1568–1625), eldest son of Pieter the Elder, was known as "Velvet Brueghel" for the texture of the rare flowers and tulips in which he specialized. **Jan van Goyen**, who also did landscapes, specialized in painting tulips (his pictures are virtual "portraits"), as well as speculating in them. It is said that the losses he incurred buying tulip bulbs during the *Tulipmania* era (see chapter "The Bulb Field Business") took him 30 years to pay/paint off. One of the most distinguished woman painters, **Rachel Ruysch** (1664–1750), who had a famed atelier, also concentrated on flower still lifes. Insects, sometimes shown devouring leaves, in addition to adding realism, can be taken to refer to the transience of life, a recurrent theme in still lifes.

**Banquet Pieces**, popular until the 1620s, were the so-called *Breakfast Pieces*, which showed the ingredients of an unpretentious Dutch meal of cheese, beer, fish, and bread on a high horizon, tilted table top. Such a painting would have been consistent with the Calvinist exhortation to moderation. The slightly later *banquet pieces* show a chaotic arrangement of half-eaten foods and overturned containers, with utensils resting unbalanced at the corner of the table. Such a scene easily could be a symbol for disharmony in life, or suggestive of the need for restraint in worldly appetites. But critics caution against a temptation to insist on symbolism in still lifes, since such a scene also could just be showing the remnants of a good party.

**Pronks** are showy still lifes of brilliant colors, rich textures, and complex compositions. They are ostentatious in their display of expensive and exotic objects: Venetian glass; lobsters and tobacco from America; rare shells from around the world. During the period from 1650 to 1675, the Dutch were the richest people in Christendom, and pronk paintings present an exhaustive account of their commercial consumption. In this era, commerce was king in Holland; Dutch merchants' home furnishings rivaled those in other countries' royal palaces. But, tucked somewhere in a pronk painting usually is some indication—perhaps a watch ticking—that points to the passage of time and the impermanence of material objects.

As the Dutch got wealthier, their lifestyle became more open to comment by the still life form known as **vanitas**, which showed little subtlety in its reference to death. The passage-of-time theme is conveyed by snuffed-out candles, hourglasses and other timepieces, rotting fruit among excessive displays of food, and elegant objects of silver and gold that warn of contamination by consumer goods. Without forcing moral judgment, the juxtaposition of objects probably were meant at least to suggest the temptations of the material world, and people's accountability to the spiritual realm.

## 19TH AND 20TH CENTURIES

Quite suddenly, the brilliance of the 17th century burned itself out. And, with the French invasion under Louis XIV in 1672–78, the entire artistic atmosphere in Holland changed. Mostly lackluster artistic overture ensued until the middle of the 19th century.

Then from Groningen, in the far north of the Netherlands, came the talented painter **Josef Israels** (1824–1911) who, after contact with the *Barbizon* group of painters in France, introduced the new "open-air" painting in The Hague. (The Barbizon painters themselves had been influenced by the 17th-century Dutch landscapists, and many had traveled from France to Holland to see their works in museums there.) Israels won esteem as a painter of Scheveningen (The Hague) fishermen, and with others founded **The Hague School**. Another notable was **J. B. Jongkind** (1819–1891), whose seascapes, filled with light and misty vapors, are reminiscent of the English painter Turner.

Painters of The Hague School returned the eyes of the Dutch to landscape. **Anton Mauve** (1838–1888) so exactly captured the effect of light and representation in his paintings that they seem almost photographic. **Hendrik Willem Mesdag** (1831–1915) was a founding member of The Hague School who also painted seascapes. The three **Maris brothers**, Jacob, Matthijs, and Willem, and **J. H. Weissenbruch** were other members. The quiet, traditional pattern of painting of The Hague School was continued into the 20th century by such painters as **G. H. Breitner** (1857–1923). A fine Hague School collection (as well as the largest Barbizon collection outside France) is displayed in the former home of H. W. Mesdag (the **Mesdag Museum,** The Hague), within walking distance of the great circular **Mesdag Panorama** scenic painting of Scheveningen.

The giant among 19th-century Dutch painters was, of course, **Vincent van Gogh** (1853–1890), a self-taught post-impressionist, whose monumental talent was just on the brink of being widely recognized when he died at the age of 37 from a self-inflicted wound in July 1890. His brother Theo supported Vincent steadfastly both financially and psychologically during the last ten years of his life when Vincent turned to art to communicate the love of humanity that he had such difficulty expressing in words (except in detailed letters to Theo, which have been preserved). Theo, who was so devastated by the death of Vincent that he lost his health, sanity, and then life all within six months of the death of his brother, had married a Dutch woman, Johanna Bonger, in April 1889, by whom he had a son they named Vincent. It is due to the efforts of Vincent van Gogh's sister-in-law Johanna and namesake nephew that so much of the artist's work (paintings, drawings, and letters with sketches) belongs to museums in Holland, principally the **Rijksmuseum Vincent van Gogh** in Amsterdam, and the **Kroller-Muller Museum** in Otterlo in the Hoge Veluwe National Park, near Arnhem.

Van Gogh's work, although much of it was realized in France, is deeply rooted in the Dutch art tradition. The first painting that Vincent considered worthy to be called one was *The Potato Eaters*, executed in Nuenen, a village in the southern Dutch province of North Brabant, where his father was a minister and where potato farming was predominant. The dark palette of earth tones harks back to the 17th century; the dark interior, lighted only indirectly, shows van Gogh's familiarity with Rembrandt's use of such effects. It is not surprising to learn that Van Gogh admired Frans Hals, when one compares the energetic quality of the two artists' brush strokes. In his five highly fruitful years of painting, Vincent explored all the aspects of Holland's great artistic traditions: *still life* (among which are wonderful irises and sunflowers); *genre* (peasants at their labors); *landscapes* (some with a low horizon and huge sky that recalls Holland); and *portraits* (in which he several times in letters to Theo expressed an interest in specializing).

Apart from his fellow countryman Rembrandt, Van Gogh scrutinized himself more searchingly through the medium of self-portraits than any other artist. Both bring the same honesty and realism to their portraits of the artists as representatives of humanity.

Although his earliest works were representational landscapes, Dutch painter **Piet Mondriaan** (1872–1944) is known as one of the chief founders of abstract art. You can see examples of the landscapes in what is the world's largest collection of Mondriaan works in The Hague's **Gemeentemuseum** (itself worth seeing, as the last work by Dutch architect H. P. Berlage, see "Architecture"). Mondriaan progressed in his paintings through Cubist works clearly influenced by Picasso and Braque until he arrived, about 1920, at the utmost austerity of a style he called *Neoplasticism*. In it, he limited himself to only the most essential use of horizontal and vertical lines and primary colors (red, yellow, blue), and non-colors (black, white, and gray). By this means he sought to achieve harmonious composition in balanced relationships. Mondriaan was a founder of the remarkably influential **De Stijl** group, which sought to exclude decoration and subjectivity from art and architecture. Other members included **Theo van Doesburg** (1883–1935), **J. P. Oud** (1890–1963), and architect **G. Rietveld** (1888–1964), one of whose houses in Utrecht can be visited. One Dutch disciple of *De Stijl*, **Willem de Kooning**, born in 1904, left Holland in 1926 to continue his creative career in the U.S.A.

The **COBRA** group (an acronym for COpenhagen, BRussels, and Amsterdam) includes founding Dutch members **Karel Appel** (born 1921) and **Constant** (born 1920). Interviewed in the group's founding year, 1948 (three years after the end of World War II), Constant said, "We have been stripped of every certainty; no faith remains but this: that we are alive and that it is part of the essence of life to manifest oneself." COBRA artists' work is characterized by spontaneity, by vivid, warm colors, and by a form and content reminiscent of children's drawing. Constant believed "a painting is not a construction of colors and lines, but an animal, a night, a scream, a human being, or all of them at once."

Appel is well represented in collections outside the Netherlands; a host of his work in Holland is in Amsterdam's **Stedelijk Museum**, one of the most influential modern art repositories in the world. Since World War II, a generous Dutch government policy towards the arts has created a lively local artistic community—as reflected in Amsterdam's well respected commercial galleries—but few figures of international stature.

## ARCHITECTURE

Julius Caesar came, saw, and conquered much of the Low Countries (which included both of what today are Holland and Belgium). He established a Roman settlement at Maastricht (in the south east corner of today's Holland) *circa* 50 B.C. Gallo-Roman remains and artifacts are located throughout the town and in Maastricht's museums.

As the Roman hold weakened during the 3rd century, Germanic-Frankish tribes began to penetrate; once the Romans departed, individualistic artistic influences of the Franks (*Rhineland* or *Rhenish*) began to have an impact on the bordering Maas (Meuse) river region. When the Frankish King Charlemagne—whom the pope had declared Emperor of the West: Denmark to Italy, and Spain to the Oder—established his court at Aachen, the move conferred increased importance on its neighbors, including Maastricht. In the territory from the Maas (Meuse) River to the east, the *Mosan* style of

**romanesque** architecture developed. Mosan architecture, in the 11th century, was, in both construction and decoration, simple, strong, and austere. An impressive example of the style's fortress-like west wall (*westwerk*) can be seen at the **Onze Lieve Vrouwekerk** in Maastricht.

The **gothic** era started more slowly and lingered longer in the Netherlands than elsewhere in Europe. Once embraced, early gothic (13th century) progressed to the more richly-detailed high gothic (14th century) and on to flamboyant gothic (15th and 16th century).

It's been suggested that prior to the second half of the 15th century, architecture in Holland hadn't taken on any specifically Dutch characteristics. But that doesn't detract from the majesty of the country's earlier *grote kerks* (great churches). **St. Jan's** at 's Hertogenbosch is considered the most important Gothic church (1336–1550) in Holland and Belgium. Utrecht's **Dom Cathedral**, one of the country's most imposing, was begun in 1254, and its detached 14th-century Cathedral Tower is, at 367 feet, the tallest in Holland. Haarlem's **St. Bavo's,** begun circa 1400, is huge enough itself not to be overshadowed by the vast size of the town's Grote Market (main square) on which it sits.

**Secular architecture** in the form of magnificently ornate municipal buildings may have been the most splendid achievement of the gothic era in Holland. The sense of independence that came with town charters and increasing commercial confidence led burghers in the Dutch Zeeland and Holland provinces to build great gothic flights of fancy—in the form of belfries, cloth halls, guild houses, and town halls—to illustrate their successes. Two of the richest examples are the *stadhuizen* (town halls) of **Middelburg** (mid-15th century), rebuilt after Nazi bombardment in 1940, and **Veere** (late-15th century). Pride and pleasure in such architectural achievements resulted in a stick-with-tradition spirit that postponed acceptance of Italian Renaissance style influence in the region.

Religious upheavals in the 16th century set in motion circumstances that shaped the long-term development of both architecture and art in Holland. The **Reformation**, which began about 1520, left men's lives and their families' fortunes in shambles if they couldn't be politic in their ecclesiastical politics. The times took a terrible toll on the artistic past, especially in Holland, where the ravagings of the *Iconoclasts* in the 1560s, furthered by the *Alteratie* of 1578—when Amsterdam, in the northern Netherlands, formally split from the

Spanish-ruled southern Netherland (today's Belgium) and officially changed from Roman Catholic to Calvinist—were responsible for the destruction of considerable church ornamentation. For example, though few pieces have survived, it is reasonable to assume that polychrome wood sculpture played a prominent part in Dutch church decoration prior to the Reformation.

By 1579 in the Dutch northern provinces, all Catholic churches were confiscated by the Protestants. Their cavernous, once ornate ecclesiastical interiors became impressive in their starkness. Altars were done away with. Their place was taken by pulpits, often beautifully carved, and placed midchurch so no church members could miss the stern Calvinist messages preached from them. The fact that strict Reform Dutch (Calvinist) Protestants didn't approve of "graven images" contributed to the fact that sculpture did not return to Holland as an art form until modern times (and then was largely secular).

An interesting architectural element arose in Dutch society early in the 17th century when certain wealthy families founded **hofjes** (almshouses) where poor women of advanced age could live independently and with dignity; housing and perhaps food, fuel, and a small allowance were included. Hofjes, small tranquil self-contained communities, provided public good while earning donors acceptable public recognition: donor names ornamented the entrances and often a richly decorated reception room, maintained as a place to conduct the business of the hofje.

Many of Holland's hofjes continue in their original role as almshouses. In some cases they are still sustained by the founding families, though most now are maintained by municipalities. Amsterdam alone has about 70 hofjes (of an estimated 200 throughout Holland), most of which are made up of a limited number of little row houses existing quietly behind a gateway, around a garden, often near the center of town. It's often possible for respectful visitors to view the central garden at many of these quaint oases. The best known is Amsterdam's **Begijnhof** (founded in 1346), which has one of the city's two remaining timber gables, this from 1460. The Begijnhof lost its religious function as a result of the *Reformation*, and it has been a municipal hofje since. It will change your ideas about "public housing."

Following the separation of the seven united northern provinces of the new Dutch Republic from the southern Netherlands (Belgium), architecture and art developed differently in the two countries. In

Holland, the 17th century took shape in buildings that showed a restrained form of *classicism*. In Belgium, the *baroque* style that had begun in Italy and was favored by the Roman Catholic church (at least partially because of its complete contrast to sober Protestant puritanism), found exuberant expression by Pieter Paul Rubens in Antwerp. After the occupation of Antwerp by the Spanish in 1585, many architects (and artists), fled north to Holland. Ghent-born **Lieven de Key,** for instance, became the municipal architect for Haarlem, building that town's **Vleeshuis** (meat hall, 1602–03), and Leiden's magnificent **Stadhuis** (1597), a last flowering of the florid 16th-century gable style. **Hendrik de Keyser** of Utrecht (1565–1621) was Holland's last major architect before a French-inspired classical influence took over. He designed Amsterdam's **Zuiderkerk** (1606–14), which was gothic with renaissance details. His **Westerkerk** (1620) made the turn toward classicism.

De Keyser was fortunate enough to be on hand during the early decades of the 1600s in Amsterdam, by which time the city's growth in prosperity and population necessitated the construction of its still-distinctive concentric canal plan. De Keyser designed a number of the canal-front town houses that continue to make Amsterdam so visually stimulating.

**Jacob van Campen** (1595–1657), from Amersfoort, placed Holland firmly under classical control with his commanding Amsterdam *Town Hall* (1648–55), today the **Royal Palace**, on the Dam at the heart of the city. An enormous structure of stone, with marvelously extensive use of marble in the interior, the building, resting on swampy land, is a terrific tribute to Amsterdam's 17th-century pile-driving people. (It rests on 13,600 piles.) Van Campen also worked in The Hague, where he designed both the 1633 *Mauritshuis* (Van Campen's pupil **Pieter Post** (1608–1669) took over the actual construction) and *Huis ten Bosch*, today used as a private family residence by Queen Beatrix.

A classical tendency continued through most of the 18th century in Holland. The French invasion of Holland in 1672 led to a fascination for all things French. **Daniel Marot** (1663–1752), a French Huguenot refugee, was employed as an architect both in Holland and at the English court by Dutch Prince William of Orange (who became the English King William III). Marot designed the interior, park and gardens for **Het Loo**. The former hunting lodge turned royal palace was restored in the late 1980s. (See "Apeldoorn" under "Central Holland.")

French influence had departed from the Dutch scene by the time **P.J.H. Cuypers** (1827–1921) arrived with his fanciful historical style. Travelers to Amsterdam are sure to see his two best-known buildings: **Centraal Station** (1885), a monumental building that at first proved too heavy for its 9000-pile foundation and partially subsided during construction, and the renowned **Rijksmuseum** (1885).

There was no looking back by the time **H.P. Berlage** (1856–1934) built the **Beurs van Berlage**, Amsterdam's *Commodity and Stock Exchange* (1899–1903). It severed every connection with historical stylistic principles and served as a turning point in Dutch architecture with its rational approach amid monumental allure. The *Beurs*, one of the largest buildings in the world at the time of its construction— the facade along the Damrak in the heart of Amsterdam is 460 feet long—has been compared to "a New York skyscraper laid on its side." The ingenious interior design, which reveals the structure of steel and construction elements of glass, brick, and stone, now serves as headquarters for the *Netherlands Philharmonic Orchestra*. A unique "glass cube" performance hall-within-a-hall, which premiered in 1990, has created great concert acoustics while leaving Berlage's architectural details intact and in view. Berlage's last building was the *Gemeetemuseum* in The Hague.

Among the outstanding European outcrops of **art deco**, a style that began in Paris in the 1910s, are two in Amsterdam. The 1918–21 *Tuschinski Theater*, on Reguliersbreestraat, between the Munt Tower and Rembrandtsplein, which opened with the silent Hollywood film *"The Old West"* accompanied by a full theater orchestra, is an exuberant center-city example. If you don't fancy a film—today there are five screens, most showing features in English with Dutch subtitles—ask the usher at the door if you can just take a look at the lobby. There's a lobby bar to lean against as you admire the marvelous wealth of detail, all in excellent repair since the theater was restored in 1984. Another art deco treasure is one of Amsterdam's great meeting places, the deliciously decorated **Café Americain** in the **American Hotel** (which couldn't be more European) located just off the Leidseplein. Your eyes will have a feast just walking into the cafe, but you'll probably want to sit and sip or sup to give yourself more time to look.

Between 1915 and 1925 a style of building flourished in Amsterdam that became known internationally as the **Amsterdam School**, notable for its whimsical and imaginative design, iron and brickwork decorative details, and many differently shaped windows. Examples are especially prevalent as working class housing in *Zuid* (southern)

*Amsterdam.* The two most acclaimed advocates of the school were **Michel de Klerk** (1884–1923) and **Pieter Kramer** (1881–1961). The Amsterdam VVV has a self-guided walking tour brochure in English on the Amsterdam School.

Holland was occupied by the Nazis during World War II, resulting in damage that changed the architectural face of the region. Nowhere is this more apparent than in Rotterdam, which suffered saturation bombing by the Nazis on May 14, 1940. The city *centrum* was bombed so heavily that you can count on one hand the salvaged buildings. Since the war, city planners have employed many innovative and acclaimed architectural means to recreate a livable center for Rotterdam. One of the most imaginative and successful is the "cube-shaped" complex of houses at tree-top level overlooking Rotterdam's lovely cafe-rimmed **Oudehaven** (old harbor). An adventurous project in low-to-moderate priced housing, each three-story sky-lighted "cube" rests on one of its points. Until you visit the model "cube" (see "Rotterdam, What To See and Do"), it's hard to imagine from the outside how floors can be flat inside.

# DECORATIVE ARTS AND TRADITIONAL CRAFTS

## *DUTCH DELFTWARE*

Many of us recall that **blue-and-white ware**—which remains remarkably popular in kitchenware from Woolworth's to delicate place settings in prestigious patterns—originally came from China: The dragons and pagodas in the enduring "willow pattern" are a helpful hint. In fact, blue-and-white porcelain existed in China for centuries before finally being brought to Europe. There it eventually was produced in and became so closely associated with the Dutch town of Delft that the two names have been nearly synonymous ever since.

It was during the early 13th-century reign of Genghis Khan, after Mongol traders returned from their travels with cobalt from Persia—where the metallic dyestuff was used to give a deep lapis lazuli color to pottery—that artisans at the imperial porcelain works in the city of Jingdezhen produced China's first blue-and-white ware. It proved easy to produce in quantity since, while other colors or polychromes required five or more firings, the blue could do with just two. Late that same 13th century, **Marco Polo** returned home to Italy from his legendary travels to China with a shipload of blue-and-white porcelain of a quality and color never before viewed in the West, and Venetians vied for the treasure.

It wasn't until the 16th century that the first Europeans, the Portuguese, started trading directly with China. Old cargo logs reveal that by midcentury, some 60,000 pieces of porcelain, mostly blue-and-white, were arriving annually in the home harbors of Europe's increasingly conspicuous merchant-class consumers. Toward the end of the 16th century, Holland, at war with Spain and Portugal, captured several cargos containing Chinese porcelain. In this way the Dutch were brought into contact with the Chinese product, which became highly esteemed. In 1602, the **Dutch East India Company** was founded in Delft, after which the Dutch dealt directly with China for its blue.

At the same time, efforts were taking place all over Europe to do away with dependence upon the China connection by developing high quality porcelain production at home. A breakthrough came in Holland in the early 17th century, when the Dutch developed *faience*, a refined form of earthenware. The establishment of an enviable blue-and-white ware product couldn't have come at a more fortunate time, with Holland's prosperous 17th-century Golden Age proving a success story for all producers of fine, fashionable objects. The pretty pieces of Delftware quickly proved prestigious. In the 16th century, potters lived all over Holland, but by the 17th century they had concentrated largely in Delft (and **Makkum**; see later). In Delft, in 1653, **De Porceleyne Fles** (the porcelain jar) factory was founded. Soon, some 30 factories in and around the town were producing the blue-and-white ware. In the 18th century, however, a slow but steady decline in demand for Delftware began, due partly to new pottery developments in Germany (*Meissen*) and England (*Wedgewood*) with which the Dutch couldn't seem to compete.

**De Porceleyne Fles** was Delft's only pottery to survive into and through most of the 19th century, but it barely managed to keep Delft's once prosperous pottery tradition alive. In 1876, the business was bought by Joost Thooft (his initials, a "J" crossed to form a "t" are still put on the bottom of all pieces) and a partner, Abel Labouchere (whose grandson Paul runs the firm today). Together, the men produced a renaissance for Delftware, and in 1919 a "Royal" warrant was conferred on the company. Today, trade in blue-and-white has come full circle: a factory in Taiwan makes Delftware look-alikes.

The delightful town of Delft is filled with shops selling bright blue-and-white ware, and, since the product's so pretty, the commercialism isn't offensive, although the profusion can cause confusion for buyers. While several firms in Holland mass produce blue-and-white ware (and put the name Delft on it), *De Porceleyne Fles* is the only one with history behind it. It employs some 150 artisans who produce a wide range of pieces from jugs and ginger jars to decorative dishes and vases for Dutch tulips. Visitors to the factory can see demonstrations by the potters and painters; the showroom with its historical and contemporary collections of pieces has the feel of an art gallery, and an inner court displays the surprising range of outdoor and building ceramic tiles. Predictably, the most popular Delftware design is the pattern with varying shades of blue applied on a white background (in production at De Porceleyne Fles since the 17th century), but the *Delft Polychrome*, with yellow, green, blue, and red-browns on a white background, has been around as long. *The Black Delft* pattern was inspired three centuries ago by Chinese lacquerware, and *Pijnacker* in red, blue and gold is based on 17th-century Japanese *Imari* porcelain. Those interested in buying Delftware should see the quality (and prices) of hand-painted De Porceleyne Fles pieces first, and then decide whether to invest in an original or purchase a pleasing but less expensive blue-and-white item elsewhere (also see "Shopping" under Delft).

**Royal Tichelaar Makkum**, still operating under watchful family eyes after ten generations, is the only company in Holland that continues to produce Dutch tiles (and other delftware pieces) following the same tin-glaze process it did when operations began in 1641. Makkum, a picturesque fishing village in the northern Dutch province of Friesland on the shores of what used to be the Zuiderzee (now the IJsselmeer), became the site of a pottery because of the presence of a very suitable chalk-rich clay in the delta area. In 1641, a farmer's son took his mother's inheritance and a new name, *Tichelaar* (brickmaker), and bought an existing pottery in Makkum. The white tin glaze coating, a technique introduced into the Netherlands at the end of the 16th century, opened new vistas to Holland's then active ceramic industry (80-odd potteries existed throughout the country between 1600 and 1800), but today Makkum is the only one to continue its use. The mysterious white tin glaze—which originated in the Near East, and was introduced by the Moors to the Spanish, who carried it to the Netherlands—still lends to Makkum ware a glow and brilliance that newer techniques are unable to rival. In addition to the tin glaze, all the blue and polychrome pieces are hand painted; artists use brushes made of hairs from the ears of the famous Frisian cows. There are guided tours and wonderful show/sales rooms. Three and a half centuries after its founding, the factory flourishes and the Tichelaars have another new name: *Royal* Tichelaar Makkum.

In addition to a broad selection of ornamental pieces, Makkum is particularly well known for its wide selection of tiles, many in the old Dutch designs. Makkum supplies customers throughout the world with tiles from old pattern books; decorators make astonishingly imaginative use of Makkum tiles, and company artists will execute special designs for particular settings or tile panels. Tichelaar is more and more called upon for the restoration of tiled surfaces in historic interiors. (See "Makkum" under "Old Zuiderzee Villages".)

# MUSIC

## THE BELL EPOCH: CENTURIES OF CARILLONS

The small country of Holland together with Belgium gave the world its largest musical instrument. Fittingly, of the nearly 600 carillons worldwide today, fully half are found in Holland and Belgium, where the instrument was developed, refined, and has flourished. Carillons, their bells hung high in historic tall towers, send their endearing, unavoidable voices across these Low Countries.

Carillons carry the flowery epithet of "singing towers," and there's a long-standing local saying: "If you can see the tower, you can hear the carillon." Even though they're the world's loudest musical instruments, rush-hour traffic in the heart of cities, where the centuries-old carillon towers often are located, can make that statement less than true today. But even when I have to strain to hear them, the short surges of unexpected music that spills from a spire to mark the hour invariably make me smile.

True carillon music doesn't come from the automatic mechanism that's programmed to send forth song on the hour, however. The instrument's real voice is released when a *beiaardier* (carillonneur) personally claims the keyboard, and the tons of bronze bells in the tower respond to a hands-on touch. When a master carillonneur takes command, even the uninitiated can hear the increased character in the chorus of the bells. Carillons in the playing care of professionals can deliver a surprising delicacy of sound and the room for variations of pace, power, and style in manual performances provide plenty of challenge. In addition to massive chords that crash like stormy surf, a carillonneur can coax notes as light as a length of Belgian lace from the instrument, skillfully balancing the voices of bells weighing as few as 16, or as many as 16,000, pounds. And the sounds created by these mighty metallic choirs encased in carved-stone towers can be as complex as they are compelling.

An important player in Dutch bell lore is the official *stadbeiaardier*, (town carillonneur), who is paid a salary to serve as keeper of the carillon. Job responsibilities, depending upon the size of the town and status of its carillon, include giving public concerts at set times, such as on market days and Saturdays. (Concerts often are offered more frequently in summer.) The lofty playing position high in a tower can make a stadbeiaardier something of a local celebrity. Included in the job description is upkeep of the instrument, programming the automated carillon for the tower clock whose tunes are changed periodically, and generally creating good vibrations as ambassador of the town bells.

Carillon players need strength to make music, for their art form is more physical than most other art forms. Few carillonneurs have elevators in their towers: hundreds of spiralling steps, up and down, must be negotiated for each practice and performance. (A number of towers are open to visitors who are up to the ascent.) For the able and interested, there's nothing like a close-up inspection of a bevy of bells, the automated mechanism, and the carillonneur's "cabin" with its keyboard. From it, there's usually a terrific view over the town and out across the invariably flat land of Holland to the far, low horizon.

To play, a carillonneur sits on a bench before a double-row of polished wood pegs, which serve as the "keys." These console pegs tug on a web of rods and wires (the transmission), which in turn operate metal clappers attached to each fixed-position bell. Weather conditions, particularly wet and cold, affect the metal of the bells and require the carillonneur to tinker and tune, and tighten the wires that connect the keyboard with the bells. As in the operation of an organ, a row of foot pedals is used to play a carillon's lower notes, the heavy metal sound of the big bass bells.

The carillonneur plays by striking down on the pegs with the side of his closed fist; protective leather pads are worn on the little fingers of each hand. The force of the blow is adjusted for the weight of the bell—the higher the musical note, the lighter and smaller the bell—and the intensity of sound required. Using both fists and feet, carillon players can work up a sweat. In warm weather, they may strip down to shorts for the workout of an hour-long concert. Nevertheless, playing the carillon shouldn't be too taxing an effort if the bells are properly balanced.

Though some Dutch carillon bells hang in secular buildings or belfries, many are found in church towers. However, even when they're located in a church, the tower and the bells frequently are the property of the civic authorities because during French rule of the Netherlands, Napoleon decreed that a town's bells should be the property of the citizens, in honor of the days when bells served as regulators of community life.

The fact that you can't ignore the bold sound of bells was, historically, the very point of their early use. In the Middle Ages, bells were central to the life of communities. Their use became widespread within the monastic system, in which they were rung to announce the offices, a series of services at set times of the day and night.

The use of bells in secular contexts developed with the rise of towns (which, in northern Europe, began in the Low Countries—Holland and Belgium). Belfries were built to contain the bells that signalled the start and end of the working day; announced the curfew hour when the town gates were shut and bolted for the night, and warned of the approach of important visitors, or of hostile troops. There were separate bells with varying pitches for the different alerting functions, so people could tell them apart.

Bruges, in Belgium, built one of the earliest town belfries (1299), to house its community bell **Magna Campana**. St. Rombout's church clock tower in Mechelen dates from 1372, and Ghent got its belfry in 1376. Further functions, and additional bells, were added as urban development proceeded; bells began to be used for summoning officials to public executions, publicizing a market or fish auction; raising the alarm in case of fire or a storm, and announcing the banishment of felons or the death of a citizen.

Eventually, time in towns needed to be measured more precisely, and bells began to mark the hours. The watchman, whose all-important job it was to ring the bell at the correct times, used a sundial as an aid and, later, a small simple clockwork alarm. This eventually led to the development of mechanisms that could chime the hours automatically, giving rise to tower clocks with bells.

Because the tolling of the hour in the tower tended to come unexpectedly, the idea arose of ringing a few notes of warning a few minutes in advance. Originally, this was always done on four small bells, which were struck with wooden mallets. From the name for that four-bell instrument, the **quadrillon**, came the name carillon. From four bells, the number had increased to a diatonic series of six or eight tuned bells by the beginning of the 16th century. A simple **automatic chime mechanism**—the first is thought to have been in Mons, Belgium—came into fairly general use soon thereafter.

The development that marked the true beginning of the carillon as an instrument, according to music historians, was when the procedure of striking the bells with a hand-held hammer was replaced with a rudimentary **clavier**, or keyboard, which enabled the manual playing of the bells. Once the keyboard had been developed, the warning flourishes sounded in advance of the striking of the hour were elaborated into actual music.

According to records, the town of **Oudenaarde**, a thriving medieval textile trading center, put the first carillon keyboard into use in the year 1510, thereby establishing the southern Netherlands (today's Belgium) as the birthplace of the carillon. Oudenaarde is in Belgium's Dutch-speaking northern Flemish area where, even today, most of the country's nearly 100 carillons are located. By 1541, Antwerp's Onze Lieve Vrouwekerk (Cathedral of Our Dear Lady) possessed a keyboard for its bells; this was followed by Ghent's acquisition of one in 1553.

Mechelen's St. Rombout got its first keyboard by 1556, but the church made carillon history in 1583 when it showed off the first instrument fitted out with **foot pedals**. Since that advancement, substantially little change has taken place in the mechanics of the carillon.

The 15th and 16th centuries were periods of prosperity for Flanders, and led to Holland's glittering 17th-century Golden Age. Successful merchants and ship owners living in Antwerp and Amsterdam, and many places in between, watched their treasure pile up, and wanted something to spend it on that would reflect well on their wealth. Cities and towns, too, became richer, and competed to proclaim their prosperity and prestige. An investment in carillons, the sweet singing bells that had already become closely connected with the character of the Netherlands, became a wonderful way to ring out rank.

The number of carillons increased, and bell foundries multiplied, as each prosperous town mounted a campaign to have more bells than its neighbors. The still-respected Dutch firm **Petit & Fritsen** was founded in 1660 in Aarle-Rixtel, on *Klokkengietersstraat* (Bell Casters Street). It was in these favorable times that the talented François Hemony (born in 1609 in Lorraine, France) and his brother Pierre discovered the secret of perfectly tuning carillon bells.

In this musical metier, François made the name **Hemony** synonymous with the finest sounding carillons ever cast. Francois and his brother came to Holland at the request of the city fathers of **Amster-**

**dam**, to build a carillon for the town hall on Dam Square (the present Royal Palace). Thereafter, they remained in Amsterdam in the main, setting up a casting foundry there and creating bells with the carefully-shaped insides that François Hemony—who took more individual care in the casting, while his brother Pierre was more inclined to cast ready-made carillons assembly-line style—knew to be the secret of their musicality. The shape or "profile" of bells, both inside and out, affect their sound. For example, today's English-cast bells (such as those of *John Taylor & Co.*) have a longer "ringing time," or resonance, than Dutch-made bells; this is because the inside lips of the latter are squared off, while English bells are cast absolutely rounded.

During the period 1646–1667, the Hemonys achieved great fame by producing approximately 50 exceptional carillons, each containing up to three octaves. Three octaves was a state-of-the-art standard in the Hemonys' day, though serious carillons today should have at least four octaves, 47 bells. (Contemporary instruments with fewer than 23 bells/two octaves are called "chimes".) When master bell-caster François Hemony died in 1667, his own bells pealed out at the funeral on Amsterdam's Dam Square for more than 3-1/2 hours.

Some 30 Hemony instruments can still be heard today, almost all in Holland or Belgium. And every town that has one—from Groningen to Gouda and Haarlem to Utrecht—proclaims the fact loud and clear. Sadly, none of the Hemonys' immediate successors turned out to be capable of producing such high quality bells.

A century later, between 1751–1786, **Andreas Josef van den Gheyn** of Louvain, near Brussels, rediscovered the tuning method, and the brilliance of his treble bells bested even the sound of the Hemonys. Unfortunately, few of the 23 instruments he made have survived and, with Van den Gheyn's death, history repeated itself and the art of tuning bells again disappeared for more than a century. This, and other factors, led to a decline in interest in carillons.

By the end of the 19th century, many a fine "singing tower" had fallen silent—either because its bells were gone, the instrument was in disrepair, or because there was no one left who could play. At the turn of this century, after some 400 years of musical history, even in Holland, the heartland of carillon culture, the elephantine instrument had become an endangered species.

Fortunately, the pre-First World War **Belle Époque** also became a **bell epoch**. Fortuitous forces combined to resurrect interest in and restoration of the carillon. Enthusiasm for the Netherlands' native instrument reemerged thanks to Belgian **Jef Denijn**. The son of a Mechelen town carillonneur, Jef, at the age of 19, was allowed to fill his father's shoes at the keyboard in St. Rombout when the senior Denijn lost his sight. The son quickly demonstrated such skills as a carillonneur that he became a star. The series of summer Monday evening carillon concerts that he initiated in the early years of this century became so popular that special trains had to be put on to transport audiences numbering as many as 20,000, who came from Brussels and Antwerp to hear him.

Under Denijn's direction in Mechelen, the carillon became a more popular instrument with the public than it ever had been before. He adapted music from folk songs to classics to current hits to suit the instrument, as well as composing an array of original works. During World War I, Denijn was a refugee in England, where he used his influence to awaken interest in carillons there. About this time in England, a clergyman from Sussex, **Arthur Simpson**, rediscovered the necessary knowledge to tune bells successfully, which resulted in the opening of two foundries in England. Many of the superb new carillons produced there found their way on board ship to the U.S. and Canada, where the taste for bells was on a rapid rise.

In the early 1920s, Jef Denijn, who had already been lifted to legendary status for his keyboard brillance, made a further contribution to the carillon culture. One of his greatest admirers was the United States ambassador to Belgium, William Gorham Rice, whose personal dream was to cover his own country with carillons and populate it with well-trained carillonneurs. Rice wrote books to kindle Americans' interest in bell music. He raised money from the Rockefeller Foundation, augmented by funds from the Belgian government and city officials, which enabled Denijn, in his 25th-anniversary year as Mechelen's *stadsbeiaardier*, to open the world's first carillon school in 1922. **Mechelen's Royal Carillon School**, flourishing today in its business of educating new generations of carillonneurs, has about 40 international students in attendance each year. Since 1953 there has been a highly respected second carillon school, **De Nederlandse Beiaardschool**, in Holland, in Amersfoort, near Utrecht (see "Amersfoort," under "Central Holland").

One among several U.S. graduates of Mechelen is Massachusetts resident **Sally Slade Warner**, who is especially glad for Ambassador Rice's dream of more carillons for America. A carillonneur for the *Phillips Academy, Andover* school and St. Stephen's church at Cohasset, Warner benefits professionally from living in the Massachusetts/Connecticut area, where there is a "clump" of nine carillons.

The state of Texas, too, has gathered a congregation of carillons, reaching a baker's dozen in number with the 1988 installation of a new instrument at *Baylor University.* Many of North America's carillons can be found at colleges, where they add notes of distinction to campuses. In Canada, the province of Ontario has the greatest concentration of carillons, with the 53-bell instrument in the *Peace Tower in Ottawa* considered by many musicians to be the country's best. The number of carillons in the U.S. today is approaching 200, the same number as in Holland. However, to put the density of Dutch carillons in perspective, one needs only to point out that Holland is but 1/258th the size of the U.S.

Despite superb technology of casting and tuning, over the years, certainly over centuries, bells do wear down and begin to ring false. Sally Slade Warner shows a carillonneur's soul when saying, "You learn to love the old carillons despite the jarring jangle of their worn-out sound." When the sound does go off a bit, the care of carillons can include grinding out some of the insides of a bell, which, to a limit, can get it to ring true again, though the procedure raises the pitch. That's where the famed bell founder and restorer **Eijsbouts** of Asten, Holland can play a part.

Although bells can lose their song through a crack or simply wear out with use, the material of the bells—metal: 80 percent brass, 20 percent in— historically has made them more vulnerable to war than to wear and weather. Over the centuries, many a commander of foreign troops occupying the flat resistanceless lands of Holland and Belgium has literally taken a town's toll by confiscating its carillon bells and melting them down and making them into mortar. Carillons sometimes survived such ignominious ends through the extraordinary efforts of citizens, who somehow managed to lower them to the ground and bury their bells.

Nazis who occupied Holland and Belgium during World War II followed suit. They shipped the contents of many "singing towers" back to munitions factories in Germany to keep their war machine going against the very towns who supplied the materials. A 1940 pre-invasion inventory of church and carillon bells in Holland listed 9000. Stock-taking just after the end of World War II showed that 4660 of these had disappeared, most presumably into the furnaces of Nazi armament factories. While the war took a heavy toll on big bells, replacement orders came quickly at its conclusion.

Notable Dutch carillons can be heard throughout Holland, in Delft, Dordrecht, and Breda. No Dutch city has more carillons than Amsterdam. From May to September its *Oudekerk* (Old Church) offers Saturday afternoon concerts on its recently restored Hemony-bell carillon. As I sit on the cobbled tree-shaded square in the shadow of the ancient church to listen, I like knowing that, on this occasion, culture has re-crossed the Atlantic: the Oude Kerk's carillonneur, **Todd Fair**, comes from the U.S. (Pennsylvania).

Carillon concerts offer superb occasions to sit, sip a drink, and savor the surroundings of the charming old centers of historic towns. The music cascades down the cobbled streets and rebounds from the fanciful facades—resounding everywhere at once. The joyful bursts from the carillon bells astonish and then delight listeners—before dispersing in the North Sea breezes.

## *ORGANS*

Another musical instrument that plays a major part in Dutch culture is the organ. Those with a keen interest consider Holland an organ paradise since, despite its small size, no other country in the world can claim such a treasure of historic instruments. As **James David Christie**, member of the *American Guild of Organists* and organ player with the *Boston Symphony Orchestra*, says, "It's hard to go to a city or even a town in Holland that doesn't have a great, a good, or, at the very least, an interesting organ, and often more than one." He notes that Holland, in particular, but Belgium and Luxembourg, too have a number of organs that date from the 17th, 18th, and 19th centuries, and some from the 16th.

Christie has the credentials to comment on organs in the area. In 1979, he won **The International Organ Competition** held in Bruges, Belgium, the first American ever to do so, and has returned since, to serve on the jury for the competition.

Many of the organs in Holland not only make memorable music, but are housed in handsome, historic cases. *The* outstanding example in both categories is the 5000-pipe, 1738 organ by Christiaen Muller in **St. Bavokerk** in the city of **Haarlem**. For a long period this organ was the largest and finest in existence, and still is one of the world's best known. The enormous bulk of St. Bavo, begun about 1400, rises from one end of Haarlem's **Grote Markt** (great market square). The church's cavernous, typically stark Calvinist interior is dominated at one end by a towering, grand and gilded arrangement of encased pipes adorned with figures: the most photographed organ in the world. From the time of its inaugural concert, the reputation of St. Bavo's organ grew rapidly, and foreign travelers sought out Haarlem to see the instrument. Visiting musicians included Handel and the then 10-year-old Mozart, who played at the keyboard for an hour. His father wrote back to Salzburg of the "excellent beautiful instrument with 68 stops, all pipes being made of tin, as wood is not lasting in this damp country."

Since 1800 the organ has been owned by the town of Haarlem, which employs official organists for the purpose of giving concerts. One of the two present town organists is **Albert de Klerk**, well-known in Holland for his keyboard compositions for both organ and carillon (St. Bavo's also has bells). A multitude of free municipal organ recitals provides opportunities to hear the remarkable instrument. Every even-numbered year, the city of Haarlem and St. Bavo host the **International Organ Festival** in July, including a Summer Academy for Organists and an Organ Improvisation Competition—all of which create additional occasions for public concerts.

Though they're off the well-toured track, James Christie classifies the organs in **Groningen**, capital city of Holland's northeastern-most province, as "two of the best in the world". They are at the **Martinikerk**, which dates back to 1480 and was most recently restored in 1979, and at the much-restored 15th-century **Akerk**. The Martinikerk also has a respected carillon of **Hemony bells**. For those with an abiding interest in organs and the time to explore, Christie has discovered that towns throughout the eastern regions of Holland, towards the German border, are especially rich in 16th- to 19th-century organs.

If you prefer to integrate organ-seeking with other sightseeing, head for **Alkmaar**, known mostly for its traditional and picturesque Friday morning cheese market. The town's Gothic late 15th- to early 16th-century **St. Laurenskerk** (Grote Kerk) holds an historic organ dating from 1643 and designed by Jacob van Campen, in a wonderful case painted by Cesar van Everdingen. A small organ in the north ambulatory dates from 1511, and it is one of the world's oldest organs still in regular use.

Amsterdam's **Oudekerk** (Old Church), the oldest in that city, dating from about 1300, has three organs, the most memorable being the early 18th-century Great Organ by Vater/Muller. This exceptionally interesting old church contains the tombstone of Dutch composer and former Oudekerk organist **Jan Sweelinck** (1562–1621). The works of Sweelinck (see "Composers") often are included in concerts given by current Oudekerk organist Gustav Le-onhardt.

Holland's finest organs are not all historic. A thoroughly modern four-manual ecclectic instrument adorns Rotterdam's **St. Lauren-skerk** (Grote Kerk). A new organ became necessary due to the heavy bomb damage sustained by the great 15th-century Gothic church in May 1940, when Nazis leveled the heart of Rotterdam in a single day.

Those interested in workings, as well as musical works, can have the inner world of organs opened up to them at Zaandam (located between Alkmaar and Amsterdam), with an appointment at the well-known Dutch firm **Dirk A. Flentrop Organ Builders**.

Exuberant sounds also spill from Holland's traditional **street organs**, with counterpoint provided by the owner as he shakes a container for coins at passersby. Street, or barrel, organs, with their winsome wooden figures and colorful individual designs, appear randomly on shopping streets and squares in Amsterdam and at markets in Dutch towns. Their exuberant player-scroll scripts invariably put a spring in one's step. (See also "National Museum for Musical Clocks to Street Organs" under "What To See and Do" in "Utrecht.")

## MAJOR MUSIC FESTIVALS

The largest and most diverse cultural event in the Netherlands is the **Holland Festival**, held annually over several weeks in June. Some performances are scheduled in other cities and towns throughout the country, but the majority of programs are presented in the Amsterdam area. Offerings include a mixture of contemporary Dutch music, drama (some productions in English), and dance (especially the acclaimed **Nederland Dance Theater** company, regarded as one of the best modern groups in Europe). Offerings each year include completely new opera and ballet productions, presented by the **Dutch National Opera** and the **Dutch National Ballet** in the **Muziektheater**, two companies' impressively state-of-the-art, yet intimate, year-round residence which opened in 1986. The Holland Festival, which also features guest performances by companies in neighboring European countries to round out its wide-ranging program, is acclaimed as one of Europe's major cultural events. (Tickets can be ordered by mail; contact your local Netherlands Board of Tourism for schedule information.)

Celebrating its 20th year in 1995, the **North Sea Jazz Festival**, held in The Hague for three days in July, has been proclaimed by an international jury of critics as the best non-American jazz festival. According to W. Royal Stokes, managing editor of *Jazztimes* magazine, the event offers "the most extensive variety of performing artists of any jazz festival in the world." Some 1000 musicians, including such stars as Brubeck, Benson, Blakey, Getz, Gillespie and Charles, perform in 14 venues for more than 50,000 attendees.

## CENTENNIAL COMPANY

**Amsterdam's Concertgebouworkest**: The caliber of Amsterdam's orchestra, which celebrated a centennial in 1988, combined with the world-renowned acoustics of its recently restored concert hall, make the Concertgebouw a must for classical music lovers. In September 1988, **Riccardo Chailly** succeeded Dutchman **Bernard Haitink** (who had held the position since 1960) as principal conductor. Guest orchestras and performers, as well as chamber music ensembles, present concerts in the Grote and Kleine halls. On Wednesdays from September-June, there are free lunch concerts at 12:30 p.m.

## COMPOSERS

When it comes to composers from Holland, there's a limited list of names of international stature. **Jan Sweelinck** (1562–1621) remains the best known of a host of Dutch composers who had their day and now only occasionally reappear at an organ concert. Sweelinck, after studying organ with his father, succeeded him as organist at Oudekerk in Amsterdam in 1580. In that post, his performances made him famous throughout Europe, and he attracted to Amsterdam many pupils and disciples. Sweelinck composed pieces for the organ and harpsichord that extended the then-limited aspects of the keyboard style, and helped develop such musical forms as the fantasia, fugue, and toccata.

Another Dutch composer whose works appear in concerts internationally is **Willem Pijper** (1894–1947), who graduated from the Utrecht Music School in 1915, and had his first symphony introduced by the *Concertgebouworkest* in Amsterdam in 1918. It, as well as other pieces of his early work, were influenced by the German post-romantic school, most of all Mahler, but Pijper soon dropped traditional techniques and structures for a more radical polytonal approach. His most important work in this manner is *Symphony No. 3*, introduced by the Concertgebouw in 1926. As well as being one of Holland's key creative music figures, Pijper was a music critic, taught at the Amsterdam Conservatory, and, from 1930 until his death, was director of the Rotterdam Conservatory.

# THE MUSE

Over the centuries Holland has produced its share of scholars, philosophers and authors who stand out for the vitality of their visions. Some of the finest early writing to come from the region appeared in times when the *lingua franca* of intellectuals was Latin. Literature in the language of the people became more common after the signing of the *Treaty of Utrecht* (1579), which set the Dutch-speaking northern provinces of the Netherlands on the political path of becoming a separate country. The use of Dutch by writers proliferated after the people in Holland received complete independence from Spain under the *Treaty of Munster* (1648). Poetry became a popular form of artistic expression during Holland's 17th-century Golden Age.

With the few exceptions documented further on, literary critics in more recent times have paid little attention to Dutch writers beyond their borders. A good deal of the international ignorance about contemporary Dutch literature can be attributed to the ongoing problem of language. Those in Holland (and Belgium's Flanders) who write in Dutch are rarely translated because the cost is too considerable for any but the most successful books. In order to reach a wider audience, some writers in Holland pen prose in English. This is not to suggest that Holland does not enjoy a lively literary tradition today. New first editions abound in Dutch, and plenty are published in *Frisian* (the centuries-old written and spoken language of Friesland, a northern province of Holland). As Dutch critic Adriaan van der Veen has commented : "A large audience is not a necessary condition for creating a masterpiece."

## DUTCH AUTHORS

**Willem** (13th century) was a Flemish poet who translated into Dutch the stories about *van den vos Reinarde* (Reynard the Fox)— which date from the 10th century, when they probably were compiled by monks. Originally told in rhyme, the stories had great appeal to the masses, as they parodied chivalry and satirized the rich, the courts, and the clergy. Reinarde, an outsider, was the small, physically weak but sly fox who repeatedly outwitted stronger characters such as the bear, the wolf, and the lion by turning their contempt for him into traps for them. The heroes and villains in the stories have a mixture of Dutch and French names, reflecting the language split in the Low Countries. The Dutch version of Reinarde is thought to have become the model for many later recountings of the stories, including William Caxton's English translation (1481). Later versions were used as vehicles for making political and social points: Goethe published one in 1794, as did Jacob Grimm (of the Brothers Grimm) in 1834. Perhaps the best-known character from the Reinarde tales is Chanticleer the Rooster.

**Thomas à Kempis** (1380–1471) wrote *The Imitation of Christ*, which is one of the Christian world's most widely read works of devotional literature. Though German by birth, Thomas was an Augustinian monk who, from the age of 27 until his death at 91, spent a life of meditation and writing in the Mt. St. Agnus monastery in Zwolle, in Holland. Thomas' religious meditation, written c. 1400, reflects the eloquence and ardor of the author, and it develops the idea that God is all, man is nothing, that from God flows the eternal truth, which man must seek. As early as 1420, it was in wide circulation; John Wesley was instrumental in having it translated into English.

**Everyman**, the best known of the English morality plays—an English edition by John Skot was in existence by the year 1521—is thought to be founded on, if not directly translated from, the Dutch *Elckerlijk*, attributed to **Petrus Dorlandus** of Diest about 1495. The 900-line play of dramatic verse describes the search by Everyman for a companion to accompany him to God's judgment seat after Death has fetched him. Everyman is eventually forsaken by all his friends except Good Deeds. With its decidedly explicit criticism of man's behavior on earth, it would have been difficult for medieval audiences to misinterpret the play, and thus performances of it met with Church approval. In the early 20th century, a professional English production of *Everyman* was revived and toured extensively in England and North America.

**Desiderius Erasmus** (1466?–1536) was born in Rotterdam and, by the time of his death, had become the most influential and admired writer and scholar of his time. Erasmus is best remembered for *The Praise of Folly*, an immediate and widely circulated success from its first publication, in secret, in 1511. He wrote the satirical masterpiece, which demonstrated a faith in reason that was remarkable for his times, in seven days, while recovering from an illness at the home of his English friend Sir Thomas More, to whom it was dedicated. In the work, Erasmus offers insight into problems of life that are universal, and he also gives an idea of the struggle that he and other early Humanists had in their effort to rid the world of the conventions of the Middle Ages.

An instrumental figure in the *Reformation*, Erasmus also was the leading figure of a small group of men of the times who, throughout Europe, sponsored the revival of learning that characterized the Renaissance. Throughout his life, Erasmus sought to help people break down the limitations of "the foolish traditions and customs" of the world in his day and "to help man find the road back to the true God and his true self." One of Erasmus' major works was a translation of the New Testament, which grew out of his conviction that true Christianity was hidden by a thick overlay of dogma and should be purified by a return to the Bible. The more than 3000 letters that Erasmus wrote which have been preserved give a matchless picture of his mind and his times.

**Note**: So admired was Erasmus for his learning, literary ability and tolerance that the Dutch town of Gouda, where he had his childhood schooling and near the monastery he was forced to enter by guardians and at which he was ordained in 1492—the Pope released him from the duties of his order in 1509—has documented an unusual fact to solidify its connection with the great humanist. A plaque outside the *St. Catherine Gasthuis* (now the City Museum) recalls in Latin that, though born in Rotterdam, Erasmus was conceived in Gouda. This intriguing detail is known, perhaps, because of contemporary curiosity surrounding the circumstances of his birth: at the time, Erasmus' mother was having an affair with a local priest named Gerard.

**Grotius** (1583–1645), or Hugo de Groot, a Dutch statesman and jurist who is regarded as the father of international law, was born in Delft of a prominent, learned family. He was educated in Holland at the University of Leyden (Leiden) in the classics, as suited a child of the Renaissance. Grotius, the Latinized version of his name by which he became known, established a law practice in The Hague. Later, he became the city clerk of Rotterdam and, as such, a member of the government of the province of Holland.

Despite that position, for his endorsement of a religious sect that was out of favor with Prince Maurits of Orange, a Calvinist, Grotius received a life sentence in 1618, and was imprisoned in the island-fortress of *Loevestein* (one of Holland's most evocative surviving castles, on the River Waal). Because of his reputation, Grotius was allowed some leniency while under lock and key: he could write, which he did on theological and judicial issues, adding to what became a voluminous lifetime output; and he was allowed a regular supply of books and visits from his wife, both of which contributed to what became one of Holland's favorite historic escape tales.

As the story goes, the books Grotius requested arrived from his home in a large chest and, when they had been read, were returned in the same chest, along with the prisoner's dirty linen. For a while, the prison guard carefully checked the contents each time the chest left the fortress, but, when it seemed that nothing was amiss, he grew lax. Thus, one day in 1621, during a well-planned visit, Grotius' wife Maria had her husband conceal himself beneath the dirty linens, Maria herself taking his place in the cell. By the usual custom, the family servant carried the chest off the prison island to the mainland, but then diverted to a prearranged point where a friend of Grotius' awaited him, with clothes to disguise him as a carpenter, whereupon Grotius fled to Antwerp. Maria, though threatened with imprisonment in her husband's stead when the escape was discovered, shortly was released—a heroine.

From Antwerp, Grotius went to Paris, where he became leader of the Remonstrants and, in 1625, published *De Jure Belli et Pacis*, regarded as the first document in the science of international law. Years later, he died in a shipwreck on the way to Sweden, while serving as Swedish ambassador to France. Grotius, buried in Delft, is well honored by his hometown. His tomb is in the 1381 Nieuwe Kerk (where the royal tombs of the House of Orange also rest) on the Markt, in the center of which stands a statue of this illustrious Dutchman.

**Rene Descartes**, though born in 1596 in France (and dying there in 1650), lived in Holland from 1628 to 1647, and visited frequently thereafter until his death. The French mathematician and philosopher, considered the father of the modern scientific method, lived much of his productive adult life in self-imposed exile in Holland, which he found to be "an almost ideal place to study." He went to great lengths to protect his privacy, dividing his time between Dutch cities and countryside.

Descartes' major works were written and published while he lived in Holland. He challenged the metaphysical view of the universe in his *Discourse on Method* (1639). Soon after, in one of the most influential works in the history of philosophy, *Principles of Philosophy* (1641), Descartes divided the universe into *spirit*, subject to reason, and *matter*, subject to mechanical laws.

Acknowledged as one of the greatest intellectuals in the history of thought, Descartes freed the 17th-century scientist from medieval dogma. He formulated the oft quoted principle *Cogito, ergo sum: I think, therefore I am*. Personally, Descartes' life was disrupted by the tensions of the times, torn between old and new ways of thinking. In

1642, Voetius, rector at the University of Utrecht, personalized his enmity for Descartes and his ideas by officially rejecting his "new philosophy" and summoning him to court regarding it. Failing to appear in court to respond to the charges, Descartes was found guilty of libel and sentenced to be burned at the stake, on a pyre—said to be personally requested by Voetius—"high enough to be seen for several miles." Descartes fled to The Hague and put himself under the protection of the French ambassador there. He left Holland for France in 1647, although he returned frequently until his death in 1650.

**Baruch Spinoza** (1632–1677), famed Dutch philosopher, was born in Amsterdam into a family of Jews that had fled religious persecution in their native Portugal. Regarded as the preeminent expounder of the doctrine of *pantheism*, Spinoza constructed one of the most complete metaphysical systems ever conceived, most notably put forth in *Ethics* (1677). At the base of his complex system is the concept that God exists only in his creations, that Nature *is* God, and that man's highest good is to seek knowledge of Nature, rather than to rely on faith. In 1656, Spinoza was excommunicated from Amsterdam's Portuguese Synagogue for "proclaiming dreadful heresy" by asserting that God had to be personified to be understood. His rationalist ideas struck contemporaries as heretical, but Spinoza anticipated much of the significant work of 20th-century Existentialists. Spinoza believed that whatever causes people to live in harmony with one another is good. In order to keep free of academic obligations, Spinoza earned his living by grinding optical lenses; glass dust in his lungs killed him at the age of 45.

Less well known on the international scene are the poets of Holland's 17th-century Golden Age, due largely to the lack of translated versions of their work. (Poetry, with its close connections to original language characteristics, is less successful in translation than other forms of literature.) **Joost van den Vondel** (1587–1679) is still considered Holland's greatest poet, honored by Amsterdam's popular Vondel Park, which has a suitably stately statue of the poet at its center. **Pieter Corneliszoon Hooft** (1581–1647) was a metaphysical romantic poet who encouraged contemporary creativity by entertaining a coterie of artists, authors, and musicians at his castle at Muiden. (See "Muiden" under "Northern Holland, Old Zuiderzee Villages.") His name adorns what is, perhaps, Amsterdam's most fashionable shopping street—*P.C. Hooftstraat*—near Vondel Park and in the attractive residential museum district of the city.

**Louis Couperus** (1863–1923) was the outstanding writer of the *Dutch Realism School* of fiction. With great talent and ability, Couperus probed the psychological impact of *colonialism* on Dutch life, writing of the decadence of upper-class life in The Hague with insight and attention to detail. Of his more than 30 novels, *Old People and the Things That Pass* (translated into English) is probably the finest.

# FOOD AND DRINK

*This cozy restaurant interior, the dining room of De Campveerse Toren in Veere, Zeeland dates from the 14th century.*

## FOOD

You'll find good food in Holland—whether you're being served at a cozy Dutch *eet café* ("eat café"), dining with distinction at a stellar-rated Amsterdam restaurant, or sampling street stand specialties such as *haring* (herring) that will redefine your ideas about "fast food." Throughout Holland, wherever and whenever food is concerned, high standards in ingredients, preparation and presentation prevail.

Travelers will discover that eateries in Holland in every category deliver value for money. The reason this appetizing situation exists has little to do with tourists and everything to do with the fact that the Dutch themselves like to eat well.

Although there are some differences in food tastes across the Netherlands, the use of fresh local seasonal fare is shared. Many kitchens pride themselves on regional dishes, some of which have become known far beyond regional boundaries.

The Dutch culinary calendar contains several other select seasons. For example, a six-week period in May and June is much anticipated for the white asparagus from Holland's Limburg province. It's known locally as "white gold," not because of export profits—supply can scarcely meet the local demand—but for its delicate taste. The traditional style of serving asparagus is with a sauce of melted butter, chopped hard-boiled egg and bits of cooked ham.

In the coastal areas of Holland, there's a focus on seafood, while Dutch rivers provide plentiful freshwater fish. Mussels (*moules/mosselen*) are such favored fare in Holland that the coming of a new season—in the months with a letter "R," beginning with September—is eagerly anticipated, especially near the North Sea estuaries where they are harvested. You'll look like a local while feasting on mussels—waiters keep bringing bowlsful until you beg off—if you hold a full shell in your left hand (if you're right-handed), and use an empty hinged-shell in your right hand as an eating utensil.

Years of encouragement from Dutch friends still have not enabled me to be able to report firsthand on the joys of eating *groene haring*, the first fresh catches of the delicacy brought in by the herring fleet in May. You're *supposed* to hold a raw young herring, slightly salted and dipped in chopped onion, by the tail and simply drop it "down the hatch," at any of thousands of street stands in Holland; you *may* eat it on a bread roll.

Despite the importance of seasons for some foods, the rich flat polderlands of Holland boast an incredible acreage of greenhouses, and the intensive agriculture undertaken in them now makes a healthy variety of hothouse vegetables available year-round. They supply not only shops and family tables in Holland and the rest of the EC, but supermarkets across the U.S. and Canada. Thanks to tender packing and air transport from Amsterdam's Schiphol, an appealing array finds its way to kitchens worldwide.

Appetizing appetizers, or starters, to a Dutch meal include small North Sea "grey" shrimp, which are eaten on buttered bread or as *tomates aux crevettes* (tomatoes stuffed with the tiny shrimp). Zeeland oysters are considered superior in these parts, as is eel, smoked or prepared as paling in *'t groen* (tender eel in a slightly sour green-colored sauce of spinach and multiple herbs).

You only have to see the herds of dairy cows decorating the Dutch countryside to be reminded of Holland's famous full-fat cheeses (which only *begin* with *Edam* and *Gouda*). Other rich milk products include milk, chocolate, butter, cream (*slagroom*, in its much-used whipped form), and yogurts (*quarks*) and *vla* (custard), some of which we never come upon across the Atlantic. If you search, you can find *magere* (skim) milk and yogurt in Dutch grocery stores.

In cosmopolitan centers like Amsterdam, continental/French cuisine is the rule at many restaurants, but typical Dutch dishes are found on many a menu. *Hutspot* is Dutch beef stew. Dutch beef filet (*biefstuk*) has a different taste, due to Holland's below-sea-level salt-water-fed grazing fields. An order for *filet américain* could come as a surprise; it's not Chicago steak, but steak tartar (raw chopped beef mixed with herbs). Holland's *ertwensoep* is a pea soup so substantial that many places serve it only in the cooler months. Rabbit is a mainstay on menus in Holland, and Dutch pork is lovely, lean, and plentiful.

Apart from the region's more formally prepared dishes, informal fare can be fun. First, there are the famed *frites*, potatoes double fried to what many feel is perfection, and served at stands throughout Holland in sturdy paper cones with a dollop of mayonnaise (which you may discover to be more compatible than catsup). Platter-size Dutch pancakes (*pannekoek*), fully a meal, come in dozens of sweet and savory varieties: cheese, apple and bacon; crystallized ginger and cheese (my favorite); with fruit, sugar and/or whipped cream. Another reasonably priced Dutch meal on a plate is an *uitsmijter*. Available at any cafe or pub, this simple but tasty and filling choice is two slices of buttered bread, each topped with a large slice of roast beef, ham, or cheese, and topped with a fried egg, the whole garnished with a bit of greenery.

Try before you buy at a cheese shop by sampling slices of *Gouda* at its different stages of age: *jonge, jonge belegen, belegen, extra belegen*, and *oude* (young to old, with mature in between). Orchards in Holland make fruit pastries popular; in Maastricht, in Holland's southeast province of Limburg, fruit *vlaai* (flans) are a specialty. Dutch *oliebollen* are solid round doughnuts sold at booths at weekly markets. *Gemberkoek* (ginger cake/bread) comes loaded with large chunks of ginger.

*Speculaas* in Holland are mixed spice and ginger cookies that can come as big as a baseball mitt at a *bakerij* (bakery) or packaged in more portable sizes. They can be found in many stores all year but burst upon the scene at Holland's Sinterklaas season from mid-November to December 5th. Then the cookies are baked in molds (popular souvenir items themselves) in the bishop figure of St. Nicholas (Sinterklaas) or other oversize figures.

In Holland adults can buy bonbons filled with Dutch liqueurs, and kids (of all ages) can spread chocolate flakes or *hagelslag* (chocolate "vermicelli") on buttered bread for breakfast. The Dutch also love licorice, sold at candy counters in dozens of shapes and sizes and, for when a sweet tooth needs a rest, in several *salty* varieties.

## INDONESIAN FOOD

Its colonial past has given the Dutch what may be Europe's most exotic "national" cuisine: certainly it's no exaggeration to say that Indonesian fare is Holland's most popular food. The 8000-island archipelago of Indonesia (the world's fifth most populous country, reaching between Asia and Australia in a 3000-mile arc) came under the influence of Holland by the 17th century, as a Dutch East India Company colony. The largest islands include Sumatra, Java (with the capital Jakarta), Borneo, and Celebes; Bali is still marketed as an idyllic tourist isle. Indonesia remained part of the Dutch Empire until given its independence after World War II in 1949. Over the centuries, many Dutch worked for companies in Indonesia; when they returned to Holland, they retained their taste for Indonesian fare. After independence, many Indonesians themselves moved to Holland. Thus, with demand created on all sides, Indonesian cuisine became ingrained in Holland.

While in North America there are take-out burger stands on every city block and, in the U.K., omnipresent fish and chip take-aways, in Holland, virtually every village has an Indonesian restaurant. The Dutch dine out frequently in their Indonesian eateries, indulging in a *rijsttafel* (rice table) feast if it's an occasion, or picking up a dinner of *loempia* (giant egg roll), *saté met pinda saus* (grilled pork or chicken on skewers with spicy peanut sauce), *kroepoek* (giant shrimp-flavored chips), or *nasi* or *bami goreng* (rice or noodles with meat and vegetables). A Dutch pils or Indonesian brand beer is a usual accompaniment.

The cuisine, even in Indonesia, has been influenced by others over the centuries. The Dutch introduced many vegetables and beer to it, the Chinese contributed various cooking methods and noodle-based dishes, and Indians shared their curry mixtures. Aside from the small side dishes of burning *sambals*, Indonesian food needn't be excessively spicy, and waiters can always counsel you—as they do so well at Amsterdam's much respected *Sama Sebo* Indonesian restaurant—on appropriate choices. Many dishes are very reasonably priced.

The *rijsttafel* is the grand dining event at Indonesian restaurants, although it is by no means a necessary one in order to sample the pleasures of this tasty cuisine. Among the many rijsttafel dishes—usually at least 16, including spices and "condiments" such as toasted coconut and peanuts—that are set up on hot plates on your table are a set selection of vegetables and meats in different sauces, some hot, some not, all to be accompanied with steamed white rice mounded in the center of your plate. As the dishes are passed, put small portions of as many as you want around, but not on, the rice. That way you can taste each dish separately. You can go back for favorites until either the serving dishes are empty, or you are full. In Amsterdam restaurants, a rijsttafel usually will be served for a minimum of two persons, with menus ranging from about Dfl. 40 to 75 per person.

About the rijsttafel Aldous Huxley once recounted this incident: "I took the trouble one day to count the number of dishes offered to me. Twenty-six actually appeared before me; but it was a busy day for the waiters, and I do not think I got all the dishes I was entitled to." Perhaps Huxley was reacting to *official* (nonrestaurant) rijsttafel ritual, in which the more important the guest, the more dishes served.

# DRINK

## *BEER*

**Heineken Brewery** is Holland's corporate giant. Combined with **Amstel**, which it owns, Heineken is the world's second largest brewing empire. (Heineken has a brewery conveniently located in Amsterdam that offers tours and free tastings; its shop sells a wide range of items imprinted with the brand-of-brew logo.) Dutch beer today consists largely of the light, thirst-quenching commercially produced *lager (pils)*. *Oude Bruin* (Old Brown), produced under both the Heineken and Amstel labels, is, in Holland, a slightly sweetened dark beer. As in the U.K., many pubs and cafes in Holland are sponsored by a single brewery and sell only that brand.

## DUTCH SPIRITS

A particularly Dutch drink is *jenever*, a kind of gin made from juniper that is downed neat. Jenever comes in *jonge* (young), clear-colored with less of a bite, and *oude* (old), with an amber tinge. It's largely a man's drink, though women sometimes take citron (lemon) or other flavored *jenever*, in liqueur-size servings.

Liqueurs are Holland's other forte on the alcoholic front: *Bols* and *De Kuyper* are the two most widely sold brands. The atmospheric old **Bols Taverne** in Amsterdam serves as a tasting place (and restaurant). A broad selection of Dutch liqueurs at favorable prices is sold at Amsterdam's Schiphol Airport's duty-free shop.

The most *fun* you'll probably ever have with a liqueur will be with *Advocaat*, now partaken of mostly by little old Dutch ladies. Still, it's a typical Dutch "drinking" experience that I recommend for its unusualness alone (and, personally, I like the taste). *Advocaat* is a thick, bright yellow alcoholic eggnog, served in a small juice-size glass with a dollop of *slagroom* (whipped cream) on top; it comes with a small spoon, since it's so thick that you actually eat rather than drink it. *Advocaat* also is popular as a topping for vanilla ice cream *(Coupe Advocaat)*.

# THE BULB FIELD
# BUSINESS

*Holland's bulb fields bloom to the far horizon.*

## THE DUTCH AFFAIR WITH FLOWERS

You won't be in Holland long before you notice the preeminent position flowers hold in Dutch life. Nowhere else will you see so many people carrying paper-cone-wrapped bouquets. There's hardly a happening in Holland that isn't an occasion for giving flowers: neighbors returning from vacation, friends finished redecorating their home, business associates closing a contract, the sun shining after a gray spell, or the gray spell itself. Long-standing custom encourages the bringing of flowers when visiting a Dutch home for a first time.

The flower-giving occasion to top all others is a birthday, the high point in the Dutch social calendar (and, often, a holiday from work). The celebrant invites friends and family to his or her home, and most guests arrive with—you guessed it—bright bouquets. But most Netherlanders need no excuse at all to buy fresh flowers, so it's easy to understand why flower stands are everywhere in Holland.

'Tis the tulip that's the most favored flower. A colorful history and the sweet scent of commercial success since its introduction into the country four centuries ago earned the tulip long-term endearment in Dutch hearts. Today, the flower serves a much more serious role than mere sentimental symbol of Holland.

Unknown to Western Europe until the 1550s—when Ogier Ghislain de Busbecq, an Austrian ambassador to Turkey, is recorded as having first seen the flower being cultivated in Constantinople—the tulip made its way to Holland after Busbecq presented several bulbs to Carolus Clusius, who was returning to Dutch soil from Austria to oversee the *Hortus Medicus* (medicinal garden) at the *University of Leiden*, which had been established in 1575. From the first beautiful blossoms that burst forth from Clusius' ugly-duckling bulbs in 1594, the Dutch have adored tulips. Fortuitously, nowhere else in Europe were better bulbs produced than in the distinctive beneath-sea-level Dutch soil—a mixture of sand and peat, with a touch of clay—found in the North and South Holland provinces.

The Dutch addiction to tulips created an amazing era in horticultural history. In the late 16th and early 17th centuries, Holland became "infected" with a disease known as **Tulipmania**. The growing wealth of Amsterdam merchants, who were just coming into their Golden Age of abundance and eager to acquire beautiful and fashionable consumer wares, quickly transformed tulip bulbs into "collectibles." Due to their desirability, tulips frequently were featured on still-life canvases created by the era's Dutch master artists. Reflecting the times, English essayist Joseph Addison wrote in *The Tatler* of his experience at a country inn in Holland. Sitting at dinner he overheard a discussion at the next table about Admiral Such-and-Such, General This, and Captain That. When he finally gave in to curiosity and inquired of his dining room neighbors who these impressive gentlemen might be, the reply was: "Gentlemen? Why, sir, these are no gentlemen. They are tulips of the very rarest and noblest sort."

The most valuable of the carefully cultivated tulips were those bulbs that, quite unexpectedly, produced unique flowers through "breaking," a sudden change in color or pattern now known to be the result of a virus. Once a tulip has "broken," all bulbs derived from it retain the variation. This process produced an active "futures" market for bulbs.

By the 1630s, not only noblemen and merchants, but seamen, servants, and chimney sweeps—anyone with access to even a small patch of soil—were growing and speculating in tulip bulbs. Demand far outran supply, and bulbs were considered as sound an investment as diamonds. Houses and businesses were mortgaged to acquire cash to buy more bulbs. Prices paid at auction for single tulip bulbs soared: to today's equivalent of $750 for an Admiral Liefkens, $1825 for a Viceroy, and $4000 for a Semper Augustus. Flemish artist Pieter Paul Rubens was recorded as lamenting that he could afford to give his wife only one bulb for her birthday.

Businessmen bartered for bulbs: a copy of one such transaction records an exchange of "two loads of wheat, four loads of rye, four fat oxen, eight fat pigs, 12 fat sheep, two hogsheads of wine, four barrels of eight-florin beer, two barrels of butter, 1000 pounds of cheese, a complete bed, a suit of clothes, and a silver beaker"—all for one bulb. Some of the excitement of this period was recreated by Alexandre Dumas in his book *The Black Tulip*, a melodramatic novel about a high-priced competition to breed a bulb that would yield a completely black flower.

Having lost their heads to the esteemed tulip, it was only a matter of time before some of the usually prudent Dutch lost their shirts as well. The "crash" of the tulip market occurred in 1637—and the government stepped in to regulate it. A moderated tulip mania has existed ever since in Holland. However, today it takes the form of a billion-guilder bulb business.

Spring's the season to catch Holland's version of the greatest show on *earth*: the bulb fields in bloom. Bulb season in Holland begins in late March—if the weather is seasonable—and continues through much of May. During the weeks of this natural beauty pageant, the colors in the country's carpet of vivid vegetation change frequently. First, crocuses in yellow, white, and purple patterns predominate. Later, giant stripes in the hyacinth hues of pink, white and blue stretch to the far, low horizon. Finally, rectangular fields blaze with the brilliance of tulips.The vast, varied patches of pure color may remind viewers of a vigorous Van Gogh canvas come to life, though when red or yellow, they also recall the primary color block of Dutch modern master Mondriaan. Of all bulbs, tulips come in the widest assortment of colors and bloom early and late, beginning in late April.

The easiest way to enjoy the bulb fields in bloom—my choice when time is limited—is to see them from the windows of the frequent trains that pass through the heart of the bulb district between Leiden and Haarlem, along the main Amsterdam-The Hague-Rotterdam line. The only drawback to the memorable 15-minute stretch between Haarlem and Leiden is a possible stiff neck from straining to catch every colorful field out both sides of the train. To let the spectacular sight sink in, on occasion, when I've had a Dutch railpass and the bulbs were in a particularly colorful stage, I've traveled back and forth through the fields between Haarlem and Leiden more than once, usually waiting no more than 10 minutes for a train in the return direction. To true fans, a tulip field in full bloom looks as lovely on a fifth view as the first!

If you have your heart set on it, you *can* tiptoe through the tulips or get close enough to the fields to smell the heady hyacinth scent. When you get a firsthand look at one, you'll notice paths between each row of flowers, so that the field workers can inspect the plants. It's terrifically tempting to head right into a field for a close-up look (and photo), but, remember, it's private property and bulbs are big business, so ask before you act. A rental car gives you the most flexibility. Helpful local tourism staff perform the Dutch rites of spring by signposting the **Bloemen** (flower) **Route** on roads throughout the bulb district. The route also wends its way through the region's tidy Dutch villages, where public and private gardens provide lots of local color.

If you choose to *doe het zelf* (do-it-yourself) by car, be forewarned that "Tulip Time" is Holland's most crowded tourist season. Coach tours come from all over Europe and Japan, and the Dutch, too, drive out to smell the flowers. Felicitously, in fact, Holland's national holiday, *Koningindag* (Queen's Day) falls on April 30, right in the middle of the bulb season. (It is the actual birthday of former Queen, now Princess, Juliana, and was kept as the date for the occasion by her daughter Queen Beatrix, perhaps because it gives the Dutch a day to see their own fields of flowers.) Roads in the region during bulb season have heavy traffic. Try to travel early and on weekdays, and have a decent map handy in case traffic on the Bloemen Route makes you want to take to different roads.

Another opportunity to get out among the bulb fields is to take local bus #50 or 51 from in front of the railway station, close to the VVV tourist offices, at either Leiden or Haarlem (going in the direction of the other), and get off when you see a bulb area you'd like to explore by foot. There are some fine bulb fields in and around the village of Hillegom. Dutch bus drivers invariably speak some English, so when disembarking, ask where the return bus stop is, and go and check the posted schedule (there are about two buses an hour) so that you can plan your return to town efficiently.

The bus route goes through the village of Lisse, considered the center of the bulb-growing district, where the relatively recently opened **Museum voor de Bloembollenstreek** (Museum of the Bulb District) is located. Exhibits in the small museum (old tools and utensils used in the cultivation of bulbs, technical geologic and soil composition descriptions, etc.) do not have English explanations and, without them, did not hold my interest. In this instance, you'll gather more memorable moments if you spend your valuable travel time with the flowers in the fields and at Keukenhof garden.

The adventurous can take to the bulb fields by hiring a bicycle (deposit and identification required) at either the Leiden or Haarlem train station, having procured a map of the bulb district at the local VVV. This area of Holland is as flat as its stereotype, so the cycling hazard isn't hills but wind blowing in from the North Sea.

Despite the 20th-century technology the Dutch bring to their bulb industry, when you get out into the scenic countryside of the bulb fields, it's easy to feel that you've wandered into one of the luminous 17th-century landscapes that amply adorn Holland's art museums. Many of the paintings' earthly elements are still present: restlessly roving cloud formations racing toward the distant low-slung horizon denoted by a church steeple, windmill, or haystacks. The terrain not planted in bulbs is made up of restful green grazing fields, speckled with cows and sectioned by slim, straight canals. Everywhere, the waterlogged land reflects the diffuse light that has defined such scenes for centuries.

Whether you get there independently—public trains and buses put you within walking distance—or join one of the local coach tours from nearby Amsterdam, **Keukenhof** garden in *Lisse* deserves a visit if you're in Holland during its season (late mid-March to late May; daily 8 a.m. to 7:30 p.m.; ☎ *02521-19034*; in season Bus #54 runs between Leiden and Keukenhof). One of the world's largest flower gardens, Keukenhof was created in 1949 by a group of prominent

Dutch bulb growers as a formal showcase for the local product, which is planted on nearly 40,000 acres radiating out from the village of Lisse. (More than 70,000 people in the area are employed in the Dutch flower industry.) While still serving its original export promotion purpose—orders can be placed on the premises for spring flowering bulbs (which are shipped for planting in the fall), and some summer-blooming bulbs (which require spring planting) can be bought on site—Keukenhof now also has become one of Holland's major tourist attractions. Some 800,000 visitors from around the world come during its annual two-month opening.

The 70-acre Keukenhof was designed as a natural lake and woodland setting, within which some six million bulbs bloom each spring. Each fall, those bulbs having been done up, another six million are planted, to provide a fresh landscape the following spring. In addition to ten miles of paths that wind among glorious outdoor plantings of inspirational mixes of color, texture and form, large greenhouses ensure that visitors can enjoy some 500 varieties of both early- and late-blooming tulips, even though these may not all be in flower at the same time in the outside beds. At both the outdoor and indoor floral exhibits, visitors can view a full range of bulbs in bloom: crocuses, narcissi, hyacinths, and tulips, as well as freesia, irises, lilies, dahlias, gladioli, and amaryllis.

Tulips usually triumph in public favor. The bulbs' personalities run from tall and majestic to frivolous and fringed. Their physical properties may be startling: flower heads the size of soup bowls or the color of midnight. Keukenhof's "black" tulip—the biggest draw—is actually a very deep purple. (Pure black does not occur in nature.) Holland has been exporting bulbs for centuries. The industry first prospered internationally in the 18th century when the landed gentry of England developed a preference for naturalistic park-like gardens with vast spreads of spring flowers. Mass-market retail sales opened up only after World War II. (In the country's Nazi-occupied war-torn winter of 1944—Holland's infamous "Hunger Winter," when 20,000 Dutch in Amsterdam alone died as a result of food shortages—the "more fortunate" residents of the bulb-growing district sometimes survived by eating bulbs, though the ever pragmatic Dutch preserved their best bulb-breeding stock.) When the war was over, the Dutch wanted to show gratitude to their allies, and gift boxes of bulbs seemed a perfect way. In the gift-giving process, new markets were created. Today, approximately 75 percent of Holland's bulb production is exported, to more than 100 countries. Major importing countries include West Germany, the United States, France,

Great Britain, Sweden and Italy. (The Vatican is an excellent customer.)

In the Dutch bulb fields, you see men knee-deep in flowers, intent on picking off the blooms. The irony of a bulb's beauty is that, once it reaches full flower, it's best to behead it. This allows the bulb to begin absorbing its stem as food for future flowering power.

Despite the beheadings, there are ample flowering bulbs for visitors to view. With up to five million bulbs blooming on every 10 acres, it takes awhile for the wooden-shoed field hands to get to them all. Furthermore, new bulbs burst into bloom every day, so the broad patterns of color keep constant. In shades from blazing to blushing, the oranges and pinks of one week are augmented the next by adjoining fields of reds, yellows, and purples.

When the stems and leaves die down, the bulbs are harvested. After being disinterred, they are dried, cleaned and graded into large bulbs (commercially salable) and small bulbs (planting stock). In storage areas for the salable bulbs, temperatures are regulated to coincide with the time of year flowering is desired (for instance, seasons are reversed in the southern hemisphere) and the climate of the country to which they are bound.

The successful hybridization of bulbs demands careful attention and patience. It takes at least six years to grow a first-flowering bulb from seed. It takes another ten years to produce 100 bulbs of the new variety, and yet another 10 before the million-bulb mark—considered the minimum to commercially market a new variety—is reached.

The Dutch mean to ensure their continued prominence in the field, and that means attention to old as well as new bulb stock. The **Hortus Bulborum** (*Zuiderkerklaan 23a, Limmen; open early April–mid-May, Mon–Sat. 10 a.m.–5 p.m., Sun. noon–5 p.m.; ☎ 02205-1529*) is a bulb research center that displays more than 1500 species, some of them the 17th- and 18th-century ancestors of today's crop. Open to the public from mid-April to mid-May, the center collects as many flowering-bulb species as possible. In addition, it seeks to preserve those species that are endangered in order to prevent the loss of valuable genetic material.

There's a festive spirit in Holland's bulb district in springtime. A symbol of the season and a means by which the color and scent of the bulb fields can be carried away and savored a little longer, are the plump garlands made of fresh-picked flower heads, on sale at roadside stands. Motorists decorate their cars with a cheerful chain, and tour buses often sport several.

Flower heads are not only recycled as garlands, but are also used on floats in annual flower parades. For more than 45 years on the last Saturday in April, the **Bulb District Flower Parade** has wound its way like a colorful ribbon from Haarlem to Noordwijk. The 20-mile procession passes through a dozen villages to the accompaniment of marching bands. The front gardens of houses along the route are also decked out in blooming bulbs. Millions of florets are imaginatively used on the parade's 20-odd floats, a closer inspection of which is possible in the preparation halls at Lisse the Friday afternoon preceding the parade and at Noordwijk the Sunday after it.

Blossoms not used for decorative purposes are gathered in baskets by field workers and brought aboard barges that are navigated along the narrow canals that crisscross the bulb fields. Piles of petals are shipped to perfume factories, where attempts are made to preserve their aromatic essence.

Although bulbs may be at their dramatic best in the fields in spring, flowers are not seasonal in Holland, thanks to hothouses and nurseries that produce cut flowers and house-and-garden plants around the calendar. Many are sold at flower and plant stalls that are part of the produce and general wares markets held weekly in many a handsome cobbled main square around Holland. Amsterdam's year-round **Floating Flower Market** on the Singel Canal is special, being open office hours Monday-Saturday. (From April through October, you'll also notice it at night when it's wonderfully outlined in white lights.) For more than 200 years, people have boarded its moored barges to browse among cut flowers, bouquets, bulbs and greenery. Business at Holland's outdoor flower markets is especially brisk in the spring when the Dutch plant their apartment window boxes, small front gardens, or tiny alloted plots in the *volkstuinen* (community gardens) at the edge of towns. The Dutch lavish as much care on these small garden spaces as gardeners elsewhere put into large estates.

Holland grows and exports more cut flowers per capita than any other country. Many are grown in the region around Aalsmeer, site of the world's largest flower auction. Annual Dutch flower transactions—as differentiated from bulb sales—come close to 10 billion guilders and account for some 70 percent of all international cut flower trade.

**Aalsmeer Flower Auction**, located not far south of Amsterdam's Schiphol Airport, is a 75-year-old outfit occupying a 47-acre building. That translates into floor space the equivalent to 100 American football fields, and is the largest commercial structure in the world. In it some 14 million cut flowers go on the block daily. Visitors are welcome Monday-Friday 7:30 a.m.–11 a.m. The earlier you arrive, the more activity; a public bus from Amsterdam can take you there. (See "Aalsmeer" under "Amsterdam" "In the Area.")

After orientation at the entrance, visitors are free to watch the colorful action from an observation gallery, and follow the proceedings by listening to multilingual audiotapes at key sites. Rarely does commerce create such beauty as that seen on the electronically controlled carts which daily bring more than five million flowers to market. From a viewer's vantage point in the Aalsmeer gallery, the multicolored flower carts create their own parade across the hall floor.

Each flower variety has its specific location. By 7 a.m., all flowers have been inspected and assigned lot numbers. As the five auction halls fill with as many as 1500 export and wholesale buyers—some 2600 are registered—the auctioneers read aloud pertinent data for each lot and start an auction clock. Ticking backward from 100 towards one, in a "reverse auction," the clock is stopped when a buyer is willing to pay the price shown.

The efficiency at Aalsmeer is legendary. Buyers can have the flowers they've purchased well-packed and at their disposal within 15 minutes of stopping the auction clock. Many lots are sent directly to Schiphol Airport for same-day delivery to flower shops in cities around the world.

# HOLLAND

*Mauritshuis Museum is located in the Binnenhof Parliament complex.*

## THE DUTCH LANDSCAPE

The word Holland comes from the Dutch *hol*, meaning "hollow," and the name Nederland means "low land or country." Thus, whether we call the country by the geographically correct *Netherlands* or *Holland*—the name of the historically most populous and prosperous province, now used by many foreigners to mean the country as a whole—by *definition*, it's impossible to discuss the Dutch landscape without the subject of water coming to the surface.

Left on its own, the western half of Holland, an area where 60 percent of the Dutch population lives, would be below the level of the North Sea and the region's rivers. Much of that area is 15 or more feet below the **NAP** (*Normaal Amsterdams Peil*), the world's reference point for sea level, much as Greenwich Mean Time in London is the planet's time standard. No one, not even the country's fundamentalist Calvinists, considers the saying "God made the world, but the Dutch made Holland" a sacrilege. It's simply fact that if it weren't for Holland's state-of-the-art hydroengineering, the Dutch goal—defined by one man as "to possess land where water wants to be"—couldn't be realized.

Holland occupies the delta formed over millennia at the mouths of Europe's major rivers, the Maas (Meuse) and the Rijn (Rhine). A line that runs roughly parallel to the North Sea coast divides the Dutch land mass into two more or less equal areas: the *low*, which is at or below sea level in the western, coastal part of the country, and the *high*, in the eastern half of the country. The highland, formed during the Pleistocene Ice Age, consists mostly of sand and gravel. The lowland, clay on which peat has formed, is younger, deposited less than 10,000 years ago. Much of the land was brought downstream by the continental rivers, and some was pushed into ridges by glaciers. The ebb and flow of the marshes and coastal dunes, a more recent element of the formation of Holland, continue uninterrupted today.

A good percentage of Holland today is anything but natural landscape. Rather, it's the result of shaping over centuries through human intervention. In this century alone, more than 550,000 acres of land were recovered from the bottom of the former *Zuiderzee* (South Sea). But not until the mid-20th century did the balance sheet in Holland's land-reclamation ledger break into the black. Watery as the land already was, by the 13th century the North Sea was breaching the coastal sand dunes. The job was finished by a great storm in the year 1287—which killed 50,000 people in Friesland—when the North Sea reached and flooded a former inland lake, creating the Zuiderzee. That flood, combined with such self-induced inundations as the 1944 Allied bombing of dikes in Zeeland during World War II to flush out the Nazis, gave 40,000 acres back to the sea.

General coastal erosion has cost the Dutch another 1.4 million acres of land in the past millenium. From the year 1000, when Friesland was completely diked—barricaded from the sea by earthen embankments—until World War II, all the land gained by the Dutch with dams, dikes, windmills and steam engines amounted to a little less than 1.3 million acres. A comparison of these two figures shows that if the Dutch didn't challenge the sea so incessantly, their country wouldn't simply stand still in size: it would shrink—and sink.

The Dutch struggle to contain the sea had begun long before Roman historian **Pliny**, in A.D. 50, described Frisian tribes in the north of the Netherlands as living on ground that "makes one doubt whether the soil belongs to the land or to the sea." He continued: "A miserable people lives there on high hills which they have thrown up with their own hands to a height which they know from experience to be that of the highest tide, and on these spots they have built their huts. They are like seafarers when the water covers the surrounding land, like shipwrecked people when the waves have retreated."

The Frisian mounds (*terpen*) were followed in time by **dikes**, which eroded all too easily on the side facing the sea, especially in storms. Once the durability of dikes had been improved, builders learned to channel the flow of water by the use of dams. Hydrocontrol took a significant step with the discovery that surrounding a parcel of land with dikes and installing a system of sluices permitted the discharge of excess water. Gradually, a network of canals that drained the land in the direction of the North Sea was created. In 1408, the first **windmill** for pumping water was built in Holland. Since the paddle wheel of a single windmill was capable only of raising water about five feet (1.5 meters), it was necessary to use several mills in a series *(molengang)* to raise it higher.

Such developments marked the turning point at which the Dutch could become offensive, rather than just defensive, in their efforts to control the relationship between the sea and their land. By about 1600, Jan Adriaanszoon had perfected the method of draining large lakes in order to create **polders** (drained land) of a size to support whole towns. In the process, he acquired the nickname *Leeghwater* ("empty of water"), which he liked so much that he legally adopted it. In a plan to drain the **Haarlemmermeer**, a huge inland lake southeast of Haarlem, Leeghwater, who had successfully drained smaller bodies of water, advocated the use of dikes and 160 windmills. Although the project caught the imagination of the Dutch public, it was deemed too ambitious by Dutch officials of the day.

In 1774, steam power was used for the first time for polder drainage. When the Haarlemmermeer eventually was drained in 1852, three steam pumping stations (one named for Leeghwater) were used. The three stations pumped nonstop for three years from 1849 to 1852, and pumped 800 million cubic meters of water. (See under "Haarlem" "In the Area: **Cruquius**," which is one of the original steam pumping stations, now a museum.) Today, Schiphol Airport is located on land lying 13 feet below sea level that once was at the bottom of the Haarlemmermeer. Having come from the lake bottom, the soil at Schiphol is so richly fertile that farmers cross the runways—with air traffic controllers' permission—to plant the fields between them.

Another Dutch milestone in hydrotechnology was marked in 1932, with the completion of the **Afsluitdijk** (enclosing dike), which sealed the Zuiderzee off from the salt water of the North Sea and formed the freshwater IJsselmeer lake. The project had been envisioned as early as 1667 by Hendrik Stevin, a mathematician, but only was realized nearly three centuries later by **Cornelius Lely**, a single-minded engineer who essentially devoted his life to taming the Zuiderzee. (The capital city of the polder province of Flevoland, which has been created from the former Zuiderzee seabed, carries his name: Lelystad.) The unfolding of the Zuiderzee Reclamation Act of 1918, which created by stages three large polders in 1942, 1957, and 1968, is recounted at the **Informatiecentrum Nieuw Land**. (Refer to "Lelystad" in chapter "Old Zuiderzee Villages and the New Polder Province.")

In Zeeland, the southern coastal region of the country, the Dutch have pioneered ways of water control on a grand scale to protect existing land. The **Delta Project**, more than three decades in its realization, was born as a result of a 1953 storm and accompanying tidal surge in Zeeland in which more than 1800 people perished. Most livestock vanished and nearly 500,000 acres were submerged under salt water. Much of the "give and take" with the sea in Zeeland ended in October 1986, when Queen Beatrix threw the switch on a massive storm control system that is a masterpiece of coastal hydro-engineering unmatched in the world. In basic terms, the project, through a series of giant fixed dams and sluices, reduced the Dutch coastline (and, thereby, its need for smaller, more vulnerable dikes) by 435 miles, making it more defendable. (Refer to the "Delta Project" under "Zeeland" in "Southern Holland.")

Such was the importance of water management in the region from the earliest days that responsibility for the dikes lay with the counts of Holland. Later, when land was individually owned, each man was required to maintain the dikes on his land; when he grew too old to do so, he was obliged to turn his holding over to a younger man who could. Today, Holland has a *Polder Authority*, a *Ministry of Water-works*, and a *Water Control Board* (one of the country's oldest democratic institutions), all functioning full force and having the final words over the country's water control. Of course, they are *only* words. As Amsterdam historian Louis van Gasteren has said: "The sea can never be conquered; the Dutch (just) made a contract with it. We said 'We appreciate you, we respect you, just don't surprise us.'"

## THE DUTCH PEOPLE

Beyond doubt, the Dutch character has been shaped by Holland's association with the sea. The Dutch never have had the luxury of being spontaneous: it is their deliberateness that keeps claim on the land captured from the sea. The Dutch sense of responsibility and resourcefulness seems almost to have come in on the tide. And their respectability and religiosity—spiritually, one needed always "to have one's house in order" since one never knew when the next "killer" flood might surge across the low-lying land—could have been blown in on a salty breeze.

The necessity of "constructing" the Dutch land by damming, diking and draining to wrest it from the sea before building could even begin dictated that individual living space be limited. Since land was so precious, qualities such as orderliness and organization, both in individuals and whole towns, were, and are, virtues in Holland. And after working so hard for the dry ground on which to build, it's no wonder the Dutch are home lovers.

The relatively small space in which the Dutch must subsist—with a population of 15.4 million, Holland is one of the most densely peopled places in the world—makes respect for personal privacy a must. However, the need to reassure the world (or at least the neighbors) of respectability leads many Dutch to forego privacy by leaving the curtains of front windows undrawn so that all can see how proper—and, perhaps, how prosperous—everything is inside.

In fact, the Dutch character is full of seeming contradictions. The people are both parsimonious and generous, tolerant and strict, cosmopolitan and parochial, pragmatic and sentimental. Though the Dutch, quite correctly, pride themselves on their individualism, the social climate of the country strongly supports a collective style of thinking and conformity to conventional behavior. Few Dutch can wholly avoid being concerned about what their neighbors think. Perhaps the essentially bourgeois approach to life in Holland is summed up in this translation of a Dutch saying: "Act normally, and you're conspicuous enough."

Holland's intimacy with the sea led to a Dutch predilection for shipping, which brought its sailors into contact with cultures around the world. Such exposure to many different ideas and attitudes contributed to making Holland a bastion of tolerance. In conjunction with the open-mindedness that they showed to the many displaced persons who have found solace in their society over the centuries, the Dutch insisted on personal and commercial freedoms in order to be competitive on the seven seas.

Dutch friends have pointed out what *they* consider a national character flaw: always having an opinion on how *other* countries conduct themselves. (For centuries, the Dutch have exhibited a strong sense of mission; the religious zeal at one time was such that one tenth of all the missionaries in the world came from Holland.) Frankly, I find it refreshing that the Dutch *know* and *care* about the rest of the world. And are committed to how well it works.

The Dutch people and their government have shown themselves more than willing to put money where their mouths are, which is a significant stance for a Dutch person, who often is stereotyped as being closefisted to the point of still having the first *dubbeltje* (10-cent piece) he ever earned. In fact, the Dutch population regularly responds with millions of guilders to relief appeals for natural and man-made disasters. The Dutch government, too, is capable of financial commitment to issues: several years ago, it "fell" over a decision not as to *whether* Holland was going to foot a huge bill for environmental clean-up—largely caused upstream on the Rhine River by other countries' factories—but *how* it was going to finance the enormous project.

Water, which both unites and divides Holland, even delineates its religions, though the lines have blurred in the recent past. While there has been a decline in membership in the Dutch Reformed Church (Calvinist) to less than half its former strength (about 28 percent of the population in 1989, it stood at 49 percent in 1900), a rise in the number of people who do not belong to any denomination (32 percent), and a stable percentage of Roman Catholics (36 percent), the uniquely Dutch sociopolitical phenomenon of "compartmentalization" still exists. It is the coexistence of separate organizations (political parties, newspapers, schools, social and sports clubs, hospitals, TV stations, old-age homes) whose members all are either Protestant Calvinist or Roman Catholic.

Very roughly, Protestants in Holland are most numerous in a broad band running across the country from the southwest (Zeeland) to the northeast (Groningen). Most Catholics live *below the Moerdijk*—the region south of the great river estuaries near Rotterdam—in the provinces of North Brabant and Limburg, where the sterner aspects of the Protestant work ethic are much less apparent. Although religious compartmentalization is ebbing somewhat in Holland, nowhere else in Europe—with the exception of Northern Ireland—is such a segmented societal infrastructure in place.

For all the stolid parts of the Dutch character, there's a decidedly sentimental side. The Dutch language is profuse in its use of the diminutive *je* (meaning "little"). It's added to everything from people's names to the most unlikely objects, and also conveys affection. A characteristic Dutch concept is captured in the word *gezellig* (pronounced rather like *HEH' zelick*), which is literally untranslatable, though "cozy" and "congenial" come closest. *Gezellig* might be used to describe the atmosphere of an historic house, a restaurant made romantic by candlelight, or a social gathering.

The Dutch manage to mix an appreciation for the traditional with modern applications. As much as any traveler in Holland, I love the country's cliches: tulips, dikes, windmills, and wooden shoes. But I'm always intrigued at how the Dutch update them. Tulips, no less loved for their beauty, are an enormously important export business; dikes have been developed by the Dutch into state-of-the-art hydrotechnology, and today's sleek wind turbines, though mere shadows of the sturdy windmills from former centuries, capture *and store* the energy of the wind. And just see what the wooden shoe has evolved to: still worn by workers in tulip fields and by farmers throughout Holland for their lightweight, water-resistant features, Dutch *klompen*—which perfectly describes the sound one makes walking in them—were used as the model for astronauts' "moonshoes."

## AN HISTORICAL PERSPECTIVE

During the Middle Ages, the area that today is the country named the Netherlands comprised a group of autonomous duchies (*Gelre* and *Brabant*) and counties (*Holland* and *Zeeland*) together with the bishopric of *Utrecht*. Under Emperor **Charles V** (1500–1558), those territories, in combination with what are present-day Belgium and Luxembourg, were known as *the Netherlands*, or Low Countries, and formed part of the great Burgundian-Hapsburg Empire. The Netherlanders had long been accustomed to outside rule and had no quarrel with Charles, who had been born in the Low Countries (in Ghent) and generally allowed them a degree of autonomy. However, when Charles V abdicated in 1556 (amid the spreading **Reformation**), ceding the Netherlands to his son Spanish **King Philip II**, a dictatorial, fanatical Roman Catholic, the stage was being set for the **Eighty Years' War**.

The harsh policies imposed by Philip inflamed Protestants, who also received antipapist preaching from the Calvinists. A wave of religious rebellion swept the Netherlands. The Spanish response to the Iconoclasm of 1566, during which Protestant crowds attacked the contents of Catholic churches, slashed paintings, broke sculptures, and burned all objects connected with the hated priesthood—and in the process destroyed a treasure house of medieval art—was brutal. In 1567, Philip II sent the **duke of Alva** and 10,000 troops to the Low Countries. Years of "*Spanish Fury*" followed, with town after town besieged, their citizens ravaged.

The first step toward establishing an independent Dutch state was taken in 1568, when a number of provinces banded together and rebelled under the leadership of **Prince Willem (the Silent) of Orange** (1533–1584), marking the beginning of the Eighty Years' War. Having survived sieges and other attacks, the **Seven United Provinces of the Northern Netherlands**—the most important of which was Holland—achieved a *de facto* independence from Spain in 1579, although the official *Peace of Munster* under the *Treaty of Westphalia* wasn't signed until 1648 (when the southern Netherlands—today's Belgium—also became free of Spanish rule).

Following the Dutch republic's tacit freedom from Spain, the 17th century proved a period of unequaled growth and prosperity in the northern Netherlands. The people of the Seven United Provinces set out to make the most of their considerable commercial skills, modest terrain, and chief natural resource—the sea. Herring provided both food and a major source of income from export, especially after the Dutch discovered the secret of preserving the fish with salt.

Amsterdam became the hub of a far-flung trading and financial empire under the **Dutch East India Company**, which traded with the Far East, and the **Dutch West India Company**, which went to the New World. It was responsible for, among other colonies, the establishment of Nieuw Nederland colony in America in 1623. The colony's settlement of **Nieuw Amsterdam** was later given by the Dutch to the British (who renamed it **New York**) in exchange for **Suriname** (on the northeast coast of South America). Dutch ships from the seven provinces sailed the seven seas, carrying spices, exotic goods, and, most important of all, grain from eastern Europe.

Dutch farmers, thus freed from growing grain themselves, turned to more specialized and profitable pursuits, such as dairy farming and the cultivation of commercial crops such as hemp and tulip bulbs, while employing massive drainage projects that increased the amount of land available for the propagation of such products. An extensive system of canals brought city and country closer together, providing farmers with ready markets and city dwellers with abundant and affordable produce. Economic opportunity and religious and political tolerance drew immigrants, many of them skilled, from Flanders and elsewhere in Europe.

The mix of these ingredients and the energy of the era created a society in Holland that was unique in 17th-century Europe: urban, mercantile, and democratic in spirit, with a strong sense of pride and achievement. Political power lay less with the princes of the *House of Orange* than with the Protestant mercantile elite, who dominated city councils, provincial assemblies, and the national *States General* at The Hague. There was a great flourishing of culture, particularly painting, to celebrate the increased prosperity. The era became known as the **Golden Age**. Eventually, there arose the need for wars—notably with England over sea-trade interests—to protect Dutch fortunes.

Though the tide eventually did turn on its fortune, the Netherlands remained independent—though the forces of French King Louis XIV invaded Holland in the 1670s—until 1795 when it became a vassal state of the French Empire. **Napoleon Bonaparte** put his brother **Louis Napoleon** in charge of the country in 1806. But Louis turned out to be too intent on being a decent ruler to the Dutch, and Bonaparte later deposed him and annexed Holland to France. French occupation came to an end in 1813, and the subsequent *Treaty of Vienna* (1815) established the **kingdom of the Netherlands**, consisting of Holland, Belgium, and Luxembourg.

The ruler of the new country was Dutch **King Willem I** (son of the last *Stadholder*, Willem V) of Orange, who also held the title Grand Duke of Luxembourg, in a union of hereditary roles that lasted until 1890. However, in the more than 250 years that by then had passed since the southern and northern Netherlands had been one, Holland and Belgium had grown too far apart in outlook to be able to exist as a single country. Following an uprising by its people in 1830, Belgium was awarded independence from Holland in 1839.

The Netherlands Constitution of 1814, which had decreed that the king govern and the ministers report to him, was revised in 1848. The updated Dutch Constitution created a constitutional monarchy with a parliamentary system, wherein ministers were accountable to an elected parliament rather than to the monarch. With the death of King Willem III in 1890, Holland's male succession ended and Willem's daughter **Wilhelmina** (1880–1962), whose mother, Queen Emma, acted as regent until Wilhelmina reached 18, became the first of what would be three successive Dutch queens. Queen Wilhelmina served Holland from 1890–1948, seeing her country through two world wars.

During the **First World War**, Holland remained neutral, though not without difficulty, since the Allies maintained the neutrality strictly, not wanting any supplies to fall into the hands of Germans by way of Holland. Holland continued to pursue a policy of strict neutrality right up until the outbreak of the **Second World War**. Then, without warning, it was ruthlessly invaded by the Nazis on May 10, 1940, and occupied for what would be a period just five days short of five years. After the Nazis leveled Rotterdam with a bombing blitzkrieg on May 14, Queen Wilhelmina and her ministers, believing that they could better serve the Dutch people from an unoccupied country, fled across the North Sea to England. Crown **Princess Juliana**, whose husband Prince Bernhard, though a German, served as a member of the Dutch forces and aide to his mother-in-law Wilhelmina in England, took up residence with her children in Canada for much of the war. When her third daughter, Margriet, was born there in 1943, the Canadians declared the birth location Dutch soil for the purpose of preserving the baby's royal succession rights.

In the fall of 1944, the southern part of Holland, near Maastricht, was the first region in the country to be freed by the Allies. But due to the disastrous results of the *Market Garden* operation around Arnhem, the northern part of the country remained under Nazi occupation during Holland's long, cold *Hunger Winter* of 1944–45. (To the present, *Liberation Day*, May 5, though not a legal holiday, is observed by the Dutch. At 8 p.m. on May 4, *Commemoration Day*, two minutes of silence is observed nationwide, after which the Queen lays a wreath at the War Monument on Dam Square in Amsterdam.)

Until the Second World War, Holland was a major colonial power, but after 1945 her colonies began seeking independence. **Indonesia** severed all its constitutional links with the Netherlands in 1949. **Suriname**, after taking over its domestic affairs in 1954, became a fully independent republic in 1975. The **Netherlands Antilles** (Aruba, Curaçao, Bonaire, St. Eustatius, Saba, and St. Maarten) in the Caribbean are equal partners with the Netherlands under a special charter.

On April 30, 1980, **Queen Juliana**—who had been queen since her mother Wilhelmina had abdicated in 1948—with a stroke of a pen in the palace on Dam Square, abdicated in favor of her eldest daughter **Beatrix**, who was installed as queen in a ceremony in Amsterdam's Nieuwe Kerk.

# RANDSTAD HOLLAND: AN INTRODUCTION

Whatever image you have of Holland, its realization is likely to be located in the Randstad. This relatively recently named geopolitical entity includes both the oldest and newest in Dutch urban planning, and encompasses Holland's two most distinctive features: **historic towns** with their tall, narrow, gabled houses, great churches, quaint canals, and museums laden with treasures from the 17th-century Golden Age, and classic **Dutch countryside** with cows, canals, windmills, tulip fields, and, above the far, low horizon, uninterrupted expanses of sky in which clouds create the mountains missing from the waterlogged, not so *terra firma*.

The **Randstad**, best translated as "city along the rim," is the urbanized region of low-lying western Holland. If you imagine **Amsterdam** at the left tip of the open end of a horseshoe, the rest of the Randstad cities fall roughly around its shape counterclockwise: **Haarlem**, **Leiden**, **The Hague**, **Delft**, **Rotterdam**, and **Gouda** with **Utrecht** at the right tip. The Randstad is 45 miles north to south and 40 miles across at its widest point, covering an area roughly the size of Greater London. As urbanized as it is, the Randstad is not a megalopolis or continual conurbation. But it is a chain of highly individual urban entities separated by green spaces. The "green fingers" of the Randstad (and the many "green thumbs" who live there) provide plenty of photogenic Dutch landscape within it.

Though the relative importance of Randstad cities has changed since the 17th century, all retain their historical significance and serve as major centers today. The term Randstad is an informal one, with no official status or administrative authority. Within the Netherlands, the term is used only to refer to the geographic region in general, and is never meant to minimize the historical, functional, and spatial distinctiveness of each of the component cities.

As early as the 16th century, Holland developed an urban consciousness that has marked Dutch culture ever since. By 1514, some 46 percent of the people in the province of Holland (the combined area of today's separate provinces of North and South Holland) lived in towns. By the 17th century, an estimated 50 percent of the Dutch population lived in towns, a statistic not reached in England until that country's 19th-century industrial revolution. The fact that the Randstad—with the exception of sand dunes wedged between Haarlem, Leiden, and The Hague and the coast—lies entirely below sea level and necessitated land reclamation to create permanent settlements, doubtless contributed to the early dense development of Dutch towns.

Close living conditions, forced upon the Dutch by their water-bounded landscape and the need to congregate in cities in order to be able to defend themselves against invaders of their flat, boggy, barrierless countryside, made early town planning a necessity in Holland. That the Dutch today prefer things well-ordered in all aspects of life, including their physical environment, is a natural result of their communal history.

In the 16th century, the towns of Leiden and Haarlem were larger than Amsterdam. A 1514 *Enqueste* (census), showed that Amsterdam had 2532 dwellings, while Haarlem had 2741 houses, Delft 2943, and Leiden 3017. Even at their 16th-century size, Holland's towns were not isolated entities, but a network of larger and smaller urban communities already reflecting the first form of the Randstad. Approximately half of the country's then nearly 300,000 inhabitants lived in towns, while the other half lived close to one. A similar situation holds true today, with 90 percent of the Dutch population considered urban.

In the 17th century, Amsterdam became Holland's largest city. It remains so, with a population today of about 750,000 in the city proper, one million in the greater metropolitan area. The inland towns of Haarlem and Leiden, and eventually even Delft, which had harbor rights on the River Schie at Delfshaven (today, one of the few remaining historic parts of Rotterdam), lost ground to Amsterdam because of shipping. Once "commerce became king" in 17th-century Holland, Amsterdam, with its connection to the North Sea through the Zuiderzee, and Rotterdam, located near the North Sea mouths of major rivers from the interior of continental Europe, became the most prominent cities due to their preeminent shipping lanes.

From a frame of reference *within* the Randstad, the rest of Holland is apt to be thought of as "the provinces." Nevertheless, while residents of the Randstad have an essentially metropolitan mentality, each thinks of himself or herself as being from Leiden, or Delft, or Rotterdam, and identifies with his or her own town's distinct character. (The differences in character of certain Randstad cities have been described this way: The Dutch make money in Rotterdam, spend it in Amsterdam, and talk about it in The Hague.) As regards new development, an all-important Randstad concept is to keep each major urban center separate from the others by "green" functions, such as agriculture and horticulture (businesses, true, but ones that provide a "green" look) plus natural preserves and recreational areas.

Within the Randstad is located a high percentage of the whole country's infrastructure: significant social-cultural institutions, the national government, commercial centers, six universities, and headquarters for the mass media and railroads. The density of population, economic wealth, and cultural and historical attractions is remarkably different in the Randstad than in the rest of the country, and thus this area is likely to claim much of your Dutch travel time.

Amsterdam

# AMSTERDAM

*Amsterdam's illuminated bridges and facades reflect in the canals.*

## GUIDELINES FOR AMSTERDAM

### SIGHTS

Amsterdam embodies Holland's **17th-century Golden Age**, when it was the richest, most cosmopolitan city in the world. (It still can compete for most cosmopolitan.) Many of its protected monument buildings (some 7000) date from that period, as does the distinct fan-shaped pattern of **concentric canals** that provide such a visual sense of place and pleasure. Amsterdam art museums hold numerous masterpieces, many by Dutch artists considered among the world's

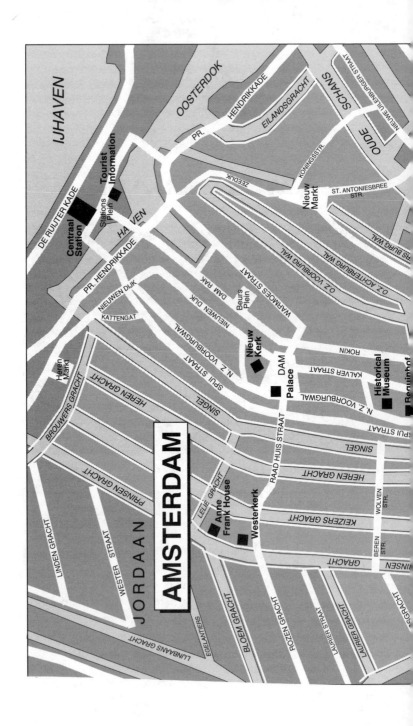

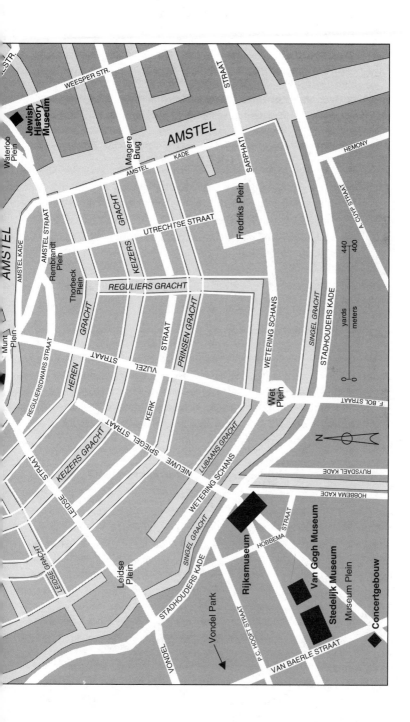

most revered painters (**Rembrandt** and **Van Gogh**, to mention the best known). The broad appeal of this fascinating city ranges from clandestine 16th-century Catholic churches to live sex shows, diamond cutters to flower markets, canalside mansion museums to cozy "brown" pub/cafes, and world-renowned performing arts companies to carillon concerts. Amsterdam turns into a veritable fantasyland at night with the tasteful, romantic illumination of canal bridges, gables and landmark facades.

## GETTING AROUND

Amsterdam is a walking city (bring comfortable shoes), not only because of its many inviting corners, but because the *Centrum* (center) is compact. A walk from Centraal Station to the Rijksmuseum (which about covers the city's tourist terrain) would take a purposeful walker 1/2 hour, though it's better to allow time for distractions along the way. The VVV (tourist information) sells a two-cassette-tape package with map for four informative **self-guided walks** (including *canal houses*, the *Jordaan* district, *old Amsterdam*, and the *Jewish quarter*); you need your own tape player. Amsterdam and its environs has a dense network of **trams**, **buses**, and **Metro**; system maps and economical, multiple-ride tickets are available from the VVV or the GVB (Amsterdam Municipal Transport), both located opposite Centraal Station. A canal cruise in one of the ubiquitous glass-enclosed boats remains one of the best introductions to the city. **Canal bikes**, with landing stages at several central city locations, provide a pedaling experience on water for up to four. **Water taxis** are expensive but **water buses** and the **museum boat** are more reasonable and provide the same picturesque mode of transportation.

## SHOPPING

Since the 17th century, when the sailing ships of the *Dutch East India Company* returned laden with exotic items for sale from the Far East, Amsterdam has been an international marketplace. Amsterdam's diamonds, Delftware, and antiques all attract shoppers' attention, as do the full complement of department stores and fashionable boutiques.

## WHERE TO STAY

Accommodations come in a wide range of standards and prices, from luxurious and very expensive to youth hostels. There's good choice in the inexpensive and moderate categories, which always include an ample Dutch breakfast.

## WHERE TO EAT

The linguistically adept Dutch claim you "can dine out in any language" in Amsterdam, and you're unlikely to come across a city where the choices of cuisine are more cosmopolitan in character. While the Dutch "kitchen" isn't overly emphasized, its traditional, fresh, well-prepared, and often hearty fare can be sampled in a number of atmospheric settings in the city. Except for the most casual eateries, a call ahead to book is a good bet, and it is essential at better restaurants.

## ENTERTAINMENT AND EVENTS

Amsterdam is home to many prestigious residential performing arts companies, which present full schedules from fall through spring. June's mostly Amsterdam-based, month-long, multifaceted **Holland Festival** is an annual cultural highlight. On the **Queen's Birthday** (April 30—a national holiday) Amsterdam becomes a crowded, city-wide, street flea market. The arrival of **Sinterklaas** by boat in mid-November is enjoyed not just by Dutch children.

## ARRIVING

Those arriving in Holland by air are likely to do so at Amsterdam's **Schiphol Airport**, which is always rated near the top of frequent international travelers' choices for best organized and operated airport in the world. Through **KLM Royal Dutch Airlines**, Holland's national carrier, and other airlines, Schiphol offers flight connections to points around the globe. A full schedule of intra European flights operates from Amsterdam's Schiphol on KLM, NLM City Hopper, and other major international carriers. Express trains leave Schiphol for central railway stations in Amsterdam, The Hague, Rotterdam and Utrecht 24 hours a day. KLM Road Transport operates shuttle bus services between Schiphol and major Amsterdam hotels (cost Dfl. 17.50). The half-hourly service is available between 6:30 a.m.–5:15 p.m.

Most **international intracity trains** from across the European continent (and from Great Britain, now that the **Euro Tunnel** under the *English Channel* is operative) serve Amsterdam, and Holland is a member of both the *Eurail Pass* and *Benelux Tourrail Pass* networks. Within Holland, Amsterdam is a major link on rail lines throughout the country. Various **ferry services** from English ports in the English Channel and on the North Sea arrive at Hoek van Holland, from which boat trains provide direct service to Amsterdam, via Rotterdam. Amsterdam is reached by Europe's principal motorways from Germany and from Belgium.

## IN THE AREA

With its excellent rail and bus connections, almost anyplace in Holland can be "in the area" for the independent traveler. A range of half- and whole-day excursions within Holland are bookable at VVVs or through individual local motorcoach tour companies. Many towns located near Amsterdam are described in detail under their own headings, but **Aalsmeer**, **Alkmaar** and **Zaanse Schans** are covered at the end of this section.

## TRAVEL TIPS

Amsterdam's hippie scenes of the '60s and '70s at the Dam Monument are no longer, though "punks" make an appearance. As in any large city, there are street people—though far fewer than in the U.S., thanks to the Dutch social welfare system. Some are homeless and some are on drugs, though hard drug use in Holland has dropped. Since these people often congregate in front of Amsterdam's *Centraal Station*, where they are particularly visible to tourists, one could get a distorted impression of the city as a whole. Violent crime in Amsterdam is rare; once you take precautions against pickpockets—see "Personal Security" under "Practical Travel Information" "Traveling in Holland"—which is an intelligent approach anywhere, including your hometown, you'll find Amsterdam refreshingly easy to enjoy. It's generally safe to stroll at night—always safest where it's well lighted and others are around—and to take public transportation anywhere.

# AMSTERDAM IN CONTEXT

While being neither the seat of government nor the residence of the queen, Amsterdam is, nevertheless, the capital and cultural center of the Netherlands. Amsterdam had its beginning when the few inhabitants along the river *Amstel* (in about the year 1270) built a dam on it that gave the town its name. A harbor, the *Damrak*, was built, and an inner harbor, the *Rokin*, was formed, around which the first trade activities developed. Not many years later (1287), a storm breached the sand dunes to the northwest, creating the *Zuiderzee* (South Sea) and giving Amsterdam easy access to the open sea. A finger of land opposite the mouth of the Amstel protected the port against the westerly winds from the North Sea, and the tidal flow of the Zuiderzee prevented the port from silting up.

As early as 1275, Amsterdam was granted exemption from paying tolls on Dutch waterways, and was thus able to focus on trade as well as fishing. In the 14th and 15th centuries, Amsterdam was the most important port between the *German Hanseatic League* towns (of which it was made a member in 1368) and Bruges, the most important trading town of the time. The favorable situation of Amsterdam led to an increase in trade with the Baltic, and the town became an important stockpiler of grain and other commodities in its many warehouses.

The cargo trade and fishing stimulated industry and attracted many laborers from the countryside. The original town along the banks of the Amstel—today that stretch of the river is the filled-in **Damrak** —expanded on each side, with the **Nieuwendijk** and **Warmoesstraat**, and then the **Oudezijds Voorburgwal** and the **Nieuwezijds Voorburgwal**. In the 15th century, the town had to be enlarged twice with new moats. The 1425 expansion added the **Singel** and the **Kloveniersburgwal**, and the town's first gateways, bastions, and brick fortress.

Amsterdam's buildings, built on soggy soil that is a thick, marshy layer of peat, at first had foundations of light timber rafts that could support a single-story wooden frame dwelling. Because of its water-confined condition, land near the center of Amsterdam was—as it remains today—at a premium. This resulted in the architectural development of narrow, deep, and increasingly tall houses. In the 15th century, bricks increasingly replaced timber as building materials due to fire risk, and in the early 16th century, thatched roofs were replaced with tiles. The resulting increase in the weight of buildings required better foundations. A system was developed in which clusters of wooden piles were driven into the ground through upper layers of mud and peat until they rested on a layer of sand. Foundation piles could go as deep as 60 feet, a fact that elicited a contemporary riddle from Rotterdam's **Erasmus** about "a city whose inhabitants live on the tops of trees like birds."

Because better foundations could also support taller houses, which meant a more intensive use of land, Amsterdam remained the same size physically from 1425 until 1580. Despite the fact that the 16th century was one of the most turbulent in the entire history of the Netherlands due to the religious and political struggles resulting from the **Reformation**, commerce there continued to expand, and Amsterdam saw a steady stream of immigrants coming for work.

It was with the fall of Antwerp to the Spanish in 1585 during the **Eighty Years' War**, however, that prosperity positively exploded in Amsterdam. Within a short period, Amsterdam took over the pre-eminence from the trading city Antwerp. Experienced Antwerp merchants and craftspeople, as well as poor Protestants and rich Portuguese Jews, sought refuge and work in Amsterdam, which gave increased impetus to trade. Amsterdam acquired a larger merchant fleet and expanded its cargo trade, especially in the Baltic, with grain from Poland and Prussia. The Dutch, through their Amsterdam port, became the "carriers" of Europe, with a fleet that was larger than those of England, Scotland, and France combined.

From 1595 onward, Amsterdam regularly embarked explorers seeking new sea routes, particularly in the East Indies, where precious spices and other exotic goods could be obtained. This led, in 1602, to the establishment of the **United East India Company**, a limited liability company that obtained a monopoly for the trade in territories east of the Cape of Good Hope in southern Africa. Soon its Dutch ships swarmed over the seven seas, and the company became the most commercially successful organization in the world, with trading posts all over the globe.

As a result of these activities, Amsterdam in the early 17th century developed into the main staple market in the world. Buffer stocks of a wide range of commodities were kept in long rows of tall, handsome warehouses that tilted slightly forward, so that bales of goods being raised by hoisting beams wouldn't brush the building. Goods —ranging from weapons to corn and spices to art treasures—could be acquired in Amsterdam. As early as 1578, Prince Willem of Orange foresaw the city's success, predicting: "Amsterdam shall prosper, and shall rise above all other cities."

With Amsterdam the busiest trading town of the 17th century, recruiting inexpensive labor became ever more important to merchants. Between 1570 and 1640, Amsterdam's population increased from 30,000 to 139,000. In 1609, a decision was reached to undertake a considerable expansion of the city, which included the construction of the **concentric pattern of canals** (*Herengracht*, *Keizersgracht*, and *Prinsengracht*) that continues to give the center city its distinctive shape. Also in 1609, the *Amsterdam Discount Bank* was established, where not only merchants, but princes, towns, and foreign governments opened accounts. Especially after the end of the *Eighty Years' War* in 1648, Amsterdam became *the* leading international center for finance, a position it maintained well into the 18th century.

With abundant commercial wealth, art, especially painting, became an accepted *and* expected form of acquisition. With an active artistic environment free of the restriction of guilds, Amsterdam was a wide-open market for painters. Among the masters most closely associated with the city were **Ferdinand Bol**, **Govert Flinck**, and **Jacob van Ruysdael**. But the grand master in Amsterdam—and widely acknowledged as such in his lifetime—was **Rembrandt**. One of Rembrandt's first major commissions came from an Amsterdam merchant family in 1631, the portrait of Nicholas Ruts (now in the *Frick Collection*, NY). By 1632, Rembrandt had moved permanently from Leiden (where he was born and raised) to Amsterdam, which offered not only a wider artistic scope, but the probability of more profitable portrait commissions. His first commission after the move was a group portrait, *The Anatomy Lesson of Professor Tulp*, for the surgeons' guild; it avoided being merely a series of posed portraits by placing guild members in a dramatic event: a human dissection in progress.

Rembrandt's Amsterdam house (see "What To See and Do") was an easy walk from the new Guildhall of the militia companies' building, the *Kloveniersdoelen* (site of the present *Doelen Karena Hotel* on *Nieuw Doelenstraat*), for which he was commissioned to paint the company of Captain Frans Banning Cocq at the precise moment that he is giving his lieutenant the command for the company to march. The work, Rembrandt's most famous and today the centerpiece of Amsterdam's Rijksmuseum, came to be called *The Night Watch*, although a major restoration in 1975 revealed it to be a daytime scene. Rembrandt never left Holland, claiming that there was enough inspiration in his native land. From Amsterdam, he took long walks out along the river Amstel finding scenery that suggested paintings and, especially, landscape drawings; he made some 250 landscape drawings and etchings in his lifetime, nearly all of them of Amsterdam and its surroundings. Having fallen on unfortunate times, Rembrandt died in Amsterdam in 1669, in relative obscurity. He is buried in the *Westerkerk* (as is his son Titus), though the specific site is unknown.

Amsterdam's prosperity lasted through the 18th century, although its port by then was surpassed in importance by London, Hamburg, and Bremen. **Napoleon Bonaparte's** army occupied Holland from 1795 through 1813. In 1806, he sent his brother **Louis Napoleon**, despite Louis' disinclination—he even pleaded that the Dutch climate would be hazardous to his health—to rule the conquered country. Living first in The Hague, then Utrecht, Louis Napoleon finally settled most happily in Amsterdam in 1806, and turned what had been the *Stadhuis* (town hall) on the *Dam* since it opened with great pomp and pageantry in 1655 into the *Royal Palace* it remains today. He filled it with a priceless collection of Empire-period furniture, most of which remained when Bonaparte, fed up with his brother's too-sympathetic approach to his subjects, recalled Louis to France in 1810. Bonaparte then solved the Dutch "situation" by absorbing the Netherlands into France.

In 1813, the French troops of Napoleon evacuated Holland, leaving it in a state of collapse, with Amsterdam's maritime glory all but gone. This stagnation lasted until 1876, when the **Noordzee Kanaal** (North Sea Canal; see also under "Haarlem" "In the Area") was cut straight through the dunes roughly along the course of **Het IJ** (pronounced "*eye*"), Amsterdam's river estuary, to give the city a short shipping connection directly to the sea. Other transportation connections also led to Amsterdam's revival. The first railway line, between it and Haarlem, was opened in 1839, and soon afterward, to Utrecht. In 1889, the grand **Centraal Station** was built on an artificial island not far from the site of Amsterdam's earliest settlement.

The upturn in the economy helped to remove one of the causes of poverty in Amsterdam, but a new *Poor Law* in 1854 was necessary. The second half of the 19th century saw an increasingly organized welfare policy implemented. Schools were seen as the gateway through which a pauper child might be transformed into a decent, upright member of society, and education soon became the city's largest item of net expense. In the early 20th century, housing, sanitation and social questions remained concerns that were actively confronted in the city.

**World War II** hit Amsterdam hard. Of the city's 86,000 Jewish residents (out of 140,000 countrywide) at the beginning of the Nazi occupation, almost all were transported outside the country to camps; fewer than 10,000 returned. The first Nazi roundup and subsequent deportation to Germany of Jews (400 men and boys) in Amsterdam took place in mid-February 1941. On February 24, workers of all religions met in Amsterdam to discuss a protest, with the dock workers in the forefront of the action. A **general work stoppage** (nothing short of treason as far as the Nazis were concerned) began the next morning. Every single factory, workshop, and office emptied; no trains, garbage or mail trucks ran, and Amsterdam fell as silent as a city can. By afternoon, the strike had spread to a 15-mile radius around Amsterdam. In response, Nazi troops were sent out in Amsterdam to arrest or shoot strikers, and within a few days they succeeded in suppressing the strike. This Amsterdam action was the single instance of broad-based support for the Jews against their oppressors in occupied Europe during the war. When the war was over, Queen Wilhelmina paid a lasting tribute to the Amsterdammers' stand by adding the words "Heroic, Resolute, Merciful" to the Amsterdam city coat of arms. Another lasting tribute to the resistence of the Amsterdammers is on the **Jonas Daniel Meijerplein**, near the site of the Jewish deportations during the war, and across from the **Jewish Historical Museum** (see "What to See and Do"): the moving, sculptured figure of *The Dock Worker* by Mari Andriessen.

Although the southern part of the Netherlands had been liberated from the Nazis by then, during the winter of 1944–45, Amsterdam and the rest of northern Holland suffered continued occupation. The period is remembered as the **Hunger Winter**. As well as there being no food, there was no fuel, electricity, or transport. Reportedly highly untasty tulips were dug up, mashed, and made into soup. Some 20,000 died of the cold and hunger in Amsterdam alone. Their bodies piled up at the *Zuiderkerk* (South Church) because it was impossible to bury the dead, with no wood for coffins and none with the strength to dig graves.

The years following the war were spent in a long process of recovery and rebuilding. Numerous urban and industrial projects were undertaken in Amsterdam, with much of the development taking place in the southeast section of the city. The plan for reclamation of land from the IJsselmeer progressed with the *Flevoland* polder province, with the *Almere* complex of cities becoming brand new "bedroom communities" to Amsterdam. Fortunately, unlike cities such as The Hague and Utrecht, Amsterdam planners avoided the process referred to by the Dutch as *cityvorming* (the building of new exclusively commercial complexes or "malls" in the *centrum*), keeping the city center instead to the traditional mixed-function urban concept. After 1960, activity in Amsterdam's harbor—which currently handles about 27 million tons annually, making it Europe's fourth busiest harbor—increasingly moved west, as a result of which the town and harbor became separated. Present town planning by the Amsterdam City Council is creating offices, museums, hotels, and housing along **Het IJ** estuary (behind the *Centraal Station*) in order to stop further migration of the harbor from the city center.

Since the 16th century, Amsterdam, as well as being a strikingly beautiful and successful commercial center for Holland, has played another important role in Dutch society, one well put into words by William Z. Shetter in his book *The Netherlands in Perspective*. (See "Random Readings on Holland".) He writes, "Amsterdam is called a *lastige stad*, a term that is difficult to translate, because although *lastig* means something like 'bothersome,' the phrase is used in a way that emphasizes the city's vital role in being on the progressive, and even radical, cutting edge, however uncomfortable that may be."

## GUIDEPOSTS

**Telephone Code 020**

**Tourist Info** • VVV, Stationplein 10, ☎ *06-34034066, FAX 6252869*; open daily Easter–Sept. Mon.–Sat. 9 a.m.–11 p.m., Sun. 9 a.m.–9 p.m. (except 11 p.m. July–Aug.); Oct.–Easter Mon.–Sat. 9 a.m.–6 p.m. (Sat. 5 p.m.), Sun. 10 a.m.–1 p.m. and 2–5 p.m. A small VVV office is at Leidseplein: slightly shorter hours.

**City Transport** • GVB (tram, bus, Metro information): Stationplein: Daily 7 a.m.–10:30 p.m. (except Sat. and Sun. 8 a.m.).

**Trains** • Central Station Information Office: Mon.–Fri. 8 a.m.–10 p.m., Sat., Sun., holidays 9 a.m.–6 p.m.; ☎ *6202266* (international), ☎ *06-8991121* (national).

**Emergency** • Medical, central doctors service: ☎ *6642111*. Police: ☎ *6222222*; main police station: Elandsgracht 117, ☎ *5569111*.

**Post Office** • Postkantoor (main post office): Singel 250-256; ☎ *5563311*; Mon.–Fri. 8:30 a.m.–6 p.m. (Thurs. til 8:30 p.m.), Sat. 9 a.m.–noon.

**Telephone/Fax** • Telehouse Amsterdam (international calls, telegrams, FAX, money orders): near Dam Square; 24-hrs. daily.

**Taxis** • Taxicentrale: ☎ *6777777*. It's best not to count on being able to hail a cab. There are taxi ranks at the Centraal Station, Rembrandtsplein, Leidseplein (across from the Concertgebouw at Museumplein), and at major hotels.

**Tours** • Holland International, Dam 6; ☎ *5512812*. American Express, Damrak 66; ☎ *5207777* Keytours Holland, Dam 19; ☎ *6247310*.

**Books** • The American Discount Book Center (specializing in books from the U.S. and U.K.) is at Kalverstraat 185; ☎ *6255537*. The Atheneum Bookstore on the *Spui* has books in English; the Atheneum Newsstand next to it has a large selection of magazines from around the world.

## WHAT TO SEE AND DO

It would be impossible to provide information on all there is to see and enjoy in Amsterdam. And many of your lasting impressions won't come from specific attractions, but from activities as offhand as an evening drink at a canalside cafe with a wondrous view of light-outlined bridges. From about mid-March through October, bridges, facades, towers and trees along sections of the city's renowned ring of canals and other historic buildings are illuminated from sunset to 11:30 p.m. (somewhat later at midsummer when, because of northern latitude, it remains light until nearly 11 p.m.). Many more, though not all museums now are open Mondays in Amsterdam. Some close January 1, Christmas, and April 30 (Holland's National Day).

The Amsterdam VVV publishes a number of informative, interesting walking-tour brochures in English, including a *Walk Through* series for *Maritime Amsterdam, Jewish Amsterdam,* and the *Jordaan.* The booklet, *Amsterdam in the Footsteps of Vincent van Gogh,* (who lived in Amsterdam for more than a year in 1877-78, returned many times thereafter, and made his love for Amsterdam plain in letters to his brother Theo) covers places associated with the artist. Prices are about Dfl. 3.75 a piece.

Knowing the key transportation and entertainment hubs will facilitate familiarity with Amsterdam. **Centraal Station (CS)** is an arrival point for many: all who travel by train and those who fly into Schiphol Airport and take the excellent rail connection into the city. A substantial number of city tram lines originate at the CS. Straight down the **Damrak** from the CS is **Dam Square**, with its *Monument, Royal Palace,* and *Nieuwe Kerk.* The Damrak continues as the **Rokin** to **Muntplein**, with the *Munt Tower* and its carillon (concerts Fri. noon–1 p.m.). Midpoint on the Rokin, where the road narrows, and the Amstel river to here out from the center has been left unfilled, a right turn brings one to the **Spui** and the **Beguinhof**.

With the Rokin at one's back, a *left* turn from the Munt into *Reguliersbreestraat* leads shortly to **Rembrandtsplein**, with its congregation of cafes. Carrying on, one comes to the **Blauwbrug** across the Amstel. To the left is the **Stopera** (the combined new *Stadhuis,* or town hall, and **Muziektheater**, behind which is **Rembrandt's House**). Straight ahead across the bridge is **Waterlooplein**, and the **Jewish Historical Museum**.

Turning *right* at the Munt, one can enjoy the block-long **floating flower market** before arriving at *Leidsestraat.* A left turn onto it leads, after crossing the city's three concentric canals (**Herengracht, Keizersgracht** and **Prisengracht**) to **Leidseplein**, a center of Amsterdam social life, with terrace cafes that are the best place from which to watch the people parade. Just beyond, past the landmark American Hotel, is the Singelgracht, over which a left brings one to the **Rijksmuseum** and **Museumplein**.

### Rijksmuseum    ★★★

*Stadhouderskade 42; Tues.–Sat. 10 a.m.–5 p.m., Sun. and holidays 1–5 p.m.; closed Mon.;* ☎ *6732121; trams 5, 6, 7, 10.* Built in 1885 by P.J.H. Cuypers, the Rijksmuseum is the cornerstone of Holland's permanent art exhibits, with the largest and finest collection of Dutch paintings in the world. The museum dates from an 1808 decree by then ruler Frenchman Louis Bonaparte, brother of Napoleon, and was first housed at the Dam, in the former Stadhuis, turned into the Royal Palace by Louis. Rembrandt's *Night Watch*, the artist's best-known work, around which the museum was designed, has its own room (Room 224, top floor) with interpretive exhibits located nearby and other rooms of his works, including *The Jewish Bride* and *Self-Portrait as the Apostle Paul.* The top floor is where the masterpieces of Dutch

15th- through 17th-century painting are, with rooms allocated to multiple works by **Frans Hals** (including *Merry Drinker*), **Jan Steen** (including *Feast of St. Nicholas*), **Vermeer** (*The Milk Maid, Woman Reading a Letter, The Love Letter, The Little Street*), and **Jacob van Ruisdael** (*Windmill at Wijk bij Duurstede* and *View of Haarlem*), **Pieter de Hooch** (*Woman with a Child in a Pantry* and *Courtyard behind a House*), and **Nicolaes Maes** (*Old Woman at Prayer*).

Also on the top floor are Flemish works ( **Rubens, Van Dyck** ), Spanish (including Dutch-born **Anthony Moro, Goya**, and **Murillo** ) and Italian (**Fra Angelico, Tiepolo**). In the Applied Arts section, there are three rooms of Delftware. Dutch painting of the 18th and 19th centuries, including Impressionism, The Hague School, and the Amsterdam School are on the ground floor. If you have time to see more, the Rijkmuseum has sections on Dutch history, Asiatic art, sculpture, and applied arts (including Flemish and Dutch tapestries). There are detailed floor plans, brochures and catalogs available in English, a museum shop, and a restaurant.

### Rijksmuseum Vincent van Gogh                    ★★★

*Paulus Potterstraat 7; daily. 10 a.m.–5 p.m.* ☎ *5705200; trams 2 and 5 from CS.* Opened in 1973 as a permanent home for a Vincent van Gogh (1853–1890) collection of more than 200 paintings, 500 drawings, graphic art, and letters, and some works by his friends and contemporaries, including Gauguin and Toulouse-Lautrec. Van Gogh, who had a troubled, truncated life, and created most of his marvelous works in a mere five years just prior to his death more than a century ago at age 37, today is as popular a painter as any who ever lived. Although he executed many of his most memorable pieces outside Holland, primarily in France, his work is deeply rooted in the Dutch artistic tradition. He dropped the name *Van Gogh*, signing only Vincent to the paintings he considered worthy, because he found that outside of Holland no one could pronounce it correctly. Among the best-known paintings at the museum are *The Potato Eaters, Vase with Sunflowers, The Bedroom/Arles*, and *Crows in the Wheatfields* (for other Van Gogh works in Holland, see the Kroller Muller Museum, Otterlo).

### Stedelijk Museum                    ★★★

*Paulus Potterstraat 13, corner Van Baerle Straat; Mon.–Sun. 11 a.m.–5 p.m.;* ☎ *5732911; trams 2 and 5 from CS.* Opened at the end of the 19th century, in the 1950s the Stedelijk became one of the first museums in Europe to collect and exhibit contemporary art. Today, it is one of the most influential modern art museums in the world. Chronologically, the collection begins with works of "classic" modern artists, **Manet, Monet, Cezanne, Van Gogh, Matisse, Chagall, Picasso**, and advances through the early decades of the 20th century, when new visual "vocabulary" replaced the traditional use of perspective and began letting go of ties to visible reality in favor of the abstract, nonrepresentational art of Dutch-born **Mondriaan**, and **Malevich**. Shown through the sweep of the Stedelijk collection, such changes can be seen as logical, even inevitable. Since the early 70s, when the Van Gogh Museum was opened next door and most of that artist's work moved to it, the Stedelijk has been devoted exclusively to modern art, and new acquisitions always strive to present the latest developments in visual art. The Stedelijk began collecting photography in 1958, following the museum's highly successful exhibit of *The Family of Man* by Luxembourg-born **Edward Steichen**. (See "Clervaux Castle, Luxembourg, the Family of Man exhibit".) Saturdays at the Stedelijk at 3 p.m. Sept.-June, there are free concerts in the series *Music of Today*; films, videos, lectures, and performance art are frequently offered. Basic floor plan in English; museum shop.

### Oude Kerk ★★

*Oudekerksplein; April–Oct. Mon.–Sat. 11 a.m.–5 p.m., Sun. 1:30–5 p.m., Nov.–March Mon.–Sat. 1–3 p.m., Sun. 1:30–3 p.m.; tower accessible Jun 1–Sept. 15 Mon., Thurs. 2–5 p.m., Tues., Wed. 11 a.m.–2 p.m.;* ☎ *6249183; year-round concerts Sat. 4–5 p.m. on 47-bell Hemony* ★★ *carillon (restored 1990), one of the finest in Holland; frequent summer evening organ concerts.* The earliest parish church in Amsterdam (c. 1300), the Oude Kerk was built on an artifical mound close to the Amstel. Various rebuildings brought the church to its large present size by the first half of the 16th century and, with the 1578 *Alteration,* the Oude Kerk was transferred from the Catholic to Protestant rite. Closed temporarily in 1951 because of the imminent danger of its collapse, the Oude Kerk was completely restored between 1955 and 1979. The medieval church has the largest wooden roof (15th century, painted) in the Netherlands. **Dirck Crabeth** is credited with some of the fine 16th- and 17th-century stained glass windows; the **Vater/ Muller organ** (the sound is exceptional) dates from 1724–36. Rembrandt's wife **Saskia** was buried beneath the stone that reads: Saskia 19 Juni 1642. Among the interior details, note the antique-decorated **Kerkmeesters Kamer** (vestry room). The Oude Kerk rests in a Linden-tree-shaded cobbled square in the oldest part of Amsterdam, complete with cafes, bicycle and pedestrian traffic, and a few red-light district "shop-windows."

### Koninklijk Paleis (Royal Palace) ★★

*Dam; daily June 15–August, 12:30–5 p.m., call for possible additional times;* ☎ *6248698.* When the *Peace of Munster* was signed in 1648, finally officially ending the *Eighty Years' War* with Spain, Amsterdam was the wealthiest city in the world. Laying the foundation stone late the same year for a monumental Stadhuis (today the Royal Palace on Dam Square) was an appropriate proclamation. Built on 13,000 piles, the massive, free-standing sandstone (all imported and virtually "emptying" two quarries) neoclassical Jacob van Campen building was called by contemporary poet Constantijn Huygens the "**eighth wonder of the world**" (a tired phrase today but one that carried more weight in the 17th century). The Stadhuis was filled with the works of the Golden Age's finest sculptors and artists. Atop the facade, Atlas shoulders the world, as the Dutch then undoubtedly felt they did economically; inside, one flight up, the huge marble Citizens Hall has maps of the two hemispheres inlaid in the floor, so that visitors to the Stadhuis could appreciate how much of the world was Dutch. Many large allegorical sculptures decorate the hall, and frescoes and paintings are inclined to subjects favoring Greek and Roman gods.

Nowhere are the moral lessons in the decorative work of the building more evident than in the Bankruptcy Office, where, in addition to reliefs showing rats gnawing at unpaid bills, the decor features the fatal Fall of Icarus. Perhaps **Meindart Hobbema** (1638–1709), one of the last born of the great 17th-century Dutch artists, should have taken note. Hobbema painted many excellent rural landscapes as a young man, but marriage seems to have changed his style. As a result of his wife, who was hired as cook to the Burgomaster of Amsterdam, who resided in the Stadhuis and entertained in great style there, Hobbema was able to get the job of wine-measurer for the city. Perhaps life became too easy, for Hobbema didn't paint much after that and, it is said, he and his wife died with little to show for it. The "classical" treatment in the Royal Palace is even carried to the softly piped-in music. The handsomely furnished former Magistrate Court Room and Burgomaster's Chamber can be visited, as well as rooms where pieces of the valuable Empire furniture collection that Louis Napoleon, installed as king of Holland in 1808 by his brother Bonaparte, used to decorate the building when he confiscated it as a royal palace. Louis' rule was too sympathetic to Dutch ideas, for which Napoleon removed him from the post, but the famous furniture and the status of the building as a royal palace remain. A good brochure in English is given out, and there is an explanatory video.

### Dam

In the center of Dam Square, which has been the heart of Amsterdam since its founding c. 1270, is the **Nationaal Monument**, which commemorates all who died from 1940–45. The queen lays a memorial wreath there on May 4th, on the eve of Liberation Day, May 5th.

### Nieuwe Kerk                                                    ★

*Dam; open conditionally Mon.–Sun. 11 a.m.–5 p.m.; ☎ 6268168; concerts on the 1655 organ in summer.* Since it was begun about the year 1400, the "new" in its name comes only in reference to the century-older Oude Kerk. The deed of foundation was signed in 1408 by Frederik van Blankenheim, bishop of Utrecht, who thus seems to have approved the division of the growing town of Amsterdam into two parishes: the Old Side, with the Oude Kerk, and the New Side, with the Nieuwe Kerk. The progressive enlargement of the church seems to have been stimulated by the unedifying rivalry between the Old and New parishes. In 1565, when the Oude Kerk acquired its magnificent tower and carillon, the Nieuwe Kerk reacted by laying up a massive foundation for a tower of its own. The project was delayed by the *Eighty Years' War.* Finally, after being badly damaged by fire in 1645 (as a result of which few interior furnishings date from before then), rebuilding plans called for the construction of a tower for the Nieuwe Kerk. But the ending of the Eighty Years' War caused a burst of building fever for a *Stadhuis* (Town Hall, now the Royal Palace) from 1648–55, and, when not enough funds could be found for that grandiose structure next door to it, the Nieuwe Kerk seems to have lost its last chance for a tower.

In addition to the wonderfully painted classical cases of the two 17th-century organs designed by Jacob van Campen, and the huge carved pulpit, placed mid-church, Calvinist-style, is the monumental black marble tomb of **Admiral de Ruyter** (1607–1676), who died in a naval battle in Sicily while defeating the French fleet, was embalmed, and then sent home to Amsterdam, where thousands attended his funeral at the Nieuwe Kerk in 1677. Though now a "decommissioned" church, all reigning Dutch monarchs since King Willem I in 1815 (through Queen Beatrix, 1980) have been inaugurated in the Nieuwe Kerk, a city honor upon which Amsterdam rests its claim of being the country's capital. In the narrow ★ **Gravenstraat** behind the Nieuwe Kerk are a number of tiny old shops. Do peek into # 18, *De Drie Fleschjes* (the three little bottles), a small 17th-century pub.

### Amsterdam Historisch Museum ★★

*Entered via decorative archway at Kalverstraat 92, from St. Luciensteeg 27, or through the Beguinhof (see following item); daily 11 a.m.–5 p.m.;* ☎ *5231822.* Whichever route one takes to it, the Amsterdam Historical Museum, with its extensive complex of buildings and courtyards, is a delightful discovery. Perhaps the pleasant surprise unfolds best from Kalverstraat, coming through the site occupied in 1414 by the sisters of the order of St. Lucy. The cow barn of their convent is now the museum cafe **In de Oude Goliath** (to the right), inside of which is a giant wooden sculpture of Goliath, which from about 1650 to 1862 was a major attraction in an amusement park in Amsterdam's **Jordaan** district. To the left, one sees a courtyard wall with lockers for the belongings of boys of the Burgher Orphanage, which was established here in 1580 after the convent was taken over by the city under the 1578 Dutch law that confiscated all Catholic Church property. The Amsterdam Burgher Orphanage occupied the site until 1960, when it moved to new quarters on the edge of town. The building was then extensively restored, and opened as the historical museum in 1975.

To the left of the entrance, which is in a courtyard at the end of the passageway through the orphanage, is one of the most exciting public pedestrian passageways one could ever hope to encounter: the ★★★ **Civic Guard Gallery**. The large-scale minimuseum walkway contains a priceless collection of huge civic guard and guild portraits, mounted on the outside brick walls of the handsome old institution, all safely encased under glass. The "museum street" is a stunningly effective and innovative use of space. Inside is a basically chronological treatment of Amsterdam's 700-plus-years history. Borrow a guide written in English at the ticket counter for the general idea behind the exhibits, although many are multimedia or wonderful works of art (old views of Amsterdam, maps, prints) that have been donated to the museum or which came from former city institutions. Some of the Amsterdam themes that are imaginatively covered are city expansions, trade and industry in the 14th and 15th centuries, navigation in the Golden Age, and the history of the Dam as the center of public life since the city was first settled. Retrace your steps to the Civic Guard Gallery and head through it for the Begijnhof.

### Begijnhof                                         ★ ★ ★

*Accessible from the Spui or from the Amsterdam Historical Museum's Civic Guard Gallery; daily, use Spui entrance after museum hours.* The full diversity of Amsterdam's sights becomes evident when one enters this peaceful, picturesque place, inhabited since 1346, when it was established as a pious community by the Sisters of St. Begga. Unlike those at the neighboring St. Lucy Convent, the Beguines were left in peace after the Alteration of 1578. Most of the houses in the courtyard were privately owned, either by Beguines or outsiders, and the city did not confiscate this private property, especially since many of the Beguines belonged to prominent Amsterdam families. The Beguine Church, which had been consecrated in 1419, was another matter, however, and it was taken over by the town. After years of being rented out as a warehouse, the city leased the church to the Presbyterians, Scottish, and English Calvinist separatists living in Amsterdam who did not want to join the Church of England (it remains the Scottish/English church today).

Some of the English pilgrims worshipped here in 1608, moving to Leiden in 1609; some of them sailed from Delfshaven in 1620 (depicted in a stained glass window), boarding the *Mayflower* in England and reaching Plymouth in the New World. The Beguines continued to live and worship in their garden square, but the mass had to be celebrated in secret, and different houses were used. In 1655, the parish priest bought two houses and converted them into a permanent chapel for the Beguines. (City permission was granted on condition that outwardly nothing would betray the presence of a church.) Today, the Catholic Chapel can claim its identity in the Begijnhof. The land in the center of the garden-like Begijnhof was used as a bleaching field until at least the mid-18th century. It is surrounded today by 17th- and 18th-century (restored) house fronts, with old gables (neck- clock- and step-style) and old gablestones, some of which have been set in a wall near No. 34. This is the **Houden Huis** (wooden house), with its original wooden exterior, c. 1475, Amsterdam's oldest surviving house.

## Anne Frank House

*Prinsengracht 263; Mon.–Sat. 9 a.m.–5 p.m., Sun. and most holidays 10 a.m.–5 p.m.; in June, July, Aug. open all days until 7 p.m.; ☎ 6264533; trams 13 and 17.* Anne Frank, who would have celebrated her 64th birthday in 1993, died of typhus at the age of 16 in the Bergen-Belsen Nazi concentration camp. Because of a diary she kept during the two years that she, her family, and four others lived in the secret annex upstairs in this 200-year-old canal house, Anne Frank has a face among the millions of Jews who died during the Second World War. Visitors can see the small secret annex in the upper back of the house, where eight people had to endure two years in close confines before their whereabouts were disclosed to the Nazis. Among the touching details are black-and-white magazine pictures of movie stars and young English Princess Elizabeth that Anne had pasted on her bedroom wall. There are two flights of very steep stairs to enter the museum. A video and brochure, in English, set the scene historically, and visitors then go "behind the bookcase" and up to the hidden rooms. Exhibits on the lower floors show photographs of Anne and her family before they fled into hiding and convey details of the Nazi occupation in Amsterdam and life in the concentration camps. The Anne Frank Foundation seeks to prevent discrimination and violations of human rights in the world.

Not long before the group in hiding was betrayed to the Nazis, Anne wrote in her diary: "It's really a wonder that I haven't dropped all of my ideals because they seem so absurd and impossible to carry out. Yet I keep them, because in spite of everything I still believe that people are really good at heart."

**NOTE:** This is one of the most popular sites in Amsterdam, and waiting lines can be long; plan an early arrival to avoid them.

## Westerkerk ★

*Prinsengracht, corner Raadhuisstraat and Westermarkt; May 15–Sept. 15, Mon.–Sat. 10 a.m.–4 p.m.; tower accessible June–Sept. Tues., Wed., Fri., Sat. 2–5 p.m.; carillon concerts Tues. from noon–1 p.m.; ☎ 6247766; tram 13, 17.* Built between 1620 and 1630 in the Dutch Renaissance style, it is considered to be the masterpiece of architect **Hendrick de Keyser**. The distinctive 265-foot (85 meter) ★★ tower is topped with the Imperial Crown of Maximilian of Austria, a right that Amsterdam received from the Hapsburg Court in 1489. Rembrandt's unmarked grave, and that of his son Titus, are in the Westerkerk. (From 1660 until his death in 1669, the artist lived in modest quarters at Rozengracht 184, nearby.) Standing at the corner of the church is a small modern sculpture of Anne Frank, which often has fresh flowers laid at its feet. Rising high above the statue is the colorfully crowned steeple of the Westerkerk, which, though only doors away from the windows of Anne's Secret Annex, could not be seen by neighbors. But its 47-bell carillon was a comfort to Anne, who wrote in her diary of "the (chiming) clock at the Westertoren which I always find so reassuring."

On the Keizersgracht side of the Westerkerk is Amsterdam's simple triangle-shaped pink granite **Homomonument** (Gay Monument). Nazis required that homosexuals in occupied Holland wear a pink triangle badge.

### Jordaan ★

Across from the Westerkerk on the Prinsengracht is a canal bike dock, and on the far side of the Prinsengracht the distinctive Jordaan neighborhood begins. Noted now for the bohemian, bizarre and beautiful, and its relaxed and creative character, the Jordaan was developed in the early 17th century, at the same time as the **Grachtengordel** (canal belt), but was purposefully left unplanned in comparison with the great concentric pattern, and allowed to grow up as a working class, artisan, tradesman, and, very early on, immigrant district, with smaller and squatter houses, and narrower streets and canals. *Jordaan* probably comes from the French "*jardin*" (garden), since many of its streets have horticultural names. Before long, it deteriorated into an overcrowded slum, a scene of repeated bubonic plague epidemics, and extreme poverty; in the 1890s, with 90,000 inhabitants, it was Europe's most densely populated city quarter. A century later, with 19,000 residents, the Jordaan has been gently gentrified, fortunately not to the point of losing its unique character. Bounded by the Prinsengracht, Rozengracht, Lijnbaansgracht and the delightful Brouwersgracht, the Jordaan contains some of the city's most characterful cafes, small boutiques and bistros, and hidden *hofjes* (almshouses). The ★★**Brouwersgracht** (brewers' canal) is the point from which construction on the three concentric canals began about 1600.

### Willet-Holthuysen Museum ★★

*Herengracht 605; Mon.–Sun. 11 a.m.–5 p.m.;* ☎ *5231870.* Built for the daughter of one of Amsterdam's burgomasters in 1689 and left by the Holthuysen family to the State in 1889, this double-width canal house has furnished rooms reflecting the 18th and 19th centuries and a fine tiled and brass and copper-utensil-adorned 18th-century basement kitchen. One room features a painted ceiling by Jacob de Wit (c. 1740), another an Aubusson wall covering. Two lounges are virtual art galleries. Be sure to reach the top floor, which has a cozy and intimate feel. The back bedroom, overlooking the garden, is set for sewing, a task lighted from the largest window I've ever seen in a house. The floor-to-ceiling windows of the enchanting garden room are on the first floor at the rear. The formal French-style garden behind the house also can be viewed (through iron railings) from Amstelstraat (between Rembrandtsplein and the Blauwbrug).

### Museum van Loon ★★

*Keizersgracht 672; year-round Mon. 10 a.m.–5 p.m., Sun. 1–5 p.m., closed rest of week;* ☎ *6245255.* At least the severely limited hours for this finely furnished late 17th-century canal house come on a day when some of Amsterdam's other museums are closed. One is free to wander around the house at will, with the help of a detailed explanatory booklet (in English). Built in 1671–72, the first tenant of the house was the successful painter **Ferdinand Bol** (once a pupil of Rembrandt). The French influence in the decor of the personable house reflects that style's popularity in the early 1800's because of Napoleon's rule (1795–1813) of the country. The house has been restored to its late 18th-, early 19th-century state as much as possible. The garden behind the house also has French flavor in its formal style.

### Nederlands Theater Museum

*Herengracht 168; Tues.–Sun. and holidays 11 a.m.–5 p.m., closed Mon.;* ☎ *6235104.* Exhibits primarily concern Dutch theater tradition, and downstairs is a miniature theater from 1781. The real reason for you to visit, however, is the 1638 canal house's exquisite decor detail, particularly wall and ceiling paintings and plaster work in the marble hall and monumental staircase from when it was rebuilt in the Louis XIV-style in the 18th century.

### Amsterdam Stadhuis

*Amstel 1; Mon.–Fri. 8 a.m.–6 p.m., Sat. 10 a.m.–6 p.m., Sun. and holidays noon–6 p.m.;* ☎ *5523458.* The ★**Normaal Amsterdams Peil** (N.A.P.) a.k.a. **Amsterdam Ordnance Datum** (A.O.D.), was established three centuries ago and based on the average high watermark of the Zuiderzee, which was then Amsterdam's connection to the North Sea; it is still the "water table" referral point for all construction in the Netherlands. The A.O.D. bronze knob, mounted in a passage of the Stadhuis, marks ground zero level; the three water columns on view show the high or low tide of the North Sea at the particular moment at IJmuiden; the high or low tide at Vlissingen (in Zeeland, to the south); and the highest level reached during the Zeeland floods in 1953. The Stadhuis shares its setting on the Amstel with the ★**Muziektheater**, from which there's a splendid view of the evening illuminations along the river during intermission and after performances.

### Rembrandt House                                              ★★

*Jodenbreestraat 4; Mon.–Sat. 10 a.m.–5 p.m., Sun. and holidays 1–5 p.m.;* ☎ *6249486.* Holland's most famous artist lived here from 1639–1660, and the house, which dates from 1606, contains a nearly complete record of Rembrandt's etchings. Rembrandt's development in etching, a form for which he is less familiar, can be seen in the works displayed. The museum also shows some paintings by his own teacher, Pieter Lastman, and his pupils.

### Jewish Historical Museum                                      ★★

*Jonas Daniel Meijerplein; daily 11 a.m.–5 p.m., closed Yom Kippur;* ☎ *6269945; tram 9 from CS, Metro to Waterlooplein.* Across from the Portuguese Synagogue on the J.D. Meijerplein is the Ashkenazic Synagogue Complex, four components dating from 1670 to 1752 and now forming the Jewish Historical Museum. The museum, which opened in 1987 and won the 1989 Council of Europe Museum Prize for its imaginative architectural restoration, stands in the former Amsterdam neighborhood Vlooyenburg (built about 1600), into which were moved large numbers of Sephardic Jews from Portugal and Ashkenazic Jews from Germany. A glass-roofed passage connects the four synagogues, added as the Amsterdam Jewish community expanded. One, the Grand (1670), is the oldest public synagogue in western Europe. Exhibits cover the Jewish life cycle and highlight the social history of the Jews in the Netherlands. English brochure, museum shop, Kosher coffee shop. Outside, on the Meijerplein, seek out *De Dokwerker* (*The Dock Worker*—see "Amsterdam in Context"), a Mari Andriessen statue, at once powerful and powerless.

### Nederlands Scheepvaart Museum (Netherlands Maritime Museum) ★ ★

*Kattenburgenplein 1; Tues. –Sat. 10 a.m.–5 p.m., Sun. and holidays. 1–5 p.m., closed Mon.;* ☎ *5232222; bus 22 or 28 from CS.* Located in the 1656 former arsenal of the Admiralty of Amsterdam, the national maritime museum was opened in 1973. The museum aims to present an overall picture of Dutch shipping, past and present, with a focus on overseas trade, naval warfare (and fine, stirring paintings), navigation and cartography (great globes and maps). There are plenty of models of ships from the Dutch East and West Indies companies, clipper ships, up to the proud passenger liners of the Holland-American Line. Set off in a separate section is the early 18th-century, oar-powered *Royal Barge,* used as recently as 1962 for the occasion of the silver jubilee of Queen (now Princess) Juliana. Museum floor plan in English, exhibit descriptions in Dutch only. Cafe with harbor view; excellent book and gift shop.

Moored next to the museum, among several ships of interest, is the recently completed (it was five years in the construction) full-size replica of the 18th-century merchant ship of the Dutch East India Company *De Amsterdam,* which sank in the English Channel on its maiden voyage in 1749. The interior has been recreated as authentically as possible to give visitors an insight into what life would have been like aboard the vessel.

### Museum Amstelkring "Our Lord In The Attic"                    ★ ★

*Oudezijds Voorburgwal 40: Mon.–Sat. 10 a.m.–5 p.m., Sun. and holidays 1–5 p.m.;* ☎ *6246604.* Located in the attics of three contiguous mid-17th-century canal houses in the oldest section of Amsterdam is a full-scale richly decorated Roman Catholic Church—in hiding. With the coming of the **Alteration** in 1578, which made Protestantism preeminent, and Catholicism technically illegal, the city of Amsterdam, governed by business interests, in general ducked the issue of religion by allowing the practice of the Catholic religion–as long as it wasn't obvious. This led to the rise of the so-called "hidden churches," of which this is the last in Amsterdam. (There were once about 60.) A museum since 1888 and appearing much as it did in 1735, **Our Lord in the Attic** has a poker face exterior and downstairs parlor. There is little to prepare one for the visual shock of the three large adjoining attics at the top of an unprepossessing staircase: a baroque altarpiece (with Jacob de Wit paintings), pews and a balcony, confessional, stowaway pulpit, and separate sacristy, all on a scale substantial enough to have supported a full-time resident priest. One of the many intriguing items in the church is a small silver box in the shape of a coffin. Since Catholics at the time could not be buried in consecrated ground, hallowed earth was kept in the box and scattered, three spoonfuls per person, over the bodies of deceased Catholics before their coffins were closed.

### Red-Light District

Examples of Amsterdam's traditional tolerance abound around the **Our Lord in the Attic** church, which is located in the center of the city's red-light district, which has been sanctioned in the same area (adjacent to the town's original site on the Dam) since the 14th century. How a city manages its sin may be a good measure of its maturity. In Amsterdam, one senses an unruffled, reasoned approach to prostitution, rather than the over-reactive, adolescent attitudes which prevail in many other places that do nothing to improve the situation. Along and in the streets off the quaint, canaled **Oudezijds Voorburgwal**, women sit in small shop-like windows, offering themselves as merchandise. The process may be shockingly direct to some, but it keeps the business of sin behind plate glass, limiting its spillage onto streets and normal city life. Medical checkups and other professional aid and advice for prostitutes are encouraged by officials (and made wide use of), and the *Red Thread* organization works to protect the women's dignity. Thus, in Amsterdam, for all concerned, including tourists, there's a certain safety associated with the practice of "the world's oldest profession."

## SHOPPING

As you'd expect with such long-established pragmatic practitioners of trade, prices are set in Holland. No need to think about bargaining (except at flea and antique markets). Prices shown always include the 17.5 percent VAT or btw tax. Basic hours are 9 a.m.– 6 p.m. except Saturday when most close at 5 p.m. Virtually all are closed all day Sunday, and many don't open until 1 p.m. Monday. Late-night shopping is Thursday, till 9 p.m.

Amsterdam has been in the diamond trade since 1586, and the *Amsterdam cut* is known for its quality. The **Amsterdam Diamond Center** (*Rokin 1; open daily,* ☎ *6245787*) and several other diamond-cutting houses can be visited for free tours and demonstrations of the "four Cs" qualities of the shining gemstones. Many sell jewelry, as well as unmounted stones, in their showrooms.

In the European city that has done more to protect its historic architectural heritage than any other, you'd expect to find an active antique trade.

More than 100 antique shops can be found on and just off Amsterdam's short **Nieuwe Spiegelstraat**. As an appropriate backdrop to the *objets d'art* in the shop windows is the Rijksmuseum, which dominates the view at the end of the street. Art and antiques have kept close company in Amsterdam since the opening of the Rijksmuseum in 1885, within a couple years of which the first antique shop had opened on Nieuwe Spiegelstraat. Amsterdam has more than 140 art galleries, most of which specialize in contemporary art, for which the city is considered one of the leaders in Europe. The galleries are scattered throughout the Centrum.

One of Amsterdam's main shopping areas is the pedestrian **Kalverstraat** (it means "bullock street," and cattle were once driven to market along it), one of the city's earliest streets. Interesting and upscale shops have made the restored former *post office* a success as the **Magna Plaza** enclosed shopping center just behind the Royal Palace off the Dam. Running parallel to the Rokin, between the Dam (location of the prestigious **De Bijenkorf** store) and the Munt Tower, it has major department stores (**Vroom and Dreesman**) and many boutiques. Just beyond the Munt Tower, which is home to a **De Porceleyne Fles** Delftware shop, on Reguliersbreestraat, is **Hema**, for colorful, imaginative housewares and, from its small food section, the makings of a picnic: fresh bread, cheese, sandwiches, *vin ordinaire*.

The Kalverstraat has Centrum convenience but not quite the cachet of **P.C. Hooftstraat** and **Van Baerlestraat** in the museum quarter, which have boutiques carrying fashionable internationally renown names. **Focke and Meltzer** on P.C. Hooftstraat carries the delftware of **De Porceleyne Fles** and other fine china and crystal. The enjoyable Jordaan district has small shops with diverse wares tucked here and there.

You'll probably run across enough typical Dutch souvenirs during your strolls around the city, but a cut-above-the-average and a useful congregation of Dutch artisans and their output can be found in a complex, near the Amsterdam Renaissance Hotel. Nearby is **De Klompenboer** (wooden shoe farm) at Nieuwezijds Voorburgwal 20, in case you want to purchase a pair.

Amsterdam's markets include the **flower market** at Singel Canal, between Koningsplein and Muntplein *(Mon.–Sat. 9 a.m.–5 p.m.)*. The city's largest general goods and produce street market is on **Albert Cuypstraat** *(Mon.-Sat. 9 a.m.–5 p.m.)*. The long-standing flea market, not quite what it once was, is at **Waterlooplein** *(Mon.-Sat. 10 a.m.–7 p.m.)*. Sundays, go to **Nieuwemarkt** for open-air antiques *(May-Oct., 10 a.m.–4 p.m.)*. The enclosed many-stalled **Antique Market de Looier** is at Elandsgracht 109 *(Sat.–Thurs. 11 a.m.–5 p.m., closed Fri.)*. Nearby, at Looiersgracht 38, is **Rommelmarkt** (flea market), same hours. A **stamp market** (*Postzegelmarkt*) lends character to the scene by Nieuwezijds Voorburgwal 280 *(Wed. and Sat. from 1–4 p.m)*. Artists offer diverse works at the Spui and on Thorbeckeplein *(Apr.–Oct., Sun. 11 a.m.–6 p.m.)*.

## WHERE TO STAY

Some of the most charming hotels, often on canals in Amsterdam—and other Dutch cities—have been made out of one or several attached one-time private houses. These have lots of character and lots of steep stairs since it's often difficult (and always expensive) to install elevators. Staff help with luggage, so *that* needn't be a concern when you consider whether or not to avail yourself of this distinctively Dutch-style accommodation. In the selection of hotels here, both convenience of location and setting have been strongly weighed. Because business travelers are inclined to be absent on weekends, inquire about weekend discount rates, which may be as much as 50 percent off. Some hotels offer winter rates at substantial savings between Nov. 15 and March 15. At more moderate hotels, always inquire when booking if/ which credit cards are accepted.

## VERY EXPENSIVE

**De L'Europe** ★★★★★

*Nieuwe Doelenstraat 2-8, 1012 CP;* ☎ *6234836, FAX 6242962.* Approaching a centennial on its superb site, arguably the best combination of scenery and convenience of any hotel in the city, the Hotel de l'Europe faces the *Amstel River* and *Munt Tower* in the confident knowledge that she is an Amsterdam grande dame. The hotel, housed behind a fine six-story Victorian facade, is old world, but not old-fashioned; attentive service is a tradition. The excellent reputation of its **Excelsior** restaurant is well deserved. There's been recent renovation and redecoration: there's dining, afternoon tea, and drinks served on a wraparound, canal-level terrace and a health club with pool (in surprising classic Roman bath-style) and sauna. You need to ask for a water view; facing the Muziektheater instead of the Munt is quieter. The hotel has 101 rooms; seats in the elegant elevators; bidets in the bath; minibars; in-room safes.

**Pulitzer** ★★★★★

*Prinsengracht 315-331, 1016 GZ;* ☎ *5235235, FAX 6276753.* Since being acquired by the Italian Ciga Group, the Pulitzer continues to please guests with its assemblage of historic buildings (19 of them, mostly 17th-century) and its imaginative integration of them into an inviting whole, complete with glass-enclosed connecting corridors and central tree-shaded garden courtyard. Much of the art and furniture is modern, as is the plumbing, but despite those changes, there's a timeless charm to this Pulitzer prize. (In fact, it takes its name from Joseph Pulitzer's grandson, who had a vision for the then-decaying canalside houses and opened the hotel in 1971.) The 195 guest rooms are all unique, with old beams, brick, and, at least until recently, a rather rustic charm. A full range of amenities and services are provided. The canalside coffee shop is highly pleasant, as is the cozy bar. The location puts one in the center of the picturesque and close to much else of interest in Amsterdam.

**The Grand** ★★★★★

*Oudezuids Voorburgwal 197, 1001 EX;* ☎ *5553111, FAX 5553222.* This 182 guest room canal front hotel occupies Amsterdam's former town hall. Parts date from 1660, when it was headquarters for the

Dutch Admiralty, others from this century's art deco era; both received authentic restoration and feature period decor. Appealingly grand, though not austere, public rooms enclose a central garden with trellises, a fountain, trees, seating areas, and those for coffee, afternoon tea, drinks when the weather cooperates. Guest rooms are high-ceilinged, large-windowed. Staff members are friendly and helpful. Special function rooms include the former mayor's office, council chamber and civil Marriage Chamber (which can be used for its original purpose again). The usual 5-star amenities, plus parking, indoor pool, sauna.

### Amstel Inter-Continental                    ★ ★ ★ ★ ★

*Professor Tulpplein 1;* ☎ *6226060, FAX 6225808, reservations U.S. and Can.* ☎ *800-327-0200.* This highly regarded Amsterdam hotel landmark, fronting on the Amstel, has undergone a top-to-toe renovation into a deluxe 80-unit all-suite property (very expensive). The historic and handsome features of the foyer have been retained, while a health spa with swimming pool and a business center have been added. **Le Rive** restaurant has been expanded and continues to serve elegeant European cuisine with a river view. The **Terrace Bar** and formal afternoon tea on the river terrace are other enjoyable options at this hostelry *just* beyond the bustle of central Amsterdam.

### Forte Crest Apollo                    ★ ★ ★ ★ ★

*Apollolaan 2, 1077 BA;* ☎ *6735922, FAX 5705744, U.S. and Canada* ☎ *800-225-5843.* This gracious, contemporary hotel, with its picture-windowed, country house-like lounge, sits at the confluence of three tree-lined canals. The 217 rooms are smart in appearance, generous in size, and have the range of amenities you'd expect, along with 24-hour room service. Ask for an even number if you want to face the canals. The Apollo, situated in a quiet, out-of-the-center corner of town, offers free parking, friendly and helpful front-desk service, and has informal, formal, and terrace cafe restaurants facing the canals. It's a three-block walk to the nearest tram into the Centrum.

## EXPENSIVE

### Ambassade                    ★ ★ ★

*Herengracht 335-353, 1016 AZ;* ☎ *6262333, FAX 6245321.* Centrally located in seven 17th-century patrician canalside houses, the Ambassade is a delight from one's first step into the elegant, welcoming lobby. Though somewhat less stylish than the public rooms (there's an elegant French-style salon), each of the 47 bedrooms (some 65 percent of which face the canal, made cheerful with p.m. sun) is distinct and immaculate, decorated with pretty prints and antiques. Breakfast (included) in an elegant canal-front room; light meals available from the 24-hour room service. Very popular with those who have discovered it, so reserve as far ahead as possible.

**American Hotel**

*Leidsekade 97, 1017 PN;* ☎ *6245322, FAX 6253236.* The thoroughly European-American Hotel has occupied its prominent canaled corner of Amsterdam, just off the Leidseplein, since the 1880s. The 188 comfortable guest rooms are replete with *art deco* details, as is the two-story lobby. Amenities include fitness center (sauna, weight machines), newsstand, room service, and character-filled cafes; terrace, canalside, and the Nightwatch bar. Its most famous feature is the flagrantly art deco **Café Americain** (open 11 a.m.–2 a.m.), a roomy rendezvous favored by the Dutch, and enjoyed by all, for coffee with newspapers, pastry, light and full meals, and after dinner drinks.

**Grand Hotel Krasnapolsky**

*Dam 9, 1012 JS;* ☎ *5549111, FAX 6383269.* The location couldn't be more in the heart of Amsterdam for this traditionally Dutch hotel, which will boast 420 rooms with the addition of 98 new ones in a renovated adjacent building due to open in April 1995, complete with fitness center. Brought back to its 1880 airy elegance is the **Winter Garden** restaurant where breakfast (included) is served. In the lobby cafe/bar, which overlooks Dam Square and across to the Royal Palace, one sits close to the heart of the city, but a bit removed from its bustle. The property's conference center is the most extensive such hotel facility in Amsterdam. Concierge; 24-hour room service; hotel parking garage.

**Golden Tulip Barbizon Palace**

*Prins Hendrikkade 59-72, 1012 AD;* ☎ *5564564, FAX 6243353, reservations U.S. and Can.* ☎ *800-333-1212.* Located in the oldest part of Amsterdam, the Barbizon Palace is one of the newest and most successful of the city's modern hotel/historic house marriages. Incorporating 19 monument facades, including one of Amsterdam's only two remaining timber houses at Zeedijk 1 (c. 1550), the Palace presents a highly individual face to the Centraal Station across from it; architects created an elegant interior with a blend of Dutch, French, and even Roman elements. Marble floors, columns and balustrades give the lobby a stately look, completed by an arched transparent roof. More than half of the 263 guest rooms are contained in the old houses and are split-level with old oak beams. Minibar, in-room safe, hair dryer, telephone with modem hook-up, health club, VIP club room, and 24-hour room service are among the amenities. The gourmet restaurant **Vermeer** has a 17th-century ambiance, and there's a typically Dutch pub. The hotel recently acquired and restored the 1638 *St. Olaf's Chapel* next door to it to serve as a conference and special events facility.

**Amsterdam Renaissance**

*Kattengat 1, 1012 SZ;* ☎ *6212223, FAX 6275245, U.S. and Can.* ☎ *800-228-9898.* Located in one of the city's oldest neighborhoods, with crooked, cobbled streets, it is dominated by the great green dome of the desanctified 17th-century *Round Lutheran Church* (*Koepelkapel*), which serves as the hotel's unique conference center and special events venue. (**Note**: Extensive fire damage suffered by the church in 1993 will be repaired by April 1995.) The Renaissance is located in a 1975 building that incorporates historic monuments into the property. The 425 guest rooms feature rich contemporary materials and furnishings, and five-star amenities. Amsterdammers, as well as guests, enjoy the hotel's public facilities: the authentic "brown" **Koepel Cafe** (with outside terrace in nice weather), the Sunday morning **Koepel concerts** in the Round Lutheran Church (see "Entertainment and Events"), the nightclub, and **Splash** health club.

### Doelen Karena Hotel

*Nieuwe Doelenstraat 24, 1012 CP;* ☎ *6262922, FAX 6221084, U.S. and Can.* ☎ *800-365-6935.* The outer walls of the 17th-century Doelen Hall, once the civic guard hall for which Rembrandt's huge Night Watch was commissioned (in 1638) and where it hung (until moved to the town hall on the Dam in 1715), were incorporated into the present hotel, which opened in 1883. The original richly ornamented marble lobby, the superb views of the Amstel and Kloveniersburgwal canal (which half of its 86 guest rooms overlook), and setting in one of the most scenic sections of Amsterdam, give the hotel plenty of character. Many of the guest rooms have been renovated and have a light, modern appearance; many have sitting areas, all have pants press, hair dryer, minibar, in-room coffee/tea maker. Small restaurant overlooks canal; cozy bar, also with views, has old Dutch ambiance.

### Schiller Karena

*Rembrandtplein 26-36, 1017 CV;* ☎ *6231660, FAX 6240098, U.S. and Can.* ☎ *800-365-6935.* Built in 1892, with art nouveau detail in the stained glass, chandeliers and mirrors of the large, gracious, plant-filled lobby lounge and restaurant, the Schiller is a historic landmark on the Rembrandtplein. The rooms are all different; some have balconies overlooking the large green, cafe-rimmed square. Pants press and coffee tray among amenities in rather standard but comfortable rooms. A glass-enclosed terrace cafe fronts the hotel along the Rembrandtplein.

### Jan Luyken

*Jan Luykenstraat 54, 1071 CS;* ☎ *5730730, FAX 6763841.* Located in three former houses on a tree-shaded street, the hotel has a quiet location near the art museums, shopping, Concertgebouw, and beyond the sounds of, but close to, the lively Leidseplein. The property's 65-room (all with bath—though I saw some very small tubs—minibars, and in-room safes) size means personal attention from the very pleasant, helpful staff at the front desk. Elevators, though some rooms are a fair distance from them. There's an attractive breakfast (only, included) room, and a typically Dutch-style cozy lobby bar with small garden terrace where snacks, soup and toasted sandwiches are served.

**Marriott** ★★★★★

*Stadhouderskade 21, 1054 ES;*  *6075555, FAX 6075511, U.S. and Can.*  *800-228-9290.* Sometimes the lobby seems as animated as the Leidseplein, which the hotel overlooks, and you can watch the street scene from **The Terrace** glass-enclosed sidewalk cafe. A cozy, quieter nook is **De Library** lobby cocktail bar, and there are both informal and more formal restaurants. Museums, shops, trams, and other restaurants are within an easy jaunt. The 400 spacious rooms and baths come with all the service (24-hours) and amenities (minibars, air conditioning, etc.) that you associate with the name Marriott. The best views are in the front rooms on upper floors.

**Victoria Hotel Amsterdam** ★★★★

*Damrak 1-6, 1012 LG;*  *6234255, FAX 6252997.* Almost every visitor to Amsterdam since 1890 has seen the stately Victorian facade of the Victoria Hotel. Steps from Centraal Station yet in the city stream, the hotel has 321 traditional, comfortable rooms; those in the original building are larger, more gracious; nonsmoking rooms and executive floor available. Business center; health club; parking garage.

## MODERATE

**Het Canal House** ★★★

*Keizergracht 148, 1015 CX;*  *6225182, FAX 6241317.* These two charming mid-17th-century mansions (26 rooms, all with modern tile baths) are filled with an eclectic collection of auction-acquired antiques and Dutch prints belonging to the friendly American long-time owner. Convenient, prestigious location. Breakfast (only) served in a quite stately garden-view salon. Rooms overlook canal or garden (illuminated at night). Elevator to most rooms, small lobby bar.

**Borgmann (Villa)** ★★★

*Koningslaan 48, 1075 AE;*  *6735252, FAX 6762580.* From the terrace tables behind this roomy 1902 home, one is surrounded by the greenery and bird songs from Vondelpark. The big windows almost bring the outside in to the luxurious, but fresh and cheerful country-house-like lounge, where breakfast (only) is served, and bar service is available. The 15 twin rooms (rooms in back or front of house are largest) and three singles each have a minifridge, trouser press, hair dryer, TV, telephone and bath or shower. Very friendly service. No elevator. On-street parking. Nearby tram, museum district.

**Owl Hotel** ★★★

*Roemer Visscherstraat 1, 1054 EV;*  *6189484, FAX 6189441.* A block from the Leidseplein, and just behind the Marriott Hotel, this light, bright contemporarily decorated 34-room hotel has a quiet location, with a small plant-filled relaxing lounge and bar that open onto a garden. The five-floor, 100-year-old building has an elevator; the generous-sized double rooms all have shower (some bath), TV, telephone; breakfast (only) is included. Very central, near art museums, trams.

### Avenue ★★★

*Nieuwezijds Voorburgwal 27, 1012 RD;* ☎ *6238307, FAX 6383946.* Located in a restored warehouse of the United East India Company, the six-story hotel has 38 rooms (12 superior—recommended because of larger size), and a pleasing contemporary wicker and wood look, some beamed ceilings. Breakfast included; restaurant; elevator; credit cards; hair dryers in all rooms. On tram lines; easy walk to Centraal Station, Damrak.

### Vondel ★★

*Vondelstraat 28-30, 1054 GE;* ☎ *6120120, FAX 6854321.* This mid-19th century, family-run house-hotel has 30 rooms, all with private bath or shower, telephone and color TV. Located less than a block from the lively Leidseplein, the hotel itself has a quiet location, and has only light bar service in the lounge. Within walking distance of museums; trams at Leidseplein to Centrum and CS. Breakfast (included) room; two saunas in garden; personal attention. No elevator, but several rooms on ground level.

### Amsterdam Wiechmann ★★

*Prinsengracht 328, 1016 HX;* ☎ *6263321.* Located in two restored canal houses, the cheerful, family style hotel has 36 simply decorated rooms, all with telephone, toilet, bath/shower, many have canal views; TV in cozy lobby lounge. There's a wonderful corner breakfast (included) cafe with wide windows overlooking two canals. Three stories, steep narrow stairs, long corridors, no elevators, but help with baggage. No credit cards.

### Atlas ★★★★

*Van Eeghenstraat 64, 1071 GK;* ☎ *6766336, FAX 6717633.* Situated in a quiet, leafy neighborhood at the edge of Vondelpark, the Atlas' 23 all-different rooms are housed in a large traditional Dutch art nouveau residence. A block from tram to Centrum, within walking distance of art museums, shopping, restaurants, Leidseplein cafes. Huge windows in reasonable rooms, each with modern bath. Elevator, friendly 24-hour room service, laundry service, safes at front desk, small lobby restaurant-bar, credit cards accepted.

### Toro Hotel ★★★

*Koningslaan 64, 1075 AG;* ☎ *6737223, FAX 6750031.* The 23 recently renovated rooms in this turn-of-the-century mansion on a quiet avenue overlooking Vondelpark are comfortable in size, decor, and in-room amenities: minibar, TV, telephone, hair dryer. Public rooms have charming details, antiques, chandeliers, stained glass windows, a terrace, and garden. Breakfast room (or served in your room) and lobby lounge with drinks service; credit cards; elevator; on-street parking; two blocks to tram to Centrum.

### Estherea ★★★★

*Singel 303-309, 1012 WJ;* ☎ *6245146, FAX 6239001.* This very centrally located canalside hotel attracts a pleasantly international clientele. Its 75 modest, modernly-furnished rooms are spread through several centrally-adjoining towntowns, whose common fine 17th-century facade is attractively floodlit after dark. The ground floor breakfast (only, included) room doubles as a lobby lounge (with daily international newspapers) and hotel bar. Helpful front desk staff is on duty 24 hours. Winter rates (*Moderate* price category) in effect Nov. 16–March 14.

### Ibis Amsterdam Centre ★★★

*Stationsplein 49, 1012 AB*  *6389999, FAX 6200156.* This newly built, seven-story hotel sits next door to Amsterdam's *Centraal Station.* Typical of all Ibis properties, rooms are utilitarian, comfortable, basic but cheerful, small but well designed. All have telephone, TV, tiled stall showers. Front rooms have center-city canal views, back ones are practically on the train tracks; specify! There's attractive indoor/outdoor carpeting throughout, and a light, attractive breakfast (Dfl. 15 extra) room which serves snacks and bar drinks the rest of the day. Reception desk staffed 24 hours daily. Public parking opposite hotel.

## INEXPENSIVE

### Washington ★

*Frans van Mierisstraat 10, 1071 RS;*  *6796754, FAX 6734435.* The generous sized rooms (both with and without private modern marble bath facilities) in this recently renovated house-hotel, decorated with antiques and orientals, ornamented with wood wainscoting and other details, are often filled with the sound of musicians, guest performers at the nearby Concertgebouw. On a residential street, close to museums and trams, the hotel features friendly service, breakfast (only); no elevator; guests have own front door key.

### Agora Hotel ★★

*Singel 462, 1017 AW;*  *6272200, FAX 6272202.* Great location on a canal, steps from the flower market, the Spui, and the Beguinhof. You do need to be able to handle steep stairs (help with luggage) to be able to take advantage of the Agora. The small Dutch-style canal-view lobby evolves to a cheerful breakfast (only) room farther back, where coffee and soft drinks are served during the day. The traditionally decorated bedrooms, all different and with private facilities, are inclined to get more interesting architecturally the higher up you go, but it's a hike; ask to be nearer ground level if you prefer. Close to sights, shops, trams.

### Rho ★★★

*Nes 11-23, 1012 KC;*  *6207371, FAX 6207826.* It's not lovely to look at from the outside, though the location, just steps from the Dam, couldn't be more convenient. Once you step into the lobby of this 1908 former theater (renovated as a hotel in 1989), with its soaring, curved skylit ceiling, you're bound to be intrigued. The 61 rooms are very functional, often generous in size, as are the tile bathrooms (open showers with curtains), and feature telephone, TV, and mini-bars. Elevator (four floors), private parking available. The intriguing former theater lobby is the breakfast (only) room, light and airy, with potted palms, stained glass, globe lights. Take a drink up to the balcony from the lobby bar to see further signs of the building's past life as a theater.

### Seven Bridges ★

*Reguliersgracht 31, 1017 LK;* ☎ *6231329.* Located on a lovely canal, close to but beyond the sound of the lively Thorbeck and Rembrandtsplein, this 200-year-old house is clean, bright, and cheerful. Most of the rooms have private shower, all have radio, some TV, no telephones. Room 3 on the garden is especially nice. Breakfast served in rooms.

### The Bridge ★★★

*Amstel 107, 1018 EM;* ☎ *6237068, FAX 6241565.* The scenic location on the Amstel, near the "Skinny Bridge," is only viewed from two rooms (large and old-fashioned), but at the far end of the long corridor on the ground-floor, on which all 26 rooms are located, are eight cozy, modern, quiet rooms facing the "unknown canal" that represent good value. All rooms have private bath facilities, toilet, and telephone (no TV); continental breakfast included (in the Italian restaurant next door). Drinks available off small unusual lobby created in days when the hotel was a marble factory.

### Rokin Hotel ★★

*Rokin 73, 1012 KL;* ☎ *6267456; FAX 6256453.* Very centrally located, close to the Dam. For both quiet and comfort above the very basic decor of its other rooms, ask for one of the ten better standard doubles located in a canal house at the back of the hotel (where there are also hotel "apartments" for longer stays). No elevator; breakfast (only) included. Major credit cards (except Diners).

## *WHERE TO EAT*

The Dutch invariably breakfast at home, so visitors will find few places that serve more than coffee early in the morning except hotels, which begin serving by 7 a.m. A Dutch buffet breakfast (*ontbijt*) will include various breads, sliced cheeses and meats, juices, cereals, milk, perhaps boiled eggs yogurt, fresh fruit, and coffee or tea. A picturesque little cafe on a tree-shaded square on the Singel canal that does serve breakfast (with eggs), outside in good weather, is the **Cafe-Eethuisje De Roef** (*Stromarkt 4, 8:30 a.m.–9 p.m.;* ☎ *6274515; inexpensive*), at end of Kattengat, just past the Amsterdam Renaissance Hotel. Breakfast is also served at **Greenwoods** (*Singel 103; Mon.– Fri. 9 a.m.–7 p.m., Sat., Sun. 11 a.m.–7 p.m.;* ☎ *6237071; inexpensive*), as well as light lunch and tea in the big-windowed, canalside, cozy, crowded cafe. Remember that dinner is taken relatively early in Holland, and even in the best restaurants, many kitchens close by 9:30 p.m. The better the restaurant, the better idea it is to make reservations.

Even if Amsterdam does boast that you "can eat out in any language" there, its Dutch restaurants deserve to come first. **Haesje Claes** *(Spuistraat 275/other entrance N.Z. Voorburgwal 318; open Mon.-Sat. noon-midnight, kitchen closes at 10 p.m., Sun from 5–9:30 p.m.; ☎ 6249998; inexpensive)* offers the Dfl. 19.75 tourist menu in an appealing dark wood, gezellig atmosphere dating from 1520 that makes it a favorite in the neighborhood. Hearty (including Dutch pea soup, *hutspot*) to simple (omelets) choices. Also offering the Tourist Menu and Dutch flavor and fare is **Oud Holland** *(Nieuwe Zijds Voorburgwal 105; Mon.-Sat. from noon, lunch and dinner; ☎ 6246848; inexpensive).* **De Roode Leeuw** hotel-restaurant *(Damrak 93; open from noon for lunch and dinner daily; ☎ 6249683; inexpensive)* offers a Dutch kitchen and a front-row view of the city from its glass-enclosed terrace.

**Die Port van Cleve** *(Nieuwe Zijds Voorburgwal 178; ☎ 6240047)*, which had been serving meals for nearly a century before it added 100 hotel rooms, offers a choice of two fine Dutch restaurants. **De Poort Restaurant** *(from 11 a.m. daily, lunch and dinner; inexpensive)* is the more relaxed, with plants, stained glass, and an old tiled fireplace; a specialty is Dutch *biefstuk* (beef steak) and every one served since 1870 has been numbered: if yours ends in 00, it's free, and so's the wine. Across the hall is the **De Blauwe Parade** *(daily, lunch from noon, dinner from 6 p.m.; expensive)*, traditional with its solid old oak and leather furniture; it was a tasting room in the mid-1500s for the beer brewery that became *Heineken*, but has become even more notable, since 1886, for its wonderful Delft blue and white *De Porceleyne Fles* wall tile tableaux of children in 17th-century court dress celebrating the gathering of grapes for wine. (The restaurant *does*, appropriately, have a fine wine cellar to accompany the excellent Dutch cuisine.)

The welcome return of one of Amsterdam's longest established traditional Dutch eateries has occurred at the **Holiday Inn Crowne Plaza**, which now houses the resurrected restaurant **Dorrius** *(N.Z. Voorburgwal, lunch and dinner daily ☎ 4202224, moderate)*, which dates from 1890. Dorrius offers such fabled Dutch fare as *IJsselmeer* eel, Zeeland oyster and mussels, Texel lamb, rabbit and *Erwtersoep*. **Hollands Glorie** *(Kerkstraat 220; daily from 5–10 p.m., closed Mon. Nov.-Mar.; ☎ 6244764; inexpensive)* is small and pleasantly cluttered with old copper and brass utensils, tiles and antiques, with candles lighted at each table. À la carte choices include mussel cocktail, smoked eel, pork cutlet and beef steak, and there's a *prix-fixe* menu. **Restaurant Bodega Keyser** *(Van Baerlestraat 96; Mon.-Sat., noon–11:30 p.m., closed Sun; ☎ 6711441; moderate)* opened in 1905 next door to the still-new **Concertgebouw** and has been inseparably associated with concertgoers ever since (so much so that its clocks are set slightly ahead so patrons won't miss the first movement of the program, and its kitchen remains open for post-concert dinners). Keyser's is also convenient for patrons of the neighborhood's fashionable shops and art museums. The typical Dutch decor of the front-of-the-house cafe, with its wood furniture, carpets on the table, brass lamps, newspapers and outside tables when the weather's warmish, is also open for morning coffee. Fresh Dutch seafood, especially *Sole à la Meuniere*, is a specialty served at the clothed and candlelit tables in the rear. Last, but certainly not least in Dutch atmosphere, is **D'Vijff Vlieghan** *(Spuisstraat 294; daily from 5 p.m.;* ☎ *6248369; very expensive)*, situated in five 17th-century canal houses. The series of seven dining rooms, each furnished in a different Renaissance-style, creates an intimate whole, upstairs and off passageways, most cozy in candlelight. The traditional Dutch cuisine has recently improved, the result of *nouvelle* nuances.

Even more than traditional Dutch dishes, Indonesian fare seems to be the national food of Holland; most Dutch have a favorite restaurant for it, and the selections are located in various sections of the city. Waiters are usually very helpful in explaining the dishes, and many restaurants have menus translated into English. A perennially popular choice is **Sama Sebo** *(P.C. Hooftstraat 27; daily lunch, dinner;* ☎ *6628146; inexpensive)* very friendly, helpful service, small, authentic, and on everyone's list of one of the best Indonesian restaurants in Amsterdam. **Indonesia** *(Korte Leidsedwarsstraat 18; open daily from noon;* ☎ *4203300; inexpensive)*, moved from its long established site at the Muntplein to just off the Leidseplein, serves tasty, traditional fare in a gracious, almost colonial style, with the aid of a helpful Indonesian staff. In the Jordaan neighborhood is **Speciaal** *(Nieuwe Leliestraat 142;* ☎ *6249706)*, which looks far more special and intimate inside than out. This is where many Amsterdammers "in the know" go for Indonesian.

You certainly don't have to head to a seafood restaurant for fish in this sea-minded country, but it's nice to know where the Dutch choose to go. **Lucius   Visrestaurant**   *(Spuitstraat 247, open daily noon–midnight,* ☎ *6241831; moderate/inexpensive menu)* is an unpretentious, very pleasant place that offers six or seven sorts of fresh fish daily, posted on a blackboard, as well as fish soup, salads, and sandwiches until 5 p.m. Fish charts are on the blue and white tiled walls, white cloths are on dark-wood tables. **Le Pecheur** *(Reguliersdwarsstraat 32; Mon.–Fri. lunch and dinner, Sat. and Sun. dinner only, from 5 p.m.;* ☎ *6243121; moderate)* has a trendy, tasteful interior, and a wonderful garden terrace with a view of townhouses for outdoor dining.

French/continental cuisine is served at some of the most highly regarded restaurants in Amsterdam. **'T Swarte Schaep** *(The Black Sheep; Korte Leidsedwarsstraat 24; open daily from noon;* ☎ *6223021; expensive)*. A calm traditional Dutch backdrop for continental cuisine and singular service, its leather-chair comfort quite removed from the casual liveliness of the Leidseplein cafes it overlooks. Lunch (set menu) and dinner (kitchen open until 11 p.m., late by Dutch standards). **Le Ciel Bleu** *(Hotel Okura, Ferdinand Bolstraat 333; open from 6:30 p.m.;* ☎ *6787111; expensive)* offers fine French cuisine with the most far-reaching view over Amsterdam. **Le Ciel Bleu Bar** *(6 p.m.–1 a.m.)* is a bar atop the Okura, highest view of the night lights. Hotel de l'Europe's exclusive **Excelsior** *(Nieuwe Doelenstraat 208;*

*daily, lunch from 12:30 p.m., dinner from 6 p.m.;* ☎ *6234836; expensive)* serves a menu de la saison, a gourmet alliance menu and, since the opening of the nearby Muziektheater, a theater menu. For post-theater and later, less expensive dining, The L'Europe's **Le Relais** is a fine choice. **De Silver-en Spiegel** *(Kattengat 4; Mon.–Sat. lunch and dinner, closed Sun.;* ☎ *6246589; expensive)* is situated in an enchanting 17th-century house opposite the Ramada Hotel's Koepel Cafe, whose patrons benefit from having a view of the restaurant. The decor of either dining floor does justice to the fine French food. The appealing old **Restaurant De Bols Taverne** *(Rozengracht 106; Mon.– Sat. noon to midnight;* ☎ *6245752; moderate)* serves a good choice of international dishes, as well as a very broad selection of the liqueurs made by the company from which it takes its name, and other Dutch drinks.

All the world seems interested now, but Amsterdam for many years has had a great following for Japanese food. The city's best Japanese restaurant is **Yamazato** *(Hotel Okura, Ferdinand Bolstraat 333; open daily for lunch, from noon, and dinner, from 6 p.m.;* ☎ *6787111; expensive)*, which overlooks a miniature Japanese garden and serves a wide range of traditional Japanese dishes. The Japanese-owned Okura emits an Oriental calm that's complemented by its somewhat out-of-center canalside locale. The hotel also has the **Sazanka Teppan-Yaki** steak house (lunch/dinner; expensive) and a sushi bar.

Cafes seem to sprout on Amsterdam sidewalks whenever the weather comes even close to cooperating. The word "cafe" also indicates a restaurant of a certain style, so some of the establishments listed below may focus more on food, others on setting (menus are always posted, so you'll know which is which). Its location surprises people, but the **le Klas Grand Cafe Restaurant** *(Spoor/platform 2b; daily 9:30 a.m.–11 p.m., Sun. 10:30 a.m.;* ☎ *6250131; inexpensive)*, once the first-class waiting room and now restored to past lofty-ceiling splendor, and a dark-wood cafe next door, also serves a more-than-acceptable menu, within sound of the pleasant rumble of the trains. A thoroughly European setting. Sat. 7–10 p.m. live jazz, Sun. brunch with live classical music. **De Knijp** *( Van Baerlestraat 134; daily noon-3 p.m., 5:30 p.m.-midnight;* ☎ *6714248; inexpensive)*, close to the Concertgebouw and museums, is a light-hearted, art deco/brown cafe combination that is a neighborhood charmer. The eclectic, cozy decor matches the menu: Zeeland oysters to sauté, paté to pasteries.

**Het Land van Walem** *(Keizersgracht 449; daily from mid-morning;* ☎ *6253544; inexpensive)* is an artsy, reading-newspapers sort of coffeehouse, and it sprawls along the canal at small tables when the weather warrants. There's a charming courtyard garden sometimes used for dining. The delightful dowager-Dutch **Royal Cafe De Kroon** *(Rembrandtsplein 15; daily 10 a.m.–1 a.m.;* ☎ *6252011; inexpensive)* is up two flights of graceful curving 1898 steps to the huge airy rooms and glassed-in balcony overlooking the tree tops of Rembrandtsplein. For tea, sweets, or more substantial treats. The **Cafe de Jaren** *(Nieuwe Doelenstraat 20; daily 10 a.m.–1 a.m., 2 a.m. Fri., Sat.; inexpensive)*, resting between the *De l'Eu-*

*rope* and *Doelen Karena* hotels, has a wonderful view over the Amstel to the Musiektheater, from terrace level and upstairs. Serving soups, salads, sandwiches, and more substantial fare. Located at the edge of the colorful Jordaan neighborhood on one of the loveliest stretches of canal in the city, **De Belhamel** *(Brouwersgracht 60; daily noon-midnight, kitchen open noon–2:30 p.m., dinner 6–10 p.m.;* ☎ *6221095; inexpensive)* serves as a special stop for a drink, with an intriguing intimate two-tier interior with faux marble columns and art nouveau details. Informal menus, daily specials, desserts. Two other cafes worth noting, as much for location as for the edible offerings, although those are certainly worthy, are **Cafe Luxembourg**, facing squarely on the Spui, and **De Beiaard**, *(daily 11 a.m.—11 p.m.)*, on the coner, with split views of the Spui and the Singel. For food before or after a visit to the Rijksmuseum, or an antique expedition in the shops of the Nieuwe Spiegelstraat, stop at the Cafe **Hans en Grietje** *(Spiegelgracht 27; lunch 11:30 a.m.–5:30 p.m., open til 1 a.m. for light fare;* ☎ *6246782; inexpensive)*. The cheerful canalside cafe, which serves sate, omelets, *uitsmijters*, and hamburgers, has a wonderful view of the Rijksmuseum.

For platter-size Dutch pancakes, savory or sweet, head for either **The Pancake Bakery** *(Prinsengracht 191; daily noon–9:30 p.m.;* ☎ *6251333)* in the roomy beamed and bricked basement of an old canalside warehouse or tiny, four-tabled **Upstairs** *(Grimburgwal 2; Tues.-Sun. 9 a.m.–7 p.m., closed Mon.;* ☎ *6265603)* up two steep flights. For tasty, quick *broodjes* (sandwiches), follow in the tracks of Amsterdammers to **Eetsalon van Dobben** *(Korte Reguliersdwarsstraat 5; daily, from 9:30 a.m., 11:30 Sun.;* ☎ *6244200)*, near the Rembrandtplein, or one of **Broodje van Kootje's** two locations: Leidseplein 20 and Spui 28, open daily 9:30 a.m. until late.

Although you'll seek them out more for their atmospheric flavor and drinks than for food, most of Amsterdam's famous "**brown cafes**" (or *bruine kroeg*) do serve snacks. The name brown cafe comes from the tobacco-stained walls and ceilings, cozy carpeted tables, and perhaps sawdust on the floor, and the "*gezellig*" ambiance of it all. You'll probably find them to be a cross between an English pub, a French cafe, and an American bar, and although the atmosphere of many may feel like the home of loosely knit family, the ranks are usually open to strangers, and of course everyone will be able to hold an avid conversation in English. Although visitors will find their own favorites, the following are certainly among the most interesting. It is said that around 1600 a coffin maker, selling drinks to earn a little extra money, marked the beginnings of **Papeneiland** *(Prinsengracht 2; 11 a.m.–1 a.m.;* ☎ *6241989)*. The Prinsengracht is home to several other brown cafes: **De Eland** *(#296; noon–1 a.m.)* and **Van Puffelen** *(#377; 11 a.m.–1 a.m.)*, but **Pieper** *(#424; 10:30 a.m.–1 a.m.;* ☎ *6264775)* is one of the most famous. **Frascati** *(Nes 59; 10 a.m.–1 a.m.;* ☎ *6241324)*, near Dam Square, is fashionable, and particularly comfortable for women to visit. And **Hoppe** *(Spui 18; 8 a.m.–1 a.m.;* ☎ *6237849)* has a split personality; *Hoppe zit*, the saloon-like seated section of the 1670 establishment, located on the left-hand side, and, on the right, *Hoppe staan*, a standing bar, with sawdust on the floor inside and a rack for drinks outside in season. In the

Jordaan is **Cafe Nol** *(Westerstraat 109; open 8 p.m.–2 a.m.;* ☎ *6245380),* a splendidly decorated cafe, where, especially on Friday and Saturday nights, amazing scenes occur. Those who like *kitsch* should not miss this.

## ENTERTAINMENT AND EVENTS

English-speaking tourists can avail themselves (at the VVV, Dfl. 2.50) of the bi-monthly magazine *What's On in Amsterdam* or *Amsterdam This Week,* for daily calendars of entertainment events, as well as listings of museums, galleries, rental car agencies, etc. The **Amsterdams Uit Buro (AUB)** on the Leidseplein and the **VVV's Theaterbespreekbureau**, Stationsplein, open Mon.–Sat. 10 a.m.–4 p.m., will book seats in advance for most concert, opera, ballet, and theater performances (in-person sales only).

**Concertgebouw** *(Van Baerlestraat 98; Box Office* ☎ *6718345; trams 2, 5 from CS).* Recently renovated in honor of its centennial, the Concertgebouw, celebrated worldwide for its acoustics, is home to Amsterdam's renowned **Concertgebouworkest** (Conductor Riccardo Chailly). Concerts by it and visiting companies and performers regularly sell out; contact or visit the box office to see what's available. Chamber music is presented in the Kleine Zaal. From Sept. to June, there are free Wed. lunchtime concerts (12:30–1:15 p.m.); varied programs from full symphony to duets.

**Beurs de Berlage** *(Damrak 62A;* ☎ *6265257)* is the architecturally intriguing home *(English tours on request at* ☎ *6258908)* of the 140-musician **Netherlands Philharmonic Orchestra**. The Netherlands Chamber Orchestra and other guest artists perform in the new "glass box" Aga Zaal there. **Muziektheater** *(Waterlooplein 22;* ☎ *6255455)* This white-marble-and-glass rounded building at a curve on the Amstel in the heart of the city is Amsterdam's latest cultural landmark. The amazingly intimate, 1600 red-plush-seat Musiektheater is the home for the **Netherlands Opera Company** (Director Pierre Audi), and the **Dutch National Ballet** (both of which create whole new productions each year for the June-long Holland Festival). Some tickets for every performance are reserved for same-day sale at the Musiektheater Box Office. Schedules for the **Holland Festival**, whose varied cultural programs are focused in Amsterdam, are available in advance from Netherlands Board of Tourism offices.

From approximately late April 1995 the year-round moderately-priced 11 a.m. Sunday morning concerts at the Amsterdam Renaissance Hotel's landmark domed 1668 **Round Lutheran Kerk Koepelzaal** will resume (following extensive repair required following a 1993 fire). For schedule contact hotel; ☎ *6212223.*) Very popular with the Dutch, they are always well-attended, and a *kopje koffie* (cup of coffee) beforehand is included in the Dfl. 6 price. During July and August, **organ concerts**—Amsterdam has 42 historic church organs—are given in the following churches: Oude Kerk, Nieuwe Kerk *(Dam)*, Engelse Kerk *(Beguinhof)*, Oude Lutherse Kerk *(Spui, part of University of Amsterdam)*, Westerkerk, and Sint Nicolaaskerk. Consult the VVV or events calendar listings for details.

Amsterdam's only casino, **Holland Casino Amsterdam** (which replaced the one formerly in the Hilton Hotel) is located near the **Leidseplein**, at

*Max Euweplein 62.* Playing time is daily 1:30 p.m.–2 a.m. Admission is Dfl. 5 ( for a day card). Visitors must be at least 18 years of age, suitably dressed (no T-shirts, sport shoes, etc.), and by Dutch law must produce a passport or driver's license. No bags, shopping or otherwise, may be brought into or checked at the casino. Games include *French, American,* and *twin roulette, Black Jack,* and *Punto Banco.* A useful booklet in English, *Rules of the Game,* is available free. The cafe-restaurant and bar on the premises is open from 1 p.m.–3 a.m.

## IN THE AREA

Several tour operators—their offices are congregated along the *Damrak,* opposite the *Beurs van Berlage*—offer half- and whole-day motorcoach excursions to various places in the area. Look carefully at the respective brochures or itineraries and ask questions as to how much time you will actually have at the sights you most want to see. It's possible to get to the major places on your own on public transportation, so consider that alternative. **Alkmaar** (see later), an architecturally appealing old town on any occasion, most warrants a visit on Friday mornings (*May–Sept.*) for its colorful (usually crowded) cheese market activities. On many commercial tours from Amsterdam are the former fishing towns of **Volendam** and **Marken**. I cannot recommend them (*especially* Volendam, since they exist almost exclusively to fulfill tourists' expectations: locals in traditional costumes worn just for you; you can wear one and have *your* photo taken; wooden shoe factories; and other gimmicky offerings). It's a pretty successful show, but Holland offers far more authenticity of atmosphere elsewhere.

### Bloemenveiling Aalsmeer (Aalsmeer Flower Auction)          ★ ★

*Aalsmeer, Legmeerdijk 313;* ☎ *(02977) 32185; open Mon.–Fri. 7:30–11 a.m., closed Sat., Sun., holidays; fee.* Catch a bus to Aalsmeer—ten miles—from near the front of Amsterdam's *Centraal Station,* beginning at 6 a.m.; there's a short bus transfer in Aalsmeer to the flower auction (ask driver for details). Allow 1 to 1-1/2 hours to get there. A return (round trip) bus ticket is the best buy.

Never have tourism and commerce combined more beautifully than at Aalsmeer. The Aalsmeer complex covers 47 acres. (It's so big that many workers "commute" within it on bicycles). A special **visitors' gallery** has been erected, from which visitors can watch the colorful auction spectacle (*the action is the best from 8–9 a.m.*). An explanatory brochure to help you understand the unique Dutch auction process is given out on arrival. There are multilingual information signs and push-button commentary around the route. Trains of carts with bundles of cut flowers wind through the building on computerized rails, each variety in its own area. The whole process proves it's possible to put a pretty face on business. (See also "The Bulb Field Business" chapter.)

**Zaanse Schans** ★★

*Kraaienest 2, Zaandam; site open at all times, special attractions open daily year-round, though not all are open in winter, 10a.m.–5p.m.* ☎ *(075) 168218; no fee.* Located nine miles (15 km.) northwest of Amsterdam near Zaandam, Zaanse Schans (established as a museum village in 1960) is a picturesque and pleasant 17th-century Dutch six-windmill country village on the river Zaan, a truly "living" museum since its houses have inhabitants. Characteristic of the community, which faithfully mirrors the one in Zaan c. 1700, are the tidy green-with-white-trim wooden houses. Among the points of interest to be visited are a cheese farm, a wooden-shoe workshop, an old grocery store, a clock museum, a tin artisan, two windmills, and an antique shop. There are boat excursions on the river. There is a Dutch pancake house, **De Kraai** *(daily 9 a.m.–6 p.m. Feb.–Sept., 10 a.m.–5 p.m. Oct.–Nov., closed Mon. in Nov.),* on the premises, as well as the restaurant **De Hoop op d'Swarte Walvis** *(Mon.–Sat. lunch noon–2:30 p.m., dinner 6–10 p.m., closed Sun.;* ☎ *(075) 165540, FAX (075) 162476; expensive)* with a well-respected kitchen (one Michelin star) and atmospheric antique interior, with terrace dining in good weather. From Amsterdam CS, it's a 15-minute train ride to *Station Koog-Zaandijk* (in the direction of Alkmaar), from which it's about a ten-minute walk to Zaanse Schans. Half-day coach excursions to Zaanse Schans are available from Amsterdam.

If you are traveling by car, some of the lovely waterland villages to include are Westzaan, De Rijp, Wormer, and Jisp. In Zaandam, now quite urbanized, is the Czar Peter cottage, lived in by Peter the Great in 1697, when he came to Holland to learn shipbuilding. He created such a stir that he had to remove himself to Amsterdam, where he could remain relatively anonymous as he learned the trade.

**Alkmaar Cheese Market** ★★

*Waagplein (Weigh House Square); Fri. mid-April–mid-Sept. 10 a.m.–noon; approximately 1/2 hour by train from Amsterdam CS, more than 1/2 mile from Alkmaar station to town center.* The attractive old town of Alkmaar, which received its charter in 1254, was frequently caught in the crossfire of struggles involving the Dutch provinces of Holland, Friesland, and Gelder. But Alkmaar is still proud of its citizens' successful stand against the Spanish seige in 1573. The moated and canaled sections of "inner" Alkmaar, within the old grassy green ramparts, retain much of the look they would have had then. While it's probably not the place for an overnight stay, Alkmaar is much more than its cheese market; however, since many of the town's other attractions open to coincide with the market, Friday mornings are the recommended time for a visit.

The cheese market usually attracts large crowds around the Waagplein to watch the colorful carryings-on. Plan to arrive enough in advance to get the good tourist information in English (walking town-tour

brochures, background on cheese market tradition and procedure,
map) available from the VVV (☎ *072-114284)* located in the **Waaggebouw** (weigh house), which also houses a **cheese museum** *(April–Oct.,
Mon.–Sat. 10 a.m.–4 p.m., Fri. from 9 a.m.;* ☎ *072-114284*). Cheese
begins arriving at the market after 7 a.m., and the market manager
allocates certain sections of the square to various sellers. The four
companies of porters are dressed in white costumes and lacquered
straw hats in red, green, blue, or yellow according to their company,
and are members of the Cheese-Carriers' Guild, which dates back to
the early 17th century, although cheese was being weighed in Alkmaar
as early as 1365. The market undoubtedly is continued in its present
form largely for tourists, but the business conducted is serious none-
theless. After inspection and weighing, the lots of cheese (primarily
the cannonball-shaped Edamms here in their natural wax covering,
not wrapped in red cellophane for export) are carried off on wide
wooden barrows to the buyers' warehouses. Payment is likely to take
place over coffee or something stronger in the cafes around the
square.

The Waaggebouw dates back to 1341 and served both as a chapel and
hostel for needy wayfarers. In 1581, Prince Willem the Silent of
Orange restored to the town so-called weighing-rights (in part to
reward the town for its brave stand against the Spanish in the 1573
seige); the need for more market space caused the chapel (which probably had been turned over to the town when the Protestant Dutch
Reformed Church became the declared religion in 1578) to be rebuilt
as the still active weigh house. The 1599 tower has a **carillon** *(concerts
on Fri. 11 a.m.–noon during cheese market season, year-round Sat., market
day, noon–1 p.m.).* The tower clock has a pair of jousting knights who
charge each other on the hour chime. Plan to stay and wander awhile
in town after the cheese market: Enjoy the early 16th-century dou-
ble-stairway Stadhuis, the Vismarkt (fish market), the picturesque old
facades along the Oude Gracht, the small narrow streets, canal
bridges, and hofjes. The Gothic Grote Kerk (St. Laurens) 1470–1520,
which contains the tomb of Count Floris V (died 1296), is noted for
its small organ (1511), one of the oldest in regular use, and the 1643
organ designed by Jacob van Campen.

## WHERE TO STAY AND EAT IN THE AREA

**Chateau Marquette**                                    ★ ★ ★ ★
*Marquettelaan 34, 1968 JT, Heemskerk;* ☎ *02510-41414, FAX
02510-45508; moderate.* Located between Alkmaar and Zaanse Schans
is a gracious country castle restaurant-hotel. Chateau Marquette's 68
tasteful contemporary guest rooms, all with spacious modern bath and
full amenities, were added in a separate building from the castle. Bicycles available for guests; sand dune trails only 1.5 miles away. The à la
carte restaurant, open daily from 6 p.m., Sunday brunch from 11:30
a.m., is located in the moated castle, whose dining rooms and salons

have superb architectural details and antique furniture. The kitchen prepares continental cuisine and offers several menus.

Haarlem

# HAARLEM

*Group portraits by Frans Hals are a highlight in Haarlem.*

## GUIDELINES FOR HAARLEM

### SIGHTS

**The Frans Hals Museum** and, on Haarlem's gargantuan Grote Markt, **St. Bavokerk** (St. Bavo's church, 1400–1550) with its famed organ, are the city's stellar stops. Throughout the appealing city, fine architecture from the 17th and earlier centuries, both on grand and smaller scales, is in evidence.

## GETTING AROUND

Once you get to the **Grote Markt**, the heart of Haarlem, a 15-minute walk from the train station, prime sights are located pretty compactly, the Frans Hals Museum being the farthest point, about a 10-minute walk. Several bus routes from the station stop near the Grote Markt; #50 and #51 pass through villages in the bulb fields to Leiden and there are taxis at the station. Bike rental at the station (Family Pieters, for reservations ☎ *317066*).

## SHOPPING

Old print, antique, and other shops are located around St. Bavo's church along the Oude Groenmarkt, and in the streets that radiate out from the Grote Markt. There also are shops in the Frans Hals Museum and in St. Bavo's church. During the growing season, there's a Saturday flower market on the Oude Groenmarkt.

## WHERE TO STAY

Hotels in town are limited, but there's a choice of two comfortable properties with fairly convenient city locations.

## WHERE TO EAT

The variety of settings and types of food available will match travelers' taste, time, and pocketbook preferences.

## ENTERTAINMENT AND EVENTS

In 1995 the city of Haarlem celebrates its 750th anniversary with special events throughout the year. Contact **Haarlem 750 jaar** (*Grote Markt 2,* ☎ *171750 for information*).

With Keukenhof gardens and the bulb fields nearby, the spring season (*Apr. 1–end May*) is easily the area's busiest. There are weekly evening concerts on the **St. Bavokerk Christian Muller organ** *mid-May–mid-Oct.*, with an additional afternoon concert a week in July and Aug. Concerts by participants in Haarlem's biennial (1994, 1996, etc.) *International Organ Improvisation Competition* are played nearly daily in July on the St. Bavo's organ. Concerts on the third Sundays of the months of Sept.–May and on occasional candlelight evenings (call for specifics and reservations) are given at the Frans Hals Museum. In early June (check with VVV for date), Haarlem holds its annual **Luilak**, an all-night giant flower and plant sale on the Grote Markt (*4 p.m.–8 a.m.*).

## ARRIVING

Haarlem is on the main Amsterdam-Rotterdam rail line, some 15 minutes from Amsterdam by frequent service; its 1908 station is a historic monument. Haarlem has good road and motorway connections.

## IN THE AREA

Several intriguing attractions are located close to Haarlem: to the south are the **bulb fields** and **Keukenhof** garden, **Zandvoort**, a favorite North Sea resort, and **Cruquius**, an old steam water pumping station, with a museum that shows how the Haarlemmermeer was drained. To the north, pretty **Spaarndam** village has a statue that illustrates the tale of the boy with his finger plugging a dike. The busy trio of locks at **IJmuiden** sends ships up the *Noordzee Kanaal* to Amsterdam. West of Haarlem are bicycle paths through the dunes at the **National Park de Kennemerduinen** and footpaths (only) in the dunes of **Amsterdamse Waterleiding** reservoir south of Zandvoort.

## TRAVEL TIPS

It's not necessary to overnight in Haarlem to attend an evening organ concert at St. Bavo's; evening trains regularly scheduled until nearly midnight provide plenty of time to return to Amsterdam, Rotterdam, or points in between. The Frans Hals Museum, unlike many in Holland, is open Mondays.

# HAARLEM IN CONTEXT

By the 10th century, Haarlem had become a township on the Spaarne River, on which the counts of Holland levied tolls. The counts' early fortification here is recalled in the name **Gravenstenenbrug** (counts' fortress bridge) that spans the Spaarne today. By the 13th century, Haarlem had acquired considerable status, as reflected in its coat of arms: a silver sword among four stars, crowned by a cross. The crown and sword had been presented to Haarlem by German Emperor Frederick II as reward for the city's help in occupying Damiata in 1219 during the Second Crusade. The "Damiaatjes," a set of chimes in St. Bavo's belfry, are a further recognition.

In 1245, Count Willem II, from the precincts of his hunting lodge on the 't Zand (now the Grote Markt), where jousting tournaments were held, presented Haarlem with a city charter. Eventually the site of the lodge, destroyed by city fires in 1347 and 1351, was given to the town, which built a Stadhuis (town hall) there by the end of the 14th century. From the 15th through the early 17th century, there were many alterations and additions to the Stadhuis; City Architect Lieven de Key designed the wing along Zijlstraat in 1620-22, and drew up plans for the last major rebuilding (1633), which gave the facade the Italian Renaissance elements it still shows. Haarlem's couples today have their civil marriages in the medieval Knights' Hall (Gravenzaal), which visitors can view when ceremonies aren't on the calendar. Facing the Stadhuis, the entrance is around the corner on the left. Behind the Stadhuis is a monastery, destroyed by the 14th-century city fires, now somewhat restored. The name *Prinsenhof* there refers to a residence built on the site in 1590 by the Prince of Orange after the monastery's church had been plundered and damaged beyond repair in 1578 during Reformation tumult.

A significant piece of Haarlem's 15th-century history is kept alive by a statue on the Grote Markt near St. Bavo's of **Lourens Coster** (1370–1440), a native with a well-substantiated claim (in 1423) to being at least a co-inventor (with Germany's Gutenberg) of the art of printing with moveable type. Coster is buried in St. Bavo's, the exact location unknown. Holland's first newspapers were published in Haarlem, and more than 570 years after Coster's typesetting here, Haarlem remains a printing center full of book publishers, editors, and newspapers. Also calling Haarlem home is the firm *Enschede*, which prints postage stamps and paper currency, not just for Holland but other governments too. (In case you hadn't noticed, Haarlem artist Frans Hals' portrait appears on the Dutch blue 10-guilder note.

As with the rest of Holland, 16th-century Haarlem was keenly affected by the northern Netherlands revolt against Spain, known as the Eighty Years' War. In 1572, with a population of 20,000, Haarlem was larger and more important than Amsterdam—not until the 17th century did Amsterdam eclipse Haarlem—and thus served as a symbol of resistance for the Dutch. In December 1572, Haarlem was besieged by Spanish troops, under Frederick of Toledo, son of the dread Duke of Alva. For a while, the Haarlemmers held out, managing to ice skate in and out of town on canals and rivers to acquire supplies. The Spanish were ordered to wear iron cleats to be able to pursue and stop them, but proved unable to. However, spring came, the canals and river melted, and the Spanish gradually gained the upper hand.

The Spanish Navy stationed in the Haarlemmermeer to the north of the town effectively blocked the town's only outside line of supply. Subsequent attempts by Willem the Silent to provide relief, and heroic efforts by the Haarlem women under the leadership of Kenau Simons Hasselaer, proved unsuccessful. In July 1573 the citizens agreed to surrender on condition that a general amnesty be granted if 57 of the town's leaders were handed over. The terms were accepted, but several days later the Spanish wrought wholesale massacre in

Haarlem, killing some 1800 of the Holland garrison stationed there, all the Calvinist leaders, and many other Dutch. Several months later, Haarlem's surviving citizens at least had the satisfaction of knowing they had made victory costly for the Spanish: unable to equip their forces adequately after the expenditures at Haarlem, the Spanish, in their subsequent attempt to subdue the nearby town of Alkmaar by siege, failed. This marked the beginning of a downturn in the Spanish domination of Holland.

Haarlem had more to suffer during the drastic decade of the 1570s. While still under Spanish rule in 1576—Haarlem remained occupied by the Spanish for five years following its siege—fire destroyed large parts of the town. Shortly after the Spanish vacated Haarlem in 1578, Dutch Protestant purges in the town succeeded in destroying the treasures in churches and religious houses that had survived the flames. St. Bavo's church, which had escaped the fire, passed into Protestant hands.

But the Reformation also produced positive results for Haarlem. After the Spanish conquest of Antwerp in the southern Netherlands in 1585, many Flemish and Wallonian Protestant refugees fled north. The specialized skills and capital of the many Flemings who settled in Haarlem significantly affected Holland's social, cultural, and economic development, and helped pave the way for Holland's soon-to-appear 17th-century "Golden Age."

In the 17th century, Haarlem occupied a fairly small, narrow strip of land, bordered on the west by a row of dunes that separated the town from the North Sea, and on the east by the large Haarlemmer-meer lake, which was drained in the 19th century. (See "Cruquius" "In The Area" at the end of the chapter.) The river Spaarne, which flows through the town south to north, passes through the east side of Haarlem. Boatyards, breweries, and numerous windmills that served as sawmills and in the baking, brewing, tannery, and cloth trades, lined its banks. Due to the generally poor road conditions, transportation then was mainly by water, and the Spaarne formed a vital link between towns in the northern and southern regions of the Holland province. A canal from Haarlem to Amsterdam was dug in 1632, and one to Leiden in 1656. The canals linked up with others, forming an extensive waterway network. The waterways were bordered by bridle paths along which horses towed barges. Hourly boats between Haarlem and Amsterdam ran on Europe's earliest published transportation schedules.

The clean, fresh water of the Spaarne was partly responsible for the success of two of the city's major early industries. Water sources were important in the production of **beer**, and by 1628 the number of breweries in Haarlem had reached 50. The number would reach 150, though none remain today. The quantity of low-alcohol beer consumed in this period, not only in Haarlem but elsewhere in Holland, was high because the quality of most drinking water was poor.

A second significant industry was **linen**. Haarlem damask graced tables in several European courts, where its sheen, patterns, and whiteness were much admired. The latter quality was the result of lengthy bleaching in the grasslands near Haarlem, where the linen, after many rinsings in the river Spaarne, was spread out to bleach in the clear coastal light. Unfortunately, town linen-makers eventually polluted the river, which ruined the quality of Haarlem beer, causing brewers to begin using the clean, naturally filtered, dune water outside of town.

The same coastal light that so successfully bleached Haarlem's linen attracted artists. In the 17th century, a specialty of the **Haarlem School** was landscapes. But the town's major art figure concentrated on portraits. **Frans Hals**, who had been born in Antwerp about 1580, and whose family came north from Flanders to find freedom from the Spanish, spent the rest of his long life working in Haarlem.

Possibly because so little is known about Frans Hals—*much less* than has actually been written about him—even late 17th-century biographers were highly imaginative in reconstructing his life. Myths that have been perpetuated are exceedingly hard to correct. One glaring inaccuracy is that Hals as an old man lived in the *Oudemannenhuis* (old men's almshouse), whose Governors' group portraits he painted. Hals never lived at the almshouse; the rented house in which he lived at the time of his death (1666) is known to have been in Ridderstraat (off Kruis Straat). In an historical twist, the Oudemannenhuis today is the *Frans Hals Museum*.

Also arriving from Flanders was Ghent-born architect **Lieven de Key** (c. 1560–1627), who by 1593 had been appointed Haarlem's city stonemason and bricklayer. Probably well before he oversaw the construction of the Oudemannenhuis in 1608, he had been elevated to Haarlem's city architect. His *Vleeshal* (Meat Hall), built on the Grote Markt in 1602/03, is one of the outstanding works of the Dutch Renaissance style. Built in brick with gray stone decorative detail, the Vleeshal has a strong horizontal element in its facade design, which keeps it down to earth, in contrast to its Grote Markt neighbor, the gothic Grote Kerk (St. Bavo's church), that reaches for heaven. On the St. Bavo side of the Vleeshal, note the ornamental steer and rams heads sculpted in expensive imported Belgium stone (Holland has no stone quarries) to show what business was conducted within. Today, the restored Vleeshal is a part of the Frans Hals Museum and used for special exhibits and lectures. This is also true for the *Vishal* (1768), which abuts St. Bavo's.

With the arrival of Lieven de Key, southern Netherlands renaissance architecture was introduced to Haarlem. De Key's buildings, and those built under his supervision, show many elements typical of the Flemish style: porches, prominent towers, balconies, balustrades, projecting sandstone cornerstones on facades, gable recesses, and scroll and iron mounting work. These ingredients are found in many buildings on and in the vicinity of the Grote Markt as well as in the Bakensserkerk, the Nieuwekerk, and De Waag (weigh house). The Grote Markt itself is the only such "southern Netherlands-style" square north of Holland's major rivers, thus confirming Haarlem as the most Flemish-appearing city in the northern Netherlands.

**Neuwe Gracht** was dug in the 17th century to give Haarlem the substantial enlargement of city limits it needed. With an expanding population in the 17th century, Haarlem's churches were no longer capable of caring for the increasing number of needy: the Golden Age meant prosperity for Holland overall, but its benefits didn't necessarily trickle down to all people. Haarlem's prosperous private citizens without children, sensitive to the plight of the poor, often provided material assistance in the form of **hofjes**, modest individual almshouses around a central courtyard. Twenty hofjes existed in the city by the end of the 17th century, and 18 remain to be seen by visitors today.

One of Haarlem's most unusual hofjes is the 18th-century (1768) **Hofje van Oorschot** with the usual family coat of arms over the door of the main building that houses the Governors' Room. Unlike most hofjes that are sheltered from the street behind an enclosing courtyard wall, Oorschot is on view from the street (Kruis Straat) through a tall open iron railing. This was the result of objections from a rich merchant living across the street who didn't want to look out on a bare brick wall. Architectural arrangements were duly made for the hofje and its garden to be open on three sides to the street.

In the 19th and 20th centuries, Haarlem has quietly prospered, growing in population to 150,000, and content in its role as provincial capital of Noord Holland.

## GUIDEPOSTS

**Telephone Code 023**

**Tourist Information** • VVV, Stationplein 1; ☎ *319059, FAX 340537.*

**Parking** • Limited meter parking at the station by the VVV; inquire there
about car parks near the sights you plan to visit.

**Trains** • Schedules and information in the station.

**Buses** • Local buses 1, 2, and 3 stop at the Grote Markt.

**NZH Buses** • Bus stops for most routes (including bulb fields, Keukenhof
garden, Zandvoort beaches) are in front of train station.

**Bike rental** • At train station.

**Taxis** • Available in front of station.

## WHAT TO SEE AND DO

If ever a small city brought body and soul together in a single place,
Haarlem does so as its **Grote Markt**. Expansive is scarcely a sufficient word
for the enormous brick paved main square, around the reaches of which are
some of the town's most memorable buildings, including the soaring gothic Grote Kerk (St. Bavo's), which is large enough *not* to be swallowed up
by the size of its setting. The Haarlem we enjoy today is a proud product
of Holland's 17th-century Golden Age, when only Amsterdam competed
with it as an art center.

**Frans Hals Museum**

*Groot Heiligland 62; open Mon.–Sat. 11 a.m.–5 p.m., Sun. & holidays 1–5
p.m.; closed Christmas and New Year's;* ☎ *319180, fee.* The *Oudemen-
nenhuis* (old men's house), built in 1608 under the supervision of
municipal architect Lieven de Key from the proceeds of a public lot-
tery held in Haarlem in 1606, served as an almshouse for 200 years,
and then as an orphanage for another 100, until opening as a museum
in 1913 restored to its 17th-century architectural authenticity. Of particular note is the magnificent Renaissance-style corridor, whose
squared black and white marble floors, edged with blue and white
tiles, seem to recreate one of the delicate Dutch interiors painted by
Vermeer of Delft. The reconstruction of the 17th-century garden
accentuates the harmony of the whole museum, a fortunate combination of the skill of an architect and the genius of a painter from the
same period.

The greater part of the life work of Frans Hals has, alas, been scattered
around the world. Nevertheless, particularly in group portraiture,
considered one of the crowning accomplishments of the Dutch school
of painting, Hals is well represented here. There is a series of five Civic
Guard group portraits, most notably the *Banquet of the Officers of the
Civic Guard of St. Adrian* (1633), a striking contrast to the group portraits of the *Governors of St. Elizabeth Gasthuis* (1641), and the

well-known governors and governesses of the Oudemannenhuis (the museum when it was an almshouse), both painted in 1664, when Hals was older than 80. These important works show the bold, fluent brushstrokes that gave Hals' portraits (Hals captured all segments of Haarlem society from prosperous merchants and military officers to fisherboys and pub crawlers), in particular, such a feeling of the moment. French Impressionists Manet and Monet made special journeys to Haarlem to see these paintings. And Vincent van Gogh, obviously influenced by Hals' remarkable rapid and free brushstroke style, wrote: "What a joy it is to see a Frans Hals, how very different from paintings in which everything is carefully and uniformly smooth."

Hals is the centerpiece of the museum, but many other outstanding Dutch painters and styles (landscapes, seascapes, still lifes, everyday life scenes, and church interiors) are on view. Since Haarlem is so close to the bulb-growing district, in one area of the museum, paintings, drawings and tiles have been assembled and designated the **tulip route** (with English brochure) to show the enthusiasm (and madness) that the flower has caused. (See "Tulipmania" in "The Bulb Field Business" chapter.) And there's a *Doll House* (never meant to be used by children) dating from 1750, filled with more than 3000 tiny decorative and artistic treasures.

### St. Bavo's/Grote Kerk ★★★

*Entrance on Oude Groenmarkt 23; Mon.–Sat. 10 a.m.–4 p.m.;* ☎ *324399.* Built between 1390 and 1520 (the date on the face of its tower clock), Haarlem's gothic Grote Kerk is one of the largest in Holland. Construction of the church was not constant; work often had to be suspended due to lack of funds. Considering the number of individuals who orchestrated the work, St. Bavo's shows a remarkable harmony. A stone lantern tower designed by Keldermans was built in 1506, but had to be pulled down in 1514 because it was judged to be too heavy. In 1518 a new tiered tower was erected, constructed of wood and covered in lead. The most recent major restoration of the church was completed in 1985.

Approaching the entrance (#23) on Oude Groenmarkt (old vegetable market), one sees centuries-old small shuttered shops snuggled into the sides of St. Bavo; with pure Dutch practicality, the shutters open from top to bottom to form a shelf upon which to display wares. The church is entered through a narrow passage beautifully adorned with old blue and white tiles. For centuries after it was built, the church was always open and used by Haarlemmers as a passage from one part of the city to another. Such unhindered entrance was the reason for Dog Whippers (who have a chapel in the church), whose job it was to remove troublesome dogs from the premises. The town brewers also had a chapel.

Among other church aspects of interest are the *Graf van Frans Hals* (the artist's grave), on view through the choir screen, a masterpiece of medieval craftsmanship made in 1517 by Jan Fyerens, a brass founder from Mechelen (Belgium). When candles are mounted in the screen and lit, it resembles the *Burning Bush*. The tomb of the well-known painter of Holland's hulking Protestant church interiors, **Pieter Saenredam**, is elsewhere in the church. Sticking half-way into one church wall is a cannon ball, left as a reminder of the Spanish siege in 1572-73. The carved oak pulpit, always center stage in Dutch Protestant churches, dates from 1679; its brass hand rails are in the shape of snakes slithering down, and meant to represent Satan fleeing from the Gospel.

*St. Bavo's church dominates Haarlem's Grote Markt.*

It's hard to turn away from the 5068-pipe Christian Muller 1748 organ, considered one of the most important instruments in the world, and certainly one of the most beautiful, in its towering (almost 100 ft. high), sculpted case. Handel played the organ on two visits, prior to Mozart's in 1766 at the age of 10; Dr. Albert Schweitzer, a fine organist, has sat at the console, too. When the organ was installed, the huge stained glass window that had decorated the wall had to be bricked over (observable from the exterior, by the Vleeshal). There are guided tours of the church May–Sept. Sat. 11 a.m. and 2 p.m. Free one-hour organ concerts are offered Tues. nights 8:15 p.m. mid- May-mid-Sept., and Thurs. 3 p.m. in July and Aug. ( Confirm schedule and times.)

### Teylers Museum                                           ★

*Spaarne 16, open Tues.–Sat. 10 a.m.–5 p.m., Sun. 1–5 p.m., closed Mon.;* ☎ *319010, fee.* This is Holland's oldest museum, with a musty, archives-like 18th-century atmosphere to support the fact. It was founded in 1778 by a wealthy silk merchant who had no family to inherit his eclectic arts and sciences collection. The original five directors left the accumulated results of their hobbies and individual interests to the museum, and Teylers left enough money in his will so that future directors could keep on acquiring assorted stuff. Teylers is quite famous for its fossils, and plays tribute to the Age of Enlightenment (in which Teylers lived) with its physics exhibits (limited English explanation on scientific exhibits). But perhaps of most interest is its exceptional selection of master drawings by Michelangelo, Raphael, Rembrandt, Jacob van Ruysdael, Correggio, Claude Lorrain, and paintings of The Hague School. The Oval Room, where minerals are displayed, is of visual interest, and the entire museum is, according with Teylers' wishes, lit only with natural light.

### Corrie ten Boom Huis

*Barteljorisstraat 19 (Ten Boom Clock and Watch Shop); Mon.–Sat. 10 a.m.–4:30 p.m. Nov. –Apr. 11 a.m.–3:30 p.m., closed Sun. and holidays;* ☎ *310823.* This is a different edition of Anne Frank's secret annex living space in Amsterdam during the World War II Nazis occupation of Holland. In the ten Boom home, above the ground floor family watch repair shop, Corrie ten Boom, then in her 50s, served as the leader of a Dutch resistance group of 80 people, and offered a "safe" house to fugitives, Jews, and other people hunted by the Nazis, smuggling them on to other havens through an underground network that saved many lives. Eventually the ten Boom family of Haarlem was betrayed, with the Gestapo raiding the house and arresting six family members, three of whom died as prisoners. Corrie survived Ravensbruck concentration camp and, for the rest of her life, traveled the world with her "calling," testifying of God's love. She died in 1983 at the age of 91.

The house, a typical Dutch town dwelling, has been left as it was for much of Corrie's life. The carefully created hiding places are preserved, and the whole story is told in Corrie's book *The Hiding Place* (see "Bibliography"). There's no fee for the 45-minute guided tours (a clock sign on the watch shop door tells the time of the next one), though at the end you get a bit of proselytizing, and a donation toward the spiritual ten Boom Foundation is welcomed.

## WHERE TO STAY

### EXPENSIVE

**Carlton Square**
*Baan 7, 2012 DB;* ☎ *319091, FAX 329853, U.S. Sales Office* ☎ *800-223-9815.* Haarlem's newest, largest (97 rooms), and most luxurious hotel is located out of the center, facing a park but within fairly reasonable walking distance of the Grote Markt. The restaurant **Cafe de la Paix** is à la carte, and the **Whiskey Bar** has a British ambiance.

### MODERATE

**Golden Tulip Lion D'Or**
*Kruisweg 34, 2011 LC;* ☎ *321750, FAX 329543, U.S. sales office* ☎ *800-333-1212.* This long-established hotel is located close to the railway station and across from the bus terminal. (Front rooms will get noise.) Rooms are more or less similar in layout, but make sure you ask for a modernized one with lighter, brighter colors and decor. Lobby lounge has Scandinavian-style modern furniture, perfectly cheerful though not luxurious.

### INEXPENSIVE

**Amadeus**
*Grote Markt 10, 2011 RD;* ☎ *324530, FAX 322328.* This 15-room, friendly service-oriented family-owned hotel is situated directly on Haarlem's immense and majestic main square. All rooms have toilet, shower, TV and telephone. A single steep flight of stairs leads from the street level to the hotel lobby—staff will help with luggage if asked—from which there's an elevator to the rest of the floors. A Dutch buffet breakfast (included) is served in the attractive dark-beamed, tile-hearthed lobby/bar, which overlooks the Grote Markt. All major credit cards accepted; credit card number required to hold reservations.

## WHERE TO EAT

Sooner or later you'll be on Haarlem's Grote Markt wanting "a little something," and the **Cafe Restaurant Brinkmann** *(Grote Markt; open daily 9 a.m.–midnight, kitchen closes at 11 p.m.; inexpensive)* could hit the spot. A Delft tile tableau, mounted to mark the cafe's 50th anniversary in 1929, decorates the entryway to the art nouveau/continental-style place, with lighted candles at the table even at lunch, stained glass, plants. If you take a window seat, while you partake of something off the varied menu of sandwiches, uitsmijters, pizza or pasta, burgers or steak with salad, quiche, or just coffee and pastry, you can enjoy a great view of the Grote Markt out the grote windows. Just a few doors away is **Cafe Mephisto** *(Grote Markt 29; Mon.-Sat. 9 a.m.– 9 p.m., closed Sun.,* ☎ *329742; inexpensive)*, a trendy, pleasant place with art nouveau details such as a stained glass ceiling, mirrors, lamps, dark wood and fresh flowers. Omelettes, uitsmijters and other tasty light meal fare.

If you're coming from the train, you won't even have to wait for the Grote Markt, since you'll pass several good choices along the route. *Kruisweg* becomes *Kruis Straat* before becoming pedestrianized as *Barteljorisstraat*, which runs into the Grote Markt. **Cafe 1900** *(Barteljorisstraat 10, open daily 9a.m.– 5 p.m., except Thurs. and Sun. to 7 p.m.* ☎ *318183; inexpensive)* is a trendy but basic art deco delight, a copy of a Parisian cafe, with dark wood detail, little marble tables and straight wooden cafe chairs and interesting lighting fixtures. Good choice for informal fare from coffee to uitsmijters. Walk a few doors down to satisfy your sweet tooth at **Tearoom H. Ferd. Kuipers** *(Barteljorisstraat 22; open Mon.-Sat. 9 a.m.–5:30 p.m., Thurs. til 9 p.m., closed Sun.,* ☎ *310114).* As Haarlem's best pastry shop, it's where Dutch women "of a certain age" share a pick-me-up pause while shopping.

For a proper sit-down meal—for which you'll want to allow time—on the Frans Hals Museum side of the Grote Markt is **Restaurant Peter Cuyper** *(Kleine Houtstraat 70; open Tues.-Sat. noon–3 p.m. and 6–10 p.m., closed Sun., and Mon.;* ☎ *320885; moderate)*, situated in restored 16th-century townhouse with courtyard (dining outside in decent weather). Lots of Dutch atmosphere with candles, fresh flowers, copper lamps, amid the architectural details and oak furniture. The cuisine is French (preparation a cross between classic and nouvelle), the food Dutch: local salmon, lamb and chocolate from Haarlem's own factory.

## IN THE AREA

### Spaarndam

In this picturesque old Dutch fishing village with 17th-century houses and gables, built along a typical Dutch dike, a 600-year-old lock on the river Spaarne (which flows through Haarlem) is decorated with a small bronze statue that represents the tale of the boy who plugged a hole in a dike with his finger. Most Americans grew up with the story (most Dutch didn't) of the brave boy who, seeing a small leak in a dike, saved Haarlem from inundation by thrusting his finger into the hole, staying there all night until he was discovered in the morning and the hole could be properly plugged. The tale is told in the 1865 novel *Hans Brinker or The Silver Skates* by American Mary Mapes Dodge, though it wasn't Hans Brinker himself who performed the supposed heroic deed (so implausible that perhaps that is why the Dutch have never paid it much heed). Nevertheless, after nearly a century of American visitors inquiring about the location of the brave act, Dutch tourism officials took over. In June 1950, while several hundred Haarlem school children sang, Princess Margriet (sister of Queen Beatrix), then 7, performed her first public function by unveiling the sculpture designed to satisfy the inquirers.

## Cruquius Museum                                                       ★

*Cruquiusdijk 27/32, south of Haarlem, just to east of Heemstede; open March–Oct. Mon.–Thurs. 10 a.m.–5 p.m., Sat., Sun. and holidays 11 a.m.–5 p.m., closes at 4 p.m. in Oct.; closed Fri. and Nov.–Feb;* ☎ *023-285704.* As early as 1641, plans had been drawn up to drain the huge Haarlemmermeer (lake), although they called for no fewer than 166 windmills to do the job, which wasn't considered feasible. Not until 1839 did the Dutch Parliament put into action a drainage plan that could be followed through. Cruquius was one of three steam-driven pumping stations used to reclaim the polder land between 1849 and 1852. Made redundant in 1933, Cruquius, a monument in Holland's history of hydraulic engineering and a relic of the Steam Age, was given new life as a main exhibit in a museum providing insight into Holland's perpetual push to gain land from the sea.

An interesting model shows what the Netherlands without its dikes and drained polder land would look like: for starters, there'd be lots less of it. Also shown are the stages by which Holland has reclaimed land from the sea, the earliest in 1456 near Alkmaar. The Haarlemmermeer project of the 19th century drained the land (13 feet below sea level) on which Schiphol Airport now rests. There are also maps and models showing the history of pumping land dry with windmills (some in the region are still used for that). There's an English translation of exhibit notes that visitors can carry around with them. Tickets and refreshments from the tea house in the former chief engineer's cottage next door. Cruquius is accessible by bus from Haarlem.

## Ijmuiden                                                              ★

The *Noordzee Kanaal,* dug (by hand) from 1865–1876 along the early course of the IJ river to preserve Amsterdam's future as a deep-water port, links that city with the sea at IJmuiden, a distance of 13 miles (22 km). The three locks (dating from 1876, 1896, and 1930, respectively) make for interesting viewing; the 1930 Noordersluis is one of the largest in the world: 1300 ft. long, 50 ft. deep, 160 ft. wide, and the Noordzee Kanaal as a whole is larger than the Panama Canal. The steady stream of huge containers led by tiny tugs, barges, and other craft, seen closer at hand here than at Rotterdam (see "Harbor Cruises" under "Rotterdam"), impresses one with the supreme economic importance of sea trade to Holland. A free, continually running (allowing for ship traffic, which has the right of way) 24-hour 5-minute car ferry crosses the Noordzee Kanaal near Velsen-Zuid (the entire old village center of which is registered as a national monument). If you aren't heading farther north, turn left when driving off the car ferry for a fascinating drive back across the Noordzee Kanaal atop the locks: Pay attention to the traffic lights! On the south side of the canal, at the IJmuiden fishing harbor (largest in the country), visitors are welcome Mon.–Fri. 7–10 a.m. at the fish auctions, and any time at one of several **fresh fish restaurants**.

## Frans Roozen Bulb Growers

*Vogelenzangseweg 49, Vogelenzang; Apr. and May, daily 8:00 a.m.–6 p.m., July–Oct. Mon.–Fri. 9 a.m.–6 p.m.;* ☎ *02502-47245.* South of Haarlem is the "old" bulb district. (It's old only in relation to the "new" bulb district, less well-known to visitors, that has been developed in the far north of Noord Holland province.) Among the many professional bulb nurseries that were established around Haarlem in the 1780s was that of the Frans Roozen family, still a pioneer in cultivating and marketing bulbs. During April and May, in the Frans Roozen greenhouses, show gardens and bulb fields, some 1000 varieties of bulbs (700 of which are tulips) are grown as a "living catalog:" bulbs can be ordered for home delivery. The place isn't overly commercial (albeit a bit gimmicky with its small windmill in the middle of the garden), is free and, with its close-up view of bulb fields in bloom, makes a good supplement to Keukenhof in the spring. From July–Oct., many summer flowering bulbs are on display in the garden and greenhouses.

## Zandvoort

Second only to Scheveningen (The Hague) as a Dutch beach resort, and the favorite with Amsterdammers, Zandvoort is well-served by both train and bus from Haarlem and Amsterdam. There are 38 pavilions along the lively broad sandy beachfront, as well as a section reserved for nude bathers. Recreational facilities range from bike paths in the dunes to the north (bike rental at Zandvoort train station, reservations recommended in summer season) to a casino.

# LEIDEN

*This dark-beamed room with period decor is in the 17th century former Cloth Guild hall, now the Lakenhal Museum.*

## GUIDELINES FOR LEIDEN

### SIGHTS

Leiden has the timeless Dutch beauty that comes with canals, picturesque gables and a working windmill in the center. **Leiden University** (Holland's oldest, 1575), numerous bookshops, cafes, sites associated with America's **Pilgrim Fathers** who lived here 11 years before sailing for the New World, landmarks from Rembrandt's early life, and interesting museums, give the town broad appeal.

## GETTING AROUND

Walking is the best way to see the town, even though its historic center is not as compact as some. Public buses or taxis from the station can supplement your feet. One-hour canal cruises (June, July, Aug. only) pass some of the main sights. The VVV offers guided walking tours of the city Sun. afternoons, June to Sept.

## SHOPPING

Leiden serves as the main shopping town for the surrounding region, and has a full range of department and smaller stores. Late-night shopping (*til 9 p.m.*) Thurs.; general market along *Nieuwe Rijn* in the city center Wed. and Sat. 9 a.m.–5 p.m.

## WHERE TO STAY

In-town hotels are limited in number, but run from modern first-class accommodations to moderate old canal-fronted townhouses.

## WHERE TO EAT

There's a full range of fare, from formal French and cozy candlelit bistros to casual cafes catering to students.

## ENTERTAINMENT AND EVENTS

Leiden is a lively student town with "brown" cafes and some music clubs. The VVV prints a monthly events calendar. Oct. 3 is celebrated annually in observance of the end of the *siege of the city* by the Spanish in 1574. A church service on the U.S.'s *Thanksgiving Day* in St. Pieterskerk commemorates the Pilgrim Fathers' 12-year stay in Leiden.

## ARRIVING

Leiden lies more or less midway on the main Amsterdam-Rotterdam train line, with Haarlem 15 minutes to the north, The Hague 15 minutes to the south. There are trains every quarter-hour in each direction, and several hourly to/from Schiphol Airport. Leiden is located just off the A 4 motorway. Leiden's canals account for the many one-way and pedestrianized streets, making driving complicated. Your best bet is to arrive by train; if you come by car, park it (legally) and forget it.

## IN THE AREA

Leiden lies at the southern boundary of Holland's main **bulb field district**, which normally is in bloom from early April to late May. The main train line from Leiden north to Haarlem towards Amsterdam (*not* the Schiphol/Amsterdam line) passes through the fields. Bus #54 from Leiden station stops at Keukenhof gardens; buses #50 and 51 travel through the bulb district between Leiden and Haarlem. Windmill cruises (three hours, mid-June to early Sept.) depart from Leiden and take in the surrounding countryside.

## TRAVEL TIPS

Leiden's university students are assertive cyclists who assume the right-of-way, even over pedestrians.

# LEIDEN IN CONTEXT

Much of what distinquishes Leiden—the same *Leyden* as it was written in periods past— stems from events that took place in 1574, though the town has a considerably longer history. Traces of Roman settlements have been found near Leiden, but essentially the region remained one of almost inaccessible below-sea-level marsh through much of the first millennium after Christ. One wonders why the Vikings bothered to plunder so persistently. About the year 1000, a stronghold and refuge from high water was built on a small island between two branches of the Rhine River. Around this *Burcht*, which still stands in the center of town, a village grew. By the 11th century, when the counts of Holland settled there, Leiden's continuance was confirmed.

About 1100, the danger of flooding from the Rhine at Leiden— the name means *place on the waterways*—was diminished by the construction of its first dikes, which also served as city walls. Gradually, craftsmen and brewers augmented the population of farmers and fishermen, and Leiden became the most important market town in the area. In 1266, Count of Holland Floris V awarded Leiden a city charter with extra all-important privileges, including toll-freedom and exemption from certain taxes, which further fostered growth in trade and population.

By the early 14th century, new canals had been dug to encompass the larger town. And Leiden's textile industry, having received a boost from immigrating Flemish weavers, had become famous far afield for the excellent quality of the woolen cloth it produced. In common with much of Europe, Leiden was plagued in the second half of the 14th century by outbreaks of the Black Death, which severely reduced its population. Nevertheless, the city enjoyed relative prosperity until succumbing to a long-lasting economic recession about 1500 that was led by a decline in the cloth trade.

In 1572, Leiden, together with 11 other important cities in the northern Netherlands, joined **Willem (the Silent)**, Prince of Orange, in opposing Spanish rule of the Low Countries. Such support ran the risk of confrontation: In 1573, Spaniards laid siege to Haarlem (successfully), then Alkmaar (unsuccessfully), and the Leijenaars prepared themselves. The town's earliest corn mills lay outside the city, but early in 1573 these were all demolished to keep them from falling to the Spanish. Eight new mills were built on the city walls. Large supplies of food were stored within the town in anticipation of a **siege**, and, late in 1573, Spanish troops did indeed surround Leiden. But the town's preparation paid off, and citizens suffered little deprivation before the Spanish, quite suddenly, withdrew in March 1574. Just as unexpectedly, however—the troops having only temporarily been needed to fight elsewhere—the Spanish reappeared in late May at the city walls. Food stores, so carefully set aside the previous year, had not been replenished, and this time food shortages in Leiden occurred alarmingly soon after the onset of the siege.

In what is the most famous Dutch stance during the *Eighty Years' War* with Spain, Leijenaars held their ground courageously. As August advanced to September, food shortages reduced many in the city to eating rats. Willem of Orange had pledged help to Leiden and, though severely ill with a fever at his residence in Delft, he directed defense plans, partly with the communications aid of carrier pigeons from the Leiden home of three brothers at 94 Rapenburg (still known as *Het Duyvenhuis*, the pigeon house). Knowing he had 200 Dutch vessels on the North Sea ready to rout the Spanish, still camped in relative comfort around the walls of Leiden, Willem made what was a drastic decision for a Dutchman: to breach the dikes that had been built over centuries to defend Leiden from the sea. The desperate deed was done: the dikes were cut in 16 places, and the sunken land surrounding Leiden flooded. But the water didn't come in deeply enough to sail the ships—which required a minimum 28-inch draught—over the countryside fields to Leiden. In fact, the wind changed direction, blowing the sea *away* from Leiden.

Within the city, the situation worsened by the day, as *hundreds* of starved-to-death citizens became *thousands*. Edible leaves were stripped from the trees. Horses, then dogs and cats, and finally cows—kept until they were too emanciated to produce milk—were slaughtered and distributed in as widely as possible among the population. When such conditions brought the plague, some people finally seemed ready to capitulate, since it had been weeks since the dikes had been severed, and no relief was in sight. It was reported that Leiden's Burgemeester (mayor) Adriaan van der Werf, who preferred death by starvation to dishonorable surrender, offered the restive citizens his own body for food "as far as it will go," thus stunning and/or shaming the citizens into continuing their resistance.

A full two months after the dikes had been damaged, 131 days after Leiden's siege had begun, with at least 6000 citizens dead, a fierce southwest storm swept Holland on the night of October 2, 1574. The North Sea surged, finally carrying Willem's Dutch naval fleet through the broken dikes to within striking distance of the Spanish. The relief of Leiden finally was realized.

In the morning of October 3, during a search of the abandoned Spanish encampments, one city marksman, Ghijsbert Corneliszoon Schaek, found a huge kettle of *hutspot*, a stew of beef, carrots, potatoes, and onions, which gave survivors of the siege their first fresh food in months. (The reputed iron kettle, often attributed to having been found by an orphan—it makes a more poignant story—is on display at Leiden's *Lakenhal Museum*.) Shortly thereafter, "seabeggars" arrived from south of the city on the river Vliet with ships loaded with white bread and herring for the starving citizens. To this day, those are the favored foods during Leiden's annual October 3 city celebrations.

For their brave endurance of the siege, Willem offered the people of Leiden exemption from taxes for a certain period or the establishment of a university. Despite what citizens in heavily-taxed Holland might do today, Leiden residents then took a long-range view and chose the first Dutch university. Its inauguration took place in February 1575, with an elaborate parade and a float procession on the river. Leiden quickly became the most important Protestant university in Europe, attracting the finest minds in Europe, and making Holland a leading center of scientific learning and art.

Deservingly, Leiden experienced better times following the siege. The manufacture of cloth once more became the driving force of the city's economy. Ironically, this was somewhat due to the Roman Catholic Spanish, who still occupied the southern Netherlands (today's Belgium). After they overtook Antwerp in 1585, among the many Protestant Flemish refugees who fled north to Holland were numerous skilled textile workers who settled in Leiden and provided fresh impulse for that industry. Leiden entered the 17th-century Golden Age as one of Holland's most industrialized places, and possibly Europe's largest textile manufacturing town. The impressive 1597 *Stadhuis* on Breestraat (whose facade fortunately survived a 1929 fire) was designed by Lieven de Key to reflect the prosperity of Leiden at this period.

Because Leiden had successfully struggled with Spain for its own spiritual freedom, and because the town had gained a special reputation for welcoming exiles fleeing persecution in other lands, it seems quite natural that English "separatists," seeking to escape the rigid edicts of King James I, wanted to settle there. After months of trying to arrange passage to religiously tolerant Holland, one group of English managed, after several false, near fatal starts, to escape from Boston, England, across the North Sea to Amsterdam. Among that group of "pilgrims" were 18-year-old **William Bradford**, who would later serve as governor of Plymouth Colony (Massachusetts) for many years, and **William Brewster**, who had served in Holland in 1587 with Queen Elizabeth's secretary of state, and would later become the pilgrims' spiritual leader in the New World.

They and others, upon discovering disagreements among the English separatists in Amsterdam, petitioned the liberal Leiden leaders for residence permits for 100. These were granted, "provided such persons behaved themselves," and by May 1, 1609, the pilgrims had moved to Leiden. A measure of Leiden's true support is the lack of attention the city burgemeester paid to English authorities who, learning that Leiden had admitted the "separatists," protested for their return.

Trained for the most part only in farming, the Leiden English exiles in many cases had to accept jobs of physical labor, particularly in the textile industry, which employed most workers in town. Having lost much of their personal property through theft or seizure while trying to get from England to Holland, many had to work long hours at subsistence level just to survive. So hard did they have to work that, despite their strong religious conviction, they were unable to establish their own meeting house until May 1611.

At that time they bought **De Groenpoort** ("the green gate"), which stood on a site that has been occupied since 1683 by the **Jean Pesijnhofje** almshouse, across from the great Pieterskerk (church). The Groenpoort served as the pilgrims' church and as a parsonage for their English religious leader, John Robinson, and his family. Small "cottages" were built around its courtyard as houses for the least well-off members of the English congregation. A plaque near the gate of the Pesijnhofje indicates that here "John Robinson lived, taught, and died—1625." The lovely enclosed garden, surrounded by small houses that today are rented to students and elderly couples, is open to the public.

Unlike many of his pilgrim parish peers, William Brewster was well educated. He was able to tutor in English at Leiden University, and eventually established a small printing press—an evangelical enterprise. The *Pilgrim Press* was located near Pieterskerk on Stincksteeg (Stink Alley, now renamed William Brewster Alley), and is indicated today by an explanatory tablet.

Continued poverty and concern about the corruption of their youth, who were growing up without English identity and under the less religiously strict influence of Dutch neighbors, caused growing discontent among the pilgrims. When William Brewster had to flee Holland to escape arrest for one of his Pilgrim Press religious essays —James I's officials had tracked down the typeface—he returned to England under the surname of Williamson. There, he began making arrangements for the pilgrims' passage to the New World. The separatists in Leiden would probably have read Captain John Smith's enthusiastic *A Description of New England*, published in 1616, and hoped to have better success with "converting" the natives there to their religious outlook than they had had in Holland. Recalled William Bradford later in his *History of Plymouth Plantation*, the young and strong pilgrims who, with him, left "Leyden, a fair and bewtifull citie," did so "not out of any newfangledness or such like giddy humor—but for sundry weighty and solid reasons."

On the last day of July 1620, 54 of the English group from Leiden—35 of them "saints," those going for religious reasons, the remaining "strangers," those who sought commercial opportunity in the New World—boarded barges by the Vlietbrug (near the present **Pilgrim Documentation Center**, see "What To See and Do"), and sailed south down the Vliet to Delftshaven (now a picturesque old harbor in a quiet corner of Rotterdam). There, they departed, after prayer, aboard the *Speedwell* for England, where they met up with the good ship *Mayflower*.

John Robinson, the pilgrims' spiritual leader in Leiden, remained behind, since the majority of his parish had not opted for the rigors of the New World. He had hoped to follow eventually, but died in 1625 and was buried in the Pieterskerk. A memorial on the outside wall of the massive old church reads: "... whence at his prompting went forth the Pilgrim Fathers to settle New England." As the pilgrims had foreseen, many of the English who remained in Leiden became assimilated into Dutch society. Robinson's son Isaac was one of the last of the Leiden pilgrims to emigrate to Plymouth (Massachusetts), in 1632.

Dutch influence on the pilgrims who established America's first permanent English colony at Plymouth is hard to pinpoint, but there can be little doubt that some of the Dutch civil laws and precedents the pilgrims had experienced in Leiden were incorporated into the idea of the separation of church and state that, even under the religious-minded pilgrims, was established in America from the start at Plymouth. Some might see a connection between the pilgrims' celebration of a Thanksgiving feast with the Indians, and the annual three days of feasting and prayer in thanksgiving for the relief of Leiden from the Spanish siege that they would have observed each October 3rd. Today, Thanksgiving services are held for both occasions in Leiden's Pieterskerk, on October 3, and on the U.S. Thanksgiving Day in November. The ecumenical service is a meaningful remembrance of the pilgrims' past.

Leiden was one of Holland's thriving centers for painting, and the birthplace of **Lucas van Leyden** (1489?–1533). During Holland's Golden Age, many important painters were born or developed their artistic lives in Leiden: **Jan van Goyen** (1596–1656); **Rembrandt** (1606–1669); **Willem van der Velde the Elder and the Younger** (1611–1693) and (1633–1707); **Gerrit Dou** (1613–1675); **Jan Steen** (1625/26–1679); **Gabriel Metsu** (1629–1667); and **Frans van Meiris** (1635–1681). Jan Steen, son of a Leiden brewer, and trained as one himself, is known to have owned a tavern in 1672 on the *Lange Brug*. It is reputed—though so much inaccurate biographical data has been perpetuated about Holland's great masters that this story needs to be taken as perhaps just another good tale—that, because Steen was his tavern's own best customer, the tavern that was meant to support him at his art in fact produced bills that had to be paid for in paintings. One biographer wrote, "For a long time his works were to be found only in the hands of dealers in wine." Steen is buried in the Pieterskerk.

**Rembrandt** is Leiden's greatest son. His father was a fairly prosperous miller, whose surname **Van Rijn** indicates that the family had lived for some generations beside or near the Rhine River, as it did in Rembrandt's day. (His birthplace and residence for most of his 26 years in Leiden, on Weddesteeg near the *Rembrandt Bridge*, is marked by a tablet.) The eighth of nine children, Rembrandt seems to have been the most promising, and was sent to Leiden's Latin School. (In the egalitarian Dutch provinces, it was not unthinkable that a miller's son could aspire to a profession.) The Latin School (built by Lieven de Key in 1599 and used as a school until 1864) is located near the Pieterskerk and, since Rembrandt would have been receiving his schooling in the same period as the pilgrims' sojourn in Leiden, he might easily have passed one or another of them on the street. The purpose of the Latin School was to prepare young men for Leiden University, then the equal of any in Europe. Although Rembrandt matriculated there, he seems to have left shortly thereafter, having determined to pursue painting.

Rembrandt's first Leiden art instructor is unknown. The second, under whom he served a three-year apprenticeship, was the Leiden painter Jacob van Swanenburgh, who taught Rembrandt the fundamentals, but seems not to have made an important impression upon his pupil; his specialties of architectural scenes and views of hell were two subjects to which Rembrandt never subsequently turned his hand. With Rembrandt showing great talent, his father sent him to Amsterdam for further study under **Pieter Lastman**, then one of the Netherlands' foremost painters of historical scenes. At the age of 18 or 19, Rembrandt returned to Leiden and set himself up as an independent master, developing rapidly as a painter, perfecting his etching technique, and soon surpassing most other Dutch artists.

Leiden was a bustling town during the six or seven years that Rembrandt had his studio there, working closely with artist Jan Lievens (who had also studied under Lastman in Amsterdam). Rembrandt had several students in Leiden, **Gerrit Dou** being the most important. With 50,000 people in 1620 (and 70,000 by 1670), the city of Leiden was then second in size in Holland only to Amsterdam (110,000). Architecturally, Leiden was typically Dutch: narrow houses, with gabled roofs and bright-colored shutters, lined the canals and streets, but if Rembrandt recorded them, no such scenes have survived. Visitors found Leiden conspicuous for its cleanliness, even in well-scrubbed Holland, but, paradoxically, the town also had an abominable stench rising from almost currentless canals that often were clogged with sewage, which perhaps contributed to Leiden's periodic outbreaks of the plague (several deadly epidemic diseases). Some years the death toll was so high that the town's earthen ramparts had to be used as supplemental cemeteries.

In the Leiden of the 1620s, almost all workers, mostly illiterate and underpaid, were associated with the town's textile trade; their living conditions would have fostered Rembrandt's great sense of humanity. He also felt the full influence of the variety of population at Leiden University, where he saw a parade of students and philosophical professors from countries throughout Europe, many from noble families, whose foreign clothes fed his eye for the picturesque, exotic, and sumptuous details in dress that he inserted in his paintings the rest of his life. In 1632, Rembrandt left Leiden for Amsterdam, where he won almost immediate fame and wealth.

Scientifically, especially due to its university, Leiden attained and maintained a position of prominence in Europe during the Age of Reason, and on into the Enlightenment. The **Museum Boerhaave** pays tribute to **Christian Huygens,** a 17th-century scholar whose most notable achievement was the invention of the pendulum clock, which improved significantly the accuracy of navigation for the all-important Dutch East India Company ships. Also honored is **Antony van Leeuwenhoek,** who invented the first microscope, which is on display.

A century-and-a-half after the pilgrims departed Leiden, another piece of early American history was connected with the town. Under initial encouragement from the province of Friesland, the Dutch were the first to recognize the thirteen colonies' proclamation of freedom from Britain, and to send them much-needed financial aid. (Pragmatic Dutch commercial shipping companies operating out of the Caribbean during the American Revolution actually sold supplies to both sides.) When the war was over, George Washington appointed **John Adams** of Massachusetts (a descendant of *Mayflower* pilgrim John Alden and who later became the 2nd president of the U.S.) the first U.S. ambassador to Holland. Adams, his wife, Abigail, and son John Quincy (who would be 6th U.S. president) came to Holland in 1781, at which time John Quincy, then 14, was enrolled at Leiden University. Abigail Adams wrote in a 1786 letter of a visit to the Pieterkerk: "I visited the church at Leyden, in which our forefathers worshipped ... I felt a respect upon entering the doors."

By the time of the Adams' appointment to Holland, Leiden's economy was on the wane again, the population reduced to 30,000, the town in physical disrepair. Economic conditions ebbed and flowed during the 19th and 20th centuries, but today, Leiden, population 109,000, appears as lovely as it ever has. Many of the town's fine old buildings, saved from urban-renewal razing because of improverished periods, have seen recent renovations, and several reconstructions have been completed. Leiden is enjoying a promising present, while preserving its past.

## GUIDEPOSTS

**Telephone code 071**

**Tourist Info** • VVV, Stationplein 210, 2312 AR, ☎ *146846, FAX 125318*; year-round Mon.–Fri. 9 a.m.–5:30 p.m., Sat. 10 a.m.–4 p.m.; Sun. closed.

**Bike rental** • Bicycle depot next to railway station, ☎ *131304*; Van der Laan, Merelstraat 13, ☎ *155915*.

**Rowboat rental** • Jac. Veringa, near Rembrandtbrug, ☎ *149790*.

**Canal cruises** • Noord-Zuid, Quay Beestenmarkt

**Parking** • Carparks indicated on VVV city map; at Stationplein (across from VVV), including Beestenmarkt, Lammermarkt (near De Valk, convenient to De Lakenhal Museum).

**Auto. Assn.** • ANWB, Stationweg 2, ☎ *146241*.

**Train** • Information in station hall.

**Bus** • NZH (local and regional bus services), Stationplein 5, ☎ *national number (fee) 06-9292*.

**Emergencies** • Police ☎ *06-11, or 258888*; medical ☎ *233233*.

**Shopping** • Pedestrianized Haarlemmer Straat, Breestraat, and side streets.

**Taxis** • Listed in VVV city brochure. Available at train station.

## WHAT TO SEE AND DO

Leiden is worthy of a more lingering look than many travelers allow time for. The activities of university students, who live throughout the city, give Leiden a lively evening atmosphere. Leiden is also centrally located, making it a good choice as an overnight alternative, which make it a useful, less expensive base from which to make Dutch day trips. No matter how short your stay, start it at the VVV across from the train station. In addition to a map, which you'll find necessary, it has other excellent English-language booklets on city sights and services, the pilgrims, town history, museums, and several self-guiding walking tour brochures: *A Pilgrimage through Leiden (free); Leiden, a true Dutch Heritage;* and *Following in Rembrandt's Footsteps;* each covers many of the town's major landmarks and costs Dfl. 3.50.

### Municipal Museum "de Lakenhal" ★★

*Oude Singel 32; open Tues.–Fri. 10 a.m.–5 p.m., Sat., Sun. and holidays; noon—5 p.m., closed Mondays and Jan. 1, Dec. 25;* ☎ *165360.* The handsome Lakenhal (Cloth Hall) was built in 1640 to serve as the center of Leiden's wool textile industry and headquarters for the preeminent Cloth Guild. Aspects of the cloth trade are shown in five sculptured plaques on the building's facade; the courtyard was used for the rigorous inspection of the cloth that preserved its high reputation. Turned into Leiden's municipal museum in 1874, the Lakenhal now houses displays in elegant rooms with beamed ceilings, tiled fireplaces, and oak floors. The historic section covers the *Siege of Leiden*, and includes a huge wall tapestry map of the city in the 16th century, and the famed siege *hutspot.* Wonderful period rooms include a delightful 17th-century Dutch-tiled kitchen and the distinguished *Governors' Room* with fine antique furniture. The excellent painting collection has works by famous artists associated with Leiden: Lucas van Leyden, Rembrandt, Jan Steen, Gerrit Dou, and Jan van Goyen's *View of Leyden*, which shows what the town looked like at the time the pilgrims lived here.

### St. Pieterskerk                                              ★★

*Pieterskerkhof; ask at the VVV about opening times.* This elephantine 15th-century edifice, the sometime house of worship for the English separatist pilgrims, has been restored and now functions as a conference center and setting for Leiden student exams, as well as special church services (particularly on *October 3* in memory of the end of Leiden's siege of 1574, and *Thanksgiving Day* to commemorate the pilgrim connection). The "minimalist" Protestant ★ interior includes many interesting grave slabs that lie flush with the floor. On the exterior is a memorial to John Robinson, religious leader of the pilgrims.

Opposite that memorial is the restored ★ **Jean Pesijnhofje**, an almshouse built in 1683 on the site of the English pilgrims' **De Groene Poort**, still in use as housing for old and student couples. Near the Pieterskerk, on ★ **Pieterskerkchoorsteeg** (Peter's Church Choir Alley) is a plaque over the door to **William Brewster Alley**, where his **Pilgrim Press** operated.

### Pilgrim Fathers Document Center                              ★★

*Vliet 45; open Mon.–Fri. 9:30 a.m.–4:30 p.m., closed Sat., Sun., holidays, and Oct. 3;*  *120191.* The center houses a permanent exhibition of photocopies of personal records documenting details of the pilgrims' lives in Leiden. Marriage and tax records, an edition from *Brewster's Pilgrim Press*, and other items pertaining to Leiden's entire 17th-century English community—with tags designating those who sailed to the New World on the *Mayflower*—can be examined. An informative ★★ 20-minute film in English can be seen on the pilgrims and the religious times in which they lived.

### Leiden University                                            ★

*Rapenburg 73;*  *277242.* In 1581—shortly after its founding in 1575—all Catholic property was confiscated in Holland, and the University's adminstrative headquarters became housed in the former convent of the White Nuns on Rapenburg canal (at the *Nonnenbrug*, Nuns' Bridge). It may be possible to enter the university building at that entrance, in which case seek out the examination waiting room with its walls covered with the names and dates of those who have agonized there. Of possible interest is the **University History Museum** *(open Tues.–Thurs. 1–5 p.m., closed Oct. 3, holidays)*, which contains exhibits regarding the history of university student life.

Founded in 1587, the University's ★ **Hortus Botanicus** (Botanic Gardens, entrance Rapenburg 73), among the oldest in Europe, was under the initial directorship of Carolus Clusius, who had been presented in Vienna with the first tulip bulbs to reach Dutch soil. (See earlier chapter "The Bulb Field Business.") *(Open daily Mon.–Sat. 9 a.m.–5 p.m., Sun. 10 a.m.–5 p.m., closed Sat. Oct. 1–Apr. 1, Oct. 3, Dec. 25–Jan. 1.)* In addition to ancient trees, gardens, and canal, there are extensive greenhouses with wide-ranging plants from around the world in climate-controlled environments.

*De Valk Windmill Museum is centrally located in Leiden.*

## Windmill Museum De Valk ★★

*Binnenvestgracht; open Tues.–Sat. 10 a.m.–5 p.m., Sun. and holidays 1–5 p.m.; closed Mon., Jan 1, Oct. 3, Dec. 25;*  *165353; fee.* I've always found *De Valk* (the falcon) to be one of Leiden's most interesting sights and the best windmill museum in Holland. A tower-style flour mill dating from 1734, *De Valk* is seven stories, beginning with a former miller's living quarters on the ground floor. Everyone can enjoy the furnished miller's rooms, though the exhibits on higher stories can only be reached via narrow flights of ship-steep stairs. Heading up, one passes the all-wood working mill parts, a self-service slide show (in English) about Leiden and windmills—some 70 of the country's approximately 900 remaining windmills (9000 once existed in Holland) are located in the greater Leiden region—and exhibits on the historic function and importance of windmills (much of the information in English), before reaching the reefing stage (5th flight). Here, 45 feet up, on the wide wooden outside platform (from which there's a 360-degree view), is the wheel by which the miller turns the sails (which have a span of 88 feet) into the wind. Wonderfully, the sails at *De Valk* are set to the wind most afternoons from Apr. 1 to Oct. 1.

For those settling into Leiden with lots of time, there are several other respected museums that can be visited, including the **National Museum of Ethnology**, and the **National Museum of Antiquities**, which has the Egyptian A.D. first century Temple of Taffeh, presented to the Dutch in 1969 in thanks for their contribution to rescuing Nubian treasures that would have been lost due to the construction of the Aswan Dam. The **National Museum of Natural History** is closed until further notice.

## WHERE TO STAY

The hotels listed are all centrally located. With the exception of the new Golden Tulip property, all are in old townhouses. Guesthouses, which may not be in the center of town, can be booked at the VVV.

### EXPENSIVE

**Golden Tulip Leiden**                              ★★★★

*Schipholweg 3, 2316 XB;* ☎ *221121, FAX 226675,* ☎ *1 (800) 333-1212.* This is Leiden's newest, largest (102 beds), most modern, luxurious, center city hotel, situated across from the railway station, on the right (center city) side of the tracks.

### MODERATE

**De Doelen**                                       ★★★

*Rapenburg 2, 2311 EV.* ☎ *120527, FAX 128453.* A handsome building on a handsome canal near the university, this nine-room hotel still has the feel of the 15th-century patrician house it was converted from, with features such as old beams, antique tiled fireplaces, dark oak wainscotting and other old Dutch details in its nooks and crannies. There's no elevator and, needless to say, no two rooms are alike (prices vary somewhat too). A couple of rooms overlook the canal. Some rooms are old-fashioned, decorated in a dark old Dutch style, while others are lighter, more modern, and have less character. The hotel's restaurant is well respected locally and has a walled garden cafe.

### Hotel Mayflower ★★★

*Beestenmarkt 2, 2312 CC;*  *142641, FAX 128516.* This 14-room family-run hotel has modern decor with touches of Dutch: stain glass, tiles, paintings in the bright, comfortable little lobby, off of which are a breakfast room and bar. Large modern baths and light wood furniture produce an airy feel to bedrooms. Two rooms have views of the canal and the square the hotel faces, but rooms in the back will prove quieter in this very centrally located hotel, four blocks from station. Elevator.

## INEXPENSIVE

### Nieuw Minerva ★★

*Boommarkt 23, 2311 EA,*  *126358, FAX 142674.* Eight former townhouses, c. 1600, provide 40 rooms that vary considerably. Some in the older part are cozy and nice, some are modernized and very ordinary; all have private toilet and shower. Though one was rumored to be coming, there was no elevator *yet* on my most recent visit. Cozy, friendly, slightly tired, eclectic Dutch-style lobby. The hotel has two locally popular restaurants (moderate and inexpensively priced), one with less formal menu, quicker service; both serve lunch and dinner.

## *WHERE TO EAT*

Though limited in number, the restaurants in Leiden will certainly serve your needs. Hotel restaurants and cafes should be kept in mind, since they need to be of a high enough standard to attract a local clientele as well as overnight guests. The "three-course fixed-price menus" and "dish-of-the-day" will represent the best values. If you're looking for a proper restaurant meal, it's always a good idea to call for reservations, since seating capacities can be small and service deliberately unrushed.

A Leiden standard because of its longevity, location, looks, and food is **Oudt Leyden** *(Steenstraat 51-53; restaurant only closed Sun.;* ☎ *133144; restaurant expensive, pancake house inexpensive/moderate);* where you get two choices at one address. Long established in a trio of town houses on the main street from the station into the Centrum, the restaurant offers nouvelle-style continental cuisine, with attentive service and handsome atmosphere. The **'t Pannekoekenhuysje** at the left entrance offers the typical Dutch platter-size pancakes and other traditional Dutch specialties.

Sharing space on the same alley just a few doors from the Pieterskerk, where the pilgrims sometimes prayed, are two of Leiden's best bistros, which may put tables out in front when the weather's nice. **De Bisschop** *(Kloksteeg 7;* ☎ *125024; expensive)* offers a pleasant dining space replete with flowers and a prix-fixe menu, among the à la carte dishes. At **La Cloche** *(Kloksteeg 3;* ☎ *123053; expensive),* fare is apt to be fresh and French in an old house that has been most successfully "smartened" with white rattan and other tasteful details.

Two *eet-cafes* recommended for informal fare and touching shoulders with students are **De Grote Beer** *(Rembrandtstraat 27)* and **Pardoeza** *(Doe-*

*zastraat 43).* According to residents, the town's best Indonesian food can be had at **Surakarta** *(Noordeinde 51;* ☎ *123524; inexpensive).*

The Hague

# THE HAGUE

*A resort pier stretches out over The North Sea at Scheveninghen.*

## GUIDELINES FOR THE HAGUE

### SIGHTS

The Hague, the seat of government for Holland and residence of
H.M. Queen Beatrix—though not the country's capital—has much
appeal for all ages and interests. Several art museums include the exquisite **Mauritshuis** mansion with its masterpices of 17th-century
Golden Age painting, and the **Gemeentemuseum**, with the largest
collection of twentieth-century Dutch artist Mondriaan's works in
the world. Other choices range from a museum of instruments of

torture, a composite Dutch town constructed at 1:25 scale (**Maduro-dam**), the **Peace Palace**, and the Parliament's **Ridderzaal**, one of Europe's best preserved pieces of gothic architecture. In appearance, The Hague differs considerably from a typical Dutch town of canals and narrow gabled houses: being a diplomatic center throughout its history— more than 60 nations have embassies or consulates there —led to a more expansive, park-like layout. The "downtown" deco-rum in The Hague is contrasted at its coast, where **Scheveningen**'s North Sea resort trappings include a **pier**, **promenade**, casino, and even a nudist beach.

## GETTING AROUND

As you'd expect in a city its size (population 450,000), sights in The Hague are spread out, but many are bunched in the **Centrum** (city center) and can be reached on foot from the **Centraal Station** (CS). The Hague has a fine **tram** and **bus** network, and the CS is close to stops on several routes, including the tram to Delft, less than five miles away. Trams also run from the center of town, and from The Hague's **Hollands Spoor** (HS) station on to the North Sea-side and Scheveningen. The 1-, 2-, and 3-day local transportation passes, tickets, and maps of the city system are available at the information (" *i* ") booth at the CS; the city's main **VVV** tourist office is next door in the Babylon Shopping Complex. Though you may see less ortho-dox bureaucrats in business suits riding bicycles to work, The Hague's two-wheeler traffic isn't as distracting as in some other Dutch cities; bike rentals are at the HS station (**Cycle Garage**; ☎ *3890830; Dfl. 8 per day, Dfl. 100 deposit*) and in Scheveningen (**Cycle Rental du Nord**, *Keizerstraat 27;* ☎ *3554060; Dfl. 9 per day, Dfl. 50 deposit*). Cycling route maps available from VVV offices.

## SHOPPING

A cosmopolitan diplomatic capital, The Hague is a sophisticated shopping center. There's a focus on antiques and boutiques, but op-portunities run the gamut from market stalls to quality department stores featuring avant-garde goods.

## WHERE TO STAY

From the seaside at Scheveningen to the heart of The Hague, choices range from rooms in grand, century-old "establishments" with superb service to small home-like hotels.

## WHERE TO EAT

Indonesian food is in plentiful supply, since The Hague is home to the Indonesian community in Holland. But from *hutspot* (stew) to

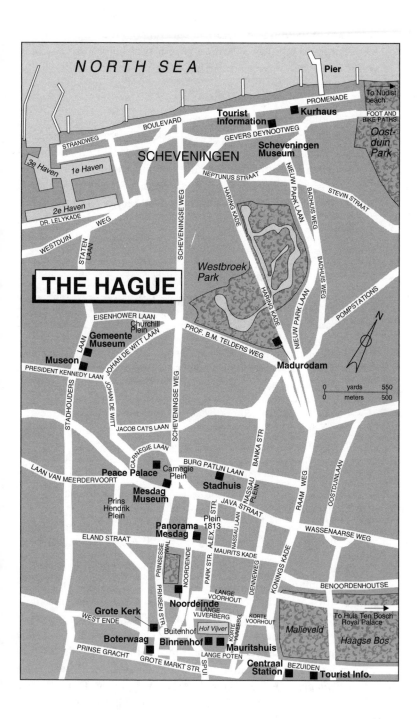

NORTH SEA

Pier

To Nudist beach

PROMENADE

Tourist Information

Kurhaus

BOULEVARD

FOOT AND BIKE PATHS

GEVERS DEYNOOTWEG

STRANDWEG

Oost-duin Park

SCHEVENINGEN

Scheveningen Museum

3e Haven

1e Haven

NEPTUNUS STRAAT

NIEUW PARK LAAN

STEVIN STRAAT

2e Haven

DR. LELYKADE

WEG

HARING KADE

BADHUIS WEG

WESTDUIN

STATEN LAAN

SCHEVENINGSE WEG

Westbroek Park

**THE HAGUE**

BADHUIS WEG

POMPSTATIONS

EISENHOWER LAAN

Churchill Plein

Gemeente Museum

JOHAN DE WITT LAAN

PROF. B.M. TELDERS WEG

NIEUW PARK LAAN

N

Museon

LAAN

PRESIDENT KENNEDY LAAN

JOHAN DE WITT

Madurodam

0       yards      550
0       meters      500

STADHOUDERS

JACOB CATS LAAN

SCHEVENINGSE WEG

BANKA STR.

OOSTDUINLAAN

CARNEGIE LAAN

BURG PATIJN LAAN

LAAN VAN MEERDERVOORT

Peace Palace

Carnegie Plein

NASSAU PLEIN

RAAM WEG

Stadhuis

Mesdag Museum

JAVA STRAAT

WASSENAARSE WEG

Prins Hendrik Plein

Panorama Mesdag

Plein 1813

STR. ALEX.

MAURITS KADE

KONINGS KADE

ELAND STRAAT

PRINSESSE WAL

NOORDEINDE

PARK STR.

NASSAU STRAAT

DENNEWEG

BENOORDENHOUTSE

PRINSEN STR.

LANGE VOORHOUT

Noordeinde

LANGE VIJVERBERG

KORTE VOORHOUT

To Huis Ten Bosch Royal Palace

Grote Kerk

WEST ENDE

Buitenhof

Hof Vijver

KORTE VIJVERBG.

Malieveld

Haagse Bos

Boterwaag

Binnenhof

Mauritshuis

PRINSE GRACHT

GROTE MARKT STR.

LANGE POTEN

SPUI

Centraal Station

BEZUIDEN

Tourist Info.

haute cuisine, and from *nieuwe haring* (fresh herring) stands in the courtyard of the Binnenhof Parliament compound to fine seafood in view of the fishing fleet at Scheveningen, you'll find most anything you want in the way of eating in The Hague.

## ARRIVING

The Hague is somewhat closer to Rotterdam than Amsterdam on the main rail line between those two cities (a trip which takes slightly over an hour). Trains run in both directions several times hourly, as do trains to and from Schiphol Airport (a half-hour ride). For purposes of visiting The Hague by foot, **Centraal Station** (CS) should be your stop, although there's more frequent service to the **Hollands Spoor** (HS), from which there are trams and buses to the *Centrum*, about one mile. The Hague can be reached via motorway and other major roads.

## ENTERTAINMENT AND EVENTS

### MONDRIAAN EXHIBIT
### TO RUN THROUGH APRIL 30, 1995

Few artists have had trademarks as readily recognizable—or as influential—as the unmistakable black lines and primary color blocks of modern Dutch master Piet Mondriaan. Opening December 17, 1994, in honor of the 50th anniversary of the artist's death, The Hague's Gemeentemuseum—which has the world's largest collection of Mondriaan's works—has mounted a major retrospective devoted to this key figure in the development of *abstraction*, founding member of the *De Stijl* group, and inventor of *neoplasticism*. The exhibit is the first to represent a complete review of Mondriaan's life *oeuvre*, from figurative to abstract. It includes loaned works from his last period when he lived in the United States.

Nearly 100 paintings and 150 drawings by Mondriaan are contained in the Mondriaan exhibition that runs at the Gemeentemuseum through April 1995. Dated and timed tickets are available in advance. Other special events related to Mondriaan also are on offer.

In addition to the ongoing, afterdark illumination of main buildings (Binnenhof, Mauritshuis, etc.), The Hague/Scheveningen have a number of colorful occasions worth noting. The VVV publishes a monthly events booklet (*VVV Info*), and will book tickets (in person only) for performances in The Hague and elsewhere in Holland. The **Nederlands Dans Theater**, a dance company that has acquired an excellent international reputation, and the **Residentie Orkest** (*Den Haag Philharmonic*), are housed, respectively, in the Dutch Dance Theater and the Dr. Anton Philips Hall, a successful and striking cultural complex on the Spui in the center of the city.

## TRAVEL TIPS

The center of The Hague tends to be quiet and relatively unpeopled at night, though it's safe to wander around.

## THE HAGUE IN CONTEXT

More than 750 years ago the counts of Holland built a structure on the site where soon would rise the **Binnenhof** (Inner Court), the building that remains the seat of government for the Netherlands' vigorous democracy. The original building, probably a hunting lodge, situated by a pond in woods lying between coastal dunes and waterlogged land, was begun by Floris IV, count of Holland from 1222 to 1234. The place is first mentioned in 1242 as *Die Haghe* ("the hedge"), from which comes the city's formal name, *'s-Gravenhage* ("the counts' hedge"); most Dutch shorten it back again to *Den Haag*. Though he never lived there, Floris' son Count Willem II, elected king of the Romans and German emperor at Aachen in 1247, who was impressed with the German nobility's regal standard of living, began to build a castle more in keeping with his status. Willem's son Floris V, who by then also numbered Zeeland among his territorial possessions, was able to add the **Ridderzaal** (Hall of Knights), an impressive Scheldt-style gothic building, by selling off his inherited rights to the Scottish throne for a handsome fee. The building complex became the Binnenhof and was the count's preferred residence by his death in 1296.

The first counts of Holland to occupy the Binnenhof with their entire court and families were Albrecht of Bavaria and his son Willem VI, in about 1400. The settlement immediately surrounding the palace was greatly expanded at the time since it had to be largely self-sufficient. Stables, livestock, vegetable gardens (planted on what today is the *Plein*), a saddlery, smithy, bottling room, bakery, and chapel all existed within the Binnenhof. Outside the core settlement was the *Buitenhof* (Outer Court), where crafts- and trades-people kept close, in hope of commissions. Today's *Plaats* was a meeting place just outside the court gate (now the Prison Gate or *Gevangenpoort*). The *Vijverberg* once was a playground among the trees, and the *Kneuterdijk* served as tournament grounds. The yet tree-lined *Lange Voorhout*, then an entry into the *Haage Bos* (Hague Woods), often was brightened with the canopies of tents in which camped court guests who could not be accommodated at the Binnenhof palace. When farms grew up slightly farther afield, The Hague could actually be called a village.

Holland and Zeeland, together with the rest of the Netherlands (which then included what today is Belgium), came under the rule of the dukes of Burgundy during the mid-15th century, but day-to-day administration remained with the Stadholder (regional ruler), who resided in The Hague. The Burgundian dukes kept court in Brussels, but the peripatetic nature of their business brought them regularly to the Binnenhof. On two occasions Philip the Good held magnificent banquets in the Ridderzaal for the knights of the *Order of the Golden Fleece* (who also attended services in 1456 at the Grote Kerk near the Buitenhof).

Early in the 16th century, sovereignty over the Netherlands had passed to Emperor Charles V. By then The Hague was a prosperous "open" place, with many mansions among its parks. To this day, The Hague looks unlike most other old Dutch towns. This is the result of it never having been a city-wall-enclosed, fortified town where space was scarce. (In many Dutch towns, taxes on homeowners to pay for the upkeep of the town walls were based on the width of a dwelling, which led to the building of narrow, deep, tall houses.) Without the space constrictions imposed by city walls, The Hague was set out with wide, tree-lined avenues and mansions amid park settings. Emperor Charles V, who was also ruler of Spain, Burgundy, and the Low Countries, found The Hague pleasing and sought to protect its natural beauty. His son Philip II, however, had little love for any part of Holland and had other things on his mind when he sent his Spanish forces through The Hague.

Its lack of defensive walls came home to haunt The Hague during Holland's *Eighty Years' War* with the Spanish. When the Spanish marched north, the government in the *Binnenhof* under Stadholder **Willem the Silent**, Prince of Orange, fled to nearby, somewhat safer Delft, which was walled. The Hague lay in the pathway to the Dutch cities—Leiden, Haarlem, and Alkmaar—destined for siege by the Spanish, and passing troops, friend and foe, burned and abused it. At one point, Delft burghers proposed burning down what remained of The Hague in order to force the Spanish out of their camping site in the area *Haagse Bos* (Hague Woods). But Willem defused the idea, suspecting it to be inspired by selfish motives to move the government to Delft.

After Willem's Spanish-inspired assassination in Delft in 1574, the executive of the *States of Holland* resolved to meet only in The Hague. (Their decision was politic since The Hague had never had a seat in the Assembly of the States because it had never received a town charter, and thus it aroused less jealousy than the selection of any *official* town as the seat of government would have). In 1588 the *States General,* which represented all the seven united Dutch provinces, selected The Hague as its headquarters for the same diplomatic reason. Thenceforth, nearly all bodies associated with the government of the Netherlands have located themselves in or around the *Binnenhof.*

As The Hague entered the 17th century, it quickly grew in importance, attracting nobility, merchants, musicians, craftsmen, and architects to its democratic court. The Hague became one of the most important diplomatic posts for foreigners, a prime gathering point for international statesmen. So much so that one contemporary Englishman wrote of it as "the whispering gallery" of Europe by the time the Republic of the United Netherlands had won full recognition when the *Eighty Years' War* was officially ended by the *Peace of Munster* in 1648.

When **Willem II** died in 1650, several Dutch provinces including powerful Holland, decided not to appoint a new Stadholder. Instead, a role of *Grand Pensionary* was instituted, the holder of that title being the effective leader of the Dutch Republic. **Johan de Witt** served with distinction in the office of Grand Pensionary, and during his leadership the Dutch overseas empire increased substantially. Simultaneously, Johan's brother **Cornelius** distinguished himself as a naval commander against the English and French fleets.

Despite this, the brothers' policies became unpopular in 1672, and Cornelius de Witt, unjustly accused of plotting against young Willem, Prince of Orange, was imprisoned in the *Gevangenpoort.* In one of Holland's least laudable incidents, political enemies sent a message to Johan under Cornelius' name asking him to come to the prison. Though friends and his daughter feared a trap and urged him not to go, the loyal Johan felt he had a duty to his brother if he were in need. The message had indeed been false, and now both brothers were under arrest. De Witt disparagers plied the impassioned masses assembled outside the prison with brandy and wine, maneuvering them into a riotous mood. Although legitimate cavalry troops were sent to control the crowd, they were cleverly tricked into leaving, and storming of the prison by an enraged, drunken mob commenced.

Once inside the prison, the rioters found Cornelius lying down, racked with pain from days of torture, unable to stand, and his brother Johan reading to him from the Bible. Both brothers were hauled from the cell, shoved down the prison stairs, and became separated from each other. In the street below, Cornelius was struck on the head and trampled to death. Johan lasted a few minutes longer before a pike was driven into his face and he was shot in the neck. It is said that as he fell he managed to clasp his hands in the direction of heaven. Steps from the Gevangenpoort prison (now a museum where the de Witt cell is on view), on the *Plaats*, is a statue of Johan de Witt.

Later in 1672, when France invaded Holland and threats along its coast came from the combined fleets of the French and English navies, the *States General* once again turned to the *House of Orange* for leadership. They called for **Prince Willem III** (1650-1702), who, in addition to being the Dutch Stadholder, was also to become **King William of England** and **Ireland** (through marriage to **Mary**, daughter of James II, with whom he became joint English ruler). Naturally, Willem's joint position made The Hague even more of an international meeting center for diplomats and merchants. Even after Willem's death in 1702, splendor continued at the court in The Hague. The pomp and pageantry included mock sea battles on the *Hofvijver* lake by the Binnenhof, royal processions through the streets with flaming torches, fireworks displays, and seafront outings at Scheveningen.

During the French rule of the Netherlands from 1795 to 1813, the matter of The Hague not being an official town was rectified by an unexpected supporter. In 1806, Napoleon had his brother **Louis Bonaparte**—who had tried to resist the invitation—come to Holland to act in his place as ruler. Louis arrived at The Hague, which doesn't seem to have suited him. But before he left, first for Utrecht and then Amsterdam, Louis awarded The Hague its first full civic charter.

In 1818, one Jacob Pronk opened a wooden "bathing machine" establishment on the dunes at The Hague's seaside neighbor village of Scheveningen. This consisted of guests "curing" themselves by sitting in sheltered tubs of "seawater with healing power" atop the dunes. Later, Pronk placed two bathing machines right in the surf, with attendants close at hand to help the daring participants. The business was so profitable that it was taken over by Scheveningen village leaders in 1828, and seaside resort activities have been a main business ever since.

Scheveningen's outer and first inner harbor were dug in 1904, and fishing remains a mainstay of the economy. The harbor is home to one of the largest herring fleets in Holland. For the opening of the fishing season in May on *Vlaggetjesdag* (flag day), the fleet is decked out in colorful pennants and more fishermen's wives than usual wear the local costume (long black dress, striped apron, black shawl, and ornamented starched-white headcover). It's still a tradition that the first barrel of *nieuwe haring* (fresh young herring) is delivered with great ceremony to the queen.

The **Peace Palace**, completed in 1913, was an outgrowth of a call for international peace by **Czar Nicholas II of Russia** on August 28, 1898, during a conference that he held in The Hague. In the U.S., **Andrew Carnegie** heeded the call and donated $1.5 million for a building to house various international institutions.

As the seat of government, The Hague had responsibility for, and a resulting influence over the administration of Dutch colonies, particularly the supremely important **Indonesia**. The island archipelago of Indonesia (today, the fourth largest country in the world based on population) gained its independence in 1949 at which time Indonesian nationals were given the opportunity to move to Holland. The majority who did so settled in The Hague, as did a number of retired Dutch military officers who had served in Indonesia, as well as returning executives who had worked in corporations there.

Though its population today has reached 450,000, in certain respects The Hague remains a small town. Nevertheless, its stores and restaurants and their clientele, reflect the cosmopolitan character of the town that the *International Court of Justice* calls home. The city also has another instance of "split personality." The Hague favors diplomacy, dignity and decorum, royal residences and elegant townhouses, well-endowed museums and well-tended lawns. In The Hague, the Dutch prefer to stand on ceremony and take pride and pleasure in their history and heraldry. Yet, mere minutes from the staid, stately center of the city proper is its seaside escape valve: Scheveningen.

At **Scheveningen** (pronounced *approximately* SCKAY-ven-ing), propriety can be dropped—though some *Hagenaars* don't, as attested to by those who stride the North Sea strand (beach) in business suits and shoes. Scheveningen boasts resort amenities and activities, from wind-screened cafes *on* the sand and sunbathing pits *in* the sand to a gambling casino. From the seafront **promenade** and **entertainment pier** that reaches out over the waves, it's a few minutes' walk north to a naturist (nudist) beach; just to the south is the centuries-old fishing village where fishermen's wives still wear their traditional Dutch costume.

In The Hague, there's larger-than-life pageantry when royal resident **Queen Beatrix** arrives in a golden coach drawn by eight matched horses and uniformed honor guard to open Parliament in September. In another corner of the city, ordinary mortals can play *Gulliver* among the *Lilliputians* in the 1:25 scale miniature Holland at **Madurodam**. But everywhere it's evident that The Hague celebrates rather than suffers its split personality.

## GUIDEPOSTS

**Telephone Code 070**

**Tourist Info VVV** • *In The Hague:* Koningin Julianaplein 30 (in Babylon shopping center, next to CS): open year-round. Mon.–Sat. 9 a.m.–6 p.m., Sun. 10 a.m.–5 p.m.; closed Jan. 1, Dec. 25 and 26; *In Scheveningen*: Gevers Deynootweg 1134; same hours as above; ☎ *06-34035051, FAX 3615459.*

**Emergencies** • Police: ☎ *3104911.* Physician (general info) ☎ *3455300.* Dentist (day, night, weekend) ☎ *3974491.* Pharmacies (evenings and weekends) ☎ *3451000.*

**Lost & Found** • Police (Mon.–Fri. 9 a.m.–3:30 p.m.: ☎ *3108015.*

**Transport Info** • HMT (public transport) ☎ *06-9292.*

**Money** • Exchange office at Centraal Station open daily 7:30 a.m.–9 p.m. (*Sat. from 8 a.m., Sun. from 10 a.m.*).

**Books** • American Discount Book Centers (for U.S. and U.K. titles): Spuistraat 72; ☎ *3642742.*

## WHAT TO SEE AND DO

Because attractions in The Hague are spread out, they are grouped below by location. Those listed under *The Hague Centrum* are all within roughly a mile of one another. A booklet from the VVV, a self-guided walking tour *Along Seven Centuries of Hague Architecture* (Dfl. 3.50), begins at Het Plein, behind the *Binnenhof*, and discusses some 45 sites en route.

## THE HAGUE CENTRUM TO PEACE PALACE

**Mauritshuis**                                    ★★★
*Korte Vijverberg 8; Tues.–Sat. 10 a.m.–5 p.m., Sun. 11 a.m.–5 p.m., closed Mon.;* ☎ *3469244; fee.* Adjoining the Binnenhof and facing the Hofvijver, a small lake with swans, a fountain jet, flowing flower boxes, and tree-shaded banks, is the recently restored Mauritshuis, acknowledged as one of the finest small museums in the world. Ensconced in a small 17th-century classical mansion, the Mauritshuis imparts a sense of intimacy and welcome, making you feel as if you're visiting an extraordinary private collection. The Mauritshuis owns about 900 works, of which some 350 are exhibited at any one time (head for the

upper floor for the Golden Age favorites). The core of the collection, which numbers 10 Jan Steens, three Vermeers (including *View of Delft*) and 14 Rembrandts (including *The Anatomy Lesson*), consists of paintings acquired since the 18th century by the princes of the House of Orange. Some of the paintings were seized by Napoleon in 1795, but returned in 1816 after his defeat at Waterloo in Belgium. In 1822, the paintings were first put on display in the Mauritshuis, where they could be seen on Wednesdays and Saturday mornings by anyone "who was well-dressed and not accompanied by children." There is a fine museum shop and cafe in the basement. An oddity the museum enjoys is the payment of your entry fee when you exit.

**Note**: A major exhibit of 20 of Vermeer's paintings (two-thirds of his known existant oeuvre) will open at the Mauritshuis on March 1, 1996. The exhibit, whose only other venue is the National Gallery in Washington D.C. (Nov. '95 - Feb. '96) contains two of the three Vermeer paintings in the Mauritshuis collection, *View of Delft* and *Head of a Girl*, both of which have been restored for the exhibition.

### Binnenhof ★★
*Information Center, Binnenhof 8a; Mon.–Sat. 10 a.m.–4 p.m., closed Sun; holidays; for booking conducted tours* ☎ *3646144.* The heart of The Hague is the historic Binnenhof, a complex of portals, courtyards and palaces built beginning in the 13th century, which is the home of the Dutch Parliament. Tours include 1st and 2nd Chambers when Parliament is not in session, and the ★★ **Ridderzaal** (*Hall of the Knights*), a huge, high-ceiling banqueting room which is one of Europe's medieval architectural treasures. Its decorations include 17th-century  Flemish tapestries, a large rose window with the coats of arms of Netherlands' counts and dukes, leaded-glass windows with the coats of arms of the principal Dutch cities, and the flags of the 12 Dutch provinces. Today used as the throne room for the queen's annual *State Opening of Parliament* and state receptions, the Ridderzaal was used by Napoleon as a stable. The ★ *Information Center* has a slide show in English and permanent exhibitions on Holland's government and the royal family.

### The Royal Tour
*Mon.–Sat. mid-April–mid-Sept., except third Tues. Sept., reservations from VVV* ☎ *3546200; 1:45 p.m.; fee Dfl. 19.* This is a 2.5-hour afternoon coach excursion that passes the palaces and other points of interest connected with the House of Orange in The Hague, and includes a half-hour visit to the **Ridderzaal** (Knight's Hall) at the Binnenhof.

### Lange Voorhout ★
This grassy L-shaped mall in the center of The Hague is lined with theaters, banking houses, embassies, and the landmark **Hotel des Indes**. Purple crocuses carpet it in the spring and, in summer, it's the setting for alfresco antique markets. The beauty of this midcity green space has long been cherished; it's said that early in the 16th century,

while he was still ruler of the Low Countries, Emperor Charles V sought to ensure the continuation of the Lange Voorhout's loveliness by ordering that any man who cut down a tree along the avenue would have his right hand cut off as punishment. All but one of the buildings along the Lange Voorhout give it an architectural elegance; the modern **United States Embassy** sticks out like a nonclassic sore thumb.

## Lange Voorhout Palace                                    ★

*Lange Voorhout 74; open Tues.–Sun., aa a.m.–5 p.m. during exhibitions only;* ☎ *3381111; Trams 1, 9, and 12.* The palace, completed in 1764 and the home of Queen Emma betwwen 1901 and 1934, has been renovated to host special exhibits in connection with The Hague's **Gemeentemuseum**. There's a museum cafe and shop.

## The Hague Historical Museum                              ★

*Korte Vijverberg 7; Tues.–Fri., 11 a.m.–5 p.m., Sat. and Sun.. noon–5 p.m.; closed Mon.;* ☎ *3646940; fee.* Opened as a museum only a few years ago, this restored mansion is worth stepping inside just for the lovely views out its huge windows overlooking the Hofvijver lake and Lange Voorhout. There's an explanatory floor plan to the exhibits of paintings, portraits, townscapes of The Hague (still recognizable centuries later), and other memorabilia detailing the history of The Hague (plan in English but not exhibit notes). Nevertheless, the museum is interesting overall, and its setting superb. There's a museum shop.

## Museum Bredius                                           ★

*Lange Vijverberg 14; Tues.-Sun. noon–5 p.m.;* ☎ *3620729.* Consisting of the fine private painting collection of **Abraham Bredius**, a former director of the *Mauritshuis Museum*, the recently reopened Bredius Museum is in new quarters, a beautifully restored manor house facing the Mauritshuis, across the *Binnenhof's* picturesque *Hofvijver* lake, which is lined with large, pink-blossomed (in May), horse chestnut trees. Bredius collected works by Dutch painters, particularly those of the 17th century; pieces on display include those by Rembrandt, Steen, van Ostade, and several wonderful ones by Dutch "little masters," lesser known artists of the period to whom Bredius attached particular importance, for he saw them as bearing witness to the very high standard of Dutch painting generally during the 17th century. The museum is furnished with fine period antiques and objets d'art.

## Gevangenpoort (Prison Gate)                              ★

*Buitenhof 33; year-round Mon.–Fri. 10 a.m.–4 p.m., Sun. 1–4 p.m., closed Sat., Jan. 1, Dec. 25 and 26;* ☎ *3460861; fee. Guided tours every hour on the hour; last tour at 4 p.m., extra tours in July and Aug.; 10-minute narrated (English) color-slide show.* Located across from the Binnenhof is the 14th-century former main gate to the complex, which doubled as a prison until 1828. Since then it has served as a museum, containing what is possibly Europe's most comprehensive collection of torture instruments (not that Holland's early treatment of prisoners was more heartless than elsewhere in Europe). A fascinating and frightening insight into the dispensing of justice in earlier days is quietly made very real by the excellent English-speaking guide. He explained that innocents unfortunate enough to find themselves imprisoned often had to suffer through torture before they were believed, and even if an innocent were to survive three days of torture on the rack, the stretcher, thumb screws, etc., he would probably have been an invalid for the rest of his life. If one were guilty, there was no reason not to confess before torture: beheading provided a more humane ending. Simple confinement was relatively rare, and the rich could often buy their way out, say by purchasing bricks to repair a city wall.

### Schilderijenzall (Prince Willem V Picture Gallery)

*Buitenhof 35; Tues.–Sun. 11 a.m.–4 p.m.;* ☎ *3182487; fee.* By 1771 Stadholder Prince Willem V of Orange, an enthusiastic art collector, had outgrown his Binnenhof living quarters because of his paintings and bibelots. He bought this house across the street, had the first floor converted to a picture gallery in 1773, and opened it to the public on certain days (making it Holland's first public museum). Only a few of the paintings here now were in Willem's original collection; he donated much of it to the State in 1815, and the paintings wound up in the Mauritshuis, which had been bought especially for the purpose of displaying the collection. Most paintings on view are 17th-century Dutch but reflect 18th-century tastes (idealized landscapes, opulent still lifes, and sophisticated genre paintings) and layout, arranged frame-to-frame from floor to ceiling.

### Grote Kerk

*Grote Kerk Plein 10; call regarding opening hours;* ☎ *3658665.* West along the Groenmarkt (vegetable market) from the Buitenhof is the Grote Kerk (St. Jacobskerk), which suffered from fires in 1402 and 1539 but still can be said to date largely from the mid-15th century. In the choir are two stained-glass windows thought to be the work of Gouda artist **Dick Crabeth** (16th century). **The Huygens** (*Constantijn* and his astronomer son *Christiaan*) family vault is in the church. Next to the Grote Kerk, dating from 1565, though enlarged twice since then, is the picturesque **Oude Stadhuis** (old town hall). It is used for civil wedding ceremonies and is not usually open to visitors.

### Noordeinde Palace Garden

*Public entrance at rear of palace on Prinsessewal; open at all hours.* The garden (good-sized and gracefully landscaped with a lake) and royal stables are behind the **Palace Noordeinde**, a neoclassic in-town palace built in 1563, where the widow of Willem the Silent and her children lived after his assassination in 1584 (see "Delft," "What to See and Do: Prinsenhof"). Since 1984, Queen Beatrix and her staff have had their offices in the elegant Palace Noordeinde, from which the queen leaves in her golden horse- drawn coach on **Prinsjesdag** (third Tues.

in Sept.) to open Parliament. The palace also has guest rooms for state visitors.

Facing the palace is an equestrian statue of Willem the Silent, and across from it, a statue of former Queen Wilhelmina dominates the small square where, under the spreading chestnut tree, there is a stamp market on Wed. p.m. and Sat. a.m. Its proximity to the palace makes *Noordeinde* one of The Hague's most elegant shopping streets. Following Noordeinde northwest, the road becomes *Zeestraat*. (See "Panorama Mesday.") Just to the east is *Plein 1813*, a monumental roundabout that celebrates Dutch independence from the French. Radiating from it are symmetrical tree-lined avenues that form the heart of The Hague's embassy area.

### Panorama Mesday                                         ★ ★

*Zeestraat 65b; Mon.–Sat. 10 a.m.–5 p.m., Sun., holidays from noon;* ☎ *3642563, trams 7 and 8.* One of the founding figures of The Hague School was H. W. Mesdag. (See "Mesdag Museum.") In 1880, he and a group of artist friends painted a protest against authorities who had decided to cart away the sand dunes at Scheveningen to construct a housing project. The result: the protest made its point, and what is probably the largest canvas in the world—45 feet high, 400 feet in circumference—remains housed in the Panorama Mesdag Museum, specifically designed to display the recently restored painting. At the museum, after progressing through several rooms of smaller works by Mesdag (his subject was almost always Scheveningen: its seascape, fishing fleet, and classic views of women in the local costume waiting on the shore) and his wife (Sina van Houten), visitors pass through a tunnel, and emerge at the top of a flight of stairs in the center of a painted in-the-round scene as seen from atop the dunes at Scheveningen. The details of Dutch fisherfolk life as it was a century ago are marvelous. A taped commentary (multilingual, with English) gives some history on panoramas (cycloramas), a popular painting form from the period (though few have survived), appreciated both as a work of art and as a historical document. Panorama Mesday, in which the sense of optical illusion is extraordinary, is made even more realistic since it employs no artificial light. When it's gloomy outside, the beach scene inside is appropriately gray, since the only light that enters the museum comes through a glass dome.

**Note:** The panorama is being re-backed during 1994-95, and after that will be cleaned, but is expected to remain open throughout the process.

### Mesdag Museum                                              ★

*Laan van Meerdervoort 7F; at press time the museum was expected to remain closed in 1995 for restoration of the building and the collection; check locally with the VVV for updated information;* ☎ *3635450.* The nearby H. W. Mesdag Museum is the late Dutch painter's private collection displayed in the townhouse that was his studio. A former banker, **Mesdag** (1831-1915) became a painter (winning a gold medal for a seascape at the 1870 Paris Salon) in a group that collectively became known as The Hague School (and included Jozef Israels, Anton Mauve, J. W. Bilders, Paul Gabriel, Willem Maris, Willem Roelofs). Not only an avid painter, Mesdag also supported other artists financially, and was a fervent collector. The museum, now a part of the Van Gogh Museum in Amsterdam, has the most important collection of paintings of the *Barbizon School* (Corot, Millet, Daubigny, Rousseau) outside of France, as well as many works from the Hague School, which was much influenced by the Barbizons.

## Peace Palace                                    ★

*Carnegieplein 2; from May–Oct. Mon.–Fri. 10 a.m.–4 p.m., rest of year closes at 3 p.m.; guided tours at 10, 11, 2, 3 ( and from May–Sept. at 4p.m.); ☎ 3469680; take Tram #7, 8.* Despite its relatively recent appearance on the scene (completed in 1913), the Peace Palace has become a symbol of The Hague. Home of the Permanent Court of International Law (since 1922) and the Academy of International Law (since 1923), the Peace Palace was built with a $1.5 million donation by Scottish-American steel magnate Andrew Carnegie after the first international conference for the suppression of war was held in The Hague (at Huis ten Bosch) at the insistence of Czar Nicholas II of Russia. As a result of the conference, the Permanent Court of Arbitration was established, and its need for a suitable home reached the ears of Carnegie. The foundation stone was laid in 1907, during a second peace conference in The Hague (held in the Ridderzaal). The Peace Palace is built in the Flemish Renaissance style (by architect Louis Cordonnier of Lille, France, whose design won out over 200 competitors). The ornate interior is rich in contributions of materials and national craftmanship from dozens of countries. The bronze entrance door is from Belgium, the marble statue Justice by Peace from the U.S., the stained-glass windows in the Great Hall from the U.K.

# EN ROUTE TO SCHEVENINGEN

## Gemeentemuseum                               ★ ★

*Stadhouderslaan 41; Tues.–Sun. 11 a.m.–5 p.m., closed Mon.; ☎ 3381120; fee; take Tram #8, 10.* The paintings of a relatively recent Dutch master are highlighted at the Gemeentemuseum (municipal museum), which has the world's largest collection (154) of works by **Piet Mondriaan** (1872-1944)—see details of major Mondriaan exhibit opening here in December 1994 under "Guidelines" "Entertainment and Events." The unique group is particularly strong in Mondriaan's early works, which show his movement from early dark landscapes, through his "blue" period, to the totally abstract primary color blocks and black-line pieces for which he is most known, and was most influential. Dutch painter **Karel Appel**, a member of the COBRA group who has lived in New York for many years, has donated more than 50 drawings to the museum. The building (1935) itself was the swan song of the grand old man of modern Dutch architecture, **H. P. Ber-lage**. The **Hall**, with its concrete skeleton visible, is the hub of the museum, whose tiles, lighting (all natural, even in the showcases), colors, and other details all bear the Berlage stamp. The 19th- and 20th-century collections contain paintings and sculpture from many European masters, as well as from The Hague School.

### Museon ★

*Stadhouderslaan 41, Tues.–Fri. 10 a.m.–5 p.m., Sat., Sun., holidays noon–5 p.m., closed Mon.; ☎ 3381338; fee; take Tram # 8 or 10.* This remarkable museum, whose exhibitions cover "every aspect of life" is "typically Dutch" in terms of its well-done displays and overall philosophy, which stresses equality with the idea that "the more you know about people, the more tolerant you'll be." *The Earth, Our Home* is a hit exhibit, and those on human activities on the planet might be something like *So Many People, So Many Hats,* a collection of hats from around the world, or *Everyone has a Right to a Home,* with examples from Bedouin tents to temples to townhouses. Most exhibits have English explanations and, even without them, the message would be meaningful.

### Madurodam ★★

*Haringkade 175; daily 9 a.m.–10:30 p.m. except closes 11 p.m. June–Aug., 9:30 p.m. Sept. 6 p.m. Oct–early Jan., closed early Jan. to late-March; ☎ 3553900; fee; Trams #1, 9.* The Hague's most whimsical attraction, Madurodam, is located midway between the town's seat of power and the sea. A miniature man-made Holland, at 1/25 scale, Madurodam fills four acres with replicas of 150 of Holland's most famous buildings (including The Hague's Binnenhof), arranged into a tiny working town complete with trains, minimarching bands, a bicycle jam, a small Schiphol airport with KLM craft, and a pint-size port of Rotterdam. Madurodam is expanding in 1995, among the new mini-size attractions will be examples of Holland's striking contemporary architecture and the Delta Works. The attention to detail at Madurodam delights the child in every adult, and children are enchanted to feel as big as *Gulliver* among the *Lilliputians* at Madurodam.

**Note**: Madurodam's endearing detail is not as visible under the mini–town's night lights, and the script of its evening **sound and light** show, which I had looked forward to, seemed contrived. I recommend a daylight visit to Madurodam and a visit to the real *Binnenhof* for its romantic after-dark illumination.

## SCHEVENINGEN

If you find the name of this seaside resort hard to pronounce, apparently you're in the company of almost everyone in the world who isn't Dutch. And the Dutch have even put their lives on the line over that fact. During Holland's World War II occupation by the Nazis, in order to determine if the person to whom they were speaking was Dutch or German, members of the Dutch resistance asked the other person to pronounce *Scheveningen*—it's the "sch" sound that makes or breaks it. If the person did so satisfactorily, it was assumed he was Dutch. (A backup tongue-twisting test sometimes used by the Dutch to test the Nazis was the word *Massachusetts*: now *that's* internationalism for you.)

## Kurhaus ★★

*Steigenberger Kurhaus Hotel (see "Where to Stay"), Gevers Deynootplein 30;* ☎ *4162636.* The 1885 Kurhaus is as much a Scheveningen monument as it is a five-star hotel. The magnificent and enormous Kurzaal, with its restored frescoed, gilted, and skylighted domed ceiling, and Corinthian columns supporting the balcony, has been the scene of many memorable events in the past century. Many important people, either performing in the concerts that have long been a tradition in the Kurzaal—the Berlin Philharmonic (under the baton of von Karajan), Bruno Walter, Stokowsky, violinist Yehudi Menuhin, Leonard Bernstein (who wielded his baton here in his European debut), singer Marlene Dietrich, Edith Piaf, Jacques Brel, Maurice Chevalier, Vladimir Horowitz, Charles Aznavour, to name a few—or passing through the great hall to meetings or other business—Churchill, Truman, Crawford, Kissinger, Brandt, Hepburn, NATO meeting attendees—have filled more than one leather-bound hotel guestbook. So, whether you're a guest or not, this is the one interior that's a "must see" in Scheveningen.

## Promenade/Boulevard ★

The broad Promenade/Boulevard, which runs for a mile or more parallel to the beach and open North Sea, just above the sandy Strand, is lined with glass-encased, wind-sheltered cafes and coffee houses, souvenir and snack kiosks, and a huge, heated, artificial wave swimming pool/exercise complex.

## The Pier ★

*At the Promenade;* ☎ *3543677.* The present pier, which opened in 1961, rebuilt after the preceding pleasure jetty had been deep-sixed by the Nazis, is being restored, but it will keep its distinctive European appearance. The pier, reaching out more than 400 yards over the North Sea, offers dining, sun terraces, a 45-meter-high **belvedere** (viewing tower), a fishing platform, and shops on its four "islands." There are **fireworks** from the pier on Friday nights at 11 p.m. in summer. A quiet corner in one of the eateries at its end is a good place from which to watch the sun sink into the North Sea at day's end.

## Museum Scheveningen

*Neptunusstraat 92; Tues.–Sat. 10 a.m.–5 p.m., also open Mon. April–Sept.;* ☎ *3500830; fee; Tram #1,7, or 9.* Located in an old school, the museum, since its formation in 1952, has been about the fishing life and history of Scheveningen for Scheveningers. There's a focus on the fishing way of life, photos of old Scheveningen, and local traditional costumes. Coffee is available at an authentic old fishermen's pub on the premises.

## *SHOPPING*

*The Hague has many handsome pedestrian shopping streets.*

Most department and clothing stores are located in the *Centrum* (around and off *Spui Straat, Hoog Straat, Grote Markt Straat*), which has a number of pedestrian streets. The **Passage** is an elegant enclosed shopping arcade. Antiques shops line the **Denneweg**, behind the *Hotel des Indes* on *Lange Voorhout,* and **Noordeinde**, the street named for the palace on it that serves as the queen's official office. There are some 100 to haunt in The Hague. (Ask at the VVV for the brochure *Antique Walk.*) Antiques, curios, art, books and bric-a-brac also are sold at the **open-air market** on *Lange Voor-*

*hout* Thursday and Sunday, mid-May–end September, 9 a.m.–9 p.m. From October 1–mid-May, the market is Thursday only, and moves to the near-by *Plein*. Late night shopping (9 p.m.) in The Hague is Thursday, with most stores closed Sunday. In Scheveningen, especially on and near the beach, opening hours for the plentiful casual shops are longer: seven days a week year-round and, from Easter through mid-October, up until 10 p.m.

## WHERE TO STAY

The two deluxe properties described here won't save you much over similar properties in Amsterdam, but both have stellar settings; the character and charm that can come with over 100 years of history; and standards of service on which they pride themselves. If you'll have to be content just to walk through their lobbies, make sure you do. There's no lack of other comfortable corners to book yourself into, keeping in mind that pleasant, less expensive small hotels in Scheveningen—most of them are family establishments—in summer are in high demand from Dutch, German and many other tourists, since this is Holland's premier coastal resort. Make reservations as far ahead as possible, and check about minimum length-of-stay requirements in summer. Especially busy is the second weekend in July, when the **North Sea Jazz Festival** (four days) fills the town with music and fans. The VVV will help with accommodations if you decide on the spot you want to stay overnight. Hotels have been separated under The Hague and Scheveningen.

## THE HAGUE

### Hotel des Indes (Inter-Continental)    ★★★★★

*Lange Voorhout 54, 2514 EG;* ☎ *3632932, FAX 3451721, reservations U.S. and Can.* ☎ *800-327-0200.* Kings, presidents and statesmen from many countries can attest to the fact that the *Hotel des Indes* has always held a grand position in The Hague. Built as a lavish town house by a baron, upon his death the family sold it to a local hotelier, and the palatial building was born as the Hotel des Indes (a name chosen to combine both French chic and the exoticism of the Dutch East Indies). Many of the baron's original furnishings remain intact in public rooms: massive crystal chandeliers, glittering mirrors, and rich brocade wall coverings. The magnificent central lounge, still *the* place to take tea, has seen many special guests pass through: Lindbergh, Czar Nicholas II, Eisenhower, Stravinsky, the Dutch spy Mata Hari, and Bing Crosby. The great Russian ballerina Anna Pavlova died here of pneumonia. With only 77 rooms, service can be as attentive as you expect, and the location in this "city of royal residence" on the lovely Lange Voorhout is superb. **Le Restaurant**, with its white-glove service, is well-regarded for its classical French flair and fare. The lobby bar is a cosmopolitan meeting place, and the lobby an after theater or symphony rendezvous. Parking available.    *Very Expensive.*

### Hotel Corona ★ ★ ★ ★

*Buitenhof 39-42, 2513 AH;* ☎ *3637930, FAX 3615785, reservations U.S.*
☎ *800-221-1074, reservations Can.* ☎ *800-344-4034.* Parliament is
just around the corner, and with a handsome marble and mahogany
public lobby for those who want to be seen and heard, and
widely-spaced tables at the hotel's fine restaurant for those who don't,
the Corona is understandably popular with Dutch politicians. The
hotel, with its 26 rooms, all of which were recently renovated in contemporary style with pastel colors, dates from the early 1900s
(although the building in the 18th century was a lively coffee house).
Parking available close to hotel.                              *Expensive.*

### Park Hotel Den Haag ★ ★ ★ ★

*Molenstraat 53, 2513 BJ;* ☎ *3624371, FAX 3614525.* Built in 1910 as a
hotel, the breakfast (included) room overlooks the Noordeinde Palace
gardens; some of the 114 guest rooms have balconies with views on to
the garden. The Park is conveniently tucked into an antique-and-
print-shop-lined street near the center of The Hague. Dignity, not
flash, dictates the decor, which has a mix of modern and traditional
furniture, and some nice architectural details, including a *Jugenstil* (art
nouveau) five-story stairwell in yellow brick. Rooms are spacious, and
have large marble baths. There's a lobby bar, but no in-hotel restaurant since there are so many others in the vicinity. The hotel has its
own parking garage.                                           *Moderate.*

## SCHEVENINGEN

### Kurhaus Hotel (Steigenberger) ★ ★ ★ ★ ★

*Gevers Deynootplein 30, Scheveningen 2586 CK;* ☎ *4162636,*
*FAX 4162646, reservations U.S.* ☎ *800-777-5848.* Scheveningen's
Grande Dame by the Sea, the Kurhaus went from the very real threat
of the wrecker's ball (in the early 1970s) to a glittering celebratory
ball in honor of its salvation, complete renovation, and centennial in
1985. The huge **Kurzaal**, with its magnificent painted, skylit ceiling,
the dome of which seems to reach halfway to heaven, is headquarters
and highlight of the hotel, and the wonderful North Sea views out the
enormous windows simply reinforce the sense of being someplace special. And I love the unlikely and light-hearted contrast of the blue
sculpture of a mermaid sitting in an easy chair reading a book amid the
grandeur. The ambiance of the evening buffet in the Kurzaal is ineffa-
bly European: live piano music floats into the lofty space, and you can
enjoy an eating experience that can be drawn out to save the setting.
(A breakfast buffet in the same superb setting is included for overnight
guests). Of the Kurhaus' 241 guest rooms, the best ones face the sea,
with French windows opening out onto small wrought-iron balconies.
A number of rooms are modest in size, but there's plenty of room to
spread out on the property. There's a terrace cafe from which to survey the sea and the pier, and large wave pool, sauna, and exercise complex.                                                    *Very expensive.*

Off the Kurzaal, under a red awning, is **Casino Scheveningen,** (*daily 1:30 p.m.–2 a.m.; minimum age 18; passport identification required; dress code*) which, while perfectly enjoyable if you like casinos, isn't as elegant as the Kurzaal; there are 24 tables for French and American roulette, blackjack, and baccarat for the big spenders. The **Kandinsky Restaurant**, in a striking *art deco* room with six original lithographs by the artist, is the hotel's à la carte restaurant, with many of its 60 seats overlooking the sea.

### Carlton Beach Hotel

*Gevers Deynootweg 201, 2586 HZ;* ☎ *3541414, FAX 3520020, reservations U.S.* ☎ *800-223-9815.* This 108-room, 76-apartment modern eight-floor hotel fronts directly on the North Sea (moderate supplement for full sea view), and all rooms have balconies. It is located at the end of Scheveningen's built-up beach, and has a pleasantly remote feeling by being the last property before the long line of sand dunes north on up the coast for as far as you can see. Two restaurants, bar, and an indoor fitness center (exercise machines, sauna, steam bath, swimming pool) are among its facilities, and there's free parking for guests. Near all tram lines to The Hague. All rooms have hair dryers, minibar or kitchenette. Buffet breakfast included. *Expensive.*

### Hotel Petit

*Grote Hertoginnelaan 42, 2517 EH;* ☎ *3465500, FAX 3463257.* This is a family-style hotel not far from the Peace Palace, on the Scheveningen side. The late 19th-century house (18 rooms) was renovated in 1988; rooms are generous in size and have desks and sitting areas; all have shower or bath and minibar. The house is three floors (elevator to top floor), with stained glass in the stairwell. In a nice residential area (on tram and bus route) near embassies, and guests are of many nationalities. Terrace cafe in front in season; restaurant.

*Moderate.*

### Bel Park

*Belgischeplein 38, 2587 AT;* ☎ *3505000, FAX 3523242.* Two rambling turn-of-the-century homes, on a green roundabout, in a residential neighborhood make this a homey, pleasant choice. It's a 15-minute walk to the pier, with a tram nearby. Airy, light, and freshly painted, all 14 rooms (and a two-room suite) have shower and toilet, with price varying somewhat with size. No elevator, but wide straight stairs. Free on-street parking. *Moderate.*

### Aquarius

*Zeekant 107, 2586 JJ;* ☎ *3543543, FAX 3543684.* Only a road separates these three connected houses that have been made into a 21-room hotel from the boulevard and beach. Some rooms front sea, several have balconies from which one gets a view of the pier. Room decor is fairly basic; all rooms have private toilet and curtained shower. There's a breakfast room, pleasant restaurant with three-course menus, and a few tables on the seafront terrace outside. No elevator. Near trams. Parking available.                    *Moderate.*

### City Hotel                                                    ★★★

*Renbaanstraat 1-3, 2586 EW;* ☎ *3557966, FAX 3540503.* Above the restaurant, with terrace cafe, several blocks from the beach and VVV, are six rooms, small, clean, decorated in white wicker with pastel floral prints. Around the corner in this residential quarter of Scheveningen are two houses with some 20 rooms, owned by the hotel, with pay phone and antiques in the small lobby (you are given your own front door key, no elevators). Breakfast is served at restaurant.    *Moderate.*

### Esquire                                                       ★★★

*Van Aerssenstraat 43-65, 2582 JG;* ☎ *3522341, FAX 3520195.* Several blocks from the Scheveningen inner harbor (with its fish restaurants), this family-run hotel has 30 rooms in seven small houses on a quiet residential street. No elevators, but eight of the rooms are on the ground floor. Rooms have modern utilitarian furniture, and modern tile baths. Breakfast is served under a skylight behind the bar and restaurant (where you can "just say what you'd like" according to the owner).                                               *Moderate.*

### Hotel Seinduin                                                ★★

*Seinpostduin 15, 2586 EA;* ☎ *3551971, FAX 3505829.* Located a block from the boulevard along the beach (near the point from which Mesdag painted the Panorama), a pleasant walk to the pier. All 18 rooms have shower, toilet, telephone, TV, and minibar. Convenient to VVV and trams. Basic but pleasant. On-street parking.

## *WHERE TO EAT*

Several of the hotels mentioned in the previous section have highly-regarded restaurants, and these should be considered among your dining choices in The Hague. Booking is recommended for the better restaurants. An appetizing aspect of the Dutch colonial inheritance is the large number of Indonesian restaurants; this is especially true in The Hague, which has as many as a hundred. **Garoeda** (*Kneuterdijk 18a; open daily; reservations* ☎ *3465319; inexpensive*) is the one Indonesians themselves, and Hagenaars who have lived there, consider the best, and its location couldn't be much more in the center of things. The dignified atmosphere lends itself to the ceremony of the *rijsttaffel*, but you can dine with fewer dishes if you desire. For Indonesian fare in a smaller, more informal setting, head for **Djawa** (*Mallemolen 12A; open daily 5:30–11 p.m.;* ☎ *3635763, reservation suggested; inexpensive*), which is owner-overseen, off the standard tourist tract, with authentic decor, just ten tables, and an assortment of mixed-selection menus and rijsttafels, including a vegetarian one. Also highly regarded locally for authentic Indonesian fare is **Tampat Senang** (*Laan van Meerdervoort 6;* ☎ *3636787; inexpensive*). Located by the picturesque Oude Stadhuis (and in appropriate weather with a terrace cafe out front from which to view it) is **'t Goude Hooft** (*Groenmarkt 13; open daily;*

☎ *3469713; moderate*) which, in addition to the outdoor tables, has a cozy colonial atmosphere. There's a bar, where live music is featured, in response to the recent addition of trendy cafes in the area. Without music, but a setting right in the center of the Hague is **Juliana's** cafe (*Plaats*), with outside seating in the center of a pedestrian square in fair weather. Whether or not you attend a performance in The Hague's Music and Dance Hall, **Cafe Piccolo Mondo** ("small world") at the Dr. Anton Philipszaal proves intriguing, since it's shaped like an ice cream cone.

For dignified dining outside or in on the Lange Voorhout, visit **Le Bis-troquet** (*Lange Voorhout 98;* ☎ *3601170; moderate*) where food has a French flavor. For contrast, behind the Lange Voorhout is the cozy **Oud Haagsch Pannekoekhuis** (*Maliestraat 10, off Denneweg;* ☎ *3462474; closed Sun. and Mon.; inexpensive*), where you can treat yourself to a plate-size pancake, sweet or savory (my favorite is cheese and chunk ginger) amid a typical old Dutch decor of red-and-white-checked tablecloths and old brass and copper utensils. You can almost count on seeing a Dutch grandmother treating the family. Finish the meal with coffee or a Heineken on the terrace of the pub a few doors down, overlooking a picturesque, unusual canaled corner of The Hague. Even if you're on the hunt for Dutch or English antiques along the Denneweg, you might get the taste for Italian. If so, you won't have far to go to find **Panino Teca** (*Denneweg 41; open daily,* ☎ *3652026; inexpensive*).

In Scheveningen, local patrons love the **Vispaleis** (fish palace): it's their favorite herring stand at the second inner harbor (Dr. Lelykade). Close at hand are **Ducdalf** (*Dr. Lelykade 5; open daily;* ☎ *3557692; moderate*) offering a wide variety of seafood (herring, sole, North Sea gray shrimp, Zeeland oysters), and it would be hard for it to be fresher, since the fishing fleet and fish auction house are at the next harbor over. To round off a day or evening with conviviality in Scheveningen, **De Vliegh** (*Badhuisweg 2;* ☎ *3559314; closed Mon.; inexpensive*) offers French fare, fish, and steak from *4 p.m.–2:30 a.m.* in its restaurant or glass-screened terrace to the sound of soft jazz. The jazz gets jouncier on *Friday and Saturday night from 11 p.m.–3 a.m.*

## VOORBURG

### Vreudg & Rust Restaurant-Hotel ★★★★

*Oosteinde 14, 2271 EH, Voorburg; open daily for lunch noon–2:30 p.m., dinner 6:30-10:00 p.m.; restaurant expensive/very expensive, hotel moderate; for reservations* ☎ *070-3872081, FAX 070-387771.* This highly-touted restaurant, within walking distance of the charming old center of Voorburg, a suburb of The Hague, is a 1751 mansion that sits on parkland that runs down to the river Vliet. Refurbished in 1989, the 14 rooms feature such individual details as beamed ceilings, red marble baths with heated marble floors, fine plaster work, and crystal sconces.

# WASSENAAR

**Auberge de Kievet**                                    ★★★★

*Stoeplaan 27, Wassenaar-Zuid; open daily lunch noon–3 p.m., dinner 6–10
p.m.; restaurant expensive/very expensive, hotel expensive; for reservations
☎ (01751) 19232, FAX. 10969.* A countrified mansion-inn in a fashionable, wooded suburb of The Hague, Auberge de Kievet is known
first for its restaurant, though the 26 guest rooms are no less comfortable for that.

## ENTERTAINMENT AND EVENTS

**Queen's Birthday**, *30th April*, This national holiday is celebrated in the
queen's hometown with a fun fair and street festivities on the Lange Voorhout. Shops are open.

**Vlaggetjesdag (Flag Day)**, *a Saturday in mid/late-May at Scheveningen harbor.* The opening of the herring season, with "dressed" fishing fleet ships,
food, music, traditional crafts, and boat trips.

**Fireworks**, *11 p.m. from Scheveningen Pier Fri. evenings July-mid-Aug.; late
Aug.* International Firework Festival with several shows per night (check
for dates and time).

**North Sea Jazz Festival**, *July*, This three-day event at various venues in
The Hague is the most prominent jazz festival outside the U.S. 1994
marks its 19th-annual celebration.

**State Opening of Parliament (Prinsjesdag)**, *third Tues. in Sept.* Queen
Beatrix, a resident of The Hague, arrives at the Binnenhof in a golden
coach drawn by eight matched horses, attended by an honor guard, to give
the details of the government's plans for the coming year in a speech to the
first session of Parliament in the Ridderzaal.

**The Hague Christmas Market** Ten days in the middle of December on
Het Plein.

## CONCERTS

Inquire at the VVV about Friday evening **organ concerts** at various
churches in The Hague, and about concerts in the Kurzaal at the Kurhaus
in Scheveningen.

# DELFT

*Hand painting of blue and white delftware continues at Delft's De Porceleyne Fles, established 1653.*

## GUIDELINES FOR DELFT

### SIGHTS

Delft's intimate old center is dense with delicate impressions. Along stretches of its tranquil tree-shaded canals, the luminescence seems to have been supplied by the town's 17th-century master painters, and charming street scenes of daily life that served as subjects for those artists can still be seen. Delft's ancient **Grote Markt** (the main market square), one of Holland's most magnificent, is anchored by the **Nieuwe Kerk** (new church, from 1381), and the **Stadhuis**. The **Prinsenhof**, where Willem the Silent (*Father of the Fatherland*) lived, and was slain in 1584, is an atmospheric in-town "palace" museum, just steps from a canalside mansion museum filled with old Dutch tiles. Most visitors head for **De Porceleyne Fles**, the only one of Delft's famous blue and white ware factories to have survived from the 17th century.

## GETTING AROUND

Delft is definitely a place to slow your touring pace to a saunter. To be seen and savored as it should, you must walk the compact, canal-laced town. Tuesdays at 2 p.m. April–September (and in July and August also on Fridays) there are 1.5 hour guided walking tours from the VVV (*Dfl. 7.50*, five person minimum, reservations necessary, ☎ *126100*.) Buses and trams serve the surrounding suburbs, but not the Centrum (old center). Canal boat excursions and tours by horse-drawn tram can supplement, but shouldn't substitute for, your feet in old Delft, especially in and around the **Grote Markt**, and along the **Oude Delft**, **Hippolytusbuurt**, **Voldersgracht**, and **Koornmarkt** canals. For a unique view (and great photographs) of Delft, create your own canal cruise on rented pedal boats and kayaks. If you want to join the bicycle brigades—Delft is a university town with 16,000 students and corresponding number of two-wheelers—rent one at the rail station. That's where taxis are too.

## SHOPPING

Delftware, the blue and white porcelain that's virtually synonymous with the town, should rightly top your shopping list, which is just as well since it's hard to avoid it in the shops on and just off the **Grote Markt**. The product's so pretty that the commercialism isn't offensive, though the profusion of choice (and range of quality and price) can cause confusion for the buyer.

## WHERE TO STAY

There's an adequate choice of moderately priced, friendly canal-front hotels in the center of old Delft.

## WHERE TO EAT

In Delft, you can dine as well as anywhere in Holland. Or catch quicker nourishment around the Markt or along a canal, at one of the many cafes; some offer outside tables when the weather warrants.

## ENTERTAINMENT AND EVENTS

The VVV tourist office, located on the Markt, will have the latest listings, but you can count on live carillon concerts on the famed Hemony bells of the Nieuwe Kerk on Tues., Thurs., and Sat., 11 a.m.-noon; in summer, there's also a weekly evening carillon concert (check with VVV for details). Buy a coffee or beer at one of the outside cafes to secure the equivalent of a front-row seat at the Oude Kerk. Confirm at the VVV the organ concert schedule at the Oude Kerk, Fridays June–Aug. 2–3 p.m., and Thurs. 8:15 p.m. every second week (free with admission to church Dfl. 2.50). Alternate Thurs. Summer evenings organ concerts at Niewe Kerk on the Markt. Delft's annual *Art and Antique Fair* (ten days in mid-Oct.), held at the Prinsenhof, is considered one of Europe's most prestigious.

## ARRIVING

Located between Rotterdam and The Hague, Delft is an inter-city stop on the frequently serviced main Rotterdam-The Hague-Amsterdam rail line. The Delft station, at Van Leeuwenhoeksingel 41, is slightly outside the center, a 10- or 15-minute walk to the Grote Markt. Regional buses and taxis congregate conveniently at the station. Tram #1, which connects Delft with the center of The Hague and Scheveningen (5 miles), has a Delft stop on Phoenixstraat, a 5-10-minute walk to the Markt. If arriving by car, take exit Delft-Noord or Delft Pijnacker off the A13(E19) motorway. Non-metered parking is available on the Phoenixstraat (just outside the old center).

## TRAVEL TIPS

Though *not* recommended as the best way to see Delft, if **De Porceleyne Fles** is on your "must see" list and your time very limited, it's wise to get a taxi from the rail station to the factory (a fair walk, none of it within the pretty old center). The factory (at which there is on-street parking if you arrive by car) will call a taxi when you're ready to leave, and you could ask the driver for a quick ride through old Delft before being dropped back at the station.

# DELFT IN CONTEXT

Although a small settlement existed previously, the real history of Delft begins with the arrival in 1075 of Duke Godfried van Lotharingen, called Govert the Hunchback, who built a fortress, probably on the site where the Stadhuis is today. He had the first canals of Delft dug, the patterns of which remain essentially the same today.

Under the administration of successive counts of Holland, Delft became a center for the exchange of agricultural goods between the village and surrounding countryside by the early 13th century. In 1226 under Count Willem II, Delft received its first charter, which included the right to hold a weekly market, which it still does (Thursday on the Grote Markt). The name *Beesten* (animal) *Markt*, recalls when pigs were sold on that square, though today its atmosphere, especially in the evening, is more like Paris' *place du Tertre*. Delft was granted permission in 1389 to excavate the Delfshavense Schie, which provided a direct water connection with the Maas River at Rotterdam, an undertaking that contributed substantially to the inland town's prosperity.

As early as the 13th century, brewing beer had developed into an important industry in Delft. By the second half of the 14th century, Delft beer boasted markets not only in Holland, but also in Flanders and Germany. The water in Delft's canals, it seems, was especially well-suited to the preparation of beer and, by the 15th century, Delft had nearly 200 beer breweries.

Another Delft industry of the day, second in success only to brewing, was cloth weaving. It expanded to the manufacture of tapestries (see the "Tapestry Hall" "Prinsenhof" under "What to See and Do") and carpets in the 16th century when emigrating Flemish weavers, fleeing difficulties caused by Catholic Spanish rulers there, settled in Delft. Street names are reminders of those days: *Voldersgracht* (Fullers Canal); *Raam* (Frame); and *Versersdijk* (Dyers' Dike).

As well as being distinguished as a center of resistance and headquarters for Dutch leader **Willem** (*the Silent*) **of Orange** during the *Eighty Years War* with the Spanish, Delft was the birthplace of some of the developing Dutch nation's proudest figures. Admirals **Piet Hein** (1577–1629) and **Marten Tromp** (1598–1653), who achieved national victories that still warm the hearts of Dutch sailors; both are buried with appropriate monuments in Delft's Oude Kerk. The town's **Hugo de Groot** (Grotius) (1583–1645), jurist and statesman who established the principles of international law (see "The Dutch Cultural Legacy, The Muse"), is singled out by a statue in the center of Delft's Markt. When Holland wrested its territory free from the Spanish in the late 16th century and began to flourish, Delft was well-positioned to share in the prosperity.

In 1572, during the *Eighty Years' War* engagements with the Spanish on Dutch soil in Holland, military leader Willem took up residence at the **Prinsenhof** in Delft (relocating from the Binnenhof in The Hague, which was less protected). Having the Prince of Orange residing within its walls conferred great prestige on Delft. He'd been an inspiring leader when Holland's major towns rose with him to resist the Spanish in the early, most trying years of the Eighty Years' War. While living in Delft, he became generally known affectionately as Father Willem and, more grandly, *Het Vader de het Vaderland* (Father of the Fatherland), the true and trusted leader of the newly Protestant northern Netherlands.

Thus the events of July 10, 1584—a date familiar to all Dutch—at Delft's Prinsenhof were especially tragic. That night, heading to the dining room with his wife Louise de Coligny and guests, Willem passed a man whom he had previously received as a Protestant emissary from the French court. In fact, unbeknownst to Willem, the man, **Balthasar Gerard** (or Geraerts), had been to the Prinsenhof the Sunday before, lingering in the courtyard. When a guard asked what his business was, Gerard, remaining anonymous, gave the seemingly guileless reply that he had no business there, that what he really wanted was to be in the church opposite (the Waalse Church, still used today), but lacked appropriate stockings and shoes. The guard kindly conveyed Gerard's need to Willem, who had given the guard money for the would-be worshipper. As was later revealed, however, Gerard did not buy footwear with the prince's money. Instead, he made a long-planned purchase of pistols and bullets, for he was no Protestant emissary from France, but a Catholic fanatic from Burgundy who was out to collect the reward that the Spanish King Philip II had put on Willem's head.

That July evening, Gerard, having obtained entry to the Prinsenhof under false pretenses, waited in hiding. Their dinner done, Willem, leading his party up to his chambers, had only mounted two steps when Gerard stepped out from behind a curtain and fired three bullets, two of which hit Willem, passing through his body, leaving holes in the wall behind him. The beloved 51-year-old leader of the Dutch people fell, his supposed final words still learned by all schoolchildren—"My God, have pity on me and my poor people." The *teychenen derkoogelen* (marks of the bullets), visible at the bottom of the stairs in the Prinsenhof, have been so enlarged by Dutch visitors touching them that they are now protected behind glass.

Gerard, who had escaped in the ensuing confusion, was soon captured by guards and taken to the prison cell in Delft's *Stadhuis* on the nearby Markt. In the belfry there—which survived a fire in the Stadhuis in 1618 and was incorporated into the replacement, built in

1620—Gerard was imprisoned to await trial and sentencing in a cell that required him to remain constantly in a prone position. Four days later, on the Grote Markt, Gerard was drawn, quartered, and beheaded, his head later placed on a pike and displayed in public.

Holland's 17th-century **Golden Age** glowed in Delft. In 1602, the *Dutch East India Company* established its headquarters here. The owners began to make trading arrangements with China to import that country's popular blue-and-white ware to Europe. Millions of pieces reached Holland through the Delft-based company between 1602 and 1657. Delft artisans, in trying to imitate the pretty pieces to get in on the profits, developed their own fine product, and the town's fledgling pottery industry took off. By the middle of the 17th century nearly 30 factories were producing blue-and-white ware, as well as other patterns, all of which became known simply as **Delft-ware**. The manufacture of tiles took an enormous upturn, and they can still be seen in old homes, restaurants, and taverns throughout Holland on fireplaces, in kitchens, and to edge walls where they meet the floor. Tiles became so typical in homes that they can be seen in many of Delft artist Vermeer's paintings.

Moving at a parallel with the 17th-century momentum of the pottery industry in Delft was painting. The greatest masters of the **Delft School** were **Jan Vermeer** (1632–1675) and **Pieter de Hoogh** (1629–1684). De Hoogh, a genius at genre, was born in Rotterdam and had moved to Amsterdam by the time of his death, but he called Delft home during the most productive period of his life when he created his memorable and intimate interpretations of domestic life. Genre painter **Jan Steen** also lived for a while in Delft, though he did not belong to the Delft School; for some years from 1654 onward, he managed the beer brewery *De Slange* on the *Oude Delft* canal. Several significant local painters, **Anthonie Palamedeszoon** (genre scenes), **Paulus Potte** (famous for his landscapes with animals), **Gerrit van Houckgeest**, **Cornelis van Vliet**, and **Emanuel White** (known for their church interior paintings) served as harbingers for Delft's Golden Age legacy of art.

Most important of all was **Carel Fabritius** (1622–1654), Rembrandt's most accomplished student, and a painter who had a strong influence on Vermeer (although no proof of any formal painter/pupil relationship exists). Already recognized, and considered a painter of enormous potential, Carel Fabritius was killed at the age of 32 in the 1654 Delft calamity, the *Delft Thunderclap*. At half past ten the morning of October 12, a gunpowder magazine (located in the northern part of the old town) containing some 80,000 pounds of powder left over from the Dutch war with the Spanish, blew up. It killed hundreds of people and completely destroyed or did great damage to at least half the buildings in Delft. The blast buckled the stout walls of the Nieuwe Kerk, which stood diagonally across the street from *Mechelen*, the house on the Delft's Grote Markt (roughly where #62 is today) where Vermeer lived most of his life, and which he used as the setting for, and where he created, most of his paintings. In the explosion, Carel Fabritius was buried beneath the rubble of his house, along with his family and a man who was there sitting for his portrait.

**Johannes** (Jan) **Vermeer** is the artist we associate most closely today with Delft. It has been suggested that the high finish of Vermeer's enamel-smooth paintings reflects the glaze of Delft porcelain, which would have been an omnipresent influence in the town during his lifetime. In the autumn of 1632, Vermeer, the second child of Reynier Janszoon Vos and his wife Dymphna, was listed in the baptism register of Delft's Nieuwe Kerk. The family home, *Mechelen*, on Delft's Grote Markt, was an active establishment: his father kept a tavern there, and designed and sold cloth. The year before Jan's birth, his father had been registered by the *Guild of St. Luke* as a Master Art-Dealer. Vermeer was undoubtedly influenced by the paintings his father handled as an art dealer. Many of the works that he bought and sold would have come from nearby Utrecht, a Catholic city whose school of artists were more closely connected to Italy, and with *Caravaggio*, known for his dramatic use of light. Young Jan would also have seen the works of artists at studios in Delft. Although nothing is known of his art education, it is likely that Vermeer began as an apprentice at about the age of 15. The register at Delft's Stadhuis notes his marriage on April 5, 1653, to Catharina Bolnes, who came from a prosperous family in Gouda. Jan and his wife lived with his parents at *Mechelen*, remaining there for most of their marriage (which produced 11 children in 20 years). In December 1653, Vermeer was listed as a Master Painter in the local *Guild of St. Luke*.

We know of Vermeer's interest in music from the subjects of his paintings. Living as he did across from the Nieuwe Kerk, the installation in the tower there of a carillon of 36 Hemony Brothers bells—"the latest thing"—in 1663 must have been of interest, perhaps even inspiration, since he would have heard them all day long.

Vermeer was well-respected by his contemporaries: twice he served two-year terms on the board of the Guild of St. Luke. Because the Dutch have always kept meticulous records of financial transactions, it can be deduced that Vermeer lived a frugal life, but his financial condition deteriorated near the end of his life. In 1672, he and his family were forced to rent out *Mechelen* and move to a smaller house (on nearby *Oude Langedijk*). When he died three years later in 1675—and was buried in the Oude Kerk—Vermeer left his wife and eight minor children with almost no money.

Of the several dozen paintings—there was little else—his wife Catharina possessed at the time of his death, some 29 were Vermeer's own (only 32 paintings of his entire life's work are known to exist today). Catharina seems to have made great efforts to keep her husband's paintings, but there was no way to make ends meet, and she declared herself bankrupt in April 1676. Designated as receiver for the estate was Delft native **Antonie van Leeuwenhoek**, a clerk to the Delft bailiff who, on the side, liked to muse over matter under the microscope. (Through his improvements on that instrument, Leeuwenhoek is credited with giving the world the first accurate description of red blood corpuscles, and is responsible for the first drawing of bacteria, in 1683. Although *his* works aren't in as many museums as Vermeer's, some are on view at the *Museum Boerhaave* in Leiden.)

Leeuwenhoek seems to have been unsympathetic in his dealings with Vermeer's widow. At the sale of the bankrupt estate, a woman merchant named Jannetje Stevens managed to have 26 paintings by Vermeer seized and held as security against a family debt of 500 guilders "for groceries supplied." Catharina protested, and it was agreed that if she immediately paid 342 guilders, the art works would be returned to her. But there are no records that tell whether Catharina ever saw her husband's paintings again.

In 1696, an Amsterdam auction catalogue listed 21 paintings by Vermeer, with an average asking price of 70 guilders. That catalogue comprises one of the few historical records that critics have for determining genuine Vermeers. The 1696 auction in Amsterdam marked the last time for nearly 200 years that Vermeer's work received any but the most incidental public attention. Vermeer was all but ignored during the 18th and much of the 19th century; even detailed scholarly volumes about the painters of Holland's remarkable 17th-century *Golden Age* of art gave no mention his work. Attention to Vermeer didn't begin again until 1842, when the French aristocrat **Thore-Burger**, during a visit to Holland chanced to see *View of Delft*, which hung in a gallery in The Hague. He was so impressed by the painting that he devoted much of the rest of his life to making Vermeer well known.

By the time Vermeer died in Delft in 1675, Amsterdam and Rotterdam, because of the superior size and location of their ports, had progressively taken over the Dutch nation's trade. Although its famous pottery industry continued strong, the rest of Delft slowed down. The number of breweries in the city shrank from 200 to 15. Just before Vermeer's death, Holland as a whole had experienced a complete change in its political fortune. In 1672, Louis XIV of France, who resented the Dutch for their prosperity and coveted their Rhine River ports at the North Sea, sent his armies into the Dutch Republic. In a matter of months, they had swept through most of the country. The French invasion closed the books on the Golden Age, and the country went into a decline that affected every phase of life, including the art market, which completely collapsed. Delft's economy came to a standstill. In the 18th century, even Delftware was in decline, and most of Delft's pottery factories closed. The town became one of retired residents, and a bastion of conservative Calvinism.

A dormant Delft saw the dawn of a new age in the mid-19th century—fostered by the founding of the *Koninklijke Akademie* (Royal Academy), now the **Technical Academy,** in 1842, and the linking of the town to the national railway network in 1847. For the sake of expansion, ancient town ramparts were sacrificed, but powerful protests against further mutilation of the old town—the Oude Delft canal had been threatened with being filled in to make way for a tram track in the center—in large measure prevailed.

Today, as you cruise along prosperous Delft's flower box-decorated canals, or absorb the sights on foot, you see well-preserved historic monuments: the former **East India Company** headquarters (originally three 16th-century houses); the former **St. Barbara Cloister**, founded in 1405, and the 1650 **Vleeshal** (now both renovated as student clubs); the 1770 **Waag** (Weigh House, used today as a theater), the **Visbanken** (still in use as a fish market, since 1342); and the picturesque **Oostpoort** (the last remaining of Delft's eight 14th-century city gates). Delft's population, which had been 23,000 during the days of Vermeer but had fallen to 13,000 by the beginning of the 19th century, now numbers 90,000 for greater Delft, with its 16,000 Technical University students making a lively contribution to contemporary life.

## GUIDEPOSTS

**Telephone Code 015**

**Tourist info** • VVV Markt 85, 2611 GS; ☎ *126100;* open Mon.–Fri. 9 a.m.–6 p.m., Sat. 9 a.m.–5 p.m., Sun. 10 a.m.–3 p.m. (from Oct. 1–March 31 closed Sun.).

**Markets** • Thursdays. general market on the Markt, 8:30 a.m.–5 p.m. (poultry to produce, nuts to knick-knacks); flower market at same time along Hippolytusbuurt canal. Flea market along canals in town center Sat. May–Sept., often to the accompaniment of barrel organs and street musicians.

**Parking** • Metered parking on the Markt (except during Thursday market), near to the VVV, which has map showing other in-town locations. Free parking on Phoenixstraat by windmill, just outside of old town to west.

**Canal Cruises** • *Rondvaart Delft* on Koornmarkt; April–Oct.; daily 10:30 a.m.–5:30 p.m.; 45 mins.; ☎ *126385.*

**Pedal Boats and Kayak Rental** • Rotterdamseweg 148 (near **De Porceleyne Fles**); rentals by the hour; ☎ *571504.*

**Horse-drawn Tram** • On the Markt; Easter–Sept.; daily except Thursday (market day); ☎ *561828.*

**Bike Rental** • At the station. Maps of ANWB signposted cycling routes (Delfland and Westland) available at VVV.

## WHAT TO SEE AND DO

Delft is a destination deserving of an overnight stay, even though it's practically in The Hague's backyard. During the day, explore quiet courtyards, quaint interiors, gardens, and gables. Sunlight sifting through ancient trees highlights fascinating Dutch facades and produces fantastic reflections in the waters (green in summer, dark in winter) of the canals, crossed by humpbacked bridges—all redefined by Delft's special quality of light. After the motorcoach crowds have called it a day, a medieval atmosphere moves back to the ★★ **Grote Markt**, and seeing the monuments around its expanse illuminated ★★ after dark is a special experience. The Markt, the showplace of Delft, is marked in the center by a statue of native son Hugo de Groot (Grotius), who is most definitely meant to be honored but is unintentionally dwarfed by the scale of the long marketplace (still used as such on Thursday). The Markt has one grouping of Delft's premier attractions, while a cluster of others can be found on the lovely ★★ **Oude Delft** canal, only several interesting walking blocks away. On national Dutch holidays, opening hours are different, so check with the Delft VVV.

*One of Delft's many 17th-century canal houses.*

## Prinsenhof ★★

*St. Agathaplein 1 (entrance off Oude Delft); open Tues.–Sat. 10 a.m.–
5 p.m., Sun. and holidays. 1-5 p.m., closed Mons., during Delft's antique
dealer's exhibition in Oct., on Jan. 1 and Dec 25;*  *602358.* The Prinsenhof is one of the Dutch nation's most historic buildings, and one
of Delft's loveliest, just off the Oude Delft canal in the St. Agathaplein. An old cobbled courtyard with chestnut trees, a 15th-century
chapel, and an ambiance of Burgundian days, when the earliest sections of the building were erected as a cloister. The Prinsenhof has the
sad celebrity of being the place where **Prince Willem the Silent**, having
lived there from 1572 when he became the leader of the Dutch Protestant revolt against the ravages of Spanish Catholic rule in the early
days of the *Eighty Years' War*, died from an assassin's bullet in 1584.

The event gives the buildings its credentials as the "cradle of Dutch liberty" (see "Delft in Context"). The fascinating building is a labyrinth of rooms and corridors of unusual beauty, filled with fresh flowers and antique portraits, paintings, and furniture, primarily reflecting Delft's history, particularly in the period of the *Eighty Years' War*. At the reception desk is a detailed English text with the history, layout of building, and description of exhibits, which you can take around with you.

### Museum Lambert van Meerten                                    ★ ★

*Oude Delft 199; hours same as Prinsenhof, except not closed during annual October Antiques Fair;* ☎ *602358.* Nearby on the Oude Delft canal is a charming, old patrician, canal-side mansion, whose owner Lambert van Meerten set out to make a museum of the decorative arts at the end of the last century. The core of the collection is old Dutch tiles. The tiles, whole walls' worth of individual squares, or grouped together in tableaux (there's a 200-tile representation of a naval victory set in the wall above the stairs that lead from the spacious entry hall), show the full range of artisans' skill and imagination in this traditional Dutch medium from the 16th–18th century. The house has lovely details, heavy oak shutters, leaded window glass, lovely carved wood molding and wainscoting, oak-beamed alcoves, 17th-century Hindeloppen paneling from Friesland, and the so-called Leyden room, whose atmosphere is reminiscent of Vermeer. This is a truly delightful corner of old Delft.

### Oude Kerk (Old Church)                                        ★ ★

*Heilige Geestkerkhof; April –Oct., Mon.–Sat. 10 a.m.–5 p.m.;* ☎ *123015.* The foundations were first laid in 1240, though the stone church and tower one sees today dates from about 1500. The squat, squared tower leans noticeably, more than six feet (two meters) off the perpendicular. During a dozen-year restoration, which was completed in 1961, glazier Joep Nicolas, who had worked in the U.S., was commissioned to make entirely new windows for the church. The church's largest bell, Bourdon by name, cast in 1570 and weighing ten tons, is rung only on the most important occasions, the last being the funeral in Delft of Wilhelmina, the former queen, in 1962. Among the prominent persons buried in the Oude Kerk is Vermeer (a simple stone); there's a memorial to Leeuwenhoek, and impressive tombs of the great Dutch naval heroes Piet Hein and Maarten Tromp. Hein's tomb, a marble effigy of the captor of the Spanish silver fleet (1628) in a chapel with doric columns of black and white marble, is the work of Pieter de Keyser, eldest son of the famous architect Hendrick de Keyser, who had designed Willem the Silent's mausoleum in the Nieuwe Kerk. Tromp's memorial, a baroque monument executed by Pieter de Keyser's brother Willem from a design by Jacob van Campen, features an effigy in full armor, with a relief of the naval battle at Terheyde, in which Tromp met his death. (In Dutch sea lore, Admiral Tromp is remembered for supposedly once hoisting a broom to his masthead to proclaim that he had swept the seas clear of the English.)

### Het Wapen van Savoye
### (Gemeentelijke Archiefdienst or Municipal Archives)
*Oude Delft 169; Tues.–Fri. 9 a.m.–4 p.m. (Thurs. til 9 p.m.);* ☎ *602341.* This former 16th-century house now exhibits changing displays related to Delft's history. A shop sells reproductions of old paintings, drawings, and maps in notepaper and postcard form. Also note next door *the Gemeenlandshuis van Delfland* (Delfland Water Authority) at *Oude Delft 176.* This former home (no visits) is Holland's finest surviving example of 16th-century gothic architecture.

### Nieuwe Kerk   ★
*Markt; Apr.–Oct., Mon.–Sat. 9 a.m.–5 p.m., closed Sun., Nov.–Mar., Mon.–Sat. 11 a.m.–4 p.m.;* ☎ *123025.* The Niewe Kerk, begun in 1381 and completed in 1496, is designated the "new church" only in comparison with Delft's tilting-towered Oude Kerk, with origins that go back to the year 1240. In the Niewe Kerk crypt are buried all members of the Dutch royal family, the House of Orange. There are permanent exhibits on members of the Royal Family and on the building itself. Willem the Silent's mausoleum, designed by Hendrick de Keyser, and years in the making at a staggering cost, shows a white marble recumbent figure, at the foot of which is the effigy of his devoted dog. So the story goes, Willem's dog refused food and water after his master's death, and died within days. Willem's monument is directly above the House of Orange royal burial vaults (not open to the public). The most recent ruler to be put to rest was former Queen Wilhelmina, who died in 1962 and, at her own decree, had an all-white funeral.

For visitors interested in an energetic climb, the 357-foot tower is open: *year-round Mon.–Sat. 10 a.m.–4:00 p.m.* The ★panorama of the Dutch countryside from atop 365 steps reveals flat green grazing fields speckled with cows, rooftops in The Hague nearby and, beyond, sand dunes and the thin blue line of the North Sea. In the Niewe Kerk tower is a ★★Hemony 48-bell carillon, one of the finest in Holland.

### Stadhuis   ★★
*Markt 87; open Mon-Fri. 9 a.m.–noon, 2-5 p.m. if no official ceremonies are scheduled;* ☎ *602960.* At one end of the Markt stands the magnificent 17th-century Stadhuis, or town hall. The tower dates from the 15th century, saved from a fire (1618) that destroyed the rest of the building. Inside, a massive marble staircase leads to the council chamber, which also serves as the site for the civil wedding ceremonies that are required by Dutch law. Among the items on display is a 17th-century map of Delft, showing a remarkably similar layout to what it is today. If timing is fortunate, you might see a wedding party arriving at the Stadhuis in horse-drawn carriages.

### Paul Tetar van Elven Museum

*Koornmarkt 67; May–mid Oct., Tues.–Sat., 1-5 p.m.;* ☎ *124206.* This 18th-century canalside patrician house was the home of Delft painter **Paul Tetar van Elven** (1823-1896), who was born in Antwerp, and taught drawing at Delft. It retains a 19th-century atmosphere in its interior. Contents in the period rooms include a fine collection of porcelain, an artist's studio furnished in the old Dutch manner, ceiling frescoes, and paintings and drawings by the former owner.

### Royal Dutch Army and Arms Museum

*Korte Geer 1, Tues.–Sat. 10 a.m.–5 p.m., Sun. 1–5 p.m.;* ☎ *150500.* While museum contents, exhibits revealing Dutch military history through realistic figures (and armies of "toy" soldiers), stylish suits of armor and more modern military dress and paraphernalia, and dioramas (no English descriptions) won't be of interest to everyone, the building (a handsome renovated 17th-century arsenal) and location may well be. The arsenal is located on an extension of the west side of Delft's Koornmarkt, just across the curve of a canal from the Zuidwal (south wall), the place from which Vermeer took his *View of Delft*, which shows the museum, town towers, the soft, reflective light, and huge sky, hovering somewhere between full sun and showers. (The *View of Delft* is at the *Mauritshuis* in The Hague.)

### Nusantara Museum of Ethnology

*Sint Agathaplein 4, Tues.–Sat. 10 a.m.–5 p.m., Sun. and holidays, 1–5 p.m.;* ☎ *602358.* Located across from the Prinsenhof, this museum has a collection of objects from the Dutch East Indies (Indonesia). It particularly focuses on the range of arts and crafts representing the diverse cultures within Indonesia, the former Dutch colony which gained its independence in 1949.

## *SHOPPING*

There's a full complement of department and other stores at in-town *In de Veste*, pedestrian shopping center. In and near the Markt are smaller, more personalized shops, such as the butcher and the baker. But, since this *is* Delft, presumably it's the candlestick maker (of blue-and-white ware) that you've come to see. Begin with at least a look at the best: De Porceleyne Fles handpainted works. You'll notice the difference in quality of decoration between these pieces and the factory-made ware at the many shops that line the Markt, and also the difference in price.

### Royal Delftware Factory De Porceleyne Fles     ★★

*Rotterdamseweg 196. Apr.–Oct., Mon.–Sat. 9 a.m.–5 p.m., Sun. and holidays. 10 a.m.–4 p.m.; Nov.–Mar., Mon.–Fri. 9 a.m.–5 p.m., Sat. 10 a.m.–4 p.m., closed Sun.;* ☎ *569214, FAX 625635.* De Porceleyne Fles (the porcelain bottle), founded in 1653, schedules potter's wheel and handpainting demonstrations (by one of the firm's 150 artists) frequently during the day, to give you an idea of the personal attention that goes into producing each piece of the factory's ware, distinguished on the bottom by the mark of a jar and initials "JT" to attest to its authenticity. The showrooms are so prettily arrayed that it feels like a museum (and indeed, some of the unique pieces are as expensive as museum objects). Around tiled fireplaces and in a superb display cabinet presented by the Dutch King William III sit blue-and-white (and other polychrome patterns) jugs and ginger jars, bowls and bud vases, and tiles and teapots.

There are some seconds (25-40 percent off) on sale at the factory, although the Royal Delft store with the largest selection of seconds in town (also with a good selection of first quality pieces) is **De Backer vd Hoeck** (*Markt 62, open daily 9 a.m.–5:30 p.m.,* ☎ *123171*), which will mail purchases anywhere. There is also a branch of the shop at *Markt 30* (*open year-round; demonstration of hand-decoration*), in the back room of which is a fine collection of colorful tiles. Many are seconds, but with careful inspection, you'll find ones that are fine for yourself or as gifts.

### Atelier de Candelaer

*Kerkstraat 14, Apr. 1-Sept. 30: Mon.–Fri. 9 a.m.–6 p.m., Sat. 9 a.m.–5 p.m., Sun. 10 a.m.–6 p.m.; Oct. 1-Mar. 31 Mon.–Sat. 10 a.m.–5 p.m.* ☎ *131848*. In a picturesque corner of Delft just off the Markt behind the Nieuwe Kerk, this two-person studio sells the fine pieces of hand-made Delft produced on-site.

## WHERE TO STAY

The hotels listed are all very centrally located, only a short walk from the Markt, but on residential streets with canals. Staffs are friendly and very able in English.

## MODERATE

### Delft Museumhotel                                ★★★★

*Oude Delft 189, 2611 HD;* ☎ *140930, FAX 140935*. This is Delft's most recent hotel, though it's in two contiguous 17th-century houses. The traditional brick, big-windowed, dignified facade shelters a friendly staff and lobby and public rooms that are updated in ambiance. Each of the 28 guest rooms in the hotel proper is different, many with original details. There are 25 additional rooms in a new addition at the back, which are larger and slightly more expensive, that offer views of the gardens. There is a lobby cafe for breakfast (no restaurant) and snacks during the day, and a bar-lounge (that looks out on Delft's Oude Kerk). Prices vary slightly with room view (eight face canal, or garden) or suite, all with modern tiled bath and shower. Nice sense of character, winding corridors.

### De Ark                                ★★★★

*Koornmarkt 59-65, 2611 EC;* ☎ *157999, FAX 144997.* Housed in three restored canal houses in a lovely residential section of central old Delft are 16 rooms (seven with canal view, others face garden). All different, large, often sunny, and neat, though with rather nondescript modern furniture. Never mind. There's plenty of Dutch gezellig (coziness) about the place, and the friendly front desk is staffed 24 hours. The bricked, beamed dining room with corner fireplace provides a Dutch buffet breakfast, and well-prepared, tasty dinners if you desire. There's parking for a fee, and several one-bedroom suites in the annex across the street (canal).

### Leeuwenbrug                                           ★★★

*Koornmarkt 16, 2611 EE; 147741, FAX 159759.* Also on the same charming canal (quite quiet, one-way traffic), all 33 rooms in this three-floor elevatored hotel, which has a mix of traditional and modern decor and details, are different, some with beams, mantels, or other details; five face the canal; each with modern bath and/or shower; five rooms are in the new additional canal townhouse next door, with huge windows. There's a cozy lobby lounge with newspapers, books, and TV (also in all rooms), that faces canal. Breakfast only, but there's a lobby bar that's open til 1 a.m. Pay parking next to hotel.

## WHERE TO EAT

You can dine handsomely (and historically) in Delft. But if you prefer a simply savory or sweet snack, you won't have to forgo a scenic setting to do so.

### Restaurant De Prinsenkelder, or the Princes' Cellar

*Prinsenhof, entrance Schoolstraat 11; Mon.–Fri. noon–2:30 p.m., and 6-9:30 p.m., dinner only on Sat., closed Sun.;* ☎ *121860; expensive.* This restaurant is in the attractive brick vaulted basement of the Prinsenhof. Meathooks can still be seen in the ceiling, which shows that while the building served as a cloister and as the home of Willem the Silent, this was the food and wine cellar. The atmosphere for the first class, local Dutch food carefully prepared and presented in the French style (fresh sauteed eel, fillet of tuna with Dutch shrimp, ginger with cream) is historic, romantic, very Dutch, and definitely Delft.

### Restaurant "Het Straatje van Vermeer"

*Molslaan 18; Tues.–Sat. 6-10 p.m.; reservations at* ☎ *126466; expensive.* For another touch of Old Delft, try the cozy ambiance of Dutch decor with antiques, old tiles and copies of Vermeer paintings on the walls found here. Reserve for dinner, since the restaurant does serve groups, and you want to be seated in a room with other individual parties. Menus and à la carte choices include a full range of continental and Dutch dishes.

### Monopole

*Markt 48, daily 9 a.m.–10 p.m.;* ☎ *123059; inexpensive.* This is a good example of the informal fare available at the Markt. Just one of many cafes there, it helps to fill the vast space with outdoor tables and chairs when the weather warrants, and provides an excellent vantage point from which to survey the superb setting. You can sit as long as you want over a coffee, juice or beer. Maybe you'll be thinking you're in heaven if the carillon in the Nieuwe Kerk begins a concert (Tuesday, Thursday—market day and quite a different scene—and Saturday at 11 a.m.). Light meals and snacks available from early morning until well into the evening.

### Banketbakkerij

*Corner of J. Gerritstraat, open Mon.–Sat. til 5:30 p.m.;* ☎ *123388.* Across the Markt from Monopole, about midway along its length, is this pastry shop, which also sells bread, chocolates and Holland's *hopjes* (coffee-flavored caramels). Head for the back of the shop, up a few stairs, to the tiny tea room (where you only need buy a cup of coffee). It has four check-clothed tables, a huge old tiled fireplace, walls hung with old wooden cookie molds, all overlooking a little canal.

### Kleyweg's Stads-Koffyhuis

*Oude Delft 133; Mon.–Fri. 9–7 p.m., Sat. 6 p.m.;* ☎ *124625; closed Sun.* On the lovely Oude Delft canal, you'll find this local favorite, for breakfast, lunch, dinner, or coffee. Served outside on a barge moored along Delft's oldest, possibly most picturesque, canal if you like. A tasty variety of sandwiches, pancakes, and other light meals is served.

### Stadspannekoeckhuys

*Oude Delft 113,* ☎ *130193, open daily noon–9 p.m., closed Mon. in winter.* Another local favorite and neighbor to Kleyweg's is this good choice for platter-size Dutch pancakes and quick meals.

### Koffiekelder de Nonnerie

*St. Agathaplein, off Oude Delft, open to 5 p.m.;* ☎ *121860, closed Mon.* Back at the Prisenhof Museum, this cafe serves coffee and lunch in the cellar, or in the garden when the weather's right.

# ROTTERDAM

## GUIDELINES FOR ROTTERDAM

### SIGHTS

Despite a history as lengthy as its neighboring Dutch towns, Rotterdam has an entirely different appearance and personality, largely as a result of the leveling of its center by the German *Luftwaffe* on May 14, 1940. Rotterdam's city skyline, especially at the waterfront, is strikingly contemporary. Sections along its **port**, the largest and busiest in the world, look like a grown-up Erector Set, with cranes locked in their skyward saluting position. Commentary during harbor cruises points out just how state-of-the-art Rotterdam's port is. On land and water, imaginative planning is much in evidence, as you'll discover when visiting the several excellent **museums** and exceptional examples of **modern architecture**. Rotterdam's one preserved historic section has U.S. ties: picturesque **Delfshaven** is the port from which English Separatists who had been living in Leiden departed by ship for a pilgrimage to the New World where they established Plymouth Colony.

### GETTING AROUND

The broad boulevard **Coolsingel**, running north/south through modern Rotterdam's center and continuing to the port as **Schiedamsedijk** from the point where **West Blaak** and **Blaak** make an east/west crossing, provides a basic orientation to the city. Many of the major sights are on or near these streets; too far to reach on foot, there's a good **tram/bus/Metro** network (and helpful system map). A day-pass (Dfl. 8.25) is available from the city transportation booth on Stationplein.

The VVV has a city information booth at Centraal Station. From Easter–Sept. at 1:30 p.m. Mon.–Sat., a comprehensive two-hour city overview **motorcoach tour** that shows off Rotterdam's monuments as well as its modern architecture, and includes a look at the port, parks, and Delfthaven, departs from Coolsingel opposite City Hall, near the main VVV office there, where tickets (Dfl. 20) are available. At **ArchiCenter Rotterdam**, a special department of, and located at, the VVV, you can get verbal information, maps, and suggested self-guided walk brochures in English about Rotterdam's acclaimed modern architecture. **Spido Havenrondvaarten/harborcruises** (*Willemsplein at waterfront;* ☎ *4135400; tram 5 from CS, Metro: Leuvehaven*) has a selection of frequently scheduled port cruises (1-1/4 and 2-1/4 hours and longer, multilingual commentary). A combination tram/cruise package takes approximately 2-1/2 hours.

## SHOPPING

**Lijnbaan** (opened in 1953), the first center-city pedestrianized shopping precinct in Europe, was a truly revolutionary concept in its era, with more than a mile-long mix of shops, boutiques, and cafes, some under cover; it remains a pleasant shopping area and city passageway, with gardens and sculpture. Major department and clothing stores are found on and around the **Beursplein**, by the bold blue-green *World Trade Center* on Coolsingel. On **Nieuwe** and **Oude Binnenweg** and **Karel Doormanstraat** are a number of antique and curio shops; in Delfshaven on Voorhaven is **Adriaan Groenewond Antiques**, considered the best of its kind in the city. Stores are generally closed Mon. until 1 p.m.; late night shopping is Fri. until 9 p.m. Rotterdam's **general market**, also with antiques and curiosities, is Holland's largest: Tues. and Sat. 9 a.m.–5 p.m. on the Mariniersweg and surrounding streets. There's also a book, stamp, and coin market on Grotekerkplein, Tues. and Sat., 9:30 a.m.–4 p.m.

## WHERE TO STAY

There's variety enough to meet your personal comfort/cost ratio, from five-star international to cozy neighborhood two-star.

## WHERE TO EAT

All aspects of Rotterdam are present in its restaurants. There are architecturally intriguing, contemporary or cozy historic settings for continental or typical Dutch cuisine, and all the flavors of foreign kitchens you'd expect to find in an international port.

## ENTERTAINMENT AND EVENTS

Rotterdam's monthly events and exhibitions calendar *Agenda* (in Dutch only) is available from the VVV or hotels, where someone can translate the listings for you. The **Rotterdams Philharmonisch Orkest** (James Conlon, Conductor) resides in **De Doelen**, which opened in 1966 in the center of the city (box office ☎ *217171*). (In the 1980s, acclaimed English conductor Simon Rattle, was principal guest conductor for Rotterdam, a musical company he describes as "exciting.") On Wednesday, October through May, free half-hour **lunch concerts** are presented at De Doelen, beginning at 12:45 p.m. Lunchtime **organ concerts** (12:45–1:15 p.m.) are held in St. Laurenskerk Fridays, with other musical performances in the church on Thursday (except January and February). The annual international **Rotterdam Film Festival** is held in January and February.

## ARRIVING

Rotterdam is served at least four times hourly by train on the main Amsterdam-The Hague-Rotterdam line, a branch of which runs to Schiphol Airport. Rotterdam also connects by rail directly to Gouda and Utrecht; all trains use **Centraal Station**. The city's **Zestienhoven Airport** offers various intra-European air connections. Travelers arriving via ferry from England at **Hoek van Holland** can take the boat train directly to Rotterdam (about a half hour) for ongoing destinations. By motorway, Rotterdam is 76 km (47 mi.) south of Amsterdam, 103 km (62 mi.) north of Antwerp in Belgium. Because of the massive size of its port, two tunnels (the *Benelux* and the *Maas*) are part of the complex highway system that serves and encircles Rotterdam.

## IN THE AREA

**Kinderdijk**, in the countryside near Rotterdam, provides windmill fans with 19 in a single scenic setting. The picturesque old port of **Dordrecht**, 20 km (12 mi.) south of Rotterdam, sometimes considered the southernmost city of the Randstad, lies somewhat off today's main tourism track, at the crossroads of Holland's inland waterways. **Spido Cruises** to the waterworks and waterways of the region are available from Rotterdam, as are maps for self-driving routes of the extensive Rotterdam port from the city to the North Sea.

## TRAVEL TIPS

Rotterdam is surrounded by an efficient but complex motorway network that is dense with drivers determined to get where they are going as rapidly as possible; it can be confusing for the uninitiated motorist. Arrival in the city by train is recommended. If you do come by car, get specific *place names* to look for on exit ramp signs.

# ROTTERDAM IN CONTEXT

Rotterdam, like Rome, wasn't built in a day. But it was laid waste in one. In the very year Rotterdam should have been celebrating its 600th anniversary—festivities commemorating its having received civic rights in 1340 had been planned—the sudden events of a single day, May 14, 1940, overshadowed the city's entire history. Mere minutes of Nazi air bombardment leveled six centuries of civilization in Rotterdam. It destroyed more than 20,000 homes and historically significant buildings, killed hundreds, and left another 78,000 homeless.

A city's history is reflected in its facades, and you can count on one hand the buildings in the center of Rotterdam that predate 1940: the *Stadhuis* (built in 1920 in the Dutch Renaissance style), the main *Post Office*, the *Schielandhuis* (see "What To See and Do"), and *St. Laurenskerk* (*Grote Kerk*). Of all the other historic monuments destroyed, only the cinder-sided St. Laurens church, with its scarred but still-standing tower, a symbol to the city, was cast to play a phoenix in Rotterdam; it was resurrected from the rubble, and re-constructed to rise again on the city skyline.

For the rest of its rebuilding, in striking contrast to the postwar plans of Europe's other badly bombed cities, Rotterdam opted for a radical and imaginative concept: creating a whole new contemporary city from the ashes of the old. **Lewis Mumsford**, the American architect and city-planning critic, wrote in his classic book *The City in History*, "Not every (bombed) city rose to the challenge of its destruction as determinedly and as skillfully as Rotterdam," adding, "The word 'renewal' is a tame one to describe the resurgence of Rotterdam."

Such a fresh start was made possible by the foresight of the Rotterdam city government, which, almost immediately after the 1940 Nazi bombing, expropriated the sites of the bombed buildings, becoming sole proprietor of 415 acres in the heart of Rotterdam. Former owners received fair compensation for the value of their property as of May 9, 1940, the day before the May 10 Nazi invasion of Holland. A year after the official end of the war, the provisional city council of Rotterdam approved the so-called "Basic Scheme" for the city, which banned industry from the center, cut by two-thirds the number of residences in what had been a severely overcrowded city center, and built in spaciousness by widening downtown streets and planting plenty of flowers. As for the centralized pedestrian **Lijnbaan** shopping plaza, first of its kind in the world, Mumford reviewed it as "exemplary in almost every way." (The Lijnbaan may appear pleasant but ordinary to today's visitors, but it should be appreciated for its conceptual contribution to the present worldwide multimalled landscape.)

Its citizens' reputation for hard work is evident in the half-kidding comment by the Dutch that in Rotterdam "shirts are sold with the sleeves already rolled up." Never was their shirt-sleeve stamina needed more than after the Second World War. Within five weeks of the liberation of Rotterdam, work on reconstruction of the port had begun—the Nazis had blown up half the port's machinery and equipment in 1944. There was no argument from citizens that the port took precedence over other rebuilding, since the prosperity of the city and, indeed, much of the country, depended upon shipping.

In his own times, as he remains in the 20th century, **Erasmus** (1466–1536) was Rotterdam's favorite native son, albeit an illegitimate one since his father was a priest. (See "Erasmus" under "The Dutch Cultural Legacy: The Muse".) Fortunately, he didn't let that happenstance hamper his life, obviously believing the words he later wrote: "No one is injured save by himself." Erasmus was one of the first persons since the end of the Roman Empire to earn his living by the pen, and Rotterdammers past and present seem to see their own straightforward selves in many of his words. His *Adages*, sayings adapted from antiquity, are familiar to us all: "As plain as the nose on your face;" "Call a spade a spade;" "Caught in his own snare;" and "In the country of the blind, the one-eyed man is king."

A brief look back to its beginnings reveals that Rotterdam was first settled in about the year 1000, at a dam on the small river Rotte, where peasants and fishermen gradually became involved with local trade and fishing. A flood in 1164 swept away the wooden huts of the early hamlet, but residents were determined to fight for its survival come hell or high water. In 1299, Rotterdam was officially recognized by its feudal overlord, Wolfert van Borsselen, as an urban entity after citizens in the 19-feet-below-sea-level town protected themselves with dikes and had become adept at driving stilts (wooden piles) into silt for building foundations. The Counts of Holland gave Rotterdam city rights in 1340. Almost completely consumed by fire in 1563, Rotterdam barely had time to rebuild before it joined other Dutch cities in support of Willem I (the Silent) against the Spanish in 1568.

Rotterdam's physical location, on the delta of two significant river systems, the *Rijn* (Rhine) and the *Maas* (Meuse), played the leading part in its prominence, but history had a supporting role. At the end of the *Eighty Years' War*, under the *Peace of Westphalia* (1648), the *River Scheldt* and *Antwerp's port* in the southern Netherlands (to-day's Belgium) were closed. Thereafter, sea traffic turned north to Rotterdam (and Amsterdam). From that time Rotterdam, until then just one of the "small towns" of Holland, and its port gradually began to grow.

Another substantial boost for its shipping trade came Rotterdam's way when Holland blockaded the River Scheldt—which had been reopened by Napoleon Bonaparte—from 1830–39, after Belgium seceded from the **Kingdom of the Netherlands** that had been established in 1815 by the **Congress of Vienna**. Much of what had been Antwerp's shipping trade, mostly with the Dutch colonies, again was diverted north to Rotterdam. With this incentive, the harbor at Rotterdam developed further, but was hindered by silt at the mouth of the Maas, which prevented the entrance of large vessels. This was more than inconvenient as Europe progressed through the *Industrial Revolution* and into an age empowered by steam. The present-day preeminence of Rotterdam's port is due to the construction of the **Nieuwe Waterweg** (1863–1872) and a subsequent plan of continual dredging. Since 1872, Rotterdam has offered ships a 30-km. lock-free entry from the North sea to the city.

Beginning in the 20th century, Rotterdam has carried out successive programs of **port development**, water management, and industrialization that have made the city the powerhouse of the Dutch economy. Overcoming the damage done during the Second World War, the port of Rotterdam quickly regained its prewar tonnage. Ironically, Rotterdam's recovery largely grew out of its role as the main furnisher of raw materials by river barge to West Germany during that country's postwar "economic miracle." The process of digging new deepwater harbors—the reverse of Holland's more usual land-filling efforts—produced the port/industrial complexes of *Botlek* and *Europort*, and put the port at *Pernis* on its way to becoming the largest oil refinery complex on the continent. By 1962, Rotterdam had edged up on and surpassed New York in total tonnage to become the busiest port in the world. Radar facilities were installed to enable ships to enter the port from the North Sea even in zero-visibility fog. Actually 20 miles (37 km.) inland from the North Sea, Rotterdam is, more accurately, a series of ports along that length, which is lockless and bridgefree; two major motorway tunnels, the *Benelux* and the *Maas*, pass under the river port in the city.

Today Rotterdam services more than 32,000 seagoing vessels and 180,000 inland waterway barges annually, handling nearly 300 million metric tons of bulk cargo, putting it well ahead of its two nearest international rivals, Kobe, Japan, and New York. In Europe, the port of Rotterdam handles more trade than the ports of Le Havre, Bremen, Hamburg, Antwerp, and Amsterdam combined. More crucial for its future, since the onward travel of goods from the port is as important as their initial arrival by ship, Rotterdam is the best-equipped transport, distribution, and trade center in Europe, and is linked to the continental hinterland by a sophisticated network of waterways, roads, railways, and pipelines. As the needs of the transport world evolve, Rotterdam is prepared to meet the challenge of offering the best and most efficient harbor service to exporters and importers of both raw materials and manufactured goods.

Apart from its "no contest" victory in comparative port size, Rotterdam's competition with the city of Amsterdam is keen. There's no casualness in the two cities' confrontation in *voetbal* (pronounced "football,"—in America called soccer), when Rotterdam's *Feynoord* team faces off with Amsterdam's *Ajax*.

Since its original postwar rebuilding, Rotterdam has had a chance to come full circle in city-planning concepts. And, again, the city is taking the lead by reevaluating some of its earlier ground-breaking urban planning ideals and ideas. **Waterstad** (water city) is the name of the combined new recreational attractions along the riverfront: **Tropicana** with its indoor swimming pool and subtropical environment; open-air museum of inland shipping; Sunday art market; **IMAX** theater; **National Econocenter**; and assorted pubs and restaurants at the attractive **Oude Haven** (Old Harbor). The words "stronger through strife" were added to the city's shield after the war, and Rotterdam's "sleeves-up" citizens—who now number 575,000 and come from some 125 countries—seem to have proved themselves to be just that.

## GUIDEPOSTS

**Telephone Code 010**

**Tourist Info** • VVV, Main Office, Coolsingel 67. Open year-round Mon.–Thurs. 9 a.m.–5:30 p.m., Fri. to 9 p.m., Sat. 9 a.m.–5 p.m.,

Sun. 10 a.m.–4 p.m. (closed Sun. Oct.–Mar.). Closed Dec. 25, 26, Jan. 1. VVV at Centraal Station (Rotterdam info. only) open daily 9 a.m.–10 p.m. Sun. open 10 a.m.), closed Dec. 25, Jan. 1. ☎ *06-34034065, (Dfl. 0.50 per minute)*. The VVV has a gift shop.

**Port Tours** • Spido Havenrondvaarten, Willemsplein; ☎ *4135400*. The 1-1/4 hr. harbor tour is offered year-round, varying schedule; additional cruises daily Apr.–Sept.

**Emergencies** • Police, ambulance: ☎ *06-11*.

**Post Office** • Coolsingel 42, ☎ *4542220*. Open Mon.–Thurs. 8:30 a.m.–7 p.m. (Fri. 8:30 a.m.–8:30 p.m.).

**ANWB** • AAA associate organization: Westblaak 210, ☎ *4140000*.

**Parking** • Public garages (look for "**P**" signs) in center around Centraal Station, Lijnbaan.

**Transport** • Information on public transportation in Rotterdam and greater region: Stationplein, ☎ *4546890*.

**Taxi** • Rotterdam Taxi Base: ☎ *4626060*; taxi ranks at Centraal Station, Hilton, on Coolsingel.

## WHAT TO SEE AND DO

During its postwar, mid-20th-century rebuilding, Rotterdam humanized its contemporary core with plenty of public sculpture, though the most moving piece is a wrenching reminder of WWII: *Devastated City* (by **Ossip Zadkine**, 1952, on *Plein 1940*, behind the Maritime Museum). The human figure, with a gaping hole in its torso that simultaneously symbolizes a "person without a heart" and a "city without a center," its hands raised to the sky, expresses both horror and hope. Far less thought-provoking, but a perennial personal favorite, is the shy yet sturdy *Monsieur Jacques* by **L.O. Wenckebach**, 1959, on Coolsingel (whose "twin" greets visitors at the entrance to the Kroller-Muller Museum in Otterlo). **Rodin's** *L'homme qui marche* meets shoppers at the pedestrianized Korte Lijnbaan. On Grotekerkplein is one of Rotterdam's most beloved sculptures, of native son *Erasmus*, who was born near this square in October 1469. The statue (by **Hendrik de Keyser**, 17th century), which thankfully survived the Nazi bombing and thereafter was safely sequestered for the duration of the war, portrays Erasmus reading a book. **Umberto Mastrianni's** *Kiss* near Centraal Station has been renamed *Goodbye* locally. Many of Rotterdam's museums are free on Wednesday (and for children under 16 at all times).

### Boymans-van Beuningen Museum                    ★★★
*Mathenesserlaan 18; Tues.–Sat. 10 a.m.–5 p.m., Sun. and hols. 11 a.m.–5 p.m., closed Mon., Jan. 1, Apr. 30.;* ☎ *4419400; Tram 5, Metro: Eendrachtsplein* There are few museums in the world where one can find works by artists **Van Eyck**, **Da Vinci**, **Van Gogh**, and **Andy Warhol** under one roof. As well as offering their works, the Boymans-van Beuningen Museum is the only one in Holland with collections of both fine and

applied art from the 14th century to the present. The museum's 250,000-piece collection is well respected worldwide, a well-blended result of private donations (many from local Rotterdam families) and selective acquisitions. One of the showpieces is **Pieter Bruegel the Elder's** *The Tower of Babel* (c. 1563), and another is **Rembrandt's** portrait of his son Titus. (Because the Boymans has so many of his drawings, the institution and scholars associated with it have become leading authorities in studies on attributions to Rembrandt.) Among artists represented in the Old Masters department are Hieronymous Bosch, Pieter Paul Rubens, Lucas van Leyden, Jan Steen, Jan van Goyen, Karel Fabritius, and Frans Hals. The print and graphics galleries contain important works by artists from Durer to Dali; among many renowned representatives in between are Picasso, Magritte, Max Ernst, Man Ray, Kokoschka, and Kandinsky. There is a large bookstore, and reproductions are available in many forms; the coffee shop has a garden terrace.

The Boymans Museum was an interested party in an intriguing chapter of art history that involved a modern Dutch "master painter." **Hans van Meegeren** wielded his brush so well that he created six "Vermeers" that even experts became convinced were long-missing works by that 17th-century Dutch master. In 1937, the Boymans paid $286,000 for one of them. During World War II, Nazi German Field Marshall Hermann Goring, an avid art collector, acquired another. When the war was over, Van Meegeren was criminally charged with having cooperated with the Nazis by sending a Vermeer out of Holland to Goring; this forced him to decide which was worse: to be charged as a *forger* or denounced as a *collaborator*. In the country's postwar climate, it seemed far safer to be a forger, so Van Meegeren admitted that Goring's "Vermeer" was a fake. Yet experts on Dutch master artists, studying the works that Van Meegeren said were his, still refused to believe that the paintings weren't genuine. Only by actually painting a *new* Old Master *before* the eyes of the court judges was Van Meegeren able to convince the art world that he was a master forger. Finally, he was believed, then convicted, and given a year in prison. Van Meegeren died of a heart attack before he was able to serve his sentence.

The Boymans is situated in what is known as **Museumpark,** which houses a total of five museums also in a landscaped garden setting that is used for outdoor theater and music feativals in season. One, the **Nederlands Architectuurinstituut** (☎ *4401200*), housed in a striking building that will be of more interest for most visitors than its specialized collection of working architectural drawings, etc., is one of the largest architectural centers in the world. Another park museum is the **Kunsthal** (☎ *4400300*), an intriguing contemporary hall for special art exhibits.

### Delfshaven                                              ★★

*Trams 4, 6, Metro: Delfshaven.* This picturesque old district (a protected historic area since the late 1960s and largely restored) was incorporated into Rotterdam in 1866, but it was created as a port for the town of **Delft** in the 14th century. Inland Delft, which needed a port to maintain its economic viability, received permission to create a shipping channel along the river *Schie* to the *Maas* in 1389. The port served its purpose until it was sacked in 1488, after which it barely survived. Delfshaven became important again in the 17th century for Delft's **East India Company** ships, but leaders in Delft proper began to be protective of their town, and refused to let Delfshaven develop. Dutch naval hero **Piet Hein** was born here (*Piet Heynstraat #10*) in 1577. (Not surprisingly, a statue of him stands nearby.)

Perhaps Delfshaven's most memorable moment in history came August 1, 1620 (on the Gregorian calendar), when the so-called **Pilgrim Fathers**, English Separatists, who had been living in Leiden, set sail from here aboard the *Speedwell*, to England, where they met up with the more seaworthy *Mayflower*. The *Mayflower* eventually reached America where the pilgrims established Plymouth Colony. The 16th-century **Oude Kerk** (*Aelbrechtskolk 20;* ☎ *4774156*), where the pilgrims most probably prayed before their departure, is rarely open to individuals (there is a service on Thanksgiving Day), but there's a commemorative plaque by the door. Inside is a stained glass window of the *Speedwell* and a memorial dedicated to the pilgrims. A **Hemony carillon** was placed in the tower of the restored Regency-style church in 1963; inquire at the Rotterdam VVV about summer carillon and organ concerts. Next door to the Oude Kerk is the **Raadhuis** (town hall), dating from 1580 and the days when Delfshaven was independent. In the attractive old **Zakkendragershuisje** (Sack Carriers house), *Voorstraat 13*, is a pewter artisan's shop. At the end of Voorhaven is a working, grain-grinding **windmill** that can be visited, including its outside "balcony," from which there's a nice view.

### De Dubbelde Palmboom                                    ★★

*Voorhaven 12; Tues.–Sat. 10 a.m.—5 p.m., Sun. & hols. 11 a.m.–5 p.m., closed Mon., Jan. 1, Apr. 30;*  *4761533; tram 6 from Coolsingel, Metro: Delfshaven.* This is a part of the Rotterdam Historical Museum. Located in a restored 19th-century warehouse with brick floors and beamed ceilings, the museum has interesting exhibits on living and working in the Rotterdam region in the pre- and post-industrial eras, attractively arranged in rooms on nine levels connected by wooden ramps (and elevators) working their way up into the eaves, where the cafe **De Bonte Hond** is housed. There are cards in English explaining exhibits in each room.

### Prins Hendrik Maritime Museum                           ★★

*Leuvehaven 1; Tues.–Sat. 10 a.m.—5 p.m., Sun. and hols. 11 a.m.–5 p.m., closed Mon., Jan. 1, Apr. 30, Dec. 25;*  *4132680; Trams 3, 6, 7; Metro:*

*Beurs/Churchillplein.* Meant to provide insight into maritime history as a whole and the story of shipping in Europe, the Netherlands, and Rotterdam in particular, the Maritime Museum fulfills its mandate by multimedia means: a series of diverting five-minute videos on shipping that bypass the need for language, old paintings and prints, charts showing the comparative sizes of seagoing craft, equipment (there's a highly popular periscope and a complete ship's bridge), and ship models of all sorts. (Kits for even smaller models of ships such as the **Holland America Line's** *Rotterdam* are on sale in the excellent museum shop, which also sells old shipping posters, books in English, etc.) Ramps (good for accessibility) from one floor to another are suggestive of ship gangways, and pass windows with fine views out to the museum's adjoining water-berthed exhibits: steam tugs, sailing vessels, and the restored Royal Dutch Navy warship *De Buffel.* As shipshape as you'd expect a Dutch crew to keep her, *De Buffel* sailed under steam from 1868 to 1896, though the engine and copper tubing gleam as if new. You'd expect the deluxe quarters of the Commandant and officers, but what was truly progressive for its day was the impressive living standards for the sailors. As for the brig in *De Buffel's* bowels, I've *paid* to sail transatlantic in cabins less large. Rotterdam's Maritime Museum shows that—as with music—ships and the sea stir emotions that transcend language.

Newly opened near the Maritime Museum on the south side of Wijn-haven is the **Museum Schepen uit Verre Landen** (*Ships from Far Countries*), a permanent, under cover, in-water collection of 25 different boat types from around the world. Contact the VVV for more details.

### St. Laurens or Grotekerk ★

*Grotekerkplein; June–Sept. Tues.–Sat. 10 a.m.–4 p.m., Oct.–May Thurs. only noon–2 p.m.;* ☎ *4131494.* Built in the 14th and 15th centuries in the Dutch late-gothic style, with wide, lofty aisles and timber barrel vaults, St. Laurenskerk was badly damaged in the Nazi bombing of Rotterdam on May 14, 1940. Throughout the war, St. Laurens' burnt shell and tower stood as a solitary sentinel on the bare *Grotekerkplein.* A particularly important link between Rotterdam's past and present, St. Laurenskerk was the only historic reconstruction of a building that the citizens opted for following the war. The church rebuilding was completed in 1968. A new organ (one of the church's three) was dedicated in 1973.

### Kijk-Kubus (Public Cube House) ★

*Overblaak 70; open Tues.–Fri. 10 a.m.–5 p.m., Sat. and Sun. 11 a.m.–5 p.m., Closed Mon.;* ☎ *4142285; Tram 3, 6, and 7, Metro Blaak.* The ★★group of 38 "cube" houses, of which the Public Cube is one, situated in the central Rotterdam city district of Blaak, are collectively called "Het Blaakse Bos" (the Blaak Woods) due to the houses' other nickname, "tree dwellings." Seeing them, I didn't find it surprising that the cube houses had garnered so many descriptive names, since they are so unexpected, so imaginative, in their shape and setting. Designed by architect Piet Blom and built in 1984, the cube houses serve as an upper-level "bridge," linking the waterfront, particularly the picturesque and popular pub-lined ★ ★ **Oude Haven**, to the town: Rotterdam's **Centraal Library**, the general street market's Marinier-sweg, and older post- WWII residential areas. As you wander beneath the cube-shaped houses, tipped 'til they're resting on one corner point, you can't help wondering what they're like as for-real living spaces: can the floors possibly be level? All is answered in a visit to the intriguing "model" cube. I will say that the windowed top point of the cube made me want to spend a night lying on the floor looking up at the stars.

Another building that deserves your notice is **the Pencil**, so-called because the building, with its steeply graded, lead-colored roof, does resemble a point-up stubby pencil. The aforementioned ★ **Centraal Library** (*Hoogstraat 110; Tues–Sat. 10 a.m.–9 p.m., Mon. 12:30–9 p.m., Sat. 10 a.m.–5 p.m., closed Sun;* ☎ *4338911*) has a bit of Paris' *Pompideau Center* about it, with large, bright-yellow exterior ventilation tubes branching off to various floors. Architects Bakema and van den Broek built the seven building layers with a sloping glass front and each floor getting smaller, appearing like a pyramid when viewed from the interior ground floor. Central escalators are designed to cascade down like a tiered waterfall.

### Euromast & Spacetower                                              ★

*Parkhaven 20; Euromast open daily year-round, April—Sept. 10 a.m.–7 p.m., Oct.– Mar. 10 a.m.–5 p.m., in July and Aug. until 10:30 p.m. Tues.—Sat.; Spacetower may be closed at any time due to weather conditions;* ☎ *4364811; Tram 6 or 9, Metro Dijkzigt, bus 39.* Today an established silhouette on the city skyline, the Euromast was built in 1960. In 1970 the Spacetower was added, since the 27-story *Erasmus University Medical Faculty* (the large gleaming white, rather shiplike structure on West Zeedijk), built in the interim, had robbed the Euromast of the 360-degree view that it advertised. At 600 feet (185 meters), the Spacetower's unmarred views over city and port now seem secure. The ★ ★ panorama from the Spacecabin's comfortable couch seating, aimed outward as it ascends and descends (in a total of five minutes) while slowly revolving, is wonderful in good weather. And, I was told, you can stay seated and go up and down again for the original price of admission. Note that there's an outside flight of stairs (and observation deck) at the Euromast level (340 feet) to reach the Spacecabin. In the Euromast are both formal and informal restaurants, and at the base there's a gift shop.

The Euromast sits in portside **Het Park**, site of the 1960 *Floriade* exhibition. Just to the east, also abutting the harbor, is **Het Nieuwe Werk,** a gracious, gardened section of the city. This is the neighborhood where shipping companies have their corporate headquarters and countries their consulates, especially in the mansions along **Park Laan**. The lovely mansion at #14 is a **Museum of Taxation**, and the avenue's other inhabitants make jokes about that being where the *real* resources of Rotterdam are. Next door is the **Veerhaven**, the harbor from which Rotterdam's much-admired Admiral Piet Hein (1577–1629) sailed and later made his legendary seizure of the Spanish silver fleet. Across the Nieuwe Maas from here, the massive green copper-topped building that looks as if it's on an island, is **Kop van Zuid**, the former embarkation halls for Holland-America Line's transatlantic and other oceangoing liners.

### Schielandshuis Museum of History                                 ★

*Korte Hoogstraat 31, Tues.–Sat. 10 a.m.–5 p.m., Sun. and hols. 11 a.m.—5 p.m., closed Mon., Jan. 1, Apr. 30;* ☎ *4334188; Tram 1, 3, 6, Metro Beurs/Churchillplein.* Housed in the recently restored, classical-facaded **Schielandshuis** (1665), the only historic building to survive the destruction of the city center by Nazi bombers in 1940, this section of Rotterdam's Historical Museum sticks out in the cityscape in a most welcome way. It was in this building, probably built from a design by architect Pieter Post, that the original Boymans collection of art had been installed in 1849; it was completely destroyed in an 1864 fire, which also badly damaged the building. The Schielandshuis has only recently recovered from an overly hasty restoration following that fire, when it was needed to house the City Archives as well as the Boymans collection renaissance. (The Boymans collection burgeoned to such a size as to require quarters of its own by 1938.)

Today, Schielandhuis exhibits focus on the development and cultural and art history of Rotterdam. A section on the May 1940 bombing shows the far-reaching effects that had on the city. Among the museum's art work are the **Atlas van Stolk collection** of prints and drawings on the history of the Netherlands, two panels of a 1540 altarpiece from the St. Laurenskerk when it was still a Roman Church, and a two-meter model by Hendrik de Keyser of the wooden steeple that topped the church between 1619 and 1645. Famed jurist **Hugo de Groot** (Grotius), who once served in the position of *Pensionary for Rotterdam*, is represented by the leather bricklayer's doublet he wore on his flight to Antwerp after his escape from Loevestein Castle. (See "The Dutch Cultural Legacy: The Muse.") The top floor is devoted to antique items of everyday living. There is also a museum shop (with English language museum guide), garden courtyard cafe, and restaurant, **De Pappegay**. (See "Where to Eat.")

## *WHERE TO STAY*

## VERY EXPENSIVE

### Hilton International Rotterdam                            ★★★★★
*Weena 10, 3012 CM;* ☎ *4144044, FAX 4118884, U.S.* ☎ *800-445-8667, Canada* ☎ *800-268-9275.* This is where you come

in Rotterdam for turn-down service, and 24-hour room service. The lobby is one of the gathering places in the city. The 254 rooms, including nonsmoking rooms, some with views of the Stadhuis handsomely illuminated at night, are decorated in the muted tones of high-quality, first-class international decor, with hair dryers and minibars. **Le Restaurant** serves Dutch and international cuisine. Full business center and corporate well-designed rooms; parking available.

## EXPENSIVE

### Parkhotel　　　　　　　　　　　★★★★
*Westersingel 70, 3015 LB;*  *4363611, FAX 4364212,U.S.*  *800-223-6510, Canada*  *800-424-5500.* Predominantly a business hotel during the week, the Park is located by Museumpark, not far from the Boymans Museum, and within walking distance of transportation, shopping, and most central sights. Of the 154 rooms, 60 are in the new wing, upgraded with air conditioning, minisafes, double-glazed windows, and lightwood decor. Nonsmoking rooms available. An art work passage connects the new and old sections of the hotel, which has a library corner in its modern lounge with fireplace. The well-kept, less expensive (moving them down into the moderate-price category) rooms in the older part of the building have larger bedrooms and baths, luxurious spreads, minibars, hair dryers. Fitness facilities available, free parking behind hotel; room service 6 a.m.–1 a.m. There's an à la carte restaurant and a casual grill-cafe.

### Atlanta　　　　　　　　　　　★★★★
*Aert van Nesstraat 4, 3012 CA;*  *4110420, FAX 4135320.* Very centrally located, on the corner of the Coolsingel, though the convenience could bring some traffic noise (quieter rooms at back). The Atlanta is, of course, a postwar construction, with a traditional lobby that's elegant in an old Dutch way, with a cozy "brownish" bar with leather chairs and couches; the restaurant serves 6-10 p.m. The 170 rooms are comfortable and reasonably roomy, with the largest on the sixth floor.

## MODERATE

### Hotel Inntel　　　　　　　　　　　★★★★
*Leuvehaven 80, 3011 EA;*  *4134139, FAX 4133222.* One of Rotterdam's recent additions on the hotel front comes with harbor and port views, a location from which all city attractions are walkable or within a quick hop on the tram located across the street. The 150 light, tidy rooms, all with small, modern bathrooms with tubs and wall-mounted showers, remote TV and telephone, feature big windows. Red leather couches, marble, mirrors, stainless steel, recessed lighting, and windows are the ingredients of the cheerful lobby. There's a lobby restaurant, where breakfast (included) also is served; the **Waterway Bar** has snacks 5 p.m.–1 a.m., with a harbor view and skyline lights after dark.

The top-floor fitness center has a pool with large windows facing harbor, sauna, solarium. No room service. In all, a very pleasant place.

### Hotel New York                ★★★★
*Koninginnenhoofd 1, 3072 AD;* ☎ *4390500, FAX 4842701.* Situated midharbor on an island in Rotterdam's busy River Maas, Hotel New York occupies the newly restored, early 20th-century, art nouveau-style building that served as head office for the **Holland America Line** until its ocean liners discontinued transatlantic service to New York City in the early '70s. The remarkable location of the landmark building—its cafe-cum-restaurant looks out mid-river on the world's largest port, across to Rotterdam's dramatically modern skyline—makes the present limited access worth overcoming. In decent traffic, it's a ten-minute taxi ride to the hotel from center city. (In 1996 a new bridge over the Maas will connect downtown with the end of the hotel pier, where a Metro stop also is planned.) The 74 rooms are spacious, with high ceilings; most have river views; windows can be opened. Many rooms have attractive newly-made wooden "steamer" trunks that serve as closets. Other amenities include a winter garden, belvedere observation tower, gym and public parking.

### Van Walsum                ★★★
*Mathenesserlaan 199, 3014 HC;* ☎ *4363275, FAX 4364410.* Built 100 years ago as a house, this family-owned-and-operated hotel, with flower boxes on the front, is situated on a pleasant tree-lined neighborhood avenue, near public transportation, and, for walkers, within range of Delfshaven and the Euromast. The 26 rooms, many with old plaster details on ceiling, all have modern tile shower (some with bath), TV, telephone; some have a minifridge in the room. The warm, welcoming Dutch atmosphere carries from the lobby bar and small restaurant; secluded garden terrace, where drinks and breakfast (included) can be served in summer. Parking available.

## INEXPENSIVE

### Bienvenue                ★★
*Spoorsingel 24, 3033 GL;* ☎ *4669394, FAX 4677475.* Located two blocks out the rear door of the Centraal Station, on a residential street fronting a quiet canal, this 1920s house has ten rooms, half with private shower and toilet. The cheerful, family run hotel is basic but very clean and neat; beds have firm mattresses. Front rooms overlook canal and lawns, there's a garden in the back. No elevator; pay telephone at reception. The lobby lounge/reception/breakfast (only) room is one flight up, with window boxes, canal view.

## *WHERE TO EAT*

**Restaurant Old Dutch** (*Rochussenstraat 20; Mon.–Fri. 11:30 a.m.–midnight, closed Sat., Sun.;* ☎ *4360344; very expensive*) has an authentic old Dutch atmosphere, right down to the stale smell of cigars. If you don't mind that or the rather steep prices, the Old Dutch will provide traditional

(Dutch/ French cuisine) and tasty dining. Located in Het Park, not far from the Euromast, with views of the Nieuwe Maas, **Restaurant Parkheuvel** (*Heuvellaan 21; lunch noon–3 p.m., dinner 6–10 p.m., closed Sun.;* ☎ *4360766; moderate*) also serves nouvelle cuisine that ranks among the best in Holland, complemented by an excellent wine list. **Zochers'** (*Baden Powell Laan 12; open daily for lunch, dinner 'til 10 p.m.;* ☎ *4364249; inexpensive*) also is located in Het Park, in the former mansion of the restaurant's landscape architect namesake. Varied fare, snacks, exotic drinks, and a Sunday morning brunch buffet with classical music. Outside dining terrace overlooks the formal box gardens.

For dining with an impressive view day or night, there's the **Panorama**, 320 feet high in the Euromast (*Parkhaven 20; daily noon–7 p.m., 5 p.m. in winter;* ☎ *4364811; inexpensive*) for buffet lunches and dinner, or lighter fare. **Silhouet** (*open until 10 p.m., closed Sun., Mon.;* ☎ *4364811; moderate/expensive*) is the à la carte restaurant (also aperitif bar) in the Spacecabin, serving French-accented continental cuisine. There's also a meal with a view right in the center of the city, on the 23rd story of the **World Trade Center Restaurant** (*Beursplein 37; Mon.–Fri. noon–9:30 p.m., closed holidays, Sat., Sun.;* ☎ *4054465; moderate*). And in the basement of the Schielandshuis Historical Museum, is **De Pappegay** (*Korte Hoogstraat 31; lunch noon–3 p.m., closed Mon.;* ☎ *4117232; moderate*).

At Delfshaven, there are several dining choices. For fish or mussels, head for **Le Harve** (*Havenstraat 9a; daily, lunch, dinner 'til 10 p.m.;* ☎ *4257172; moderate*), and speak up for a window table. **Eethuis de Parel**, or *the Pearl*, (*Voorhaven 54; Wed.–Sun. 5–11 p.m., kitchen till 9 p.m., closed Mon., Tues.; moderate*) will offer fish, but also meat and vegetarian dishes, overlooking the canal from which the Pilgrim Fathers sailed. **Cafe "Oude Sluis"** (*Havenstraat 7; daily;* ☎ *4773068; inexpensive*) has real working class "brown cafe" character and, from the small back terrace or tables on the bridge, a great view of the old harbor.

Grand cafes, dignified, high-ceilinged spaces that offer international newspapers and a full range of food choices, are good places to mix with the Dutch. **Dudok** (*Meent 88; cafe open Mon.–Sat. 8 a.m.–1 a.m., Sun. from 10 a.m., restaurant 6–10 p.m.;* ☎ *4333102; inexpensive*) serves breakfast items until 4 p.m., and salads, soups, sandwiches non-stop. Restaurant/cafe **Loos** (at Veerhaven) is another option popular with Rotterdammers, with outside tables across from one of the city's many harbor inlets.

If you want to dine in the area of the city that Rotterdammers are most fond of, head for the **Oude Haven**. There, against an eclectic architectural backdrop of the Cube Houses, the Pencil, and the boats in the picturesque harbor, is a neighborhood conglomerate of pubs and restaurants, most of which spill out onto the terraces in good weather. The establishments located around the Oude Haven each have their own character. Facing Oude Haven and the attractive recently restored old buildings along Wijnhaven is **De Wagon** cafe/restaurant (*Geldersekade 10; open daily 11 a.m.–1 a.m.;* ☎ *4331728; inexpensive/moderate*), which occupies a restored 1928 railway car. The ten-tabled dining area serves a well-prepared assorted menu in a setting of soft lights, white clothed tables with fresh flowers and candles. There's a bar car for drinks and, in season, outside terrace seating facing the scenic old harbor.

## IN THE AREA

### Kinderdijk ★★

☎ *01859-30925.* At no other single site in the world will you find as many windmills as in the Dutch town of Kinderdijk (near Alblasserdam), nine miles SE of Rotterdam. In about 1740, 19 mills were built here to drain excess water from the Alblasserwaard polders. Although nowadays power-driven pumping engines do the job, the mills remain well-preserved. The rural Kinderdijk site is always open (no fee) and, though often crowded during the day in season, is an essentially unspoiled setting. From April–September, one of the mills is open to visitors daily, except Sunday, 9:30 a.m.–5:30 p.m., showing its antique interior with furnishings and mechanical workings. Every Saturday afternoon in July and August, the mills are put into operation. During the second complete week in September, the mills are illuminated at night. From May–September, there's the possibility of a cruise in the mill region.

### Dordrecht ★

From the **Groothoofd** gate of this handsome old port city (town rights were granted in 1220), one overlooks the *Merwede* and the *Oude Maas*, the busiest river junction in the world. A walk along **Wijnstraat** (named for the staple rights awarded in 1299, which meant that all the wine brought to Holland by ship had to be first unloaded in Dordrecht) passes many delightful 16th- and 17th-century Dutch facades, decorated with lace curtains at the windows. Along ★**Nieuwe Haven**, one gets an idea of life aboard a barge, a large number of which are moored here. The ★**Museum Mr. Simon van Gijn** (*Tues.–Sat. 10 a.m.–5 p.m., Sun. and holidays. 1–5 p.m.;* ☎ *078-133793*) here is a patrician house with period rooms including an 1800 kitchen, tapestries, silver, tiles, and pewter. The **Statenzaal** (States Hall) in the **Hof** (Court) was the site of the signing of the first documented resistance to the Spanish in 1572. The ★**Dordrechts Museum** (*Museumstraat 40; Tues.–Sat. 10:00 a.m.–5 p.m., Sun. and holidays. 1–5 p.m.;* ☎ *078-134100*) has a 17th-century collection that includes works by Nicolaes Maes, Jan van Goyen, and Aelbert Cuyp, and paintings of The Hague School and those of Dordt artist Ary Scheffer. The ★**Grote Kerk** (*April–Oct.., Tues.–Sat. 10:30 a.m.–4:30 p.m., Sun. noon–4 p.m.* ☎ *078-144660*) mostly dates from the late 15th century, although the massive tower was begun in 1339 in the Brabant Gothic style. The 1626, 49-bell carillon usually is played Friday 11 a.m.–noon, and Sat. 2–3 p.m.; the organ dates from 1671. There is a fine marble pulpit (1756) with a magnificent wooden canopy.

### Rotterdamse Havenroute

The **ANWB** (Royal Dutch Auto Club), in conjunction with the Port of

Rotterdam, publishes a **Rotterdam Port Route** booklet in English, with detailed information and directions intended to give the automobile-driving traveler the clearest possible picture of the vast installation. Inquire at ANWB or the VVV.

### Spido's Delta Works and Seven Waterways Cruise     ★

☎ *010-4135400*. In July and August, Spido runs nine hour (beginning at 10 a.m.) excursions from Rotterdam that take in, by way of water, locations including the Nieuwe Maas, Oude Maas, Haringvliet, Hollands Diep, the Pernis Oil refineries, the sluices near Hellevoetsluis, Willemstad, Dordrecht, and the windmills of Kinderdijk, as well as a visit to the ★★**Delta Works** (see "Delta Expo" in "Southern Holland: Zeeland").

Gouda

# GOUDA

*Lives once hung in the balance of these scales in the Witches' Museum.*

## GUIDELINES FOR GOUDA

### SIGHTS

Gouda's lovely **Grote Markt** (market square) is one of the largest in Holland, and at its center stands the **Stadhuis**, which may be the oldest gothic town hall (1450) in the country. St. Janskerk (Grote Kerk), with the longest nave in the Netherlands and some of the country's most remarkable stained glass windows, abuts the Markt and is just across the street from **St. Catherina Gasthuis** museum.

Much of the center of the canal-laced town has been designated an historic district.

## GETTING AROUND

Walking is the best way to get a feel for this pleasant town and the only way to see the very center. The train station, just outside the old canal-encircled town, is within reasonable walking distance of the Grote Markt. Taxis and regional buses are based at the station.

## SHOPPING

This town of 61,000 is the shopping center for a much greater regional population. Local specialties include clay pipes (both decorative and practical), candles, pottery, and what travelers most associate with the name of the town: cheese.

## WHERE TO STAY

Hotels in Gouda are very limited, your best bet being **Keizerskroon** (*Keizerstraat 11-13,* ☎ *28096; inexpensive*), with a dozen or so bedrooms, some with private toilet and shower. Located in the old center, just a few minutes' walk from the Grote Markt, it is clean, VVV-approved, has a restaurant, car park, TV in rooms, and accepts major credit cards. The VVV office may be able to suggest alternatives if there is no room at this inn.

## WHERE TO EAT

For informal munching as you meander, buy some *Goudse Siroopwafels* (treacle-filled waffles), which, though sold all over Holland, originated here. For sit-down casual fare, try **Old Dutch** (*Markt 25; inexpensive*). **De Zes Starren** (*Achter 14; Mon.–Sat. noon–3 p.m., 5–9 p.m., closed Sun.;* ☎ *16095; moderate*) is a small, stylishly old Dutch-decorated restaurant in the former kitchen of *Het Catherina Gasthuis Museum.* **Mallemolen** (*Oosthaven 72; Tues.–Sun. 5–9:30 p.m., closed Mon.;* ☎ *15430; expensive*), used by local Dutch when they want to celebrate in style, has an intimate old Dutch atmosphere and serves traditional French dishes.

## ENTERTAINMENT AND EVENTS

From late June to late August, a **cheese and old handicrafts market** joins the year-round general one on the **Markt** from 9:30 a.m.–noon Thursday. The rest of the year, area cheesemakers mostly sell their great homemade wheels of Gouda informally off the backs of farm trucks parked near the **Waag** (weigh house) during the Thursday and Saturday markets. Concerts on St. Jan's 49-bell 1676 Hemony carillon are played by the town carillonneur Thursday 10-

11 a.m., Saturday 11:30 a.m.–12:30 p.m. from April-September. **Organ concerts** are presented by visiting players on St. Jan's great organ, a 3850-pipe instrument built between 1732 and 1736 by Jacob Francois Moreau of Rotterdam.

**Gouda bij Kaarstlicht** (Gouda By Candlelight) takes place annually on a Tuesday evening between December 13 and 20 from 7–9 p.m. During it, the darkened windows of the Stadhuis and buildings surrounding the Markt are gradually lighted in sequence with candles, while Christmas carols are sung by Gouda choirs and a large public crowd standing in the square. The memorable event was initiated a number of years ago when, on the occasion of its 100th anniversary, the **Gouda candle factory** made a presentation to the town of a substantial number of candles and this ceremony was conceived for their use.

## ARRIVING

Gouda is located about 15 miles (25 km) northeast of Rotterdam and 21 miles (35 km) southwest of Utrecht. There are trains to Gouda from both cities; trains from Amsterdam connect through Utrecht. If you are traveling in the area by car, there are many pleasant country roads to and from Gouda, especially the route from Gouda to Schoonhoven (see below) via **Haastrecht** (with its lovely 17th-century, stepped-gable Stadhuis) and along the **Vlist** river.

## IN THE AREA

**Oudewater** has an intriguing witch story to tell and small streets with appealing 16th-century Dutch Renaissance facades. **Schoohoven** is a pleasing old place with a long tradition of silver craftmanship. Both are located in the pretty countryside surrounding Gouda, much of which is traversed on roads built along the tops of dikes. Both towns are accessible by bus from Gouda.

## TRAVEL TIPS

If you plan a trip to Gouda on a summer Thursday morning, you'll catch a morning carillon concert, as well as the only opportunity in the year to see *inside* the Waag (weigh house), as part of the cheese market. Although the market ends for the day by 12:30 p.m., plan to stay longer to savor the city's other sights.

# GOUDA IN CONTEXT

Gouda (pronounced HOW da), long a merchant town, was granted a charter in 1272 by Count Floris V. During the 14th and 15th centuries, it was a center for the cloth trade, and in subsequent centuries became prominent in the production of a variety of other items, including clay smoking pipes, pottery (today, much blue and white delftware is produced in Gouda), candles, and cheese.

The Rotterdam-born humanist and theologian **Erasmus** was educated in Gouda—and probably conceived here. According to a plaque at **Het Catherina Gasthuis** in scholarly Latin: *Desiderius Erasmus Goudae Conceptus Rotterodami Natus Anno 1457.* What the plaque doesn't add is that his father was a Roman Catholic priest.

## GUIDEPOSTS

**Telephone code 01820**

**Tourist Info** VVV • Gouda, *Markt 27*; Mon.–Fri. 9 a.m.–5 p.m., Sat. 10 a.m.–4 p.m.; ☎ *13666.*

**Bike Rental** • Railway station, *Stationplein*; ☎ *19751.*

**Markets** • *On the Markt*, Thurs. 9 a.m.–1 p.m., Sat. 9 a.m.–5 p.m.

**Buses** • Bus station *near rail station*, just outside old center to the north. Bus 85 goes to Oudewater (seven miles, about 25 mins.) through pretty typical Dutch countryside approximately half-hourly during the day; Bus 197 to Schoonhoven is through equally interesting Dutch scenery.

**Parking** • *Parkon Markt* on nonmarket days. Metered parking behind Waag (weight house) and by Kleiwegplein, near station.

## WHAT TO SEE AND DO

The heart of Gouda is the slice-of-pie-shaped ★★**Markt**, on or near which are most of the major places of interest. The handsome **Stadhuis** (town hall) stands at its center. Gouda is very pleasant to explore on foot, especially the area behind the **St. Janskerk** and **Het Catherina Gasthuis**, where one finds small canals, bridges, gardens, and hofjes (almhouses) tucked away. The public library and municipal archives, housed in a former orphanage (1643) at *Spieringstraat 1*, are particularly appealing, as is the **Willem Vroesenhuis** (1614), a former old men's hofje. The old **Vismarkt** (fish market) and corn exchange sit on the *Lange Gouwe* canal, just a short way from the Markt.

**St. Janskerk**                                                              ★

*Achter de Kerk—behind the church; March-Oct. Mon.–Sat. 9 a.m.–5 p.m., Nov.–Feb. 10 a.m.–4 p.m.;* ☎ *12684.* Although the original stone church on the site was 14th century, the cross-shaped church with the wooden arched roof that we see today is mostly 16th century, rebuilt after substantial destruction was caused to the earlier structure by lightning in 1552. The present church has the longest nave (123 meters/403 feet) in the Netherlands; its dramatic length so dominates the town that Gouda has been described as "a church with a town." The main reason most people visit St. Jans (dedicated to John the

Baptist) is to see its stunning ★★**stained glass windows**. Numbering some 70 in all, the earliest windows date from 1555 and were in many cases given as bequests by the citizens of Gouda, who had raised money to rebuild the structure following a 1552 fire. As well as showing scenes from the Bible (especially the life of John the Baptist and Christ: Nos. 9-19), the windows also are a record of Dutch history. The brothers **Wouter** and **Dirck Crabeth** designed and executed the best windows, these being world famous for their size (up to 20 meters/66 feet high), brightness (the huge windows catch lots of light), color composition, and perspective. Since Holland was still a Roman Catholic country at the time the church was being rebuilt, it was appropriate that the first person to respond to the request to donate a window was the Bishop of Utrecht, whose gift, *The Baptism of Christ by John* (Dirck Crabeth), was placed in the center of the choir in 1555. Philip II of Spain, who ruled Holland at the time, also gave a window in which he and his consort, English Queen Mary Tudor, are portrayed. St. Jans remained Catholic until 1571, and in that period 22 windows were installed, 14 by the Crabeth brothers. In 1572, the town of Gouda joined the conflict on the side of the *Protestant Reformation*. Although no new windows were installed for 20 years because of the troubled religious times, fortunately the church escaped *Iconoclastic* backlashes and destruction. Not only did the windows survive, but between 1593 and 1603, Protestants finished the project begun by the Catholics, though from this point the windows reflect more the history of Holland than the story of the Bible. *The Relief of Leiden* is depicted in window 25 and shows Willem the Silent. Forward-thinking city fathers saw the windows as being threatened in 1939 and removed them in anticipation of war with Nazi Germany. They were stored first in the cellars of local farms, then later removed to bunkers beneath sand dunes for greater safety. After the liberation, it seemed fitting to add another window as a witness to both the occupation and its liberation. A detailed booklet about the windows is available in the church. The Dutch Reformed Church services are held Sun. at 10 a.m. and 5 p.m.

## Het Catherina Gasthuis                                      ★

*Achter de Kerk 32 or Oosthaven 9; Mon.–Sat. 10 a.m.–5 p.m., Sun., holidays noon–5 p.m.;* ☎ *88440.* A former hospital for transients and the local needy, functioning from the 14th century until 1910 and in places dating back to the 14th and 16th centuries, the building is largely from the mid-17th century. As the town museum, it contains the usual regional historical material, as well as religious art (including 16th-century altarpieces, a *Doubting Thomas* by Wouter Crabeth, and other works from Gouda churches) and paintings (including an important collection of Barbizon and Hague School works from the 19th and 20th centuries). A chalice and eucharist dish of silver-gilt with enamel decoration, presented by Jacqueline of Bavaria to the Gouda Civic Guard in 1425, is one of the museum's treasures. Plenty of pleasure comes from the building itself. Rooms of interest include an old dispensary, a kitchen equipped in the late 18th-century manner, an originally furnished 17th-century women's Regents' Room, and a torture room in the cellar. There's also a "mad room" for the troublesomely insane; once numerous, this is the last of such rooms intact in Holland. At the Oosthaven entrance, an English booklet on the museum is available.

### Stadhuis                                                          ★★

*Markt; Mon.–Fri. 9 a.m.–noon, 2-4 p.m., 11 a.m.–3 p.m. Sat., closed Sun;* ☎ *88475.* An extensive restoration completed in 1952 resulted in the reappearance of the facade of Gouda's freestanding 1450 Gothic Town Hall, the side walls distinctive with shutters in Gouda's colors of red and white. The Stadhuis was built by **Jan Kelderman**, probably a member of the famous family of sculptors and architects by that name in the southern Netherlands (today Belgium) city of Mechelen. The front is ornamented with a double set of steps (1603) and representations of counts and countesses of the House of Burgundy, while the rear, which faces the Waag (weigh house) has a handsome stepped gable and had a scaffold, used as late as 1860, now the balcony for the civic wedding chamber behind it. Though always meant to house the town authorities, the building also originally served as a meat hall at ground level, since keeping a close eye on the slaughter of animals so as to prevent contamination was an important task of city leaders. At the corner of the front facade toward St. Janskerk is a sundial. Near it is a modern carillon that plays a tune every half hour, upon which the figure of Court Floris appears to reenact his presentation to Gouda of its city charter in 1272.

### Waag                                                               ★

*Markt; last week of June to last week of Aug. Thurs. 9:30 a.m.–noon only, not open at other times.* Built by architect Pieter Post in 1668, Gouda's weigh house is used for its original function during the summer Thursday morning cheese markets. It is distinguished by a fine ★ sculptured relief on the front by Batholomeus Eggers that shows the weighing of cheese.

### De Moriaan

*Westhaven 29; Mon.–Fri. 10 a.m.–5 p.m., Sat. 10 a.m.–12:30 p.m. and 1:30 p.m.–5 p.m., Sun. & holidays noon–5 p.m.;* ☎ *88444.* This 17th-century merchant's house is set up as an old tobacco shop: Inventory is on marble shelves in black-and-white containers; the floor is of black-and-white tiles. De Moriaan has an impressive collection of old Dutch tiles and Gouda pottery (even now there are nearly 100 potters in town). There's also a first-rate collection of old smoking pipes, from the funny and frivolous to the fine and beautiful. Clay pipes actually were introduced to Gouda by English soldiers stationed here circa 1600; an English soldier founded the first pipe factory, after which the Dutch adopted the trade that has become a tradition in the town.

## SHOPPING

The famous Gouda cheese (*Goudse kaas*) carries the name of the town and has more ages than man—as you'll see at **Hoogendoorn**, a cheese-and-wine delicatessen on the Markt. Beginning with the youngest (*extra jonge*), the taste gets somewhat sharper with each aged stage: *jonge, jonge belegen, belegen, extra belegen*, and *oude* to *overjarig* (which crumbles in your hand). The shop works closely with the town cheese board, and sells all sorts of factory and local farmers' cheeses (*boerenkaas*). The place to find the town's well-known candles is **Gouda Kaarsen** (*Achter de Kerk 9*). The city's celebrated clay pipe-making and decorating are demonstrated at **Adrie Moerings** (*Peperstraat 76; Mon.–Sat. 9 a.m.–5 p.m.;* ☎ *12842*), a personable potter whose hand-made pipes and hand-thrown pots are for sale.

## IN THE AREA

Heading toward Schoonhoven from Gouda, via Haastrecht, you will be on the northeast edge of a region called the **Krimpenerwaard**, real Dutch polder countryside. Along the river **Vlist**, on this stretch of which there are two well-restored windmills, are beautiful willow trees and reeds. Behind the high dikes, along the tops of which one drives, it's a "downward" look onto old thatched farm houses. The lush meadows feed the cattle from whose milk is made the *Boerenkaas*, which one sees *Te Koop* (for sale) along the roadsides. This is good bicycling country.

## ★ OUDEWATER

This quaint, quiet town (pop. 7000) of mostly late 16th-century Dutch Renaissance buildings with fascinating facades, tiled roofs, step gables, and brick bridges crossing the canal that runs between cobbled streets down the middle of the elongated Markt, is nothing if not peaceful. And that's quite a contrast to the days when Oudewater was visited by tens of thousands of women during a lengthy European wide **witch hunt** primarily in the 15th and 16th centuries that left nearly a million dead before the fear and fury were spent. To understand that furor, and the significance of Oudewater to those accused of being witches, you'll need to dip into *diabology* with me for a moment.

Belief in the "existence" of witches was first officially acknowledged at the time of the *Inquisition*, a tribunal established by the Roman Catholic Church in the 13th century for the discovery, suppression, and punishment of heretics. From that, there arose an elaborate diabology, or devil lore. Thirteenth-century Italian scholar **St. Thomas Aquinas** was the first to dogmatize the belief in witches, who were thought to be handmaidens of the Devil. Much fear was attached to possible association with witches, who were believed capable of causing thunder, crop failure, even the *Black Death*, all certain signs of Satan's strength.

Following the *Spanish* version of the *Inquisition*—the reorganization of the Catholic Church under the Spanish sovereigns in 1478—belief in and

fear of witches reached epidemic dimensions. In 1490, a book appeared
that codified the campaign for exterminating witches. Published under the
auspices of Pope Innocent VIII and Emperor Maximilian, *Malleus Mallefi-
carum (Hammer of the Witches)* was written by righteous men who sincerely
believed it was better for the innocent to suffer than for the guilty to escape. It defied all present-day criteria for acceptable evidence, presumed
guilt, advocated torture to obtain confessions, and suggested ways to con-
fuse prisoners. If accusers wished to remain anonymous, they were allowed
to do so, since witch-sleuthing was considered a service to God that justi-
fied every expedient. Those accused were hunted down and exterminated
like vermin. With mere rumor basis enough for accusation, whole regions
could be quickly infested by witch fever. Whether his determination to get
a divorce (the idea had been inconceivable before then) by fair means or
foul gave other men ideas during the height of the witch craze is unknown,
but no less a heavyweight than **Henry VIII** (1491–1547) probably was instrumental in putting into some men's minds the thought of ridding
themselves of no-longer-loved wives by planting an anonymous accusation
of witchcraft against their spouse.

The era is notorious for cruel and prolonged torture to wring confessions from those suspected of witchcraft, usually women. So agonizing
could the torture be that one inquisitor is said to have boasted that he
would be able to extort a confession from the Pope himself. Often, under
torture, body and soul literally came apart. In addition to torture, three
tests were used to determine if the accused was a witch. The test of **tears**
was based on the well-known "fact" that witches couldn't cry. A priest or
judge placed his hand on the suspect's head and told her to shed tears; if
she couldn't, she was bound to be burned at the stake. In the **water** test,
the suspect was bound by rope and lowered into a river. If the woman sank,
although she also most probably drowned, she was proclaimed innocent. If
she floated, that was considered proof that she also was light enough to fly
at night on the Devil's business.

It was believed that the Devil gave witches the supernatural power to fly,
and assumed that those who had been given this Satanic gift must be light
enough to get airborne. Thus, **weight** was the third and perhaps most
widespread test for witchcraft. Public scales were set up all over Europe,
each with its own official weighmaster. Women who weighed less than an
arbitrarily agreed upon amount were pronounced witches and sentenced to
the stake. With court-ordered weighing being literally a matter of life or
death to the accused, many weighmasters became masters of bribes. Some
became so greedy that if *not* offered pay-offs, they would "rig" the scales
so that the accused would not weigh enough to be set free. There are even
recorded cases in which vengeful unbribed officials signed certificates stating a woman to be completely weightless.

In Oudewater, trial by weighing was the only one used in witchcraft
cases. When a suspect came in to be weighed, she went into a dressing
room with the town midwife, and was stripped and searched to determine
if she had any hidden weights on her person. When this check was complet-

ed, the suspect had to put on a long white robe and was then measured for height. She was required to weigh in kilograms at least the number of centimeters she measured over one meter. However, at Oudewater, her body's build was also taken into consideration. Only at Oudewater, if her weight was judged to be in accordance with the natural proportions of the body, even if she was very light, was a woman given a certificate that acquitted her of witchcraft. Furthermore, the weighmasters at Oudewater had a reputation for being honest and unsusceptible to bribery.

In 1545, near the height of the witch craze in Europe, Spanish King and Holy Roman Emperor Charles V himself grew concerned over the devilish storm that had been unleashed by the extremism of the *Spanish Inquisition.* In Holland, he had occasion to attend a witch trial in Polsbroek. A suspect was being weighed there and the weighmaster, who had not been bribed, declared that the woman weighed only 2.5 kilos (5.5 lbs.). The emperor did not believe this, and took the woman with him to Oudewater. There, he even surreptitiously enticed the weighmaster with gold ducats, but they were refused, and when the woman was weighed she was found to be 50 kilos and acquitted. Impressed with the honesty, Charles V gave Oudewater the privilege of issuing certificates, valid throughout his vast European empire, which stated that the bearer of one could never again be accused of witchcraft.

No one had been before, or ever was thereafter, judged to be a witch for weighing too little at Oudewater. After Charles V's pronouncement, thousands upon thousands of women came from as far away as Sweden and Sicily, Poland and Gibraltar to pay the set fee to step onto the scales in Oudewater and to step off free from further accusation.

In 1613, the government of the Seven Provinces, having declared themselves free of the Spanish who still ruled the southern Netherlands (today's Belgium), abolished all witch trials. But, in actual fact, the last certificate issued for the Oudewater *heksenwaag* (witches' scale) was dated June 12, 1729.

Though witches weren't burned at Oudewater, the town—which received its rights in 1295—itself went up in flames in 1575. Hence, the handsome ★★**Heksenwaag Museum** (*Leeuweringerstraat 2; Apr.–Oct. Tues.–Sat.10 a.m.–5 p.m., Sun. noon–5 p.m.;* ☎ *03486-3400*) dates from the late 16th century, as does much else in the town. Entering the building, one immediately notices the huge wooden scale, which was not destroyed in the fire and is the Oudewater original. Should you choose to step on the scales (almost everyone does, even former Queen Juliana couldn't resist), the weighmaster will be discrete with the results, which surprise nonmetric Americans by taking off 10 percent of their poundage. Your souvenir copy of the *Testimony of the Act of Weighing in the Weigh-House at Oudewater* certificate will be in English. Most exhibits in the museum of witch documentation upstairs aren't, but with the background provided here you should be able to find items of interest.

Next to the Waag, at *Markt Oostzijde 14,* is the step-gabled **de Boerenbakker**, a bakery and tea room with a terrace cafe in front and a few tables in back overlooking a garden. Ask for the local butter cookie specialty, *Heksenwaagjes.* On the other side of the Heksenwaag is an *ijs salon* (ice cream shop), in front of which are two canalside benches, one *always* occupied by a family that sits in sculptured silence. Save time to browse about town: the lovely Stadhuis dates from 1588 (although its tower is 14th century, a survivor of the fire), and there are several antique shops.

## ★ SCHOONHOVEN

A small, attractive old fortress (pop. 11,000) on the banks of the River Lek that has been known as "silver town" for the several centuries that silver craftspeople have made it their place of business. Particularly in the 18th and 19th centuries, the silver industry flourished here manufacturing silver articles, especially the ornaments worn with traditional costumes. The **★ Nederlands Goud, Zilver, en Klokkermuseum** (*Kazerneplein 4; Tues.–Sun. and holidays noon–5 p.m.;* ☎ *01823-85612*) has a fine collection of Dutch silver, including some rare pieces made in Schoonhoven as early as the 17th century. As well as silver tea sets, decorative boxes, "sewing things," and some gold objects on display, there's an outfitted silversmith's workshop and a history of hallmarks in the Assay Office. The clock room collection, with timepieces from all over Holland, ranges from small pocket watches as old as 17th century to the substantial 16th-century works of a tower clock from Breda. The **Waag** (1616) on the Dam in front of the museum, with a wide overhanging roof where open carriages of goods waiting to be weighed could remain dry, is now used as a *pannekoekhuis* (pancake house) in summer.

The VVV, which has a map and walking guide to the town in English, resides in the basement of the **Stadhuis**, begun in 1452, with a 50-bell carillon (1775) in the steeple. In front of the Stadhuis, which is on the in-town **Haven** (harbor), Schoonhoven has preserved the site of a 1597 witch-burning, in which the victim was Marrigje Ariens, a woman who sought to cure people with the herbs she gathered and prepared; a circle of stones marks the sad spot. (The "honor" of Holland's last case of witch burning, in 1608, probably goes to nearby Gorinchem. That date was relatively civilized by contemporary standards. The Salem witch trials in Massachusetts took place in the 1690s; the last English witch was burned in 1716, and the last witch known to have died at the stake in Europe did so in Switzerland in 1782.) Following the harbor down from the Stadhuis to the river leads to the **Veerpoort** (1601), the only remaining original town gate.

# UTRECHT

*Cafés line the Oudegracht at water level.*

## GUIDELINES FOR UTRECHT

### SIGHTS

The Randstad's easternmost city is the country's fourth largest (pop. 230,000), capital of the province of Utrecht, carrying Roman-origin credentials. Utrecht (pronounced EW *trecht*) was in medieval times the only center of importance in the northern Netherlands, a history that shows in its attractive, atmospheric, well-preserved old center. An ancient bishopric and present archbishopric, Utrecht has a bevy of beautiful old churches, including the city-symbol, **Dom Tower**, and its slightly separated cathedral. Utrecht also offers a unique system of lower-than-street-level canals whose quays are set with inviting cafes; musical and other unusual museums; and a historic university (the largest in Holland), whose students lend a lively perspective to the city.

## GETTING AROUND

Utrecht is served by buses and trams, though you won't need them in the old center where most attractions are located. Every Sunday **Bus Line M** makes the attractive *Museum and Green Line* run through Utrecht. Sundays from mid-May to mid-Sept. there's a **VVV guided walking tour** on different themes (*courtyards and almshouses, canals and wharves, churches around the Dom, etc.*) in the center of Utrecht, beginning at 10:30 a.m. (also at 1:30 p.m. from late June-late July), departing from **Stadkasteel Oudaen** (Oudegracht 99). In July and Aug. the VVV organizes various **bus tours** that provide an overview of the various districts of the city. At the VVV you can rent a **self-guided cassette tour**, and buy a tour brochure to the churches of this one-time ecclesiastical capital. **Canal tours** and **canal bikes** offer different views of Utrecht.

## SHOPPING

For shopping in high style, Utrecht's **La Vie** enclosed complex with fountain and waterfall offers a wide range of luxury wares at elegant department stores such as **De Bijenkorf** (sometimes called the "Harrod's of Holland"); exclusive boutiques abound on Vie Straat and Oudkerkhof. Other major Dutch and European stores (**Vroom & Dreesmann, C & A**, etc.) are on adjoining Vredenburg and in the **Hoog Catharijne** center by Centraal Station. **Hema** can be found on the **Oudegracht**, as can **De Sleate**, a Dutch chain that sells remaindered and other books (plenty in English) and posters. **Lichte Gaard** and **Vismarkt** are streets with ample antique shops. A large general market is held on the Vredenburg Wed. and Sat.

## WHERE TO STAY

Utrecht, a venue for major international trade congresses and industry fairs—many held at the *Royal Exhibition Center* (*Jaarbeurs*), the largest trade marketplace in Europe—has several modern international chain hotels to serve trade show attendees, who number nearly a million annually. Thus, there's no lack of hotel rooms (though the city *can* be completely booked during major fairs), but properties that are cozy, comfortable and central are limited.

## WHERE TO EAT

Being a genial gathering spot for both students and business and pleasure travelers, Utrecht has a broad assortment of restaurants and cafes.

## ENTERTAINMENT AND EVENTS

Concerts of all kinds are presented in the **Muziekcentrum**, where the VVV has its offices. Programs and events are listed in the biweekly guide (in Dutch) *Uit in Utrecht*. **Concerts** by Utrecht's carillonneur can be heard year-round Sat. 11 a.m.–noon at the Dom Tower, which has the largest and one of the finest instruments (dating from 1669) in The Netherlands. Frequent organ concerts are held in summer in the city's many churches. In June, there's the **Festival Theater a/d Werf** with street and indoor theater and musical performances along the canals. Sept. brings a festival of ancient music.

## ARRIVING

With its location in the center of the Netherlands, Utrecht is the country's main rail junction. (As such, it's the logical location as headquarters for the country's railroads and the **Dutch Railway Museum**, see "What To See and Do"). Amsterdam, to the northwest, is about 30 minutes away on frequent trains; Rotterdam, to the southwest, is a bit farther. Utrecht has rail connections to Schiphol Airport. Buses serve Utrecht province, but a car is recommended (and may be necessary) for reaching many of the region's castles, riverside villages, and quiet spots of scenic beauty.

## TRAVEL TIPS

If you didn't come to Utrecht to see its city shopping malls (however fine they may be), don't be discouraged as you come out of the super-modern **Centraal Station** and have to negotiate through the **Hoog Catharijne** (the largest covered shopping center in Holland, and one of the largest commercial centers in Europe—so big it's been divided into *kwartiers/*quarters as if it were a city unto itself) to reach the VVV at its far end. Once at the VVV, it's only a brief two blocks to the **Oudegracht**, and all the old canalized center-city picturesqueness you could want. Utrecht's evening appeal, with light and laughter emanating from the waterside cafes, should also be experienced.

## IN THE AREA

If you're traveling by car to the northwest of Utrecht (in the direction of Amsterdam), there are a couple of Holland's best known midcountry castles, and the many-mansioned banks of the **Vecht River** through the delightful villages of **Breukelen**, **Loenen**, and **Ouderkerk** along your route.

## UTRECHT IN CONTEXT

Utrecht received its name indirectly from that of its Roman predecessor *Trajectum ad Rhenum* (ford on the Rhine), which was founded in A.D. 48 on the site now occupied by the city's **Dom Plein**. The settlement came into disuse after a flood in 839 rerouted the waters of the Rhine into the Lek River, and the place name became *Oude Trecht* (old ford), eventually shortened to *Utrecht*.

Well before that flood, circa 500, Frankish King Clovis had constructed a church here. But the beginnings of real importance for the province arrived with **St. Willibrord**, a monastic native of Northumbria, England, who became the first **bishop of Utrecht** in 696. He became so influential that the town was known for some period thereafter within the Frankish and Frisian parts of the considerable Utrecht bishopric territory as *Wiltaburg*. About the year 700, St. Willibrord had two churches built in Utrecht, the one dedicated to St. Martin proving to be a predecessor to the present Domkerk. From his base in Utrecht, Willibrord converted most of the north of the Netherlands to Christianity. After the destruction from raids by Norsemen and Frisians (who sacked the city in the early 10th century) was stemmed by erecting defenses that provided a sense of security which attracted a growing population, Willibrord's successors became increasingly powerful as overlords to large land holdings.

Utrecht was under the protection of the Germanic **Holy Roman Empire** (and often served as an imperial residence), which meant its powerful *Prince Bishops* were a constant challenge to the authority of the *counts of Holland*. Increasingly, the politically-minded prelates also alienated the growing wealthy Dutch merchant class. In 1527, Emperor Charles V bought the secular rights in the substantial Utrecht territory from Bishop Henry of Bavaria. Charles proceeded to build a castle for himself in Utrecht on what is today the **Vredenburg** (the castle was demolished in 1577 in a citizens' revolt against the unpopular Spanish Roman Catholic rule of the Netherlands by Philip II, son of Charles V).

As a youth, Charles, who had been born in the southern Netherlands in Ghent, had as his tutor **Adrian Florisz**, a native of Utrecht who was one of the most educated men of his era. While later serving as bishop in Tortosa, Spain, he was elected **Pope Adrian VI**

(1522). In Utrecht, there was great rejoicing over the honor of having a man from the city chosen pope (Adrian remains the only Dutch pope and, until 1978, had been the last non-Italian pontiff). In 1517, Adrian had a house built for himself in Utrecht (the **Paushuise** or Pope's House, corner of *Kromme Nieuwe Gracht* and *Nieuwe Gracht*) and wanted nothing more than to return to it and his city, but died in Rome (Sept. 14, 1523) not long after his papal election without ever having seen the house, which today is used for official city functions.

Practically from its founding, Utrecht has been a city of churches and bishops. About the year 1025, Bishop Adelbold built a new church on the site originally chosen by St. Willbrord for his **St. Martin's** (site of today's Domkerk). His successor, Bishop Bernold, used the site as the centerpiece for his enterprising undertaking of a *kerkenkruis* (cross of churches), in which four churches built through the city, with Adelbold's ecclesistical edifice at the crossing point, formed the shape of a cross. The four new churches, named for the four major churches in Rome at the time, are **St. Pieter's** at the east arm of the cross, **St. Jan's** in the north and **St. Paul's** in the south, with **Mariakerk** (St. Mary's) on the west; the "cross" was completed in 1080. Fire, the Reformation, and other city troubles took a toll over the centuries, but the basic plan is still in evidence. However, no sole church structure has in its foundations more of Utrecht's history than the **Domkerk** (see "Domkerk" under "What to See and Do").

The **University of Utrecht**, second in age in Holland only to Leiden and today the largest in the country, was founded in 1636 near the Domkerk. In the 17th and 18th centuries, the university was popular with Scottish students, including **James Boswell**, who studied civil law here in 1763. Having the Dutch *House of Orange* on the English throne in the person of **William III** (joint ruler with Mary, daughter of James II) led to many ties between the two countries: Utrecht native son **Godert de Ginkel** (1630–1703), later Earl of Athlone, was a general in William III's forces in Ireland.

Utrecht university's present auditorium is the Dom Cathedral's former Chapterhouse, which was the site for the signing of the **Union of Utrecht** (1579), which made the northern Netherlands officially Protestant. The bells of the Domtoren rang out when the Union was signed here by **Count Jan van Nassau**, brother of **Willem the Silent**, for the province of Holland, and by other representatives for the provinces of Zeeland and Utrecht. William originally disapproved of the Union, feeling, in his broad-minded way, that it overlooked too many of the interests of the Roman Catholic people. With Utrecht's strong Catholic presence, understandably there had been opposition to overcome by those ecclesiastics who feared a close alliance with Holland, where the Protestant Calvinists were in control. Utrecht supporters of the Union went so far as to literally lock up one of the Catholic priests of a Counter-Union movement until the *Union of Utrecht* had been duly signed on January 23. On May 3rd, Willem finally expressed cautious approval of the Union, having been persuaded that no better union was possible under the given circumstances. Although not originally intended as such, the 1579 Union of Utrecht virtually became the constitution for the **Republic of the Seven United Netherlands** (1588–1795.)

In 1559, the Roman Catholic church in Rome raised the bishops of Utrecht to archepiscopal rank, but the honor turned out to be short term. Within a year of the signing of the *Union of Utrecht*, the Catholic see in Holland was dissolved. Under French Napoleonic rule of Holland (1795–1813) the Roman Catholic Church's legal status was restored, although the archbishopric was not revived until 1851. When Louis Bonaparte ruled as king of Holland (1806–1810) for his brother Napoleon, he reigned from Utrecht for a brief period, using what is now the library of the university as his palace.

Today, the Dutch Roman Catholic archbishopric of Utrecht is alive and well. And inclined to cause the Vatican consternation with the independence of its ideas.

## GUIDEPOSTS

**Telephone code 030**

**Tourist Info** • VVV Utrecht, Vredenburg 90 (in the Muziekcentrum); Mon.- Fri. 9 a.m.–6 p.m., Sat. and holidays 9 a.m.–4 p.m.; ☎ *314132*, or ☎ *06-34034085.*

**Canal cruises** • Utrechts Rondvaartbedrijf, Schuttevaer, ☎ *319377.*

**Canal Bike** • Oudegracht 14, opposite Stadhuis; ☎ *020-6265574*; Apr.–Sept., 9 a.m.–7 p.m., closed Monday.

**City Transport** • Information can be obtained at the GVU kiosk on Stationplein; Mon.–Fri. 6:30 a.m.–8:30 p.m., Sat. & Sun. 8:30 a.m.–6:30 p.m.; ☎ *317962.* Also at the VVV.

**Post/Telephone** • Neude, Mon.–Fri. 8:30 a.m.–7 p.m. (Thurs. to 8:30 p.m.), Sat. 9 a.m.–4 p.m.

**Police** • Kroonstraat 25, ☎ *325911.* Lost property, ☎ *325272.*

## WHAT TO SEE AND DO

Utrecht's below-the-street wharfs, built beginning in the 12th century when the water level of the river and canals through the city was still changeable, provide a unique and distinctive look to the center.

### Domkerk (Dom Church)                                    ★★

*Domplein; daily May–Sept. 10 a.m.–5 p.m., Oct.–Apr. Mon.–Sat. 11 a.m.–4 p.m., Sun. 2–4 p.m., guided tours Dfl. 2.25;*  *310403.* Entrance to the lacy-facaded, flying-buttressed Gothic St. Martin's Church (Dom Cathedral), whose foundation stone was laid in 1254 (atop the site where St. Willibrord had built a church, which in turn had topped the city's original Roman settlement site), is in the remaining section of the structure's once-lengthy nave. The nave was said to be completed in 1505, though this did not include a roof. A temporary one was placed on the nave between 1505 and 1512, after which work on the cathedral was suspended. Not for the first time, but this time—due to war and economic difficulties, forever. The Reformation and rise of the Dutch Republic culminated in 1579 with the Dom's conversion from Cathedral of a Catholic Archbishop to an "ordinary" Dutch Reform Protestant church. On August 1, 1674, Utrecht was hit by a tornado, and the double-aisled nave of the Dom collapsed. The Dom tower, which by plan had always been basically detached structurally from the church, was undamaged by the storm, but thereafter stood much more distinctly separated. For undocumented reasons, the rubble that resulted from the "whirlwind" destruction of the nave was not cleared away until 1826 (when you think of the *generations* that lived their whole lives with that massive mess, it certainly puts a new perspective on a month's worth of dust under your bed back home). Once the rubble *was* removed, the Domplein was laid out with tinted stones showing the outline of the collapsed nave.

For centuries, the play of light in the soaring, spacious Choir and High Choir has been the glory of the Dom. The most recent restoration, begun in 1979, was completed in 1988. The picturesque *cloisters* ★★ (14th and 15th century) connect the cathedral with the former Chapterhouse (1495), in which the *Union of Utrecht* was signed in 1579. Over the windows in the cloister, a popular place to rest or listen to a carillon concert from the Domtoren, are carved scenes from the life of St. Martin.

### Domtoren (Dom Tower)                                    ★★

*Domplein; Apr.–Oct. Mon.–Fri. 10 a.m.–5 p.m. (last tour 4 p.m.) year-round Sat.and Sun. noon–5 p.m.;*  *919540.* When the 112-meter/367-foot Domtoren was finished in 1382—from the beginning, the plan had been to attach it only superficially to the church, on which construction was expected to last much longer—only four churches in Europe had taller towers: England's Salisbury; Bruges' Our Dear Lady, and the churches of Freiburg and Lubeck in Germany. Its straight lines to the sky are possible because the buttresses are within the body of the structure. Many climb the 465-step tower, beginning at the deceptively broad, straight, stately stair, which was built for the bishop to reach the St. Michael's Chapel near the base. Rising up the Domtoren, one gets a close–up look at the 50-bell carillon. The Domtoren has served as model for a number of other church towers in Holland.

### Van Speelklok tot Pierement                                    ★ ★

*National Museum for Musical Clocks to Street Organs. Buurkerkhof 10; multilingual guided tours on the hour Tues.–Sat. 10 a.m.–5 p.m., Sun. and holidays 1–5 p.m., closed Mon., most major holidays;* ☎ *312789.* In the 1980s, Utrecht's 15th-century "citizens' church" or **Buurkerk**, the largest gothic parish church in Holland, took a new lease on life. A 500-year lease, in fact, as a museum in which "everything makes music." In it, Holland celebrates its singing-tower (carillon) clocks and street organs in a collection that includes automatic musical instruments from the 18th-20th centuries. These are true musical instruments, with some form of "program" replacing the musically-skilled human hand. In principle, any musical instrument can be automated, and throughout history many attempts—both successful and unsuccessful—have been made. The earliest efforts were in the 14th century in the Netherlands with the development of mechanical clocks and striking works. This is definitely a museum where you'll want to join a tour—tours strike every hour, on the hour, for about an hour—since during one you get to hear up to 20 of the enchanting exhibits play.

There are multimelody mantel clocks and marvelous music boxes that play disks (forerunners of CDs); automated chamber and church organs; and pneumatically operated pianolas, whose player-rolls reproduce actual performances of famous master pianists such as Saint-Saens, Chopin, and Fauré. Instruments range in size from the miniature mechanisms in musical watches to the large barrel-operated *orchestrions*, meant to replicate an entire orchestra's sound. Also at the museum is a collection of barrel organs, from early 17th-century examples of portable ones to the still-popular street-style Dutch specialty (early each June, Utrecht stages a street organ day), to the huge, handsomely carved and painted fairground organs (a German and French musical tradition) and dance hall organs. The museum has a video that shows more instruments in action if you haven't heard enough, and there's a cafe and shop. The rise of radio and gramophones in the post-1929 depression period brought an end to the 400-year era of string-playing automatic instruments.

The Buurkerk is a building worth enjoying in its own right, since its careful restoration and conversion to a museum imaginatively conserved its architectural integrity and valuable frescoes. The innovative interior design created acoustically independent galleries in a free-standing form so that the church could be returned to its original con-

dition at any time. That shouldn't be soon, since the museum really
did sign a 500-year lease.

## Centraal Museum

*Agnietenstraat 1; Tues.–Sat. 10 a.m.–5 p.m., Sun. and holidays noon–5
p.m.;* ☎ *362362.* Holland's oldest municipal museum (1838), the
Centraal has a rich resource in its half-dozen 17th- and 18th-century
period rooms. **Jan Scorel** (1495–1562) is one of the leading lights
among the Utrecht painters represented; others include **Abraham
Bloemaert** (1564–1651) and sons, and **Gerrit van Honthorst**
(1590–1656).

## Het Catharijneconvent ★

*Nieuwegracht 63; Tues.–Fri. 10 a.m.–5 p.m., Sat., Sun., and holidays 11
a.m.–5 p.m., closed Mon.;* ☎ *317296.* Two years after it opened in
1979, the *International Council of Museums* presented Het Catharijne-
convent with its *Museum-of-the-Year* prize. With Utrecht a past and
present Dutch ecclesiastical center, the contents appropriately cover
the country's history of Christianity (both Roman Catholic and Protestant); they represent the largest collection of medieval art, sculpture, paintings, illuminated mss., breviaries, religious relics, and
vestments in Holland.

## Nederlands Spoorwegmuseum (Dutch Railway Museum) ★

*Maliebaan station; Tues.–Sat. 10 a.m.–5 p.m., Sun. and some holidays 1–5
p.m., closed Mon.;* ☎ *306206.* You can catch a special 10-minute train
from Utrecht's Centraal Station, or walk from the Centrum to the
1874 *Maliebaan,* a "retired" station where exhibits keep track of Holland's more than 150 years of rail history. (The country's first line
opened in 1839 between Amsterdam and Haarlem.) On three covered
platforms and five tracks are beautifully restored rolling stock, steam,
electric, and some horse-drawn tramway cars; on Spoor 1 (platform
one) stands a row of seven locomotives; both the beginning (1864)
and end engine (1945) are British achievements. Nostalgic paintings
and prints decorate part of the old railway hall. This is a well-done
museum at Holland's rail crossroads that even non-train buffs will find
interesting, considering that trains are such a tradition in Europe.
There's a comprehensive booklet available in English on all aspects of
Dutch trains, from the historic to the futuristic, and refreshments
await in the old **Wagons-Lits** restaurant car.

## Rietveld-Schroderhuis ★

*Hendriklaan 50A; Weds.–Sat. 11 a.m.–5 p.m., Sun. 12–5 p.m.: visits only
with prior reservation by telephone* ☎ *362310; bus #4 (De Hoogstraat
stop).* Despite Holland's many buildings of interest across several centuries, this is the *one* example of Dutch architecture to be
incorporated in the *World List of Protected Buildings.* An important
monument in the Dutch art movement **De Stijl**, the house was built in
1924 by architect and furniture designer **Gerrit Rietveld**, and contains
both his simple bold lines, brightly colored geometrical chairs, and

other furniture he designated for it. Visits must be arranged ahead of time because of the limited space inside the house.

### Museum voor het Kruideniersbedrijf (Grocery Museum) ★

*Hoogt 6; Tues.–Sat. 12:30-4:30 p.m.;* ☎ *316628.* This is the Dutch equivalent of an old penny-candy store, with women in aprons serving choices of sweets from great glass jars (there are some 25 different kinds of licorice, a favorite in Holland). A free museum of sorts, with old kitchen and cooking utensils, is upstairs, but the real delight is downstairs, especially if a crowd of Dutch children come in on the way home from school. For sale are tins of tea and biscuits, prettily decorated with Dutch scenes.

## WHERE TO STAY

## EXPENSIVE

### Scandic Crown Hotel

*Westplein 50, 3531 BL;* ☎ *925200, FAX* ☎ *925199.* Located on the non-historic side of the tracks, though only steps from **Centraal Station**, the gleaming glass 120-room Scandic Crown is convenient to the **Jaarbeurs Complex** for trade fairs, a short walk to the VVV, and not much farther from Utrecht's old center. Its Scandinavian style is carried through from room decor and restaurant specialties to a sauna in the fitness room. Non-smoking rooms, parking available.

### Smits

*Vredenburg 14, 3511 BA;* ☎ *331232, FAX* ☎ *328451.* Sitting close to the site of Charles V's short-lived 16th-century castle on the Vredenburg, this recently renovated five-story, 87-room property is close to the station, sights, and shopping. All rooms have shower; ask for a tub/shower if you want one. Since the hotel faces the **Vredenburg**, where the Wed. and Sat. markets get an early start, rooms on the back are a quieter choice. There's an attractive lounge bar (with live piano music many nights) and a restaurant that serves all three meals (buffet breakfast included for guests). Elevator, major credit cards.

### Malie

*Maliestraat 2, 3581 SL;* ☎ *316424, FAX* ☎ *340661.* This friendly, stylish hotel with 30 rooms in adjoining restored houses, is owned and operated by a young couple who are trained in hotel management and show it. The residential neighborhood property is a short bus ride, or longish walk, to the city center. Each airy, neat, individual room has shower, TV, telephone, reading lamps; several overlook the garden, and two have private terraces. Prices vary only slightly with size—so, splurge! The breakfast (only, included) room looks on to the garden; there's a lobby bar with comfortable leather couches, magazines. Elevator, bus #4 to Centrum.

## WHERE TO EAT

The starting and stopping point for eating and drinking in Utrecht is the **Oudegracht** with its cafes on the canal terraces and eateries within the wharfs (in which case their address reads *onder*, or under, the building on the main street level above). With menus posted and prices kept pretty reasonable by the city's student population, making a choice here isn't very chancy. Nevertheless, you might want to know that **Il Pozzo** is *the* Oudegracht's largest and most famous terrace cafe. Locally, it's the place to be seen, although crowds also tend to follow the sun in their search for a cafe. Il Pozzo's name reflects the strong Italian influence in Utrecht, as does **Venezia** (*Oudegracht 105;* ☎ *319135; closed Oct. 15–Feb. 15*), the Oudegracht location for Italian *ijs* (ice cream). **La Pizzeria** (*Voorstraat 23; noon–2 p.m., 5–11 p.m., closed Sun. and Mon. 'til 5 p.m., closed holidays;* ☎ *316021; inexpensive)* claims the honor of being Utrecht's oldest Italian restaurant, and dishes up pasta, veal in a variety of styles, and Italian wines, as well as pizza.

**Café de Paris** (*Drierharingstraat 16; noon–2 p.m., 5:30–10 p.m., closed Sun. and holidays;* ☎ *317503; moderate)* is an enterprise of one of the enterprising *Fagel brothers*, who operate a handful of highly respected individual restaurants in Holland. The menu is limited but choice, French-influenced, and served in a Belle Époch setting. Also offering a good range of French fare is **Grand Café Polman's** (*Keistraat 2; daily noon–11 p.m.;* ☎ *313368; inexpensive)*, which occupies a desanctified 17th-century church with art deco accents and huge floor-to-ceiling mirrors; music is served up most evenings. Another historic setting for supping is the restored medieval mansion (which also had a life as an old men's home), **Stadskasteel Oudaen** (*Oudegracht 99; daily 5:30–11 p.m.;* ☎ *311864; moderate)*, whose upstairs restaurant serves continental cuisine and a four-course menu. At ground floor is a fashionable bar and a cafe, both of which are open for morning coffee.

Back on the Oudegracht, or rather one level down from it, look for **Tantes Bistro** (*Oudegracht a/d Werf 61; daily 5 p.m.–1 a.m.;* ☎ *312191; inexpensive)* that serves French-style food, but also Dutch dishes, in an old vaulted canalside cellar. Nearby is **De Werfkring** (*Oudegracht a/d Werf 123; Mon.–Sat. noon to 8 p.m., closed Sun. and holidays;* ☎ *311752; inexpensive)*, where the vegetarian dishes are healthy, tasty, and priced for a student's pocket. That's also true of the plate-size delicious Dutch *pannekoeken* (pancakes) and other light items at the 14th-century **De Oude Muntkelder** (*Oudegracht a/d Werf 112, beneath the main Post Office; Tues.–Sat. noon–10 p.m.;* ☎ *316773; inexpensive)*, at which there's outside canalside terrace or inside seating. At **Victor Consael** (*Neude; open 10 a.m.–10 p.m. in summer, 8 p.m. winter; closed Mon.;* ☎ *316377; inexpensive)*, a Utrecht family institution since 1850, you can get poffertjes (rather like doughnut holes sprinkled with sugar) and waffles, as well as pancakes.

For a snack "to go," stop at the Jewish bakery **De Tarwebol** on Zadelstraat, near the Buurkerk. To end the day on a completely different note, you might drop in to **Fellini** (*Stadhuisbrug; Wed.–Sun. 10 p.m.–4 a.m.),* a disco located in the extensive ancient cellars underneath the *Stadhuis* (town hall). The restoration has made the cellars truly beautiful, and, even if you don't plan to dance, it's a special place to stop for a drink.

## IN THE AREA

### Slot Zuylen                                                    ★★

*Signposted to the right on east bank of Amsterdam-Rijn Kanaal, five km./three miles northwest of Utrecht, near Maarssen, Tournooiveld 1, Oud Zuilen; mid-Mar.-mid-Nov. daily, tours at 10 and 11 a.m., 2, 3 and 4 p.m., Sun. 2, 3, and 4 p.m., closed Mon.;* ☎ *030-440255.* A castle with a substantial moat surrounded by woods, it originally was built in the late 12th century but given a facelift in the 18th; it is still one of Holland's most characteristic medieval castles. Contents include fine furniture, tapestry, porcelain, and pictures. James Boswell visited and established a long-lasting friendship with Isabella van Zuylen here in 1763-64 while he was a student at Utrecht University; she later married a Swiss and became known as a novelist under her married name Isabelle de Charriere. A main feature of the fine garden, to which the public has free access, is a serpentine wall.

### Kasteel De Haar                                                 ★★

*5 km./3 miles further north at Vleuten-Haarzuilens; Kasteellaan 1; March-mid-Aug and Oct.-mid-Nov., tours more or less hourly 10:30 a.m.–4:30 p.m., Sun. 1:30 p.m., closed Mon.;* ☎ *03407-1275.* Flamboyant-by-design, neo-gothic **De Haar**, which definitely lives up to its brochure claim of being "an unexpected occurrence in this down-to-earth Dutch landscape," dates from the turn of this century, having been first built in 1165. It was enlarged in 1287, destroyed in 1482, rebuilt in 1505, and badly damaged by the French in 1672, after which it was left relatively alone and in ruins. Marriage of the heir (Baron Etienne van Zuylen van Nyevelt van de Haar) in 1887 to a Baroness de Rothschild provided funds to restore the ancestral home. In 1892, the commission was given to **P.J.H. Cuypers**, the famous, prolific, and authoritative architect of Amsterdam's *Rijksmuseum* and *Centraal Station.* During the renovations there were altercations as well as alterations, more over matters of taste than finance; funds seem to have been almost unlimited, since hundreds of laborers and artists worked, sometimes day and night from 1892 through 1912 to complete the task. To ensure the necessary supply of bricks the Baron built a brick factory. He also dismantled the entire village that had grown up near the castle over the centuries but was by then, he felt, too near the castle to allow for the forested hunting grounds and gardens he had planned, and moved it two kilometers away. He "built" a forest by transporting and transplanting only mature trees.

While the castle was being rebuilt, the owners took a sort of second honeymoon around the world, buying whatever they liked as furnishings to stock it. Architect Cuypers felt it was all too eclectic, and expressed his thoughts by weaving into the library decoration such sayings as "Nothing in excess" and "I hope you won't regret it." In fact, the castle contains valuable works of art, none more worthy than the dining room's 17th-century Flemish **tapestries** after a design by David Teniers the Younger. The hall is a lofty landmark of the castle: a celebration of van Zuylen prominence in the Middle Ages, it features ten family statues set into the carved sandstone, towering, tiered galleries that rise to a gilted oakwood ceiling based on one at the Palace of Justice in Rouen, France. Stained glass windows in the hall have scenes from the de Haar history. It isn't an *Everyman's* idea of home, but one has to say it's impressive. The family anecdotal tours, which include details about the style of living when the family and its high-society guests take up residence each Sept. (the castle is centrally heated and the plumbing thoroughly modernized), cover the grand rooms on the ground floor and a bedroom or two. Allow time to enjoy the lovely Versailles-style formal gardens. There's revival in Haarzuilens village—which can be reached by a walk through the woods from the castle if you like—at cafe-restaurant **De Vier Balken** (*Brinkstraat 3;* ☎ *03407-1268; open noon–9 p.m., closed Mon.*), a pleasingly rustic atmosphere with tasty Dutch dishes from salads to steaks.

★ ★ **The River Vecht** flows from Utrecht almost to Amsterdam and, during medieval days, nobility from **Het Sticht** (the old name for the province of Utrecht) and the bishops of Utrecht built fortress-castles along it in order to defend the region from attacks by provocators from the province of Holland. During the devastating time of the French occupation of the region (1672-73), virtually the entire region of the Vecht was destroyed. Many Amsterdam merchants, however, retained enough riches from the East Indies trade of the Golden Age to line the river once again with marvelous buildings—this time ornate summer mansions with landscaped lawns and teahouses. (The daily ceremony for tea, first introduced in Holland c. 1610, became wildly popular in the course of the 17th century; as engaged in at these riverfront gazebos, and visible to "sightseers on the water" the occasion was meant to be showy.) Although few mansions are open to the public, the exteriors can be enjoyed by those traveling in the area by car, cruise boat or bicycle.

One of the most beautiful villages on the Vecht is ★ ★ **Breukelen**, from which the New York City borough "Brooklyn" gets its name. Yes, there's a bridge here, a pretty little drawbridge, though no one mentions selling it. Breukelen, too, was largely demolished by Louis XIV's forces in 1672, with the stones being used to build defensive works. However, the subsequent rebuilding doesn't seem to have cost the village much of its narrow-streeted charm.

South of Breukelen, on the west side of the Vecht, is the **Restaurant-Hotel Hofstede Slangevegt** (*Straatweg 40, Breukelen; lunch noon–2 p.m., dinner 5:30–9:30 p.m.;* ☎ *03462-61525; moderate*), an elegantly cozy traditional restaurant with river terrace and conservatory. The locally popular restaurant has three-course prix-fixe lunches and dinners. If you don't mind mixing with the family owners, there are several rather ordinary rooms (*inexpensive*); two face the river, with balconies, private shower/ toilet.

Another village long on loveliness is ★★ **Loenen** (pop. 7000), with its many 18th-century houses. The design for the 15th-16th-century Dutch Reform Church tower was taken from Utrecht's Domtoren, though in 1741 the foundation had to be propped up with peat to correct a lean, which from some angles is still noticeable. Two intimate and tempting local dining choices are **Tante Koosje** (*Kerkstraat 1; ☎ 02943-3201; closed Wed.*) in a house beside the church, and **Restaurant 't Amsterdammertje** (*Rijksstraatweg 119; ☎ 02943-4813*), cozy with wooden tables, candles, and ivy draped around the mirrors. Continue on toward Amsterdam through **Ouderkerk aan de Amstel** (Old Church on the Amstel), another authentic old Dutch village that's a pleasant place to pause for refreshment at one of the riverside cafe terraces.

# NORTHERN HOLLAND

## AN INTRODUCTION

The north of the Netherlands includes the provinces of Friesland, Groningen and Drenthe. The northern provinces are anchored by the cities of Leeuwarden, capital of Friesland, and Groningen, capital of its same-name province.

**Friesland** has an atmosphere of landed nobility and wealth. Cows (the famous *Frisian black and whites*, bred and exported around the world) have for centuries been so important to the province's economy that a statue of one (named *Us Mem*—"Our Mother") stands near the station in the center of Leeuwarden. The countryside is studded with prosperous farmhouses, distinctive in that the family living quarters and barns are often sheltered under a single huge roof. Black glazed tiles—as distinguished from the more common ones in orange terra cotta—were symbols of wealth and used over the home section of the structure.

The Frisians were early settlers of the sea-embattled land in the north, living first on man-made mounds (*terps*) meant to keep them above the high water level; by the year 1000, they had developed an extensive network of dikes. Friesland has always seemed separate from the rest of the Netherlands, its location on the far side of the former **Zuiderzee** (now the enclosed *IJsselmeer*) adding to its sense of remoteness. The road atop the enclosing **Afsluitdijk** (opened in 1932) provided a more accessible driving route to the province and opened Friesland to more outside influence, but, even today, few residents of Holland, and fewer visitors, know much about this interesting and attractive area.

In addition to Dutch, Friesland has had its own language (today, a compulsory course in the province's primary schools) and body of literature for centuries; *Frisian* is described as being "a brother to the English language and a cousin to Dutch." The Frisian people have long been friends of the United States. In 1782, while still an independent province, Friesland was the first government to recognize the newly formed United States of America as a country; there's a plaque stating that fact in the historic Provincial House in Leeuwarden. The Frisians also strongly urged the Dutch government to loan the young America some much-needed capital.

**Groningen**, at the "top" of Holland, has far-stretching fields, rows of poplars permanently bent by the winds off the shallow *Waddenzee*, and horizons marked by "mountains" of clouds. The only town of any size in the province, Groningen was a center of activity by the 11th century, and today retains the inner-city waterways that were its moats in earlier eras. The landmark of the attractive historic city center is **Martinikerk**, a lovely church, largely 15th century in appearance, though begun in the 13th. The distinguished **University of Groningen** was founded in 1614.

*Mooi* **Drenthe** ("lovely Drenthe") is the way this northeastern province, the least well-known of the country's twelve, often is described. With Drenthe's heathland, inland sandbanks, peat fens, and woods, the phrase is apt—and certainly more appealing than Drenthe's other epithet: "the forgotten province." The most intriguing attractions in Drenthe are reminders of its prehistoric (c. 3000 B.C.) inhabitants: great megalithic burial chambers known as *Hunebeds*, many of which survive, especially along the Hondsrug ridge that runs northwest from Emmen.

As interesting as the "far" north of Holland may be, it is the "near" north with its picturesque old fishing villages around what formerly was the **Zuiderzee** (South Sea, now the **IJsselmeer lake**) that usually is most rewarding for visitors. Of particular interest are **West Friesland** (the northeast section of today's North Holland province) and, across the Afsluitdijk that closed off the Zuiderzee, the **southwest corner of Friesland**. Most visitors also want to know how the new polder province of **Flevoland**, which exists in a region that until 1932 was under the tidal waters of the Zuiderzee, came to be reclaimed.

# OLD ZUIDERZEE VILLAGES AND THE NEW POLDER PROVINCE

Following two centuries of topographic turmoil—sinking land, rising seas, and mounting floods—the **great storm of 1287** breached the sand dune barrier between the North Sea and what had been an inland lake north of Amsterdam. The flood produced by the storm (which killed 50,000 people in Friesland) created the **Zuiderzee**, whose tidal shores became the site for the many flourishing fishing villages and seafaring towns that gave the region its identity. Their Zuiderzee connection became the characteristic quality of these quaint, often handsome, seashore communities. So strong was the shaping force of the Zuiderzee on life around its rim, that 60 years after the great **Afsluitdijk** (barrier dam) sealed it off from the open water of the North Sea once again in 1932, you can still sense the salt in the air of the picturesque old ports, now mostly filled with recreational sailboats instead of commercial sailing ships.

For many visitors to the area, sentimental regret for the passing of the "sailing on the tide" seafaring tradition of the Zuiderzee villages is offset by fascination with the story of the creation of a whole new province of polderland from what used to be the bottom of the sea. The tale is exceptionally well told—in multiple languages—at the **Informatiecentrum Nieuw Land** located in **Lelystad**, capital of the new **Flevoland** polder province.

## *GUIDELINES FOR OLD ZUIDERZEE VILLAGES AND THE NEW POLDER PROVINCE*

### SIGHTS

There's a great deal of scenic variety in the region covered in this chapter, from compact waterland villages to prosperous towns that sent forth sea captains around the world in the 17th century. The open-air **Zuiderzee Museum** at Enkhuizen gives an impression of daily life and work in the Zuiderzee region during the period of 1880-1930. The 350 year-old craft of making Dutch tiles and porcelain can be seen in **Makkum**, and Hoorn's **West Fries Museum** is one of the area's most attractive sources of local history. You can also encounter traditional costumes, thatched farmhouses, a village where farmers ferry cattle from one grazing field to another on flat-bottomed boats, castles, and cloudscapes above Friesland's vast and verdant reaches that will make you catch your breath.

## GETTING AROUND

To reach the sights in this section requires a car, although certain places are served by train: Hoorn, Enkhuizen, and Lelystad, more or less conveniently from Amsterdam. Groningen, Leeuwarden, Harlingen, and Kampen can be reached on trains via Utrecht. An historic steam train runs between Medemblik–Hooin–Enkhuizin from May –Sept. (☎ *02290-16653*). Local and regional buses go to literally every village, but a traveler with limited time will not want to waste it waiting at remote countryside crossroads to make a bus connection. A word of caution about driving on the provincial roads. Many are single lane in each direction; the flatness of the polder terrain, combined with the speed at which local drivers go, can fool you about on-coming car distances, so be wary when planning to pass. Also, the smaller the rental car you can manage with, the easier it will be to navigate on tight turns in tiny villages.

## SHOPPING

The larger towns on this route (Hoorn, Harlingen, Kampen) have the most varied selection of shops for basic and specialty goods. There's a museum shop with gift items at Enkhuizen's **Zuiderzee Museum**. **Hindeloopen**, once famed for its painted furniture, has a number of shops with smaller items in its distinctive style. **Makkum** has stores selling its traditional Dutch tiles and porcelain.

## ENTERTAINMENT AND EVENTS

Wednesdays from early July to mid-August, there are **folklore markets** in Hoorn. Thursdays (mid-June to mid-August), the West Frisian Folklore markets are held in Schagen. Also on Thursday afternoons in July and August, in both Enkhuizen and at the **Zuiderzee Museum**, large groups from various Zuiderzee villages dress in traditional costume and perform live music. From mid-April–late May, **bulb fields** bloom around West Friesland; those at Anna Paulowna are the largest unbroken stretches of flowers in the country. Every 3rd Sunday of the month from Easter to September Naarden celebrates **Civil Guard days** in medieval costume at its Vesting Museum. In Purmerend on Thurs. in July and Aug. from 11 a.m.–1 p.m. a small **cheese market** with handicrafts is held. The Dutch are fond of taking guided hikes through the **Waddenzee mud flats** in summer.

## WHERE TO STAY

Given the limited quantity and size of hotels in the area, reservations are suggested, and are a must in the summer months when the

Dutch and other Europeans come here on holiday. (Even those arriving by private sailboat—which many do—often opt for a hotel hot
shower.)

## WHERE TO EAT

Seafood is bound to come to mind as you circle the former
Zuiderzee and see the wealth that fishing brought to its villages and
towns. Most hotels have a more-than-reputable restaurant.

## TRAVEL TIPS

Keep a stash of *guilders* and *kwartjes* (25-cent pieces) on hand for
parking meters, so you can make the most of short stops in towns.

## *THE ROUTE*

This exploration of old Zuiderzee villages, including places of interest inland and the new polder province of Flevoland, heads north
from Amsterdam, following the map in a roughly clockwise route.
After visiting the fishing villages of **Monnickendam, Marken**, and
**Edam**, it then proceeds up the west side of what today is the
**IJsselmeer** to the important towns of **Hoorn**—explorer Willem
Schouten put his hometown's name on the map by naming the
southern tip of South America *Cape Horn*—and **Enkhuizen**. After
crossing the **Afsluitdijk** into Friesland, and making stops at **Harlingen** and **Franeker**—from which a motorway continues northeast to
Leeuwarden and Groningen—the route drops south to the small
and picturesque ports of **Makkum** and **Hindeloopen** that lie along the
northern coast to the IJsselmeer. Then it's inland southeast to lovely
little **Sloten**, the smallest of Friesland's 11 towns. Without neglect-
ing **Blozijl** (now bound into the mainland by polder), and the pleasing oddities of **Giethoorn** and **Staphorst**, the road continues to **Urk**,
once an island, but now also absorbed into the mainland. Both **Kampen** and the well-preserved formerly fortified town of **Elburg** have
roads leading onto **Flevoland**, the new polder province. The *Informatiecentrum Nieuw Land*, in the capital **Lelystad**, details how Holland has reclaimed over 400,000 acres from the former Zuiderzee in
the last 50 years. As you leave the new land, there are last looks at the
old: fortifications and castles at **Naarden** and **Muiden**, almost at Amsterdam's door. The mileage for the entire route is remarkably man-
ageable, and even the rural roads are well paved and signposted. You
can easily meander for much of a week, or take the shortcut dike-top
road from Enkhuizen across the IJsselmeer to Lelystad (Rt. N302,
28 kms./17 mi.) for an edited edition of the tour.

## ON THE ROAD

Leaving Amsterdam *Centrum* via the **IJ Tunnel** north, look for signs for **N247** (or **Volendam**) in the next few miles, and exit there. That's the end of motorways for the remainder of the route, unless you choose otherwise on select stretches.

## ★ BROEK-IN-WATERLAND

About six miles from Amsterdam—less than a half hour by car, even if you're negotiating heavy central Amsterdam traffic out of the city—you'll arrive in *Waterland*, a lovely water-logged region of canals and small villages with typical wooden houses often painted green with white trim. With its large wooden houses, ornamental summer and domed tea houses, and gracious gardens, the village of Broek-in-Waterland (pop. 3000) is a charming witness to 18th-century prosperity. At the far end of the village, just past the church, built in 1628 and recently restored (*open from May–mid–Sept. 10 a.m.–4 p.m.*), there are several wooden shoe (*klompen*) and cheese-maker shops (*De Domme Dirk*) that are friendly and non- commercial in comparison with the ones you'll see on the road to Volendam. Broek was the setting for the 1865 story **Hans Brinker**, or **The Silver Skates**. Hans and friends regularly *skated* into Amsterdam, but today there's an attractive sea dike cyclists' route from Amsterdam along the IJsselmeer to Broek and Monnickendam; inquire at the Amsterdam VVV for the *Waterland Cycle Route* (English) booklet.

Broek-in-Waterland is so convenient to, yet such a complete change from, Amsterdam that one of its restaurants (**Neeltje Pater**) is a luncheon favorite out of the city for chauffer-driven business clients. Across the road is the more reasonably priced **De Witte Swaen** (*noon-9 p.m., closed Mon.*) for Dutch pancakes.

## ★ MONNICKENDAM

**VVV** • *In the 15th-century* **Grote Kerk**, *the first building you come to; April–Oct. Mon–Sat. 10 a.m.–noon, 2–5 p.m., rest of year 4 p.m.; pop. 10,000.*

Just 12 km./7 mi. north of Amsterdam. Monnickendam's center is the Middendam, with the 17th-century **De Waegh** (Weighhouse), now a pleasant **panneloekhuis**, *(11 a.m.–10 p.m. daily April 1–Oct. 31; open Fri.–Sun. only Nov. 1–Mar 31;* ☎ *02995-1241; inexpensive).* Nearby is the 16th-century **Spleeltoren**, with the second oldest carillon in Holland. **Restaurant "De Posthoorn"** (*Noordeinde 39;* ☎ *02995-1471; inexpensive/moderate*) has a quietly stylish attractive antique-decorated traditional old Dutch interior, with candlelit tables even at lunch, and serves three-course luncheon menus that feature such favorite starters as Zeeland oysters, smoked eel, eel soup, and fish or chicken salad, but will also prepare a light choice of omelet or salad. With a terrace on the harbor, near the herring smoke-houses, is the **Cafe-Restaurant Stuttenburgh** (*Haringburgwal 2;* ☎ *02995-1869; inexpensive)* which features service from 10 a.m. of pancakes to fresh fish and a *gezellig* (cozy) interior filled with antique music boxes.

# ★ MARKEN

From Monnickendam, you can drive atop a dike to the former island of Marken, whose land was resurrected from the Zuiderzee by nuns and monks in the 13th century. Since the mid-1900s, it has been connected to the mainland by causeway. The village's typical green wood and white-trim cottages sit in a crescent facing what used to be open sea; they retain a far-reaching waterview across the *IJsselmeer*. If you arrive in the late afternoon or evening, and linger over a drink at **De Taanderij** (*Havenbuurt 1;* ☎ *02966-1364*), a terrace cafe at one end of the crescent, you may get a personal impression of the tiny village, where traditional costumes are worn for the tourists. Perhaps one shouldn't fault the villagers for their successful "switch-to-tourism-to-survive" business sense, since their former sea fishing industry foundered with the sealing off of the Zuiderzee in 1932. There's a **Marken Museum** (*Kerkbuurt 44; Easter–Nov. 1, daily 1 a.m.–5 p.m.; Sun. noon–4 p.m.*), fitted out as a typical fishing family would have lived up to about 1932. You may manage a pleasant visit to Marken: tour buses have to park outside the village, which itself is mostly pedestrian. The commercialism at the nearby, much larger town of **Volendam** is harder to ignore, however, and can be avoided.

# ★★ EDAM

**VVV** • *1737 Stadhuis on the 1569 Damplein; Mon.–Sat., Apr.–Oct., 10 a.m.–5 p.m.; Nov.–Mar., 1 a.m.–12:30 p.m., Mon.–Sat.; closed Sun;* ☎ *02993-71727; pop. 25,000.*

Its name is familiar for having originated, centuries ago, the recipe for the regions' most widely produced type of cheese. Edam's cheese market (*Wed. mid-July–mid.-Aug., 10 a.m.–noon*), at the 18th-century **Kaaswaag** (itself open daily 10 a.m.–5 p.m.), is a small, tourist-oriented affair. (Alkmaar is the main cheese market for the cannonball shaped edams see "Amsterdam, In the Area".) However, the wonderfully picturesque town merits much meandering to see its canals, drawbridges, grassy ramparts, and many fine facades; it's conveniently small, but always seems to offer another enticing corner to turn. Edam received its town rights in 1357, at which time it was walled and had a toll-free canal to the Zuiderzee constructed. From 1573–1922, an important weekly cheese market was held there (records from 1649 show that Edam exported a half-million cheeses that year), and its cheese-aging warehouses are still active.★**Dam Square** is the center, but recently restored 15th-century ★★**Grote Kerk** (*Grote kerkstraat; April-Oct., daily 2–4:30 p.m.*), tucked in the corner of the town, is perhaps Edam's proudest possession. It is the largest triple-ridged church in Europe, with a fine carved-oak choir screen, and has 30 early-17th-century windows that give the lovely lighting. Edam's oldest brick house (c. 1530) is now the **Town Museum** (*Damplein 8; April–Oct., Mon.–Sat., 10 a.m.–4 p.m., Sun. 2-4 p.m.*); inside you can see the typical construction, which must be sturdy to support its "floating cellar," a brick box-shaped room that floats freely on ground water that is rumored to have been devised by a retired sea captain-owner who wanted to sleep rocking on water. The

VVV sells *A Stroll through Edam* in English. If no other restaurants have already caught your eye on your tour about town **"Rimi"** *(Prinsenstraat 5;* ☎ *02993-71630)* is recommended locally for casual fare, while the **Cafe-Restaurant "Hof van Holland"** *(Lingerzijde 69;* ☎ *02993-72546)* has a more elegant decor and exrtensive menu.

## WHERE TO STAY

### Hotel "De Fortuna"                                       ★★★

> *Spuistrat 1;* ☎ *02993-71671; inexpensive.* This cozy complex of five restored 17th-century houses (about 30 rooms) around a garden and flowered terrace overlooks a canal at the edge of the historic town. Most rooms have a private shower and toilet, many have a TV and telephone with cheerful modern room decor; there are steep stairs (no elevators) to negotiate in some cases. Breakfast (included) is served, but not other meals; drinks are available to guests only. On-street parking.

## ★★ HOORN

**VVV** • *1613 stepped-gable "Statenpoort," Niewstraat 23, year round, Tues.-Fri., 10 a.m.–12:30 p.m. and 1:30 p.m.–5 p.m., Sat. 10 a.m.–2 p.m., Mon. 1:30–5 p.m., closed Sun., except Jul. and Aug., Mon.-Sat. until 6 p.m.;* ☎ *02290-18342; pop. 56,000, 5,000 in old center; 20 km./12 mi. north of Edam.*

In the 12th century Hoorn was a shipping stopover between Denmark and Bruges in Flanders. In the 14th century, it received town rights, after which markets and a legal system were established. With the local economy strong in sea trade in the 5th, 16th and 17th centuries, especially from the Dutch East and West Indies companies, Hoorn embellished its mansions, warehouses, hofjes, and admiralty buildings to reflect the prosperity of those times. A building in the old center that can't help but hold your attention with its fanciful Dutch Renaissance facade is the 1632 provincial government building that now houses the ★★**West Fries Museum** *(Rode Steen 1; Mon.-Fri. 11 a.m.–5 p.m., Sat., Sun., hols. 2-5 p.m.,* ☎ *02290-15783).* Also intriguing on the inside, the handsome museum houses period rooms (including a tiled kitchen and loft), with furniture, fine and decorative arts, old maps and ship models, old paneling tapestries, and civic guard portraits, and has a charming garden. Many Dutch "naive-style" painters have come from the West Fries section of Holland, and a permanent display of their delightful art recently was added to the museum. Walk from the museum down to the ★**Old Haven**, where the striking semi-circular 1532 (restored 1905), **Hoofdtoren** (old defense tower) dominates what is a yacht harbor. Across from it is the terrace cafe **Het Schippershuis** (☎ *02290–15202*) for a drink or lunch with a view. The VVV has a brochure in English (*Walking in Hoorn*) that features the harbor and *hofjies* (almhouses, of which there are many in Hoorn, founded by the wealthy merchants), and gives a map, descriptions of sights, and a good bit of history. During the first half of the 17th century, Hoorn and Holland, may have become too prosperous for their own good. In the second half of the

17th century, Hoorn's prosperity began to decline, partially as a result of the **Anglo-Dutch Wars** which reflected an English attitude expressed by Samuel Pepys in his diary of 1665 that "all were mad for a 'Dutch war' which would, it was hoped, ruin Dutch trade."

## ★★ ENKHUIZEN

VVV • *Stationplein 1; ☎ 02280-13164; pop. 20,000; 16 km./9 mi. northeast of Hoorn.*

How appropriate that a museum dedicated to life as it was around the former Zuiderzee should be reached by boat—and boat alone. From Enkhuizen's train station (parking included in museum admission) boats embark every few minutes for the few-minute cruise past the steepled skyline of the town to the ★★★**Zuiderzee Museum** (*Wierdijk 12; outdoor museum open April–Oct., daily 10 a.m.–5 p.m., last admission 4 p.m.; indoor museum open daily year-round 10 a.m.–5 p.m. ☎ 02280–10122).* The site of the Zuiderzee Museum, which opened in 1983 and promptly won the *European Museum of the Year Award,* is the former working harbor site from which the 35 km./21 mi. dam/road from Enkhuizen to Lelystad (on the then-new East Flevoland polder on the other side of the IJsselmeer) was built in 1965. The Zuiderzee Museum is dedicated to the sociohistoric purpose of recreating work and domestic life as it was in the region during the half century prior to the 1932 construction of the Afsluitdijk. Through its 135 houses and workplaces, collected from Zuiderzee villages and towns, the museum has been assembled to create a complete and charming urban setting, with canals, churches, alleyways, and gardens. There's a detailed, color-illustrated guidebook in English that describes the specific buildings and also provides interesting background tidbits, such as: rain water, used for drinking and cooking (well water being good enough only for cleaning and outdoor needs), was most pure when it ran into collection barrels off roofs made of tiles that were glazed, and hence didn't grow moss. As you wander through this Zuiderzee "village" you'll find many folk more than willing to chat about about their activities: the man in the smokehouse bending over his hot oakwood fire; a fisherman sitting on a lawn "doing penance" (mending nets); or the attendant at ★**Apotheek De Grote Gaper** ("The Big Yawner"). Having explained that the large carved wooden head with mouth open and tongue stuck out was typical of Dutch signage used since the Middle Ages to indicate a drugstore or chemist's shop, he made sure I didn't miss the wonderful collection of 40 such heads in the room behind "his" old shop, originally from Hoorn. There are several eateries at the museum, including the Pannoekenhis Taveerne de Meermin (☎ *02280-10291*) which features light meals, a menu, and soup of the day, in addition to pancakes, and a pub with an outdoor terrace overlooking the IJsselmeer.

The actual town of Enkhuizen, to which you can return by foot from the exit (*uitgang*) of the museum if you wish, is a historic treasure itself, dating back almost a millennium. Coming on foot from the museum, you'll see the restored Peperhuis (1625), which was owned by the Dutch East India

Company from 1682. Walk along the tree-shaded, sun-speckled Zuider Havendijk, and the Zuiderspui, which ends at a white pedestrian draw-bridge that crosses to the 1540 ★ Drommedaris Tower with its 1677 Hemony carillon (concerts Sat. 4–5 p.m.), both easily enjoyed from the terraced cafes opposite. Enkhuizen has a second Hemony carillon in the green copper-crowned Zuiderkerk (1450), with additional concerts. In summer, Enkhuizen is the Dutch port with the largest number of traditional sailing ships: large-masted old wooden craft that can make a fine sight when under sail in the IJsselmeer, which you can view from atop the town's grassy ramparts.

## WHERE TO STAY AND EAT

### Die Port van Cleve

*Dijk 74;* ☎ *02280–12510; inexpensive.* This friendly, slightly old-fashioned, 20-room family hotel is cozy and pleasantly located in the old town facing the old port, an easy walk to the most interesting part of town and still not far from the station if you've come by train. Bedrooms are functional, with tile toilets/showers. Its old Dutch decor restaurant and terrace cafe are congregating places for visitors and town dwellers alike.

### Restaurant Die Drie Haringhe

*Dijk 28; noon–2 p.m., 5 p.m.–10 p.m., closed Tues.; for reservations* ☎ *02280–18610; moderate.* Offers fare from *lapin* (rabbit) to *lotte à la gember* (lotte fish with ginger) in an upstairs setting of old brick, wood beams, and candlelight on the white-light-strung old harbor, across from the illuminated Drommedaris, whose carillon chimes the quarter hours. There's a cafe in the **Drommedaris** evenings.

From Enkhuizen, enroute to the Afsluitdijk, to the south and north are some of the ★★**bulb fields** that increasingly have been planted in the northern part of North Holland province around *Anna Paulowna* if you're here in season (more or less mid-April–mid-May), keep your eyes open. You also might make a turn into tiny **Twisk**, a pretty village entirely under preservation. Among the noteworthy buildings are distinctive dome-shaped farmhouses, a 14th-century church, mansions with particularly elegant front doors and chimneys, and the requisite canal bridges. If you are tracking down all tempting touring options, consider that from **Den Helder**, home of the *Netherlands Royal Navy*, and **Het Torentje**, the museum that documents its history from 1813. ★**Texel** (pronounced TES sel), the first and largest of the **Waddenzee islands** off the northwest coast of Holland, is only a quick car ferry away (departing Den Helder every hour on the hour 6 a.m.–10 p.m.; ☎ 02220-69600). Texel is well known for its birds (especially spoonbills) and sheep (its lamb is advertised in many a Dutch restaurant), and there are some bulb growing fields in-season. Surrounded by sand dunes, Texel's several towns (the capital is Den Burg) are a popular place for summer and camping holidays. In the Texelstroom, at the leeward side of the island (opposite what used to be the mouth of the

Zuiderzee), the heavy-laden ships of the *Dutch East India Company* rode out rough seas three centuries ago.

## ★★ THE AFSLUITDIJK

The 30-kilometer/19 mile Afsluitdijk (*barrier dam*), which runs from Wieringen to the coast of Friesland and sealed the mouth of the **Zuiderzee** (South Sea), was built between 1927 and 1933 using traditional methods with contemporary technology. No hydraulic engineering project—not even the mammoth and amazing *Delta Plan* in Zeeland, whose planning began 20 years later and was 30 years in the actual execution—has ever appealed so much to the imagination of the Dutch people as the Afsluitdijk. It also impressed the *American Society of Civil Engineers*, though members took their time (50 years) to put the fact on a plaque there. Plans for damming the Zuiderzee and reclaiming large sections of the land within the enclosed area date back to 1667 and one Hendric Stevin. Many highly ambitious schemes surfaced during the 19th century, but it was the plan of Dr. Cornelis Lely that eventually met with approval from Parliament (finally pushed into action by burst dikes and floods that did great damage around the Zuiderzee in 1916). Dredged clay loam, sand, stone, straw and reeds were the ingredients that sealed off the sea five years after the dam was begun, the last gap closed in the presence of Queen Wilhelmina. The long blast of ships' horns sounded the sea's death toll midday on the 28th of May, 1932. Soon the dam was topped off with a two-lane road and cycle path. Locks allow ships to pass in and out to the Waddenzee and sluices discharge excess water. Today, it's a four-lane motorway that runs between North Holland and Friesland. At the point at which the last gap was filled, there is a lookout tower with visitor parking, cafe, a pedestrian crossover (and vehicle turnaround), and monuments. Be prepared for stiff breezes at this highly-exposed piece of man-made real estate.

## ★ HARLINGEN

**VVV** • *Voorstraat 34; Mon.–Fri. 9 a.m.–6 p.m., Sat. 9 a.m.–1 p.m. & 2–5 p.m.;* ☎ *05178-17222; pop. 16,000; 100 km./60 mi. from Amsterdam.*

Arriving on the mainland after crossing the Afsluitdijk, head north on Rt. N 31/A 31 for Harlingen, which, since the construction of that barrier, has the distinction of being Friesland's only seaport (the town is situated outside the dam). Since it is still a bustling seaport, it has a commercial look at first, with its piers and port, but head into the old center to ★★ **Noorderhaven**, and dispose of your car at one of the parking meters there. The entire Noorderhaven, several blocks of buildings with fine 16th–18th-century facades on both sides of this in-the-town harbor, is a preserved historic monument, with the 1736 Stadhuis at #86. One block away is Voorstraat, the town's attractive tree-lined main street, on which is located the ★**Hannemahuis** #56, *open April–Sept., inquire at VVV #34 for hours*. This is an imposing patrician house museum with the local treasure trove, among which will be found mementos from the whaling expeditions from the 16th century onwards (which originated from Harlingen), a silver collection (much of it the work of members of a guild founded here in

1648), and locally-produced tiles from the 16th-20th centuries. Makkum (see following) was only one of many Friesland tile factories in the 16th and 17th centuries, and Harlingen tiles were well known after 1600. Having disappeared long ago, the craft was revived in 1973 by the **Aardewerk en Tegelfabriek** (*Voorstraat 84*). The Hannemahuis also has a lovely garden. A walk atop Harlingen's several piers affords a fine view of the Frisian landscape, as well as across the Waddenzee with its shipping traffic.

## FRANEKER

**VVV** • *In the 17th- and 18th-century 't Coopmanhus Municipal Museum, Voorstraat 51; pop. 13,000.*

Heading inland from the sea only a short distance is **Franeker**, another historic town which from 1585 was the proud possessor of a university until Napoleon suppressed it in 1811. **Pieter Stuyvesant** (1592-1672), a Frisian, studied there *before his travels* to Nieuw Amsterdam (New York). The VVV in the **'t Coopmanhus Museum** (which has exhibits of local history and objects, but only a brief explanation sheet in English) can supply a town map and English-language leaflet on the highlights in the town. Certainly Franeker's (and one of Holland's) most unusual attractions is located in the old and intimate house of self-educated Eise Eisinga. Sitting across from the 1591 **Stadhuis** on Raadhuisplein, a sign on the facade reads: ★ **Planetarium** *(April–Sept., Tues.–Sat. 10 a.m.–12:30 p.m., 1:30–5 p.m., May–Aug., also Mon. 1–5 p.m.;* ☎ *05170-93070)*, and that is what Eisinga built in the ceiling of his living room here between 1774 and 1781. Once you know (from the excellent booklet in English on sale at the planetarium and tour given by the custodian) that Eisinga wrote a 600-page volume on mathematics at age 16 and was calculating eclipses at age 18, his accomplishment can be understood as the work of a genius. After an extraordinary planetary alignment in 1774 had led a Friesland minister to predict that two planets would collide and destroy the universe, Eisinga decided to build a planetarium that would give his contemporaries a better insight into the science, rather than superstition, of the sky. Keeping his everyday job as a wool comber, he spent seven years at night by candlelight with amazing accuracy and complexity, creating dials for day and year, movement of the planets, moon and sun, the date, all with cogwheel clockwork. Since its completion, it has been open to the public because Eisinga wanted to convince the public that the solar system would not collapse. Astonomers and engineers from around the world, even NASA officials, still come to see it. Eisinga's own star rose and set: from rising through Franeker ranks as officer of the civic guard and member of the town council, he became embroiled, against his will, in civil discord and could preserve his personal liberty only by going abroad, away from his planetarium and family. For eight years he remained in exile but finally returned to teach at Franeker's university. Eventually, Eisinga wound up with a State stipend for himself, and his son upon his death, as caretaker of the planetarium, which the government had bought.

From Franeker, ★ **Leeuwarden** *(VVV, Stationplein 1;* ☎ *058-132224)* is only 20 km./12 mi. As well as being an interesting historic and canaled destination and the provincial capital, it is a departure point for the far northern Friesland coast that is a natural recreational region dear to the hearts of many Dutch.

## WADLOPEN

Wadlopen is not a place name. Rather, it's an **activity** that provides an encounter with a unique ecosystem that summons up the senses: a sense of accomplishment, perhaps even a sense of survival; the sensations of sight, smell, hearing; and, particularly, a sense of touch, since while wadlopen one's skin comes into contact with much mud!

Wadlopen is the crossing on foot of the tidal mud flats between the coast of northern Friesland and the near offshore Frisian Islands in the Waddenzee (sea). When the daylight tide is out—it recedes 10 to 15 miles—the flats become feeding and resting places for a variety of wildlife, especially birds, and a recreational area for those whose purpose is to complete a "walk" to an island before the tide comes in. For some, wad walking is a nature hike through a vastly different terrain, the first impression of which can be of an eerie no-man's landscape that is, literally, the bottom of the sea. The mud flats can be remarkably colorful when the sun comes out, though fog can roll in swiftly, and be decidedly disorienting. For all participants, wadlopen is a sporting feat, a physically consuming, strength-testing—not to mention slippery—experience making progress through knee-high mud. The only equipment requirements are woolen knee socks underneath laced high top sneakers; the vacuum-like mud would suck off any other footgear. The physical demands of wad walking are reinforced by a constant competition with time, since the turning tide waits for no man or woman who can't keep up the pace necessary to gain non-tidal shoreland before the waters cover the sea bed once more.

Because of its potential treacherousness in facing the elements, wad walking should be undertaken only under the direction of experienced guides, all of whom speak English, who share their extensive knowledge of the environment. The very reasonably priced guided walks are scheduled from May–September from the mainland to Schiermonnikoog, Ameland, and Engelsmanplaat islands; return is by boat. Participants should be in good physical shape; walks are graded from beginner to advanced and last from 2.5 to 4 hours. For information contact **Wadloopcentrum** *(Pieterburen, Postbus 1, 9968 ZG Pieterburen, Friesland, The Nederlands;* ☎ *05952-8300).*

## WHERE TO STAY

**Oranje Hotel** ★★★★★
*Stationsweg 4; Leeuwarden;* ☎ *058-126241, FAX 058-121441; moderate.* The hotel, the only five-star property in Friesland, was practically rebuilt for its reopening in 1986, with 78 thoroughly modern guest and bright, pleasant public rooms. The lobby lounge/bar is the community congregation point, and its **L'Orangerie** restaurant (*dinner*

*only; moderate/expensive*) has both *prix-fixe* menus and *à la carte* choices. The **Taverne** offers more casual meals. The hotel is within sight, but out of sound of the station, and a short walk from the historic center.

## ★★ MAKKUM

**VVV** • *1698 Waaggebouw at Pruikmakershoek 2;* ☎ *05158-1422; pop. of greater area 3,500.*

With a sharp turn south at the end of the Afsluitdijk, you're almost immediately in Makkum. A delightful former Zuiderzee fishing village, Makkum now has mostly pleasure craft in its harbor. Makkum made its name in ceramics because of the particular quality of the sea clay found here (see "The Dutch Cultural Legacy: Decorative Arts and Traditional Crafts"). Tichelaar's Koninklijke Makkumer Aardewerk en Tegelfabriek or, more simply, ★★★ **Royal Makkum** *(Turfmarkt 57; Mon.–Fri. 9 a.m.–5:30 p.m., Sat. until 4 p.m.; guided tours Mon.–Thurs. 10–11:30 a.m. and 1–4 p.m., Fri. until 3 p.m.; salesrooms open Mon.–Fri. 9 a.m.–5:30 p.m., Sat. 9 a.m.–4 p.m.;* ☎ *05158-1341)* is a ten-generational ceramic factory that was awarded use of the title "Royal" in 1960. Guided tours (approx. a half-hour long) of the factory's biscuit-fired and hand-painted process are given Mon.- Thurs., 10 a.m.–4 p.m., and on Fri. until 3 p.m. Makkum ware comes in several multicolored patterns, without emphasis on the blue and white of Delftware. In addition to many practical and ornamental items, a wide variety of historic-patterned and modern tiles are produced. The shops at the factory and in the center *(Het Makkumer Tegelhuis, Markt 19)* charge the same substantial prices for their first quality ware that you'll find in Amsterdam or The Hague, but do ask about the "seconds" for sale. The VVV, which distributes a small map of the town, is located in what is the local museum, worth a visit if you have time after first taking an explorative turn around the pretty canaled- corners of this atmospheric town.

## ★ WORKUM

**VVV** • *1650 Waag at Merk 4;* ☎ *05151-1300; pop. of greater area 4,500.*

A seaport in the 15th century, Workum is centered around an attractive cobbled main square (the **Merk**) on which stands the Stadhuis (15–18th century), and the **Waag**, which is decorated with grotesque statuary. Leaving the Merk via the Begine drawbridge, you'll come to the Doltewal, a canal lined with pleasure craft at the back of the village. **De Gulden Leeuw** is a pleasant terrace cafe at Merk 2.

## ★★ HINDELOOPEN

**VVV** • *1619 Oostertoren at the Haven;* ☎ *05142-2550; pop. 900.*

This exceptionally charming village is worth allowing plenty of time in which to wander and wonder. Once occupied by captains who sailed the seven seas from its small harbor, and formerly famed for the decorative painted wooden furniture that carried the town's name, Hindeloopen claims neither distinction today. Nevertheless, the legacies of both activities—sea commanders' homes and *likhuzen* (small houses behind the captains' main homes used by wives and children during the summer in the absence of the masters, a feature unique to the village), and ateliers, where smaller items painted in the historic Hindeloopen style are crafted and sold, will hold your attention. There's one essential stop, the ★★**Hidde Nijland** museum (*Dijkweg 1; March–Oct, Mon.–Sat., 10 a.m.–5 p.m., Sun. and holidays, 1:30–5 p.m.* ☎ *05142-1420*) in the former *Stadhuis* (begun in 1683). Here you'll see what you can't buy anymore: the Scandinavian/Oriental-influenced genuine Hindeloopen painted furniture. The rooms reveal a variety of furniture, wall panelling, and utensils painted in both traditional and mourning colors. Visit the VVV for a leaflet in English with map and town sights; it will indicate the 18th-century mansion that now has a cafe in a canalside garden. Parking is outside the village, either at the Hidde Nijland museum, from which you can walk into town "by the back door," or at the other end of town just before the Haven; blue "**P**" signs are posted.

## STAVOREN

**VVV** • *Voorstraat 80;* ☎ *05149-1616; pop. 1,000.*

Lying on the projecting southwest point of Friesland, Stavoren isn't on the way to anywhere, except the passenger (only) ferry to Enkhuizen. Its harbor is a stopover point for summer sailors. Stavoren is pleasant but unexceptional; however, since hotels are limited in southwest Friesland, it's worth mentioning the one here.

## *WHERE TO STAY*

**De Vrouw van Stavoren**                          ★★

*Havenweg 1, 8715 EM;* ☎ *05149-1202, FAX 05149-1205; moderate.*
This place has a dozen basic tidy rooms, some with private toilets and showers. There's a pleasant restaurant inside, and dining alfresco on the rear patio. The name of the hotel refers to a statue across from it of the "Vrouwe (woman) of Stavoren," who looks out to the offshore reed-grown sandbank known as the **Vrouwezand.** As the popular local story goes, a rich merchant's wife asked a ship captain to bring back from his distant destination the most precious cargo he could find. The captain returned with a hull full of wheat from Danzig (Poland), a commodity which made the Netherlands very wealthy in the 16th and 17th century. However, such mundane merchandise was obviously not what the woman had hoped for; in a fury, she ordered the ship's contents tipped into the Zuiderzee at the Stavoren harbor mouth. It is said that the wheat, when it germinated, caused the formation of the sandbank that eventually ruined Stavoren's harbor.

## ★★ SLOTEN

**VVV** • *Dubbelstgraat 125;* ☎ *05143-583; pop. 600.*

This is the smallest of the Friesland's 11 towns, a fact which gives its attributes—a moat, dike (on which is a high-water warning cannon), canal through the cobbled center of town (open to residents' cars only), old sluice gates, and 17th- and 18th-century facades and step-gabled houses—all the more appeal. The Stadhuis dates from 1757 and, under its Fries name **Stedhus Sleat,** contains a museum *(Heerenwal 48; Easter–Sept.; Tues.–Fri. 10 a.m.–noon, 2–5 p.m., Sat. and Sun. 2–5 p.m.),* which only shows that no place is too small to have one.

## ★★ GIETHOORN

**VVV** • *Beulakerweg a/b ark;* ☎ *05216-1248; pop. 2500.*

Known for its tree-lined canals—there are no roads, only foot/bicycle paths along the canals, and arched bridges over them—on which most everything in the many-islanded village must be transported in flat-bottom boats, tiny rural Giethoorn is without doubt picturesque. The first inhabitants in the mid-13th century named the place *Geytenhorn* for the masses of wild goat horns they found, probably the result of the animals' drowning deaths in earlier floods. The village acquired its characteristic appearance from haphazard peat digging. Earlier residents cut peat turfs in the most accessible places, making hollows that filled with rain, forming ponds and lakes—and required further ditches and canals to be dug to transport the peat. The area became a series of islands, with short, steeply arched footbridges built to connect them, yet allow for boats to pass beneath them. In the fields on the fringes of Giethoorn, reeds are grown for thatch (cut in spring), which is seen on many a local roof, and sold for that purpose all over Holland. Open, covered, motorized, manual, group tour or self-hire "punters" are prominent in Giethoorn, which can get very crowded (especially on summer weekends), reducing its otherwise quite considerable charm. One way to avoid the crowds is to stay overnight on the fringe of the village and walk to it in the evening or early morning. There are car parks outside the village, which is accessible only by foot or boat. Various residents tout home-exhibits as museums, though none is necessary to see, as the grassy green and gardened village houses are artful and interesting enough. A stop at one of the terrace cafes along the paved, footpathed, main canal is as good a way as any to set the scene in your mind.

### *WHERE TO STAY*

**Hotel-Pension De Jonge**                                      ★

*Beulakerweg 30, 8355 AH;* ☎ *05216-1360; inexpensive.* This basic but clean and modern 20-bed property has central heating, some rooms with private facilities, and a restaurant (breakfast, included) that at lunch and dinner specializes in *pannekoeken* (Dutch pancakes). No elevator, two floors.

## ★★ BLOKZIJL

**VVV** • *Kerkstraat 12; June 1–September 1, Monday–Saturday, 9 a.m.–6 p.m.;* ☎ *05272-414 or 286.*

Once directly on the coast but now land-bound as part of the *Noordoostpolder* (northeast polder), Blokzijl, like so many former Zuiderzee towns, today has mostly pleasure craft in its harbor, which by a system of canals remains connected to the recreational waters of the IJsselmeer. Blokzijl's cobbled alleyways, steepled church, and harbor crescent rimmed by 17th-century merchant houses topped with typical step, neck, or bell gables, tell a tale of one-time prosperous trading days. Nearby ★ **Vollenhove** is another former Zuiderzee town which offers 17th-century appeal around its port.

## WHERE TO STAY

### Hotel Kaatje bij de Sluis ★★★★

*Zuiderstraat 1;* ☎ *05272-1833, FAX 05272-1835; hotel is closed Mon. and Tues. nights, month of Feb.; expensive.* Located beside the town's busy lock (Room 2 looks straight out at it), this light-hearted, light-colored, 8-room, three-story, townhouse-hotel understandably requires reservations (at least a month in advance in summer). Rooms, decorated in pastels and white, with minibar, terry robes, hair dryers, in-room coffee makers, old map prints, and appealing gray and pink tile in the bath and toilet, can be better than a home-away-from-home. Breakfast (included) is served in the garden terrace, shaded by old trees, or glass-enclosed room overlooking the garden and sluice (where coffee and drinks are available during the day). Upon checking in, hotel guests invariably make reservations for a meal at the hotel's renown restaurant—*see below.*

## WHERE TO EAT

### Kaatje bij de Sluis
*Brouwerstraat 20; noon–2:30 p.m., 6–10 p.m., closed for lunch Sat., closed Mon. and Tues. and month of Feb.; for restaurant* ☎ *05272-1833, FAX 05272-1836; expensive.* Just across the drawbridge (which goes up and stops traffic on a regular basis) from the hotel is its restaurant, possibly the better known of the two establishments. The award-winning cuisine is served in a romantic, but spirited setting appropriate for the imaginative dishes from soup to sweets: *Soupe de courgettes aux Escalopes de Poissons* (zuchini soup with assorted fish), *Tarte a l'Ananas et Sorbet au Citron* (pineapple tart and lemon sherbert).

## STAPHORST

This inland town, a bit off the beaten track, has a reputation for traditional costumes and old-time religion in strict Protestant Dutch Reform style. The pattern of Dutch life represented in this strictest of Calvinist farming communities is a significant part of the country's heritage, but the elements can be experienced elsewhere under easier circumstances. The people in Staphorst don't want you taking pictures of them in costume (women and children, and some males regularly wear traditional attire) on any day of the week, and don't even want you in town on the Sabbath Sunday, when they march to church and back home on several occasions—and when they might do physical damage to your camera. Staphorst's lengthy main street is lined with large old thatched farmhouses (which once served for both owners and their animals) set amid modern store fronts and milk factories. If you're looking for coziness to accompany the quaintness of the lifestyle, this isn't the place to look, and your curiosity isn't appreciated. But it will undoubtedly be fed from hearing stories of Staphorst behavior, such as the public shaming of adulterous members of the community by parading the hand-bound couple through town in a manure cart while people lining the street pelt them with dung. And, there's the "open bedroom window" policy for suitors of eligible daughters, who can't get married in the Reformed Association Church in Staphorst until they are pregnant. In this closed community, where marriage with outsiders is forbidden, women accept the circumstances as expressed in local farming paraphrase: "No farmer can buy a cow until he is sure of the calf." There's a farming museum **Museumboerderij** *(Gemeenteweg 67; April 1–Nov. 1, 10 a.m.–7 p.m., Mon.–Sat.;* ☎ *05225-2526)* that shows the typical Staphorst style of decor, costumes and the local weaving of material for them, a *klompen* or clog maker, and has a garden.

## URK

**VVV** • *in Museum "Het Oude Raadhuis," Wijk 2, April 1–Sept. 30, Mon.– Fri., 10 a.m.–5 p.m., Sat. 10 a.m.–1 p.m.; Feb., Mar.–Oct., Mon.–Fri. 10 a.m.–1 p.m.; closed Nov.–Jan.;* ☎ *05277-4040; pop. 12,000.*

Since the reclamation of the northeast polder in the IJsselmeer, the greater part of Urk, once an island in the Zuiderzee, has been enclosed by the new land and become land-bound. The sealing off of the Zuiderzee did not bring about the decline of Urk that had been predicted. Determined to continue with sea fishing, Urk fishermen expanded their field of activity (their catch now comes from as far afield as the Danish and Spanish coasts) by building one of the largest and most modern fleets in the world, and using the sluices in the Afsluitdijk for access to the North Sea. Two generations ago fishing was a job learned at sea, but nowadays no Urk fisherman goes to sea without thorough training at the local nautical college. Urk also developed an important fish auction, and is flourishing with fish processing factories. A busy harbor with more than 150 "beam-trawler" fishing vessels gives Urk an air of modernity about its quays, though visitors can enjoy the contrast of seeing an old man in his baggy black ★**traditional costume** sharing the setting. In the small residential streets of this architecturally varied town, the more brightly colored dress of the old women (the only ones who regularly wear the costume these days) may be seen as they chat in the front gardens of their homes; church on Sunday brings out the greatest number of costumes.

For some time in the 17th and 18th century, the island of Urk belonged to the city of Amsterdam, which had bought it in order to maintain its important Zuiderzee coastal navigational marks (such as the first light beacon in 1617), in order to avoid the treacherous "Shallow of Enkhuizen" sandbank. Near the newer present lighthouse landmark (beyond which is a long line of modern "turbine" windmills) is the **Kerkje aan de Zee** (little church on the sea), inside which a plaque lists all the ministers who have served there since 1629. Nearby, also sharing the point of land that overlooks today's IJsselmeer, is Urk's ★**Vissersmonument,** a statue of a wind-blown woman in Urk costume looking out to what still appears to be open sea. Just down the road in **Het Oude Raadhuis** is the town museum showing Urk's long history with the Zuiderzee. Quite naturally, fish is the specialty at most Urk restaurants. A cozy local favorite, with lace at the curtains indoors and an outside terrace with IJsselmeer views, is **De Kaap** *(Wijk 1, daily lunch to 10 p.m.,* ☎ *05277-1509, inexpensive)*, with its well-known "all you can eat" fish plates. A passenger ferry (no cars, but bicycles allowed) sails between Urk and Enkhuizen several times daily in season *(early May-early Sept. daily except Sun.; 1.5 hours one-way;* ☎ *05277-3407)*.

## ★ KAMPEN

*VVV Oudestraat 85;* ☎ *05202-13500.* **Kampen** is a former Hanseatic town with a well-preserved town center that was begun in the 13th century. Among the sights to seek out is the Stadhuis with its remarkable ★ ★ **Magistrates Hall** dating from the 16th century (English booklet), and displaying a complete set of full-length portraits of members of the royal Dutch *House of Orange* from Willem the Silent. St. Nicolaaskerk dates from c. 1500 in its present shape and size, and has a famous organ from 1742, on which summer concerts are held *(Sat. in July and Aug. at 3 p.m.)*.

## ★ ZWOLLE

*VVV Grote Kerkplein 14;* ☎ *038-213900.* **Zwolle** also is an old Hanse town, whose golden age was the 15th century. It has appealing remnants of two sets of fortification walls, bastions, towers, and old town gates. In 1980, Zwolle was instrumental in renewing the *Hanseatic League* association (some 70 northern European towns were trading partner members in the period from the 1200s to 1669) and members now meet regularly in those cities on a rotating basis.

### WHERE TO STAY

**Grand Hotel Wientjes**                                ★ ★ ★ ★
*Stationsweg 7;* ☎ *038-254254, FAX 038-254260; moderate.* This 50-room, third-generation, family-owned and managed hotel has been a landmark on the regional scene since its opening in 1929 in a former burgomaster's residence. Guest rooms are comfortable and the young staff friendly and service-minded. The Grand Wientjes' kitchen is also well-regarded.

## ★ ELBURG

**VVV** • *Jufferenstraat 9;* ☎ *05250-1520; pop. 750 inside the moat.*

Elburg is a monument in itself, one of the best-preserved towns in Holland. Its appearance is in large part from the 16th century, but there are many touches from the 14th, when Elburg was one of the earliest members of the **Hanseatic League**. At the end of the 14th century, Elberg moved inland, behind walls, and its unique rectangular town design was laid out by Arent thoe Boecop, steward of the duke of Gelders. You can enjoy the original moat around the old center by walking atop the grassy and wooded ★★**ramparts** that rim most of the town; a section of old city wall still has houses built into it. If you can manage the climb up the ★**St. Nicolas** church tower (156 steps), you'll be rewarded with a remarkable view down on this picture-tempting compact, intact town, in good weather, a 20-mile vista across the flat, flat land of neighboring Flevoland. The church has carillon concerts on Saturdays from 3-4 p.m., and the Elburg Town Choir Boys sing there Wednesdays in July and Aug. from 11 a.m.–1:45 p.m. The VVV has a *Do-It Yourself Guided Tour of Elburg* booklet in English and a map. Across the street from the VVV is the 15th-century ★**St. Agnes Convent**, housing Elburg's interesting local museum. The heart of the town is the **Vismarkt** (concert bands Wed. evenings in summer), with terrace cafes and restaurants spread out at every corner.

## WHERE TO STAY

### Het Smeede Hotel                                          ★★

*Smedestraat 5;* ☎ *05250-3877; inexpensive.* Located in a well-restored old house in the heart of historic Elburg, the spotlessly clean, 14 crisp-yet-cozy bedrooms are walk-up (help with the luggage if needed), with private facilities, telephone, writing table, and TV. There is no lobby to speak of in this friendly, family-owned-and-operated hotel; breakfast only (included) is served on the ground floor.

## HARDERWIJK

**VVV** • *Havendam 58;* ☎ *03410-26666.*

★**The Veluws Museum** in this former Hanseatic town on the Zuiderzee *(Donkerstraat 4; May–Sept., Mon.–Fri., 10 a.m.–5 p.m., Sat. 1-4 p.m., closed Sun., and Sat. during rest of year;* ☎ *03410-14468),* located in an 18th-century merchant's house, offers a 12-minute slide show in English that presents a history of Harderwijk. The ★**Markt**, the former fish market, is an attractive cobbled rectangle, tree-shaded and surrounded by fine facades, in the soul of the old center of the town; you'll find a quiet terrace cafe or two. Whether or not you stop in Harderwijk, take the **N302** from it across the *Veluwe meer* (the very edge of the old Zuiderzee) to the new Dutch polder province of Flevoland.

## FLEVOLAND

**VVV** • *Lelystad, Agorahof 4;* ☎ *03200-43444; 50 km./30 mi. from Amsterdam.*

Flevoland province was established on January 1, 1986, its polders (reclaimed land) adding more than 238,000 acres to the small country's total. The "new" area consists of the eastern section ("dried" between 1950–1957) and the southern (1959–1968). The entire **Zuiderzee Project** has produced five polders and 616,730 acres since 1930. Today, Flevoland sometimes is spoken of as the granary of western Europe for its corn fields that grow golden in summer. Other Flevoland crops of particular importance are oilseed rape (which blankets the fields in brilliant yellow in May), pearl onions (which you can smell in the air), sugar beets, potatoes, and flower bulbs (there's a Flevoland bulb-field route). Flevoland's capital

**Lelystad** is named for Cornelius Lely (1854–1929), who developed the plan for the Zuiderzee Project. His original objectives (developed in the 19th century) were finally adopted and set out in the *Zuiderzee Act of 1918*: To reduce the length of coastline, thereby reducing the risk of flooding; to improve water management, including the creation of a fresh-water basin; to improve the lines of communication (roads), and to increase the area of agricultural land. The first three of these goals were met in large measure upon the completion of the **Afsluitdijk** in 1932. The agricultural needs could be met only upon the production of polderland. The place to head for an appreciation of the technology that went into making this polder province lies just outside Lelystad, ★★ **Informatiecentrum Nieuw Land** (*signposted: Oostvaardersdijk 1–13, year-round Mon.–Fri. 10 a.m.–5 p.m., from April–Oct. also Sat. and Sun 11:30 a.m.–5 p.m.;* ☎ *03200- 60799; full exhibit information in English*).

Begin your visit by watching the excellent slide show (English and other language versions) with background on the formation and control of the Zuiderzee and the polderland. The center also has lots of English language literature; for those who want the whole story, ask for the publication *Planning and Creation of an Environment*. Exhibits tell a highly interesting story about the creation of polderland in Holland from the 13th to the 20th century and detail the actual "drying" process of a Dutch polder. As an underwater dike is built, electric and diesel pumping stations work round the clock to drain the area. The main waterways planned for the finished polder are dredged while the polder is still submerged; smaller canals and dividing ditches are dug after the polder has been drained. Immediately following drainage, the swampy soil is sown by airplane with reed seed; reed serves to break up and ripen the soil for cultivation while also preventing the growth of weeds. Following the reclamation phase, agricultural engineers usually grow field crops on the new soil for about five years, a transition period needed for the soil to mature and become suitable for later use. Rapeseed usually is the first crop sown because its deep roots promote soil aeration. Later crops may be flax, grass, peas, and dwarf beans. After the maturation period, when the land is destined for farming and fruit-growing, it is let to private individuals for those purposes on a short or perpetual lease (actual ownership of the land is retained by the Dutch government). Large expanses of woods also have been planted in Flevoland.

The uses to which the new polderland have been put were carefully considered. Agriculture was the primary purpose to which the earlier North-East polder, created between 1937–1942, was put. This also was the case with East Flevoland, which was dry by 1957, although towns, too, were planned. The first inhabitants of Lelystad, pioneers who had to build a whole community from scratch, picked up the keys to their brand new homes in September 1967. The very high birth rate and resulting population crunch in Holland in the 1960s led to the South Flevoland polder (dry by 1968) being planned for more heavy urbanization. By 1975, the dike road between Enkhuizen and Lelystad was completed. It was meant to serve not only as a means of transportation across the Ijsselmeer, but as part of the drainage process for the last scheduled element of Lely's original plan, the **Maarkerwaard** polder. The Dutch, however, began raising their voices over the need for preserving open areas for water recreation (especially their beloved sailing). The demands, accompanied by a decline in the 1980s of Holland's birth rate and an increase in intensive agriculture production elsewhere in Holland (not to mention agricultural surpluses mounting throughout the European Community), have put plans for draining Markerwaard on hold for the time being.

Adjacent to the Informatiecentrum Nieuw Land, the VOC-ship **Batavia** *(Oostvaardersdijk 1- 9; boatyard open daily 10 a.m.–5 p.m., closed Dec. 25; Tel: 03200-61409)*, an exact replica of one of the proud merchant craft owned by the Dutch East India Company in the 17th century, is in the process of being built.

## ★ NAARDEN

**VVV** • *Adr. Dortsmanplein 1b;* ☎ *02159-42836; pop. 16,000.*

When you've had your fill of polders, head southwest for Amsterdam. Past the polder city complex of Almere, back on the "mainland," are two more chances for a look at old Zuiderzee villages. First, head for **Naarden**, a fortress town dating from 1350. Its distinctive ★ six-pointed star bastion, ramparts, and double-moated fortifications took shape when the Dutch rebuilt the town after the troops of Louis XIV, who had captured it in 1672, were forced out in 1673 by Willem III. A visit to the ★ **Vesting museum** *(Turfpoortbastion; Easter–Oct., Mon.–Fri., 10 a.m.–4:30 p.m., Sat. & Sun., noon–5 p.m.)* takes you into the casements, which display dioramas, old prints, and cannon, and offer an opportunity to mount the grassy ramparts for a view. (There's fine dining under the management of one of the famous Dutch Fagel family restauranteurs in the gunworks of the fort.)

An even better view of the fortification pattern comes from atop the ★ tower of the **Grote Kerk** *(April 30–Sept. 30, Sat.–Thurs., on the hour from 1–4 p.m.)*. The late Gothic Grote Kerk (essentially 15th century) is worth seeing inside for its 20 Old and New Testament ceiling panels, painted between 1510 and 1518. In 1572 the Spaniards massacred the entire population of Naarden, ransacked the city, and partly burned it down, but spared the church. Noted for its acoustics, it is the site of a renowned annual performance of **J.S. Bach's** *St. Mathew's Passion* on Good Friday. Ask the VVV about weekly evening organ concerts in summer. The VVV has several brochures with information in English, including the self-guiding *Naarden Gabletour.* A bus from the nearest railway station serves Naarden.

## ★ MUIDEN

**VVV** • *Kazernestraat 10;* ☎ *02942-4754; pop. 7,000.*

Also a former fortress town on the Zuiderzee, with locks and a harbor now filled with private pleasure craft. Muiden is best known for its romantic-looking castle ★ ★ **Muiderslot** *(Herengracht 1; April 1–Sept. 30, Mon.-Fri., 10 a.m.–5 p.m., Sun. 1–5 p.m., Oct. 1–Mar. 31 until 4 p.m., 1-hour guided* *tours only, depart several times an hour, last tour an hour before closing).* Built by Count Floris V in the 13th century, it is decorated with a valuable collection of furniture and paintings from the 17th century, the period when the great Dutch poet and historian **Pieter Corneliszoon Hooft** lived here as sheriff of Muiden and castellan of Muiderslot. P.C. Hooft gathered about him here a group of leading artistic figures and scholars (including **Grotius**, the poet **Vondel**, and **Constantijn Huygens**) which became known as the Muiden Circle. Guided tours (which require climbing a fairly steep flight of hollowed brick stairs at the beginning but otherwise is easy) are pleasantly anecdotal and unrushed. There's an herbal garden in front of the castle. Muiden is close enough to Amsterdam (public transportation available), and popular enough with Dutch from even further afield, for its cafes and pubs to be busy; on warm nights, terrace tables are spread out along the little harbor, in sight of Muiderslot.

## WHERE TO EAT

**Eethuys-Cafe Graaf Floris V van Muiden** *(Herengracht 72; 11 a.m.–10 p.m.; till midnight for drinks;* ☎ *02942-1296; inexpensive),* an atmospheric old brown cafe and a short walk form Muiderslot, makes a good stop for salads, soups, fish and tasty snacks.

# CENTRAL HOLLAND

## AN INTRODUCTION

One of the most noticeable characteristics of the countryside in the central part of Holland is that east of Utrecht most of the land lies above sea level. The landscape has large stands of primeval forest that haven't undergone the scourge of centuries of saltwater floods. Thousands of acres of trees adorn Apeldoorn's **Royal Park** and the **National Park De Hoge Veluwe**, both of which fill much of the triangle formed by three of the principal cities in the center of Holland: **Arnhem**, **Apeldoorn** and **Amersfoort**. In addition to old trees, the landscape in this region is lightly rolling, rather than water-surface flat as in the west of the country.

Within the Netherlands, province names tend to be used to define districts, which is not particularly helpful for the unfamiliar traveler. In any case, in the center of the country the most outstanding attractions cut across provincial boundaries, although many lie within the largest and largely rural Dutch province of **Gelderland**. The city of **Utrecht** has a central location in the country, but since it is also a component of *Randstad Holland*, it has been included in that section. Also, for the purpose of travel logistics, some smaller places often considered "central" Holland are covered in this book in the "Old Zuiderzee Village-New Polderland Province" chapter. Center of Holland sights lying *bezuiden de Moerdijk* ("below the rivers") have been included in the **Southern Holland** section under "North

Brabant province." (The index at the back of the book is a quick reference.)

# ARNHEM, APELDOORN AND AMERSFOORT

## GUIDELINES FOR ARNHEM, APELDOORN AND AMERSFOORT

### SIGHTS

Several of the most interesting and important museums in the country are situated in central Holland, in or near the towns of Arnhem, Apeldoorn, and Amersfoort, which is how they are arranged here. The rich fruit orchards of the **Betuwe** ("good land") and the country's largest national park, **De Hoge Veluwe** ("bad land"), with its drifting sand dunes, heathland (in bloom late August through September), and woods, add another scenic dimension.

### GETTING AROUND

The three main cities are served by train. From the rail station in each there are local buses that serve most of the other attractions, towns, and villages covered. However, it must be mentioned that depending upon public transportation, reliable though it is in Holland,  will slow you down. A car is recommended if you want to cover more than one of the major sites, included here, in one day. Taxis, while practical within Arnhem from the station, or for Het Loo from the Apeldoorn station, will be expensive to the **Kroller-Muller Museum** because of its rural location. Bicycle hire is possible at the city train stations, though again here an assessment of time and distance will need to be made. If you take a public bus (from Arnhem station), check with VVV for season and specific times: usually there is a direct bus to the museum July-September, year-round public bus to Otterlo or Hoenderloo (3.4 and 4.0 km./approximately 2 mi., respectively, to Visitor Center), from which bicycle rental and taxis are available. At the **Visitor Center** (*Bezoekerscentrum*) in the center of  the national park **De Hoge Veluwe**, one of the famous little fleet of 400 "white bikes" (one speed, no basket or provision for parcels, no time limit) is available to you for free (a service to cut down on car traffic in the national park) on a first-come basis; weekends can be busy, but there's also back-up paid bicycle hire on the premises. The **Kroller-Muller Museum** is an easy and enjoyable bike ride from the park Visitor Center, and there are plenty of paved cycle routes of different duration in De Hoge Veluwe.

## SHOPPING

The three cities in this chapter are the main shopping centers in the region. **Het Loo** palace has an excellent gift shop; the museum shop at the **Kroller-Muller** has a wide selection of art books, prints, and cards; there's a gift shop at the Arnhem **Openluchtmuseum**.

## ENTERTAINMENT AND EVENTS

Check with VVV about the Amersfoort carillon concerts in the **Onze Lieve Vrouwetoren** and **Belgian Monument** and the organ concerts in the **1534 St. Joriskerk**. In **Spakenburg**, traditional costume and crafts fairs take place on the last two Wednesdays in July and the first two in August.

## WHERE TO STAY

With the assumption that many of you will be traveling by car in this region, several country castles and inns have been included. With the exception of the **Keizerskroon** across from Het Loo in Apeldoorn, country accommodations in the area will prove more interesting than their in-town counterparts.

## WHERE TO EAT

Many museums discussed in this chapter have a cafe and/or restaurant (as is often the case, especially in museums outside of cities, throughout Holland). There are some fine country restaurants in the region, located in settings from sophisticated rustic to castles.

## ARRIVING

Holland's public transportation and information coordination will impress you anew. At **Arnhem** (pop. 130,000), local and regional buses and the VVV (*Stationplein 45,* ☎ *085-420330*) are located at the train station, as is true in **Amersfoort** (*VVV Stationplein 27,* ☎ *033-635151, pop. 100,000*) and **Apeldoorn** (*VVV Stationplein 6,* ☎ *055-788421, pop. 144,000*).

## IN THE AREA

Many visitors come via Arnhem to visit the exceptional **Kroller-Muller Museum** (with its 278 Van Goghs and other great 19th-and 20th-century paintings and sculpture) set in the Dutch national park **De Hoge Veluwe**. **Oosterbeck** has an **Airborne Museum** about the Market-Garden operation of September 1944. The more geographically spread-out smaller attractions in the center of the country have been included under the most appropriate of the three cities.

## TRAVEL TIPS

Remember that throughout Holland VVVs in major towns and cities (identified with an "*i*" sign) can supply you with quite detailed and up-to-date information about museum hours and public transportation in other regions. That way you can plan a day trip ahead of time with the help of your "home base" VVV; having the details about public transportation/opening hours, etc. for your destination beforehand will result in more time to enjoy what you came to see and do.

# ARNHEM

Even though the soaring-towered 15th-century ★**Grote Kerk**, whose 230-foot tower (with 54-bell carillon, concerts 10 a.m. Friday), restored after its destruction in 1944, includes flying buttresses embellished with modern gargoyles resembling Mickey Mouse, Donald Duck, and the local pastor (whose dispute with the stonecutter inspired this "tribute") makes Arnhem infamous; despite its lovely parks, fountains, and squares, such as the attractive ★**Korenmarkt**, a lively scene of cafes and students whenever the sun shines, and even though vistas over the Rhine River beckon, Arnhem is most closely associated with the eight-day September 1944 battle that bears its name.

"In Britain, the epic fight of the 1st Airborne Division at Arnhem tends to be thought of as a separate action. In fact it was only a part of a much larger operation spread over more than 50 miles and involving far larger forces than a single division. It was, moreover, Hitler's last victory and one he should never have been given the chance to win. It was the end-product of inter-allied rivalries and, above all, of the arrogance and vanity of the newly promoted Field Marshal Montgomery." This is how Michael Glover opens his chapter on Arnhem and Operation Market-Garden in his book *A New Guide to the Battlefields of Northern France and the Low Countries* (see "Bibliography" "Random Readings").

Although it saw small successes, Operation Market-Garden was largely doomed to failure from the start; that failure came with the battle of Arnhem. From the Belgium border, the advance had to take place along a single main road that ran for most of the distance on a causeway with no possibility of vehicles moving off it, essentially creating a front of one tank. Market-Garden was envisioned by Allied planners as a final push over German troops that were seen as irredeemably broken for a swift capture of the German Ruhr, due east, and final victory in the war. The Market aspect of the two-part operation (drawn up separately in Belgium and England) was the dropping of the Airborne Corps to advance over the Arnhem bridge, while the advance was the Garden. It was understood from the start that only total success would serve the purpose, a point that emphasized the risky nature of the project, risky even before allowing for such events as the breakdown of radio communication (which among other things led to the landing of a large supply drop straight into the hands of the Nazis) and bad weather that delayed the dropping of the Polish Parachute Brigade. Two days before it was set to be implemented, General Eisenhower, originally a supporter of Market-Garden, was so convinced that it had become inoperative that he sent his chief of staff Lieutenant General Bedell Smith to dissuade Montgomery from undertaking it. Having been accused of being overcautious in the Normandy campaign, Montgomery was out to demonstrate that he could take risks and was "the greatest general in the world." Comments Michael Glover, "Fifteen thousand allied casualties was a high price to pay to prove that he was wrong." Glover continues, "The courage and endurance of everyone engaged—British, American, Polish, German and, in particular, the members of the Dutch Resistance—should not blind anyone to the fact that Market-Garden was a disastrous failure. What is worse is that it was a predictable failure."

In the center of Arnhem, only a short distance from Arnhem's 15th-century Stadhuis and Grote Kerk, is **Airborne Plein**, a sunken garden traffic rotary with some ruins from the city bearing the date 17 September 1944, that leads into Nijmeegseweg (the road south to Nijmegen), which shortly crosses the Rhine River over "the bridge too far." The in-town end of the now rebuilt and renamed **John Frost Bridge** (also still known as the **Rijnbrug**) was taken and defended gallantly for three days and four nights by the 2nd Battalion of the 1st Parachute Brigade, but in the end for nought.

### Nederlands Openluchtmuseum                             ★★★

*Netherlands Open-Air Museum; Schelmseweg 89, at northern edge of Arnhem, off the A12/E35 road, or north from the Willemsplein by Arnhem train station on Zijpendaalseweg on bus #3; daily Apr.–Oct. 9:30 a.m.–5 p.m., Sat. from 10 a.m., Sun. from 11 a.m.;* ☎ *085-576111.* Admired as one of the world's best open-air museums, this Dutch edition was founded in 1912 with a half-dozen houses. Since then, it has grown to 75 buildings, dismantled brick by brick, stone by stone, or peat turf by turf in their original locations throughout the country and reassembled with the same care at the museum, representing all walks of ordinary life as practiced in the not-so-distant past. There are no guided tours, which is just as well since you want to be at leisure to explore at will, sampling the authentic settings, sometimes through "hands-on" means, as the mood strikes. There is an excellent English guide, with a map, both short and detailed descriptions of each site, and recommended routes for one- to four-hour length visits. But essentially it's an informal place that invites you to stroll at will, by the windmills, in the herb garden, through the traditional costume exhibit. The distinctly different farmsteads from various regions around Holland, separated by beech woods, garden plots, a drawbridge perhaps, are well worth visiting, from a day laborer's one-room cottage (c. 1700 *los hoes* without a dividing between the barn and human living space), to a prosperous 18th-century Frisian "head, neck, and body" building. There's a one-room school building, dovecote, eelmonger's hut, and c. 1820 tradesman's house from Zaandam that does double duty as a gift shop. A restaurant, pleasant pancake cafe, and snack stall on the beechwooded landscaped acres will keep you refreshed.

## IN THE AREA

Since it was central to the Arnhem action of the Market-Garden Operation, Oosterbeek is the place with the most to see. Leaving Arnhem from the Willemplein in front of the station via the **Utrechtstraat**, along which (at No. 85) a plaque notes that this was the German security headquarters for the area from 1940-1944, and opposite No. 68 is the Dutch war memorial. Crossing into **Oosterbeek** (*VVV Utrechtseweg 216*), passing many of the parachute and glider landing fields (the **Airborne Monument** stands at the edge of them), the cumulative memorials, historical markers, museum, and, finally, the war cemetery, provide a haunting commentary on the events of September 1944.

### Oosterbeek Airborne Museum                                    ★

*Utrechtseweg 232 in Oosterbeek suburb west of the city; Mon.–Sat., 11 a.m.–5 p.m., Sun. and holidays, noon-5 p.m., closed Christmas and Jan 1;* ☎ *085-337710.* Located in the former Hotel Hartenstein, which served as the headquarters for both armies at one time or other, the Airborne Museum recreates the circumstances and situations of the battle by means of excellent audiovisual (in English) presentations, dioramas, photographs, and other materials that recount the downhill course of the misguided mission. Next to the museum is the **Klein Hartenstein** (*Utrechtseweg 226,* ☎ *085-342121*), an excellent cafe-restaurant with bar, fireplace, and terrace. In Oosterbeek, Stationweg leads north to the **Oosterbeek War Cemetery**, (*Limburg stirumweg; open sunrise–sunset;* ☎ *085-336265*), where the majority of Allied casualties from Market-Garden rest. The **Tafelberg Hotel**, which can also be visited, was used as the emergency hospital in the film *A Bridge Too Far* about the battle.

### National Park De Hoge Veluwe                                ★ ★

*Bezoekerscentrum or Visitor Center; Marchantplein; daily year-round 8 a.m.–sunset;* ☎ *08382-1627.* Much of the land contained by the rough triangle formed by Arnhem, Apeldoorn and Amersfoort is made up of Holland's largest national park, **De Hoge Veluwe**. In the center, near the village of Otterlo, is one of the country's most outstanding art museums. The 13,300 acres of natural parkland of heath, woodland, sand dunes, and fen, as well as the magnificent collection of man-made treasures, were a gift to the Dutch nation from Anton Kroller, a business success story in Rotterdam, and his wife, Helene Muller, who turned her attention to collecting art (see "Kroller-Muller Museum"). They lived in the ★ **St. Hubertus Hunting Lodge** (*in park 6.5 km./4 mi. from Visitor Center; May 1–October 31, 10–11:30 a.m. and 2–4:30 p.m. daily*), after it was designed in 1913 by Dutch architect H. P. Berlage to be a stone visualization of the 8th-century life of Belgian St. Hubert, patron of the hunters (Kroller originally purchased De Hoge Veluwe as his own private hunting domain, and the fauna, including red deer, roe, and wild boar, are still protected in the park). One of the design considerations of the equally individualistic interior was the control of light and brightness to correspond to the level of "enlightenment" in St. Hubert's life at the stage a given room is meant to portray. Berlage also designed much of the furniture (Henri van de Velde, architect of the Kroller-Muller Museum, collaborated on some pieces) and the pond in front of the lodge. Among the many park services offered are free ★ ★ *white bikes* (*near Visitor Center; daily 8 a.m.–sunset, Apr. 1–Oct. 31*) for use on a first-come basis within the park to visitors who arrive by car or public transportation in order to cut down on motorized traffic in the park; the **Koperen Kop Restaurant** (*near Visitor Center; daily 9:30 a.m.–6:30 p.m., except 4:30 p.m. Nov. 1–Mar. 31*) with a spacious dining room and sunny terrace; the **Groene Winkel** (green shop), by the visitor center, which sells books, posters, "green" souvenirs; miles of walking and cycle paths; and an observation high stand "hide" from which to watch male deer at close range.

### Kroller-Muller Museum ★★★

*Hoge Veluwe National Park; Tues.–Sun., 10 a.m.–5 p.m., except 11 a.m.– 5 p.m. on Sun. & hols. from Nov.–March; closed Jan. 1 and Mon.; sculpture garden: April–Oct. 10 a.m.–4:30 p.m.; ☎ 08382-1041.* Much more than the tip but scarcely the entire iceberg of art in this museum is the collection of 278 works by Vincent van Gogh. There are too many treasures in the superb, predominantly 19th- and 20th-century collection for them to all be on display at one time, but many of the major paintings by Van Gogh, including *The Potato Eaters* (and other peasant protraits from his Dutch period in Nuenen—see "North Brabant"), *Sunflowers*, and *Self Portrait, 1887*, as well as several Arles-era scenes, are kept on view. The museum opened in this Belgian Henry van de Velde-designed building in 1938, built by the Dutch nation in exchange for the gift of the contents by Helene Muller. The museum was extended by W. G. Quist in 1977. In addition to **Van Gogh**, there are pre-Impressionists, including **Corot** and **Courbet**; Impressionists such as **Seurat, Renoir,** and the Dutch **Jongkind**; post-Impressionists, and many later modernists including **Picasso, Mondriaan, Braque, Gris,** and **Leger**.

There are a small number of Old Masters as well. The Kroller-Muller ★ ★ **sculpture garden** is Europe's largest (47 acres) and its pieces begin pleasing from the front lawn of the museum. At the start of the path is Wenchebach's endearing hat-in-hand *Monsieur Jacques* (whom you might have been introduced to in Rotterdam). Among the many nature-ensconced works are ones by **Rodin, Henry Moore, Epstein, Giacometti, Lipchitz, Maillol, Nevelson, Serra,** and **Oldenburg**; an open pavilion by **Rietveld** houses several works by **Barbara Hepworth**.

# APELDOORN

Although the name Apeldoorn is first documented in 793, it wasn't until the building of the ★ ★ ★ **Royal Palace Het Loo** (1685–1692) that the city attracted any attention. From that time, the construction of comfortable houses began because many wanted to live in the shadow of Dutch royalty. The burgeoning park-like city remains surrounded by the king's former hunting ground, the *Royal Forest* (nearly 25,000 acres). Het Loo had unusual appeal because Dutch society did not traditionally support an ostentatious royal court lifestyle, which is understandable given their essential Protestant Calvinist character. In fact, as the building of Het Loo began, Dutch painters were creating the "*Vanitas*," still lifes that warned against a concentration on possessions above considerations of the soul. And, in case you're recalling the splendid marble Royal Palace on the Dam in Amsterdam (1648–1655), remember that it wasn't built as a royal palace at all, but as the Stadhuis for a flourishing city in which "commerce was king" and thereby worthy of such a tasteful display of wealth. In fact, it was the influence of history and English royalty that helped hasten Het Loo (meaning "open place in the woods") palace into being. Mary (daughter of James II of England) and her Dutch husband Willem accepted an invitation to undertake an armed expedition to England against her Catholic father in 1688. James had forfeited support in England by his Catholic and unconstitutional rule, and on his flight, Willem and Mary were invited to be joint rulers as King and Queen of England, Scotland, and Ireland. (Again, in 1690, Dutch Protestant Willem of Orange, as England's King William III, was called upon to battle Catholic James II, then on Irish soil, in the *Battle of the Boyne*. The orange band on the Irish flag comes from this encounter with Holland's House of Orange.) In 1684 Willem had purchased the 15th-century manor house now called **Het Oude Loo** (*restored, open to public, as are its gardens in*

*April and May*) as a hunting lodge. In 1685, Willem and Mary lay the foundation stone of **Het Nieuwe Loo**. Perhaps even the new palace would have seemed small by Mary's English standards, a "come down" unless she appreciated its intimate scale. Het Loo did, however, have some amenities that most English castles of the time wouldn't have had: indoor plumbing and sliding windows. The decoration of the interior and the layout of the gardens were designed by **Daniel Marot** (1661–1752, and, incidentally, an ancestor of the late actress Audrey Hepburn), a French Huguenot who fled to the Netherlands in 1685. Once he became king of England, Willem competed with contemporary Louis XIV of France (who was at war with Holland at the time). In the royal rivalry, at least for the loveliness of its gardens, Het Loo was said to surpass *Versailles*. Two globes, one of heaven and one of earth, served as water fountains, and were fed by the waters of the Rhine. Symmetry was the word for both the building and garden design.

Het Loo was drastically altered in 1807–09 when it was designated a summer residence by **Louis Bonapart**, whose brother Napoleon had him installed as king of Holland from 1806–1810 during the French occupation from 1795–1814. The garden was changed to the then-fashionable English landscape style, and the facade was altered with Empire-style shuttered windows. The Dfl. 80 million restoration from 1975–1984 was undertaken with the idea of restoring both the palace and gardens to their original design.

Het Loo is a palace of subdued splendor compared to some of the continent's castles, but that actually makes it easier to relate to and imagine people actually living there. In fact, Het Loo was renovated with the idea of accurately depicting its three centuries of royal residency by the House of Orange, from Willem III and Mary II through frequent use as a royal family summer residence over the centuries, to **Queen Wilhelmina** (1880–1962), who came to live year-round at Het Loo after a 50-year reign, following her 1948 abdication in favor of her daughter Juliana (whose own country house-like palace **Soestdijk**—no visitors, but clearly visible from the road—is located in nearby Baarn). Wilhelmina lived at Het Loo until her death, after which she lay in state in the palace chapel. After the 1953 hurricane, Wilhelmina offered shelter at Het Loo to flood victims (see "Southern Holland, Zeeland"), and also provided aid there to Dutch nationals forced to flee from Indonesia under President Sukarno (1945–1967). The last royal resident of the palace was **Princess Margriet** (sister of Queen Beatrix) who, with her husband, Mr. Pieter Vollenhoven, and their four sons, departed in 1975 so that the extensive restoration process prior to Het Loo's reopening as a national museum could be accomplished.

During restoration, Het Loo was painstakingly brought back to the original design of the celebrated Daniel Marot, who had overseen every detail, from the sculpted marble garden urns down to the many different damask wall coverings. Wall and ceiling panels and marble and faux marble (fashionable then) floors and columns were uncovered, tapestries were restored. Visitors are struck by the lack of corridors at Het Loo; one apartment leads directly to another as was the 17th-century style. Although the 17th century predominates, some of the rooms used by the royal family in the late 19th and 20th centuries have been left as they were enjoyed by more contemporary members of the House of Orange (some of Wilhelmina's childhood toys have been left in one room), and a tour of Het Loo can be made in a roughly chronological order.

Appropriately, among the first apartments one is led to are those of Willem and Mary. Much of the furniture in their two separate apartments (between which is located the Audience Hall) is not the original (though the pieces are period) because a great deal of destruction occurred during the two French occupations. The king's and queen's gardens, carefully planned for the view out their respective windows, couldn't have brought much more pleasure to Willem and Mary than they bring visitors today. Rooms of particular interest because of their intimacy include Mary's Cabinet, a bright tiny corner room overlooking gardens on two sides, with pieces of the blue and white Delftware that she collected on the mantel, and Willem's corner-room library, which contains dark-wood cases between the windows and a mirrored and plastered oval ceiling. The long Picture Gallery also offers a view out onto the garden, where the formal box-hedged parterres ringed with flowers appear as large flowered Dutch tiles at that distance. A typical Dutch detail at Het Loo is the bountiful use of fresh flowers in wonderful arrangements displayed throughout the palace.

Your visit to Het Loo is self-guided (plentiful English-language documentation on interior and garden available, descriptions on actual exhibits in Dutch only). From April 1–Oct. 31, a recommended ★★25-minute video film in English is shown in the Delft-blue-decorated Grotto as an introduction on aspects of Het Loo's history, restoration, interior design, and furnishings. Concerts are held in Het Loo the last Friday of every month at 8:15 p.m. and the last Sunday of every month from 2–4 p.m. (restaurant and tickets required, contact the palace or VVV). A map of marked, varied-length walking routes in the palace park is available at the museum entrance.

Two dining possibilities are offered at Het Loo. The **Balzaal Paleis Het Loo** (*10 a.m.–5 p.m., closed Mon. and Nov.–April;* ☎ *055-212244; inexpensive*) is located in part of the West Wing; the restaurant takes its name from the fact that the space was a ballroom in the early 20th century. Its ceiling and paneling remain as decor for your dining. On the walls of the restaurant are five gold-leather hunting scenes of c. 1650 Flemish origin, representing the hunting of lion, boar, deer, heron, and women. **Theehuis Paleis Het Loo** (*10 a.m.–5 p.m., closed Mon.; inexpensive*) is a self-service restaurant in one of the "garages" of the royal stables that house the vintage carriages, coaches, and cars once used at Het Loo.

## WHERE TO STAY

### Hotel De Keizerskroon                                  ★★★★★
*Koningstraat 7, 7315 HR;* ☎ *055-217744, FAX 055-214737, for restaurant in U.S.* ☎ *800-223-6510, in Canada* ☎ *800-424-5500; expensive.* De Keizerskroon ("the emperor's crown") came by its name legitimately, when Czar Peter the Great, visiting royalty at Het Loo, ignored the protocol of staying at the palace and stayed instead with his servants at the inn next door which advertised "*A l'auberge, on traite proprement*" (at the inn everyone is treated well). That's still the case today, though the hotel has burnt and been rebuilt since Peter's days and now is a modernized hotel with 100 well-lit, colorful rooms, with windows that open, some with balconies, all with hair dryers and a basketful of amenities in the bath. The cozy, leather-bound-furniture lobby has a modern fireplace, at the corner of which is a charming sculpture of a girl reading. The hotel has a parking garage and an indoor swimming pool. The hotel **De Keizersgrill** (*noon-10:30 p.m.; moderate*) is bright and beckoning, with painted wall panels of Het Loo's gardens.

## WHERE TO EAT

**De Echoput** *Amersfoortseweg 86, Hoog Soeren: 10 a.m.–midnight, kitchen closes 10 p.m.; 9:30 p.m. Sun., closed Mon. and Sat. for lunch; for reservations* ☎ *05769-248; expensive.* A Member of Alliance Gastronomique and Relais Gourmand, this place may be somewhat unprepossessing in appearance, but wait for the palate to pass judgment. The "nouvelle with solid French classic base" (as the owner describes it) highlights the several *prix-fixe* menus and à la carte dishes, of which game is a specialty in-season. If the weather cooperates, you can dine on the terrace surrounded by the royal forests of neighboring Apeldoorn.

## IN THE AREA

**Deventer**

*VVV Brink 5, pop. 65,000.* A short distance to the northeast from Apeldoorn is an old Hanseatic League town with a well-preserved ★ historic center, often called the **Bergkwartier**, with many houses in the Gelderland-Overijssel style of the 12th–16th centuries. The **Waag** (weigh house, 1528) has a museum of local history. Across from the essentially 15th-century Grote Kerk is the late 17th-century **Stadhuis**, in which hangs a picture of a Deventer town council meeting painted by Gerard Terborch (1617–1681) who, as burgomaster then, appears presiding over the meeting.

**Zutphen**

*VVV in the 14th-century Wijnhuis—with Hemony carillon—on Groenmarkt, pop. 32,000.* To the southeast of Apeldoorn is Zutphen, also a former Hanse town with an attractive ★★historic center. **St. Walburgskerk** (*Grote Kerk*), noted for the 15th- and 16th-century wall and ceiling paintings, is also renowned for its Gothic chained library (where original manuscripts remain fastened to old reading desks), the oldest in western Europe, in the former chapter house (1564).

# AMERSFOORT

The lovely medieval heart of Amersfoort (*VVV Stationplein 27;* ☎ *033-63515; greater pop. 100,000*) was first fortified after receiving enfranchisement in 1259 from Henry of Vianden (Luxembourg), then bishop of Utrecht. Amersfoort has the picturesque distinction of being the only city in Europe to have a double ring of canals around its old center. Described in one source as making "no significant appearance in Netherlands history," Amersfoort is and appears ancient enough to have provided the settings and props for any number of dramatic historical roles (such as the one neighboring Arnhem was cast for in World War II), but certainly is better preserved today for the fact that it didn't. For example, the so-called  *muurhuizen* (wall houses) were built where the first town walls (1381) were dismantled in 1451 when a larger second wall had been completed, and are a unique feature from early Amersfoort. Much within those second walls preserves a medieval picture. ★★**Het Havik**, the former harbor of Amersfoort and center of the old town, is now a canal lined with beautiful house facades (and a flower market on Friday mornings). There's also a ★ **Friday morning fish market** on Groenmarkt by St. Joriskerk, at which women in traditional costume from nearby Spakenburg (see "In the Area") may be preparing and selling their fresh wares.

## Onze Lieve Vrouwetoren

*Onze Lieve Vrouwekerkhof; check with VVV for summer hours of admission.* The 100-meter (328-foot) church tower dates from the 15th century, although it has been restored several times since; it has a 47 mostly Hemony-bell carillon that used to belong to an attached chapel until that unfavored building blew up in 1787 while being used as an arsenal. The unlucky chapel's outline was put into the pavement in the square when it was redone. There's a Friday morning carillon concert from 10–11 a.m. for market day.

## Museum Flehite

*Westsingel 50; Tues.–Fri. 10 a.m.–5 p.m., Sat. and Sun. 2–5 p.m., closed Mon.* The museum, which is housed in three old wall houses, the right-hand one of which is in large part original, has exhibits on the history of Amersfoort and its surroundings, and has a large model of the historic town center. The restored ★ ★ **Pieters en Bloklands Gasthuis** (hospital), located diagonally across the road from the Flehite, is also a part of the museum (ask about access). The men's ward, dating from the early 16th century, has retained its original character, including its wooden bedsteads or sleeping cupboards, old tiles, and locked oaken chests where individuals kept their earthly belongings. It is unique in Holland and well-worth the effort to visit.

## De Keppelpoort

*Grote Spui; June 24–Sept. 1, Mon–Fri. 10 a.m.–5 p.m., Sat. and Sun. noon–5 p.m.* Built at the beginning of the 15th century as part of the second town rampart, **De Koppelpoort** is a combination land and water gate by the River Eem. The restored treadmill inside was powered by men to lift and lower the heavy partition gate.

## De Nederlandse Beiaardschool

*The Dutch National Carillon School; Grote Spui 11, 3811 Ga;* ☎ *033-752638 with a reservation open to the public during Flehite Museum hours in summer, other seasons by special arrangement, contact VVV.* The Amersfoort school, and the one in Mechelen, Belgium, are the only carillon schools in the world (see chapter on "Carillons"). Since its founding in 1953, Amersfoort has had more than 250 students from 11 countries, who have in the course of their studies played on most of Holland's 182 carillons. The main school building, in a particularly attractive part of the old center, houses offices, campanological display, library, and practice keyboards. The school has keyboard computers on which students are encouraged to compose contemporary carillon music. Although the Onze Lieve Vrouwetoren carillon is close by, most playing lessons and practice time are scheduled at the **Belgian Monument** at the Amersfoortse Berg (woods) at the southeast edge of town. The Monument, which commemorates Belgium's gratitude to Holland for helping with its refugees during World War I, has a light four-octave Eijsbouts carillon. Director of the school, Jacques Maassen, is the *stadsbeiaard* for the town of Breda, and

American Todd Fair, carillonneur for Amsterdam's Oude Kerk, is on the faculty. Diplomas and performing artists' diplomas are granted; a week-long summer academy is held.

## IN THE AREA

South of Amersfoort are a castle and a village worthy of attention if you are ambling by auto (also accessible by bus from rail stations in Amersfoort and Utrecht CS). To the north is the "costume town" of Spakenburg. A couple of castle hotels and a renowned restaurant are also there.

### Kasteel Huis Doorn                                              ★

*Langbroekerweg 10, Doorn 3941 MT, 13 km. south of Amersfoort; Mar. 15–Sept. 1, Mon.–Sat., 9:30 a.m.–5 p.m., Sun. 1–5 p.m.; ☎ 03430-12244.* When Germany's Kaiser Wilhelm II was forced into exile in 1918, being a cousin of Dutch Queen Wilhelmina, he turned to Holland for help and Parliament gave him permission to settle in. He bought this 14th-century, largely reconstructed in the 18th-century house from the late actress Audrey Hepburn's great aunt, a Dutch baroness. Although it's a pleasant mansion, it certainly must have seemed a great come-down to Wilhelm when he arrived with his 58 wagon-loads of belongings from the palaces of Germany, including two loads of silver (some of the elaborate pieces are on display). Other treasures with which the Kaiser arrived are the **Gobelin tapestries** in the dining room, and display cases with an exceptional collection of *snuff boxes* that once belonged to Frederik the Great of Prussia. Huis Doorn is decorated in 1920s style and has been left largely as it was when the former emperor, who lived here from 1920 to 1941, died. (When he died, Nazi forces then occupied Holland, and Hitler ordered a full military funeral for him). Wilhelm was a proud man and placed plenty of pictures of himself all over the house; the magnificent crystal-edged mirror in his bedroom must have framed his image nicely. Perhaps pleasure in his face was compensation for having been born with a much shorter left arm, which shows quite clearly from his military uniforms on display. Be sure to see Wilhelm's study/library, a lovely, liveable book-lined round room with views of the grounds in three directions. Most remarkable is the riding saddle on stilts in which he sat while working at the stand-up desk; Wilhelm believed that no man could be mentally alert unless he was sitting absolutely erect. The park surrounding the castle provides for pleasant strolling among old oaks and beech trees and groves of rhododendrons. From the terrace of the former **Orangerie**, now a tea room, there's a pleasant view back to the castle.

### Wijk bij Duurstede                                             ★

*VVV Markt 24, in the 1662 former Stadhuis; ☎ 03435-75995, open Mon. 1–4 p.m., Tues.–Sat. 10 a.m.–noon, 1–4:30 p.m.; pop. 15,000.* The Dutch visit this lovely old town largely to enjoy its *gastronomy* and *galleries*, and just in case you think it might ring a bit hollow with that description, local residents say that "people never leave because it is so pleasant here." There are no set sights save for the ancient tree-shaded ★ ★ Markt, and small cozy streets (printed walking-tour in English available from the VVV), though many visitors make their way to the romantic ruin of 12th-century moated ★ **Duurstede Castle**, with its historic restored square **Donjon** (defensive dwelling tower), a typical early construction in the region. David of Burgundy, bastard son of Philip the Good, became Bishop of Utrecht in 1456 and took possession of Duurstede Castle, intending to make the fine John the Baptist church (recently restored) on the Markt equal to the Utrecht Dom in splendor, but failed to finish his plan. Down by the dijks on the rivers (Wijk is where the Neder Rhine becomes the River Lek) is Holland's only still existing windmill built on a gate in the city wall, and carries the name **Rijn en Lek** (Rhine and Lek, 1659). Many people mistakenly think it is the windmill in the marvelous moody-skied masterpiece painting by Jacob van Ruisdael entitled "Molen at Wijk bij Duurstede" (c. 1665) in Amsterdam's Rijksmuseum. That specific windmill, which stood close by, was demolished in the first half of the 19th century, but you can ask to have the **windmill base** pointed out to you as you walk along the bank to enjoy the river views.

## WHERE TO EAT

### Restaurant Duurstede

*Maleborduurstraat 7; noon–2 p.m. and 6–10 p.m., closed Wed.;* ☎ *03435-72946, FAX 03435-74614; moderate.* Chef and owner **Paul Fagel** (one of eight brothers who cook in the famed Dutch family of restaurateurs) has housed his well-regarded kitchen in an ancient stone building, in a pleasant home-like split-level setting, with bar in the basement and dining room upstairs. The old beamed ceilings, bright contemporary art and decorative details are as imaginative a combination as Fagel's *prix-fixe* and *à la carte* offerings, which show Italian and seafood influences.

### Restaurant 'T Schippershuys

*Dijkstraat 5; Tues.–Sun., 10 a.m.–9 p.m., closed Mon.;* ☎ *03435-71538; inexpensive.* This stylish 1840s space with wood floors, high ceilings, big windows and a terrace on the Rhine/Lek riverfront across the street is close to the site of the Ruysdael windmill base and the picturesque existing city wall windmill. Tasty menu choices include omelettes, uitsmijters, salad nicoise, and pancakes.

### Cafe-Bar 't Hoff

*Markt 15a; daily, lunch to late night;* ☎ *03435-74848; inexpensive.* It's not surprising that there's the aroma of beer in the air of this small pub, since it's been serving the same since the end of the 15th century. Light dishes and snacks are served inside under the ancient wooden ceiling or on the terrace at the back, where there's a view to the town's castle and a *jeu de boules* may be brewing.

## IN THE AREA

### Spakenburg

*11 km./7 mi. north of Amersfoort, served by public VAD bus from station
every half hour.* A former Zuiderzee fishing village, whose fishermen
have mostly taken to eel fishing, building and chartering traditional
Dutch sailing boats (which keeps the little harbor full of ship masts),
and also preparing and selling fish in costume at weekly markets all
over Holland. About 800 women in the village (out of a population of
about 20,000 for the combined township of Spakenburg and Bunschoten, which is inland and therefore has a farming character) wear
traditional costume every day, the youngest doing so about the age of
40. Most have inherited some of the costume parts from family members, and so the clothing is antique and valuable, as well as sentimental. One woman explained to me that those who wear traditional
costume in Spakenburg daily "really wouldn't feel dressed in anything
else." These women even wear the costume on holiday in other countries on the continent. Others in the village will wear the dresses on
special occasions, such as family weddings, birthdays, anniversaries,
and also tourist ones, such as the last two Wednesdays in July and first
two in August when Spakenburg hosts its annual market and traditional crafts days. While not extreme, the community is very religious
and there are those who don't even watch television on Sundays.
However, such is the passion for *voetbal* (soccer) across all segments
of Dutch society that when there's an important match being shown,
if a Spakenburger for religious reasons can't bring himself to watch
the match on Sunday, he'll record it on his VCR for Monday viewing.

### Museum 't Vurhuus ★

*Oude Schans 47; end April–mid Oct. Mon.–Sat. 10 a.m.–5 p.m.;*
☎ *03499-83319.* This appealing little museum is arranged to show
the various intricacies associated with traditional costumes and their
evolution (for adults and children) in Spakenburg and next-door
neighbor village Bunschoten in c. 1915 setting of shop and typical
fisherman family living room, which also includes interesting household decorative details, such as the tiled fireplace.

## WHERE TO STAY AND TO EAT IN THE AREA

### Kasteel 't Kerchebosch Hotel-Restaurant ★★★

*Arnhemse bovenweg 31, Zeist;* ☎ *03404-14734, FAX 03404-13114;*
*hotel: expensive.* A turn-of-the-century, neo-Gothic, former country
house of a nobleman, who created the eclectic decor from antique
details and materials gathered from old monasteries, castles, and
churches (such as doors from Utrecht's Dom cathedral). Set in quiet
park surroundings, the 30 rooms include 14 in the house and the rest
in a new wing added at the rear in 1976; all have moderate amenities,
although there is no elevator, which accounts for the only-three-star
rating. Among the facilities (open to the public) are a bar lounge *(daily*

*8 a.m.–12:30 a.m.)*, bistro *(Wed.–Sun., 6–10 p.m.)*, and specialty restaurant, where breakfast (included) is served, open for lunch and dinner daily.

## Kasteel De Hooge Vuursche Hotel-Restaurant ★★★★

*Hilversumsestraatweg 14, Baarn;*  *02154-12541,* ☎ *02154-23288; hotel: expensive.* This Cuypers-designed late 19th-century house, a hotel now, has retained a residential graciousness. The public rooms have hardwood floors, high ceiling elegance, and delicate architectural details. There are garden and fountain views out the large lounge windows, and each of the 20 guest rooms has its own restful, uncluttered character amid a soft-colored decor. There's 24-hour room service and luxury amenities in the rooms. The formal traditional French cuisine à la carte restaurant is open for lunch and dinner daily, and there are tables on the terrace overlooking the lake.

## Auberge de Hoefslag ★★★★

*Vossenlaan 28, Bosch en Duin; for restaurant* ☎ *030-251051, FAX 030-285821; hotel: expensive; restaurant open noon–2 p.m., 6–9:30 p.m., closed Sun., expensive to very expensive.* A countryside restaurant of charm and style that works wonders with local market produce, all created by **Martin Fagel** of the renowned Dutch restaurant family. If you're expecting to be too pleasantly satiated after dining to drive, De Hoefslag also is an inn, with 34 rooms; breakfast included.

# SOUTHERN HOLLAND

*Veere's waterside De CampVeerse Toren dates from the 14th century.*

## AN INTRODUCTION

In its use here, Southern Holland includes the provinces of **Zeeland**, **North Brabant** and **Limburg**, all lying "below" the great *Rhine*, *Maas* and *Waal* rivers, which flow from the interior of the European continent to empty into the North Sea near Rotterdam.

Even Dutch tourism officials use the term "Southern Holland" in their foreign-language literature, since it's a convenient phrase for referring to this less-well-traveled section of the country. However, it's precisely in this region that the resident Dutch want to make the point that their country is **the Netherlands**, *not* Holland—which, technically, is only two provinces, North Holland and South Holland. Travelers in these southern provinces who use the word "Holland" when speaking of the country may encounter occasional explanations (always given with a smile). When I'm in Zeeland, North Brabant, or Limburg, I attempt to be sensitive to the issue by trying to remember—not always successfully—to use the name "Netherlands."

The Dutch provinces in the south of the Netherlands are linked by ties to Belgium, on which they all border. Here, history left the boundaries a bit blurred, not (since the mid-19th century) politically but psychologically. Rule by the Burgundians and the Spanish lasted longer in the once so-called **southern Netherlands** (today's Belgium), and the cross-cultivation across the southern Dutch border —which, in any case, shifted regularly for centuries—left a greater impact upon the personality of the people there than elsewhere in today's Netherlands. The differences between the Dutch in the north of the country and those in the south may not leap out at you, but only the most casual passer-through will not notice the change in mentality and mood between the Holland "north of the rivers" and the Netherlands south of them.

# ZEELAND

Well-named, **Zeeland** ("sea land") is as much water as land, and much of what is land lies below sea level. The southern section of Zeeland, **Zeeuwsch Vlaanderen**, is connected to the European continent at Belgium's border, but to the rest of its own province only by car ferries across the watery finger of the **Westerschelde**, which points inland to the Belgian port of Antwerp. **Walcheren**, with the provincial capital **Middelburg**, and **Noorde** and **Zuid Beveland**, form Zeeland's largest "island grouping," some linked by modern dikes and dams, and others, once attached to the mainland, now sliced from it by canals but reconnected by bridges. **Zeelandbrug**, Europe's longest bridge at 5022 meters/3.1 miles, reaches gracefully across the **Oosterschelde**, the mouth of which has been given "the teeth" of the massive 65-concrete-pier *Stormvloedkering* (storm surge barrier), the final complex part of the most impressive hydraulic engineering plan ever undertaken in the world. (See the "Delta Expo".) Interest in that project has brought a new public to beachblessed Zeeland, though the remote-seeming province's contact with the greater world still comes mostly in the form of summer holiday makers.

From an early date, Zeeland shared in the trade prominence and prosperity that its access to the sea provided. Historically, the province of Holland (today's North and South Holland combined) also included Zeeland, which had been annexed by Holland in 1323, following long disputes over its territory by the counts of Holland and Flanders. Basically, Zeeland, Holland, and Flanders shared a similar history for some 500 years up until 1436, at which time Holland itself was annexed into the wide holdings of Duke Philip of Burgundy. Early trade in *wool* and *cloth* with England and Scotland created wealth for the region, a fact attested to by richly adorned public buildings such as the **Middelburg** and **Veere stadhuizen**. It certainly was a boon for Zeeland business when, in 1444, Lord of Veere Wolfert van Borssele married Mary, one of the six daughters of James I of Scotland, a match which led the way to Veere's monopoly in the **Scottish wool trade**, which lasted until the French occupation of Holland of 1795.

Meanwhile, many Zeeland towns were involved in the sieges of the Dutch seven-province struggle against the Spanish. **Vlissingen**, an ancient town of little previous importance, was chosen in 1556 as embarkation port by Spanish King Philip II, who left the Netherlands embittered against his Dutch subjects, accusing Willem the Silent of treachery. When the Spanish attacked in the 1570s, Vlissingen was one of the first towns to revolt against them.

Lowlying Zeeland has a long history of floods. One of the worst was the St. Elizabeth Flood of 1421, which destroyed 72 Zeeland villages and drowned some 10,000 inhabitants. Though fewer human lives (1835) were lost during the **hurricane of February 1, 1953**, which breached many of Zeeland's dikes, 200,000 livestock died, some 485,000 acres of the country's most fertile farmland were submerged in salt water, and 48,000 homes were damaged, many beyond repair. That catastrophic storm, combined with the degree to which the Dutch had raised the science of hydraulic engineering, resulted in a "never-again" stance that subsequently produced the **Delta Project**. (In February 1990 a hurricane again struck the coast of Holland—the same storm caused death and devastation also in the U.K., Belgium, and inland in Luxembourg—but, with the Delta Project in place, it was only beaches, not breaches, that required repair from sea damage.)

What must have made the disastrous hurricane of 1953 even more devastating for Zeeland was that it came so soon after the enormous flood damage sustained by the province during World War II's deliberate **bombing** by the RAF in September/October 1944 to unearth the Nazis from their bunkered positions in Walcheren, from which they controlled the Westerschelde entrance to the port of Antwerp. (Following the successful Normandy invasion in June 1944, the Allies had a particular need for Antwerp as a port for landing supplies for the rest of their continental campaign.) Beginning in September, bombs rained down on Walcheren's dikes, the aim being to breach them and literally flood the Nazis out. By the end of October 1944, the RAF had succeeded in causing several serious breaches in the dikes at Westkapelle, Veere, Vlissingen, and Rammekens. Most of Walcheren lay under sea water (where it remained for more than 13 months, during which time most trees, as well as all other vegetation, died). Walcheren was freed by Allied troops (including the *2nd Canadian Division*), landing at **Vlissingen** and **Westkapelle** (*Landing Monument* and other memorials) on November 1, 1944. By the end of 1944, work was begun on repairing the breaches, although it wasn't until February 1946 that the last gap in the dikes of Zeeland closed. And the entire job of reconstruction had not been fully completed when the 1953 hurricane struck.

Today it's possible for travelers as well as residents to put to rest that troubled past and enjoy Zeeland's peaceful rural setting of dignified farms, remote sand dunes, quaint quiet old towns, a quality of light that's a delight, and long-repaired dikes lined with full-grown rows of fast growing "replacement" poplars.

## GUIDELINES FOR ZEELAND

### SIGHTS

Situated in the southwest of the Netherlands, cut by the Eastern and Western Scheldt river arms, Zeeland is made up of areas that originally were islands. That geographical fact created a certain isolation which, while mitigated today by connecting roads resulting from the Delta Project, produces within the province more vestiges of older customs (such as *traditional costumes*) than are visible in Randstad Holland. Zeeland's location between Flanders and Holland involved it in important mercantile enterprises in the 15th to 17th centuries, a fact reflected in rich and refined buildings such as the *stadhuizen* in **Middelburg** and the villages of Veere.

Other historic towns such as **Zierikzee**, **Goes**, **Tholen**, and **Sluis** will make your camera-shutter finger itchy. **Vlissingen** is a busy long-established port and resort. Today Zeeland's beaches are busy in summer, and her former sea fishermen have turned their focus to cultivating the famous *Zeeuws oysters* and *mussels*. The ingenious **Delta Expo**, the definitive protection for the province against a too-assertive sea, attracts visitors from around the world.

### GETTING AROUND

Without question, a **car** is the best way to capture the essence of the area. There's a quite extensive Zeeland provincial **bus** service: tiny Veere can be reached from Middelburg, for instance. Inclusive day **train** trips from major stations to the **Delta Expo** are run by the

Netherlands Spoorwegen several times weekly. **Bicycle** rentals are available at Middelburg station (reservations in summer suggested) and many private locations throughout Zeeland. Two-wheelers are common commuting means for Zeelanders, and you're liable to come across Walcheren women in traditional dress (cap with lace "blinkers" and golden coils, black shawl, voluminous skirts, and black and white overskirt) pedaling with a full load of parcels.

## SHOPPING

The main shopping centers in the region are Middelburg, Vlissingen, Zierikzee, Goes, and Hulst. Some shops close for lunch (*generally 12:30–1:30 p.m.*); most are closed on Sunday, although there's an exception for shops in some towns in Zeeuwsch-Vlaanderen, which keep open to compete with the nearby Belgium shops that open Sundays.

## ENTERTAINMENT AND EVENTS

Although *traditional costumes* are seen less and less frequently in Zeeland, they are still worn with some regularity in Walcheren and South-Beveland, the best bet to see them being at the **weekly general markets** (in *Goes* on Tuesday, *Middelburg* and *Zierikzee* on Thursday, *Vlissingen* on Friday) or Sunday mornings en route to a rural church. **Tilting at the Ring**, a traditional "tournament" game with horses (that also amounts to something of a flower festival), is held once in July and once in August. (Check with the VVV for specific dates.)

## WHERE TO STAY

One should book well ahead during the peak summer season. Vlissingen has the most hotels and the most liveliness, no doubt because of its port. Most Zeeland hotels are the small, family-run sort. The **Zeeland Provinciale VVV**, upstairs from the Middelburg VVV on the Markt, (*Mon.–Fri. 8:30 a.m.–noon and 1:15–5 p.m.;* ☎ *01180-33051*) can help with bed-and-breakfast-type accommodations (most plentiful and most heavily booked in summer).

## WHERE TO EAT

There's nothing more appropriate—or fresher and more varied— to grace the tables in Zeeland than the "fruits of the sea." Specialties are shellfish: oysters, mussels, North Sea "gray" shrimp, lobsters, winkles. A number of fish also are landed here (sole, turbot, eel). Traditional, locally produced sweets include *bolus* (sweet rolls) and *babelaars* (buttery candies). Do not neglect the restaurants in hotels in Zeeland since it is through customers' stomachs that those establishments often attract overnight guests.

## ARRIVING

Zeeland borders on Belgian Flanders, and it is an easy driving distance from the Flemish cities of Bruges, Ghent, and Antwerp. Daily **car-ferries** run between Sheerness in Kent, England and Vlissingen (Flushing) in Zeeland. Locations in Zeeland that can be reached by **train** are limited to Middelburg, Goes, and Vlissingen, **via Roosendaal** on a main line south from Rotterdam.

## TRAVEL TIPS

If you visit Zeeland by car or car ferry to Vlissingen, a glance at a Benelux map will show it's only a short drive across the border to Belgium's Flemish "art" cities: Bruges, Ghent, and Antwerp. If you come to Middelburg by train, a plan to combine that Zeeland city with a Flemish itinerary is equally sound: retrace your rail route to Rosendaal, and hop a quick direct train south to Antwerp-Mechelen-Brussels, etc.

## *ON THE ROAD*
### ★MIDDELBURG

**VVV** • *Markt 65, population 39,000; telephone code* ☎ *01180.*

Bombed by Nazis on May 17, 1940 (three days after the leveling of Rotterdam), Middelburg's center lay largely destroyed at the end of the war. The town, sitting on the slightly elevated land that makes its Lange Jan tower visible from afar, did, however, escape the flooding that followed the 1944 Allied bombing. With careful postwar rebuilding, the devastation disappeared, and today Middelburg goes about its business with an appealing, quietly proud air. ★ **Lange Jan** (*Easter–Oct., Mon.–Sat., 10 a.m.–5 p.m.;* ☎ *75450*). The tall (90-meter/295-foot, 207-stair), crown-topped, "singing" tower of the abbey (Abbey Tower) is the landmark not only of the town, but the whole of Walcheren, from most parts of which it is visible. Its carillon (concerts Thursdays noon-1 p.m., extras in summer) sounds rebound about the pedestrian streets, and it's impossible to tell where the wonderful music is coming from if you don't know; the enclosed Abbey courtyard (with cafe) is a fine place for listening. Originally constructed in the first half of the 14th century, the tower burnt down many times, most recently in the Nazi bombing of May 1940, when in its flaming crash it also wrecked the **Abdijkerken** (Abbey churches) near its base. The three churches were rebuilt as one, complete with *Lange Jan*, reconstructed and recrowned.

### Stadhuis ★★

*Stadhuisstraat 2; guided tours Mon.–Fri. 10:30 and 11:30 a.m., 1:30 and 4:00 p.m.;* ☎ *75450.* Middelburg's other outstanding monument, her

Stadhuis, stands at a corner of the cafe-rimmed Markt. The original of this opulently sculpted Gothic edifice was begun in 1452. With carved oak moldings and high vaulted ceilings, it was an impressive headquarters for the town's important cloth guild. When the Nazis bombed the center of Middelburg on May 17, 1944, it's said that the Stadhuis continued to burn for two weeks, keeping the ground around it too hot to walk on. The re-creation of the marvelous, many-figured (25 counts and countesses of Holland and Zeeland) facade, which originally had taken several generations of the Flemish architect family Keldermans of Mechelen to finish, was completed in 1967. The hall has a number of antiques to admire, including Delft vases and 17th-century Makkum tiles. The civic wedding room has two Brussels tapestries (c. 1600), and there are two more from Bruges in the large Banqueting Hall, which was originally used as the first cloth market in the Netherlands. The"star" of the Aldermen's room, generally considered the most beautiful in the Stadhuis, is a large 17th-century Dutch "cushion" cupboard of rosewood and ebony.

### The Abbey Complex                                          ★

*Multilingual tours , May 1–Nov. 1, Mon.–Sat. 1:30 and 3 p.m.; also at 11 a.m., Tues.–Fri., July and Aug.* The Abbey was founded by canons from Belgium in 1127, occupying buildings on this site from 1150 until 1574, when Willem the Silent's troops "secularized" it by turning the complex over to the States of Zeeland. The Abbey churches were required to change from Catholic to Protestant practices. The 1940 bombings almost entirely destroyed the Abbey buildings, but they have been faithfully restored. Zeeland's provincial goverment meets in the Council Chamber of the Abbey each month, and other organizations share quarters. One is the **Roosevelt Study Center** *(Abbey 9; Wed. and Thurs. 9:30 a.m.–12:30 p.m., 1:30–4:30 p.m.;* ☎ *01180-31011)*, a research resource that also has a permanent exhibit of photographs, clippings and other memorabilia on Theodore (especially his 1910 trip to Europe as reported in the Dutch newspapers—translated bits), Franklin (his roles in the WPA and World War II), and Eleanor ("First Lady of the World"). Claes Maertenszoon van Rosevelt and his wife Jannetje sailed from Zeeland in the 1640s, settling in the colony of Nieuw Nederland in the city of Nieuw Amsterdam (New York), and became the founders of an American dynasty.

### Zeeland Museum

*Abbey 3; year-round Tues.–Fri. 10 a.m.–5 p.m., Sat. and Sun. 1:30–5 p.m., closed Mon.;* ☎ *01180-26655.* Located in the 16th-century "canons' quarters" wing since 1972, the museum's core collection of curiosities was assembled by the Zeeland Society beginning in 1769. The ★★ **tapestry** room may be considered the highlight. The seven tapestries, each 4 meters/13 feet high, with a combined total length of 30 meters/99 feet, were made around 1600 by Flemish weavers working in Middelburg. They were commissioned by the States of Zeeland, who decided that the battle between the Zeelanders and the Spanish should be recorded for posterity in a memorable manner. The two largest depict dramatic sea battles off Bergen op Zoom and Rammekens. The remaining beautifully colored and bordered tapestries, whose size permits a remarkable wealth of detail, have all been restored in recent decades (a process that took much more time than the ten years it originally took for their creation). The ★ folklore room, in the beamed, steep-roofed attic, shows the regional traditional dress, how it has been modified over time, and the differences between the Catholic and Protestant costumes. There is also a display of objects related to the cultivation of the *madder plant*, whose roots yield a red dye that was an important ingredient in the region's cloth trade. In the 17th- and 18th-century rooms are elegant examples of furniture, Delft blue, and a striking portrait of Admiral de Ruyter by Ferdinand Bol (1667). Although the museum exhibits themselves are described only in Dutch, an English-language explanation sheet is available.

## WHERE TO STAY

**Le Beau Rivage**                                             ★ ★ ★
*Loskade 19, 4331 HW;* ☎ *01180-38060; inexpensive.* This is a friendly house-size hotel, well located along the town side of the Walcheren Kanaal, within walking distance of the station or town center. It has a small restaurant and lounge-bar; nine rooms, all individual, with bath; parking; no elevator.

**Hotel Du Commerce**                                         ★ ★ ★ ★
*Loskade 1; 4331 HV;* ☎ *01180-36051, FAX 01180-12386; inexpensive.* This is on the Walcheren Kanaal (canal), across from the station. The 40 bedrooms have a basic but comfortable decor, all with private shower/bath. The hotel has a restaurant and bar.

## WHERE TO EAT

**Het Groot Paradijs** *(Damplein 13; noon–2 p.m., 6-9 p.m., closed Sun., Mon.;* ☎ *26764; moderate)* occupies a fine house on a handsome square, and it serves select seafood and other carefully prepared cuisine in a setting of beamed ceilings and brass chandeliers. **De Huifkar** *(Markt 19; noon–11 p.m., closed Sun. in winter;* ☎ *2998; inexpensive to moderate)* provides a rustic touch in the center of town, with brick, beams, candlelight, and ladder-back chairs. Zeeland's seafood is also a specialty here; sole and mussels merit attention. Close by is **De Ploeg** *(Markt 55; noon–9 p.m., closed Wed. in winter;* ☎ *34690; inexpensive)* with outside tables (in season) from which to view Middelburg's marvelous Stadhuis and sample the varied menu.

**De Kabouterhut Pannekoekhuis** *(Oostkerkplein 7; noon–9 p.m., closed Mon. except school vacations;* ☎ *12276; inexpensive)* is an informal, friendly place where lines are liable to form for its platter-size fare. **De Abidij** *(Abdijplein 5; 10 a.m.–3 p.m., closed Sun.;* ☎ *35022; inexpensive)* is a pleasant resting point for coffee, snacks, or light lunch, amid the museums of the Abbey complex.

## ★★VEERE

**VVV** • *Markt 21, pop. 1000.*

When Veere, four miles northeast of Middelburg, was at the height of its importance, thanks to a marriage bond between Mary, a daughter of James I of Scotland, and Wolfert van Borssele, lord of Veere, in 1444, the population of this wonderfully quiet (if there's no tour bus making a quick stop) backwater reached 9000. It later (1541) become a "staple port" whereby all Scottish trade to Europe had to pass through its harbor. From the grassy ramparts and brick paths that encircle much of this petite patrician village, one can observe the lingering legacy of those prosperous days, though the red roof tiles may be muted in the mist. The *Delta Project* ended Veere's days as a sea fishing port, but sailing and watersports have taken over on the Veerse Meer (Veere Lake), and the village sports a yacht harbor instead of a fishing one. Standing by the Veerse Meer by the 14th-century ★★**De Campveerse Toren**, the 14th-century **Grote Kerk** is an elephantine hulk on the horizon on the other side of the village. The Cisterne, or village well, was constructed in 1551 on the orders of Maximilian of Burgundy, who had promised the Scottish wool merchants a supply of good drinking water; the well stored the rain water collected off the roof of the Grote Kerk. The gothic ★**Stadhuis** (*Markt;* ☎ *01181-253*), dating from 1474, and slender Renaissance steeple topped with a gilded ship weather vane (added in 1599), are still recognizable as they appear in old prints. The ★★facade, renovated in the 1930s and suffering no damage during the subsequent war, is decorated with statues of lords and ladies of Veere. Inside is a museum containing objects related to town history and a celebrated cup left by Maximilian when he came to inspect the Cisterne; the council chamber is adorned with **Gobelin** tapestries and paintings.

### Schotse Huizen                                                        ★★

*Scottish Houses; Kaai 25 and 27; April –Oct. Mon. 1–5 p.m., Tues.– Sat. 10 a.m.–5 p.m., closed Sun.;* ☎ *01181-1744.* In exchange for Veere having a monopoly on all importing, storing, and trading of Scottish wool, Scottish traders living there received certain privileges: their own legal system, their own chapel in the Grote Kerk, and housing. The Schotse Huizen are the only two buildings occupied by Scottish traders to have been preserved from this period (which ended with the Napoleonic occupation in 1795). In addition to being private houses, they also served as business premises. **Het Lemmeken** ("the little lamb," which refers to the gablestone decoration indicating the wool trade), the finer of the two houses, was built in 1539 and is an important example of 16th-century Dutch architecture with its wall clamps, fanlight, and adorned arches above the windows. The museum is entered next door via the front room of **De Struys** (once a twin to "Het Lemmeken" but losing out in later remodeling), where one is greeted by one of the finest pieces in the collection: the late 17th-century Zeeland "star cabinet," which is inlaid with ivory and many varieties of wood. There is an interesting set of sculptures by a Mechelen artist (c. 1516) of lords and ladies of Veere that originally were painted in bright colors and mounted on the Stadhuis facade. Among the pieces of fine furniture, porcelain, jewelry, and old watercolors of Veere when it was a trading and fishing port, one also appreciates details of the setting: the huge blue and white tiled hearth hung with brass and copper utensils, high beamed ceilings, shiny tile floors, brick walls, and, from the top floor, which is a fishing museum, the wind whistling in the gables as one looks out over the tiled roofs and gardens of the town and the wide waters of the Veerse Meer.

## WHERE TO STAY AND EAT

### De Campveerse Toren ★★

*Kade 2, 4351 AA;*  *01181-1291, FAX 01181-1695; inexpensive.* Dating from the mid-14th century, when it was built as part of Veere's fortifications, **De Campveerse Toren** became an inn not long afterwards. A favorite place with the Dutch for their civil marriage ceremonies, the Restaurant-Auberge, open year-round, has six basic rooms in the ancient inn building (No. 1 has a curved end wall with windows onto water and ramparts on three sides) and 11 in historic next-door annexes; most rooms have view of harbor; many have private bath. Centuries ago, the inn advertised: "simple night's accommodations but an absolute night's rest."

### De Campveerse Toren Restaurant

*See above; moderate to expensive.* De Campveerse Toren is renowned as a romantic (window booths with views on the water, beams, brick, candlelight, and a walk-in fireplace) setting for remarkable food, far more than for its hotel (although I recommend both). England's Edward IV enjoyed his food and stay here in 1471. Breakfast must not have been included in the price of his bed (as it would be today), however, because records note that Edward, presented with the bill for his boiled eggs for breakfast, felt that he had been overcharged. "Are eggs so rare in Holland?" he is said to have asked the innkeeper. "No," was the reply, "but kings are."

Also well-documented (the menu and bill rest in the town archives) is a banquet enjoyed here on June 21, 1575, by Willem the Silent, Prince of Orange, and 30 guests on the occasion of his marriage (his third) to Charlotte de Bourbon. The royal repast included two peacocks and two heron, three pheasant, an undisclosed number of suckling pigs, a whole calf, hams, joints of beef, lobster, and turbot, washed down with a river of Rhine wine (156 liters/165 quarts) and an additional 268 liters/284 quarts of assorted French wine and beer. Included in the bill were charges for candles, peat for the fires, the hire of cutlery and several serving wenches, a lost napkin, the innkeeper's time and trouble, and broken glasses (reported to be a fair number). De Campveerse Toren obviously oversaw a successful affair, since eight years later Willem returned for a repeat with his fourth wife, Louisa de Coligny. De Campveerse Toren's romantic and royal restaurant reputation has continued. Prince Rainier of Monaco brought Princess Grace here for a leisurely evening meal shortly after they were married. Wonderful food and well-garnished dishes, from smoked eel, "sea vegetables,"and seafood to anything else off the continental menu.

### D'Ouwe Werf

*Bastion 2; lunch and dinner;* ☎ *01181-493; moderate.* Attractively noticeable across the narrow harbor via a little bridge—a white house with a usually well-peopled terrace in front for a lovely view back over Veere, *prix-fixe* menu, and fresh à la carte seafood and shellfish.

## ★ GOES

**VVV** • *At station, pop. 31,000*

This is the main town of Zuid Beveland, with a large rectangular Grote Markt with some fine facades. The West and Oost singels (canals) mark the old moats and ramparts around the old center. To the east of Goes is Yerseke, renowned in Holland for its *Yerseksche Oesterbank* (oyster beds) and mussel beds too, which rest up against the Zuid Beveland banks of the Oosterschelde.

## ★ ★ DELTA EXPO

*On Neeltje Jans island, follow signs for Burgh-Haamstede/Oosterscheldewerken from Brouwersdam or Zierikzee; daily April–Oct. 10 a.m.–5 p.m., Nov.–Mar. same hours but closed Mon. and Tues. and Christmas; 50-minute boat trips in the Oosterschelde near the Storm Barrier from April–Oct. only, every hour from 11:30 a.m.–4 p.m., reservations necessary* ☎ *01115-2702.* The immediate impetus for the most extensive hydraulic engineering project ever undertaken in history was the hurricane of February 1, 1953, in which 1835 people drowned in Zeeland; the sea came within inches of overreaching sandbagged dikes near Vlaardingen, the result of which would have been to send the bottled-up water that surged through the English Channel and across the North Sea barreling over the Randstad, flooding Rotterdam, The Hague, Leiden, and dampening the threshold of Amsterdam. Exhibits at the Delta Expo, located on the former construction island for the final stage of the 30-year Delta Project, make real the need for such a system, and show the state-of-the-art engineering expertise used in its realization.

Hydroengineering, a science of which the Dutch have become the undisputed international masters—Dutch consultants were prominent in developing England's **Thames Barrier** and are now widely sought as consultants worldwide in areas vulnerable to the impacts of an accelerating sea-level rise, as under the "greenhouse effect"—is presented in a brief historical perspective at the Delta Expo that gives visitors a 2000-year overview of Dutch-style sea water management from pre-Roman times to the present. Landscape maquettes and "wet" tidal models, slide presentations, instruments, and other multimedia assemblages also bring the mammoth Delta Project into focus.

A good starting point for visitors is the ★introductory film (in Dutch, with English subtitles—and there's an excellent multilingual leaflet for the whole Expo). The film explains that the Delta Project called for a series of dams that would reduce the length of the Zeeland coastline by some 700 kms./420 mi., thus eliminating the need for and risk from damage to the many smaller dikes and dams previously required to keep the sea at bay. (A similar concept had been envisaged 400 years earlier but had to bide its time.) The film shows that it took a complex combination of equipment, computers, cables, underwater TV cameras, purpose-built boats, and many quality control experts to complete the huge storm barrier. Construction of the 65 18,000-ton (dry weight) underwater piers required the round-the-clock pouring of concrete from March 1979 until the beginning of 1983 to ensure that the quality of the materials was uniform and the tight construction schedule met. Special "mattresses" were laid once the shifting sands were scrapped down to the rock bed, and upon these rested the enormous concrete piers, 40 meters/130 feet high, fitted to centimeter-precision. Movable steel barriers (each 42 meters/138 feet wide) are suspended between the piers and, in normal circumstances, remain open, allowing the tide to flow through. If the water level increases to a dangerous level, all 62 barriers can be closed in about an hour. The Storm Surge Barrier, which can, when necessary, halt the flow of the 1.1 billion cubic meters of water that pass through the Oosterschelde with each turn of the tide, was opened in October 1986 by Queen Beatrix in ceremonies that inspired awe and relief.

The other dam constructions of the Delta Project had to be completed before that final and most complicated segment, the Oosterschelde storm barrier between Schouwen and Noord Beveland, could be completed. When the project was begun in the late 1950s, preserving the environment hadn't yet become a concern. But by the second half of the 1960s, environmental groups and representatives of the fishing industry pointed out that permanently damming the Oosterschelde would mean the end of a unique natural environment, as well as the loss of the financially significant trade in oysters, mussels, and fish. The Dutch Parliament decided to take another look at the expensive segment already underway. A special committee was commissioned to perform a new study, and it came back with a new concept: the Oosterschelde should not be permanently closed off and in fact should be kept open most of the time, but be able to be closed when there was a risk of flooding. That decision saved a highly developed ecosystem, many species of fauna and flora, allowed for the existing salt and fresh water areas to remain stable, and, of course, kept the economically important shellfish and fishing industries alive.

The roof of the exhibition center (which has a cafe and restaurant) affords a magnificent view over the mouth of the Oosterschelde. Your visit to Delta Expo should include a walk into the interior of one of the great concrete piers of the ★storm barrier, an experience that reinforces the enormity of the work and the force of the water it seeks to control. Now it's tourists who flood this section of Zeeland.

# ★ZIERIKZEE

**VVV** • *Havenpark 29;* ☎ *01110-12450*

At the north end of the Zeelandbrug, in Duiveland, is a long, narrow town, with carillons that strike the hours at either end. Head for the ★★ **Oude Haven**, with its park and road leading to a picturesque drawbridge and old towers. Zierikzee has three towers (Nobelpoort, Noord and Zuidhavenpoort) which date from the early 14th-century extension of the town along the harbor.

### Stadhuismuseum                                                    ★

*Meelstraat 6; May 1–Sept. 30 Mon.–Fri. 10 a.m.–noon and 1–5 p.m.;* ☎ *01110-13151.* Located in the spired 1554 building, among its historical exhibits and traditional costumes, the town hall is particularly noted for its Schutterszaal (Militia Room), which features an impressive "overturned" original oak roof that resembles the massive hull of a ship. It is also noted for its municipal silver collection, recalling the days from the 14th-18th centuries when the town was an official assayer of silver.

### The Maritiem Museum                                              ★

*Mol 25; April–Oct., and school holidays, Mon.–Sat. 10 a.m.–5 p.m.; Sun. and hols. noon–5 p.m.;* ☎ *01110-13151.* Housed in the restored brick, step-gabled 1526 Gravensteen, whose facade is decorated with wrought iron latticework. This old prison's original cells are preserved, and other exhibits tell of the rise and fall of Zierikzee's fishing and merchant shipping industries.

## WHERE TO STAY AND TO EAT

### Hotel Mondragon                                          ★ ★ ★

*Havenpark 21, 4301 JG;* ☎ *01110-13051; inexpensive.* With just under a dozen rooms, most with private bath, the Mondragon is wonderfully situated in the loveliest part of pretty old Zierikzee, by the park, old harbor, and historic towers. The hotel has a restaurant and bar just down the street.

### Restaurant Mondragon

*Oude Haven 13; daily lunch and dinner;* ☎ *01110-2670; moderate.* Scenically situated on the old harbor and has a lovely traditional decor. Seafood's the suggestion, starting with the freshest oysters you've ever likely to slide down.

To the north of Zierikzee, ★**Dreischor** is worth a visit. It is the most attractive of several unusual *ring-villages*: its church (1340–1475) sits in the center of the village on a moat-surrounded grassy circle. The village's small stadhuis dates from 1637. **Brouwershaven** is a small interesting town, the center of which (the broad **Markt**) includes the small port where Count Floris V built a dam in 1285. Willem the Silent had it walled in 1582 (now dismantled). The facade of the **Stadhuis** is from 1559, a young face on an older building, and the **Grote Kerk** is basically the result of rebuilding in

the 14th and 15th centuries. Silting, the result of flooding in 1682, rele-
gated the town to its present sleepy but pleasing status.

# NORTH BRABANT

Brabant was born as a part of the duchy of Lower Lorraine, which was created in the 10th century amid the territorial reshufflings that followed Charlemagne's death. In 1190, Lower Lorraine ruler Duke Henry I took upon himself the new title Duke of Brabant. The **Duchy of Brabant** (which included much of what today is the Dutch province of North Brabant and the Belgian provinces of Brabant and Antwerp) lasted from then until 1430, when Duke Anthony died childless, leaving the title to Duke Philip the Good of Burgundy. From that time, Brabant's history merged with the Netherlands.

During the *Eighty Years' War* (1568–1648), Brabant was split in two, the southern section being retained by Spain (and eventually becoming the Belgian provinces of Brabant and Antwerp), while the northern portion was merged with Willem the Silent's Dutch Protestant rebellion. North Brabant became part of the United Provinces under the *Treaty of Munster* (1648), but only as a "land," not a self-governing province. During the occupation of the Netherlands by Napoleon (1795–1814), the two Brabants were reunited. But, with the establishment of the Kingdom of the Netherlands in 1815, Brabant was again separated into its Dutch and Belgian parts, this time North Brabant having full status as a Dutch province.

Historically, the people in North Brabant have been predominantly Roman Catholic. (Today 85 percent are so "on paper, not in practice," was the way it was put to me.) After the rebellion of the Dutch against Spanish rule in the northern Netherlands, the success of Protestants there led to difficulties for North Brabant's Catholics.

They felt that the Protestant leaders of Holland's *States General* in The Hague regarded them as a "colonial" territory, and that the economic well- being of the region was largely neglected.

Traditionally a "poor" province, in that the sand and clay soil from the region's rivers is not fertile enough to support the population economically, North Brabant has come into economic strength in this century largely due to development at **Eindhoven**. There, in 1891, Dr. Anton Philips founded a firm that produced electric light bulbs. As **Philips**, now a world-recognized name in electronic products, grew, Eindhoven became a "company town," such was the firm's influence in attracting talented people and bringing related industry to the region.

## GUIDELINES FOR NORTH BRABANT
### SIGHTS

Special places of interest are spread out in North Brabant, a roomy province, much of it woodlands, heath, and peat fen, extending west to east along the Belgian border from the Scheldt River to Limburg, and north to the Merwede and Maas river boundary. In **Eindhoven** (*VVV Stationplein 17,* ☎ *040-449231; pop. 192,000*), there's 20th-century art at the respected **Van Abbemuseum**. Places where the past is palpable are the small fortified river towns of **Willemstad** in the west of the province, **Woudrichem** in the center, and **Grave**, **Ravenstein**, and **Megen** to the east. From Woudrichem it's possible to take a boat to **Loevestein** (*in summer, Mon.–Fri. once an hour from 10:30 a.m.–4:30 p.m.; from 12:30 p.m. Sat.; no boats Sun.*), the c. 1360 castle/prison (*open April–Oct., Mon.–Fri. 10 a.m.–5 p.m.; Sat.–Sun., 1–5 p.m., guided tours every half hour, last 4 p.m.*) from which Grotius made his famous escape (see "The Dutch Cultural Legacy: The Muse"). **Oirschot** (northwest of Eindhoven) has the most attractive and best preserved market square in Brabant (with cobblestones, shady old trees, gas lamps, and the dignified calm of centuries), and the entire town center is a national monument, including the Stadhuis (1463) and Gothic St. Pieterskerk (1465- 1500). **Bergen op Zoom**, a historic town in the west of North Brabant, where the dunes meet the heath, has a Grote Markt that's carefree with cafes in summer, and buildings that reflect its past, including the last 15th-century **Markiezenhof Palace**, now a museum.

### GETTING AROUND

Since sights of interest to the traveler are scattered, a car is nearly necessary for seeing your selected sites in a reasonable time frame. As everywhere in Holland, there is excellent provincial bus service, but it is time-consuming. Trains serve the major towns: **'s Hertogen-bosch (Den Bosch)**; **Breda**; **Eindhoven**; **Bergen op Zoom**. Boat cruises (☎ *566773*) from Den Bosch to **Heusden** *(Tues., Thurs., Sat. 11 a.m. mid-June through Aug.)* and **Woudrichem** *(daily at 10 a.m. mid-June to late Aug.)* leave from the Dommel, near the town's train station.

## SHOPPING

Branches of main Dutch stores can be found in the centers of cities and major towns; many will be located on now-pedestrianized streets.

## ENTERTAINMENT AND EVENTS

Breda celebrates the pre-Lenten **Carnival** with the most vigor in North Brabant, though Bergen op Zoom and Den Bosch hold their own. In addition to its annual **Art and Antiques Fair**, Breda hosts the colorful military **National Taptoe (Tattoo)** at the end of each August, and a jazz festival then as well, with performances set mostly in the Grote Kerk. In mid-August, the Grote Kerk is decked out in flowers for *Breda Flora*. Den Bosch has an important annual vocalist competition, and in September Tilburg and Eindhoven have jazz festivals.

## WHERE TO STAY

While there are pleasant town and country choices in the two, three, and, occasionally, four-star categories, five-star luxury in the area is not available (except at a business hotel in Eindhoven). As elsewhere in Holland, the local VVVs are the most up-to-date accommodations authorities.

## WHERE TO EAT

Anchovies from Bergen op Zoom can raise a thirst for Brabant-brewed beer. In May and June, asparagus is the traditional treat, and locally favored sweet specialties include the Den Bosch "Bossche koek" (cake). Both rural bistros and highly regarded restaurants reflect a Burgundian fondness for fine food.

## TRAVEL TIPS

When exploring by car in regions near rivers, check your map carefully and ask questions locally, to make sure of the location of bridge and/or car ferry crossings.

## ON THE ROAD
### ★ 'S HERTOGENBOSCH

**VVV** • *Markt 77; Mon–Fri. 9 a.m.–5 p.m., Sat. 4 p.m.,* ☎ *123071; pop. 90,000; telephone code 073.*

North Brabant's provincial town is the pleasant smaller city of **'s Herto-genbosch** (**Den Bosch**, pronounced Den BOSS). Its center is the enclosed triangle of the **Markt**, which has a bronze statue of painter **Hieronymus Bosch** (1450–1516), who was born there. The Markt plays host to Wednesday and Saturday morning markets (on Wed. accompanied on the **Stadhuis Hemony carillon** from 10–11 a.m.). The Stadhuis has a remodeled classic Dutch facade (1670) and interior wall paintings, tapestries, and other objects in the Council Chamber worth seeing (normally open during business hours).

The village of 's Hertogenbosch ("the dukes' woods") grew up around the early 13th-century ★ **De Moriaan**, built by Henry I, duke of Brabant (who conferred a charter on the town in 1185), as a hunting lodge. It now houses the VVV on the Markt. There, you can pick up a leaflet *Wandering around Old Den Bosch*, which will send you to, among other places, the restored ★ **Uilenburg Quarter**, a canal, arched bridge, gallery, boutique, and bistro pedestrian neighborhood not far from the Markt. Much of the core of the city is closed to vehicular traffic, and public sculptures along the way make the walk to the town's most outstanding attraction a pleasure.

### Sint Janskathedraal                                         ★★★

(*St. Janskerkhof; check at VVV for hours*). This is the finest example of late gothic architecture in Holland, and could be your sole reason for a visit to Den Bosch, especially since it was fully restored to splendor not long ago. Sint Jan's, built between 1380 and 1552 under the auspices of the Bishop of Liège, took its share of shuttling back and forth between Catholic and Protestant rites, but finally settled with Catholicism (thanks to Napoleon) in 1810; in 1929 the pope conferred the status of basilica upon the structure. The building's blend of Romanesque brickwork and Perpendicular-style carved stonework has been compared to that of England's Lincoln Cathedral. Sint Jan's tower's progression through various architectural ages can be seen as it ascends, from Romanesque base to slender 17th-century baroque spire, with Gothic bringing up the midsection. The small figures, a hundred individual gargoyles groping about the buttresses, are one of the most distinguishing details of the exterior (copies of some of the small figures are sold as souvenirs in town). Inside, the double-aisled nave, which appears especially lofty owing to the lack of capitals in the main arcade, carries one's view to the choir. Among the specifics that warrant attention are the solid copper 1492 font, the many restored flat floor tombs, the north transept's two grisaille works by **Hieronymus Bosch**, and, near the south transept, the *Altar of Passion*, an Antwerp retable from 1500. The monumental 17th-century organ casing by Symons and Schysler, with an 18th-century instrument by Heyneman, is one of the largest and most beautiful in Europe. Concerts on the 48-bell carillon are given Wed. noon–1 p.m., and the tower can be climbed on certain days in summer (inquire within).

**Noord Brabant Museum**

*Verwersstraat 41; Tues.–Fri., 10 a.m.–5 p.m., Sat. and Sun., noon– 5 p.m.*
Established in 1837, and moved into the restored and enlarged 1769
Government House palace (until recently the residence for provincial
governors) a hundred and fifty years later, the museum has displays on
all facets of North Brabant life as befits a building with the Brabant
coat of arms on its facade. Among the many exhibits are two early
"dark" period Van Gogh's painted in Brabant, and views of Den
Bosch over its long history.

## WHERE TO STAY

**Golden Tulip Central** ★★★★

*Markt 51, entrance Mr. Loeffplein 98, 5211 RX;* ☎ *125151, FAX
145699; res. in U.S.A.* ☎ *800-333-1212; moderate.* A modern hotel
with a fine location on the Markt (entrance at the back), the Central
has 122 rooms; many on the higher floors have fine views of the
square. Breakfast (not included) is served in the hotel's 14th-century
vaulted cellar. The comfortable indoor-outdoor lobby cafe fronts the
Markt. There's also a restaurant. Parking garage next door.

## WHERE TO EAT

**Raadskelder**

*Stadhuis cellar;* ☎ *136919; moderate.* This restaurant in the venerable
brick vaults of the Stadhuis basement serves a full menu of well-
prepared, traditional fare in the soft light of wrought-iron chandeliers.
There's a bar-lounge if you want the atmosphere but just a drink.

**Pumpke**

*Parade 37; daily; inexpensive.* From outside tables on a square, you can
face the splendid structure of St. Jans. Enjoy the view over coffee or a
light meal.

## ★ HEUSDEN

**VVV** • *Engstraat 4, daily in summer 10 a.m.–5 p.m.,* ☎ *04162-2100; pop.
2,000 within fortified town.*

Here there are no "must-see" museums, just the pleasure of enjoying an
enchanting old fortified town on the river Maas with more than 400 historic buildings that have been recently and lovingly restored. The centuries-old streets, cobbled market, tucked-away squares, step gables, gable
stones, the windmill by the little former fishing harbor (now for yachts),
and, of course, the view across the river and over the canals of this former
Roman settlement won't fall short of your scenic needs. There are un-
earthed ramparts and town walls from the 17th century on which to walk
around the town. Heusden has bus service to/from Den Bosch.

## WHERE TO STAY

**"In Den Verdwaalde Koogel" Hotel-Restaurant** ★★★

*Vismarkt 1, 5256 BC;* ☎ *04162-1933, FAX 04162-1295; inexpensive/*

*moderate.* This is a step-gabled delight dating from the 17th century; all of its 13 rooms restored outside and inside, each individually decorated, with private toilet and shower, TV, telephone, and minibar. The spirit of service of the management ("In North Brabant, you're only a stranger once"), setting (an interior of tasteful contemporary furnishings amid brick and old beams), and a terrace cafe on the lovely main square in sight of the historic harbor windmill, all assure a pleasant stay. And so does the reputable kitchen of the restaurant (*lunch and dinner daily, noon–2:30 p.m., 6–9:30 p.m.*), which offers various multicourse daily menus, and full à la carte selection, especially the house pâte lamb, and the lovely, lean, local pork. (The province has 3.2 pigs for every person.)

## WHERE TO EAT

### De Pannenkoekbakker
*Vismarkt 4;* ☎ *04162-2100.* For savory or sweet meal-on-a-plate Dutch pancakes.

### Café Havenzicht
*Vismarkt 2;* ☎ *04162-2723.* For a variety of appealing informal fare on the square or inside. Has an excellent harbor view.

## BREDA

**VVV** • *near station, Willemstraat 17, Mon.–Sat. 9 a.m.–6 p.m., 5 p.m. Sat.;* ☎ *222444; pop. 120,000; telephone code 076.*

One of the chief, and most attractive towns in the province, with most of its monuments in the old center, Breda has a long, turbulent history as a fortified town near the border of Belgium. There has always been a quiet corner in Breda, however, at the **Begijnhof**, whose history goes back to 1267, and whose situation on the present site dates from 1531. Small brick houses, restored in 1980, encircle the ancient garden courtyard, decorated with a delightful contemporary statue of two Beguines by Amsterdam sculptor Hans Bayens. Behind the Beguinhof is Breda's large in-town Valkenberg Park.

The **Castle of Breda** grew from the first stronghold built by the *Heren* (Lords) *of Breda* on the site in 1198, and was later enlarged into a grand palace by the famous Italian architect Tomaso Vincidor of Bologna. From the castle, **Charles II**, who had lived in Breda in exile for some time, set forth in the *Declaration of Breda* (1660) the terms upon which he would sit on the throne of England. The *Treaty of Breda* (1667), also signed at the castle, awarded the colony of *Nieuw Amsterdam* (New York) to the English. Since 1828, the castle has housed Breda's important **Royal Military Academy** (no visitors except during the late August evening performances of the colorful ★★**National Tattoo** in the forecourt). The lords of Breda who lived in the castle were the scions of the Netherlands' House of Oranje-Nassau. Count Hendrik III of Nassau, a tutor and counselor to Emperor Charles V, was an influential ruler in the early 16th century, and did much to aid the reconstruction of Breda following the town's great fire in 1534.

Not far from the castle is the ★**Spanjaardsgat** (Spaniards Gate), two heptagonal towers with watergate that were added to the 16th-century fortifications of the city in 1610. Its name stems from an inaccurate association with a historic event that took place in Breda on Shrove Tuesday in 1590. In 1581 Breda had been occupied by the Spanish, who had a stronghold in the nearby southern Netherlands (now Belgium). The surprise attack was probably in retaliation for the town's role in the *Compromise of Breda* (1566), the first document signed by Dutch noblemen denouncing Spanish dominion. However, in 1590, in a Trojan-horse kind of caper, Maurice of Nassau was able to retake the town when 80 of his men, hidden under peat turfs in the barge of Adriaen van Bergen (who supplied the Spanish garrison with fuel), were towed into the center of town under the unknowing noses of the occupying forces, who were quickly overpowered. (The Spanish retook Breda in 1625.)

The heart of Breda is the ★**Grote Markt**, where the citizens go to market Tuesday and Friday mornings, drink beer at the many cafes, and, for one long weekend of the year, revel at *Carnival*. In the **Stadhuis** (1767) is a large reproduction of the famous Velasquez painting, *Las Lanzas*, which shows the surrender of Breda to the Spanish commander Spinola in 1625. At Grote Markt 19 is ★**Het Lam**, an exceptional 17th-century building that houses the municipal museum *(Wed.–Sat., 10:30 a.m.–1 p.m., Tues., Sun., holidays 1–5 p.m.)*. The neighboring former meat hall carries sculpted heads of cattle on its facade.

At the northern end of the Markt is the **Grote Kerk**, begun in the 13th century and noted for its many monuments, a triptych by **Jan van Scorel** (1495–1562), and copper latticework. The church has played an important role in the history of the Oranje-Nassau dynasty; all the related lords of Breda prior to Willem the Silent are buried here, their tombs memorials to history as well as works of art. Beneath the magnificent alabaster mausoleum of Count Engelbert II (who died in 1504) is buried his grandson, **Rene de Chalons**, the first prince of Oranje-Nassau (died 1544). In 1552 his successor Willem the Silent, prince of Orange, who became known as the "Father of the Fatherland," had the vault enlarged, probably for himself. However, when Willem was assassinated at the Prinsenhof in Delft in 1584, Breda was still held by the Spanish, and thus Delft's Nieuwe Kerk became the burial site for Willem and all succeeding members of the House of Orange. The church's lacy-looking tower (97 meters/318 feet) has a carillon (concerts twice a week), and can be climbed (276 steps). A 25-year renovation was completed in 1969; originally built in 1509, the tower burned when struck by lighting in 1694, and was replaced as a gift by King Willem III.

## WHERE TO STAY

**De Klok** ★★★

*Grote Markt 26, 4811 XR;* ☎ *214082, FAX 143463; inexpensive/ moderate.* If you want to be in the midst of the grandeur of the Grote Markt, stay in a front-facing room at this small (23 room) unpretentious hotel, which has its own cafe and bar, and private facilities in most rooms, TV in all. There's an elevator, but no parking.

## WHERE TO EAT

### Auberge de Arent

*Schoolstraat 2; lunch and dinner; for reservations* ☎ *144601; moderate.* Offering a view of the Grote Kerk, this bistro has a superb Renaissance setting of its own and exceptional food (a combination that's hard to beat). The dining space includes a high, painted ceiling, a baroque fireplace, and fresh-flower-decorated tables set out on a black-and-white checkerboard marble floor. French and Dutch-inspired dishes, well-served from a choice of *prix-fixe* or the *à la carte* menus. The **Cafe Franciskaner** (*Grote Markt 23; daily; inexpensive*), only one of a number of establishments on the congenial, cafe-cluttered square, is a local favorite for *koffie en gebak* (coffee and pastry) or other snacks.

## BAARLE-NASSAU/BAARLE-HERTOG

**VVV** • *St. Annaplein 10,* ☎ *04257-9921; pop. 7,500; bus service from Breda, 19 km/12 mi.*

This *one town-two countries* place arouses the curiosity of almost everyone who hears about it, and the civic complications that arise from its geopolitical status raises smiles in those of us for whom the world is overly bureaucratic. Parts of the town are legally Dutch and others legally Belgian. Different laws apply in the two sectors. Thus, there are two burgomasters, two stadhuizen, two police forces, two school systems, and two tax systems; townsfolk buying chocolate and cigars go to Belgian shops, where a lower rate makes them cheaper. The nationality of a house that straddles both Belgian and Dutch territory—a common occurrence, since the town's numerous small enclaves of land crisscross all over the map—is determined by the location of the front door; a house number plate indicates by its design which country one's in. Naturally, there's at least one edifice in which the front door itself opens on both Belgian and Dutch soil. One such building, **Het Huis op Loveren 2 en 19**, is the former Swan Inn, whose records show that **Grotius** (see "The Muse" under "The Dutch Cultural Legacy") spent the night of March 22–23, 1631, en route on his escape from Loevestein prison to Antwerp. Even jurists as learned as Grotius (considered the father of international law) haven't solved all the problems associated with Baarle-style situations: When the going gets complicated, transactions take place at the **Café Het Hoekske**—through which the national frontier runs, as indicated by a painting on the outside wall—in the presence of both a Dutch and a Belgian notary.

Historians aren't entirely sure why Belgian enclaves exist in Dutch territory, though the confusing condition is said to have its roots in inheritance disputes in 1198, between Duke Henry I of Brabant, who had the Baarle-Hertog lands, and Godfrey, lord of Breda, who, with the additional identity of count of Nassau, held the Baarle-Nassau estates. At the *Peace of*

*Westphalia* (1648), the Baarle that had belonged to Nassau was given to the northern Dutch United Provinces, and the part that had belonged to the duke (Hertog) was awarded to the southern Netherlands (now Belgium). This singular situation remained unchanged even after 1843, when the frontier of the at-long-last legally separated countries of Holland and Belgium was formally established. Over the centuries many attempts have been made to find a remedy for what outsiders consider an abnormal and untenable condition, but which some of the local populace refer to as a "precious inheritance." Its circumstances did save Baarle-Hertog from the German occupation suffered by the rest of Belgium in World War I. Then, in spite of Dutch Baarle surrounding itself with barbed-wire fencing to signal its neutrality, Belgian Baarle in October 1915 established a radio station which made the village an important outpost for Allied espionage.

## NUENEN

Ardent fans of **Vincent van Gogh** will find interest in this otherwise ordinary town of 20,000, a suburb to the southwest of Eindhoven. The **★Van Gogh Documentation Center** *(Papenvoort 15; Mon.–Fri., 9 a.m.–noon and 2–4 p.m., except closed the first and third Fri. of the month;* ☎ *040-631668)* gives a picture of the period when Van Gogh lived and worked here, with exhibits of photographs, reproductions, and numerous original works of art produced during his Nuenen period. The center, opened by Van Gogh's nephew Vincent (son of the artist's supportive brother Theo) in 1976, has a self- guiding brochure to the places in Nuenen that are associated with Van Gogh. Many have hardly changed and are recognizable in his paintings and drawings. The artist Vincent came to Nuenen, where his father was minister of the Protestant Dutch Reformed Church on Papenvoort, in 1883, at the age of 30. He lived at #26 on the Main Road (still standing, dated 1764 in iron numbers, today the church rectory) with his parents for much of that period, until 1885 when he left the town. His parents furnished a shed in their back garden (visible from the road behind the house) as a studio for Vincent, who worked intensely on his art while he lived in Nuenen. At the time, this Kempen region of Brabant relied mainly on agriculture and weaving, and Vincent often helped with tilling the soil. His admiration increased for the peasants and the way in which they literally ploughed their way through their heavy work and their hard life, and he created many well-known paintings and drawings of them. It was in Nuenen that Van Gogh produced the works of his early "dark" Dutch period, under the influence of Rembrandt's effects of light and shadow (*chiaroscuro*), and painted his first masterpiece (both in Vincent's and art historians' opinion): *The Potato Eaters* (April 1885). He left Nuenen (then a community of about 2000 people who, other than the peasant workers he befriended, generally regarded Van Gogh as an odd character) after a painful love affair that was ended by the family of his beloved, Margot Begemann, who then tried to take her own life.

**Note:** Van Gogh was born in the North Brabant town of **Zundert** (several miles south of Breda, close to the Belgian border), but his childhood home has been demolished (although near the site is the small Vincent van Gogh Plein, with a statue *Vincent and Theo* by **Ossip Zadkine**). There's little else to see except, in the graveyard of the church where his father was minister, a marker for a year-older brother *Vincent* who died in infancy. (The reuse of a Christian name under such circumstances was quite common in those days.)

# LIMBURG PROVINCE

*Maastricht's Vrijthof square is lined with cafes.*

Limburg Province is an essentially north-south strip of land that stretches roughly 50 kms./30 miles in the southeast corner of the country along the border that Holland shares with Germany. The Dutch Limburg forms a wedge into Belgium's Limburg province. The two Limburgs once were one, under the early bishoprics of Tongeren, then Maastricht, and finally Liège. Under the *Treaty of Munster* in 1648, the Spanish kept the southern portion of Limburg, but the Dutch United Provinces in the northern Netherlands received Maastricht and all Limburg east of the Maas (Meuse) River. In 1814, the two Limburgs were rejoined under the short-lived

Dutch-Belgian United Kingdom of the Netherlands. In 1830, all of Limburg except Maastricht joined in the Belgian uprising against Dutch rule. Thereafter, Limburgers in the north regarded themselves as Belgian until divided again by the 1839 *Treaty of London*, under which the borders of the present Dutch Limburg province were set.

The northern part of Limburg province is made up largely of small industrial towns with rather uninspiring landscape, and travelers will find few sights of sufficient interest to warrant a stop. Exceptions include **Thorn**, cobbled, medieval, and known as the "white village," an epithet derived from its all-white-painted buildings. There's an interesting 13th-century gothic abbey church with baroque interior (*open daily, 9 a.m.–6 p.m., Easter–Oct.*). Also worthy of a visit is the old center of **Sittard**, around whose spacious Markt (parking, terrace cafes, shops) stand a number of 16th-century half-timbered structures. In the town center of **Heerlen** is the **Thermen Museum** (*Tues.– Fri., 10 a.m.–5 p.m., Sat., Sun., holidays 2–5 p.m.;* ☎ *045-764581*) with Roman baths, excavated in the 1970s, imaginatively on view from a bridge above. On display are related exhibits (descriptions in English) and maps of the important Roman roads that led through Heerlen.

Southern Limburg is by far the more physically attractive portion of the province, with wooded rolling hills unlike the landscape anywhere else in Holland. The summer holiday heart of the region is **Valkenburg**, a bustling, family-style place, with countless hotels, casino, and new *Thermae 2000* spa complex. But for most travelers, the most attractive, interesting, and historic place in Limburg is **Maastricht**. Only 125 miles from Amsterdam, diagonally across the country, Maastricht seems far more distant in terms of the differences in its ambience.

# MAASTRICHT

## *GUIDELINES FOR MAASTRICHT*

### SIGHTS

Maastricht, with a population of 115,000, has an appealing and compact old center, with narrow cobbled streets, quaint squares, and some 1450 protected historic monuments, the oldest from Roman days. The mellow yellow stone buildings of local marl in the restored pedestrian **Stokstraat Quarter** are from the 17th and 18th centuries, and many have sculpted gable stones. Maastricht, with its assemblage of churches (romanesque and gothic) and cafes, is ringed by

**rampart walls** (built in 1229, 1350, and 1516, respectively), atop which one can encircle much of the town on foot. The river Maas adds interest to the city, which is divided by it, but reconnected by the multiarched St. Servaas Bridge.

## GETTING AROUND

Maastricht's mood is best met on foot; walking allows for poking into picturesque corners, glancing up at gables and gable stones, and making spontaneous stops where and when your senses are engaged. The VVV offers guided 1-1/2 hr. **walking tours** of the city (*at 2 p.m. on holidays and weekends, daily during July and Aug.; Sat. only April– June and Sept.–mid Nov.*). The VVV sells the architecturally detailed book A *Walk Through Maastricht,* and supplies other self-guided walking tour literature. City buses provide coverage of the outskirts, and you can go by river cruise boat to see the St. Pietersburg caves. Taxis and rental bicycles can be had at the station.

## SHOPPING

For such a relatively small city, Maastricht has surprisingly sophisticated shops, from boutiques to bakeries. Many of the main department and other stores are located on and just off the pedestrianized **Grote Staat**, which leads to the **Vrijthof** (main square), and **Kleine Staat**. General markets are held on Marktplein in front of the Stadhuis Wednesdays and Fridays (*8 a.m.–1 p.m.*). Saturdays from 10 a.m.–4 p.m. there's a flea market on the Stationsstraat (opposite the rail station). Mondays most shops don't open until 1 p.m. (through 6 p.m.); late night shopping (9 p.m.) is on Thursday. Because of its proximity to those countries, Belgian francs and German marks are accepted in most stores.

## ENTERTAINMENT AND EVENTS

Available free from the VVV is the monthly events calendar *Maastricht Maandagenda*; there's a summary listing in English. Cafes, **concerts**, and **pub crawls** cover the favored evening activities. Maastrichtenaars enjoy the fact that their city has a church for every *week*, and a pub for every *day* in the year. A number of the pub/cafes have live music, and many remain open until 2 a.m. In summer, weekly evening organ concerts (usually Tuesday) are held at one of several churches. The well-known 150-voice male choir **Mastreechter Staar** has free open rehearsals (except July and Aug.; details from the VVV). Maastricht is in **Carnival** country, and makes much of pre-lenten festivities (some museums are closed from the Saturday before, and continuing through, *Mardi Gras*). The Burgundian food festival of **Preuvenement** fits in with the city's intense interest in cuisine.

## WHERE TO STAY

Maastricht offers a small but solid choice of hotels in the city. Some are family-owned and operated; all deliver friendly, personal service. In the surrounding Limburg countryside are several castle/manor house-style hotels with renowned restaurants.

## WHERE TO EAT

This region is the cuisine capital of the Netherlands. Fresh produce and attention to preparation make it hard to find less than fine food at any eatery, but some restaurants really star on taste tests.

## ARRIVING

Tucked into the far southeast corner of the Netherlands—which gives it almost a central continental location—Maastricht is a Dutch destination that can easily be included in an itinerary featuring France, Germany, Switzerland, and, of course, Belgium and Luxembourg. Maastricht is readily reached by rail, road, and air. There are hourly train arrivals from Amsterdam; an *Intercity* takes about 2.5 hours. Rail connections from The Hague and Rotterdam have a convenient cross-platform change at Eindhoven. Maastricht also is served hourly by trains from Belgium's Bruges, Ghent, Brussels, and Liège, and other European points. Via motorway, Maastricht is 215 kms./125 mi. by road from Amsterdam; it lies roughly halfway between Brussels and Cologne. Maastricht's modern airfield offers, among other service, several flights daily to/from Amsterdam on *NLM Cityhopper* (contact **KLM** for flight information) and to/from London.

## IN THE AREA

The only U.S. military cemetery in the Netherlands is nearby at *Margraten*. Old fortified farms, villages with half-timbered buildings, and country castles are scattered in the rolling hills of surrounding southern Limburg.

## TRAVEL TIPS

If you don't plan to have a rental car in this rural region of the Netherlands, you needn't worry about missing the province's most important historic and sightseeing highlights, since these are in Maastricht itself. The cruise along the River Maas to Liège, Belgium, (20 kms./12 mi.) is not recommended, since the riverside scenery does not justify the length of time the trip takes (several hours one way); if travelling to Liège, take a quick train instead.

## MAASTRICHT IN CONTEXT

Masstricht isn't a name that readly rolls off the tongues of tourists, even those fairly familiar with Holland. But it's been in the news a lot lately, primarily because of a treaty signed here at the end of 1991 by the leaders of the *European Community* (today, the *European Union*, EU) member countries. The so-called *Maastricht Treaty* provides for monetary union within the EU and for the adoption of a single European currency by 1999. As ratification of the treaty came up in each EU country so again did mention of Maastricht.

Maastricht is the Netherlands' oldest, southernmost (it lies well below Belgium's northern border), and most unexpected city. For starters, the largely Roman Catholic population of Maastricht practices an almost unDutch-like indulgence in the good life, exhibiting a Burgundian *joie de vivre*, and focusing on fine food, drink, and fun. As one resident put it, "We don't have a lazy mentality, but we do love life." That contrasts sharply with the "Black Stocking" attitude towards life endorsed by the dourly conservative, very religious element of the Protestant Dutch Reformed Church in the north of the country, whose numbers undoubtedly would be shocked by the view held *here*: "Catholicism allows you to enjoy yourself."

In Maastricht and surrounding Limburg, features commonly associated with Holland—waterlogged land, windmills, wooden-shoes—make way for other characteristics in the intriguing territory of this tricultured corner of the Netherlands. With **Aachen, Germany** (the ancient city inseparably associated with Charlemagne and the Holy Roman Empire), and **Liège, Belgium** (the capital of French-speaking Wallonia), each only a dozen miles (20 km.) away, Maastricht merchants have long accepted *marks* and *francs* as freely as *guilders*, providing a foretaste of the European monetary dexterity anticipated under the European Community's "single market" economic initiatives.

Maastricht's "mentality" encompasses the foreign influences of its nearby neighbors. As a guide explained, "In Maastricht we live and let live. Sometimes those who are surrounded only by their own kind become judgmental, but this doesn't happen in Maastricht where so many things mix." Many Maastrichtenaars could be called chauvinists, in that they love their city above all others, but, as one city official said, "People like us who live in places where their history has gone back and forth feel European or international, not overly nationalistic." Another expressed it this way: "We don't feel we're crossing a border when we go to Belgium or Germany, but we do feel we've come home when we get back to Maastricht."

Maastricht was founded by the **Romans** about 50 B.C. Its name derived from the Latin *Mosae Trajectum*, meaning "site where the Maas could be crossed." The settlement, which grew to become a walled *castellum* (fortified district), was located on important roads, the foremost of which ran from the English Channel and North Sea ports to Cologne, and was known as the "Appian Way of the North." Towards the end of the 4th century, after 400 years of occupation during which Maastricht became a center of Christianity, the Romans and their army withdrew to return to Rome, leaving the city vulnerable to attack by Frankish tribes. Their raids were among the first of more than twenty beseigements suffered by Maastricht over succeeding centuries, the most recent being the four-year Nazi occupation during World War II. That ended in September 1944, when the 30th Infantry "Old Hickory" Division of the *U.S. 1st. Army* made Maastricht the first town in war-ravaged Holland to be freed.

From A.D. 380 to 721, Maastricht was a bishop's seat, becoming so when **St. Servaas**, fearing the Frankish tribes, transferred the see from Tongeren (the oldest town in Belgium) to Maastricht. A small chapel was built on the site where he was buried in Maastricht, and several centuries later a cathedral named for him began taking shape there. In 721, **St. Hubert**, Maastricht's last bishop, transferred the see to Liège (which led to an era of great power for the prince-bishops there).

Maastricht came under the influence and favor of Charlemagne's Frankish Empire when the Holy Roman Emperor made his base at nearby Aachen. Having survived the turbulent centuries following the death of Charlemagne (in 814), Maastricht became, in 1204, a joint possession of the dukes of Brabant and the prince-bishops of Liège. With feudal fending required to keep itself intact, Maastricht erected its first protective ramparts in 1229. It wasn't long before the town outgrew them, and a second set of city walls was added about 1350. Sections of each still stand. These were the earliest of many bastions that eventually made Maastricht one of Europe's most strongly fortified cities. With its strategic European location, the armies of the Spanish, French, English, and Germans all too often over the centuries beat a path to the city's sturdy town gates.

In 1576, Maastricht joined with **Willem the Silent's** other Dutch supporters in rebellion against the Spanish. But in 1579, Spanish leader the duke of Parma paid the city back with a four-month seige and ruthless sacking. However, because it had the traditions of both Protestantism (through the House of Orange) and Roman Catholicism (being within the realm of the nearby Bishop of Liège), Maastricht escaped the outbursts of the *Iconoclast* and other religious outbreaks of the Reformation. Eventually, most of the citizens settled on the Catholic faith (about 90 percent of the population today).

In 1673, Maastricht fell to the French, in one of the city's most famous beseigements (due to the cast of characters). That year, French king and army commander **Louis XIV** stood on a hilltop watching his forces, which included **D'Artagnan**, (the inspiration for and a captain in Alexandre Dumas' novel *The Three Musketeers*), and 6000 troops of England's duke of Monmouth, who had pledged to fight with the French against the Dutch United Provinces. During the encounter **Captain John Churchill** (who later became duke of Marlborough, an ancestor of Winston Churchill) was rescued by D'Artagnan, who lost his life in doing so. D'Artagnan is remembered by a statue, supposedly marking the spot at which he fell, in Maastricht's **Waldeckpark**.

In 1795, the once-again occupying French made Maastricht capital of the newly created *Department of the Lower Meuse*. After Napoleon's defeat at Waterloo (1815), Belgium and the Netherlands were ordered to unite under Dutch King William I. But after battling over the union for nine years (1830–1839), the two countries adopted a partition. Perhaps because of the logic of their geographic location, some citizens in Maastricht at the time wanted to join with Belgium, but the Dutch garrison that occupied Maastricht decreed otherwise. Thus, the ancient province of Limburg was split in two, with Maastricht remaining a part of the Netherlands.

Today it's possible to say that Maastricht has the best of both countries: Dutch-style tidiness and tolerance combined with a Belgian-style appreciation for the fine art of the kitchen and "cafe-society."

## GUIDEPOSTS

**Telephone code 043**

**Tourist Info •** VVV, Het Dinghuis, Kleine Staat 1; year-round Mon.–Sat. 9 a.m.–6 p.m.; in July and August open until 7 p.m., and on Sun. 11 a.m.–3 p.m; during Carnival and on some holidays 11 a.m.–3 p.m..; ☎ *252121 (calls for information taken personally during business* *hours, recorded information only, in Dutch but with option for English afterwards).* Bookings for guided walking tours of city, tours of limited access sites, St. Pietersburg caves, casements, Derlon Museum Cellar, river cruises, day coach trips. VVV shop with maps, pamphlets, books, prints, posters, gifts.

**Parking** • Parking garage beneath Vrijthof in center.

**Post Office** • Corner of Vrijthof and Statenstraat, Mon.–Fri. 8 a.m.–7 p.m., Thurs. til 8 p.m., Sat. 9 a.m.–noon.

**Emergencies** • Police ☎ *292222*, health ☎ *293333.*

**Bike rental** • At the Railway Station bicycle stall, 6 a.m.–midnight, 1 a.m. Sat. and Sun. ☎ *211100.* Dfl. 7.50 per day, Dfl. 30 per week; Dfl. 50 deposit and ID required.

**Cruises** • Stiphout Cruises, Maaspromenade 27; daily Maas River cruises from mid-April–Sept., on the hour 10 a.m.–5 p.m., Sun. 1–5 p.m., 55 mins.; ☎ *254151.*

**Taxis** • In front of the rail station.

**Recreation** • The VVV has information on the full range of area recreational opportunities, including fishing (license required), archery, tennis, *jeu de boules* (public courts, sets can be rented), and *Kayak Tours Limburg* for kayak day trips on safe "white-water" on un-canalized stretches of the Maas.

## WHAT TO SEE AND DO

The whole of Maastricht city center is a protected area due to its wealth of historic buildings (at least 1450). New and renovated buildings by law must be adapted to their surroundings. The ★ ★ ★ old city is a strolling, cafe-sitting, settling-in at a cozy restaurant paced place. Students at the city's facilities for translation studies, music, and hotel management contribute to the city's atmosphere. ★ ★ **Vrijthof Square**, Maastricht's largest square by far, is generally considered to be the center of town. The expansive space is surrounded by interesting structures, not the least of which are an uninterrupted row of terrace cafes (sidewalk cafes) settled along its east side. Use the VVV brochure *Maastricht Fortifications Walk* as your guide for a walk on the ★ ★ city walls, the **Pesthuis** being a good place to mount the ramparts. For a good view back to the ramparts, visit **Waldeckpark**, near Tongerseplein. Note that the 17th-century Waldeck Bastion is where Chevalier D'Artagnan, the famous French musketeer, fell on June 25, 1673. **Grote Looiersstraat** (with its French-flavored, tree-shaded center mall where you may see men playing jeu de boules) and **Ezel Markt** (with its donkey sculpture and fine view of the pretty 17th-century **Huys op den Jeker**, which straddles that stream) are two delightful corners of the city. Year-round, many historic buildings are floodlit after dark, and from mid-June to mid-September and on bank holidays, additional monuments are illuminated, from dusk until the wee hours.

## Het Dinghuis

*Kleine Staat 1; same hours as VVV, given before.* Today the headquarters
of Maastricht's VVV tourist office (ground floor), Het Dinghuis, dating from about 1470, with its beautiful stone gable and a timbered
wall on the Jodenstraat side, is the most striking example of Maastricht's many saddleback buildings, with steeply slanting roofs that
provided much needed storage space for staples to ensure survival
through the sieges that have been so much a part of the city's history.

## Onze Lieve Vrouwekerk

*(Church of Our Dear Lady) Onze Lieve Vrouweplein; open daily (not dur-
ing services). Treasure-house (entrance through church) open daily 11
a.m.–5 p.m., Sun. 1–5 p.m. Easter to mid–Sept.;* ☎ *251851.* Entry to the
church from the ★★**Onze Liev Vrouwekerk square** is to the left of
the formidable ★★**westwerk** (c. A.D. 1000), an almost windowless,
fortress-like wall, via the **Stella Maris** side chapel (c. 1500). The
essence of centuries worth of incense clings to the candlelit interior,
the most notable feature of which is the choir with its richly carved
capitals. The church's treasure includes reliquaries, procession banners, church silver, and other ecclesiastical art and crafts.

## St. Pietersberg Caves

*Mount St. Pietersberg; two miles south of Maastricht; guided (only) tours,
one hour, several times daily June–mid-Sept., reduced schedule rest of year,
must be booked through VVV;* ☎ *252121.* Since the St. Pietersberg
caves were interesting enough to merit inclusion in Roman historian
Pliny's writings in A.D. 50, and have generated interest among most
of the city's guests in the two succeeding millennia—the cave walls are
a virtual "visitors' book," so we know—you can feel confident about
putting them on your list of Maastricht "musts." The limey labyrinth
of 45-foot deep galleries cut in marl-limestone (a soft chalky building
stone that hardens in the air) has numerous names, the earliest from
1037, carved in its soft walls, among them Sir Walter Scott, Voltaire,
princes of the House of Orange, and Napoleon. For a thousand years,
until 1875, the caves' stonecutters carved huge blocks of limestone
here, expanding its already considerable *natural* size to over 200 miles
of dark, silent, and cool—a constant year-round temperature of 50
degrees F.—of some 20,000 subterranean "branches." Guides delight
in telling the story of four 17th-century monks who entered
unescorted, having affixed a thread at the cave entrance to find their
way out; but the "lifeline" broke and their days ended in a search for
a way out of the caves.

For those who could find their way within them, the caves have served
as a place of refuge. In the 18th century they harbored Austrian and
Italian mercenaries hired to help the Dutch combat the French invaders. In World War II they were readied to shelter up to 50,000 people
from Nazi bombing, but were never needed. Deep in the caves, Rembrandt's *The Night Watch* was hidden from the Nazis during the war,

rolled up in a specially prepared copper drum. When the war was over and the huge 13 x 16-foot painting was being restored before being rehung in Amsterdam's **Rijksmuseum**, it was discovered that the picture, darkened from the smoke of peat fires in rooms where it had previously hung, actually showed a daytime scene.

### Bonnefanten Museum

*Ceramique District; Closed until 1995 reopening in new quarters across Maas, contact VVV for opening date and times.* The Bonnefanten, Maastricht's main museum, will reopen in an exciting new complex in 1995. The new museum, a cornerstone to a former industrial site that is being developed into a multi-purpose publicly and privately developed river-front district (linked to the historic city by a pedestrian/cyclist bridge across the Maas), has been designed by architect Aldo Rossi. The innovative building, which integrates such elements as the 1912 classified industrial monument production hall of a former stoneware factory as display space for monumental sculptures, gives the museum enlarged areas for its collections of modern and contemporary visual art, and for visiting exhibitions. The Museum's fine arts collection includes sculpture from the Romanesque and Gothic periods, Italian paintings of the 14-16th centuries, and 16th-18th-century paintings from the southern Netherlands, including several Brueghels. Also of interest is the maquette (model) of Maastricht, a modern copy of a 1748 "relief model" of the city (the original is in Paris' Hotel des Invalides) that French officers built as a military siege study, with descriptive slide show. All works will benefit from new exhibit space that has skylights that offer natural light, controlled by a new climatization system. An eye catching cyclindrical domed tower, an extension of the central wing of the Bonnefanten, will offer a belvedere, with a view of the historic city, and there will be a cafe with outdoor terrace. The permanent collection of the Bonnefanten also includes rich archaeological holdings: The Maas valley has been a timeline of cultures for more than a quarter of a million years, and Maastricht is one of the few European cities that has been inhabited continuously since the Roman period. Shown are fossils found in the area's marl caves: the tableland here was formed 80 million years ago. (Elsewhere in Maastricht, at the ★ **Natural History Museum**, are displays of the particularly wide variety of fossils that were found in the local St. Pietersberg caves. **Napoleon** once found there the fossilized head of a massive lizard, known as the "Meuse Lizard", which experts estimate must have been 20 meters/66 feet long. It was so admirable that he was willing to exchange 500 bottles of fine French wine for it.)

### Spanish Government House
*Vrijthof 18; Wed–Fri. 2–5 p.m., and every first weekend of the month Sat. and Sun. 2–5 p.m.;* ☎ *292201.* This 16th-century furnished mansion, once headquarters for Spanish officials, has a rich collection of Dutch, Flemish, French and Italian antique furnishings and decorative art.

### Derlon Museum Cellar ★★
*Hotel Derlon, Onze Lieve Vrouweplein 6; Sundays 1–5 p.m., or through*

*VVV tours.* Since there had been Roman and medieval finds in this oldest part of Maastricht before—in nearby ★ **Op de Thermae** square the outlines of a Roman bath are indicated on the pavement—prior to excavation (1983) for the most recent hotel on the site, a major archaeological investigation was carried out by the municipality. The astonishing result, the discovery of a 6-meter/20- foot deep, virtually undisturbed stratum of the city's history from the 1st century to the 14th, was in large part preserved through altered building plans; it is on public display as a unique cellar museum beneath the modern Hotel Derlon. (See "Where to Stay.") On view are a 1st-century cobbled Roman road, a 2nd-century Roman temple square, and a wall that is part of a 4th-century Roman fort (castellum) that once covered Maastricht's entire *Stokstraat quarter.*

## Stadhuis                                                       ★

*Markt 78; Mon–Fri. 8:30 a.m.–12:30 p.m. and 2–5:30 p.m.;* ☎ *292222.* Built in the years between 1659–1664, the building, currently undergoing restoration, is one of the most important works by Dutch architect **Pieter Post**. The interior (★ ★ the imposing domed entrance hall is open to the public and sometimes other rooms; inquire within), with its original antique furniture and parquet floors polished to a glowing patina, could easily be a museum in its own right. The rooms feature tapestries (Gobelins and Brussels), stucco work, painted ceilings, leather wall hangings, and mantelpieces. The Stadhuis tower dates from 1684, and contains a **carillon** (bought before the tower was even built) of 43 bells, 17 of which were cast by the Hemony brothers. It's regularly played on Fridays from 11:30 a.m.–12:30 p.m. by the town carillonneur, with additional concerts scheduled in summer. The **Markt**, the square in front of the Stadhuis, is the scene of Wednesday and Friday markets, and a 1902 sculpture with an eternal gas flame that honors the Maastricht chemist **S.P. Minckelers** (1784–1824), the inventor of gas lighting.

## St. Servaasbasiliek                                          ★ ★

*Vrijthof; daily 10 a.m.–5 p.m. (4 p.m. winter, 6 p.m. summer).* St. Servaas, a massive Romanesque church, reopened in May 1990 following several years of large-scale interior and exterior restoration that produced a magnificent result. The body of this medieval cruciform basilica dates from circa 1000, but its soul and name come from St. Servaas (St. Servatius), the first bishop of Maastricht, who moved the bishop's see from Tongeren (in Belgium) to Maastricht in the late 4th century, and was buried on the site in the year 384. The **Treasure Chamber** has been part of the basilica since A.D. 827, and its collection of reliquaries is renowned; most highly prized is the golden reliquary, an outstanding example from 1160 of the Maasland's goldsmith art, in which part of the skeleton of St. Servaas has been preserved. Another showpiece is an arm in silver that contains a supposed arm bone of the apostle Thomas, a gift from the First Crusader Godfrey of Bouillon in 1099.

### St. Janskerk

*Vrijthof Square; Easter–early Sept., Mon.–Sat. 11 a.m.–4 p.m.* St. Jan's, dating from the 14th century, is Maastricht's finest gothic church. Nevertheless, its 256-foot spire (which, rising above the plain stone building, is a surprising red color, the result of a mineral covering used to make the surface harder) is not entirely successful in matching the soaring grace of Utrecht's Domtoren, after which it was modelled. Originally built to be the parish church for the St. Servaas basilica, St. Jan's was designated a Protestant church in 1632, when much Roman Catholic property officially was taken over by Dutch Protestants. Thereafter, the alley (now much-widened) between St. Jan's and the Catholic St. Servaas has been known as "Purgatory." In clear contrast to St. Servaas' elaborate decor, the interior of St. Jan's is plainly Protestant, with bare stone walls and columns, fine old tombs set flat into the floor, and a mid-church Louis XVI pulpit. The tower ★ can be climbed.

## WHERE TO STAY

The city hotels listed below are all within a mile or so of one another, but the actual location of the property you choose will affect your experience of the city. Since Maastricht has a new convention center just outside the center and good European transportation connections, the city is increasingly attractive for congresses and conventions; hotel reservations are suggested.

For visitors wanting to use local bed and breakfasts, it's best to check with the VVV for their suggestions as to the best choices for the amenities and location desired.

## EXPENSIVE

### Hotel Derlon

*Onze Lieve Vrouweplein 6, 6211 HD;* ☎ *216770, FAX 251933; reservations in U.S.* ☎ *800-344-1212.* Located on the historic, intimate-yet-lively square that's home to Our Beloved Lady church, a street away from the restored pedestrian Stokstraat, and near the ancient city ramparts, the Derlon couldn't be better or more charmingly situated. Several bedrooms in the modern but tastefully styled, service-oriented 42-room hotel overlook the cafe-cluttered, colorful scene on the square, where patrons gather until the wee hours of warm evenings. It is a special place that rests above Roman ruins that are one of the city's most significant early sites (see "Hotel Derlon Museum Cellar" under "What To See and Do").

### Holiday Inn Crowne Plaza Maastricht

*De Ruiterij 1, 6221 EW;* ☎ *509191, FAX 509192.* Located on the banks of the Maas, facing across the river to the skyline of the historic city center (which is just a few minutes' walk across the St. Servaas Bridge), this attractive, modern, full-service 131-room property with several restaurants, including the **Kobe** Japanese steakhouse, is Maastricht's most deluxe. Some of the many river-view rooms, which feature a decor of lively colors and marble baths, have balconies, and there also are split-levels and apartment accommodations. Many rooms have new king-size beds. The terrace cafe on the river overlooks the city and the steady stream of barges heading upstream into the heart of Europe.

## MODERATE

### Hotel Du Casque
*Helmstraat 14, 6211 TA;* ☎ *214343, FAX 255155.* There has been an inn on this site on the Vrijthof since the 15th century, though the present facade and interior of this family-run 38-room (6 rooms face on square) hotel are modern renovations. The lobby is small and unprepossessing, rooms clean and spacious. Breakfast (only, included). Parking.

### Hotel Beaumont
*Wycker Brugstraat 2, 6221 EC;* ☎ *254433, FAX 253655.* This family-run (3 generations), traditional, 85-room hotel lies midway between the railway station and the old heart of Maastricht (10-minute walk). Many of the rooms have been recently refurbished. Its restaurant, **Alsacien**, off the lobby bar, is a favorite locally. Indoor parking.

### Hotel Bergere
*Stationsstraat 40, 6221 BR;* ☎ *251651, FAX 255498.* Behind the historic facade and lobby with a stylish cafe are 40 guest rooms with recently modernized amenities. It's a short walk to the railway station and a pleasant, somewhat longer one across the Maas to the old center. Elevator; free parking; nonsmoking rooms.

## INEXPENSIVE

### Maison Du Chene
*Boschstraat 104, 6211 AZ;* ☎ *213523, FAX 258082.* A hotel/restaurant since 1985, with a cozy, especially recommended French brasserie (*daily, noon–2 p.m., 6:30–10 p.m.; moderate*) on the ground floor, this hotel has 21 tidy, modernly outfitted bedrooms in three old townhouses, most with shower/bath. There's a European flavor with friendly service, and it's in an excellent location (just off the Markt with Maastricht's City Hall).

## *WHERE TO EAT*

Residents around Maastricht revel in fine dining, and this strong gastronomic tradition has resulted in the restaurants of southern Limburg province, *en masse*, garnering more recognition than those of any other region of Holland. Local Limburg food favorites include *white asparagus* (fresh in May/early June), fruit *flans* (*Limgurgse vlaai*), fresh water *trout*, game, and Belgian-style chocolate *pralines*. In cases where a restaurant has a three-course menu, that has been used for the price category.

For fine dining, **'t Hegske** *(Heggenstraat 3a; 5–11 p.m., closed Tues; for reservations* ☎ *251762; moderate)* is a tiny, antique-congested restaurant just off centrally located St. Amorsplein. The romantic six-tabled candlelit interior—with another eight under the skylighted enclosed terrace with softly splashing fountain—specializes in fish and meat prepared in the French style. **Restaurant Jean La Brouche** *(Tongersstraat 9; noon–2 p.m., 6–10 p.m., Sat. dinner only, closed Sun., Mon.; for reservations* ☎ *214609; moderate)* serves up selections such as lamb, fish, and duck salad in an intimate French country home decor. Nearby is **Pater Noster** *(Tongersstraat 42; noon–2 p.m., 5–11 p.m., closed Mon., no lunch weekends; inexpensive)* for good Dutch food. At **Au Coin des Bons Enfants** *(Ezelmarkt 4; noon–2 p.m., 6:30–10 p.m., closed Sun., and Sat. for lunch; for reservations* ☎ *212359; expensive)*, whether you opt for open log fire elegance indoors, or the rustic courtyard when the weather's fine, the French/Belgian fare will agree with the setting. Split-level **Sagittarius** *(Bredestraat 7; 6–10 p.m., closed Sun., Mon.; for reservations* ☎ *211492; moderate)* specializes in seafood (bouillabaisse, scampi, sole, smoked salmon), though the meat dishes also merit attention; both are served with a smile.

**Le Vigneron** *(Havenstraat 19; 5 p.m.–midnight, closed Sun., Mon., holidays; for reservations* ☎ *213364; inexpensive)*, a cozy darkwood bistro which offers a large selection of wines by the glass, and menus of traditional French dishes, is one of several excellent eateries clustered in the area between the lovely *Onze Lieve Vrouweplein* (on which the restaurant also offers outside terrace dining) and the *Op de Thermen* (site of old Roman baths), both just off handsome Stokstraat. **'t Plenkske** *(Plankstraat 6; noon–2:30 p.m., 6–10:30 p.m., closed Sun.; for reservations* ☎ *218456; moderate)* offers light and bright glassed-in, or outdoor patio, dining overlooking the Op de Thermen; regional dishes from Maastricht, Liège, and France fill the bill of fare. **'t Klaoske** *(Plankstraat 20; noon–3 p.m., 6–10:00 p.m., closed Sun.; for reservations* ☎ *218118; inexpensive)* has more of an old Dutch look and feel, and the traditional country cuisine makes it a long-standing local favorite; it offers weekday business luncheon specials.

There are plenty of places in Maastricht for lighter, less formal fare. The oldest pub (1673) on the vast Vrijthof is the **In Den Ouden Vogelstruys** *(The Old Ostrich; Vrijthof 15; 9:30 a.m.–2 a.m.;* ☎ *214888; inexpensive)*. This traditional cafe bar, with its rustic wooden interior and terrace cafe, has a faithful local following and is a good, yet limited choice for a hearty or light lunch or dinner of Dutch specialties (pâté, choucroute garni, soups, sandwiches of cheese and Ardennes ham). Next door is **Panaché** *(Vrijthof 14; daily 9 a.m.–midnight;* ☎ *210516; inexpensive)*, one of the restaurants that promises tasty, traditional dishes *(tournedos-poivre* to *pastries)*. Moving along the row of cafes that anchor the Vrijthof one comes to **Monopole** *(Vrijthof 3; daily 10 a.m.–10 p.m.;* ☎ *214090; inexpensive)* which features light fare and drinks on its terrace.

With more than 365 of them, Maastricht's pubs come in every variety. Many serve food (an excellent value, all *inexpensive)* amid their special and individual ambience, making them cafes as much as a bars. Without doubt

the smallest is **De Moriaan** *(Stokstraat 12; noon.–2 a.m., closed Sun., Mon.;*
☎ *211177)* with 3-1/2 tables inside, a terrace on the Op de Thermen outside, and good spaghetti. Close by is **In de Karkol** *(Stokstraat 5; noon–2
a.m., closed Sun., Mon.;* ☎ *217035).* On the extension of the Stokstraat is
**In 't Knijpke** *(St. Bernardusstraat 13; daily 5 p.m.—2 a.m.;* ☎ *216525)* which
calls itself a cafe cheese-cellar; with the brick vaulted-ceiling room candlelit, and mellow music an accompaniment to the likes of onion soup,
mussels, pâté, and escargot, need I add it's atmospheric and friendly. With
a stirring view from its terrace tables of the fortress-like west front of the
O.L. Vrouwekerk (memorably illuminated at night) across the square,
**Charlemagne** *(O.L. Vrouweplein 24; daily; 10 a.m.—2 a.m.;* ☎ *219373)* is a
popular place. At the corner of the square is **De Bobbel** *(Wolfstraat 32; 10
a.m.–midnight, closed Sun;* ☎ *217413).* **Café Sjiek** *(St. Pieterstraat 13; daily 5
p.m.–2 a.m.;* ☎ *210158)* has a cozy interior of stained glass, wood, candles,
and flowers, and in good weather customers spill out across the street to a
terrace cafe on lawns in view of fragments of ancient city walls *(terrace
kitchen hours, noon–9 p.m.).* Choices run the gamut from soups and salad
niçoise to crab and steak.

---

### IN THE AREA

## SOUTHERN LIMBURG PROVINCE

The Netherlands' Limburg Province is popular with the Dutch and
other Europeans for country (especially summer) holidays. Here are the
country's highest hills, commonly called the "Dutch Alps" (though, to put
the topography in perspective, their top elevation of 1000 feet still comes
short of New York City's *Empire State Building).* If you have a car to explore this gently rolling land, you'll find it dotted with fine old (some 17th
century) fortified farmsteads *(boerderij),* built around courtyards and
closed to the street side by gates. Villages such as Epen, Epenheide, and
Gulpen have handsome half-timbered buildings tucked into them. The castles found across the countryside originally formed a defensive line during
the area's turbulent earlier times, but once their protective elements were
no longer politically important, many were architectually embellished.
Sometimes castles and fortified farms stood side by side, as one sees at
**Kasteel Erenstein** in Kerkade. Having a car will enable you to indulge in
some of the countryside restaurants for which South Limburg is renowned.
Some are set in castles that also offer guest rooms, but frequently the establishments are sought out first and foremost for their food. Definitely reserve—for meals as much as for rooms.

**Netherlands American Military Cemetery** *(Margraten; cemetery open
year-round 8 a.m.–5 p.m., 6 p.m. in summer, information center open 9 a.m.– 5
p.m.* ☎ *04458-1208.)* The only American military cemetery in the Netherlands, the site was liberated on Sept. 13, 1944, by the *U.S. 30th Infantry Division* during the *First U.S. Army's* drive towards Germany. The cemetery
was established on Nov. 10, 1944, by the *Ninth U.S. Army* as one of the
first used for the interment of Americans who had fallen on German soil. A
peaceful resting place for 8300 (including 40 pairs of brothers buried side

by side), there is row upon row of graves marked by white Italian marble Latin crosses or Stars of David, and an observation tower (149 steps) that offers a panorama of the cemetery and countryside.

## WHERE TO STAY AND EAT IN THE AREA

### Kasteel Wittem Hotel/Restaurant　　　　　　　★★★

*Wittemerallee 3, Wittem 6268 AB; for reservations* ☎ *04450-1208, FAX 04450-1260; hotel: moderate; restaurant: expensive.* Set in a hilly landscape of ancient trees 20 kms./12 mi. from Maastricht, Castle Wittem has a history that dates back to about 1100, and Willem the Silent, prince of Orange, who rescued it from the Spanish (who, under Charles II, had shown good taste in their conquering) in 1568 and then used it as a base for counter-attack. The castle was restored in 1611 with money given in compensation for damage suffered during that struggle, and again in 1972, in cooperation with the *Commission for Ancient Monuments.* Its 12 guest rooms located atop stately staircases and winding castle corridors (no elevators) are roomy, individualistic, and mostly recently renovated with marble baths and English country-style decor. Inquire about the two tower rooms. There's a terrace for drinks by the double moat, in which a black swan swims. **Kasteel Wittem Restaurant** offers creative classic French cuisine in a setting of silver candlesticks, leather chairs, and beamed ceiling. Excellent service and wine list. Inclusive gastronomic weekends.

### Kasteel Erenstein Hotel/Restaurant　　　　　　★★★

*Oud Erensteinerweg, Kerkrade 6468 PC; for reservations* ☎ *045-461333, FAX 045-460748; hotel: moderate; restaurant: expensive, closed Sat. for lunch.* The 45 modern, well-furnished guest rooms are located in an imaginatively restored 270-year-old boerderij (a fortified farmstead built around a central courtyard), which is a protected national monument. Breakfast (not included) can be served in your room or in the glass-enclosed winter garden (former courtyard), open during the summer. There's a health club: whirlpool, sauna, steam, and hot tub (fee). Across the road, the renowned **Kasteel Erenstein Restaurant** is in the early 14th-century Renaissance chateau's grand hall (traditional, intimate, elegant); the cuisine is French, the menu *à la carte* or *prix-fixe.*

### Chateau Neercanne Restaurant

*Cannerweg 800, 2 miles outside Maastricht; daily noon–2:30 p.m., 6:30–9:30 p.m., closed Mon., and Sat. for lunch; for reservations* ☎ *043-251359; expensive.* Located on a hillside, overlooking the River Jeker and the Belgium border, Chateau Neercanne was built in 1698, and one of its first houseguests was Czar Peter the Great. Since restoration in 1955, Chateau Neercanne has elegantly housed one of the region's preeminent restaurants. The internationally-renowned French cuisine uses only fresh ingredients (in season, herbs and vegetables come from its own garden) and focuses on seasonal and regional specialty dishes for the *à la carte* and *prix-fixe* menu offerings.

In addition to the romantic setting of the dining room (Venetian glass chandeliers, baroque wallpaper, leisurely gracious service) and broad stone terrace for use in fine weather, there's an Auberge in the vaulted cellar of an adjoining building where one can have lunch. The natural marlstone cellars extending into the hillside behind the castle hold one of the most choice selections of wine in the country (and, in neighboring caves, NATO installations).

# BELGIUM

*Architectural details on Brussels' Grand Place are illuminated at night.*

## INTRODUCTION

### THE BELGIAN LANDSCAPE

For its size—30,500 sq. kilometers/11,775 sq. miles—Belgium has a remarkable variety of scenery, with countryside that can change character in two dozen miles. Clockwise from the northwest, where the North Sea fronts Belgium's sand dune and broad beach shore, the country is bordered by Holland to the north, Germany to the east, Luxembourg to the southeast, and France to the southwest.

The north (**Flanders**) and south (**Wallonia**) of Belgium are not only different from each other linguistically and culturally (see "The Belgian People"), but topographically. In general, the north is much flatter, with some areas, especially in the province of *West Flanders*, lying below sea level. There, the land had to be reclaimed from the sea. Between the 8th and 13th centuries, a 12-by-30-mile-wide strip of low-lying coastal land was, through the use of sluices, transformed from salty swamp into fine polder farmland that remains among Belgium's richest. Rows of sentinel-like trees that form wind-breakers along cross-country canals are one of the distinctive sights in this part of Flanders.

The **Kempen**, in northern Belgium, is a large section of land between the *Schelde* and the *Maas* rivers that reaches through the provinces of Antwerp and Limburg. Its terrain changes from moorland, heath, and lakes to extensive pine forests and orchards as one moves from west to east. West Flanders' **Heuvelland**, a presently peaceful district of lakes and walking trails south of Ieper, was the heart of Belgium's battlefield in World War I.

**Wallonia**, roughly the southern half of Belgium, also is varied but overall more wooded and hilly than Flanders. This section of the country has an industrial sash stretched across it from Liège to Tournai, and in the past was prominent for coal production.

A large area of Wallonia is covered by the forests of the **Ardennes**. The most elevated area (600 meters/1600 feet, with winter skiing) is the **Hautes Fagnes**, located in the mostly German-speaking **Cantons de l'Est** in the far east of Belgium near the German border. The Ardennes is bounded and intersected by the castle-fortified cliffs of the **Meuse Valley** and the smaller but equally picturesque river valleys of the **Sambre**, **Ourthe** and **Semois**. Belgium's annual rainfall is lowest on the Belgian coast and highest in the Ardennes, where it feeds the rushing rivers that have carved the countryside. The region is famous for its **caves** (see Han–Sur–Lesse under "The Meuse Valley"). Because of its natural beauty, the Ardennes has been one of Belgium's major tourist areas for several centuries, with towns such as *Spa* and *Dinant* appearing on many a "Grand European Tour" itinerary.

There are few places where rivers or mountains distinctly separate Belgium from Holland, France, Germany, or Luxembourg. This circumstance has left the country open to invasion by foreign armies for virtually all of its recorded history. Yet, internally, Belgium has a very clearly defined border: one of language. Its **language frontier**

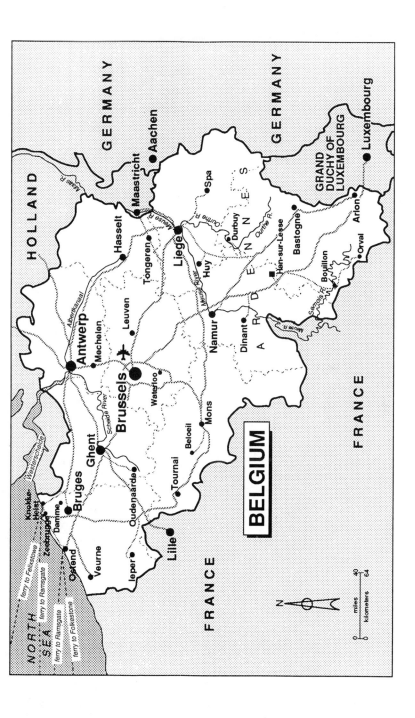

*(see map on page 357)*, running roughly east to west through the country's center, makes the single geopolitical entity of Belgium a nation *divisible* culturally.

## THE BELGIAN PEOPLE

While "England and America are two countries separated by the same language" (according to Irishman George Bernard Shaw), Belgium inherited the decidedly stickier situation of being *one country* separated by *two languages*. Stickier still, Belgium could be said not to be inhabited by Belgians. As people there say, the situation "is not so simple."

Belgium is home to both the **Flemish** in the north and the **Walloons** in the south; the former speak *Dutch*, the latter *French*. The second language of either is as likely to be English as the other of Belgium's two official tongues. Only in such crucial areas as supporting the country's team in *European Cup* football (soccer) or speaking up on behalf of its renowned cuisine, do most Belgians overcome regional identities for a national one.

While the Flemish and the Walloons can be tentative about being Belgian, the 85,000 people who live in the mostly rural Eastern Cantons (125 miles southeast of Brussels) and speak *German* (Belgium's truly "minority language") are ardent believers in Belgium. Though they live near the German border, watch German TV, and buy German products in Germany (where taxes on many items are lower), these Belgians aren't at all ambiguous about what country they are citizens of.

Belgium's internal "**language frontier**" dates back to the fifth century, quite faithfully following the line along which local tribes split into those influenced by the region's *Roman* or *Germanic* heritage. The Celtic **Belgae**, whom Julius Caesar noted as the most courageous, as well as the most troublesome tribe he had had to deal with in his conquests, adopted the Latin-based *French* language. The **Franks** remained true to their Germanic origins in the development of *Dutch/Flemish*, which are essentially identical with *Flemish* in written form.

Residents of the land that today is now Belgium were forced by history to follow a constantly changing course of leadership. The region gradually developed identity through **duchies** (such as that of the *Duke of Brabant*) and **counties** (as under the *Counts of Flanders*).

By the time northern Europe was evolving out of the Middle Ages in the mid-15th century, the people from both cultural areas had

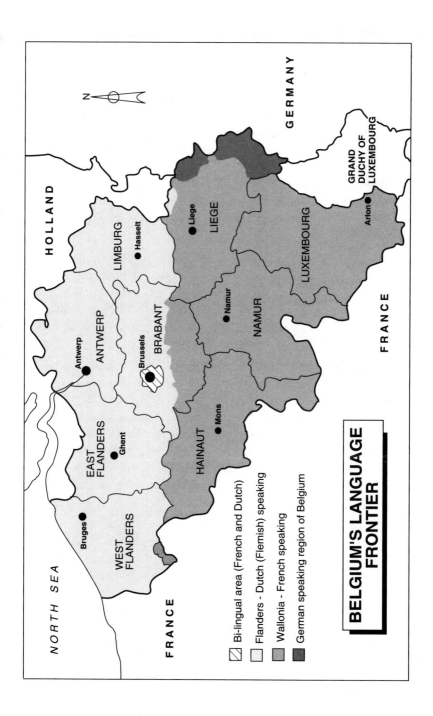

BELGIUM'S LANGUAGE FRONTIER

come under *French Burgundian* rule. French became not only the favored language of the upper class, but also a fashion copied by the educated *bourgeoisie* (a term derived from *burghers* or town citizens); a social class that virtually began in Belgium's early-to-flourish Flemish towns. (Though today "bourgeoisie" means "middle class" and often carries overtones of the ordinary, at the end of the Middle Ages being a self-supporting citizen of a town was an accomplishment in a Europe where the serf-driven feudal system still held wide sway.) Thus, at that time, it was only the uneducated peasant population in the rural countryside who used the Flemish tongue. Today, despite a plethora of sociopolitical permutations in the centuries since, Belgians still are basically bourgeois in their life style and values, and the French language still retains something of an upper hand in the country's culture.

Belgian culture developed during 2000 years of often all-too-intimate exposure to that of other—occupying—European countries. As a captive audience for its foreign leaders, Belgians absorbed certain outside fashions, but maintained their own deeply rooted qualities over the centuries, up to the relatively recent establishment of an independent Belgium in 1830.

Over centuries under foreign rule, Belgians of both cultures developed a certain indifference to government, a habit of doing their own thing. As a friend in Bruges describes it: "Even today, Belgians look for an escape clause from government because for generations of occupation foreigners made all the rules for them. Belgians are inclined to see all government, even their own, as 'foreign.' Coming from that attitude, many see our 'black money' system—under-the-table arrangements to avoid government taxes—as a kind of national sport."

Though conservative in many ways, Belgians openly admit to not liking regimentation. They may appear undisciplined because of their aversion to rules. Again, my Bruges friend traces this to Belgium's past: "Historically, since Belgians were not ruled by Belgians, they got used to ignoring leaders, and that has carried over to an avoidance of regulation. Belgians don't like following building codes or traffic signs." He's the first to admit that this "leads to disorganization," but returns to the point that it's a trait that "comes out of history."

Belgium has a population of approximately 10 million: 5.7 million are Dutch-speaking Flemish; 3.1 million are French-speaking Walloons; another 1 million are residents of Brussels (where a large majority is French-speaking). An additional half-million are foreigners: Eurocrats and diplomats (many countries post diplomatic missions in *triplicate* to Brussels, one each to the European Union, NATO, and the Belgian royal court), as well as immigrant workers (many from Africa, especially Zaire, formerly the Belgian Congo).

As the above figures show, today Belgium's Dutch-speaking Flemish population is decidedly in the majority. Until the last decade or so, however, French speakers more than overcame their numerical inferiority through their domination of the country's culture. While recent legislation on various language issues and the implementation of federalism have worked towards equalizing Belgium's two cultural communities, their "balance" remains part of the Belgian "problem."

During the Reformation in the 16th century, most of Belgium's Protestants eventually headed north to Holland to escape the harsh intolerance of the region's Roman Catholic ruler, Philip II of Spain. With nearly all the population remaining Catholic, religion served as a bridge linking Belgium's two cultures. Today a large number of Belgians still are self-professed Catholics (particularly in Flanders), but during the 20th century, anticlericalism increased so substantially (especially in Wallonia) that eventually the various religious/anti-religious movements each wanted their own political parties.

*Religion* and *politics* affect every Belgian's life, whether or not they choose to participate in either actively. Belgium's political parties represent the same ideological tendencies as those elsewhere in Europe: *Christian Democratic* (called Social Christian), *Conservative* (called Liberal), *Socialist,* and *Green.* When their community's economic situation strengthened in the 1960s, the Flemish began insisting on a stronger voice in the Belgian national government. (For more on the Flemish Movement, see "Flanders: An Introduction.") This resulted in each of the main political parties breaking into two sections, duplicating themselves along linguistic cultural community lines. Since then, *compromis à la Belge* has been an even greater fact of Belgian political life. Despite coalition governments—all but unavoidable due to the splintering of political parties—the language issue often comes ahead of other considerations, and often has led to a falling out, and subsequent "fall" of the current coalition.

Whatever cause for cursing the Flemish and Walloons have between themselves, they stand in similarly estranged circumstances with respect to their contiguous, supposedly culturally related, neighbor countries. In France, for instance, there's little acceptance of

French-speaking Walloons as French (in large measure due to their perceived inelegant pronunciation of the language). In Holland the Dutch are inclined to think of the Flemish as rather embarrassing country cousins who speak a dialect. Uncomplimentary Belgian jokes, often taking as their subject a perceived inability to properly use the French or Dutch languages, are told over the borders in both France and Holland. Thus, in the end, Belgium's internal "situation" is so peculiarly its own that it almost creates a national consciousness. Belgians, well aware of the jokes told at their expense, take them pretty well. Some Belgians even manage a smile at the irony that, for all the energy expended on gaining the right to speak their respective languages *inside* their country, *beyond* their borders, Belgians' ability to speak those languages may be regarded as laughable. In any case, only the few extremists in either community ever have thoughts of actually merging with France or Holland—though the issue was the subject of *The Times* of London's annual front-page *April Fools Day* article in 1992.

Other ironic aspects of Belgium's internal language situation can present themselves. In 1986, for example, a small farming village in Flanders, *Fourons*, that lay near the Walloon language boundary (and thus, though officially Flemish-speaking, had a large number of French-speaking residents and was a "protected French-language minority" locale), made headlines. Its French-speaking mayor, Jose Happart, regularly refused to take a required examination that would have revealed his poor knowledge of Flemish. (Fluency in both Belgian languages is legally required in order to hold any government job in Belgium.) Happart expressed his feelings with the logic: "Why should I conduct all official acts in Flemish if most people here speak French?" Flemish officials responded "because Fourons is in Flanders," a not unreasonable insistence, given their hard won right to administer affairs on *their* soil in *their* language. Through media coverage, Happart became a hero in Wallonia, a fiend in Flanders. Today Happart, an elected member of the *European Parliament*, still speaks up on Belgian issues of respective languages and region. However, after a recent lively television debate with a leading Flemish politician, Happart posed a new perspective on the subject by saying: "After all, everybody will speak English in 20 years."

With their complicated sociopolitics, it's no wonder that Belgians take fun in their folklore. Folkloric celebrations in Belgium are loosely referred to as "carnivals." *The* carnival, **Mardi Gras**, is, of course, one of the year's highlights, especially in **Binche**, 30 miles south of Brussels. Then the Walloon town teems with the prancing figures of the *Gilles*, members of a male society who break out annually in dazzling costumes, complete with elaborate eight-pound ostrich-plumed headgear. Although some of Belgium's carnivals are seriously religious—among them Bruges' **Procession of the Holy Blood** and Veurne's brown-cowled, cross-carrying participatory **Process of the Penitents**—many more are only slightly so (as in a David and Goliath-type encounter annually played out by **"giants"** at Ath). Such pagents may also be permeated with pagan traditions, reflect bygone 15th-century Burgundian days, or suggest the 16th-century influence of the Spanish empire.

Historians believe that Belgium's folkloric festivals originated in pre-Christian spring fertility rites (or sun worship—still practiced by many northern Europeans, though in costumes more appropriate for the beach). The introduction of the pageantry element into Belgian folk history can be pinpointed precisely. In response to the **Reformation**, Ghent-born Emperor Charles V, who ruled over much of continental Europe, is credited with creating festivals beginning in 1549 to show the "romance" of Roman Catholicism—in contrast to the puritanism of the Protestant approach to life. Brussels' annual July **Ommegang**, a florid Flemish historical "walkabout" in the Grand Place, is Belgium's grandest show of this kind of carnival. Ostend's **Blessing of the Sea** is a straightforward celebration of that town's fishing industry and longtime maritime flavor. Most Belgian carnival celebrations are fanciful and cheerful, but some meander into the macabre, their enactment giving a glimpse of the *grotesque*, a quality that has been reflected in the area's art over the centuries, from Bosch and Bruegel to 20th-century surrealists Ensor, Magritte, and Delvaux.

Belgians' relationships with their country can be complex, but individual passions are clear. To a person, they appreciate the good things in life, including food and drink. It's a trait said to have held since the country's Burgundian days five centuries ago. Along with a *de rigueur* fervor for football (soccer), cycle-racing stirs the souls of Belgian participants and spectators alike. The annual Flemish **Ronde van Vlaanderan** cycle race is one of the runners-up in excitement to the **Tour de France**.

Many Belgians find pleasure in specialty interests, such as radical adult puppet theater. The **Toone Puppet Theater**, tucked into Brussels' ancient *l'Ilot Sacre* district is the best known of the "establishment" puppet theaters, which dole out strong satire (though usually not in English). See under "Brussels, Entertainment and Events."

Comic strip art is so popular that there's a museum, the **Belgian Comic Strip Center**, in Brussels (see also under "What To See and Do") devoted to it. (The late Pierre Culliford, a Belgian artist better known under the professional name of "**Peyo**," was the creator of the *Smurfs*, the internationally popular little blue characters that reflect the local fondness for cartoon and comics art.)

Most unusual of all may be the near mania in certain circles for **pigeon racing**. Before becoming aware of that sport I had, most mistakenly, assumed that the caged pigeons I saw at the Sunday morning *Bird Market* on Brussels' Grand place were destined for dinner tables. The much more interesting story behind the contents of those cages is that Belgium is home to the world's largest number (some 120,000) of *colombophiles* (pigeon fanciers), who get passionate about the roughly 25,000 pigeon races held there each year. Betting on the birds can involve substantial sums.

Unlike their Dutch neighbors to the north, Belgians were not shaped by the sea. While Dutch merchants spent the 17th century garnering wealth by sailing the world, Belgians made their money as at-home industrialists. As a result the Belgian character is clothed in a bourgeois life-style and fed by conservative capitalist ideology. Belgium's prudent and productive market economy runs by methodical, nonspontaneous means. An historically strong belief in free trade results in the basically hardworking labor unions occasionally calling strikes to keep the populace aware of their contribution.

Beyond doubt, Belgians and Belgium defy easy definition. But while the country's internal situation can be frustrating and fraught with overtones for residents, visitors with a little insight into the complex nature of the country's bicultural society can enjoy observing the whole intriguing situation.

## *AN HISTORICAL PERSPECTIVE*

Between 57 and 50 B.C., Julius Caesar conquered the northern sector of tri-parted *Gaul*, the land lying in the basins of the *Scheldt* and the *Meuse* rivers. At the time, it was inhabited by Gallo-Celtic tribes, including the *Belgae*. The *Romans* named the region **Gallia Belgica** and occupied it until the 5th century. From the 3rd century, however, Rome's hold began to weaken, and the *Franks*, a loose federation of German tribes, began to penetrate the area. Eventually, the Franks colonized the lower Scheldt, which left only a thin forested stretch from the Scheldt to the Ardennes separating them from the *Wala* (Walloons, or romanized Celts). Thus was set what virtually is the same ethnic and linguistic frontier that runs through the center of Belgium today.

Once the Romans departed, **Clovis**, who was born in 465 in Tournai—then the capital of the Frankish Merovingian kings—conquered all of Gaul (except Burgundy and Provence). He then declared himself Christian, thereby gaining the support of the Roman Catholic Church. After his death in 511, the Gallic territory became splintered, with what today is Belgium becoming merely a remote corner. In 751 **Pepin the Short** ousted the last weak Merovingian ruler and founded the Carolingian dynasty. His son, **Charlemagne**, who reigned from 768 to 814, was declared Emperor of the West by the Pope in 800; his lands reached from Denmark to southern Italy and from northern Spain to the Oder. Under Charlemagne, Belgium had an important position in the empire.

Upon Charlemagne's death, however, fierce fighting broke out between his grandsons, and what had been achieved during his reign was lost in the partitioning of the region. As a result of the warring, the 843 **Treaty of Verdun** divided the "Belgian" area between Charles the Bald and Lothair. Charles, king of West Francia—France, as we more or less know it—received the territory west of the Scheldt (which would become Flanders, and included a part of what is Walloon territory today).

The dissolution of the Carolingian Empire led to the founding of numerous principalities—many of them having kept their names as modern provinces—whose powers were determined by frequently changing alliances. In 864 the **Flanders countship** came into being and, through marriage between dynasties, became strong and unified.

While much of Europe still slept in the Dark Ages—also known as the Middle Ages, lasting until about 1450—Belgium's Flanders began awaking. The **rise of towns** there led to new structures for society by redistributing the population from the countryside where the feudal system still flourished. By 1100 Flanders was firmly established, with Bruges, Ghent, and Ypres rapidly becoming city-states through the power of the privileges bestowed upon them by the Flemish counts. A mastery of mercantilism resulted in wealth that encouraged and supported an active artistic environment. In the 1200s, Ghent and Bruges had become so independent-minded that they hardly recognized the Counts of Flanders' authority, much less that of the French King, to whom Flanders was allegiance-bound.

In 1302 French King-to-be Philip the Fair decided to do away with Flanders (by invading it and overpowering the Count) in order to annex the region's riches to France. Flemish citizens quickly showed how fiercely they were willing to fight for their freedom. Led by weaver Jan Breydel and butcher Pieter de Coninck, a rough-and-ready crowd of tradesmen and craftsmen met at **Kortrijk** to confront an army of France's finest mail-clad knights. The Flemings were armed primarily with devices called *goedendags* ("how do you do's"), small spiked balls of iron that were swung on four-foot chains in circles over their heads and let loose to slash the enemy. Though the French were contemptuous of their low-born opponents, they couldn't defeat the brave Flemish citizens. At battle's end, the French dead numbered 63 nobles, including commander Robert d'Artois and 700 knights, from each of whom was removed a pair of golden spurs, ornaments which gave the battle its name. Still regularly reenacted as one of Belgium's most colorful folkloric events on the actual site in Kortrijk is the **Battle of the Golden Spurs**. It is significant for being the first occasion on which common citizens defeated well-armed and protected knights. In addition to making medieval military and social history, the battle marked the beginning of the end of the era of chivalry.

During the 14th century, various developments combined to bring about instability in Flanders. There were local guild rivalries and tyranny by the urban oligarchy over the rural peasantry. Changing trade patterns affected Flanders' all-important cloth industry and led to the emigration of many weavers to England. The marriage of Margaret (heir of Count of Flanders Louis de Male) to Philip the Bold of Burgundy resulted in the end of Flanders as a separate state and the beginning of **the Burgundian period** in 1384. The **Dukes of Burgundy**, who ruled the region until 1473, united almost the whole of the Netherlands.

Under the tenure of **Philip the Good** (1419–1467), there was an increase in trade and luxury, and the first flowering of Flemish painting occurred, (**Jan van Eyck** was court painter to Philip.) Philip was set on having monarchical status: in 1421 he bought Namur; in 1430 he inherited Brabant, Limburg, and Antwerp; in 1433, after deposing the previous ruler, he took over Hainaut, Holland, and Zeeland; and, in 1443, he bought Luxembourg. For an extra measure of authority, in 1456 Philip had his nephew Louis de Bourbon elected Bishop of Liège and made his bastard son Bishop of Utrecht. In the meantime, he forced Bruges and Ghent (which had mounted an unsuccessful revolt in response) to surrender many of their privileges. *That*, after having honored their superior wool-weaving by establishing the *Order of the Golden Fleece* in Bruges in 1430.

Philip was succeeded by his son **Charles the Bold**, the richest and most ambitious prince of his day. He, too, held the nobles and cities in check, and in his desire to be a king, married Margaret of York, sister of Edward IV of England. Overextending himself in a military campaign in Lorraine, Charles was killed at *Nancy* in 1477. He left extensive lands in turmoil to his daughter **Mary**, whom the Flemish held virtual hostage until she signed *The Great Privilege* charter that granted far-reaching rights back to the towns. In the same tempestuous year that her father died, Mary (in response to demands from the French king to marry his son) arranged to marry **Maximilian of Austria**, whereby the Netherlands passed from the Burgundians to the **Hapsburgs** of Vienna.

Mary and Maximilian had a son, **Philip the Fair**, to whom Maximilian, upon his election as *Holy Roman Emperor* in 1494, handed over the Netherlands and other lands, including Spain. Philip died young, and in 1506 the Burgundian land inheritance passed to his six-year-old son Charles, who had been born in Ghent.

**Charles**, who was to become one of the dominant figures of European history, spent his childhood under the governorship of his aunt, **Margaret of Austria**, who established herself and Charles in Mechelen. In 1515, the *Netherlands' States General* declared Charles (then 15) of age to lead their lands. In 1516 Charles also became King of Spain and, in 1519, Emperor of the Hapsburg empire, having inherited the title from his grandfather.

As Charles V (Charles Quint) and later *Holy Roman Emperor*, he ruled over greater European domains—from Spain to Hungary, and from Sicily to the Netherlands—than any single person before or since. In 1530, Charles V appointed his sister, Mary of Hungary, as regent of the Netherlands. She exacted heavy taxes in order to support the wars that Charles waged elsewhere (particularly in France) to keep his empire intact. In 1540, Ghent rebelled against paying for such wars. Charles personally suppressed the uprising and, in keeping with his aim to diminish the ancient privileges of towns that impaired the power of his crown, he rescinded many of Ghent's rights.

But the business of managing his empire militarily increasingly became overshadowed for the Roman Catholic Charles by concern about the Protestant **Reformation**. First Martin Luther in Germany (beginning in 1520), and then John Calvin in Switzerland, attacked the corruption of the Catholic Church, particularly the selling of indulgences and the self-indulgent lives of priests and the Pope. From Switzerland, the austere fundamentalist beliefs of *Calvinism* spread to Belgium (and on to Holland where, after 1550, Calvinism was the prevailing religion). In Belgium, Calvinist orators attracted and converted thousands in the forests outside towns from Bruges to Liège and Antwerp to Tournai. The number of Protestant converts increased continually. Charles tried to hold back the tide, first by prosecuting individual "heretics," and then moving to more wholesale action under the **Edict of Blood**, which decreed death for those convicted.

In 1555, an exhausted (perhaps ill—he died in 1558) Charles abdicated in favor of his son **Philip II of Spain**. A contemporary painting of the actual transfer of power ceremonial event depicts some of the main characters (**Charles** entering on the arm of **Willem the Silent** of Orange, **Philip II**, **Duke of Alva**, and the **Counts of Egmont** and **Hoorn**) for the upcoming **Eighty Years' War**. It is said that at the end of his father's abdication address in the throne room of Brussels' Coudenberg Palace, Philip, who could speak neither Dutch nor French, had his acceptance speech read by another. Philip never learned either language and wound up loathing the "Lowlanders," never setting foot in the Netherlands again after 1559, though he lived until 1598. Philip did, however, favor Flemish art. He had many works by **Hieronymus Bosch** (1474–1516) sent to him in Madrid; Utrecht-born and Belgium-educated painter **Antonio Moro** (c.1519–1576) was frequently called upon to paint Spanish court portraits.

The year prior to assuming power in the Netherlands, Philip II had married Queen **Mary Tudor of England** (1516–1558, herself a Catholic with a passion against Protestants—the treatment of whom earned her the epithet "Bloody Mary"). Philip's narrow-minded religious views fanned smouldering controversies into flames, spreading Protestantism further. He countered the Reformation in every way he could, ordering the ruthless persecution of all Protestants (and many others he accused of heresy).

For their part, Protestants participated in events such as the **Iconoclastic Fury** of 1566, a month-long spree during which hundreds of Catholic churches throughout the Netherlands were broken into, statues smashed, religious images burned, and tombs opened. Antwerp was particularly hard hit by damage from extreme Calvinists; to this day one sees churches there with empty niches and disfigured statues. It resulted in the loss of much of the Netherlands' early artistic legacy.

One extremist action provoked another. Within a year (1567), Philip sent the fanatical **Duke of Alva** (a.k.a. **Alba**) to the Netherlands with an army of 10,000 Spanish troops. He outlawed Willem of Orange, garrisoned towns with his troops, and set up the so-called **Council of Blood**, which he used as a means to execute many of the nobles, including **Counts Egmont** and **Hoorn**, who had become Protestants.

Dutch Prince **Willem (the Silent) of Orange**, who had lived in Brussels (having been brought up there at the court of Charles V), was unable to convince Philip II of Spain to follow a moderate course in the Reformation rather than persecuting Protestants. Willem left Brussels in 1568, collected troops, and headed north to Holland to lead an armed resistance from there. Protestant rebels under Willem began to see some success beginning in 1572 with the capture of Vlissingen (Flushing) in Zeeland. By the end of the year, they controlled most of the province of Holland and Willem had been declared Stadholder. The Duke of Alva concentrated on stamping out the simultaneous uprisings in the southern Netherlands (today's Belgium). In 1573, just before his return to Spain, Alva's soldiers, unpaid and mutinous, unleashed their anger in the brutal sacking of Antwerp known as the **Spanish Fury**. Alva's Spanish replacement, Luis de Requesens (who died in 1576 and was in turn replaced by the Duke of Parma), continued the fighting in the Netherlands, mostly against Willem's forces in the now Protestant-controlled north (Holland), since the south seemed ready for compromise.

In 1579, the signing of the **Union of Arras**—which declared faith in Roman Catholicism and loyalty to Philip II—by the deputies of certain southern regions ended the last hope for unity between the northern and southern Netherlands. It was followed shortly by the **Utrecht Union of the Seven United Provinces**, which established the Protestant northern Netherlands (roughly, today's Holland) as separate from the southern Netherlands (roughly, today's Belgium). Most Protestants had fled either to Holland, or England by the time the Duke of Alva had finished his reign of religious persecution. (Amsterdam had to tear down its walls and expand the city to accommodate all the immigrants).

Before his death in 1598, Philip II ceded the southern Netherlands to his daughter Isabella who, married to **Archduke Albert of Austria**, was made an archduke in her own right. The *Reign of the Archdukes* (which lasted until 1621) was a period of economic recovery and great intellectual and artistic brilliance led by Antwerp-based baroque age genius **Pieter Paul Rubens**.

The southern Netherlands was returned to Spanish rule in 1621 and became contested territory between the Hapsburgs and the Bourbons during the **Thirty Years' War** (1618–1648). The war ended with the *Treaty of Munster*, which gave official acknowledgment of the United Provinces' (Holland) complete independence, and secured Spanish agreement to the Dutch-imposed condition that the Scheldt River estuary be closed. Antwerp, predictably, went into decline, and its trade and prosperity shifted northward to Holland's North Sea ports.

During the late 17th century, it became increasingly important to France's **Louis XIV** (who had married the **Spanish Infanta**) to have the Spanish southern Netherlands subject to him. To achieve that he went so far as to invade Holland but was unsuccessful there, due to England's help in opposing the French Louis' plan. All parties wound up one way or another in the **War of the Spanish Succession** (1702–1713). In the *Treaty of Utrecht* signed in 1713, France finally abandoned all claim to the Spanish southern Netherlands, which passed to the Austrian Hapsburgs.

The Southern Netherlands remained essentially independent as the **Austrian Netherlands**, undergoing little more change than the name of the sovereign, which for much of the period was **Maria Theresa**. Her popular and enlightened Brussels representative, **Charles of Lorraine**, ushered in a period of prosperity and renewed interest in culture. Transportation networks were constructed, agriculture was modernized, and industry (especially coal) was encouraged. Maria Theresa's successor, Joseph II, was (for reasons of personality more than policy) unsuccessful in his dealings with the Austrian Netherlands. In 1792, war broke out between Austria and revolutionary France; by 1794, Austria had been defeated and the southern Netherlands once again came under French occupation.

It was with a measure of acceptance (as opposed to protest) that the southern Netherlands became a dependency of France in 1795. However, the French lost favor with the dependent nation when Napoleon introduced conscription, centralized its government, and French anti-religious revolutionaries (survivors of the French Revolution) persecuted the Roman Catholic Church. Under **Napoleon's** rule from 1799 to 1814, a few positive elements were added under his *code of civilization* (among them the metric system and the first plan for numbering buildings for street addresses). However, after the Corsican Emperor suffered final defeat in 1815 on his own soil at **Waterloo**, the idea of independence loomed large for Belgians.

But Britain had other ideas, fearing that Belgium was too weak to resist if the French made new attempts to control the region's ever-important North Sea ports. The European powers meeting at the *Congress of Vienna* ordered Belgium incorporated into the **Kingdom of the Netherlands**. The plans—described even by the diplomats of the day as being solely for "the convenience of Europe," rather than the welfare of Belgians—proved, unsurprisingly, unpopular. Two points in particular doomed it from day one. The Belgian Roman Catholic Church, especially strong in Flanders, could not tolerate the Dutch Protestant approach to religion. Secondly, Belgians refused to accept mere equal representation in the *Netherlands States General* since they had twice the population of Holland. In addition, King Willem, though Dutch, following the social form of the day, spoke French, which offended the Flemish. Also, Willem paid particular attention to the industrial development of the rich coal fields in Wallonia while virtually ignoring Flanders's economic well-being. Only the port of Antwerp, recovering rapidly after being reopened by Napoleon, benefitted by being part of the Kingdom of the Netherlands.

In 1828, the two Belgian communities, and opposing political parties, put aside their differences in common hostility to Dutch rule. Within weeks of the Revolution of 1830 in France, the Belgians held a brief one of their own, demanding from the European powers —this time successfully—that their independence and "perpetual neutrality" be recognized. The crown of the new **constitutional monarchy** was offered to and accepted by German Prince **Leopold of Saxe-Coburg**, an uncle of and strong influence over England's Queen Victoria. Holland's Willem did not give in to the arrangement willingly and, ironically, the new King Leopold I was forced to call upon France for military reinforcement to flush the Dutch out of Belgium.

No sooner had the Belgians achieved the right to be their own political leaders than they became leaders in the **Industrial Revolution**. The European continent's first steam-operated locomotive and rail line, running between Brussels and Mechelen, began in 1835. Belgians also invented the tram, and in the 19th century built tram networks all over the world.

**Leopold II**, who did much to foster Belgium's growth and transport systems, came to the throne in 1865. A colonialist to the core, he tried to get the Belgian government interested in acquiring a piece of Africa. When he couldn't, he decided to do so himself. In 1879 Leopold had H. M. Stanley (of "Dr. Livingstone, I presume" association) make agreements with some African chiefs to open up trading stations in an area he called the **Congo Free State**. Using his own resources, Leopold established what amounted to a personal fief—eight times the size of Belgium, with three times the population. The resources he realized in return—copper, cobalt, timber, diamonds, and uranium, among others—made Leopold one of the richest men in the world. Eventually, however, even his own countrymen charged him with exploitation, and, in 1908, the African territory became the **Belgian Congo** colony under a largely reluctant Belgian government rule.

In 1960, the Belgian government granted independence to the Congo. The manner in which it did so reinforced its relative uninvolvement from the start: Belgium simply walked away, leaving only a few indigenous university graduates, doctors, and trained administrators to cope with the change. Renamed **Zaire**, with the capital *Kinshasa* (it had been *Leopoldville* under the Belgians), the newly independent country began life largely in a state of political and social disarray; the internal violence that has dogged it since has been attributed by some to the unprecedented speed with which Belgium cut its colonial connection. In any case, most Belgians agreed with the independence decision at the time, despite the resulting loss of 4% of national income. Today, Zaire continues to be burdened with backwardness and political corruption, but businessmen who seek its still-considerable natural resources keep themselves largely unconcerned about the social conditions of the country.

In Belgium, the 19th century proved relatively calm and stable. A rising demand for social rights and equal education was evident in the demands of the **Flemish Movement** (see "Flanders: An Introduction"). After the *Workers' Congress* at Brussels in 1886, socialism gained a new following. Even art got into the act, as the *art nouveau* style was specifically adopted by those sympathetic to socialism. Art nouveau architect Victor Horta created a marvelous headquarters for the *Workers' Congress* in the **Maison du Peuple** (built 1895, demolished 1966).

Most other issues fell away when Belgium, whose neutrality had been guaranteed by the Great Powers in 1839, was nevertheless invaded and occupied by the Germans at the beginning of the **Great War** (World War I, 1914–1918). Belgium's "language situation" surfaced on the **Ypres Salient** in the form of the *Flemish Front Move-*

*ment.* At issue was the fact that although an estimated 80% of Belgium's trench-confined conscripts were Dutch-speaking, few of the country's disproportionately large number of French-speaking officers knew the language of their soldiers, punishing some for failing to obey commands they could not understand.

The German occupiers found that the conflict between Belgium's two language communities played into their hands. But working to keep Belgians together in battle was the brave leadership of the beloved **King Albert** and **Queen Elizabeth**, who based themselves at De Panne on the small southwest strip of Belgian soil which—with the help of hundreds of thousands of Allied troops in the trenches around Ypres—remained free for the duration.World War I devastation in Belgium included the loss of much magnificent medieval architecture (though the people eventually rebuilt many of the monuments in their original exterior splendor).

Reconstruction from World War I had not been fully completed when **World War II** began, with the Nazis invading Belgium (and Holland) on May 10, 1940. But for his death in a tragic climbing accident in 1934, King Albert I might have seen his country through another war. Instead, his son **Leopold III** was seated on the throne. Leopold had married the extremely popular Princess Astrid of Sweden in 1926, but, a year after the royal couple was crowned, Astrid died in a motor accident in a car driven by her husband. Misfortune was to rule Leopold's reign.

During World War II, many Belgians were deeply troubled by the feeling that their king was not behaving in the best interests of the nation. Leopold III, stiff and inclined to ignore his ministers' advice, probably never would have won the affection felt by the Belgians for his father, King Albert, who symbolized Belgium's strength under prolonged fire in World War I. Leopold, in contrast, surrendered his armies and permitted himself to be taken prisoner only 18 days after the Nazis invaded Belgium. His initial "wait and see" stand, probably more passive than pro-Nazi, and based on a belief that he could do more for his people from within Belgium than in exile, nevertheless proved wrong on all counts. Staunch Leopold supporters point out that, once a prisoner, he successfully pleaded with Hitler for a less restrictive occupation. (No *Gestapo* were stationed in Belgium, and conditions there were much easier than ones the Dutch had to endure.) But the bottom line was that, once a prisoner in his palace at Laeken (outside Brussles) and seen receiving mild treatment himself from the Nazis, Leopold was forever compromised in the eyes of his Belgian people. (Particularly, they contrasted his actions with those of Holland's **Queen Wilhelmina**, who escaped to England with her government after the Nazi invasion. Once the Dutch got over the shock of her fleeing, Wilhelmina was able to serve as a stirring symbol of resistance for her country.) Leopold spent the war being shifted by the Nazis from one place of imprisonment to another, eventually to Germany in 1944 for safekeeping after the Allied Normandy invasion, and finally to Salzburg, Austria, where he was found in 1945 with his 15 year-old son **Prince Baudouin**.

In exile in Switzerland, Leopold—whose brother Prince Charles had been asked to take over as regent for Belgium—knew he could not wear the Belgian crown again without the issue being resolved. Just short of ten years after the Nazis had invaded Belgium in May 1940, the **Royal Question** was posed to the people: *Should Leopold return to the Belgian throne?* He won the plebiscite, but by a 57 percent of the population that so closely followed the bicultural lines of the country—in general, he was favored by Flemish Catholics and rejected by Walloon anticlerics—that, had Leopold insisted upon reclaiming the crown, Belgium might have seen civil war. Leopold's son **Baudouin** was quietly given constitutional powers and acceded as king in 1951 when he turned 21. More than one Belgian murmured under his breath: "The crisis is dead. Long live the king."

Well before the end of the war, in 1944, from their headquarters in exile in London, the governments of Belgium, Holland, and Luxembourg began talks about a post-war border-free economic union among the three. The name coined was **BENELUX** (BElgium, NEtherlands, LUXembourg), and it marked the beginning of a new era for Europe. The promise of the Benelux association led to the six-membered **European Coal and Steel Community**, which was established to pool coal and steel production within the three Benelux countries plus France, Germany, and Italy. The 1951 plan was called by Walter Lippmann "the most audacious and constructive initiative since the end of the war."

By 1957, yet another new stage in European integration had been reached, with the signing of the *Treaty of Rome* that established the **European Economic Community** (or *Common Market*). The new international body eventually designated **Brussels** as its **capital**. (Belgium, it seems, was small enough so that the privilege conferred upon its capital did not unleash jealousies among the other larger members.) The broader-based **European Community** (EC) doubled its membership from the Coal and Steel Community days to a full dozen, and scaled new heights of European economic cooperation with the *Single Europe Act*. Today, renamed the European Union

(EU), the organization again has new members and an enlarged mandate.

The anniversary of the founding of the European Economic Community in 1950 is observed in Brussels each May 9th—Eurocrats have dubbed it "St. Schuman's Day," after Common Market co-architect Luxembourg-born Robert Schuman. As far as Belgium is concerned, it's certainly a day worth celebrating, since the EU has changed the course of the country, particularly its capital. After centuries of being a pawn of Europe's empire builders, Belgium has the satisfaction of knowing that its voice is heard as an equal in the European Union. And Belgium's crossroads capital has become virtually the capital of Europe.

Belgium is unique among the bilingual countries of the world in that its two main language groups are so nearly equal in numbers and area. Even more unusual is the extent to which bilingualism has, in the second half of the 20th century, been regulated by legislation. This process has continued under **federalism**. The introduction to Belgium of federalism, in 1988, gave important decision-making powers and regional autonomy to *Flanders, Wallonia* and *Brussels.* In April 1993, both chambers of the Belgian National Parliament voted final approval for a 35-amendment revision to the constitution to turn Belgium into a federal state, which was made official with a nod from the late King Baudouin. Federalism has helped both to stabilize Belgium's political situation and to overcome the lingering linguistic divisions. In the past, when Belgium's internal petty rivalries and hostilities have periodically ignited, it sometimes has seemed that the country would split. Though often predicted, however, that split hasn't happened and now is even less likely to under federalism.

Due to the complexity of Belgium's circumstances, a correctly calibrated federal formula is still evolving for the separate but equal regional governments of Flanders, Wallonia, and Brussels. The national parliament and central government retain responsibility for international affairs, security, defense, consumer protection, labor, social security, and overall economic and monetary policy, which must deal with Belgium's large chronic national budget deficit.

Despite an often wasteful, excessively expensive overlapping of resources, the change to federalism has been deemed largely successful. Nevertheless, a lot of energy that could go into more far-reaching endeavors is expended to maintain Belgium's bicultural balancing act. For example, bilingual switchboard operators for the Belgian Senate must say "Le Senat/De Senaat" when answering the

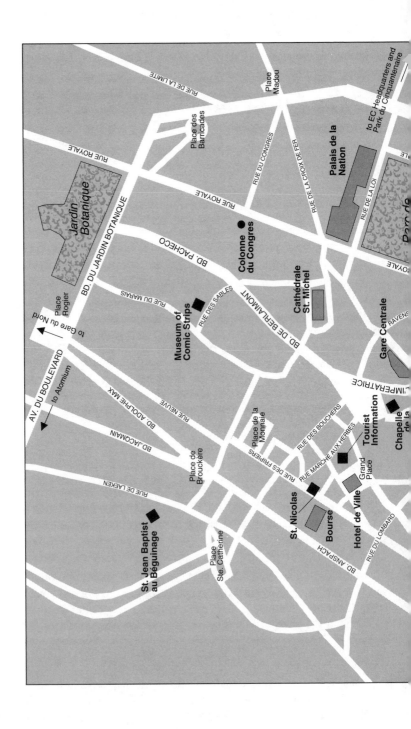

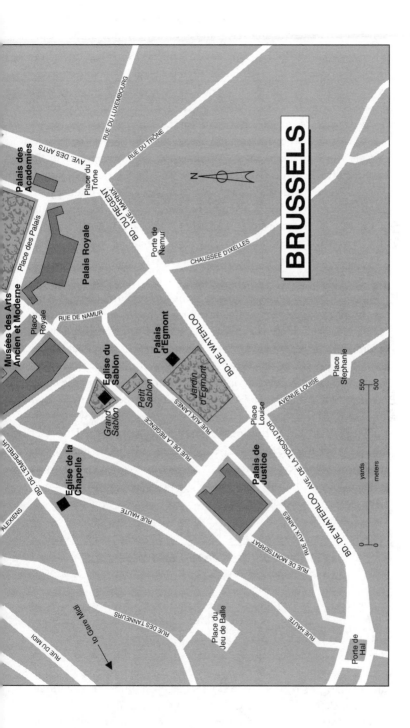

phone on Mondays, Wednesdays, and Fridays, and "De Senaat/Le Senat" on Tuesdays, Thursdays, and Saturdays. Sundays, they rest.

The recovery of the Belgian economy in the 1980s was one of the world's success stories. Despite an unemployment rate above the EU average, small 10-million-people-strong Belgium is surprisingly well poised economically for the 1990s. Eleven of the country's corporations—a mix of metals, merchandising, banking, and utilities—make it onto Forbes magazine's list of the 500 largest companies outside the U.S. Belgium is the highest *per capita* exporter in the world: fully 70 percent of the GNP leaves the country as exports. The only worry with that is, as *Forbes* points out, "If its trading partners catch colds, Belgium gets pneumonia." Belgium recently found out that, even as the seventh most active financial center in the world and the fourth largest in Europe, it isn't invulnerable to international corporate raiding. Several once proud family-run operations are now in the hands of foreigners.

Many of the internally traumatic turns of Belgium's 20th-century history have barely been noticed beyond its borders. In any case, on the world stage, they pale beside the significance that Belgium has assumed in the latter part of this century as a small but equal state in the European Union. With Brussels moving from the *de facto* to the *de jure* capital of Europe as capital of the European Union, the country has high visibility. Today, Belgium—which perhaps more than any other EU country has loosened the ties of its own nationalism—eagerly awaits Europe's economic integration. This will, among other things, further ease the exit of its exports. Belgians are the first to characterize Europe's adventure in *deregulation* an evolutionary, not revolutionary, process. The distinction suits their essentially conservative character just fine.

# BRUSSELS

## *GUIDELINES FOR BRUSSELS*
### SIGHTS

Brussels's **Grand-Place**, with its inspiring 15th-century **Hotel De Ville** (Town Hall, with **Tourist Information Brussels—T.I.B.**) and gilt-highlighted guild houses (late 17th century), is Europe's most magnificent square—and car-free at long last. It's the starting point for all city sightseeing, to be followed by the small surrounding medieval market streets of the Ilot Sacre, including the restaurant-clogged Petit rue des Bouchers. Belgium's finest collection of *Flemish "primitives"* paintings, as well as wonderful works from the

*Netherlands' 16th and 17th centuries*, and the *Belgian Surrealists*, are at the **Musées de l'Art Ancien et Moderne** on **place Royale**. The sights around the Grand Sablon include its antique shops and weekend outdoor market, art galleries, church, and the **Petit Sablon**, with its restful statue-ornamented garden. Among Brussels' varied architecture are fascinating samples of the turn-of-the-century **art nouveau** style, especially the former house of Belgium's most famous exponent, Victor Horta. City attractions are varied and sometimes surprising. The **after-dark illumination** of monuments creates lasting impressions; the Grand-Place aglow will leave you spellbound.

## GETTING AROUND

Belgium's capital city is well equipped for conveying people from one to another of its 19 *communes*. The **Metro** is the fastest, most decorative means. (See "Bourse Station/Metro Art" under "What To See and Do" below); **buses** are next best; then **trams** (colorful but slow, they're gradually being done away with since street cars interfere excessively with Brussels's notorious traffic). Metro and transportation system maps are available from the T.I.B., as are **daypasses** (BF 120) for unlimited use until midnight on the day purchased of city Metro, buses, and trams. Single rides are (BF 50), cards for 5 journeys are (BF 230), 10 journeys are (BF 305). The *Tourist Passport* includes a day pass combined with entry reduction vouchers for selected attractions for BF 220, available from T.I.B. Fares shown on taxi meters include tip. Parking in Brussels is as eventful as in any too-traffic-congested old European city; metered spaces (have BF 5 and 20 pieces handy) have varying rules. Paid car parks (indicated by blue **"P"** signs) can be found at **blvd. de Waterloo**, **place de la Monnaie**, and **place Rogier**.

## SHOPPING

Brussels isn't London, Paris, or Rome, but the best designer names from each can be found in the luxury specialty shops and designer boutiques in the *Haut de la Ville* (Upper Town) along the chic **blvd. de Waterloo** and **avenue de la Toison D'Or**. Big-name chain and department stores are clustered primarily in **blvd. Aldolphe Max** and the pedestrianized **rue Neuve**. Late-night shopping is Friday until 8 p.m., though smaller shops and grocery stores that close at lunchtime may remain open until 6:30 or 7 p.m. other nights, too. Travelers should inquire of shopkeepers about the conditions for duty-free purchases.

## ENTERTAINMENT AND EVENTS

The Tourist Information Brussels' publication, *BBB Agenda* (for sale), has a calendar of events in the city, including opera, ballet, and concerts; T.I.B. also can arrange bookings. See, too, events listings in *The Bulletin*, Brussels' English-language weekly newspaper, and especially its weekly all-Belgium entertainment supplement *What's On*. Cafes, nightclubs and cinemas (some 35, showing a varied range of films in their original language) are clustered in the upper town between porte Namur and place Louise, and in the lower town between the place de la Bourse and place Rogier.

## WHERE TO STAY

Brussels offers plentiful hotel choices in all prices—which have risen across the board in the last several years in this European capital. Because of the start-up each September of European Union meetings, as well as annual fall trade congresses and corporate conventions, hotel rooms then and in October can be scarce.

## WHERE TO EAT

If gourmets worldwide consider Brussels one of the top cities for food—restaurants number more than 1500—you'll hardly want to leave without assessing the celebrated cuisine for yourself. Whether you want *frites* (french fries) from stands, *alfresco* meals of *moules* (mussels) at tables set out along ancient alleys, *vlaams carbonada* (Belgium's beef stew in beer specialty) in an atmospheric cafe, or an extraordinary repast at an elegant dining "institution," it will be hard to find less-than-fine food in Brussels.

## ARRIVING

Those arriving by air fly into Brussels' **Zaventem Airport**, 9 mi/14 km northeast of the city. **Sabena World Airlines** is the major Belgian carrier, with both transatlantic routes and air connections onward to many European cities. There's thrice-hourly rail service from the airport into the city (20 minutes, fare BF 85), with the first stop at Brussels' **Gare du Nord** (North Station), then **Gare Centraal** (Central Station); one train an hour continues on to the **Gare du Midi** (South Station), the city's third main station. If you are arriving in Brussels by train, and already have reservations at a hotel, you'll find it helpful to know *before arrival* which train station is closest to your hotel, although the Metro links all stations, and all have taxi stands. Gare Centrale is closest to the Grand-Place, the heart of old Brussels, and to both the Brussels and the all-Belgium tourist information (*rue Marché aux Herbes 61*) offices. As the de facto capital of

Europe, Brussels is well-linked with the continent's major motorways. Ferries arriving from England at Ostend and Zeebrugge are met by Brussels-bound trains.

## IN THE AREA

Located in a magnificent building on the eastern outskirts of Brussels at Tervuren is the **Musée Royal de l'Afrique Centrale** which, formerly focused on the former *Belgian Congo* colony, now has exhibits on the whole of Africa. South of Brussels is the rural battleground at **Waterloo** where the Emperor Napoleon—much to the relief of the early 19th-century European heads of state—came but did not conquer.

## TRAVEL TIPS

Brussels' museums, offices, and other attractions often close at noon for up to two hours, so plan your midday touring accordingly. The **Art l'Ancien** and **Art Moderne** museums have coordinated their one-hour lunch closures so that one or the other of the underground-connected sections remains open.

## *BRUSSELS IN CONTEXT*

Imagine the scene, seen by an American acquaintance in Brussels, visiting his Belgian in-laws: two Bruxellois conversing, a French-speaker forming questions in his language to a Fleming, who was replying in Dutch—both continuing in that manner without missing a meaning. That's not the way the city's *official bilingualism* is meant to work, of course.

Geographically, Brussels lies well within Dutch/Flemish-speaking Flanders, but, culturally, it remains decidedly French in its orientation. According to William Z. Shetter, author of *The Netherlands in Perspective*, "The power of Brussels to radiate and extend French influence is a source of constant anxiety to the Flemish." By law, no count is made, but it's known that Brussels' French-speaking Belgian-nationality residents outnumber the city's Flemish speakers by an estimated 4 to 1. The 1962 guarantee of equal language rights for the Flemish did not erase French-outlook favoritism in Brussels, though recently Flemish has become a more accepted route to advancement in business and government there. If one could put language aside, the *Bruxellois* are more of an amalgam: while a majority may *speak* French, most *think* like the Dutch, the result being a cultured business acumen.

In addition to having to absorb the complexities of its indigenous inhabitants' bicultural concerns, Brussels, with a population of just under one million, is nearly 25 percent foreign, with many MEPs (*Members* of the *European Parliament*), diplomats, multinational corporate executives, and their families. It may sound like the making of a melting pot, but, according to Brussels-based *Financial Times* reporter Lucy Kellaway, it's not so simple. In an article in that British newspaper, Kellaway explains: "Each nationality keeps to itself, remaining true to all its prejudices, persuasions, and preferences ...Outside work they stick to themselves. They live in little pockets, send their children to national schools, and, distance permitting, go home to their own countries on weekends...While (citizens of EC) member states mix little with each other, they do not mix with the Belgians at all...Language is only partly to blame for this isolationist behaviour. After all, anyone who works in the Commission must be able to speak French, and most people can muster decent English and probably another language too."

While this picture of human nature, almost reminiscent of a colonial lifestyle, may be discouraging to those in the EC who seek to drop their narrow nationalist identities for a "big picture" of Europe, it perhaps proves reassuring to citizens of individual countries in Europe—and travelers from abroad—who have worried that the European Community's *Single Europe Act* might mean the end of an individual country's cultural idiosyncrasies.

Brussels, today one of Belgium's three federalist regions (with Flanders and Wallonia), celebrated its millenium in 1979. That puts its founding back in A.D. 979, when Charles of France, Duke of Lower Lotharingia, built a fortified structure on the island of Saint Gery on marshy land called **Bruoscella**. In 1041, ducal successors built a new castle on the highest land, becoming early residents of the **Haut de la Ville** (Upper Town) at **Coudenberg**, site of the present Royal Palace. Brussels first had fortified walls in the year 1100, and the first version of its Cathédrale Saint Michel appeared in 1225. To embrace the continuing growth, a second series of city walls—where the *inner boulevard* ring road now runs—was finished in time for Brussels' quadricentennial in 1379.

Entering the 15th century, Brussels gained in stature as a residence of the ambitious **House of Burgundy**, which became the most powerful state between France and Germany, acquiring nearly all the secular lordships of the Netherlands. The first stone of the *Hôtel de Ville* (town hall) was laid on the *Grand-Place* in 1402, in response to the need for Brussels to have grander buildings for use by the Burgundian dukes. Their court attracted large numbers of French knights to

Brussels, and the French language became fashionable among the Netherlands nobles.

In 1430, Burgundian duke **Philip the Good**, called "the equal of kings and emperors," took possession of Brabant, thereafter moving his capital from Dijon to Brussels. The city achieved remarkable economic growth by turning to the production of luxury goods: lace, paintings, tapestries, jewelry, and church furnishings. Artists and craftsmen of great renown flocked to Brussels' increasingly ostentatious court. Under Philip, **Jan van Eyck** became court painter, and **Rogier van der Weyden** (*Rogier de la Pasture*) was appointed Brussels' town painter.

**Charles V** (**Quint**) confirmed the political and administrative pre-eminence of Brussels by himself settling in the city at the palace of Coudenberg in 1515 and, in 1530, officially moving the Netherlands' court there from Mechelen. As capital of the Netherlands' 17 provinces—land that today includes much of both Belgium and Holland—and with a central location within the immense Hapsburg empire which then ruled the Netherlands, Brussels received great benefits. The original **Ommegang** (still annually reenacted on the Grand-Place) was a brilliant pageant marking the grand entry procession of Charles V, by then *Holy Roman Emperor*, and his son Philip II, King of Spain, into Brussels in 1549. But Brussels also had the unenviable inevitability of being at the center of the **Reformation**.

The stage was set for the **Eighty Years' War** by the 1555 abdication of Charles V at Brussels' Coudenberg Palace. Power over the 17 Netherlands' provinces passed to his son Philip, a fanatic Roman Catholic. In Brussels to receive rule from his father, Philip thereafter oversaw the Netherlands long distance from Spain, dispatching orders and officials to collect unpopular taxes and tributes, suppressing Protestants, and installing his half-sister Margaret, duchess of Parma, as regent in Brussels. Philip's harsh policies inflamed newly converted Protestants, who were filled with anti-papist preaching from Calvinists and Lutherans. A wave of religious rebellion swept the Netherlands. The first action of the Eighty Years' War came April 5, 1566, when hundreds of Netherlands nobles marched through the streets of Brussels to the home of Margaret of Parma to protest religious persecution. Many carried the beggars' bowls that once had signified that their support for the king would last until they were reduced to beggars. Taunted as *geuzen* (beggars) as they walked past regime loyalists, the nobles and their followers adopted the term as a rallying nickname. The year 1566 also produced extremist Protestant crowds that attacked Catholic churches and their contents.

Brussels' **Cathedrale St. Michel** suffered severe damage, and relics in the **Eglise Notre-Dame du Sablon** were destroyed.

Spanish response to the widespread destruction was brutal. In 1567, Philip II sent the **Duke of Alva** (or Alba) and 10,000 troops to the Netherlands to replace the Duchess of Parma. In Brussels, Alva established the *Council of Troubles* for trials of sedition charges against Netherlanders (who called the court the **Council of Blood**). By 1568, groups of 30 to 50 people at a time were being condemned to death, their property confiscated by the Spanish Crown. In only a short time, the tally of the dead reached 8000.

Perhaps because the earliest resistance to Spanish religious oppression had come from the Netherlands nobility, when the Dutch **Counts Egmont** and **Hoorn**—both of whom had previously served with honor in the armies of Charles V and Philip II—went to Brussels to seek relief for Holland from the persecution of the Protestants there by the Spanish king's representative, Alva wouldn't listen. At 10 a.m. on June 5, 1568, on Brussels' Grand-Place in front of the *Maison du Roi* (which never housed a king, only the Spanish law court), a silent, shocked crowd saw Egmont and Hoorn beheaded. It is said that afterward, many people pushed past the Spanish guards to dip their Belgian lace-trimmed handkerchiefs in the blood of the first martyrs of the war. (Some time later, a memorial commemorating the infamous execution was erected on the spot in front of the steps where it took place; the statues of Egmont and Hoorn and fountain from it were moved to the peaceful *place du Petit Sablon* when the garden there was laid out in 1890). The tide turned in 1576 when **Dutch Prince Willem of Orange** was able to drive the Spanish out of Brussels, and the city enacted anti-Catholic laws that virtually abolished all outward signs of the religion.

From 1585, however, by which time the religious struggles between the Spanish and the Dutch had caused a split between the northern and southern Netherlands provinces, Brussels was reoccupied by Spanish forces and named as the capital of the southern Spanish Netherlands. Thereafter, the city, and most of the rest of what is Belgium today, remained basically loyal to Spain and Roman Catholicism. The pro-Catholic **Counter-Reformation** brought a wave of Jesuits, priests, and nuns to Brussels, and the arrival of Philip II's daughter Archduchess Isabella, who, jointly with her husband Archduke Albert of Austria, was appointed ruler of the Spanish Netherlands in 1598. Life in Brussels again flowed around a fashionable court, and the city became a haven for political exiles, such as the sons of beheaded Roman Catholic English King Charles I.

As Spanish influence flagged at the end of the 17th century, French **King Louis XIV** embarked on an imperialist adventure through the Netherlands. In 1695, he ordered his 70,000-man army to fire cannon and mortars from the heights of Anderlecht on central Brussels. Forty-six hours later, Brussels had lost nearly 4000 houses, 16 churches, and many major buildings, including all those surrounding the *Grand-Place*, with the exception of the Hôtel de Ville which, miraculously, withstood the onslaught. The Bruxellois response was to build an even more magnificent main square, a goal they accomplished in four short years. French efforts to gain the southern Netherlands, in the **War of the Spanish Succession** (1701–1714), finally went down in defeat due to England's Duke of Marlborough, John Churchill (Winston's ancestor), and Austria's Prince Eugene. This brought the region under Austrian Hapsburg rule.

The Austrian era began oppressively, and social confrontations culminated in the beheading of Brussels' guild leader **Francois Anneessens** in 1719. But **Charles of Lorraine**, a genial Austrian ruler (dispatched from Vienna's Hapsburg household by then Empress Maria Theresa), oversaw the era after the 1745–1748 **War of the Austrian Succession** (during which France reconquered nearly the whole of the country before losing it *again* to Austria). Under Charles, the physical face of Brussels around the **Place Royale** changed to *neoclassical*, as the *Royal Palace*, *Palais de la Nation*, and *Parc de Bruxelles* took shape. Maria Theresa's son, Joseph II, who ruled from 1765–1790, had a well-intentioned plan for reform, but his overhasty and insensitive implementation aroused a spirit of revolt.

Under the influence of the French Revolution and the leadership of **Henri van der Noot**, the people of Brussels took arms, and in a national uprising, declared the **United Belgian States** (the first use of the "Belgian" name in modern times) in January 1790. The life of the independent republic was short-lived; by agreeing to restore some civil rights that had been rescinded by Joseph II, Austrian Emperor Leopold II was able to reoccupy the country. Between 1792–94, in yet another turnaround of rulership, the *French Revolutionary Army* under **Napoleon Bonaparte** beat the Austrians for Belgium and defeated Holland. Both the southern and northern Netherlands became dependences of France (and were united as the **Batavian Republic** from 1795 to 1808). With the exile of Napoleon to Elba in 1814, the *Congress of Vienna* was poised to bind Belgium to Holland again when its plan had to be postponed because of the reappearance of the French emperor.

Cannon fire from the fields of **Waterloo**—a dozen miles away—could be heard in Brussels during the day of the battle there, June 18, 1815. Many who had gathered lightheartedly at the Duchess of Richmond's "Waterloo" Brussels ball for guest-of-honor the English **Duke of Wellington**—who danced until dawn on June 16—were, on the 18th, sure that Napoleon would bring bloodshed all the way to Brussels. Those fortunate enough to find passage fled to Antwerp on barges.

Shortly after the Battle of Waterloo in 1815 (see "Waterloo" under "In the Area" below), despite Belgian protestations, Holland's Prince Willem became ruler of Belgium as head of the **Kingdom of the Netherlands**, since the European powers, still meeting at the *Congress of Vienna*, were anxious to keep a strong, established, buffer state between themselves and France. Brussels became co-capital (with The Hague) of the new kingdom. But, beneath the surface, Belgians breathed **revolution**, which came in 1830 in Brussels. An opera performance of Auber's *The Mute of Portici*, which carries a strongly suggestive patriotic message, inspired Belgians to take to the streets of Brussels after an August 25, 1830, performance. Some raised the Brabant flag—the same tricolor of black, gold, and red that the new country adopted soon after—over the Hôtel de Ville. Young intellectuals and others rioted, sacking the homes of government ministers, raiding bakeries for bread and bars for alcohol, and destroying machinery in factories. Brussels' Burgomaster Vanderlinden d'Hooghvorst formed an 8000-man militia that quelled the riot but couldn't stop the movement. Joined by volunteers from the provinces, the Bruxellois rebelled against 14,000 Dutch soldiers who arrived in September. The **Parc de Bruxelles**, in front of the *Palais de la Nation* where the Dutch government had its Brussels headquarters, was the scene of some of the fiercest fighting. On September 27, 1830, a free **Kingdom of Belgium** was finally declared, with Brussels named the capital. In July of 1831, the keys to the city were handed over to the new country's first King **Leopold of Saxe-Coburg**, who swore allegiance to the Belgian people on the steps of *St. Jacques sur Coudenberg* church on **place Royale**.

The energy released with the achievement of Belgian independence produced plentiful signs of progress and prosperity in the capital of the new kingdom. The **Free University of Brussels** was founded in 1834; in 1835, continental Europe's first passenger steam locomotive chugged out of Brussels (to Mechelen); and the Royal Library opened in 1837. Later in the 19th century, the covering of the Senne River took place, largely for sanitary reasons, but it made possible the construction of Brussels' central boulevards (today's **Anspach, Adolphe Max,** etc.). The **Palais du Justice** (built between 1866-1883 by Joseph Poelaert), a Greco-Roman domed domain larger than St. Peter's in Rome, if nothing else showed civic confidence. The 1880 exhibition at the **parc du Cinquantenaire** was held in celebration of the free country's 50th birthday.

In World War I the Nazis violated Belgium's declared neutrality, and used the senate chamber of Brussels' *Palais de la Nation* (Parliament Building) for its wartime tribunal. In that chamber in 1915 the *Nazi Tribunal* condemned courageous English nurse **Edith Cavell** to death by firing squad. She had been running a training school for nurses in Brussels and, uncowed by threats, had willingly harbored and further helped Belgians and Allies seeking to escape across the border to neutral Holland. (She is credited with helping 130 prisoners escape.) Brussels again was occupied in World War II (from May 1940–September 1944).

During 1944, government ministers who had fled from Belgium, Holland, and Luxembourg, and were all operating in exile from London, settled on the idea of the **BENELUX,** a mutually beneficial, barrier-free customs and trade, which, when officially instituted in 1948, helped put the devasted economies of the three countries on the fastest possible post-war recovery track. The BENELUX proved a harbinger of European evolution, and, in 1959, Brussels was selected as capital of the six-nation **European Economic Community** (Common Market). Brussels also blossomed from hosting the extremely successful **World's Fair in 1958**, with *Atomium* being the symbol of its nuclear energy theme. In 1967, Brussels was chosen capital of **NATO** (North Atlantic Treaty Organization). Those developments forever changed the face and mentality of the city. On the domestic front, in 1980, under a new Belgian form of government, Brussels found itself one of the country's three federal regions (together with Flanders and Wallonia).

While the internationalism of Brussels is intriguing to travelers— it's the "company town" for European government, and TV news anchors in countries throughout Europe begin their coverage with "Today in Brussels ..."—it also can create a certain dissatisfaction due to the resulting lack of a well-defined foreign identity. Even its own Belgian population doesn't permit Brussels to present a single cultural face to visitors—though two foreign flavors for one destination could be considered a bonus. The simple fact is that Brussels is complex.

More than with most places, Brussels is the result of its history, which includes major changes in this last decade of the 20th century. They are all revealed on the physical face of the city, nowhere as clearly as in the mixed architectural course the city has followed during the second half of this century. What some call a carelessly conserved architectural heritage, others explain by saying that Brussels wants to be more in the present, not just a pretty face from the past. That shouldn't be a worry, since Brussels, as **capital of the European Union (EU)**, heads the world's largest economic block: the 340 million citizens of an evolving *single-market Europe*.

Brussels' long-standing city symbols, the surprisingly smaller-than-life boy statue mascot **Manneken-Pis** and the **Atomium** molecule multiplied many billion times its size, both seem to have had to step slightly aside for the **EU flag** (a circle of gold stars, representing European Union member nations, on a field of blue), the city emblem one sees everywhere. But, ever interested in being innovative as well as true to its history, Brussels has adapted: Manneken-Pis' wardrobe has been updated with an official EU outfit.

## GUIDEPOSTS

**Telephone Code 02**

**Tourist Office Tourist Information Brussels (T.I.B.)** • Hôtel de Ville, Grand-Place, B-1000 Brussels; ☎ *513.89.40, FAX 514.45.38*; daily 9 a.m.–6 p.m. (from Oct. 1–March 30 closed Sun.), closed Christmas, New Year's.

**Emergencies** • Accident ☎ *100*; police ☎ *101*; doctors on duty: ☎ *479.18.18*, ☎ *648.80.00*; dentists on duty: ☎ *426.10.26, 428.58.88*.

**Airport** • General info. ☎ *02.722.30.00*; SABENA World Airlines: reservations ☎ *511.90.30*, information ☎ *720.71.67*.

**Trains** • Information for all trains in Belgium and in Europe: ☎ *219.26.40*.

**Metro, Tram, Bus** • Information day and night: ☎ *515.20.00*.

**Lost Property** • Lost property office for metro, buses, trams: ☎ *515.23.94*, ave. de la Toison d'Or 15, 9:30 a.m.–12:30 p.m.; for property lost in a taxi, apply to police station nearest point of departure. ☎ *100*

**Tours** • **ARAU City Tours** in English on such themes as **Brussels 1900, Brussels in the 1930s, Surprising parks and squares**, ☎ *513.47.61*, FAX *511.68.29*. **Sightseeing Line**: 14-seat minibus tours in English (headset) through Brussels' smaller streets, schedule, information ☎ *513.89.40* (T.I.B.).

**Taxis** • Available at taxi ranks, or by telephone order: **Taxis Oranges** ☎ *513.62.00*; **Taxis Verts** ☎ *349.49.49*; tip is included in meter price.

**Post Office** • Main office: **Centre Monnaie**, Mon.–Fri. 9 a.m.–5 p.m.; money orders, 8 a.m.–8 p.m.; stamps Sat. 9 a.m.–noon. (Sat. in July & Aug. 9 a.m.–8 p.m. for stamps only.)

**Telephone/Telex** • Main city office: blvd. de l'Imperatrice 17, daily 7 a.m.–10 p.m.; ☎ *513.44.90.*

**Local Newspaper** • *The Bulletin*, a Brussels weekly in English; events information.

**English Books** • *W. H. Smith*, blvd. Adolphe Max 71; ☎ *219.27.08.*

## WHAT TO SEE AND DO

By law, the names of Brussels' streets, buildings, etc. must appear in both of the city's official languages (as you'll see on the T.I.B. map). But here, solely for simplicity's sake—and with, I hope, the forgiveness of the Flemish—I often have used only the French. Except for scattered attractions (included at the end), major sights are grouped under three main centers: the **Grand-Place**; the **Place Royale**; and the **Grand Sablon**.

## GRAND-PLACE AND SURROUNDING AREA

**Grand-Place**                                    ★★★

*Grote Markt, main square.* It's difficult to overstate the impact the Grand-Place makes as you enter it on foot from any of the confined cobbled streets that lead there. Suddenly, you are assaulted with splendor on a staggering scale, an impression strengthened not only by the great size of the square, but by the architecturally harmonious appearance of the whole. In the disaster-turned-triumph of the 1695 French bombardment, enemy cannons leveled everything around the Grand-Place except what they sought most: the soaring spire of the Hôtel de Ville. Immediately, plans were made to build even grander guild houses and, between 1696 and 1699, many were completed. Baroque and beautifully embellished, with statue-studded gables, pilasters, and balustrades, the gold-leaf detail of the decor glowing in the sun or gleaming under night spotlights, the guild houses surround Brussels' immense (120 by 75 yards, 110 by 70 meters) main square. Most of the buildings served as headquarters for the business and social meetings of Brussels' guilds, identified by the appropriate patron saint or insignia on the facade; all have stories (inquire at the T.I.B. about its audio-tours of the Grand-Place) though none has a more varied history than the **Maison du Cygne** (swan) at No. 9.  Rebuilt in 1698 as a house for Peter Fariseau (a founder of the Brussels opera), it became in 1720 the butchers' guild house. In exile from Germany, **Karl Marx** (1818–1883) moved with his family into the building in about 1846 and, having met Friedrich Engels in Brussels, undoubtedly wrote some of their jointly published (1848 in Belgium) *Communist Manifesto* under its roof. So perhaps it's appropriate that the *Belgian Labor Party* was founded in the Maison du Cygne in 1885. Today, it houses an elegant restaurant of the same name whose prices are most certainly capitalist, not communist.

### Hôtel de Ville/ Stadhuis/Town Hall ★★★

*(Guided tours only; English Tours Tues. 11:30 a.m. and 3:30 pm, Wed. 3:15 p.m., Sun. & hols. from April–Sept. 12:15; tours cancelled in case of City Councel sessions or receptions;* ☎ *512.75.54).* This centerpiece of the Grand-Place is one of the largest (197-foot/60-meter facade) and finest Gothic buildings in the Benelux. With a 295-foot/90-meter openwork spire by Jan van Ruisbroek, topped with a figure of Archangel Michael, patron saint of the city, it was completed in 1454. Included in the guided tour of the interior are reception halls laden with decorative treasures: 16th-, 17th-, and 18th-century Brussels' tapestries, Gothic wood carvings, and fascinating full-length portraits of the likes of Charles V and Philip II.

### Museum of the City of Brussels ★★

*Maison du Roi, Grand-Place, directly opposite the Hôtel de Ville; Mon–Fri. 10 a.m.–12:30 p.m., 1:30–5 p.m. except 4 p.m. Oct. 1–Mar. 31; Sat., Sun., holidays. 10 a.m.–1 p.m.;* ☎ *511.27.42.* Despite a lack of English explanation, much here will capture your attention, including the building itself (though, singly among those on the Grand-Place, it is not as old as it looks). Destroyed in the 1695 bombing, it remained a shattered shell (and eyesore) until rebuilt in 1763, but it was reconstructed in such an ordinary and unharmonizing style that it became neglected and had to be virtually demolished and rebuilt again in 1873, under the patient efforts (22 years worth) of City Architect Victor Jamaer. He used old engravings as his guide, but added the galleries and the tower. The ground floor displays 16th- and 17th-century Brussels' tapestries, including one made from a cartoon by Rubens, 15th-century carved-wood retables, 14th- and 15th-century stonework saved from Brussels' buildings, and 18th- and 19th-century Brussels faience, all highlighted by **Pieter Breugel the Elder's** *Marriage Procession.* The first floor also presents a history of Brussels's city design and development, shown through items such as a model of the 17th-century town, and paintings and prints showing the Senne river harbor before it was filled/covered in the 19th century. The main attraction of the second floor is the display of several dozen of the 400-odd outfits in the ★★wardrobe of Brussels's mascot **Manneken-Pis**. The costumes periodically donned by the two-foot- tall statue range from Roman centurian to American cowboy. Maurice Chevalier penned and published a song to Manneken-Pis in 1949 and gave him an outfit complete with a straw hat of the type the French songster was famous for. On some dates Manneken-Pis is dressed ceremonially: each Sept. 3, in thanks for their liberation of Brussels on that date in 1944, he wears the uniform of the Welsh Guards.

### L'Ilot Sacré ★★

*The Sacred Isle.* This old section of the lower town, a network of narrow cobbled streets built on the once-marshy land where Brussels was born more than one thousand years ago, covers the area immediately north of the Grand-Place. Its pedestrian back streets carry the names of the businesses conducted here since medieval days: *Marché aux Herbes* (herb market), *rue des Bouchers* (butchers' street), *rue de Beurre* (butter street), *rue de Poivre* (pepper street). Today, L'Ilot Sacre is indeed considered to be sacred, and protected from the demolition and development that have wreaked more havoc on Brussels' buildings than the cannonballs and bombs of any war since the 17th century. One of Brussels' most appetizing tourist sights is the restaurant region of rue des Bouchers and Petit rue des Bouchers: it's often said that if visitors haven't eaten here at least once, they can barely say they've been to Brussels.

### Art in the Metro/Bourse Station ★★

*blvd. Anspach; Art in the Metro* brochure in Dutch and French only. From 1976, when the first stations of the Brussels Metro opened, until 1984, when the city's Museum of Modern Art opened on place Royale, the only real museum of contemporary art in the Belgian capital was underground in the system's shiny new stations. When Metro construction began in 1969, an art-loving politician helped direct its decoration, moving city planners to a totally innovative approach because, as one spokesman said, "we did not want to have a stereotype Metro with kitchen or bathroom-type tiles and every station the same." The Ministry of Transport not only solved much of Brussels' enormous urban traffic problem, which had come to impact the quality of life in the city, but also improved the quality-of-life dimension of the Metro stations (elsewhere so often anonymous, monotonous, user-unfriendly underground spaces). About 1 percent of the Metro budget was set aside for commissioned works from jury-invited contemporary Belgian artists who, once asked, were given freedom to express themselves in the station space and often were involved right along with the construction. Artists were asked to use materials that would stand up to the underground environment.

**Bourse** is only one of some three-dozen Metro stations that display some of the 50 works of original art, but since it's central, we'll begin a Metro art inventory there. A large oil painting of old Brussels trams, painted by Belgium's father of Surrealism **Paul Delvaux**, is quite in character for the artist who has used train stations as symbols for years. As with several stations, Bourse has more than one art work; **Pol Bury** created a *Moving Ceiling* out of 75 welded stainless steel cylinders. At the *Comte de Flandre* station, **Paul van Hoeydonck's** *16 x Icarus* group of figures "fly" from the ceiling. (Van Hoeydonck, who lived in the U.S., has the distinction of being the world's only artist to have a work on the moon: his small statue *Fallen Astronaut* was placed on the moon's surface by *Apollo 15*'s Armstrong in 1971.) Since the opening of the new **Stockel** station in 1988, riders have been delighted by artist **Van Herge's** colorful comic strip figures lining both long walls. The entire **Alma** station reflects nature: pillars are painted as tree stumps and the ceiling is a puffy cloud-filled sky. **Vandervelde** is a fantasy landscape, with the second-largest ceiling fresco in the world (following, of course, the Sistine Chapel). **Aumale** features the world's largest photographic work of art. It depicts scenes showing the Anderlecht neighborhood as it was before and after demolition to make way for the station. **Hankar** station has Roger Somville's 500-square-yard acrylic wall and ceiling painting called *Notre Temps*, showing the contradictions of "our times" in vividly colored scenes: an all-night cafe where people discuss the future of the world, motorcyclists refusing to take part in the everyday battle of life. At **Merode**, Roger Raveel's large oil panel painting *Ensor: Vive La Sociale*, with its faceless people (in the style of painter Ensor), bright colors, and mirrors, is meant to raise questions. Many of the stations feature sculptures; at **Stuyvenbergh**, **Yves Bosquet** has mounted statues of the Royal Family against one wall. With the variety of materials used (Station **Louise** has a tapestry), there are stations that do have tiles, but there's nothing of the bathroom about them: **Tomberg's** are yellow ceramics with a blue line design; **Merode** has a wonderful wall of blue, red, yellow, and brown tiles; and **Roodebeek's** tiles mix with marble in striking black and shades of gray vertical stripes.

It's nice to know that in this city, which has commissioned works from celebrated artists for more than 500 years, the Ministry of Transport is continuing the tradition today and has enabled many of Belgium's best artists to carry out work which many of the artists themselves consider of decisive importance in their careers. In addition to its aesthetic appeal, the Brussels Metro has statistics that show it has greater passenger security, less graffiti and vandalism, and fewer suicides than the underground transportation systems of comparably sized cities.

### Manneken-Pis

*rue de l'Etuve at the corner of rue du Chene, some 100 yards/90 meters southwest of the Grand-Place.* Manneken-Pis, an unexpectedly small, scarcely two-foot-tall/just over a half-meter-high statue of a naked young boy urinating into a fountain struck such a strong chord with Bruxellois that city fathers in 1619 commissioned a bronze replacement from Jerome Duquesnoy the Elder to replace a similar 15th-century stone statue. Many legends exist concerning the origins of Manneken-Pis, but, even leaving such speculations aside, the story of the statue-turned-city-symbol is absorbing.

His singular popularity and position as city mascot have made Manneken-Pis the subject of a series of kidnappings over the centuries. The first, intercepted, attempt was made by British soldiers in 1745. That effort seems to have inspired French soldiers in 1747, but their plot, too, was uncovered before it played out. However, to recompense Brussels for his soldiers' seizing of the statue, King Louis XV bestowed upon Manneken-Pis a title and gold-embroidered brocade court costume, complete with sword and feathered hat, to wear on festival days. Before long, other groups, both Belgian and foreign, were following suit, gifting Manneken-Pis with sufficient garb to make him the city's best-dressed citizen, one necessitating a wardrobe keeper. (See "Grand-Place, Maison du Roi,"). The most damaging kidnapping incident occurred in 1817 when a supposed ex-convict pulled the statue from his street-corner niche and broke it into pieces. Fortunately, the fragments were found and reassembled to form a mould from which the present statue was cast. In 1956, after yet another attempt, Manneken-Pis was bolted in place and equipped with a burglar alarm. During a snowstorm a few years later, however, the alarm bells froze, and prank-minded students from Antwerp were able to make off with him, though he was returned unharmed the next day.

### Galléries Saint Hubert ★★

*entrances off rue du Marché aux Herbes, rue des Bouchers, and rue d'Arenberg; always open.* At the end of rue des Bouchers, one enters a different era. The Industrial Age made possible the art of glass and metal that found one of its earliest and finest expressions in the skylighted Galleries Saint Hubert, Europe's first covered shopping walkway, built in 1847 by J. P. Cluysenaer. Not only was the arcade an early all-weather environment, but it also provided pedestrians with through passage in an alley area that over the centuries had become choked with impasses. The airy and attractive glass-vaulted arcade splits into the flag-festooned yet elegant **Galerie de la Reine** and **Galerie du Roi**, housing boutiques, cafes, and a theater.

### Belgian Center of the Comic Strip ★★

*rue des Sables 20; daily 10 a.m.–6 p.m., closed Mon. and Jan. 1, Nov. 1, Dec. 25;* ☎ *219.19.80.* Opened in 1989, this museum links two distinctively Belgian forms of creative expression. The setting is a 1903 former textile warehouse that was designed by Brussels's leading art nouveau exponent, architect Victor Horta; the contents are what Belgians call the Ninth Art, the social phenomenon and genuine art form of the comic strip. The museum was once the Waucquez Warehouse, the only one remaining of six art nouveau department stores that Horta built in Brussels. It, too, was very nearly lost to the wrecker's ball when the store went out of business in 1965 and buyers couldn't be found for the building, leaving it abandoned to weather and vandals until the middle of the 1980s. Fortunately, visionaries in the '80s seeking a place to gather the fantastic examples of their unusual art form saw the possibility of doing so under the historic Waucquez roof, which was subsequently restored. The displayed comic strips and audiovisual exhibits (more than 60 years of creativity are documented) usually are in French and/or Flemish only, but their visual appeal and that of the wonderful building with its magnificent lobby, ornamental grand staircase, art nouveau details, and space and light on all three floors, make the museum thoroughly worthwhile. There's also a shop with curios and posters, and an attractively ornamented brasserie (omelets, pasta, salads, chicken and seafood dishes, beverages including wine and beer, kitchen open until 3:30 p.m.). The museum's location, rue des Sables, in an area of central Brussels now in transition back to respectability, once teemed with pedestrian traffic because of the public stairs at the end of the street which still lead to the upper town.

## PLACE ROYALE AND SURROUNDING AREA

**Cathédrale Saint-Michel**

*place Sainte-Gudule; open daily Easter to Oct. 31, 7 a.m.–7 p.m. (except Sat. opens 7:30 a.m., Sun. 8 a.m.); Nov. to March, closes at 6 p.m.;* ☎ *217.83.45.* The cathedral, whose triforium is especially lovely when illuminated, has stood on its sloping site between Brussels's lower and upper town since the mid-13th century; the twin truncated towers, a rarity in Belgium, give it a strong French appearance. Overall, the massive building has a simple Brabant-Gothic style, with the nave and transept dating from the 14th and 15th centuries. Though elevated in rank to cathedral only in 1961 (when it became the seat of the Archbishop of Brussels-Mechelen), St.-Michel, long known as Belgium's national church, has been the setting for all the country's great religious occasions since the time of Duke Philip the Good of Burgundy. An extensive and extended restoration-in- progress makes uncertain what will be on view to visitors, but the 16th-century stained glass windows in the south and north transepts, created from cartoons by **Bernard van Orley**, are a treasure to search out, as are those of the same period in the **Chapel of the Blessed Sacrament** donated by Charles V and his family, whose granddaughter Archduchess Isabella and her husband are among those buried in the crypt. Also buried in the cathedral is one-time Brussels's city painter **Rogier van der Weyden** (1400–61) and Margaret of York (d. 1322), daughter of England's Edward I. A superb carved-wood baroque pulpit by Hendrik Verbruggen (1669) shows Adam and Eve being expelled from Eden, and six splendid 17th-century tapestries by Van der Borght sometimes are hung in the choir, often in summer when chamber concerts may be given in the chapel.

**Museum of Ancient Art/Art Ancien;**
**Museum of Modern Art/Art Moderne**

*rue de la Régence 3 for access to both museums; daily 10 a.m.–5 p.m.;* **Note:** *lunch closings are coordinated so that when one closes for an hour the other remains open; closed Mon., Jan. 1, May 1, Nov. 1, Nov. 11, Dec. 25, and election days;* ☎ *508.32.11; catalogues in English.* Simply stated, these museums house the most important collections in Belgium, a country noted for its art. The Museum of Ancient Art, whose focus is on the **Flemish "Primitives"** rather than classical ancients, concentrates on the art of the 15th-17th centuries in the Netherlands. There are some contemporary paintings from Italy and elsewhere included for comparison. Highlights from the rich collection, in which virtually all major Netherlands artists are represented, include *The Annunciation* by the **Master of Flemalle**, *Portrait of Anthony of Burgundy* and *The*

*Lamentation* by Brussels' mid-15th-century city painter **Rogier van der Weyden**. A room is devoted solely to five major works and a fragment by **Pieter Breughel the Elder** (the most important grouping of his works outside of Vienna). In an adjoining room are copies and adaptations of his work done by his son, **Pieter Breugel the Younger**, who was born just a short distance from the museum in 1564. Often called "Hell Breugel" for his own painted visions of life after death, he is responsible through his carefully copied versions of having preserved now-lost original works by his father (who died when his son was only five). Among the copies here are the *Massacre of the Innocents* and *Festival of Flanders* which, though not of the genius of the father's originals, are masterpieces in their own right. The great works in the 17th-century Dutch gallery are displayed in a lovely carpeted and sky-lighted setting.

The Museum of Modern Art, opened in 1984 and connected—compliments of **Alphonse Balat** (1875–1885)—to the older, neoclassical museum building by passageways and escalator, is a stunningly successful creation of ★★ multilevel exhibit space in the form of a glass half-bowl curved to catch the natural light, and set some eight levels in and beneath the courtyard of Charles of Lorraine's palace. Belgium's entire cast of 19th- and 20th-century painters and sculptors is included, along with a collection of 26 major works by **René Magritte** (*Empire of Lights* and *The Domain of Arnheim* kept by his widow until her death in 1986). A well-marked, color-coded museum plan (comprehensible even in its French/Flemish form) helps make the most of your time. There's a good shop and cafeteria.

## THE SABLON DISTRICT

### Place du Grand-Sablon/Grote Zavel ★★
*rue de la Regence, a short distance southwest of Place Royale.* Far more refined than its name in French ("sandy wasteland") suggests, the Sablon is an elegant, elongated square, encircled by smart antique and art shops, trendy bars and restaurants. It first became fashionable in the 16th century. It's at its most colorful on weekends, when the red-and-green-awninged stalls of the antiques market are set at the top of the square.

### Eglise Notre-Dame du Grand Sablon ★★
*rue de Regence 3B; Mon.–Sat. 9 a.m.–6:00 p.m., (5 p.m. Sat.), Sun., holidays 1–5 p.m., guided tour Sun. 4 p.m.;*  *511.57.41.* A lovely example of late flamboyant Gothic style, the church developed from a 1304 chapel built by the Guild of Crossbowmen. In 1615, Archduchess Isabella, using a crossbow, shot down the guild's target bird atop the church, which garnered her much admiration. The interior has some fine detail, including Gothic carvings on the cornerstones, but the church also is much admired simply for its overall harmony with the setting. The fine stained glass windows are illuminated wonderfully from ★★ within at night. Rededicated (by American organist James

David Christie) in 1990 after its rebuilding, the organ is often used for concerts.

### Place du Petit-Sablon ★★

*across rue de Regence from Notre-Dame* is a tranquil Renaissance-style garden with benches well used by area residents. Elegant effigies of counts Egmont and Hoorn (who met their death by beheading on the Grand-Place in 1568) have been given a place of honor; the Egmonts were one of the noble families who settled on the Sablon in the 16th century. The pretty park is surrounded by a wrought iron fence, with each of its 48 supporting columns topped with a small bronze statue representing one of Brussels' 16th-century guilds.

## ATTRACTIONS ELSEWHERE IN BRUSSELS

### Musées Royaux d'Art et d'Histoire ★

Royal Art and History Museums; *Parc du Cinquantenaire; year-round Tues.–Fri. 9:30 a.m.–5 p.m.; Sat., Sun. 10 a.m.–5 p.m., closed Mon. and major hols.; however, some sections of this enormous institution are staffed only on certain days, with some collections open solely on odd or even days; it's best to call ahead if you are interested in a particular exhibit;*  *741.72.11; Metro station Schuman; color-coded museum plan, exhibit notes in French/Flemish only.* The monumental museum wings, surrounded by the 90-acre/ 36-hectare **Parc du Cinquantenaire**, were built for a national exhibition held in 1880 to celebrate 50 years of Belgian independence; the triple triumphal arch that connects the two colonnaded buildings was built in 1904–05 by architect Charles Girault. The *Museums of Art and History* are in the wing on the right. Among the extensive collections that cross all eras and areas (a fine model/maquette of ancient Rome, for example) are a number of excellent Belgium-related exhibits: the remarkable Flemish Renaissance *Story of Jacob* ★★tapestry set (see "Tapestries" under "Decorative Arts and Traditional Crafts"); ★★art nouveau and art deco vases, stained glass, and jewelry; ★★Belgian lace and furniture; and porcelain from Tournai.

The wing to the left houses the Museums of the Army and Military History, which provide a general impression of the major military and historical events that have taken place on Belgian soil since 1789. Of perhaps more interest to non-Belgians, and not as dependent on non-existent English exhibit notes, are the *armored car* and *aviation* sections that focus mostly on the first and second World Wars. One huge room offers an exceptional collection of World War I fighter planes and *Battle of Britain* (1940) spitfires; gondolas from balloons and airships also are on display.

### Victor Horta House ★★

*rue Américaine 25, 1060 Saint-Gilles; year-round Tues.–Sun. 2–5:30 p.m., closed Mon., holidays;*  *537.16.92; tram 81, 92, bus, 54, 60.* From the moment you reach for the door handle, your fun has begun. Art nouveau, a style determined to do away with straight lines, puts arabesques in iron, curls in wood, and whirls and whiplashes in many materials that normally defy such shapes; its inventive practicality delights. Victor Horta (1861–1947), Belgium's leading exponent of art nouveau, trained under Alphonse Balat and, receiving commissions for houses by 1890—the earliest days of the style—in 1898 bought two plots of land on rue Americaine and began designing his house and studio. One of the few art nouveau interiors on view to the public, the whole house exudes Horta's sense of creative exhilaration and reflects the purest realization of his mature artistic concepts. Applied arts flourished in the art nouveau period and Horta, who always aspired to full unity between architecture and interior design, wrote—"in every house, I designed and created the models for each piece of furniture, for every single hinge and door handle, the carpets, and the wall decorations." Horta's art nouveau elements are organic and use a proliferation of vegetable forms, such as flower petal and leaf shapes; a ceiling may be shaped like a calla lily. Throughout the house, banisters curl up staircases like ribbons; cabinets seem to grow out of corners.

Horta based his art nouveau designs on the concept that structural elements could become artistic ones. He showed that iron and stone and bricks and wood could work together in a "human" architecture, and materials formerly used only for industrial buildings could make extra height and light possible in homes. Art nouveau sought to bring light and air into the dark and stuffy decor of the Victorian era. For light, Horta created revolutionary winter gardens by putting open stairwells in the core of a building, topped by a skylight. He often made use of the contoured opalescent glass developed by Americans **La Farge** and **Tiffany** in the 1870s for its soft effect. The pale-colored walls we take for granted are a legacy from the progressive properties of art nouveau.

Horta houses that have survived and can be viewed from the exterior include: the **Tassel House** *(rue Paul Emile Janson 6; 1893);* the **Solvay Mansion** *(avenue Louise 224; 1894);* and the **Van Eetvelde Mansion** *(avenue Palmerston 4; 1895).* Tours through **ARAU** (see "Tours" under "Guideposts"), may get you inside the astonishing, delightful, art nouveau-detailed ★ ★ Van Eetvelde mansion (originally ordered and owned by a baron who was Secretary General of the Belgian Congo in Brussels), which now serves as the offices of the **Federation de l'Industrie du Gaz.** It's located not far from EC headquarters at Rond-Point Schuman, an area worth exploring on foot for the art nouveau exteriors.

In 1916 Horta went to America, where he lectured in architecture and remained until 1919. When he returned to Brussels he began to work in **art deco**. (One of the reasons art nouveau died out as quickly as it did was that it had become so expensive.) Horta drew up the first plans for the Palais des Beaux-Arts in 1919 (undertaken in 1928) and finished final plans for Brussels *Gare Centrale* (Central Station) in 1937.

## SHOPPING

Belgium's Val Saint Lambert hand-cut crystal is on display at **Art & Selection** (*rue Marché-aux-Herbes 83*). Belgian lace (covered with a focus on Bruges in the *Decorative Arts and Traditional Crafts* section at the front of this book) is also a Brussels business of long-standing. Lace shops (with machine- as well as handmade items) are concentrated in the small streets off the Grand-Place, particularly **rue de l'Etuve** in the direction of **Manneken-Pis**; you'll also see shops selling machine-made tapestries. At rue de l'Etuve 26 and 43 are *Semal* shops, which, despite being located on Brussels' most touristic street, actually sell some good quality Belgian souvenirs. If you're looking for EC flag-bearing gear (T-shirts, carry-alls, umbrellas, and smaller items), shops here are worth checking out. Nearby **Picard** (*rue de Lombard 71*), which deals in carnival masks and other party paraphernalia, makes an amusing stop.

Its open-air markets are among Brussels' most mentioned attractions. The daily **flower market** carries on a tradition in the **Grand-Place**, which for centuries was the center of market activity in the town. The square's Sunday **bird market** (*7 a.m.–2 p.m.*) has its roots in the exploration of the 15th and 16th centuries, when previously unknown exotic and tropical species were brought to the old world from the far corners of the new. They are displayed here to the amazement of all. More diverse items tempt at the **antique and book market** held on the **Grand Sablon** Saturdays from 9 a.m.–6 p.m. and Sundays from 9 a.m.–2 p.m. Casual and avid collectors will find much to catch their attention on the canvas-awninged tables covered with antiques and almost-antiques. The genteel Sablon square, surrounded by well-kept townhouses, is a chic showplace of antique shops and art galleries with an elegant air, unbroken since the 16th century when it became a residential neighborhood for nobility.

Less pretentious but as much a microcosm of its milieu, the **Marolles** quarter, which it has operated since the 17th century, is the **Vieux Marché** (old market). The flea market takes place on the **place du Jeu de Balle** daily 7 a.m.–2 p.m., though Saturdays and Sundays are the best days; there's direct access on buses 20, 21, 48, within walking distance of tram stops at **Porte de Hal**. It's situated just off **rue Blaes**, which parallels **rue Haute** running through the center of the Marollies. For those seeking a "find," who like to bargain, and are as interested in people-watching as picking through the *brol* (acknowledged junk) and *brocante* (a better class of junk), this is the place. Many of the 200 stall-holders come from the working-class and immigrant-occupied Marolles surroundings, which gives the Vieux Marché the feeling of a neighborhood affair, even though dealers from as far away as Britain and Germany may be among the early-bird buyers doing business off the backs of trucks at 7 a.m.

## WHERE TO STAY

Because the city is dominated by the EU, NATO, trade congresses, and multinationals, Brussels' hotels in all price categories have a large business traveler clientele. With the Monday-to-Friday corporate crowd providing their bread and butter, many hotels, particularly the more expensive ones, may offer substantially reduced rates on weekends year-round, and daily during the summer business holiday months of July and August. Always ask about special rates.

## VERY EXPENSIVE

### Royal Windsor

*rue Duquesnoy 5;* ☎ *505.55.55, FAX 505.55.00; in U.S. and Canada* ☎ *1-800-223-6800.* This modern 300-room hotel with smart marble lobby is only several blocks from the Grand-Place and an equal distance from the Central Station (Gare Centraal) giving it one of the most convenient locations in Brussels. The well-furnished, wood-accent guestrooms are small but attractive, as are the marble baths. The hotel's Michelin-starred gourmet restaurant **Les 4 Saisons** offers fine French cuisine and an excellent wine list in an English-style Georgian and Regency setting. The Victorian-period English pub atmosphere Windsor Arms, is a popular local rendezvous, as is the lobby piano Waterloo Bar. Griffith's night club attracts many from throughout Brussels for its refined late night life. The hotel's fitness club offers sauna, treadmill, rowers, steppers, weights, and Lifecycle machines. Continental breakfast included; 24-hour room service; underground parking at hotel.

### Stanhope

*rue du Commerce 9;* ☎ *506.91.11, FAX 512.17.08.* Six years of renovation of three adjoining 18th-century houses produced this deluxe 50-room (25 are suites) hotel, located near the European Community center and the luxury shopping street *La Toison d'Or.* Rooms, each individually and tastefully decorated with English furniture and featuring a full range of amenities, have twice daily service, fax availability, and personal V.I.P. attention. Library-like bar; health club with sauna and exercise machines; book-lined elevators. The elegant hotel restaurant, decorated by the same craftsmen who restored the Royal Pavilion in Brighton, England, opens onto brick-walled garden. Rates (inclusive of buffet breakfast) reduced on weekends.

### Jolly Hotel du Grand Sablon

*place du Grand-Sablon;* ☎ *512.88.00, FAX 512.67.66, in U.S.* ☎ *1-800-221-2626, in Canada* ☎ *1-800-237-0319.* Opened in July 1991, in a uniquely interesting location on the Grand Sablon (at the "top," by the weekend antique market and Eglise Notre Dame du Grand Sablon), the 197-room Italian-operated hotel includes a buffet breakfast in its price. The tasteful period-decorated guestrooms in the highest of the three price categories have Jacuzzis. Restaurant, piano bar, hotel garage; 24-hour room service; shuttle service to/from airport.

### Metropole

*place de Brouckere 31;* ☎ *217.23.00, in U.S.* ☎ *1-800-THE OMNI, FAX 218.02.20.* Brussels' only remaining grand 19th-century hotel, the 410-room Metropole, opened in 1895, still is situated near the center of things, a block from the Monnaie Opera House, and an easy walk to the Grand-Place. The public rooms, worth a look even if you're not staying, are wonderful: a French Renaissance entrance hall, a reception hall with chandeliers, decorated ceilings, gilted molding details, stained glass, and polished wood; lounge/bar in the style of a gentlemen's club with deep leather sofas, marble columns, mirrors, piano and potted palms. The ground floor restaurant and cafe (whose sidewalk section is one of Brussels' premier people-watching places) offer more amazement. Rooms on five floors, served by three elevators and located along sprawling corridors (bellhop service) come in many shapes, sizes, and degrees of modernity. (Older rooms may have more atmospheric appeal.) All have minibar, private bath, color TV, 24-hour room service, 24-hour drycleaning, turn-down service. The setting is lovely, but I did find front-desk service lackadaisical on a recent visit.

## EXPENSIVE

### Amigo ★★★★★

*rue de l'Amigo 1;* ☎ *547.47.47, FAX 513.52.77.* A block from the Grote Markt, the Amigo offers Brussels' most central accommodations. The oldest part of the six-floor Spanish Renaissance-style hotel building was formerly a prison: a popular contemporary saying was that a one-night stay here made one a true citizen of Brussels. Although the most visible half of the well-blended building dates only from 1956, the Amigo feels as much like an old country home as a well-serviced hotel. The flagstone-floor lobby has been newly redone, although it still features antiques and a clubby bar. Most of the recently updated 200 traditionally furnished rooms have hair dryers, heated towel racks, alarm cords in bathrooms, and air conditioning. Continental breakfast included; restaurant; 24-hour room service; under-hotel parking. When the present-day Duke of Wellington returns to the victory scene of his ancestor, he uses the Amigo's Spanish-style suite.

### Dixseptieme

*rue de la Madeleine 25;* ☎ *502.57.44, FAX 502.64.24.* A grand residence in the neighborhood of the Grand-Place dating from the early 18th century, when it was home to the Ambassador of Spain, the Dixseptieme was carefully restored in 1990. This vintage stylish structure features many original details in its public salons and 21 individually designed guestrooms (9 suites and 12 studios with kitchenette with fridge, stove and sink): parquet floors, chandeliers, wall paintings, wooden medallions, mirrors, sconces; recorded piano music floats through handsome marble hallways. All rooms have comfortable contemporary furniture, marble baths with bathrobes, mini-bar, some with beams, functional fireplaces. Laundry room for personal use; swedish sauna; public lounge with bar service. Breakfast served in elegant dining salon. Near Centraal Station.

## MODERATE

### Manos

*chaussée de Charleroi 100, 1060 Brussels;* ☎ *537.96.82, FAX 539.36.55.* Built in the 1930s, this hotel features high ceilings and plaster molding details in many rooms. Off the small elegant marble reception area is a lounge decorated with bamboo furniture, paintings, wall panels, marble fireplace, and chandelier; there's also a small library with leather chairs, a pleasant ground floor bar, breakfast (only) room, and walled patio with white iron furniture, and resident white rabbit. All 38 guest rooms have tasteful contemporary furnishings, cable TV, small fridge, modern tile bath, hair dryer. Located on a busy street (tram to Place Royale) off fashionable avenue Louise, three blocks from the Victor Horta Museum.

### Chambord

*rue de Namur 82;* ☎ *513.41.19, FAX 514.08.47.* Located at the edge of the fashionable upper town at Porte Namur (Metro stop), the 64-room Chambord also is just a walk down the hill to the Place Royale. There's light-hearted, light-colored decor in the reasonably sized rooms, which have small marble baths, minibar, color cable TV; front rooms have small balconies. The pleasant, partially skylighted piano bar (light food service) also serves for breakfast (continental only, included). Clientele is a mix of business and leisure travelers from several nations. Safe-deposit boxes at hospitable, helpful front desk.

### Ibis Saint-Catherine Brussels Centre

*rue Joseph Plateau 2;* ☎ *513.76.20, FAX 514.22.14.* A modern 234-room hotel in an interesting, old section of central Brussels worth exploring; well-situated for the Metro, within walking distance of the Grand-Place. Rooms, in cheerful soft colors, all have compact stall/shower, toilet, remote control TV, telephone, individual heat control. Open closet rack, with built-in bench below for suitcase. Inside courtyard rooms are quieter. Buffet breakfast (only, included) served in lobby lounge/bar with nonsmoking section. Credit cards; elevator.

### Atlas

*rue du Vieux Marché aux Grains, 30;* ☎ *502.60.06, FAX 502.69.35.* Located just off Brussels' fashion house row, and a half-block from a tree-lined stretch of Vieux Graan Markt, the 88-room Atlas is a recently converted property behind a restored old facade on a convenient cobbled residential street near the historic center. Service is personable and the property's public rooms very pleasing, with original art, plants, and a cheerful color scheme. All rooms in the 4-floor hotel have baths, TV, minibar; 8 rooms under the eaves have skylights, 6 others have kitchenettes, 5 rooms take 4 persons.

### New Hotel Siru

*place Rogier, 1210 Brussels;* ☎ *217.75.80, FAX 218.33.03.* If, among other things, you are coming to Brussels to enjoy its contemporary art, you could do no better than to bed down here where many (eventually all) of the 101 rooms have been individually decorated by Belgian artists or sculptors. The contemporary furniture often fits into the scheme of the whole design: in Room 704, for example, a 3-dimensional sculptured couple is stretched over the headboard reading travel brochures and maps. The owners never asked for changes in an artist's concept, though they did reject an entire design if they believed that the resulting room might produce bad dreams. That certainly wouldn't be the case with Room 108: the ceiling fresco by painter Roger Raveel above the bed is entitled "Valium" and is a field of sheep made easy to count. Back to basics. The hotel is located at the corner of place Rogier (Metro, near North Station), and was remodeled in 1988. There's friendly desk service, breakfast (continental included) served in the attached corner cafe (continue beyond the breakfast room); elevators.

## INEXPENSIVE

### Matignon

*rue de la Bourse 10;* ☎ *511.08.88, FAX 513.69.27.* Facing the Bourse, and located above a brasserie/restaurant and terrace cafe decorated à la Belle Epoque, this hotel has 22 rooms (including five suites), all with marble bath with hairdryer, TV, telephone, double glazing for soundproofing. Beds have modern painted cane headboards and restful decor colors; lighting is pleasant and there's good closet space. The breakfast (included) room, overlooking the brasserie, is an attractive skylighted area.

### Opera

*rue Grétry 53;* ☎ *219.43.43.* Located in the heart of Brussels' ancient **L'Ilot Sacre,** this medium-size (52 rooms) clean and utilitarian property has the feel of—and is—a thoroughly European budget hotel. But it's tasteful in its way: restful tones in the decor; halls carpeted and walls papered; functional front desk with youthful English-speakers. Windows of front rooms open onto pedestrian street scenes; back rooms are quieter. Rooms include small built-in desk (can be used as luggage rack), two chairs, wardrobe closet, small curtain-enclosed shower stall. There's a button by each bedroom door to turn on hall lights. Elevator, major credit cards.

### Welcome

*rue du Reuplier 5;* ☎ *219.95.46, FAX 217.18.87.* Located just off the-

Marché aux Poissons (Fish Market with its fish restaurant row), this small hotel has just six rooms; 2 small, 2 medium, 2 large; prices vary, but all in inexpensive category. All have bath, tiled stall shower, TV, telephone, alarm/radio, and heat; larger ones have hair dryers, the largest a minibar. Friendly owner. No elevator. Continental/cooked breakfast extra: BF 250/BF350.

## WHERE TO EAT

Culinary connoisseurs frequently rate Brussels as one of the top three restaurant cities—along with Paris and Hong Kong—in the world. The chapter on *Food and Drink* at the front of this book describes traditional Belgian dishes, which are as much a part of the Brussels food scene as classic French *haute cuisine.* The background on *Belgian Beer* may prove helpful as you sample it in Brussels' cafes. Except at name restaurants, where high prices are sustained by the plethora of expense-account business travelers, restaurant costs in Brussels should not seem steep to those familiar with major cities in northeast North America, and should seem reasonable to visitors from London. Virtually all Brussels (and Belgian) restaurants pride themselves on providing value for money, and tax and service are always included in the price. Remember that selecting a *menu* (several courses for one fixed price; be sure to inquire if you don't see it listed) will always save over multicourse *à la carte* ordering. Many Brussels restaurants that are priced in the *expensive* category in the evening can be brought down to *moderate* by going there at lunch and/or ordering the *plat du jour* (daily special). Many eateries in central Brussels cater to workers at midday with three-course *menus* in the BF250–400 range.

Hotel restaurants (some of which are among Brussels' best) have not been included below, but have been mentioned under the hotel's listing. They will be open on Sundays when many independent restaurants close. For any but the most casual establishments, it's wise to at least inquire about reservations if you hope to dine at a particular place. Reservations (as far ahead as possible) are *essential* for any of the top restaurants.

Many opinions (almost as many as there are diners) exist as to which is the city's best restaurant. The Bruxellois discuss the topic among themselves as heatedly as they do sports or bicultural politics. You can count on the following selection, presented in no particular order, to include the restaurants that most experts variously purport to be the best. Unless otherwise indicated, all serve classic French cuisine in an elegant atmosphere; some are located outside the metropolitan city. To begin with a flourish:

### Comme Chez Soi

*place Rouppe 23; closed Sun. and Mon., Christmas to New Year's, and July;* ☎ *512.29.21, FAX 511.80.52; expensive/very expensive,* whose proprietor and **Chef Pierre Wynants** is nothing short of a celebrity (both in his 14-table home territory and in culinary circles around the world) remains an institution in the rarified Brussels culinary realm where dining is an *event.* To dine amid the renovated Victor Horta-style art nouveau decor, however, visitors need to be farsighted and/or favored by the gods: friends in the know tell me that reservations should be made a *minimum* of two months ahead.

It's also wise to plan as far ahead as possible for the following: **Bruneau** *(avenue Broustin 73; closed Tues. for dinner, Wed., holidays, mid-June–mid-July;* ☎ *427.69.78, FAX 425.97.26; very expensive)* serves seasonal fare with a flair in the Uccle area; **Villa Lorraine** *(avenue du Vivier d'Oie 75; closed Sun., and July;* ☎ *374.31.63, FAX 372.01.95; expensive)* delights diners with its garden-like indoor and outdoor setting in a renovated chateau on the fringe of *Bois de la Cambre* forest; **Ecailler du Palais Royal** *(rue Bodenbroek 18; closed Sun., holidays and August;* ☎ *512.87.51; expensive, plat du jour moderate),* where seafood is the speciality, is located at the top of the Grand Sablon; and **La Maison du Cygne** *(rue Charles Buls 2, off Grand-Place; closed Sat. lunch, Sun., three weeks in August, and between Christmas and New Years;* ☎ *511.82.44; expensive)* has a dream location fronting the Grand-Place.

While the above "best" restaurants are all on the expensive side, I repeat the point that it is *not* necessary to pay dearly to dine divinely in Brussels. And apart from money, for many, the reservation requirements of Brussels' stellar establishments don't leave sufficient room for spontaneous dining decisions. The ordinary mortals among us who are seeking memorable morsels *can* be more spur-of-the-moment about our meals: Brussels surely is one place where if the *carte* posted in the window and the view from the door both strike your fancy, you should feel free to follow your instincts, since almost certainly good, and perhaps great, food awaits.

Traditional Belgian fare first. In a restored, former 16th-century nobleman's world with lots of Flemish details such as the copper-hooded fireplaces, wood-paneling, and tiles is **Ravenstein** *(rue Ravenstein 1; closed Sat. lunch, Sun., and August;* ☎ *512.77.68; inexpensive/moderate),* which, in addition to local fare, specializes in seafood and continental cuisine. **Au Duc d'Arenberg** *(petit Sablon 9; daily noon–2:30 p.m., 7–10:30 p.m., closed Sun., holidays, last week of Dec.;* ☎ *511.14.75; moderate)* offers rustic decor and traditional food in its tavern/restaurant. Although eateries serving *moules* (mussels) abound in the **Ilot Sacre, Au Vieux Bruxelles** *(rue Saint-Boniface 35; closed Sun., Mon., holidays, June and July;* ☎ *513.01.81; inexpensive),* near avenue Louise, is *the* place for them as far as the Bruxellois are concerned. **Aux Armes de Bruxelles** *(rue des Bouchers 13; noon to 11:15 p.m., closed Mon., month of June;* ☎ *511.21.18; moderate, plat du jour inexpensive),* located on Brussels' "street of restaurants," is an excellent introduction to Belgian specialities, and *moules* prepared in many ways, *waterzooi de homard* (lobster stew), and *croquettes aux crevettes* (North Sea shrimp croquettes) to *carbonnades flamandes a la biere* (beef stewed in beer), in a pleasant setting. At **'t Kelderke** *(Grand-Place 15; daily noon–2 a.m.;* ☎ *513.73.44; inexpensive)* typical Belgian dishes such as *lapin* (rabbit) cooked with Brussels' *queuze* beer are offered—as well as helpful counsel about the dishes and drink—in an atmospheric 16th-century cellar. **La Roue D'Or** *(rue des Chapeliers 26; until 12:30 a.m., closed mid-July–mid-Aug.;* ☎ *514.25.54; inex-*

*pensive)* is a brasserie near the Grand-Place with a varied menu of traditional fare and daily specials.

A search for seafood in Brussels will take you to the Sainte-Catherine
district to what used to be the banks of the river Senne, still referred to as
the *March aux Poisson* (Fish Market). Virtually all the restaurants in the region feature fish, but special among them is **La Sirene d'Or** *(place Sainte-
Catherine 1A; open lunch and dinner, closed Sun., Mon., Christmas to New
Year's;* ☎ *513.51.98, FAX 502.13.05; plat du jour inexpensive, menu moderate)*, small, and quite elegant with touches of velvet, lace, and old beams in
the decor, and serving dishes such as *bouillabaisse Grand-Marius, fricassee de
homard aux asperges.* Thoroughly atmospheric is the **La Truite d'Argent**
*(quai au Bois à Brûler 23; noon–2:30 p.m., 7–11:30 p.m., closed Sat. lunch,
Sun., late July–mid- Aug.;* ☎ *219.95.46; moderate)*, whose specialty is lobster
and scallops with wild mushrooms. **Jacques** *(quai aux Briques 44;*
☎ *513.27.62; closed Sun. and in July; inexpensive)* is small, quite plain, and
apparently the perfect choice for the many Bruxellois who call it their favorite bargain fish brasserie in the Marché aux Poissons district. **Scheltema**
*(rue des Dominicains 7; 11:30 a.m.–3 p.m., 6:30 p.m.–12:00 a.m., closed Sun.
and mid-July–mid-August;* ☎ *512.20.84; moderate, lunch inexpensive)*, with
specialties like *saumon grillé à l'orange* and *jardiniere de sole*, is where locals
come for seafood (although the menu has other offerings), and to seriously
eat, not chat.

When your tastebuds want to travel beyond Belgian borders, the enormous variety of cuisines available in Brussels will be obvious. Among the
most numerous are Italian, Spanish and Chinese. And with some of the
other ethnic choices (Turkish, North African, Central African—Zaire)
available, it can sometimes seem as if the Third World is feeding the First
in Brussels. Belgium's lingering occupation by the Spanish may be one of
the reasons for the interest in that country's cuisine. In any case, Brussels'
seems to have a thriving taste for *paella valenciane*, the specialty at **Casa
Manuel** *(Grand-Place 34; daily noon until 1 a.m.;* ☎ *511.47.47; inexpensive;
musicians)*. Also highly popular among the many Spanish restaurants in the
Marolles neighborhood is **Alicante** *(rue Haute 411; daily 11 a.m.–3 p.m., 6
p.m.–midnight;* ☎ *538.25.54; inexpensive)*. A popular choice for Italian is **Al
Piccolo Mondo** *(rue Jourdan 19; daily 11:30 a.m.–3 p.m. and 6 p.m.–midnight,
closed in August;* ☎ *538.87.94; inexpensive)*, just off trendy avenue Louise
near Waterloo boulevard. It has a cozy, if non-Italian, environment of
brick walls and arches, wood-burning fireplaces, and oil paintings. Dishes
such as *saltimbocca alla romana, veal cutlets Milanaise*, and *pastas* are served.

You'll come across pleasant places to pause for liquid refreshment or
light cafe fare at every stop of your way around Brussels. On the Grand Sablon, try **Au Vieux Saint Martin** *(Grand Sablon 38; daily noon–midnight;*
☎ *512.64.76; inexpensive)* for sandwiches, omelets, salads, and some heart-
ier fare on the square, and **Les Jardins du Sablon** *(Grand Sablon 36;*
☎ *512.55.37; closed Mondays; moderate)* inside the skylighted upmarket
complex of art galleries, book shops, and antique shops. On the
Grand-Place, a favorite with the Bruxellois is **La Brouette** *(Grand-Place 2;*

*lunch to late evening;* ☎ *511.54.94; inexpensive)* for sandwiches and salads, and special plates served inside or on the cafe's terrace in the shadow of the Hôtel de Ville and full view of the glorious square.

When dining out becomes a drag, as it sometimes does—*temporarily*—during travels, head to block-long **Rue Tabora** near the Bourse for the makings of a fine picnic from its shops: a fromagerie, a charcuterie, a boulangerie, a traiteur, ecailler (deli), and a wine merchant. To satisfy your sweet tooth in traditional Belgian style, you can start simply, following the smell of vanilla in the air to any of the street-front waffle (*gaufre*) shops on and off the appropriately-named **rue au Beurre** (Butter Street) off Grand-Place. While on the street, at least visit **Biscuiterie Dandoy** *(rue au Beurre 31, daily 8:30 a.m.–6:30 p.m., Sun. 10:30 a.m.–6:30 p.m.)* to see its large wooden *speculoos* (spiced cookie) molds, and sample the marvelous (smaller) cookies available by 100-gram servings. **Le pain à la Grecque** (despite its name, a Belgian specialty) is another famed sweet treat at this 1829 institution. There's a second **Dandoy** *(rue Charles Buls)*, off the Grand-Place in the direction of *Manneken-Pis*. For the height of self-indulgence, head to fashionable **Wittamer** *(place du Grand Sablon 12;* ☎ *512.37.42; daily 8 a.m.–7 p.m., Sun. 7:30 a.m.–6 p.m., closed Monday)* for Brussels' most outrageous *pralines* (handmade, filled chocolates), *manons* (fresh cream- filled chocolates), Viennoise and French pastries, and caramelized fruits.

Although they usually also serve traditional, informal Belgian dishes (and great *frites* with almost anything), **cafes** offer the opportunity to sample Belgium's amazing beers, especially Brussels' own *gueuze, kriek, and lambic.* There could be no better place to begin than at **Falstaff** *(rue Henri Maus 17;* ☎ *511.87.89; daily 7 a.m. til 4 a.m.),* with its art nouveau interior, and large open, overhead-heated outdoor terrace facing the Bourse. Close to the Grand-Place in the opposite direction is **La Mort Subite** *(rue Montagne- aux-Herbes-Potageres 7; noon–1 a.m., closed Suns.,*☎ *513.13.18),* whose name means *sudden death,* though the place is life to many regulars for its large selection of Belgian beers. Featuring another memorable name is **De Ultieme Hallucinatie** *(Koningsstraat/rue Royale 316;* ☎ *217.06.14; open until 3 a.m.),* a former house, with three rooms front to back, each with a different character, each a treasure trove of rational-style *art nouveau* detail, each serving cafe or restaurant fare. **L'evasion** *(chaussée de Haecht 165;* ☎ *218.09.77)* is said to serve the city's largest selection of beers, up to 300, including "seasonal" specials. **La Becasse** *(rue Tabora 11; open daily from 10:30 a.m. -11 p.m.;* ☎ *511.00.06),* down an alley near the Bourse, is known for its jugs of beer served by stiff-aproned waiters. **La Fleur En Papier Dore** *(rue des Alexiens 55;* ☎ *511.16.59)* has been called a temple of surrealism, though it's also a favorite quiet tavern. Offering a typical Brussels evening of cafe theater and music (mostly jazz) is **Chez LaGaffe** *(rue de l'Epee 4;* ☎ *511.76.39; music from 9 p.m.),* located in the Marolles neighborhood.

**Note:** To insure that your cafe hopping is entirely pleasant, here's a reminder—valid for cities everywhere—**not** to hang your purse or camera on the back of your chair or put them on the ground, especially when outside on a terrace.

## ENTERTAINMENT AND EVENTS

The **Palais des Beaux-Arts** *(rue Ravenstein 23 and rue Royale 10; Mon.–Sat. 10 a.m.–10 p.m., Sun. 10 a.m.–6 p.m.; program information* ☎ *507.82.00)*, built between 1922 and 1929 to the design of art nouveau architect Victor Horta, is one of Brussels' most important cultural complexes, with concerts halls, art galleries, cinema, and cafes. It is highly regarded for the organ and acoustics in the 2,200-seat main hall. Both it and the **Brussels Conservatory of Music** are settings for the prestigious **Queen Elizabeth of Belgium International Music Competition**. Organized by the late monarch in 1951 for violinists (Queen Elizabeth herself was an accomplished one), the competition was later expanded to include piano, composition, and, in 1988, voice. All concerts of the competition, which welcomes contestants from around the world and takes place before an international jury of musicians, are open to the public (from elimination rounds to finals, and special Laureate performances). The competition begins in early May and lasts until mid-June. It is held three out of four years. The cycle, which repeats itself, is as follows: first year—violin; second year—nothing; third year—piano; fourth year—composition and voice. The year 1995 falls into the third year of the cycle, piano.

**Note:** Near the beginning of the 1980 American film *The Competition*, about competing pianists in a fictional, San-Francisco-based situation not unlike the Queen Elizabeth Competition, the character Heidi (Amy Irving) asks Paul (Richard Dreyfuss) if he had gone to compete at Brussels as planned.

The **Palais des Beaux-Arts**, the **Conservatory**, and the **Cathédrale Saint-Michel** are all used as venues for Brussels' performances in the annual September–October **Festival of Flanders** concerts. The Cathédrale has *Musical Sundays* from late June through September, with special music (Gregorian Chant, Scarlatti, Haydn, Mozart, Palestrina, Britten, Fauré) at the 10 a.m. Mass (information: ☎ 217.83.45). Check with the Tourist Office about scheduled concerts on the superb and newly restored organ of the **Eglise Notre- Dame du Sablon** (see *Organs* under "Music" section of "Belgian Cultural Legacy" chapter).

The **Theatre Royal de la Monnaie** *(place de la Monnaie; open Tues.–Sat. 11 a.m.–6 p.m., closed July–mid-Aug.;* ☎ *218.12.11/217.22.11)* is notable for its acoustics and recent lavish renovation. Designated the National Opera House in 1963, it is home to the opera company that bears its name; during the late September-April season, artistic director Anne-Theresa Dekeersmaeker stages widely acclaimed, original language productions with international casts. Ballet productions are also presented at the Monnaie.

One of Brussels's entertainment institutions is **Toone VII Puppet Theater** *(impasse Schuddeveld 6, off Petite rue des Bouchers 21; performances at 8:30 p.m., puppet museum open free during intervals between sketches, cafe on premises open noon-midnight; reservations recommended:* ☎ *511.71.37,*

*513.54.86).* It began with Toone I who, from 1835 to 1880, performed with puppets in a cellar in the Marolles district, and introduced the character **Woltje**, a Brussels street urchin in a checked jacket and jaunty angled cap who speaks the Marolle-Brussels dialect. Toone, the VIIth of the tradition, opened in the present theater in 1966, and continues the use of the Brussels dialect, which makes it unlikely you'll understand much of the dialogue (and piquant asides) in the *Cyrano, Faust, The Three Musketeers, Nativity,* or *Massacre of the Innocents* fare on the program—though that may not matter if you want to see something true to Brussels. The tradition of puppet plays here actually goes back long before Toone—to Spanish times. When the occupying Spanish had heard all they cared to of the criticism and insults hurled at them from the legitimate stage, they closed the theaters. But imaginative minds came up with the idea of using highly portable (and easily hidden) puppets as a means of reaching the population with revilements for the foreign forces. Puppet theater in Brussels is still a place for provocative political and social commentary.

Events from Brussels' annual calendar include the late-April, early May openings of the **Royal Greenhouses** at Laeken. The twice-in-early-July **Ommegang** (which comes from a Flemish word meaning "walkabout") is a splendidly costumed reenactment of the festivities staged in 1549 for the entrance into Brussels of Charles V, his son Philip II (then Duke of Brabant), and his sisters—performed on the floodlit Grand-Place, which is a source of wonderment even for those blasé bureaucrats inclined to call Brussels boring. 1995 dates are July 4 and 6; 1996 dates: July 2 and 4. From April–Sept. there are free nightly **music and light** shows after dark on the Grand-Place. Laid out on the Grand-Place for three days over a mid-August weekend in even years is a fabulous **Flower Carpet** (next in 1996). On odd years (1995), when there is no flower carpet, a "Flower Symphony" is held for three days over a mid-August weekend inside the town hall. From late July to late August the annual **Brussels Fair** is held in the Midi, and September brings **Bruegel festivities**. In December, there's a traditional **Christmas market** on the Sablon (always the second weekend of the month). In addition to the longstanding traditional nativity scene and Christmas tree on the Grand-Place, there's a new, free holiday offering on that grand square: **Music and Light** shows of carols from EU countries nightly at 7:30–8 p.m.

## IN THE AREA

### Musée Royal de l'Afrique Centrale                                      ★
*Royal Museum of Central Africa; Leuvensesteenweg 13; Tervuren; daily mid-Mar.–mid-Oct. 9 a.m.–5:30 p.m., mid-Oct.–mid-Mar. 10 a.m.–4:30 p.m.; ☎ 769.52.11; Brussels' metro to* **Montgomery**, *then Tram 44 through the lovely 10,000-acre ancient beech tree* **Forest de Soignes***; museum plan but no exhibit descriptions in English.* Begun in 1898 as the **Musée du Congo**, this museum was an important scientific institute where the information of the Congo could be collected and synthesized. In 1960, the year of the Belgian Congo's independence, its

scope was extended to cover all of Africa. Exhibits are arranged in sections covering anthropology, history, and economy. There are zoological dioramas, ethnic sculpture, and souvenirs of the great explorers; of particular interest are those on mineralogy and art, including jewelry and tribal ornaments. The museum—housed in a Charles Girault-designed Louis XVI-style palace built for Leopold II and surrounded by exceptional French gardens—is located in **Tervuren Park**, which also features scenic lakes, the picturesque **Moulin de Gordeal** (windmill), an Arboretum, a Renaissance chapel to Saint Hubert (patron saint of hunters), and stables remaining from the 17th-century castle of Austrian-Hapsburg ruler Charles of Lorraine.

### Waterloo

*Town of 25,000, 12 mi./20 km. south of Brussels on Charleroi Road; public bus W from Brussels'* **place Rouppe** *twice hourly, takes about an hour.* Today a pleasant Brussels suburb where many resident-alien Americans live, *Waterloo* is also a household word for *defeat* that joined our vocabulary after the retreat of **Napoleon Bonaparte** from the 1815 battle fought there that determined the future of Europe. No one who has seen the magnificent gifts (on display at **Apsley House** in London) presented to Englishman Arthur Wellesley, **Duke of Wellington**, by European leaders after he defeated Napoleon's armies, can doubt their relief at the fall of the charismatic Corsican.

To set the stage: After taking over the leadership of the French forces that had occupied the Netherlands, north and south, in the late 18th century (and showing himself to be a well-rounded genius by introducing such modern measures as the metric system and house numbers for addresses), Napoleon arranged to have himself pronounced Emperor of France in the presence of the Pope in 1804. He continued to turn Europe inside-out with a series of successful military campaigns, before overextending himself in 1812. From the Royal Palace at Laeken outside Brussels, Napoleon signed the order for the advance of his 600,000-strong army into Russia, where climate, unorthodox opponents, and sheer distance defeated him. Back in Central Europe in 1814, Napoleon again met more than his match, and was exiled to the island of Elba off Italy by the allied powers of Austria, Prussia, Russia, and England, who then convened the **Congress of Vienna** to restructure the political entities of Europe. It was settled that the Belgian territory would be bonded to Holland, but before the details had been dealt with, word came to the diplomats in Vienna that Napoleon had escaped from Elba. Bonaparte made his way to Paris without a shot being fired, easily and quickly rallying the French forces still faithful to him. Newly installed King Louis XVIII fled to Belgium's Ghent. Of the European armies, which quickly regrouped to confront the Corsican, it was the troops of England's **Duke of Wellington**, Prussia's 73-year-old **General Marshal Blucher**, and Holland's **Prince Willem of Orange**, gathered in central Belgium, who would fight the inevitable battle.

Ironically, only a year before, the Duke of Wellington had passed through Waterloo and made the statement that if he were ever to fight in the Netherlands, he would choose the fields at Waterloo for the battle. Yet, it was Napoleon, beating a path to Brussels, which he hoped to recapture (believing, as, indeed, even many of his political opponents did, that Belgium rightfully belonged to France), whose actions largely established the farming village of Waterloo as the site where scores of thousands of soldiers would meet history head-on.

The opposing forces that squared off at Waterloo on Sunday, June 18, were headed by two men of great stature but slight height: Napoleon stood 5 feet 3 inches tall; Wellington measured in at 5 feet. Napoleon commanded 72,000 men and had more heavy hardware than Wellington, who as supreme commander for the British, Dutch, Belgian, and German forces, had 60,000 (though the Prussian reinforcements who arrived progressively during the day numbered nearly another 45,000). But, as in many battles, Waterloo's outcome was as much the result of weather and the health of its leaders as it was other elements. Through the night before the battle it rained heavily, and Napoleon postponed the beginning of battle until late the following morning to give the ground some time to dry (maneuvering heavy artillery through mud was unwieldy). But those elapsed morning hours later in the battle day added enough time for Marshal Blucher to get to the battlefront with fresh Prussian troops for Wellington. Although the two generals were the same age (45) at Waterloo, Wellington was well and Napoleon was not (suffering so badly from hemorrhoids that he spent most of the battle day outside the house, **Caillou**, he used as headquarters, in a chair from which the seat had been removed for his comfort). Wellington spent it on his horse, Copenhagen, constantly traversing the undulating terrain that hid battlefield hollows and allowed no single good vantage point for the action, and encouraging his troops. (So close to the action did Wellington stay that day that many of his soldiers were amazed that he survived.)

An account from the diary of a Waterloo resident that cloudy Sunday of June 18, 1815, reads: "The whole morning, soldiers pass in mass formation. Towards 10 o'clock a heavy silence reigns around us. Everyone is struck dumb with the approach of the events which are due to take place." At about 11:30 a.m., Napoleon's forces opened battle against the more securely positioned Wellington forces. (Napoleon later said of Wellington, "In the management of an army he is full equal to myself with the advantage of possessing more prudence.") Napoleon, uncharacteristically, tried to apply head-to-head brute force while waiting for reinforcements from a division he had previously sent after the Prussian Blucher. Wellington, having to endure the full force of the French attack alone for far longer than expected, was waiting for Blucher himself, who had met with him at 2 that morning and promised troops. Movement on the distant horizon at about 1 p.m. raised hopes on both sides, but it turned out to be Blucher progressing very slowly because of the mud.

From that time on, Napoleon (who hadn't expected Blucher to be a factor in the fight) was in a race against time. At 4 p.m., he launched a massive cavalry charge, but Wellington's "squares" held. Later, however, a breakthrough for the French seemed possible, and the Duke of Wellington worried, "Night or the Prussians must come." Afterwards, an officer said, "I never heard yet of a battle in which every one was killed, but this seemed likely to be an exception." The French marshal who was trying to effect the turnaround requested reinforcements, but Napoleon, thinking of the Prussians marching ever closer, delayed an hour before finally sending the marshal his final reserve, the impressive Imperial Guard. By then, however, they were tactically too late; Wellington had had a chance to regroup and, after the Prussians arrived about 7:30 p.m., what was considered Napoleon's finest force was routed during the general charge mounted against it at 8:15 p.m.

Taking less than 10 hours, Waterloo was a short battle that was long and decisive enough to produce something like peace—at a great cost, however, and only for a short time. The toll for both sides was more than 50,000 casualties. Some 7000 in Wellington's army were killed or wounded, and the Prussians lost nearly the same number. An accurate count of French army losses was impossible to come by after the final rout, during which many of the men simply slipped away. But a minimum of 30,000 were killed, wounded, or captured. Ten days after the battle, the wounded were still being brought into Brussels.

Tourists sought out Waterloo from the start. That very year, the king of England came to view the battlefield, and on the first anniversary a crowd from many countries gathered in commemoration. **Lord Byron** wrote of Waterloo in his poem *Childe Harold*, and **Victor Hugo** walked the battleground 40 years later seeking inspiration for the Waterloo scenes in *Les Miserables*. Today, from atop the ★ **Butte du Lion** *(Lion Mound; 3 miles south of Waterloo center; 226 steps; daily, same hours as Waterloo Visitor's Center, below)*, visitors have a panoramic view of the Waterloo terrain that neither commander nor any combatant on the battle day had. The vast circular Lion Mound was built as a Dutch memorial between 1823–1826 on the site along Wellington's line where the Dutch **Willem of Orange** (who would be crowned king of the less-than-pleased Belgians only three months after Waterloo) was wounded in the shoulder. At the base of Lion Mound is the ★ ★ **Waterloo Visitor's Center** *(route du Lion 252; daily April–Sept., 9:30 a.m.–6:30 p.m.; in Oct. 9:30 a.m–5:30 p.m., Nov.–Feb. 10:30 a.m.–4 p.m., March 10:30 a.m.–5 p.m., closed New Year's and Christmas;* ☎ *02/385.19.12; English-language materials and exhibits)*, a well-executed and welcome addition to the site. The 40-minute program includes a sound and light model that retraces the main phases of the fighting, and a 200-slide show that—with its imaginative script and extracts from Columbia's Bondartchouk-directed film *Waterloo*—involves viewers in the experience of the battle. The center has maps and illustrations that give visitors a better grasp of where and how the fighting took place. Interactive computerized information terminals have a data base that enables you to ask questions (in English) about the battle. Items in the gift/book shop featuring the losing leader vastly outnumber those concerned with the winner at Waterloo.

Next door is the hard-to-miss round building that houses the ★ **Panorama**, which dates back to 1912. Definitely old-fashioned (though restored), this nostalgic in-the-round art work is a 360-degree, 360-foot/110-meter, 40-foot/12-meter painting by Frenchman Louis Dumoulin, his art assistants, and military consultant that places you literally in the center of Waterloo's French calvary charge. Standing on the viewing platform at the center, you can't help but be involved, from the cloudy sky from the recent rain, clouds of smoke from the cannon, and foreground of three-dimensional figures (a wounded horse, soldiers, fences, dirt) that all lend verisimilitude to the scene. Unless you're addicted to such attractions, the **Wax Museum** across the road isn't a necessary stop, though the cafe **Bivodac de L'Empereur** next to it might be.

An alternative site at which to begin your visit to Waterloo is in the town at the ★ **Wellington Museum** *(chaussée de Bruxelles 147; daily April–Oct. 9:30 a.m.–6:30 p.m., Nov.–Mar. 10 a.m.–5 p.m., closed Christmas and New Years;* ☎ *354.78.06; booklet, exhibit notes, and other items in English).* Of the many items of interest in the several rooms of this old coaching inn (at which Wellington spent the night before and the night after the battle), none is more meaningful than the duke's own bedroom. In it, in the pre-dawn hours of the 18th, he received confirmation that the Prussians would join him in battle against Napoleon later that day, at which point he definitely decided on undertaking the task at Waterloo. And it was to this room that he returned after battle to write the report that was published in *The Times* in London on June 22. In the wing to the rear of the museum are illuminated battle-phase maps that show the relative positions of units at each stage of the struggle.

Next door is the **Tourist Information** office for Waterloo *(chaussée de Bruxelles 149;* ☎ *354.99.10)*, which can provide specific information about rental bicycles, the sightseeing train which during July and August links up with Waterloo train station, and hours/details about other Waterloo sights. Across the street is the domed 17th-century **Royal Chapel/St. Joseph's Church** (restored). The only object in its large rotunda is a white marble bust of the duke of Wellington; many burial plaques and other memorials are exhibited on the side walls of the church.

If you are traveling by car to Waterloo and want to see every sight, there's **Caillou**, a farm where Napoleon spent the night before the battle. **La Belle Alliance** is where Napoleon spent much of the day of the battle, and Wellington and Blucher met in happy victory at the end of the battle. From it you can realize how little Napoleon can have known of what was happening on the actual battle front. Various division monuments are located along the sides of roads in the region.

## WHERE TO STAY AND EAT IN THE AREA

**Chateau du Lac** ★★★★

*ave. du Lac 87, Genval;* ☎ *654.11.22, FAX 653.62.00; very expensive.* This is a lakeside castle hotel 20 minutes south of Brussels, not far cross-country from Waterloo. Fine contemporary decor in an elegant setting, with a good selection of recreational facilities (tennis, golf, riding, watersports). The hotel's restaurant **Le Trefle** *(closed Mon., Tues.; expensive)* is considered one of nearby Brussels' best.

# FLANDERS: AN INTRODUCTION

Belgium's 5.7 million Flemish (*de Vlamingen* to themselves, *les Flamands* to the French-speaking Walloons) constitute nearly 60 percent of the country's total population, who live in the northern five provinces of **West** and **East Flanders**, **Antwerp**, **Limburg**, and **Flemish Brabant**. With the exception of Brabant, each province borders on Holland, with whom Flanders shares the Dutch language.

Despite an attractive beach-bound North Sea coastline—all of Belgium's seashore is located in the province of West Flanders—Flanders' main appeal to overseas visitors is its medieval mercantile towns. Flanders' **Ghent**, **Bruges**, **Antwerp**, and **Brussels**—all cloth manufacturing and trading centers with a prosperous burgher class—formed the early core of the Low Countries' (Netherlands') culture. Noted for their prosperity, Flemish towns attracted artisans and became treasure-troves of 14th-, 15th-, and 16th-century architecture and painting. If you've provided yourself generously with time for touring Belgium, you'll find additional examples of sacred and secular structures in Flanders' fascinating flamboyant Gothic style—exuberant evidence of an opulent past—in **Ypres**, **Louvain**, **Mechelen**, and **Oudenaarde**.

While Flanders' early urbanized areas virtually *demand* the attention of travelers, the region also has a variety of rural landscape: moor and heath in the *Kempen,* modest height in the *Flemish Ardennes,* and rich flat *polderland* just behind the *coastal dunes.* Farming has long been a prime livelihood in Flanders, on both its rich and poor soil. The open-air museum of **Bokrijk** *(in Bokrijk,* *northeast of Hasselt; open daily Easter–Oct. 10 a.m.–6 p.m.;* ☎ *(011) 22.27.11*) pays homage to Flanders' farming heritage.

# ANTWERP

## *GUIDELINES FOR ANTWERP*

### SIGHTS

Three "must-see" sights in Antwerp (Antwerpen, Anvers) are baroque painter **Pieter Paul Rubens' house**, the **Plantin-Moretus house** and the **Gothic cathedral** (Belgium's largest). Other major attractions include the **Royal Museum of Fine Arts**, the **Diamond Museum**, and the **port**.

One of the remarkable aspects about art in Antwerp is that so much of it remains in the specific spaces for which it originally was created: **city churches** and **patrician townhouses** (several now furnished museums) of contemporaries of Rubens. Old Antwerp, around the grand **Grote Markt**, is linked by appealing streets (many pedestrian-only), quaint cobbled alleys, and quiet old squares. Belgium's proud port city is inextricably tied to the **river Scheldt**, the riverfront of interest for its ancient fortress/prison **Steen** (now the **Maritime Museum**), the **Flandria** cruise boat pier, riverbank promenades, and a pedestrian tunnel under the water that leads to a fine view of Antwerp from the far bank. There's striking **after-dark illumination** of the cathedral, the Stadhuis on the Grote Markt, and other buildings and monuments. Most museums are closed Mondays, including holidays that fall on Monday.

### GETTING AROUND

Antwerp (with a core city population of 250,000, greater city 500,000) sprawls, but several important sights are within a few blocks of the centrally located **Grote Markt**, on which is located the main **city tourist office**. Most others are within walking distance either north or south of **Meir** (pronounced *mare,* as in horse), Antwerp's confusingly multiple-named, but essentially straight, main midcity street, running from **Centraal Station** to the river **Scheldt**. More than 25 percent of the city center is now pedestrianized, including the Grote Markt. The city's public transport network includes trams, metro, and buses (system map at tourist office); tickets are sold by 10-ride strip, 24-hour day pass, or single ride. Near the cathedral and Grote Markt, several tram and bus lines converge at **Groenplaats** (identifiable by its statue of Rubens), beneath which is a stop on the metro line, which runs under Meir to the Centraal Station. Groenplaats, and **Koning Astridplein** in front of Centraal Station, have taxi stands. Antwerp has a reasonable number of paid parking lots; those in cars should avoid the area around the Grote Markt, which has the most pedestrian-only and congested streets. For sightseers afoot, the tourist office has produced a brochure in English: *City of Antwerp: Walk Centre* (BF 30).

*Antwerp's cathedral, here illuminated at night, and also by day, is the city's most majestic landmark.*

## SHOPPING

Antwerp provides sophisticated shopping, with all the expected Belgian and European department, clothing, and specialty stores, most located along **Meir** (Fridays until 9 p.m., other nights until 6 p.m.). The city is noted as an innovative international fashion design center thanks to the styles of the so-called **Antwerp Six**. Dries van Noten's boutique *Modepaleis* on Nationale Straat and the shop of three other designers, including Ann DeMeulemeester, *Louis* at *Lombaardenstraat 2*, have attracted other fashion boutiques to the district. Antique and secondhand shops are scattered throughout the city, and with Antwerp's history as an international trading hub, one never knows what objects might turn up. The 16th-century cobbled **Vlaeykensgang alleyway** off Oude Koornmarkt is as much worth seeking out for its picturesqueness as its antiques. Art galleries continue to open in Antwerp, many branches of Brussels' establishments. Antwerp's brilliantly cut diamonds are sold wholesale and retail in nondescript shops along the side of **Centraal Station**; prices for unset stones are some 40 percent off those in the U.S. If you're looking for a gem, though not necessarily a jewel, save Sunday mornings (8:30 a.m.-1 p.m.) for the **Vogelmarkt** or bird market, a 600-year tradition on the site (near the City Theater). Originally solely geese and chickens were sold, hence its name, but today it's also a flea market. Saturdays (10 a.m.-6 p.m.) from Easter through Sept. there's an antiques market on *Lijnwaadmarkt*, north of the cathedral. Wednesday and Friday mornings at the **Vrijdagmarkt** there are public auctions of secondhand furniture and household goods.

## ENTERTAINMENT AND EVENTS

A remarkably cosmopolitan and cultured city, Antwerp offers its citizens and visitors a wide variety of regularly scheduled and special events. The monthly *Kalender Antwerpen* (available from the tourist office) lists programs for the city's concert, opera, ballet, and theater companies, as well as the 50-odd cinemas (where films are shown in the original language—many in English—with Dutch subtitles), cabaret, exhibitions, and other events. Upon request, the tourist office will provide a free computer printout of the events for the day.

## WHERE TO STAY

In addition to modern international chain business hotels outside the city center, Antwerp offers a limited but interesting selection of pleasant in-town properties. Since central Antwerp is spread out, no hotel will be convenient to all attractions, though most are near public transport.

## WHERE TO EAT

Antwerpians like to dine with wine. With an estimated 800 cafes and restaurants and perhaps 2000 pubs, there's no lack of places for visitors to fit in with local food fashion. Tasters' choices range from a traditional Flemish stew pot to a melting pot of ethnic eateries to meet the culinary preferences of Antwerp's cosmopolitan population. You can satisfy a sweet tooth for Antwerp's *pralines* (filled, handmade chocolates) least expensively at small sidewalk shops, and most imaginatively at **H. Burie** (where white chocolate is molded in *stalks* resembling Belgium's famed white asparagus ☎ *232.36.88*). Antwerpse *handjes* ("little hands") are rich butter and almond cookies that honor the city's *Brabo* legend. (See "Antwerp in Context.")

## ARRIVING

There is frequent half-hour train service between Antwerp's **Centraal Station** (the so-called "railway cathedral") and all three Brussels' stations. Belgium's dense rail network also makes Antwerp easily accessible from elsewhere in the country and from most anywhere in Europe (connections through Brussels). Antwerp is less than three hours from Amsterdam on numerous direct trains. Belgium's **SABENA World Airlines** runs regularly scheduled buses between Antwerp and Brussels' **Zaventem Airport**. Buses leaving Antwerp for Zaventem (bus stop on Keyserlei across from the Alfa de Keyser Hotel, near Centraal Station) depart daily every hour on the hour from 7 a.m.–10 p.m. Those arriving from England by North Sea ferry at Ostend or Zeebrugge can reach Antwerp by rail with a transfer either at Ghent or Brussels (Gare du Nord). Antwerp is well served on the Belgium/European motorway system.

## IN THE AREA

A short bus ride from Centraal Station to a southern Antwerp neighborhood brings you to the **Middelheim Open-Air Museum**, one of the world's finest sculpture gardens. Also accessible by bus, the streets **Cogels-Osylei** in the city's southeast district of Berchem offer a turn-of-the-century architectural free-for-all, with plenty of fanciful *jugendstil* ("art nouveau"). Less than 15 minutes by frequent train from Antwerp is attractive **Mechelen**, city of carillon concerts, tapestry tradition, and once a historic Hapsburg Court.

## TRAVEL TRIPS

In 1993 Antwerp was spotlighted as the European Community's Cultural Capital. For the occasion, Antwerp polished itself citywide as carefully as it would one of its own fine diamonds. Visitors in

1995 will continue to reap the results—completed restorations of the *Cathedral, Bourla Theatre* and *Centraal Station* are among the permanent improvements to the city—without the extra crowds.

## ANTWERP IN CONTEXT

Antwerp's most famous son, artist Pieter Paul Rubens, once observed: "It is not a question of living long, but of living well." Rubens may not have been referring to cities, but his historic and handsome home town has nevertheless seen fit to follow the suggestion. Antwerp, which dates from Roman days, not only lives graciously with its long and prestigious past, but enjoys an enviably lively and prosperous present.

Although it is by Belgian standards a populous city, with a half million inhabitants, Antwerp retains the feeling and friendliness of a small town. And though Antwerp is one of the world's premier ports and the diamond capital of the world, its ambiance is akin to a cosmopolitan village. Antwerpians have devised a life-style of their own, and seem to identify more with their city than with the rest of Flanders, let alone Belgium. Some residents claim that a lingering influence from the days of Spanish occupation accounts for Antwerpians' being more intuitive and emotional than most northern Europeans. One told me, "In Antwerp we have our own way of life, but we are xenophiles, not xenophobes." Antwerp's agreeably integrated population proves it: some 117 nationalities make up the mix.

The inevitable influence of its port (the fifth largest in the world, and a regular port of call or home port for approximately 300 shipping lines from more than 100 countries) adds more foreign flavor. Some who first came to Antwerp to discuss international trade found the city so well suited to living well that they returned to stay. Those fortunate enough to be native Antwerpians, though healthily chauvinistic, also are an outlooking lot, having grown up with the tradition of the seven seas on their doorstep. But of the many who leave to see something else of the world, most return to Antwerp's exceptional environment.

Antwerp calls the 16th century its **Golden Age**. The period was the most prosperous of any in Antwerp's history—though the present could come to rival it: currently, the city of Antwerp provides the country of Belgium with close to half the Gross National Product (GNP).

Antwerp's prosperity has always been linked to its port on the Scheldt. More than one Antwerpian may quote the old saying: "The town owes its river to God, but everything else it owes to its river."

The Scheldt features in a favorite fable about the city's Roman days. The river at Antwerp, so it is told, was ruled by a giant who demanded tolls from passing ships. Sailors who didn't pay had their hands cut off. Finally, a Roman soldier named **Brabo** decided to defy the giant. In a struggle reminiscent of David and Goliath's, Brabo defeated the giant, whose huge hand he cut off and threw into the river (the very action captured in the *Brabo Fountain* sculpture on the Grote Markt). From this tale, the source of the name Antwerp, from the Flemish *handwerpen* ("throwing the hand") has been suggested. But the more prosaic, and probable, derivation is *aanwerp* ("a promontory in the river"), which describes the present site of **the Steen**, where Antwerp's earliest settlement was founded.

Battered even earlier by Norsemen and Normans, Antwerp was noted as a port by A.D. 1031. In the 12th century, the city gained municipal rights from the dukes of Brabant. The **Hanseatic League** set up an establishment here in 1313 and Antwerp also acquired the important right of staple for English wool. Both events brought foreign merchants to the town on the Scheldt in increasing numbers. Residence in Antwerp by the *counts of Flanders* (who became unified with Brabant under the Burgundians in 1406) marked the beginning of a period of even greater commercial recognition. While benefitting from association with Brabant's economic progress, Antwerp also gained at the expense of the once flourishing Flemish city of Bruges. That town lost its access to the North Sea as the river Zwin silted up, while Antwerp's access increased as the mouth of the Scheldt was considerably widened by flooding in Zeeland.

By the end of the 15th century Antwerp had become the chief port in all the Netherlands. Major sources of trade were sugar, soap, beer, diamonds, and textiles. (The city had gained control of *alum*, a substance indispensable to the cloth industry, by imposing a stage tax for it on the Scheldt.) In 1454, Philip the Good established the Antwerp **Guild of St. Luke** for the encouragement of painting, an act which served as a foundation for the *Flemish School*. The guild played host to Albrecht Durer during his stay in Antwerp in 1520–1521.

In the 16th century, Antwerp continued to grow as an important trading center for spices and staples, and by then, Antwerp's diamond industry had been in business for a century. Merchants from many cultures—English, German, Italian, Spanish, and Portuguese—met and mingled in the port city. The city's financial establishments lent money to kings and emperors dealing at Europe's first international exchange building, which opened in Antwerp in 1460 (and served as a model for subsequent exchanges in London and elsewhere in Europe). Antwerp became the continent's foremost center of commerce, navigation, finance, and art. Up to 300 vessels put in and out of Antwerp's port daily, and more than 1,000 foreign trading concerns had offices here. Even a Venetian ambassador to the city called Antwerp "the first trading center of the world." Another dubbed the port "the most noble warehouse of the whole world."

Finally there was enough money to finish Antwerp's cathedral, whose construction, begun in 1352, had frequently floundered thereafter for lack of funds. Its magnificent tower (400 feet/123 meters), added in 1518, marked the completion of the largest Gothic church in the Netherlands. In 1514, Antwerp had a population of 40,000 (which, even then, made it as large as London, and three times the size of any town in Holland). By 1560, the city had exploded to 100,000. Truly, it was a Golden Age.

But Emperor Charles V, who had ruled the Netherlands through the opening phases of the rapidly spreading **Reformation**, abdicated in 1555 to his son Philip II of Spain. Philip's response to the Protestants practically decreed that prosperous times in Antwerp, by then rent with religious dissent, would not survive his reign. Antwerp's cathedral and other churches were pillaged by Protestant Calvinists in the 1566 *Iconoclast*, which took a great toll on the city's artistic achievements. The 1576 *Spanish Fury's* toll was in lives, when the city was sacked, and 7000 citizens were killed in an attack by angry Spanish soldiers, mutinous from not having received their pay from the **duke of Alva**. (The Spanish Fury caused many Protestants to flee for their lives, including one **Jan Rubens**, a Lutheran lawyer whose son **Pieter Paul** was born the next year in exile in Westphalia, Germany.) In 1577, with help from Holland's **Prince Willem (the Silent) of Orange**, whose rebel forces were for a while headquartered in Flanders, Antwerp, stood up to the Spanish so successfully that for the next eight years the open practice of Roman Catholicism in the city was forbidden. (The Rubens' family wasn't yet able to return from Germany because Pieter Paul's mother was Catholic.)

In 1585, after a two-year siege, the duke of Parma recaptured Antwerp for Spain. This turn of fortune established that Antwerp's future would be with the Spanish or southern Netherlands (the future Belgium) rather than the northern Netherlands (Holland). The firm establishment of Antwerp as a Roman Catholic city under Spanish rule drove thousands more Protestants to Holland: diamond cutters went to Amsterdam, tile workers found employment in Delft, and the family of five-year-old **Frans Hals** left for Haarlem. (Finally, his Protestant father having died, Pieter Paul Rubens and his mother returned to Antwerp.) The many Antwerp artisans and artists who emigrated north to Holland can truly be said to have had a hand in that country's upcoming golden 17th century.

The relatively peaceful reign of the equally-entitled **archdukes** (Isabella, daughter of Philip II, and her husband Albert) from 1598–1621 was a period of economic recovery for Antwerp and its port. Baroque art blossomed under **Pieter Paul Rubens,** whose students, studio helpers, and collaborators included **Jacob Jordaens**, **Anthony Van Dyck**, **Adriaen Brouwer**, and **David Teniers Elder** and **Younger**. At the same time an intellectual coterie, which included Rubens, arose around the brilliant **Balthasar Moretus** of the printing house *Plantin-Moretus.* The period left a physical imprint upon Antwerp that visitors can see today. In 1620, using almost touristic terms, Jan Woverius, humanist, town-clerk, and one-time learned counsellor to the archdukes, wrote: "Our City of Antwerp is happy to possess two such great citizens as Rubens and Moretus...their houses will evoke the astonishment and admiration of visitors."

No end to an era could be more definitive than that which came to Antwerp with the signing of the 1648 *Peace of Westphalia.* In the agreement that officially ended the 80-year Spanish/Netherlands war, the Spanish accepted the Dutch terms that demanded the **closing of the Scheldt** to ships. (The banks on both sides of the river estuary are in Dutch territory.) The Dutch move to do away with competition for the port of Amsterdam by closing the Scheldt effectively closed the port at Antwerp. As it happened, the port would not be reopened for a century and a half. Cut off from sea trade, Antwerp foundered. Its population plummeted: by 1790, it was back to the size it had been in 1514: 40,000.

The port of Antwerp owes its revival to **Napoleon**, who in 1799 took over the reins of the *French Revolutionary Army,* which earlier in the 1790s had conquered both the southern and northern Netherlands. The French Napoleon reopened the Scheldt with an ulterior motive: to have a naval "pistol pointed at the heart of England." Between 1800 and 1803, dock basins and river quays were built; the Bonaparte Lock was inaugurated in 1811 (and still is in operation). With its port once again open to commerce, Antwerp experienced an astonishing revival.

When Napoleon was defeated at **Waterloo** in 1815, Antwerp came under Dutch rule in the *United Kingdom of the Netherlands* partnership enforced upon Belgium by outside European powers. With

Antwerp then doing business under the same flag as the Dutch, its port's revitalization was encouraged. With the improvements, Antwerp developed into the largest port in the Netherlands. Dutch trade with its colonies in Indonesia and the Caribbean provided steady traffic in and out of all Netherlands ports, but Antwerp's share of the shipping stopped with Belgium's revolt against Dutch rule in 1830. Whatever Dutch King Willem I felt about being thus "divested" of Belgium, he had no intention of giving up Antwerp's preeminent port without a fight. The Dutch dug in, and great damage was done to the port by bombardment and sieges in 1830 and 1832 before they were dislodged. (The new Belgian King **Leopold I** eventually called in the French for help.)

In the 1839 peace that finally established the present national borders, Holland was granted the the right of levying navigation dues on shipping in the Scheldt. In 1863, Antwerp, with the help of the Belgian government, bought out Holland's right to the levies for a considerable compensation. At the turn of the century, Antwerp became important as the port for the *Kongobootes* that sailed the seas to and from **Belgium's Congo colony** (now **Zaire**). When the big ships steamed into Antwerp from Africa, they always caused a stir and raised a crowd, and often attracted brass bands on the piers.

Antwerp's World War II destruction was heaviest toward the end; when retaken by the Allies, the port suffered Nazi V-1 and V-2 attacks in late 1944 and early 1945. Antwerp was the goal of Hitler's last-gasp across-Belgium campaign in the winter of 1944–45, but what became known as the *Battle of the Bulge* became bogged down where it began: in the Ardennes. That Hitler had even thought of attempting to regain Antwerp so late in the war was a testament to the port's strategic value. Its location remained important when peace came, and the two world wars proved to be only interruptions in the port's 20th-century progress.

Today, Antwerp on the Scheldt, situated some 50 mi./85 km. from the North Sea, is becoming ever more significant as an international crossroads for maritime and continental shipping and distribution. In tonnage and traffic, the city has the world's fifth largest port and, by many accounts, Europe's most efficient in turnaround time. Port pilots are taken aboard incoming ships at Holland's Vlissengen (Flushing), and in Antwerp proper, on out-sailing vessels, their knowledge is vital because of the Scheldt's shifting sandbars and waters—tidal water well above Antwerp—which rise and fall about 13 feet between tides. The 37,000-acre/15,000-hectare, state-of-the-art port, has a control tower with a computerized system to plan and control shipping, and as of 1991 the world's longest radar chain (78 mi./130 km.), stretching down the Scheldt to the North Sea.

The relative quiet along the waterfront in the center of Antwerp, where old warehouses with stylish iron pediments lie abandoned except for scenery-seeking, riverbank pedestrians, belies the port's actual activity. Increasingly after World War II, Antwerp's port spread downstream (nearer to the North Sea) to accommodate larger ocean-going vessels; it now has some 100 kilometers of wet and dry docks, extending north to the Dutch border. Along the Scheldt are five sea-locks, of which the newest, **Berendrecht Lock** (opened in 1989) is the largest in the world. Major port industries at Antwerp include oil refineries, petrochemical and automobile assembly plants, grain companies, trans-shipment yards, and multinational firms such as *Bayer* and *Montsanto*. Even segments of Antwerp's old sailors' quarter have moved on down the river, and some of the brothels and rooming houses in the city's waterfront district have been converted into apartments and artists' lofts.

Dockers' pride in their port has helped make Antwerp a highly efficient installation. Four shifts are needed to keep the river-borne, business moving during the port's 24-hour day. Antwerp's dock workers' ways are traditional, but unions, management, supervisors, and stevedores in the hiring hall haven't come up with anything they like better, and there hasn't been a strike since 1963. Being strike-free has played a big part in Antwerp's having won business away from the ports of Rotterdam and London.

There are two possibilities for visitors to see something of Antwerp's port. The boats of **Flandria** (berthed on the Scheldt near the *Steenplein* in central Antwerp), whose 50-minute cruises don't get far enough downstream to show much of the port, also offer day or evening 3-hour port excursions. For those traveling by car, the 40-mi./65-km., self-guiding *Havenroute* (map available from the tourist office), best undertaken when there's a passenger who can serve as navigator, provides insight into the workings of the port.

As visitors discover, Antwerp is a destination with many dimensions, one that integrates new ideas with older ones. The intellectual environment that blossomed as an accompaniment to the baroque art of Antwerp's Golden Age at the end of the 16th century had its birth at the beginning of that century. At that time **Thomas More** (1477–1535), an English humanist and a *Man for All Seasons*, used Antwerp as a setting for his book *Utopia*. Considered one of the most influential books in Western philosophy, *Utopia* described a mythical island off South America where wealth was divided equally and all lived in happy cooperation free of war and want.

Book One of *Utopia* opens with More recounting: "The most invincible king of England, Henry the Eighth of that name, sent me into Flanders as his spokesman (and) since my business required it, I went to Antwerp." More lived in Antwerp from May to October in 1515, and in *Utopia* speaks of his Antwerpian friend Peter Giles, whose house until recently stood just behind the *Grote Markt* at *16 Oude Beurs*. He visited it many times, since it was a prominent meeting place for fellow **humanists**, including Erasmus. Thomas More was an intimate of Rotterdam-born humanist Erasmus (with whom he founded a college at Louvain University where *Utopia* was first published in 1516). Humanism was an intellectual and cultural movement concerned with the interest and ideals of people rather than religion. In the pages of *Utopia*, Peter Giles introduces Thomas More to Raphael, who tells them both of the wonders of the world that he—Raphael—had heard recounted by explorer Amerigo Vespucci (1451–1512). At this time, in accordance with their individual beliefs, most Europeans were either entranced or alarmed by tales about overseas expeditions, but the philosophers of the day saw in the broadened horizons a fresh chance for men to create a better way of life. Hence, More, inspired by Vespucci's voyages, conceived in *Utopia* how an idealistic society might be set up in an unspoiled new world.

During his stay in Antwerp, early on in the city's Golden Age, Thomas More would have observed a metropolis that mixed material success with humanism. More than 450 years later, an antiques dealer has this to say about his city: "We are at a very similar point in history: the humanism of the Renaissance is a philosophy that suits our present." He believes that Antwerpians are open, seeking, and creative, and may well be in the midst of a renaissance that will rival the city's 16th-century glory.

## GUIDEPOSTS

**Telephone Code 03**

**Tourist Information** • City Tourist Office: Head Office: Grote Markt 15; B-2000 Antwerp; Mon.–Fri., 8:30 a.m.–6:00 p.m., Sat., Sun., holidays, 9 a.m.–5 p.m.; ☎ *232.01.03*. Office closed Christmas and New Year's Day. Free accommodations booking assistance, from youth hostels to the Hilton.

**City Transport** • De Lijn Head Office: Grotehondstraat 58; Mon.–Fri., 8:30 a.m.–4:00 p.m.; ☎ *218.14.11*.

**Trains** • Centraal Station inquiries: Mon.–Sat. 8 a.m.–10 p.m., Sun. and holidays, 9 a.m.–5 p.m. ☎ *204.20.40.*

**Port Cruises** • *Flandria*: Steenplein, ☎ *231.31.00.*

**City Tours** • *Sightseeing Line*: 13-passenger 50-minute narrated (head sets, 7 languages) mini-van tours from Grote Markt: schedule and reservations at Tourist Office. *Touristram Antwerpen* departs from Groenplaats on the hour, 11 a.m.–5 p.m.

**Consulates** • Great Britain: Korte Klarenstraat 9; ☎ *232.69.40.* Ireland: Rudolfstraat 16; ☎ *237.69.94.*

**Emergencies** • Police: ☎ *101*; accident: ☎ *100*; a list of doctors and pharmacists/chemists on night and weekend duty is published in the weekend editions of local newspapers, and available from the Tourist Office or at hotel.

**Automobile Aid** • Royal Automobile Club of Belgium: ☎ *232.16.93.*

**Lost Property** • Police headquarters: ☎ *202.55.11*; Centraal Railway Station: ☎ *204.24.16*; city tram/bus office: ☎ *218.14.11.*

**Post Office** • Main Post Office: Groenplaats 42; Mon.–Fri., 9 a.m.–6 p.m., Sat. 9 a.m.–noon; ☎ *231.06.70.*

**Telephone/Telegraph** • Head Office: Jezusstraat 1; daily 8 a.m.–8 p.m.; ☎ *232.58.10.*

## WHAT TO SEE AND DO

Central Antwerp's attractions are grouped below in three general areas, each of which can be covered fairly easily on foot. The most distant site is the Fine Arts Museum (more than a mile from the **Grote Markt**), to which most visitors take a tram or taxi. Sights start with those within walking distance of the Grote Markt (the tourist office there has maps and printed English commentary on eight suggested walking tours), and riverfront, following which are descriptions of sites south and then north of **Meir**. Local custom calls for time out at cafes along the way. Many museums in Antwerp are closed on Monday; holidays on which they are commonly closed are Jan. 1 and 2, May 1, Ascension Day, Nov. 1 and 2, Dec. 25 and 26.

## AROUND THE GROTE MARKT AND RIVERFRONT

**Grote Markt**                                            ★★★

This is the heart of Antwerp and at the great square's center; replacing the former tree of liberty is the **Brabo Fountain** (1887, sculpted by **Jef Lambeaux**). Rimming it are dignified 16th-century guild houses, each topped with a gilt-adorned patron saint appropriate to the particular craft or trade (drapers, haberdashers, coopers, and crossbows) once headquartered therein. The guild houses (some original, such as numbers 38 and 40, others reconstructions of those that once stood elsewhere, such as 15 and 25) are in Renaissance style, which gives

Antwerp's Grote Markt a less ornate appearance than Brussels' baroque-era main square. Though not used for weekly general markets, Antwerp's Grote Markt is the setting for special festival markets.

Southwest off the Grote Markt is the statue of the **Dock Worker** (by **Constantin Meunier**). Out the northeast corner across Oude Beurs, at 15 Hofstraat, is Antwerp's old **stock exchange**, a beautiful Gothic building from 1515 that now serves as the city's education office (the lovely inner courtyard can be viewed during office hours). Behind Grote Markt to the right of the **Stadhuis**, and between it and the not-distant **Vleehuis**, one finds exemplary urban renewal in one of the city's most historic sections. An extensive housing project (following the clearance deemed necessary due to ancient buildings that had become slum like) has been built to blend in scale and materials with original old city buildings.

### Stadhuis                                                    ★★

*Grote Markt; Mon.–Sat. 9 a.m.–3 p.m., except Mon. 9 a.m.–noon, Fri. noon–3 p.m., Sat. til 4 p.m., closed Sun. and holidays;* ☎ *220.82.11.* The Grote Markt is dominated by the *Stadhuis* ("town hall"), whose 247-foot facade has a coat of many colors of marble. Built from 1561–1565 by Antwerp architect Cornelis Floris, it is one of Flanders' earliest and finest buildings in the Renaissance style. During summer months the Stadhuis festively flaunts some of the flags of the more than 100 countries whose ships put into Antwerp's port. The impressive interior decoration dates mostly from the city's prosperous 19th century, many earlier works of art having been destroyed or stolen during the French occupation at the end of the 18th century. The former Lords' Chamber, now the **Leys Room**, is decorated with four historical paintings by Henri Leys representing the main privileges of Antwerp. Murals on the staircase walls and in the marriage chamber are also notable.

The statue in the center niche in the front of the Stadhuis is of the Virgin Mary, patron saint of the city, and it recalls the other Madonnas you'll see by the dozen in street corner niches. Two reasons account for their great number. During the days of the St. Luke's Guild, in order to become a *master* member, an artist had to create a *masterpiece*; often, Antwerp sculptors selected the Madonna as their subject, and later presented the completed work to the district in which they lived. Secondly, when these statuettes of the Virgin, displayed on street corners, were lighted by votives, the districts avoided the taxes that otherwise were levied on private street lights.

### Onze Lieve Vrouw/Notre Dame cathedral                      ★★★

*Groenplaats 21; Mon.– Fri. 10 a.m.–5 p.m., Sat. 10 a.m.–3 p.m., Sun. and church festivals 1–4 p.m., not accessible during church services;* ☎ *231.30.33.* Because of its position on the ground and the prominence of its steeple in the sky, Antwerp's cathedral is *the* landmark of the city. Hemmed in by buildings, the cathedral body cannot be seen as a whole, but the structure nevertheless is an omnipresence in the old center. The largest Gothic church in Belgium, the cathedral was begun in 1352 under a general design by Jan Appelmans. (See the imaginative **Appelmans Monument** by **Jef Lambeaux**, 1935, to the right of the cathedral's main door on **Handschoenmarkt**.) With construction spread out until 1521 due to erratic funding, the nave, originally Romanesque, was demolished in about 1425 and begun again in Gothic. The seven-aisle interior is of startling size, only recently (April 1993) revealed following a long-term $70 million-plus fundamental restoration. At 400 feet/123 meters, the cathedral's soaring spire, completed in 1521, is the highest in the Netherlands, resembling Belgian lace in its delicacy. Unwrapped in 1993 from scaffolding that had contained it since 1965, it brings fresh meaning to the word *inspiring.* The view from its inside out, if you aspire to climb the tower, is pure panorama.

Cathedral treasures include three of Rubens' most famous paintings: *Raising of the Cross* (triptych, 1610), *Descent from the Cross* (triptych, 1611–1614), and the impressive altarpiece *Assumption of Mary* (1626). The central panel of *Descent from the Cross*, with its strong diagonal line that draws viewers into the action and emotion of the moment, is the essence of Rubens' best baroque work. Concerts occasionally are performed on the 5625-pipe organ. Many flat tombstones can be seen in the cathedral floor; people paid a lot to be buried here because of the one-time belief that if on Judgment Day they were raised to their feet inside a church, they would fare better than if in a cemetery.

## Handschoenmarkt ★ ★

This lovely square in front of the cathedral's main door has retained its historic Frankish triangle shape, which facilitated the protective containment of cattle. At No. 13 is the house (with plaque) in which the artist **David Teniers the Younger** was born in 1610. The cafe-rimmed, square is a delightful locale for listening to concerts on the cathedral's 47-bell carillon (*Fridays from 11:30 a.m.–12:30 p.m. year-round, and Mondays from 9–10 p.m. from mid-June to mid-September*).

In the square is a stone well with a lovely ironwork canopy (c. 1495). The canopy is ascribed to **Quinten Metsys** (or *Matsys* and *Massys*, c. 1460–1530), a favorite adopted son of Antwerp, who arrived from Louvain trained as a blacksmith and with a talent for intricate ironwork. But an *artisan* wasn't good enough for the *artist* whose daughter Metsys fell in love with in his new city. As the story of the courtship is recounted, Metsys continued to visit the young lady at her home, and one day, speaking with her in her father's studio, he picked up a brush and painted a fly on a canvas that her father had left to dry. A few days later when the father had occasion to look at the painting again, he tried to brush off the fly. When he realized that it was painted and inquired of his daughter who the artist was, he was persuaded to give permission for her to marry Metsys. The Latin phrase inscribed on a tablet to Quinten Metsys on the facade of the cathedral (to the left of the door near the well) translates: "Twas love connubial taught the smith to paint." Metsys, who today is considered the first major artist of the Antwerp School, is represented by *The Lamentation of Christ Triptych*, and five other paintings in Antwerp's **Royal Fine Arts Museum** (which has none by his "artist" father-in-law).

### Steenplein and Riverfront ★

The Scheldt is nearly a third of a mile (500 meters) wide in front of the Steenplein, where a statue of **Minerva**, the Roman goddess of wisdom and industry, reflects upon the river. Though much of the shipping that makes the *Port of Antwerp's* statistics so impressive must now be accommodated downstream by facilities fit to handle it, you'll still find the flavor of river traffic in the center of the city, from the barges heading upstream on the waterway into the heart of the European continent. The entrance to the under-river pedestrian **St. Annatunnel** (built in 1933, about 1/3 mile long) is located west of the *Vrijdagmarkt* at *St. Jansvliet*.

### The Steen (National Maritime Museum) ★★

*Steenplein 1; daily 10 a.m.–5 p.m.;*  *232.08.50; exhibits with English explanation.* On the waterfront is Antwerp's oldest (12th century) edifice, the Steen, situated on the site of the city's earliest development. Built as a fortress, and for centuries used as a prison, the Steen was restored (by architects De Waghemakere and Keldermans, who had just completed work on the cathedral) about 1520 by order of Charles V, whose coat of arms can still be seen on the lovely loggia over the entrance gate. Under Charles' son Spanish King Philip II and the dread duke of Alva, however, the Steen deteriorated into a torture chamber. Today, no longer fusty or frightening, it is the fascinating setting for the National Maritime Museum. Within the wonderful building are nautical exhibits that include a copy of the state barge built in Antwerp for the Emperor Napoleon on his visit in 1810, sailors' old tatoo paraphernalia, an elaborate tile panel showing a 17th-century sea battle between the Dutch and the English, and a model of Antwerp harbor c. 1515. The widely varied exhibits are shown in 12 sections in a series of mostly small rooms separated by narrow passageways and some steep stairs. There's a cafe in the basement.

Beyond the Steen on the ★★ promenade along the Scheldt are ships and sailors from around the world, and riverfront, glass sheltered cafes at *Noorderterras* and *Zuiderterras* ("North and South terrace") where Antwerpians go to enjoy the late day sun, and the scene and setting.

## SOUTH OF MEIR

### Rubenshuis ★★★

*Wapper 9; daily 10 a.m.–5 p.m., closed major holidays.;*  *232.47.47;*

*English language guidebook available.* The best place to appreciate Pieter Paul Rubens' personality, if not his works, is the house he began building in 1610 and lived in from 1616 until his death there in 1640. The mansion, with its restrained Flemish Renaissance street-front facade, makes way for the family living quarters and the artist's exuberant statue-studded studio, linked together by an imposing portico topped with figures of the Roman gods *Mercury* and *Minerva* that appear in several of his paintings. With stature as "the prince of painters, and the painter of princes," Rubens dominated the baroque age in Antwerp.

Rubens was the son of a Lutheran lawyer who had to flee Antwerp for religious reasons. Thus Rubens was born in Westphalia, Germany in 1577, returning to Antwerp about 1585 with his Catholic mother (who converted her son to her religion). He was apprenticed successively to three Flemish artists, and in 1598 became a master in Antwerp's artists **Guild of St. Luke**, of which he later was dean. In the corner bedroom of his house is the actual chair (with the gilt lettering "PET. PAUL. RUBENS 1633" on the back) that was reserved for him in the painters' room of the guild's headquarters.

In 1600, Rubens went to Italy, staying in Rome, Venice, and Genoa, and studying with masters there. During his eight years in Italy, he also went to Spain on diplomatic business for Vincenzo Gonzaga of Mantua, a patron in whose service he worked. Rubens returned to Antwerp in 1608 because of the ill health of his mother (she died while he was enroute home). The next year, 1609, he became court painter to the Archdukes Isabella and Albert and married Isabella Brant. In 1610, he made an immense investment in land on what is now the Wapper and began designing and building a house and studio (into which he moved five years later, though the buildings were not yet finished). By 1611 he was at work on two monumental works for Antwerp cathedral where they can be seen today: the triptychs *Raising of the Cross* and *Descent from the Cross.*

The fleshy flamboyance of Rubens' figures may not be fashionable today, but the flourishing of the baroque period when and where it did is thoroughly comprehensible in the context of the times. The baroque style, with its massive forms and nearly excessive ornamentation, was embraced by the Roman Catholic Church in Europe during the Counter-Reformation, undoubtedly the more so for its being in such complete contrast to the unadorned style decreed by Calvinist Protestantism.

But though he breathed baroque with every brush stroke, Rubens himself was something of a Renaissance man. Having studied the classics until the age of 12, and having used his eight years in Italy to study archaelogy and to begin a collection of classical statuary, Rubens revealed his close identification with the ancients in the statesmen and gods whose likenesses grace his home, inside and out. Within the house, off the painting gallery where he displayed the favorites of his excellent and extensive personal collection, a marble half-pantheon or apsidal gallery served as a display case for his treasured antique busts and statues. In 1618 Rubens exchanged some of his paintings for Greek and Roman statues and other antiquities from the collection of Antwerp's English ambassador Sir Dudley Carlton. "Art above gold for investment," he believed.

Rubens' carefully acquired collection of classical art was admired by all who saw it, and he was praised as an archaeologist by learned men of his time. One wrote, "Especially with regard to antiquities, Rubens has the most universal and remarkable knowledge I ever met with. He is very well-grounded in all the branches of archaelology." A bust of the Roman Seneca rests above the door to his Great Studio, and stoicism and humanism were guiding philosophies for Rubens. In a cartouche in the portico, Rubens had inscribed in the stone a line from the Roman poet Juvenal: "Leave it to the gods to give what is fit and useful for us; man is dearer to them than to himself."

Although attempts had been made to buy the house for the city of Antwerp as early as 1762, the Rubens house became a museum only in 1946, following a major reconstruction that returned it to its original state. The furniture visitors see today did not, with rare and noted exception, belong to Rubens, but is authentic in recreating the atmosphere of a patrician house in Antwerp of the 17th century. In the house are some ten paintings by Rubens, perhaps the most interesting being one of his few self-portraits (in the dining room). The art gallery in the house was hung with the artist's favorites in a collection that numbered about 300 at the time of his death. The wide-ranging collection included many Flemish primitives, and it is a sad loss that it was scattered after the artist's death. In the collection were 17 paintings by **Adriaen Brouwer**, whose work Rubens obviously much admired. Brouwer, notorious for a dissolute life, is said to have once been released from imprisonment in the Steen due to Rubens' intercession.

Rubens loved his work and worked hard at it. But the estimated 1500–2000 paintings in his *oeuvre* could not possibly have been realized without his studio staff of students and collaborators. Often, Rubens would create the design for a painting, leave the intermediate execution of it to his pupils, and then add the finishing flourishes that gave it his touch. Such a division of work was quite common in the times, if one had sufficent commissions to warrant supporting a studio. It was in the Great Studio, where several Rubens' paintings are displayed, that several pupils would have worked on a cluster of canvases and panels. In order to assess or show to guests and clients his largest works, those destined to decorate palaces or church altars and meant to be viewed from a distance, Rubens used the *bel-etage* or first floor that looked into the Great Studio.

Rubens also had a private studio where he sketched and had models sit for him. His pupils also had their own studio. In the so-called large bedroom, though not now furnished as a bedroom, Rubens would have seen his son Nicolaas born and his first wife die (probably of the plague); he shared it with his second wife (Helene Fourmont), whom he brought there when she was 16 and he was 53. Rubens himself stayed in this bedroom when he was sick—he suffered from gout— near the end of his life, and it was here he died in May 1640.

### Plantin-Moretus House                                          ★ ★ ★

*Vrijdagmarkt 22; daily 10 a.m.–5 p.m.;* ☎ *233.02.94; English guidebook for sale.* In the elegant 16th-century Plantin-Moretus house, nine generations of the same family lived and ran a printing plant and shop between 1555 and 1876. The first three generations were the most forward-looking and contributed substantially to the intellectual environment of Antwerp, Europe, and well beyond. The founding **Plantin**, French-born Christophe (1520–1589), having been apprenticed to a bookbinder, arrived in Antwerp in 1548, during the city's gilded days. He choose Antwerp over all other cities because "no other town in the world could offer me more facilities for carrying on the trade I intend," and further cited the city's accessibility to skilled craftsmen, raw materials, and international buyers and sellers. Also, Antwerp's place in printing was already well established. In the pre-1500 *incunabula* printing period, Antwerp had been an important center, but when the prosperous early 16th-century era arrived, the city initiated a golden age for the art of mechanical printing. Between 1500 and 1540, half of all the works published in the Netherlands were produced on Antwerp presses.

Plantin turned from binding to printing, and one of his first books, published in 1559, was a volume on the funeral ceremonies of Charles V (who died in 1558) that was nearly as magnificent in its execution as the actual funeral had been. Between 1563 and 1567, Plantin's presses turned out the unheard-of average of 50 quality books a year. Probably Plantin's most outstanding undertaking was the *Biblia Polyglotta*, a reliable edition of the Bible in five languages (Latin, Greek, Hebrew, Syriac, and Chaldaic or Aramaean), with appendices on grammar, vocabulary, and culture of remarkable detail. Begun in 1568, the colossal task was finished in 1572; bound in eight big folios, it remains the most important work ever published in Belgium.

In 1572, Christophe Plantin received a monopoly from Philip II for the sale of certain liturgical works in Spain and its colonies (a monopoly which supported what became a rather stagnant printing house from the fourth generation for nearly two full centuries until the agreement finally was terminated). Production slowed but was not devastated by the 1576 *Spanish Fury* in Antwerp, and Plantin, himself a devout Catholic, managed to walk a fine line between religious factions during the Reformation/Counter-Reformation. Although he never denied the king of Spain, Plantin managed to print several anti-Spanish works and retain the favor of Dutch Protestant Willem of Orange, who was based in Antwerp for a while and visited the printing house. When he died in 1589, having published more than 1500 important works—his first and foremost concern always was the *content* of the books—of humanists, classical authors, and scientific dissertation in 34 years, Christophe Plantin was buried in the high choir of Antwerp's cathedral.

Plantin bequeathed the printing house and shop to his favorite son-in-law, **Jan Moretus**, who had entered the workshop at the age of 14. Jan's son **Balthasar** (1574–1641), who headed the printing concern from 1610 to 1641, was a man of exceptional intelligence and knowledge, the greatest of the Moretuses. During Antwerp's blossoming in the baroque era, Balthasar, an intimate of Rubens, encouraged and fostered the work of scholars and artists. (He induced Rubens to design and illustrate frontispieces for many volumes.) The books published under Balthasar were the firm's most splendid.

The Plantin-Moretus house, which became a museum in 1877, more or less reached its present form under building changes begun by Plantin and continued by Balthasar Moretus, who designed the appealing inner courtyard. Behind the characteristic 18th-century Louis XV-style facade is hidden one of Belgium's finest civic Renaissance constructions. Many rooms have their original character and, with period furniture, offer a clear picture of a rich Antwerp patrician house from the 16th-18th centuries.

What makes the Plantin-Moretus museum unique is that its working role is emphasized under the same roof: many of the original furnishings of the printing plant, the foundry and fonts, the composers' and correctors' rooms, and shop are in evidence. The house's three richly filled libraries contain about 30,000 volumes, including copies of all the publications by Plantin and the Moretuses and choice works by foreign typographers, including 150 *incunabula* among which is a two-volume Bible (c. 1401) of the Czech miniature school that belonged to King Wenceslas of Bohemia, and a priceless copy of the 36-line Gutenberg Bible, the only one in Belgium. Old sheet music, printed with square notes, is also on display. Antique furniture, art (about 150 paintings and family portraits by Flemish masters, including 18 by Rubens), some 650 drawings, a wall map of Flanders by Mercator, tapestries, walls covered with gilt leather from Mechelen, and tall tiled fireplaces round out the charm of the building. Throughout the darkwood-decorated house are large *Liège* ("Belgium") crystal chandeliers, their pendants cut as carefully as diamonds so as to reflect as much light as possible.

## Koninklijk Museum voor Schone Kunsten                    ★★
**(Royal Fine Arts Museum)** *Leopold de Waelplaats; daily 10 a.m.–5 p.m., closed Mondays;* ☎ *238.78.09; English language catalogues. Tram # 8.*

Trade brought riches to Antwerp; riches brought art; and the Museum of Fine Arts eventually reaped much of the reward. It houses an exceptional collection of works by the essentially 15th-century **Flemish "Primitives"**: Jan van Eyck, Rogier van der Weyden, Hans Memling, Dirk Bouts, and Gerard David. From the Antwerp School, founded by Quinten Metsys (1466–1530) and the Bruegel family, to the baroque age, of which Pieter Paul Rubens was the towering talent, Belgian masters are well covered. Antwerp's Fine Arts Museum has the world's finest collection of Rubens (17 paintings), and many works by his contemporaries Anthony van Dyck and Jacob Jordaens. Not only the artists of southern but also of northern Netherlands (Holland) are well represented: Hals, Rembrandt, Ter Borch.

Antwerp's nationally owned Museum of Fine Arts celebrated a centennial of residence in its neo-Gothic/neoclassic home in 1990, but the nucleus of the collection had its origins with the Antwerp **Guild of St. Luke** to which city artists belonged between 1454 and 1773. When guilds were disbanded, the paintings that St. Luke's had displayed in the *kunstkamer* (art room or gallery) of its guild house were turned over to Antwerp's *Academy of Fine Arts*, which established a museum. During the French occupations of the city in 1794 and 1796, many paintings—a total of 70, including 30 well-known works by Rubens, according to an official contemporary report—were confiscated from churches, monasteries, and public buildings, and sent to Paris. After the Battle of Waterloo in 1815, 40 were returned, of which 26 went to the museum.

During the period of the United Netherlands (1815–1830), Dutch King Willem donated several paintings to the academy, including its first work by a living artist (*The Death of Rubens* by Matthijs van Bree, who was director of the Fine Arts Academy). Willem also granted the museum a substantial subsidy for the purchase of contemporary art from the salons of Amsterdam, Brussels, Antwerp, and Ghent (though the 1830 Belgian revolution naturally nullified the grant, and it was not until 1873 that the museum began buying contemporary works). The museum's limited collection was boosted in 1840 by a bequest of 141 works from Florent van Ertborn, a former Antwerp burgomaster, who had, with flawless taste, built an exceptional collection of 15th-century paintings at a time when Flemish "primitives" were not appreciated. In 1859, the museum received another gift, 41 works consisting primarily of 17th-century Flemish and Dutch paintings. Together, these donations assured the museum's reputation. Today the collection consists of more than 3200 paintings, 3600 drawings, and 400 sculptures.

In the Department of Old Art, displayed on the upper story, the museum owns some 1200 paintings that give a survey of Flemish art from c. 1360 until the end of the 18th century, as well as covering most aspects of Dutch, Italian, German, and French art. On the ground floor is displayed a fraction of the fine arts' considerable 19th- and 20th-century collection, principally Belgian, beginning with the *romantic movement*, whose leading exponent was **Gustaf Wappers** (1803–1874). **Henri de Braekeleer** (1840–1888), represented in the fine arts by 33 paintings and 45 drawings, is considered by many to be Belgium's first significant 19th-century artistic figure. *Realism* came into being in Belgium between 1850 and 1860, and the museum is particularly well-represented in realistic landscapes. Antwerp-born sculptor **Jef Lambeaux** (1852–1908), exhibited on the streets of Antwerp as well as in the museum, shows the 19th-century move to *naturalism*. Of course, no discussion of modern Belgian art can neglect *surrealism*. Here you find 35 paintings and 606 drawings by **James Ensor** (1860–1949), the reclusive Ostender who held society up to ridicule with his "mask people." Also shown are works by **René Magritte** (1898–1967), who influenced 20th-century art internationally, and **Paul Delvaux** (b. 1897). The museum has an excellent shop.

### Provincial Diamond Museum/Diamantmusem ★★

*Lange Herentalsestraat 31; daily from 10 a.m.–5 p.m.;* ☎ *324.02.07; good guidebook in English.* A gem on Antwerp's list of attractions is the Provincial Diamond Museum where visitors can see the whole sparkling history of the stones that have engaged the attention of cutters, polishers, brokers, and buyers in Antwerp for five centuries. Once a symbol of virtue and virility, diamonds today represent value. They are a compact treasure: one ounce of high-quality diamonds is equal to 400 pounds of pure gold. With four of the world's twenty diamond bourses, Antwerp can be considered the capital for the world's diamond dealings: at least 60 percent of all diamonds traded worldwide pass through Antwerp, and the diamond business by itself represents 7 percent of Belgium's GNP.

The diamond museum, opened in 1988, offers an introductory 20-minute video (English version) on Antwerp's historic association with diamonds, and can arrange for you to see a diamond-grinding demonstration. (For more information, see "Diamonds" in "Decorative Arts and Traditional Crafts" under "The Belgian Cultural Legacy.")

## NORTH OF MEIR

### Rockox House ★★

*Keizerstraat 12; daily 10 a.m.–5 p.m., closed Mondays;* ☎ *231.47.10; English guidebook.* Also holding up a mirror to Antwerp's gilded age is the Rockox house, an opulent, splendidly restored, and period-furnished early 17th-century house owned by a former burgomaster and friend of Rubens. The Rockox house was purchased in 1970 by *Kredietbank*—banks in Antwerp make a point of supporting museums— which created a non-profit foundation for it. Nicolaas Rockox (1560–1640) was a member of Antwerp's Civic Guard, seven times alderman, nine times mayor of Antwerp, and a humanist who also was a benefactor and patron of Rubens, with whom he shared a belief in the *Counter-Reformation* and a great knowledge of classical antiquity. Among Rockox's commissions to Rubens was the 1612 *Descent from the Cross* triptych for the chapel in the cathedral of the Arquebusiers' Guild (of which he was captain); *Christ on the Cross* (now in Antwerp's Fine Arts Museum), and *Christ and St. Thomas*, with portraits of himself and his wife on the side panels. *The Adoration of the Magi*, commissioned from Rubens as soon as the artist had returned from eight years in Italy for the Chamber of State in the Antwerp Stadhuis, is now in the **Prado Museum** in Madrid.

In 1603, when Rockox became burgomaster for the first time, he bought this and an adjacent property, combining the two into a fine Flemish Renaissance-style patrician dwelling. The house and its original contents were sold at auction in 1715 (in accordance with Rockox's will, which distributed the proceeds to benefit the poor), but contemporary documents have made it possible to recreate an appropriate degree of wealth in the Rockox interior. Among the many paintings, one of the most moving is Rubens' *The Virgin in Adoration Before the Sleeping Christ Child*, in which the Virgin has the features of Rubens' first wife Isabella Brant, and the Infant Jesus those of his second son Nicolaas. Teniers the Younger, Jordaens, Van Dyck, Jan "Velvet" Brueghel, and Pieter Brueghel the Younger (whose *Proverbs* is a copy of his father's fascinating original) are all shown amid the marvelous pieces of furniture and decorative art that make the house seem so "lived in." The very special atmosphere of the inner courtyard will make you want to linger even longer.

**Note:** Normally it's only shown to groups, but inquire in any case about seeing the excellent audiovisual presentation (in English) *Nicolaas Rockox and His Time*, which beautifully communicates a feeling for Antwerp, its art, and its architecture during the period 1560–1640.

### Sint Jacobskerk (St. James Church)  ★★
*Lange Nieuwstraat 73; April 1–Oct. 31; 2–5 p.m., no visitors Sundays and during services; ☎ 232.10.32; brochure with church layout.* Begun in 1491, though not entirely completed until 1656, St. James thus shows a late Gothic/Brabant style with some Renaissance influence. After the cathedral, St. James' is the most important church in Antwerp, and surpasses it in rich baroque adornment. St. James was Rubens' parish church and his second marriage took place there in 1630. In Rubens' day, all Antwerp's leading families had their burial vaults and private chapels there. Visitors may seek out Rubens' own chapel and tomb (he died in 1640), which is situated in the ambulatory directly behind the high altar. The centerpiece of the chapel is the painting, *Our Lady Surrounded by the Saints*, executed by Rubens in 1634 specifically for his sepulchral monument, and considered one of his finest works. It is generally accepted that in the painting the figure of St. George is a self-portrait; Mary has the features of Rubens' first wife;

the infant Jesus those of his son; Mary Magdalene his second wife's face; and St. Jerome the features of his father.

Although St. James has known damaging times, in the Calvinist *Iconoclast*, the French Revolution, both world wars, and from arson in 1967, many of its treasures have been saved, and extensive exterior and interior restoration has been completed. Carved-wood confessionals by Artus Quellin the Elder, a majestic black and white marble altar topped with trumpeting angels by Artus Quellin the Younger, and two paintings each by Jordaens and Van Dyck are among the artistic treasures in the church. There are two organs: the 1727 instrument was once played by nine-year-old Mozart; the 1884 organ, set in a handsome carved 1723 organ-loft, was rebuilt into a concert-organ in 1956.

### Hendrik Conscienceplein

This charming Antwerp square is made more so by its location in front of the elaborate Rubens-designed Carrolus Borromeo church facade. Dedicated to the writer who helped raise Flemish consciousness in the 19th century—particularly with his book, *The Lion in Flanders,* see "Belgian Bibliography"—Hendrik Conscienceplein thus is the appropriate site of Antwerp's public library, which is housed in the 17th-century buildings of the former college of the Jesuits who built the church. The square draws lots of readers, at the tables of cafes that line one side, or on seats beside the statue (by Frans Joris, 1883) of the square's namesake.

## *WHERE TO STAY*

## VERY EXPENSIVE

### De Rosier

*Rosier 21, 2000;* ☎ *225.01.40, FAX 231.41.11.* On an ordinary old street in central Antwerp is a most extraordinary hotel: a remarkable antique-filled, interior designer-owner-decorated mansion that is an oasis where attentive personal service prevails. Modern art and sculpture are integrated into the richly comfortable, tastefully original guest and public rooms that feature marble, crystal chandeliers, tapestries, track-lighting, paintings, and plants. The ten individually decorated guest rooms each have private bath, TV, and telephone. Breakfast (only, extra charge), formal afternoon tea, and drinks are served in the enchanting glass-enclosed, garden-surrounded Summer-patio Room. No restaurant. Cozy bar, elevator. Advance reservations essential.

## EXPENSIVE

### De Witte Lelie

*Keizerstraat 16, 2000;* ☎ *226.19.66, FAX 234.00.19.* This recently opened four-guestroom, six-suite restored 17th-century in-town mansion, a neighbor of the Rockox House Museum, offers large, big-windowed, well-lighted rooms with antique and stylish-contemporary decor, for an elegant yet at-home ambiance. In-room amenities include complementary mini-bar, CD player, 24-channel TV, safe, good bedside reading lights, fresh flowers and Belgian chocolates, and modern baths with glass-doored shower stalls. There's 24-hour room service. Public rooms are restful and romantic. The breakfast (included) room faces a fountained courtyard. Underground parking (fee) available. This center-city oasis is better than a home-away-from-home, since home is rarely this civilized.

### Rubens ★★★★

*Oude Beurs 29;* ☎ *222.48.48, FAX 225.19.40.* Newly opened in 1993, the 36-room Rubens is situated in a restored townhouse mansion close to Antwerp's *Grote Markt.* Features include a stylish entry and green marble-floored, green plant-decorated reception area, off which is an attractive small lobby bar and lounge/breakfast (included) room. In fine weather breakfast or drinks can be enjoyed in the pinkwashed enclosed courtyard, which has trellises, tables, and a 16th-century brick watchtower in one corner. Rooms are pleasantly decorated, with rheostat controls for pleasing, effective lighting. Baths have green marble and white tiles; toilets in separate room. Windows (which open) are double glazed to keep out traffic sounds for sleeping.

## MODERATE

### Hotel Firean ★★★

*Karel Oomsstraat 6, B-2018;* ☎ *237.02.60, FAX 238.11.68.* Though beyond walking distance from any of central Antwerp's attractions (but convenient to tram lines to both the cathedral and Centraal Station), this restored, owner-operated, 12-room, 1921 house is so pleasant that it should be considered. The hospitable homelike house-hotel, with intriguing art deco details and all Belgian furnishings, features original Tiffany windows, antique tapestries, backlighted glass panels, and the additional charm of a flood-lighted rear garden (with bar service for guests). Guest rooms are uniquely furnished in soft colors, with pants press, hair dryer, minibar, toiletries, double-glazed windows (for quiet), cable TV, and extra evening housekeeping of rooms. Breakfast (included) is served indoors or on the garden patio; international morning newspapers in lobby. Room service (light food dishes) until midnight, 24-hour laundry, parking, major credit cards. Reservations well-ahead recommended.

### Classic Hotel Villa Mozart ★★★★

*Handschoenmarkt 3, 2000;* ☎ *231.30.31, FAX 231.56.85.* Opened in 1990, this hotel is Antwerp's first in the Grote Markt vicinity, and is located on the delightful Handschoenmarkt across from the cathedral. (Light sleepers take note of the carillon that strikes the hours all night long.) Behind a restored 5-story period facade, 24 guest rooms and 4 suites are tastefully decorated with cane and bamboo furniture upholstered in rich materials. Amenities include extra wide beds, luxury bath, minibar, AC, room service. The hotel's **Vivaldi** restaurant serves fine French and international cuisine based on fresh seasonal produce; there's indoor or terrace cafe seating. Buffet breakfast included; year-round discounted weekend rates; public parking garages within two blocks.

## WHERE TO EAT

Prices in Antwerp's better restaurants are generally less than in Brussels. Reservations are essential at the best restaurants, and a call to book if you have a specific place in mind is always a good bet except for the most casual eateries. A number of restaurants are closed on Sundays and holidays, and some close for personal holiday periods, particularly in August. When your're in a picnic mood, a good choice is downstairs at the **Grand Bazaar** complex on centrally-located Groenplaats for the largest in-town grocery store (open from 9 a.m.)

Consistently ranked as one of the Antwerp's most appetizing restaurants is **La Perouse** *(Steenplein; noon–2:30 p.m., 7–9:30 p.m., closed Sun., Mon., holidays, and June through mid–Sept. when it is a Scheldt-cruising restaurant for* **Flandria***;* ☎ *232.35.28; expensive).* When it isn't floating, La Perouse sits moored on the Scheldt at the foot of Suikkerui. In its ship-shape polished brass and steel atmosphere, seafood is the specialty, especially *waterzooi de poussin*, a creamy fish stew/soup and traditional Flemish dish that doesn't get any better than it is here. **Sir Anthony Van Dijck** *(Oude Koornmarkt 16; Mon.– Fri. noon–2:30 p.m., two evening seatings, reservations required; closed Sat. & Sun.;* ☎ *231.61.70; moderate),* is located in a beautiful setting of an-tiques, tapestries, candlelight, polished stone tile floors, dark beams, fire-places, and ivy-draped enclosed courtyard with the sound of dripping water from a fountain in a former burgomeester's home in the charming 16th century cobbled alley of antique shops called *Vlaeykensgang.* Recently, the owner of this regular on the rolls of the city's best restaurants got tired of being chic and snobbish and purposely let his two Michelin Star rating slide to concentrate on simpler fine cuisine and a more authentic Antwerp ambience. **Neuze Neuze** *(Wijngaardstraat 19; noon–2:15 p.m., 7–9:30 p.m., closed Sun.;* ☎ *232.57.83; moderate/expensive),* reveals Antwerp's love of juxtaposing the old and new with smart modern decor under ancient beamed ceilings and arches. The cuisine is French with the flair of its four chefs, who provide a two-course menu that's always worth consideration.

**De Peerdestal** *(Wijngaardstraat 8; noon–2:30 p.m., 6–11 p.m., closed Sun.;* ☎ *231.95.03; inexpensive),* located in a 400-year-old building in a small pe-destrian street that runs into the Hendrik Conscienceplein, offers excellent atmosphere along with its tasty traditional dishes. Good choices include *to-mate aux crevettes* (tomato stuffed with small North Sea shrimp), *fondue au fromage* (melted cheese croquette), and *moules* (mussels) in myriad ways; also served at red-check-covered, candlelighted tables, beneath old beams and beside brick walls are chicken, steak, fish, soups, and salads. There's a long friendly bar at which to eat in somewhat speedier style, or sit over a drink while reading the *International Herald-Tribune.* **In de Schaduw van de**

**Kathedraal** *(Handschoenmarkt 17; ☎ 232.40.14; inexpensive)*, whose name means "in the shadow of the cathedral," sometimes is in the sun; either way, there's always a wonderful view from the base of the lace-like steeple. In addition to the terrace cafe, inside dining is in a pleasant room amid mirrors and banquettes. Not only the setting but the cuisine is traditional Antwerp, from mussels and eel prepared in several ways to meat and potatoes (frites, of course). A very different typical Antwerp atmosphere is found at **'t Hofke** *(Oude Koornmarkt 16; daily noon–1 a.m.; ☎ 233.86.06; inexpensive)*, a tiny lunchroom-tearoom-bistro tucked into the ancient Vlaeykensgang. At the few tables in the garden—open to the sky—along the alleyway, or the several inside; salads, quiches, and larger meals are served to the sound of classical music and a caged songbird. **De Groote Witte Arend** *(Reyndersstraat 18; daily 11 a.m.–1:30 a.m.; inexpensive)*, most suitable for outdoor weather, is found through an old courtyard just doors from the house of artist Jacob Jordaens (1593–1678) at Reyndersstraat 6. Salads, pasta of the day, lasagna, waterzooi, and sandwiches are brought out to the tables and benches in the courtyard that is draped with plants, studded with statuary, and lifted by the strains of classical music. Antwerpians often sit here over a drink on Monday nights in summer to hear the carillon concert from the nearby cathedral.

**De Foyer** *(Komedieplaats 18; Mon.–Fri. noon to midnight, Sat. and Sun. 11 a.m.–6 p.m.; ☎ 233.55.17; inexpensive)* is upstairs at the exquisite curve-fronted, just restored Bourla Theater. (A bell rings in the restaurant to announce the start of performances.) Occasional live concerts held in the restaurant's neoclassic room accompany the light fare (quiche, soups, sandwiches) and salad buffet bar. Close by, located in a house just past the pleasant *Botanic Garden*, and one street over from the *Mayer van den Bergh Museum*, is **Botanica** *(Leopoldstraat 24; daily 10 a.m.–11 p.m., Fri. and Sat. 1 a.m.; ☎ 225.10.04; inexpensive)*. The cozy 49-seat interior, from which there are views of the garden, has an eclectic decor with Japanese prints, Venetian glass chandeliers, and track lighting on the art work. There's a daily three-course menu and limited à la carte offerings.

Only a block from the Scheldt, with a great view of the handsome historic Vleeshuis, is **Jan Zonder Vrees** *(Krabbenstraat 2; daily 9 a.m.–2 a.m.; ☎ 232.90.80; inexpensive/moderate)*, located in four, former 400-year-old houses. Offerings at the outside tables, at the bar, or in the fashionably decorated restaurant under brick arches, run from snacks, soup and sandwiches to steak and daily specials. **De Gulden Kroon** cafe upstairs at Antwerp's restored Centraal Station is worth a stop at least for a cup of coffee in order to be able to sit down to enjoy the splendor of the surrounding gilt and yellow and white marble walls and elaborately carved high ceilings.

Whether one drinks a pint of pils or a "bowl" of specialty beer, spending time at an atmospheric pub with one or another of Belgium's hundreds of brands of beer is an Antwerp way of life. This most typical cafe in the city is where Antwerpians rendezvous to share stadhuis—the town hall is next to it—gossip or to start an evening's drinking. The oldest pub in the Low Countries is **Quinten Matsys** *(Morriaanstraat 17; closed Thurs.;*

☎ *225.01.70)*, dating from 1565. Also in existence since Antwerp's 16th century golden age is Pegrom (*Pegrimstraat 15; daily from 11 a.m.;* ☎ *234.08.09)*, which serves bar snacks and beer in marvelous brick-vaulted, candlelit cellars well beneath its handsome stepped-gabled facade. **In Den Engel** *(3 Grote Markt)* supposedly never closes its doors, and some say it hasn't since it opened them in 1579. This most typical cafe in the city is where Antwerpians rendezvous to share stadhuis—the town hall is next to it—gossip or to start an evening's drinking. Often regarded as the best beer cafe in town, serving some 350 kinds, is Kulminator (*Vleminckveld 32; open from 11 a.m.—1 a.m., from 8:15 p.m. Mon., from 5 p.m. Sat., closed Sun. and holidays;* ☎ *232.45.38)*. Many might end the evening at **'t elfde Gebod** (*Torfburg 10; open daily til all hours;* ☎ *232.36.11)*, an ivy-draped cafe beside the cathedral whose name means "the 11th Commandment," which Antwerpians interpret to be "Thou shalt enjoy life."

## ENTERTAINMENT AND EVENTS

A continuing result of Antwerp having been the 1993 Cultural Capital of Europe are the new impulses felt there in art, theater and opera. In Zuid (South) Antwerp, near the Royal Fine Arts Museum, new art galleries, studios in former riverfront warehouses, and the Modern and Photography museums have made the area trendy, bringing new cafes. As the unofficial capital of Flanders, Antwerp is home to several performing arts companies. The **Royal Flemish Opera**, the **Flemish Chamber Opera**, the **Royal Flanders Ballet**, and the **Royal Flemish Conservatory** provide a full program. The works of the **Royal Flemish Theater** head a theater bill that is the most extensive in Belgium, although most productions are in Flemish.

Year-round, hour-long concerts are played on the cathedral's 47-bell carillon at 11:30 p.m. Fridays. Additional weekly concerts are added May—September on Sundays at 3 p.m. The weekly Monday night **carillon concerts** in July and August at 9p.m. are a highlight for Antwerpians and visitors alike. Mid-August Antwerp celebrates summer with a week-long list of events, highlighted with the **Rubens Market** and **Ommegangpageant**. Other annual events include the July **Steen Festival**, the August **Middelheim Jazz Festival**, and the November **Antwerp Diamond Awards**. The multifaceted cultural events of the **Festival van Vlaanderen** (Festival of Flanders) are held each Sept./Oct. Check with the City Tourist Office about the location for the Sept.–May Fri. 12:30 p.m. hour-long **midday concerts**. **Early music** concerts are held from Oct.–March in the Grand Studio at the *Rubenhuis* and in the *Vleeshuis* (Butchers' Hall Museum).

There are several entertainment centers in Antwerp. The **Grote Markt/ Groenplaats** area is known for its cafe terraces. (Also refer to the end of "Where To Eat".) The so-called **high town** (along *Hoogstraat* or High Street, *Pelgrimstraat, Pieter Potstraat,* and surroundings) has some of the most interesting and cozy of Antwerp's supposedly 2500 cafes and bars; "brown" pubs, bistros, and jazz clubs can be found in this area. **De Keyserlei** is visited for its boulevard-cafes, taverns, and terraces, and the adjoining

neighborhood around Centraal Station has night clubs and cinemas. The
**Quartier Latin**, near the City Theater, has artists' cafes and bars.

## IN THE AREA

### Middelheim Open-Air Museum of Sculpture                       ★ ★

*Middelheimlaan 61, outside the Kleine Ringweg/Small Ring Road, south
of center city in lovely Nachtegalen Park; daily from 10 a.m., closing hours
range from 9 p.m. in June and July to 5 p.m. in winter;* ☎ *827.15.34.* Art
in Antwerp is not limited to Old Masters. At the Middelheim Open
Air Museum of Sculpture, founded in 1950, almost every important
sculptor from **Rodin** to the present is represented by major works;
prominent among the Belgian sculptors is **Rik Wouters** (1882–1916)
and **Constantin Meunier** (1831–1905). In the early years of the
museum's development, many foreign specialists and sculptors—among them Russian-born **Ossip Zadkine** (1890–1976), whose
works are well-represented in the Benelux, and England's **Henry
Moore**—served as consultants to the museum. The collection currently consists of more than 300 works, which are exhibited in a natural outdoor park setting, to be enjoyed in the changing seasons and
weather. The **Middelheim Biennials** of modern sculpture (held during
odd-numbered years) are highly regarded both in Belgium and
abroad.

# BRUGES

## *GUIDELINES FOR BRUGES*

### SIGHTS

Bruges (*Brugge*), having become impressively important in commerce and, consequently, in culture between the 12th and 15th centuries, was then all but forgotten as circumstances combined to turn
the tide of its fortune. As a result, Bruges (population 35,000 within
the historic double encirclement of **canals**) is delightfully stuck visually and atmospherically back in medieval days; many consider it the
*best preserved medieval city in Europe*, though it's far too actively
engaged in the present to be considered a "museum town." Bruges
is small enough for you to manage all major sights on foot, but so
densely packed with enchanting places that you'd never get bored
wandering aimlessly. Bruges' **architecture** may be even more outstanding than its **art**, which features *Flemish "primitive" painters* **van
der Weyden**, **van Eyck**, **Memling**, **van der Goes**, and **Gerard David**,
often displayed in historic settings. There are also a Michelangelo
sculpture, and exhibits of the traditional town crafts of lace and tapestry. Sounds spill out over the town during the frequent concerts
played on the town carillon, high in Belgium's most beautiful **belfry**,
but reassuring silence can be found in the peaceful precincts of the

**Begijnhof**. A night walk around the intimate town, turned to magic by the tasteful illumination of monument buildings, ivy-covered brick facades, canals, and humpback bridges, is mesmerizing, and each season has special appeal. The prime season for **night illuminations** is May 1 to September 30, but many buildings now are lit year-round.

## GETTING AROUND

Many travelers arrive in Bruges by train; the station, just outside the old city to the south, near the **Minnewater** and **Begijnhof**, is about 1 mi./1.5 km. from the **Markt**, considered the center of Bruges. Close to the Markt is the **Burg**, where the **tourist office** is located. In this town of lace shops, you'll want to lace up walking shoes to enjoy the cobbled streets in comfort. Supplemental ways to see the town begin with half-hour **canal cruises** (there are several central departure piers) with multilingual commentary; the open boats afford wonderful photographic angles, and umbrellas when it's misting. A **rental bike**, though a bit bumpy on the cobbles, is a great way to see the outer edges of Bruges. **Horse-drawn carriages** congregate on the Burg and by the Begijnhof if you want to see the town to the sound of horse hooves clopping on cobblestones. A far more modern means is by **minibus tour** (English commentary on headsets) with **Sightseeing Line** (departure point in the center of the Markt). Taxi ranks are found at the station and on the Markt, and otherwise should be ordered by telephone; starting fare 80 BF, tip included. There's a public bus system (several routes have stops on the Markt), but it's unlikely you'll use it within old Bruges itself. To see the Flemish countryside beyond the borders of Bruges, take a daytrip (9:00 a.m.–4:00 p.m., Mon., Weds. or Fri., April–October) on a 22-passenger bus with **Quasimodo** tours (*Poortersstraat 47, Brugge;* ☎ *370.470; FAX 374.960*).

## SHOPPING

As the capital of West Flanders province, Bruges is well-stocked with department stores (INNO is a good choice), boutiques (the Theaterboutieks on Vlamingstraat is a recent addition), gift and art galleries. The visitor-season, canalside, weekend **outdoor antiques market** on the Dijver is popular. In Breidelstraat, which runs from the Markt to the Burg, and on the pedestrian route to the Begijnhof, **lace** and **chocolate shops** abound.

## ENTERTAINMENT AND EVENTS

The periodically published *Agenda Brugge* (free from the tourist office) gives a multilingual listing of scheduled programs and events. The scope of Bruges' entertainment options run from several *carillon concerts* weekly, and musical events staged on canals and in churches, to elaborately costumed historic pageant processions.

## WHERE TO STAY

Bruges, with 100-plus hotels, offers more rooms than any other city in Belgium except Brussels; most are in the historic town, at prices lower in all categories than those in Brussels. Reservations at any time of year are recommended, since Bruges is a highly popular place year-round for Friday and Saturday night weekend getaways for Europeans; particularly heavily booked are the three- and four-day Europe-wide spring holiday weekends at Easter and Whitsun. Bruges is also busy with visitors in July and August, but many come just for the day—a great mistake. Once the bus-borne hordes of day-trippers have left, Bruges generally has space available for overnighters midweek. If you haven't booked ahead, the tourist office offers an accommodations service; although the Tourist Office will work with you until they have found accommodations, these could be well outside of the historic center, and even of Bruges itself, if you arrive without reservations on a holiday weekend.

## WHERE TO EAT

Bruges also has more restaurants than anywhere in Belgium other than Brussels. Fine food and pleasurable settings are found in all price ranges. The traditional Flemish, fresh seafood, and French *haute cuisine* choices will satisfy most palettes. If you want something a little lighter, you're in the right place: the English word "snack" was derived from the Dutch/Flemish *snakken* ("to yearn for"), and Bruges has plenty of informal eateries that serve both indoors and outside. Bruges is chock full of **chocolate shops**, one of which, **Sukerbuyc** (*Katelijnestraat 5;* ☎ *33.08.87*), offers not only 65 kinds of handmade chocolates including *pralines* (filled chocolates), but from May–December makes *marzipan* in many fancy and unexpected forms. The delicate sweet biscuits called *dentelles de Brugge* are an edible version of local lace.

## ARRIVING

**Train** is the choice of many travelers to Bruges; the direct twice-hourly service from Brussels takes just over an hour. If you arrive by **ferry** from England at Ostend, the first stop on the **boat train**

for Brussels (or beyond) is Bruges. Historic Bruges, which has lots of winding one-way streets, was not made for cars. Should you drive, plan to park and forget it until you leave. However, when "disposing" of the car, be sure to do so correctly so you won't be towed; there's an underground garage at **'t Zand**, inside the old city via **Koning Albertlaan** from the station, which is close to major roads, or park on Bruges' ring road.

## IN THE AREA

Some 4 mi./7 km. from Bruges, along a canal lined with wind-bent poplars on polderland so flat that it takes the fertile farm fields forever to meet the huge cloud-besprinkled sky at the horizon, is Damme. You can travel by boat, bike, foot, or car to Damme, a hamlet noted for its restaurants, but whose few fine buildings are vestiges of the days centuries ago when it served as Bruges' outer port on the ill-fated Zwin and had a population of 60,000.

## TRAVEL TIPS

Bruges is one of Europe's most exceptional destinations—even in the Middle Ages, everyone who could came to see it. Bruges is only a little over an hour from Brussels by train, easy to do on an individual or commercial motorcoach day trip. But just because that's the way the vast majority of travelers see Bruges doesn't mean that you should. And that truism, evident during the day, becomes inescapable in the evening when, no matter what the season, you have the city largely to yourself. It's when the crowds have gone that Bruges will bewitch you with its medieval mystique. After dark, the reflections in its canals will capture you in a reflective mood, and almost anywhere it's safe to slow from a stride to a stroll, you'll want to stop and stare.

## *BRUGES IN CONTEXT*

In 1896, English writer Arnold Bennett noted in his *Journal*: "The difference between Bruges and other cities is that in the latter you look around for the picturesque, while in Bruges, assailed on every side by the picturesque, you look curiously for the unpicturesque, and don't find it easily." The foresight of Bruges' city fathers in the century since must be lauded; by 1904, they had established a *Commission of Urban Beauty* and imposed strictures to preserve Bruges' Middle Age aspect (even in the Middle Ages, Bruges was considered one of Europe's most beautiful cities). Although in the 20th century commercialism has reached its tentacles into many of the most remote corners tourists can travel to, Bennett's words about Bruges remain remarkably true.

Bruges is not undiscovered as a place of touristic charm. In the late 19th century, the town awoke from a nearly four-century Sleeping Beauty scenario during which relative poverty had preserved its unique architectural heritage. In the century since, Bruges has grown in popularity to the point where it has more pleasure visitors than any other place in Belgium. Paid holidays for workers (a result of the Industrial Revolution) and improved public transportation (particularly the train) in the 19th century woke Bruges to its tourism possibilities. Turn-of-the-century revitalization came, as the government made plans for the long ago silted-up city to have a port again by developing **Zeebrugge** (meaning "Bruges-on-the-sea") and constructing a cross-country canal from the town.

Bruges often is categorized as the "Venice of the North," the canals for which each is noted inviting inevitable comparison. *Bruggelingen* (residents of Bruges) quite reasonably respond that it would make just as much sense to call Venice the *"Bruges of the South."* In fact, the cities have much more in common than watery ways and byways. At their respective apexes of power, Bruges with an earlier start, but their successful 13th to early 15th centuries overlapping, both independent, wealthy city-states exerted far-reaching commercial and artistic influences. Bruges traded wool, fine cloth, lace, and tapestries to Italy in exchange for commissioned paintings. Venetians maintained important consular and trade offices in Bruges, and also commissioned paintings from the Flemish "primitive" masters. Eventually, both cities suffered change from circumstances beyond their control.

To speak again of canals—in the 1970s, when Bruges' inner city waterways had become offensive-smelling due to 20th-century industrial waste, a pipeline was constructed to bring fresh lake water into the dredged and cleaned canals, and the waste water from industry (all of which operates beyond the borders of historic Bruges) was diverted away. Today, the bad odor in Bruges' canals is gone, a situation that can't be said of Venice.

The history of Bruges began in the 9th century, when **Boudewijn** (also known as **Baldwin Iron Arm**) boldly eloped with the daughter of French King Charles the Bald. Though less than pleased, in order to provide a united family front against invading Vikings, Charles gifted his impetuous new son-in-law with the misty lands in the extreme north of Gaul (modern Flanders). To withstand the frequent Viking invasions, Boudewijn built a solid fort on the site of today's **Burg**. Soon a village arose around it, taking its name from the *brug* (bridge) he built over the Reie river. From these beginnings in Bruges, Boudewijn went on to become founder of the powerful dynasty of the counts of Flanders. (See also "Ghent in Context.") At about the time of Boudewijn, Bruges' future was for the short term, favorably influenced by a great North Sea inundation of the coast that greatly deepened an arm of water, the **Zwin**, that reached inland to the Reie.

By the 10th century, Norsemen were no longer a nuisance, and Bruges was becoming a significant business center. Old annals record the first annual trade fair—it would become the most important in Flanders—in 958, for which merchants arrived in vessels in Bruges' harbor, located where the **Minnewater** is today. During the 11th century, Bruges laid the foundations for its future commercial greatness, fortifying itself physically, and in 1089 becoming the administrative capital of the county of Flanders. Churches, hospitals, and monasteries began to be built.

Bruges established important economic relations with Germany, England, France, the Baltic, Russia, and the East, and by the 12th century, had become one of Europe's most prosperous market towns. The cloth trade was becoming highly important—also in the fellow Flemish cities of Ypres and Ghent—and the import and storage of English wool was making a fortune for Fleming nobility and merchants.

On March 2, 1127, Count of Flanders Charles the Good, was assassinated in the Burg's **St. Donatian church** (built in the 9th century, consecrated as a cathedral in 1559, and demolished by post-Revolution, antireligious French fanatics in 1799). A heated dispute over Charles' successor arose, and Bruges' wealthy shopkeepers took advantage of the situation to claim the right to participate in governing the flourishing city. From that time, the *meliores civium* ("the best citizens") in addition to the nobility, could participate, but the manual workers, weavers, and other crafts people were still excluded from the power process.

While Bruges continued to burgeon in business, by late in the 12th century, the **Zwin**, which tidal forces had earlier favored by deepening, began to be **threatened with silt**, and it was dredged between 1175 and 1200. In 1180, Count of Flanders Philip of Alsace granted town rights to the nearby (4 mi/7 km) fishing village of **Damme** on the Zwin. Damme, its harbor created by embanking the Reie in Bruges and damming it (hence its name) where it joined the Zwin, henceforth served as the port for Bruges. The **Spielgelrei**, today dead-ended at Jan van Eyckplein, once brought the waters of the

Reie from Damme right to Bruges' Markt; there, barges loaded with wool from ships too large to sail inland beyond Damme unloaded it into the Cloth Hall.

An indication of the size of the new port in Damme (see "In the Area") comes from the fact that, in 1213, Philip II of France used it for his fleet (said to number some 1000 vessels) while he pillaged the town during his war against Count Ferdinand of Flanders. However, Ferdinand's English allies burned most of Philip's fleet as it lay in Damme harbor (thereby creating a new need to dredge). Damme recovered, growing in a few years from virtual nonexistence to a population of 10,000, and gaining its own maritime law (*Zeerecht van Damme*) and valuable staple rights on wine and herring.

The early 13th century saw many foreign merchants making themselves at home in Bruges. Nobles built mansions and merchants built town houses. To proclaim its fame, fortune, and freedom, Bruges constructed an exceptionally fine **belfry**. (The first edition of the edifice was built in the early 13th century, destroyed by fire in 1280, and reconstructed in 1282–1296.) Bruges founded the **Flemish Hanseatic League of London**, through which it practically monopolized trade with England, and whose wool was vital for the Flemish cloth workers. Bruges also obtained a *kontor* from the *Teutonic Hanseatic League* and was a member of the *Hanseatic League of the Seventeen Cities*, associations which protected members' commercial links. The protection the Bruges-Hansa tie implied led many countries to set up substantial trade missions in the city. Bruges became the transit warehouse for Hansa members from the Baltic to Italy and overflowed with imports: carpets from the East, furs from Russia, velvet from Italy, metals from Poland, exotic fruits from Egypt, and spices from Arabia. The Italian cities of Venice, Florence, Genoa, and Pisa built trade houses in Bruges, which was mentioned by Italian poet **Dante Alighieri** (1265–1321) in *The Divine Comedy's Inferno*.

The growing opulence of Bruges' merchants, who monopolized all trade, contrasted sharply with the poverty of the tens of thousands of exploited workers in the city's 52 guilds. In 1280, the "blue nails" (as textile workers were known due to their dye-stained nails) led a revolt against the more privileged citizens. During this period, Count of Flanders Guy de Dampierre, who had been instrumental in developing Bruges' trade fairs, and sought to maintain Flanders' autonomy from the French crown, met strong resistance from Philip the Fair. Eventually, Philip found an excuse to imprison the rebellious count in Paris, and annexed Flanders. Burgundian **Philip the**

**Fair** came in triumph from France in 1301 to visit Bruges, then Europe's most important commercial city. Most Bruggelingen turned out to see Philip, many so luxuriously turned out that his queen, Joanne of Navarre, is said to have reacted to the sumptuous display of dress and jewels by pronouncing, "I thought that I alone was queen, but I see hundreds around me here."

Under the Burgundians, the unequally favored citizens of Bruges soon squared off into camps: the patricians, who preferred French dominion (*Leliaerts*); against the discontented common people (*Klauwaerts*), who took their name "lion's paw" from the Lion of Flanders, the count's emblem. Klauwaert **Pieter de Coninck**, a weaver, became leader of their rebellion. Philip's appointee as governor of Flanders, his uncle Jacques de Chantillon, treated the guildsmen of Bruges with such oppressive intolerance that the citizens, under Pieter de Coninck and **Jan Breydel**, revolted against Bruges' French garrison within a year. At dawn on May 18, 1302, as the bells rang for matins (the incident became known as the **Bruges Matins**), they attacked some 2000 French soldiers and patricians who had collaborated with the French. None of these could, when it was demanded of them, properly pronounce the gutteral sounds of the Flemish words *schilt ende vriendt* (shield and friend). All were slaughtered on the spot.

Six weeks later, the two Bruges guild leaders (remembered in a statue on the Markt) led Flemish burghers against French nobility, achieving victory at the *Battle of the Golden Spurs* at Kortrijk. (See "An Historical Perspective" under "Belgium.") This battle broke the control of trade by the rich merchants and patricians, and put more power in the hands of the guilds.

In 1369, the last count of Flanders, Louis de Malle, gave his only daughter's hand in marriage to duke of Burgundy, **Philip the Bold**, and the couple made Bruges their favorite residence in the Netherlands. In 1376, work began on a Stadhuis (town hall) worthy of Bruges (today, the oldest in Belgium and one of the most splendid). Philip fostered the Flemish school of painting, giving commissions to many members of the *Guild of St. Luke*. Burgundian Bruges was the meeting place of Europe's North and South, where intellectual ideas intermingled amid the easy exchange of material goods. These, unloaded on the quays at Damme, where the seagoing ships anchored, and transferred to barges, made a continuous procession up the canalized Reie to Bruges. Some 150 ships entered the Bruges/ Damme ports in a single day, and the population, which included the consuls from 20 nations and city-states, reached 150,000. But even as Bruges was at its best, Damme, too, was becoming afflicted by sand, the insidious silting preventing the deepest-draft ships from sailing to it up the Zwin, from the North Sea.

In 1429, Isabella of Portugal, whose portrait was painted by Jan van Eyck, sailed into Damme to become the bride of **Philip the Good**. The week-long wedding celebrations were the talk of the west. That same year in Bruges, Philip founded the famed *Order of the Golden Fleece*, both to highlight the splendor and stature of his House of Burgundy and in recognition of the skill of Flemish wool weavers. The Order's insignia, a limp lamb's fleece worn on a substantial gold chain around the neck of its knights—as seen in period portraits such as that of "Anthony of Burgundy" by **Rogier van der Weyden** in Brussels' **Museum of Ancient Art**—took its name from the ancient Greek myth of Jason and his Argonauts' search for the Golden Fleece. Membership in the medieval order of chivalry (limited to 24) was a great honor. Members were chosen by Philip and subsequent rulers, who would congregate the knights for consultation at chapter meetings. It was an honor, too, to be the venue for such a meeting: the carved choir stalls in Bruges' St. Saviour's Cathedral were commissioned in 1430 for the occasion of the founding of the Order, which returned there in 1478 for the Thirteenth Chapter meeting. In 1464, Philip named Bruges the meeting place for the first *States General of the Netherlands*.

Bruges' cultural high point came with the long reign of Philip the Good (1419–1467). Flemish art flowered and music played an important part in Bruges life, as shown by the numerous instruments that appear in Flemish paintings. Memling painted *The Last Judgment* as a commission for Tomasso Portunari, who was the director of the Medicis' bank at Bruges, and the same connection may have been the route by which **Hugo van der Goes's** *Nativity* found its way to Florence's Uffizzi Gallery.

By the 15th century, Bruges was a central clearing house for all European trade, as well as the warehouse for the Hanseatic League. At Vlamingstraat 35—today a business address not far from the *Markt*—in a 13th-century family mansion **Huis ter Beurze**, the entreprenurial Brugean innkeeper Joris van der Beurze served the merchants and bankers who met, dined, drank, and negotiated business deals there; an assortment of business services that amounted to the world's first currency and commodities exchange. His name *Beurze*, in the forms *bourse* and *beurs*, still is in use for stock exchanges worldwide. For his 15th-century clients, van der Beurze arranged money exchanges, since each of the states and cities that traded in

Bruges coined its own currency; he also coordinated weights, since many dominions also maintained their own measurement systems. Eventually, van der Beurze began a form of *letters of credit* which, given the weight of the all-metal money in those days, was not only safer from robbery but much easier to manage. On the former site of Huis ter Buerze is a modern bank where you can conduct your financial business.

By Philip's death in 1467, Bruges fortunes had begun to decline, though the pomp and circumstance of civic life under the dukes of Burgundy concealed its fading glory. In 1468, Damme hosted the wedding, and Bruges the month-long celebrations after, for **Charles the Bold** and the English princess **Margaret of York**, sister of English King Edward IV. By then, silting on the Zwin made even Damme unreachable by water, and arriving from England, Margaret could sail only as far as Sluis in Holland, where the port for Damme and Bruges had been moved. Nevertheless, the wedding was a grandiose occasion; the knights of the Golden Fleece gathering for a tournament which they called the **Pageant of the Golden Tree** (recreated every five years in Bruges, next in 1996). But two, too-short Burgundian reigns (Charles the Bold died in battle at Nancy in 1477, and his daughter and heir, Mary of Burgundy, only five years later from a fall incurred while falconing on horseback—both have grand mausoleums in Bruges' Onze Lieve Vrouwekerk) led to the transfer of Flemish power from the French Burgundians to the Austrian Hapsburgs through Mary's husband **Archduke Maximilian**.

Hapsburg rule was not a success for Bruges. In 1488, for a period of 11 weeks, Bruggelingen held Maximilian prisoner at the **Craenenburg** (corner of *Markt* and *Sint-Amandsstraat*). The extreme, and ultimately unwise, action was in response to what they considered unjustified infringements upon their freedom (the garrisoning of German soldiers, etc). Having thrown Maximilian in jail to stress how strongly they felt, the citizens also summarily tried and condemned to death the archduke's local right-hand counsellor, **Pieter Lanchals**, whose execution Maximilian was made to witness. A popular local story is that Maximilian, finally released from jail on the basis of promises (later largely unkept), ordered Bruggelingen to forever keep swans on their canals in remembrance of Lanchals, whose name is derived from *lange hals* meaning "long neck" and whose coat of arms bore a swan. Lanchals is buried in a chapel in Onze Lieve Vrouwekerk. Though swans (with a B for Bruges and the year of birth marked on their beaks) remain plentiful to this day, the Maximilian incident proved to be Bruges' swan song. The uprising against him had caused political instability, a serious detriment to trade; many foreign merchants, and Maximilian himself made a permanent move to Antwerp.

The Zwin, continuing to sink under sand, most certainly was a deciding factor in the death blow to Bruges, but there were others. Bruges, among other places in Flanders, had practiced overly restrictive commercial policies in the cloth industry, its merchants and guild members refusing to handle any cloth made by competitive weavers (particularly those in England). As the English industry grew and the country kept more of its own wool, the lack of the raw material led to ruin throughout the Flemish cloth industry. Many out of work Flemish weavers left for England to find new jobs.

Maximilian's grandson, Charles V, made a triumphant entry into Bruges in 1515, the year he became ruler of the Netherlands at the age of 15. But any hopes Bruggelingen had that Charles could change their downhill course ended that year when he selected Brussels as his principal residence. When Bruges perceived the full threat to her very existence, it was too late. Native son **Lancelot Blondeel** (1496–1561), primarily a painter, but also a Renaissance man with an interest in the sciences was called in by municipal officers to plan a canal to give Bruges renewed access to the sea. Blondeel threw himself into the task and eventually proposed a massive project. But such was the extent of work required that it was not implemented.

Religious struggles of the second half of the 16th century completed the process of ruin for Bruges as a commercial center. But, after Iconoclasts had pillaged, killed priests, and disfigured sacred statues, with the coming of the *Counter-Reformation* in Flanders, Bruges became a safe haven for Roman Catholic nuns and priests, many of whose institutions survive today. Wealthy burghers built *godshuizen* (almshouses) for the increasingly impoverished city's poor. Business improved somewhat in the 17th century, and a number of houses date from that period. But, basically, Bruges became a backwater.

Finally, in 1811, **Napoleon Bonaparte** employed Spanish prisoners-of-war to dig a canal between Bruges and the Scheldt—for his own purposes. He wanted to connect Bruges, via Damme, with Breskens in Holland on the Westerscheldt estuary so that his ships could sail from Antwerp to Dunkirk without having to use the North Sea, thereby avoiding the English coast—and the English Navy. But Napoleon's canal plan was interrupted by other events in 1814 and 1815. And the Industrial Revolution continued to bypass Bruges.

Between 1895–1907 the Belgian government under Leopold II built—very much along the lines of Lancelot Blondeel's 16th-century proposal—the **Boudewijn Kanaal** (230 ft/70 m wide, 26 ft/8 m deep, and 6.5 mi/10 km long) to a place on the coast that was named **Zeebrugge**. Subsequent development of the port provided a fishing harbor, an inner harbor, and an outer harbor with 245 acres of water sheltered by a crescent-shaped *mole* or jetty (with *promenade*) that reaches more than 1.5 mi/2.5 km into the North Sea. The once-open mouth of the Zwin is today but a saltwater marsh nature reserve.

Five centuries after its fall from greater glory, though the Zeebrugge port is important for regional business, tourism has placed Bruges back on the map. But Bruges is again playing a part in the history of Europe, through its *College of Europe*, founded in 1949. Today the multilingual international students of the prestigious postgraduate institution (located on the Dijver), well-grounded in cultural and scientific studies of contemporary Europe, are much in demand and serving in positions of importance as the integration process towards a single European marketplace continues.

## GUIDEPOSTS

**Telephone Code 050**

**Tourist Information (Dienst voor Toerisme)** • Burg 11, ☎ *44.86.86*, FAX *44.86.00*. Mon.–Fri., April-Sept. 9:30 a.m.–6:30 p.m.; Sat., Sun., holidays 10 a.m.-noon and 2–6:30 p.m.; Oct.–Mar., Mon.–Fri. 9:30 a.m.–5 p.m., Sat. 9:30 a.m.–noon, 2–5 p.m., closed Sun., holidays; hotel booking assistance. Guided city walking tours daily July–Aug. 3 p.m.; meeting point: tourist office.

**Rail Station** • office open daily 6:30 a.m.–10:30 p.m., ☎ *38.23.82 or 38.24.06*.

**Bus** • daily 6 a.m.–9 p.m. ☎ *(078) 11.36.63*.

**Taxis** • Taxi ranks at Station and Markt; to book ☎ *33.44.44* and *38.46.60*.

**Post Office** • Markt 5, ☎ *33.14.11*.

**Police** • Hauwerstraat 7, ☎ *44.88.44*.

**Emergency** • ☎ *100*; weekend doctors on duty (Fri. 8 p.m.–Mon. 8 a.m.) ☎ *81.38.99*.

**Rental Bikes** • Railway station: ☎ *38.58.71*; 't Koffieboontje, Hallestraat 14 (by Belfry), ☎ *33.80.27*; Eric Popelier, Hallestraat 14, ☎ *34.41.96*; bicycle tour brochure in English available.

**Canal Cruises** • Five departure points, several on Dijver and Rozenhoed-kaai; Mar.–Nov. 10 a.m.–6 p.m., Dec., Feb. weekends, holidays, closed Jan.; duration 1/2 hour.

**Horse-drawn Cab Tours** • Mar.–Nov. on Burg, 10 a.m.–8 p.m. **Sightseeing Line**, bus stop in center of Markt, schedule, reser. ☎ *31.13.55.*

**Cruises to Damme** • Departure point: Noorweegse Kaai 31, Dampoort (Bruges City bus 4); April–Sept., departures on the hour 10 a.m.–6 p.m. Info from Damme Tourist Office, ☎ *(050) 35.33.19.*

## WHAT TO SEE AND DO

What you most want to do in Bruges is look at the delightful details of this lovely little city in Gothic garb: the texture of century-smoothed cobblestones, the mellow colors of aged building bricks, lacy wrought-iron lanterns, lace curtains at the windows, and flower boxes strung along the canals. Shadings in the changeable sky and reflected creations in canal waters produce natural "special effects" that will leave you looking wonderingly (and wishing, perhaps, for the skill to capture them on film). As rewarding as the insides of Bruges' museums are—the tourist office sells combination tickets to four major museums (BF 350), a savings for visitors who intend to see them all—it may be that by stopping on bridges to gaze down a canal, you'll discover an image of Bruges that lingers in your mind. So *don't,* however little time you have in this atmospheric city, spend it all indoors—*whatever* the weather.

### Markt ★★

This has been the commercial heart of Bruges for more than a millenium (when the merchants moved the short distance from the town's fortified Burg to set up a permanent main market square). It's unusual for a Markt in the Benelux not to be home to the stadhuis/town hall; Bruges' Markt used to be, but the building burned, and an all important Cloth Hall was built on the site (where the ornate 19th-century West Flanders Provincial House now stands). A new Stadhuis was built on the **Burg**. (See "Burg".) The dominating monument on the Markt is the belfry. Around the square are the gabled facades of guildhouses and former dwellings of dukes and foreign dignitaries, many of which at street-level now support terrace cafes that burst with imbibers in pleasant weather. In the center of the Markt is a statue (1887) of **Pieter De Coninck** and **Jan Breydel**, leaders in the *Bruges Matins* and 1302 *Battle of the Golden Spurs.* To understand the full impact of the activity on the Markt during Bruges' bustling 13th and 14th centuries, keep in mind that the **Reie**, the waterway that connected Bruges to Damme and the sea, came right up to the east side of the Markt, to and under the Cloth Hall for all-weather unloading.

### Belfort/Belfry ★★★

*Entrance in courtyard of Halle; visits to tower mean climbing 366 mostly stone steps, no elevator; April–Sept., daily 9:30 a.m.–5 p.m.; Oct.–Mar., 9:30 a.m.–12:30 p.m., and 1:30–5 p.m.; English-language guide and printed booklet about tower.* The Bruges belfry (265 ft/88 m) is acknowledged to be Belgium's most beautiful. "Thrice consumed and thrice rebuilded," (noted no less a poet than Longfellow [1807–1882] in *The Belfry of Bruges*), its present post-fires square base, which rises from the roof of the Halle (market hall), dates from 1296. Used as a storage depot and market, the front dates from 1248, the sides from 1363–1365, and the back, 1561–1566. The graceful octagonal top of the belfry was added in 1487. The ★★ view from its top, well worth the effort of those up to the climb, inspired Longfellow, who climbed it one winter morning and, gazing down, imagined "pageants splendid that adorned those days of old" and "knights who bore the Golden Fleece, Lombard and Venetian merchants, with deep laden argosies" traversing the Markt. At the 55th step is the former treasure chamber, normally on view only through a wrought-iron railing dating from 1300. A typical early example of this Flemish art form, the railing has six locks. In chests in wall niches were stored the town's precious *Charter of Liberty* and *Great Seal*, both destroyed in the belfry's fire of 1280. (The written evidence of rights awarded to citizens was important; since the count of Flanders at the time was annoyed by the amount of freedom the Bruggelingen had gained, it has always been suspected that he was responsible for the fire.) At the belfry's 333rd step you come to the automatic mechanism for the tower clock. At the 352nd is the chamber with the carillon keyboard, above which, behind the uppermost arched openings, are Bruges' 47 mighty bronze carillon bells.

The carillon is attended to artistically and maintained mechanically by the present holder of the full-time paid position of *stadbeiaardier/* town carillonneur, the amiable **Aimé Lombaert**, whose talents have taken him on carillon-playing tours in the U.S., Canada, and Europe. (Perhaps surprisingly, standing by the bells when the carillon is being played won't drive you mad or make you deaf, but you actually hear the music better from below). From above, there's a splendid view across Bruges and the Flemish countryside. Blind visitors to Bruges can get an appreciation of the building from the belfry "in braille" in front of the Halle; the "hands on" model of the Belfort, also has a description of the tower in braille.

**Burg**

This, the most handsome square in Bruges, is the site of the city's founding, where Boudewijn, first count of Flanders, put up a fortified building in the 9th century. It should be any traveler's first stop, too, for the well-supplied and helpful tourist information office is located here. On the site of the present Holiday Inn Crown Plaza once sat the 9th-century St. Donatian church, broken down brick by brick by religion-hating French Revolutionary zealots in 1799. A smaller version of the statue of Jan van Eyck that stands on the nearby Jan van Eyckplein was placed here to commemorate the fact that the artist had been buried in St. Donatian. Remnants of the foundations of the church were discovered in 1955, and have been preserved in a cellar "museum" in the hotel. Several important stops face the square.

### Stadhuis ★★★
*April–Sept., daily 9:30 a.m.–5 p.m., rest of year, closes noon–2 p.m.*
Bruges' Late Gothic-style Stadhuis was begun in 1376, making it the oldest in Belgium and one of the finest. The ornate ★★facade, which took 45 years to finish, is today once again studded with statues; most of its 48 niches only recently refilled with copies of the figures of counts and countesses of Flanders that were removed and ruined by the French in their devastation of the city in 1799. The entrance hall is decorated with colorful guild banners and historic paintings. Also on display are fine antique maps of Bruges, which show that the inner city has so little changed in 400 years that you can still tour from a copy. Be sure to head upstairs to the spacious ★★**Gothic Hall**, with its superb wooden rib-arched and vaulted, vividly painted ceiling (1385–1402), an altogether worthy setting for the first council of the *States General of the Netherlands*, seated here by Burgundian Philip the Good in 1464. Town authorities met here for centuries, but now the space is reserved for civil wedding ceremonies and official receptions. The circular vault keys in the ceiling show scenes from the New Testament and ones depicting the 12 months and 4 natural elements. Restoration of the room at the turn of the century resulted in the addition of romantic wall paintings by the Flemish artists **Albert and Juliaan de Vriendt** of events in the history of Bruges. Among these are the triumphal return of Bruges warriors from the Battle of the Golden Spurs in 1302, the founding of the Order of the Golden Fleece by Philip the Good in 1429, Bruges renewing its privileges in the Hanseatic League, and the opening of the new Zwin canal in 1404.

### Groeninge Museum ★★★
*Dijver 12; April–Sept. daily 9:30 a.m.–5 p.m., Oct.–Mar. 9:30 a.m.–12:30 p.m. and 2-5 p.m., closed Tues.; booklet with English translations of the captions by the museum's works of art.* Even though they broke new artistic ground as a group, the leading Flemish "primitive" painters can be appreciated for their individual qualities: **Jan van Eyck** (1390–1441) for realism; **Rogier van der Weyden** (1399–1464) for passionate emotion; **Hans Memling** (circa 1435–1494) for delicacy and purity; and Hugo van der Goes (1440–1482) for striking dramatism; a trait duplicated by his student **Gerard David** (1460–1523), the last great master of the *Bruges School*. Its primitive paintings of the Bruges School are the museum's greatest treasure, although the pleasantly human-scale Groeninge collection shows the whole evolution of Flemish art, from the surrealism of **Hieronymous Bosch** (1450–1516) to that of **James Ensor** (1860–1949).

Among the more outstanding paintings are van Eyck's *Madonna with St. Donatian and St. George* with its superb portrait of the donor **Canon**

**van der Paele**, and *Portrait of Margarete van Eyck*, the artist's wife painted in his most realistic mode; Memling's Triptych with donors Willem Moreel, burgomaster of Bruges and his wife; van der Goes' *Death of a Virgin*; David's *Triptych* including the *Baptism of Christ*; and *Last Judgment* by the intensely individual master Hieronymous Bosch, whose contemporaries could make nothing of his spirit and technique, although a century later Breugel seemed able to. The horrifying painting *The Judgment of Cambyses* (1498) by **Gerard David** of a man being skinned alive uses the story from Herodotus of the skin of a corrupt judge being stripped from him and used to make a cushion for the chair on which his son would sit as successor. This painting is said to have been commissioned by the magistrates of Bruges in atonement for the town's execution of Maximilian's adviser *Pieter Lanchals* (see "Bruges in Context") to hang (as a copy does today) in the **Brugse Vrije**, Alderman's room of the court of justice.

At the Groeninge, you'll see many works attributed with the word "*naar*" (meaning "after" or "in the school of"), some of which may be copies (usually contemporary and often excellent—recall Pieter Bruegel the Younger's many copies of his father's works, some of the originals of which no longer exist). The number of works noted "naar" also is an indication, in a world without other methods of artistic reproduction—no art posters—of the popularity of the work in its day. The number of anonymous works ("*anoniem*") is a sign of the substantial artistic activity in Bruges during the 14th-16th-century period, during which the painter's names of some unsigned works were lost.

### Gruuthuse Museum                                    ★ ★ ★

*Dijver 17; April–Sept. daily 9:30 a.m.–5 p.m., Oct.–March closed between 12:30–2 p.m. and Tues.; numbered room plan.* This was the luxurious mansion of the **Heren van Gruuthuse** (Lords of Gruuthouse), whose fortune came from their right to impose a tax on the import of "gruut," a mixture of dried plants and flowers used by brewers to flavor beer. **Louis de Gruuthuse** (whose representation is above the door) was a counsellor to Philip the Good and Charles the Bold. Decorative art lovers will rarely have had such a wonderful place to wander around, with room after numbered room (19 in all) of tapestries, porcelain, paintings, brass, musical instruments, and antique furniture, such as the large lovely carved wooden cabinets that were built for rooms of this scale and ceiling height—and need them to be appreciated. All these are displayed in a fine 15th-century noble family's architecturally homogeneous ivy-covered mansion that alone is worth the walk inside. Among the built-in treasures are massive carved stone chimneypieces and tiled hearths, carved ceilings and moldings, and curious corners such as the one found through Room 16. It's a small ★ ★ oratory built into the wall of Onze Lieve Vrouwekerk (see below) directly overlooking the choir of the church. While the Gruut family obviously used the room as a means of "attending" mass without leaving home (a different variation of a private chapel), we spectators get a strange feeling looking down on the tourists in the church. Also worth seeking out are the 16th-century Flemish kitchen (Room 3). In the height of the house, visit the outside balcony (through Room 21) for views, dominated by the tower of Onze Lieve Vrouw, of the ★★attractive garden, canal, and St. Bonifacebrug behind the house. (The garden extends to the *Groeninge Museum* and displays a recent sculpture, *The Four Horsemen of the Apocalypse* by **Rik Poot**.) One of the many oddities in the multifaceted Gruuthuse collection is an 18th-century guillotine, for some reason left in Bruges by the French after they were defeated in the *Battle of Waterloo*. In 1989, on the occasion of the 200th anniversary of the French Revolution, this guillotine was loaned to the Bicentennial Committee in Paris because it was unable to find a real one in France because, after the revolution, they had all been ordered destroyed.

### Onze Lieve Vrouwekerk/Church of Our Lady ★
*April–Sept., Mon.–Sat. 10–11:30 a.m., 2:30–5 p.m.; Sat., 4:00 p.m., and Sun., 2:30–5 p.m.; Oct.–Mar., Mon.–Sat. 10–11:30 a.m., 2:30–4:30 p.m., except Sat. 4:00 p.m., and Sun., 2:30–4:30 p.m..* The Church of Our Lady is predominantly 13th-century Scheldt Gothic. Its 400-foot/122-meter belfry is one of the tallest brick structures in Europe. What draws many here is the ★★★ *Madonna and Child* by **Michelangelo** (1475–1564). One of the few works by the master to have left Italy during his lifetime, the Bruges Madonna was one of 15 statues Michelangelo was commissioned to sculpt for the Piccolomini altar in the Duomo of Siena. For various reasons, only four statues of the series were completed, including this one. The Brugean merchant Jan van Moeskroen is generally credited with bringing the statue to Bruges in 1506 and donating it to this, his own parish church. (He is buried beneath the altar by the statue.) The chubby Christ child and his mother, favorite subjects of Michelangelo, are made of glowing white Carrara marble and sit in a black marble niche. The half-turned pose of the child demonstrates the sculptor at his best and most typical. Though twice stolen (by the French in 1794 and the Nazis in 1944), both times the piece was recovered in good condition.

The untimely death of Mary of Burgundy, wife of Maximilian of Austria, at age 25 from a fall while horseback riding, meant the end of Burgundian rule for Bruges and all Flanders; the Hapsburgs of Austria taking over through her widower Maximilian. Mary was buried here in Bruges' most important church, where her father Charles the Bold also lay. Their life-size recumbent ★effigies atop *mausoleums* (entry fee) are among the art treasures executed here by Brussels goldsmith **Pieter de Beckere** in 1495-1502. Over the altar, which the mausoleums face, is the large 16th-century *Crucifixion* triptych by **Barend van Orley**. Other paintings in the church are by **Anthony van Dyck**, **Gerard David**, **Pieter Pourbus**. In the north ambulatory you can see the Gothic 1474 oratory of the Gruuthuse (referred to before). The ornate north portal (1465), one of the oldest preserved parts of Our

Lady, known as **paradise porch**, has been restored and is used as a baptismal chapel. *Weekend church services Sat. 5 and 6:30 p.m., Sun. 11 a.m.*

### Memling Museum/Oud Sint-Janshospitaal              ★★★

*Mariastraat 38; April–Sept., daily, 9:30 a.m.–5 p.m., Oct.–Mar. 9:30 a.m.–12:30 p.m., 2–5 p.m., closed Wed. p.m.* Across the street from the Church of Our Lady is Sint-Jans Hospitaal, founded in 1118, one of the oldest hospitals in Europe, and the longest operating at one site when it was relocated outside the town in 1965. The beautiful, spacious old hospital wards' brick buildings, largely from the 13th and 14th centuries, welcomed pilgrims, orphans, soldiers, and the sick over the centuries; on display are many early medical instruments, fascinating pieces of early furniture such as an 18th-century "carrying chair" with handles, a pedestrian ambulance. (Note: In all probability, the medieval wards will continue to be closed for major restoration in 1995.) You'll also be rewarded for time spent in the apothecary and with the paintings there. The hospital's 19th-century wards have just been restored to serve as a special art exhibition and meeting space in a handsome historic setting. On site is the restaurant/tea room **de Promenade** (☎ *34.56.76*), which has canalside terrace seating.

Set apart, in the former chapel of the hospital, are the ★★★ six sole but exceptional works of German-born, but Bruges-developed Flemish primitive artist **Hans Memling** (c. 1435–1494) that make up his museum. One of the six, the *Ursula Shrine*, actually is itself a series of six magnificent paintings, set in an intricate small Gothic church-shaped reliquary. More like the miniatures in *The Book of Hours*, they depict scenes from Ursula's martyred life. The large triptych of the *Mystical Marriage of Saint Catherine*, its wings extended fully for front and back views, is freestanding in the center of the chapel with chairs for visitors who want to take advantage of the unique opportunity to be able to concentrate on so few wonderful works at one time. *The Lamentation over Christ Triptych* was commissioned by St. Jan's hospital brother Adrian Reyns. After the multipanel pieces, it's a relief to study the single image in the *Portrait of a Woman Sibylla Sambetha*, thought to be the daughter of Moreel, one of Memling's patrons. It is fascinating for its delicacy and mere whisper of lace for the headpiece. (Note: If, in 1995, restoration work requires the closing of the Memling Museum section of Oud Sint-Jans, the paintings will remain on view at the Groeningen Museum, where they were moved for the August–November 1994 Memling Exhibition.)

**Note:** When you exit, turn right on **Mariastraat** and walk the short distance to the canal for a view of a wonderful exterior view of St. Jan's (this location has great photographic potential from cruise boats). If you continue straight on, you'll shortly see Wijngaardstraat on the right leading to the Begijnhof.

### Begijnhof/Beguinage     ★★★

*Wijngaardstraat, to Minnewater bridge and entrance gate,* is one of Bruges' most memorable spots. **Winston Churchill** was so captivated by the sight of the Begijnhof with spring daffodils in bloom that he recorded it in a watercolor (reprinted on postcards for sale in town). Since the last Begijn died here in 1930 (the first came in 1245), the Begijnhof has been in the loving care of Benedictine nuns, whom you may see strolling in traditional black-robed, flowing white head-clothed, 15th-century-style vestments. They are quietly impressive figures as they walk across the paths to the white-washed buildings of their lovely private world. Part of the Begijnhof's charm is its peacefulness, and though hundreds, perhaps thousands, of tourists may be milling around just beyond the gate on a sunny weekend day in summer, within its precincts the request for quiet usually is respected. The central lawn is dotted with tall trees and parted here and there by paths, all open to the elements; the light and sky seem always to make a fresh, frequently dramatic impression. The ★**Begijnhof church**, a triple-nave 13th-century Gothic structure (though in rebuilding after a 1584 fire, it took on more baroque lines), in addition to services on Sun. at 9:30 a.m. and Sat. at 7:15 a.m., multiple services most days. (Some have chanting and/or organ music; confirm times.)

## SHOPPING

Though a small piece of light-weight lace commands a heavy price (handmade, a four-inch square is a full day's production), it's big business in Bruges. Many shop windows are filled with lace for sale, and the product is pretty enough to counter the commercialism. If you're a potential buyer, you'll want to know what you're paying for, especially if you decide to splurge on handmade lace, as opposed to the Hong Kong machine-made variety sold in many shops. Pieces range from postcard-size scenes to bridal veils to huge tablecloths, and some shops also sell antique lace (about the only way today to get a piece of Bruges' famed *Fairy Stitch*). Most lace shops are open seven days a week in the tourist season, accept major credit cards, and advise on tax-free export purchases; at one or more you may be able to see a demonstration of lace making (otherwise, visit the **Lace Museum/Kantcentrum**).

In a different tradition, visit **Classics Kunstatelier** (*Oude Burgstraat 32*), in a 15th-century building near Simon Stevinplein, which has a huge display (up to 250 pieces) of Flemish and Brugean tapestries, wall hangings, and other decorative art. Bruges **carillon recordings** are for sale at the information desk at the base of the belfry.

## WHERE TO STAY

All hotels listed are located within canal-enclosed historic Bruges. The tourist office has a list of bed-and-breakfast establishments and can make recommendations. Although restaurants are not a rule in Bruges hotels, those in several are among the finest dining establishments in the city; for simplicity's sake, I have included details with the hotel listing.

## EXPENSIVE

### Holiday Inn Crowne Plaza

*Burg 10;* ☎ *34.58.34, in U.S. and Canada* ☎ *800-465-4329, FAX 34.56.15.* This recently opened 96-room hotel, located on Bruges' most architecturally outstanding square, has an essentially modern brick facade of controversial, but carefully-overseen design meant to match neighboring buildings in scale and materials. All guest rooms have TV, telephone, individually controlled a/c, double-glazing on windows, minibar, hair dryer, trouser press; some nonsmoking rooms are available. There's a restaurant, coffee shop with outside terrace, lobby bar, and 16-hour room service. Some space in the cellar has been set aside to show the foundations of the 9th-century St. Donatian church that once existed on the site before it was destroyed by the French in the later 1700s.

## MODERATE

### Oud Huis Amsterdam

*Spiegelrei 3;* ☎ *34.18.10, FAX 33.88.91.* These two restored 16th-century former "gentlemen's houses" with full canal frontage offer an owner-overseen oasis just a short walk from the Markt. Each of the 17 antique and old print-decorated guest rooms is furnished individually, all have remote-control TV (placed pleasantly out of view in wardrobe cupboards), telephone, modern bath (some with whirlpool), hand-held shower; there's turn-down service with a praline on your pillow. Breakfast only (included) is served overlooking Spiegelrei canal, drinks in the warm wood-panelled bar with fireplace and Cordoba-leather covered walls. There's a terrace with tables in the quiet back courtyard, and a garden (which back bedrooms overlook) with a surprising sculpture. Friendly, superior service from reception, including free horse-drawn carriage ride from April-Sept. from/to dinner at the family's excellent **'t Bourgoensche Cruyce restaurant**. Elevator; limited on-street parking.

### Romantik Pand Hotel

*Pandreitje 16;* ☎ *34.06.66, FAX 34.05.56.* This owner-run 18th-century mansion-hotel in the plane-tree shaded Pandreitje at the end of which is Bruges' most famous belfry/canal view, has an intimate, tasteful interior with plenty of personal touches in the service. The classic decor in the entry/reception hall features crystal chandeliers, marble, oriental rugs, oil paintings, plants, and lots of architectural detail. The 24 uniquely decorated rooms have TV, telephone, clock-radio, minibar, bath, and hair dryer; six are specially designed luxury rooms. The comfortable lounge has newspapers, drink service during the day; a buffet (included) is served in the garden-like breakfast drawing-room. Elevator.

### Die Swaene

*Steenhouwersdijk 1;* ☎ *34.27.98, FAX 33.66.74.* There's a homelike atmosphere to this fastidiously operated family hotel, created from three adjoining 15–17th-century houses on a particularly picturesque stretch of canal. The hotel is so central that by day cruise boats and horse-drawn carriages pass the front door, but by night its quaint corner of old Bruges is as quiet as you could want. There's a garden for pre-dinner drinks and a tapestry-hung lounge upstairs for after-dinner coffee. Hallways are filled with an eclectic collection of paintings and statues, and the cozy front lobby has English-language newspapers. The 24 guest rooms are comfortably and individually furnished, most with antiques; many face the canal; all have bath/shower, TV, telephone, minibar. Buffet breakfast included; elevator; major credit cards. The in-house **Die Swaene restaurant** (*closed Wed., Thurs. night; expensive*, menus *moderate*) sets a table fit for its superb service and celebrated continental cuisine. Specialties include fresh fish, its in-house foie gras, and homemade sorbet, served between courses, served on Belle Époque china, with soft classical music and candlelight.

### Duc de Bourgogne ★★★

*Huidenvettersplein 12;* ☎ *33.20.38, FAX 34.40.37.* Long revered for its fine food, the guest rooms at the Duc de Bourgogne shouldn't be ignored, especially since they share the same unsurpassed canalside setting in the center of Bruges for which the restaurant is noted. Of the 10 bedrooms in the 1648 building, 6 have water views; all are different in shape, size, and price. Guest-room decor, like the restaurant's, is dark wood and traditional; all rooms have bath with fixed shower head, telephone, TV; breakfast is included. No elevator; major credit cards accepted. The **Duc de Bourgogne restaurant** (*closed Sun. evening, Mon.; expensive*, menu *moderate*) has a lengthy listing of classic choices. Its large-windowed Rubenesque-decorated formal dining room overlooks one of Bruges' loveliest converging of canals, a setting that's illuminated at night, with the belfry in view. Both the hotel and restaurant are closed for the months of Jan. and July.

### Ter Brughe ★★★★

*Oost Gistelhof 2;* ☎ *34.03.24, FAX 33.88.73.* This 24-double-room hotel is a 500-year-old restored protected monument building, once a patrician mansion and canalside warehouse. A friendly staff, which makes it more a house than a hotel, welcomes guests to the traditionally decorated lobby that features large paintings of the history of Bruges. All the modern furnished rooms have tile bath, TV, telephone, minifridge; some on the top floor have ceiling beams. The handsome vaulted brick cellar where breakfast only (included) is served has huge water-level warehouse doors that swing open to greet the swans that await their breakfast. No elevator; bar; major credit cards.

# INEXPENSIVE

### Adornes                                                    ★★★

*St.-Annarei 26;* ☎ *34.13.36, FAX 34.20.85.* With a three-canal-junction location in a residential area of old Bruges, away from but within walking distance of the Markt, this 20-room hotel is situated in three restored 17th-century gabled houses. The big-windowed, small lobby is decorated comfortably with leather couches and an antique tapestry on the wall. Rooms (some on the small side; higher-priced ones on the top floor are larger and have exposed ceiling beams) have basic modern furniture, TV, telephone, clock-radio, desk, and small but cozy bathrooms with bath/hand-held shower, hair dryer. A buffet breakfast only (included) is served in a cozy dining room. Elevator.

### Bourgoensch Hof                                            ★★★

*Wollestraat 39;* ☎ *33.16.45, FAX 34.63.78.* Picturesquely situated canalside—7 of the 10 rooms face the water—on a small quiet courtyard not far from the Markt, the hotel's location may be its major amenity. While reception service is only civil, the traditionally decorated, canal-facing breakfast room is delightful. Lounge and bedrooms are a bit old-fashioned, with stuffed furniture. No TV in inexpensive category rooms (others are higher priced, with TV). In the cellar of the hotel at canal-level (and with a few outside terrace tables) is **Bistro 't Traptje** *(7 p.m.–midnight;* ☎ *33.89.18; inexpensive),* with cozy old wooden decor, brick walls, black and white tile floor, serving a small but varied menu of regional specialties.

### Botaniek                                                   ★★★

*Waalsestraat 23;* ☎ *34.14.24, FAX 34.59.39.* Opened in 1992 in a tastefully restored 18th-century townhouse, this 9-room hotel on a quiet side street is a few minutes' walk from the center of Bruges. All rooms—doubles, twins, one family with kitchenette—furnished differently; top room has view of town towers lighted at night. All rooms have stall showers, TV, radio, telephone. Breakfast (buffet, included) room with bar facilities, small attractive lounge. Elevator.

## *WHERE TO EAT*

In a country celebrated for its food, Bruges is second only to Brussels for pride of palate. Reservations are recommended for Bruges's better restaurants, a category that certainly includes **Vasquez** *(Zilverstraat 38; daily lunch, dinner, closed Wed. and Thurs. lunch;* ☎ *34.08.45; expensive),* whose adventurously classical gastronomic cuisine (not nouvelle, but unusual pairings and seasoning of traditional fresh local foods) is served in the elegant surroundings of a 15th-century emmissary of Isabella of Portugal. **DeVos** *(Zilverstraat 41; closed Tues. evening, Wed.;* ☎ *33.55.66; moderate),* a small 13th-century house originally used by traveling monks now with an art nouveau decor including a stunning 20-foot stained glass ceiling, and garden terrace, offers finely prepared regional specialties that should be lingered over. Located in the delightful, sun-filtered, leafy square just back from the Rozenhoedkaai is **Den Braamberg** *(Pandreitje 11; lunch and dinner, closed Sun. night, Thurs.;* ☎ *33.73.70; moderate)*, which serves fish and lamb specialties.

**Restaurant 't Bourgoensche Cruyce** *(Wollestraat 41, open lunch and dinner, closed Tues., April–Sept., closed Sun. and Mon. lunch Oct.–Mar.;* ☎ *33.79.26; expensive,* menu *moderate)* has a small ground floor canal-view dining room, with a few tables on a canalside courtyard terrace. It features gastronomic versions of regional specialties, with fresh in-season fare. Reserve as far ahead as possible. In a discussion of some of Bruges' best restaurants (which includes those mentioned under the **Die Swaene** and **Duc de Bourgogne** hotel listings), one must mention **De Snippe** *(Nieuwe Gentweg 53; closed Sun., Mon. lunch;* ☎ *33.70.70; expensive)* even though it is located outside the old city. Here, *haute cuisine*—caviar mousse, scallops with truffles, wild duck—is offered in an 18th-century townhouse. (It also has 7 rooms, *moderate*; 4 jr. suites, *expensive*.)

Since **De Visscherie** *(Vismarkt 8; closed Tues.;* ☎ *33.02.12; moderate)* faces the fish market, you could hardly expect it to specialize in anything else, and it does fish well with a wide choice of fresh fare. Equally central, in a casual setting just off the Burg, **Breydel-De Coninck** *(Breidelstraat 24; open noon–9 p.m., closed Tues. and Wed.;* ☎ *33.97.46; inexpensive)* is the place in Bruges for mussels, served in enormous enameled pots until you "say when."

With its charming olde world interior, and canalside view similar to the expensive **Duc de Bourgogne** next door, **'t Dreveken**, also known as **'t Huidevettershuis**, *(Huidenvettersplein 10–11; kitchen open noon–9:30 p.m., closed Tues.;* ☎ *33.95.06; moderate)* is a great choice for regional specialties. With a less historic atmosphere, but certainly in the center of things is **Den Gouden Cop** *(Steenstraat 1; inexpensive)*, one of about a dozen brasseries/terrace cafes that line two sides of the **Markt**. It and most of the others offer a continuous service of soups, sandwiches, and snacks to a full meal during the day and evening. There are both outside and glassed-in dining with a view of town activity. From the front terrace at **Craenenberg** you can have a drink on the Markt while facing the row of cafes that appear on the cover of this book. **Restaurant Belfort** *(32 Markt; inexpensive)* is another pleasant, convenient cafe with varied dishes that include such typical local fare as asparagus soup and Dutch herring.

**Tea rooms**, a name *Bruggelingen* employ, serve lighter dishes such as pancakes, snacks, and pastry, especially in the afternoon, though many also serve more substantial fare for lunch and dinner. In one of the most picturesque corners of Bruges, where the Groenerei crosses other canals, you can sit on the bricked terrace at **Uilenspiegel** *(Langestraat 2; inexpensive)* and sample a wide range of tasty snacks with a drink. At **Belle Époque** *(Zuidzandstraat 43; daily from noon through dinner;* ☎ *33.18.72; inexpensive to moderate)* there's a cozy yet chic feel to the *art nouveau* decor that accompanies the friendly service and imaginative menu (paté maison, croque monsieur, salads, waterzooi, scampi). Tea-room Restaurant **Vienna** *(Vlamingstraat, in the Theaterboutieks; cafe open daily 10 a.m.–11 p.m., restau-*

rant *11:30 a.m.–2 p.m. and 6:30–9 p.m., closed Tues. from Nov.–March;* ☎ *34.90.20; inexpensive, four-course gastronomique menu moderate)* offers excellent food from pancakes to gourmet fare in four different settings, from a casual indoor terrace cafe to a formal traditional dining room with crystal chandelier and a baby grand piano. Generously-portioned home-made soups and desserts a specialty. **Bistrot De Serre** *(Simon Stevinplein 15; kitchen open daily 11 a.m.–9:15 p.m., closed Tues. year-round, Sun. Sept.– June;* ☎ *34.22.31; inexpensive)* is tucked into a garden behind an attractive square halfway between the Begijnhof and the Markt. Dine indoors or at a marble-top table in the small garden on tasty casual fare—omdettes, salads, toast Hawaii (open-face toasted cheese and pineapple sandwich), soups—or rest from nearby shopping over a beer, wine, or coffee and a dessert crepe. Not far away is **'t Keteltje** *(Oude Burg 20; daily 11 a.m.–11 p.m., closed Thurs.;* ☎ *33.29.79; inexpensive)*, where Belgian waffles and pancakes (25 varieties of sweet and savory) are a specialty.

For a wonderful selection of regional pastries, breads, and chocolates, visit **Bakkerij Sint Paulus** *(Vlamingstraat 25; 7 a.m.–7 p.m.;* ☎ *34.85.70)*. **Panos** *(Geldmantstraat 14;* ☎ *33.83.39)* is another great patisserie in the center of Bruges. For that rarity, an inner city grocery store (that also sells basic cosmetics, nylons, etc.), where you can procure all the makings of a picnic, including beer and wine, head for **NOPRI** *(Noordzandstraat; open 9 a.m.–6:30 p.m., closed Sun.)*.

If you're looking for a place for a drink with a view, you can't do better than **'t Klein Venetie** *(Braambergstraat 1; 10:30 a.m.–2 a.m., closed Tues. from 5:30 p.m., Wed.;* ☎ *34.01.75; inexpensive)*, which offers one of the most pleasant views in Europe, across a confluence of canals and along a converging line of gables, to the belfry. For those who want to become better acquainted with Belgian beer, the helpful bar attendants at tiny **De Garre** *(tucked away at the end of the alley located between 12 and 14 Breidelstraat; 11 a.m.–1 a.m., last call accompanied by the playing of Bolero; closed Wed.)* can certainly begin your education. Courses in beer bartending are taught by the friendly owner of **'t Brugs Beertje** *(Kemelstraat 5; 4 p.m.–1 a.m.; closed Wed.;* ☎ *33.96.16)*, which serves the largest selection of beer in Bruges, more than 300 kinds. Under such conditions, the bartenders obviously have to be prepared to help you choose your Belgian brew.

## ENTERTAINMENT AND EVENTS

Bruges offers one of the most extensive programs of ★★**carillon concerts** in the world. Thanks to the talent, energy, and enthusiasm of *stadsbeiaardier* (town carillonneur) **Aimé Lombaert**, more people get to hear a carillon here than perhaps anywhere else in the world. From mid-June through Sept., hour-long concerts are played at 9 p.m. on Mon., Wed., Sat, and on Sun. at 2:15 p.m.; from Oct. 1–mid-June, afternoon concerts are played at 2:15 p.m. on Wed. and Sat. Sundays concerts are played at 2:15 p.m. year-round. For Bruggelingen, high points of the year are the 11 p.m. concerts played by Lombaert on Christmas Eve and New Year's Eve. From mid-June–September, Lombaert offers four "duplex concerts" in which he, shown at his keyboard in a big video screen on the Markt, plays the carillon in the height of the Belfort in a joint concert with a band on the ground.

The annual ★★**Festival of Flanders** (around the first two weeks of August) brings some of the continent's best classical music to Bruges in nightly competitions. Booking is strongly recommended because of local popularity. In 1995 (August 17, 18, 21, 23, 25 and 26), Bruges will stage a ★★★**Festival on the Canals** on six different nights. Historic scenes and periods are recreated in costume, music, by over 500 performers in several squares, all illuminated, continuously from 9 p.m.–midnight. It's a spectacular show for spectators, but be forewarned of crowds.

The ★★★**Procession of the Holy Blood** (on May 25 in 1995), held annually on Ascension Day, is the veneration of what is believed to be a drop or two of Christ's blood mixed with water washed from his crucified body, a relic brought to Bruges in the mid-13th century. The blood is in a rock-crystal phial which rests in a silver reliquary, presented to Bruges in 1611 by archdukes of the Spanish Netherlands Isabella and Albert. After religious services in the morning in the **Basilica of the Holy Blood** and a leisurely lunch break, celebrants carry the relic through the streets, accompanied by a costumed cast of thousands. The centuries-old tradition arose from the annual gathering of feudal lords and burghers 'round the relic to offer oaths of loyalty, and gradually evolved into a procession with the magistrates and guilds of the city in full dress for the affair. The present religious-historical affair through the decorated streets of ancient Bruges includes tableaux (groups which perform episodes from the Bible), floats, and authentically dressed groups recalling old city guilds, foreign merchants from Bruges' 14th-century golden age, the entry into Bruges of the "count of Flanders" and his richly dressed retinue of courtesans, with cortege of choirs, banners, and musical instruments. Reserved grandstand tickets on procession route available from tourist office from Feb. 1. Every Sunday in July and August, there's a free **organ concert** after the 10 a.m. service at St. Saviour's church. Friday nights at St. Saviour's in July there are concerts (fee) in conjunction with an annual international organ competition. Every evening in July and August somewhere in Bruges there is a free jazz concert as part of the Lotto Jazz Summer Days.

## IN THE AREA

### Damme

*Tourist information, Huis De Grote Sterre, Jacob van Maerlantstraat 3; Mon.–Fri. 9 a.m.–noon, 2–5 p.m., Sat. and Sun. 2–6 p.m.; ☎ (050) 35.33.19; pop. 1,000.* From its founding, Damme's history has been inextricably linked with Bruges, both the flourishing and the fall. Damme's picturesque **Marktplein** shows typical Flemish gables, and a statue of 13th-century poet Jacob van Maerlant who was born here and would have witnessed his city's great growth. The elegant **Stadhuis** *(July 1-Sept. 15 daily 10 a.m.–noon, 4–6 p.m.)* whose elegant 15th-century Gothic facade is studded with statues of counts of

Flanders; on the right are the figures of the duke of Burgundy, Charles the Bold, and English princess Margaret of York, who were married in 1468 in Damme (at St. John House, Kerkstraat 4). The original tower clock of the Stadhuis dates from 1459. Several spacious, impressive rooms usually are open inside.

## WHERE TO EAT

**Die Drie Zilveren Kannen** *(Markt 9, Damme;* ☎ *35.56.77; moderate)* offers fine Flemish dishes in a decor to match; it's wise to reserve. **Ter Kloeffe Bretoens Pannekoekhuis** *(Hoogstraat 1; closed Mon. evenings, Tues.;* ☎ *(050) 35.41.24; inexpensive)*, a less formal, typical old beamed and tiled, choice, serves savory and sweet Brittany crepes.

# GHENT

## GUIDELINES FOR GHENT

### SIGHTS

A first, and lasting, impression of Ghent (*Gent* in Flemish, *Gand* in French) is of marvelous medieval structures, whose sturdy stone facades reflect well in canal waters. Considering those monuments are mostly in shades of gray, city street scenes are surprisingly vibrant. Prime sights are central, particularly the towers of **St. Bavo's Cathedral** (which contains the famed van Eyck brothers' *The Adoration of the Mystique Lamb*), the **Belfry**, and **St. Nicolaas church**—the three almost aligned in the famous view of them from **St. Michiel's Bridge**. The bridge spans Ghent's former harbor, from the **Graslei**, with its magnificent row of early 13th- to 16th-century buildings, to the **Korenlei**, from which it's a short scenic walk to the **Castle of the Counts** (c.1180).

### GETTING AROUND

If you arrive by train at **St. Pieter's Station**, take Tram 1 (1.5 mi/2.5 km) to **Korenmarkt**, in the center of historic Ghent (population 150,000). **Tourist Information** is in the close-by **Stadhuis/** town hall crypt. From there a multi-lingual two-hour guided city tour leaves daily at 2:30 p.m., April–Oct., ☎ *233.53.11*. The bus, tram, trolley system (map available) covers the city well, but since Ghent's major sights are compactly located and its streets and squares warrant walking-speed appreciation, you're unlikely to make much use of it once you're in the center. **Sightseeing Line** offers a minibus tour (commentary in English on headset); horse-drawn carriages are available in season. Canal cruises, while affording some attractive perspectives, are limited in their course; much of the route must be retraced since many canals no longer connect with each other since early 20th-century filling in of some sections.

## SHOPPING

As the capital of East Flanders province, Ghent has long been the main market town for a large area. Major commercial streets include **Veldstraat**, which has department and larger stores, **Volderstraat** with smaller and smarter shops, and the surrounding Kouter, Nederkouter, Zonnestraat, and Brabantdam, which all attract their share of business. Ghent has many markets: **Groentenmarkt** (food and general wares) *Mon.–Sat. a.m.*, with artists' works Sun. a.m.; **Vrijdagmarkt** (new wares) *Fri. 7 a.m.–1 p.m.*, *Sat. 1 p.m.–5 p.m.*; **Kouter** (flowers) *daily 7 a.m.–1 p.m.*; and **St. Michielsplein** (food) *Sun. mornings.*

## ENTERTAINMENT AND EVENTS

From April–mid-Nov. all historic buildings and monuments are illuminated nightly from sunset to midnight; for the rest of year, they are illuminated each Friday and Saturday night. The restored **Zuid** (south) quarter of Ghent is the place to head for varied nightlife. From late June to the end of August, **carillon concerts** are played Saturdays 9–10 p.m. on the **Belfry's** 53-bell (some *Hemony*-cast) instrument by town carillonneur Jos D'Hollander and guest players from around the world (☎ *223.99.77*). For ten days each mid-July, the varied cultural and entertainment activities of the **Ghent Festivities** are held in the city's halls and streets. In July and August, St. Bavo's offers **organ concerts** Thursdays at 8 p.m. (☎ *355.91.79*). Concerts are Ghent's main events in the annual Sept.–Oct. **Festival of Flanders**; St. Bavo's, the Stadhuis, and old abbeys provide memorable settings. (Schedule is available from the middle of May, ☎ *225.77.80.*) Although staged only once every five years (1995, and then in the year 2000), **Floralia** is an internationally renowned flower show that celebrates the beauty of the blooms that annually produce good business for Ghent. Northwest of the city, *begonias* (Belgium's national flower), *azaleas*, and *roses* are cultivated in colorful fields around **Lochristi** (6 mi/9 km), the heart of the flower district.

## WHERE TO STAY

With the opening in the last few years of new properties in the center, Ghent now has a reasonable selection of hotels handy for tourists. However, major trade fairs and exhibitions held several times yearly at the *Palace of the Floralia/Congressgebouw* can fill them with business travelers.

## WHERE TO EAT

Ghent restaurants tend toward traditional rather than trendy. You won't have trouble finding historic settings in which to sup and sip.

## ARRIVING

**St. Pieter's Station** has twice hourly service to/from Brussels and Bruges, with Ghent more or less midway between them. There's hourly service to Antwerp and to the northeast. Boat trains meeting North Sea ferries from England at either Ostend or Zeebrugge pass through Ghent on the way to Brussels. Ghent is served by regional/international motorways (the E17 and E40), and is more or less equidistant (35 mi/60 km) from Antwerp, Brussels, Ostend, Tournai, and Lille (France).

## TRAVEL TIPS

Not that you wouldn't begin your visit at the tourist office anyway, but in Ghent it's particularly helpful because several city sights (the cathedral, Stadhuis and Cloth Hall) offer tours/screenings in English at set times, which are worth knowing about when planning your touring.

## *GHENT IN CONTEXT*

Many travelers will be more interested in Ghent's prosperous past than in its prosperous present, particularly the *appearance* of that past. The 12th century is conjured up in the sight of the moated **Castle of the Counts/Gravensteen**, which passes into the realm of fairy tales when floodlit at night. A castle probably was first built on the site by **Boudewijn (Baldwin, the Iron Arm)**, who visited Ghent from Bruges about 867. (Settlement in the area began in the 7th century with two abbeys, *St. Bavo* and *St. Pieter*, the later buildings of both surviving today.) Boudewijn's castle at the confluence of the *Lieve* and *Lys* rivers was originally built for defense against raids by Norsemen, who continued on up the *Scheldt* to Ghent after dropping in on Antwerp. But enlargements to this seat of the *Counts of Flanders* (of whom Boudewijn was the first) in the 11th and 12th centuries increasingly were made with an eye on managing the independently minded people in Ghent's cloth industry, which came to prominence during the 12th century. The basic structure of the castle we see today was completed about 1180.

Ghent's river port was a necessity from the start of its cloth industry, due to the need to import wool from England. The **Graslei**, on the right bank of the Lys, and **Korenlei** on the left, formed the central harbor; the oldest building on the Graslei, the **Staple House** (*Spijker*), dates from c. 1200. Early in the 13th century Ghent supplemented its natural inland waterways with canals, one being dug to Bruges, from which, by way of the Zwin, there was access to the North Sea.

In the 13th century, with the cloth business flourishing, Ghent experienced continued expansion—at the end of the 13th century Ghent had a larger population than Paris—but also increased political unrest, a situation that would continue to shape the city's history. Difficulties arose between the increasingly ambitious town citizen textile workers and Ghent's rich patricians (who generally remained loyal to their suzerain, the French king). Although the Counts of Flanders had granted a charter to Ghent in 1180 and added citizens' rights, such as election of town magistrates, heretofore appointed, in 1212, the economic success generated by the burghers led to their demanding even greater independence. In 1302, a contingent of Ghent workers led by **Jan Borluut** joined other Flemish workers (mostly weavers, particularly from Bruges) in the **Battle of the Golden Spurs** (see "An Historical Perspective" under "Belgium"), a confrontation with French nobility which the workers won.

In 1338, when the count of Flanders at the beginning of the Anglo-French **Hundred Years War** sided with France (thereby threatening Ghent's cloth trade, which depended heavily upon English wool), **Jacob van Artevelde** (1287–1345), a patrician who supported the merchants, took over the leadership of Ghent to protect business and made an independent alliance with English **King Edward III**. (Edward at the beginning of the Hundred Years War had declared *himself* king of France, a position van Artevelde supported.) In the course of the alliance, Edward visited Ghent, and his third son, **John of Gaunt** (a form of *Ghent*), was born there to Queen Philippa (of Hainaut, in Wallonia) in St. Bavo's Abbey in 1340. Both Ghent merchants and England's wool growers prospered under the arrangement, but guildsmen, unsure of van Artevelde's ambitions, murdered him in 1345.

The Hundred Years War continued with various players, including pro-French **Count of Flanders Louis De Malle** and van Artevelde's son Philip, who lost his life when the French won the battle at Westrozebeke. Upon De Malle's death in 1384, because his daughter and only heir had married **Philip of Burgundy** (in Ghent's St. Bavo's Abbey), Ghent became part of the duchy of Burgundy, and Flanders as a separate county ceased to exist.

From the middle of the 14th century, the cloth industry in Ghent—and elsewhere in Flanders—began to decline, mainly due to competition from the English, who themselves had begun making cloth from their wool. But the excellent reputation of the luxurious Ghent/Flemish cloth, which was exported throughout Europe and as far afield as North Africa and the Middle East, remained a standard: **Geoffrey Chaucer** (c.1340–1400) in his *Canterbury Tales* spoke of the skill of the wife of Bath as surpassing that of the weavers of "Ipres and Gaunt" (Ypres and Ghent). And, a century later, **Jan van Eyck**, using the new oil paint medium, finally could show well enough the texture of the brilliantly colored heavy cloth in art works such as *The Ghent Altarpiece*, so that we can appreciate the quality of the famed Flemish product.

Throughout its history Ghent has been a "fighting" town, constantly striving for both town and civilian rights. As a result, construction of buildings often was interrupted by unrest. Thus, though the city center is a veritable textbook of architectural styles from the 12th to the 20th century, several important structures begun centuries ago were completed only relatively recently. The **Cloth Hall**, started early in the 15th century, was not completed in its original design until the beginning of the 20th. In the case of the **Stadhuis**, construction, begun in the late 15th century, stretched into the 18th with exterior statues added in the 19th; the result is one Renaissance facade, one late-Gothic, and assorted-era outside ornamentation.

Under the Burgundians, who took over rule near the end of the 14th century, Ghent workers didn't alter their fighting ways. In 1453, after a five-year revolt, a humiliating loss of privileges was imposed upon them by **Philip the Good**. In 1477, however, *Gentenaars* rebounded by holding Philip's granddaughter, **Mary of Burgundy**, captive until she signed the *Great Privilege* which conferred many rights back to the people. But Mary was killed in an accident soon after, and back came her widower, **Maximilian of Austria**, who, as the first of the region's Hapsburg line of rulers, subdued Ghent again. The Netherlands-born humanist **Erasmus** (c. 1466–1536) covered both positive and negative points about Gentenaars in his words: "I do not think that one could find in the whole of Christendom a town which could compare with Ghent as for its political organization or the nature of its people."

Because of their particularly impassioned positions on civil rights, Ghent citizens, even more than those in other medieval towns, treasured their **Belfry** (1321–1380) historically, the town's most important building since it served as a safe-deposit box for its charter and rights, as well as a bell tower from which to ring warnings of danger or celebration. In Ghent's belfry hung a huge bell, around whose rim appeared the words: "My name is Roeland. When I clap there is fire. When I toll there is a storm in Flanders." Roeland itself became a player in the stormy year of 1540. By then, **Emperor Charles V**, Maximilian's grandson who was born in Ghent in 1500, had become tired of his birth town's belligerence. Angered at the disorder and defiance of the Gentenaars, Charles ordered the great 12,000-pound/6000 kg. *Roeland* removed from the belfry, an act of great symbolic significance. Then he dismantled the entire early defensive works of the city. (The 1491 medieval tower *Rabot* is all that survives.) As a result, though he was the most famous person ever born in Ghent, Charles V was disliked there for much of his lifetime.

Although by the end of the 14th century, the cloth industry had been ruined in Flanders by English competition, Ghent shipping got a new source of revenue after 1500—partly as a result of the increasing prominence of Antwerp, with whom Ghent shared the Scheldt river—from the export of grain from France. Boatmen (whose guildhalls stand on the Graslei and Korenlei) replaced cloth makers as Ghent's most important workers. The addition of the 16th-century **Corn Merchant's House** and the **Free Boatmen's Guild Hall** (1500–1531) on the Graslei reflected the new times; the forwarding and carrying trade in grain enabled Ghent to weather the loss of the cloth industry (while the Flemish cloth towns of Ypres and Bruges were not able to do so). By 1547, Ghent had cut a new canal (18.5 mi/30 km) directly north to **Terneuzen** (now in Holland), on the *Westerscheldt*, the wide Scheldt estuary that leads into the North Sea. All was well until Ghent's port was effectively closed by Dutch demands for sole control of the Scheldt estuary in the 1648 agreement with the Spanish that settled the *Eighty Years War*. Following the fate of Antwerp, whose port also was closed, Ghent remained in decline thereafter until 1795, when the French under **Napoleon Bonaparte**, then in control of the Netherlands north and south, reopened the Scheldt.

In 1814, during the six months of negotiations that preceded the signing of the **Treaty of Ghent** (see "Stadhuis" under "What To See and Do") that ended the American-English War of 1812, U.S. participant **John Quincy Adams** lived in the city. It is said that Ghent was chosen as the site of the negotiations because of the luxury of its amenities. That luxury could be one reason why, the next year, **Louis XVIII** moved to Ghent in refuge during the *Hundred Days* (March 15–June 28, 1815) from Napoleon's return to France following his escape from Elba until his final abdication after defeat in the **Battle of Waterloo**.

Under the **United Kingdom of the Netherlands**, which put Belgium and Holland together as a single country in the European realignment that followed Waterloo, Ghent fully regained the use of its port, and expanded her sea trade. With the encouragement of Dutch King Willem I, Ghent's Terneuzen canal was expanded in 1827 to handle seagoing vessels, an important development in the city's maritime history. Because of trade with Dutch overseas colonies, Ghent remained faithful to the *House of Orange* during the **Belgian Revolution** of 1830, though it lost the business after Belgium achieved independence that year.

Although its impressive 12th-century textile trade had become history during the 14th century, in the early 19th century Ghent entrepreneurs, freed from the framework of guilds—Napoleon had disbanded them—turned again to textiles. The leaders of the thriving cotton mill business became known as "cotton barons." They were enamored of an aristocratic life style: buying titles, marrying into old families, beginning art collections, and building sumptuous town mansions. Fine French-style facades from the era still line **Jan Breydelstraat**, **Koningstraat**, **Kouter**, and **Veldstraat**.

An interesting tale of industrial espionage plays a prominent part in Ghent's second textile success story. **Lieven Bauwens** (1769–1822), a tanner's son and later burgomaster, single-handedly revolutionized the cotton industry in Ghent. In the year 1789, while living in Manchester, England, Bauwens managed to "come by" a copy of the plan for the **spinning jenny** power loom, which, together with parts for an entire machine, he smuggled out of England hidden in sacks of coffee. He also enticed two technicians to join him in Ghent. (The spinning jenny, consisting of a number of spindles turned by a common wheel, worked by hand—the first machine on which a number of threads could be spun at once—was invented (c. 1767) by **James Hargreaves**, a Lancashire, England, weaver.)

Back in Ghent, Bauwens immediately set up a factory featuring his new acquisition. Such was the spinning jenny's impact that in the single subsequent decade, Ghent employees in the cotton-spinning industry jumped from next-to-none to 10,000, many to be housed in makeshift workers' camps. In England, Lieven Bauwens was sentenced to death in absentia and buried in effigy. In Ghent, he's honored with a statue on a square named for him (near St. Bavo cathedral). Belgian historians gave some slight recompense to

England by dubbing Ghent the "Manchester of the Continent." A sample of the smuggled spinning jenny is on exhibit at the **Castle of the Counts**, an appropriate location since the venerable structure was enlisted for duty as a cotton factory in the 19th century.

Ghent boomed in the industrial revolution, its population trebling between 1801 and 1900 (from 55,000 to 160,000). As the number of factories increased, so did the overcrowded conditions of the workers. Historic buildings, as well as workers, were sacrificed to the system. So was the Scheldt river, parts of which were covered, its main course diverted out of the center of Ghent. With the city sublimated to industry, its mass of workers pulled from the surrounding countryside and herded into squalid living conditions in back streets, it's little wonder that the socialist movement in Flanders began and became centered in Ghent. With the workers' movement related to the **Flemish Movement**, it was an achievement when, in 1930, the *University of Ghent*—which Willem, king of the United Netherlands had ordered established in 1817—finally became a Flemish-speaking institution.

After 1960, Ghent's economic future focused beyond textiles on the chemical and steel industries, and particularly its port. In 1968 a new lock at Terneuzen made it possible for vessels as large as 60,000 tons to use the canal, and Ghent's tonnage has increased ten fold in the intervening years. By the turn of the century ships of 125,000 tons will be able to discharge goods at its inland terminals. Ghent, Belgium's second port, has a different focus from the international outlook of its first, with Antwerp concentrating on incoming vessels that discharge cargoes to be channelled to the European hinterland by barge, road, and rail. Ghent's port provides 50,000 jobs (directly and indirectly) for the greater city population of 250,000.

While patently respecting their past, Gentenaars know that the city and its citizens have always been at their best when industry is doing well, which it is today. But never again, as in the 19th century, will Ghent neglect its historic gables at the expense of business. The medieval **Castle of the Counts** will never again have to house industry within its walls: the **Dienst Monumentenzorg en Stadsarcheologie** (city department for the care of buildings) will see to that.

## GUIDEPOSTS

**Telephone Code 09**

**Tourist Information** • Crypt of Stadhuis (Town Hall; April–Oct., daily 9:30 a.m.–6:30 p.m.; Nov.-Mar., daily, 9:30 a.m.–4:30 p.m.; ☎ *266.52.32.*

**Trains** • Main station **St. Pieter's** in SW of city, 1.5 mi./2.5 km from center.

**Bus/Tram Info** • ☎ *230.41.95.*

**Minibus Tours** • Sightseeing Line minibus tours, departure from Belfry; schedule, reservations from Bruges office: ☎ *(050) 31.13.55.*

**Canal Cruises De Bootjes van Gent** • Open boats, Korenlei, ☎ *223.88.53*; **Benelux Gent Watertoerist**; Open and covered boats, Graslei, ☎ *282.92.48*; Easter to end Oct.

**Post Office** • Main office: Korenmarkt.

## WHAT TO SEE AND DO

Ghent's major sights are covered more or less in order of their significance. Conveniently, the most important also are the most centrally located. From the end of April through Oct., and Fri. and Sat. the rest of the year, Ghent's historic buildings are illuminated nightly from 8 p.m. (or dark, which can be as late as 10 p.m. in June, July, and Aug., 9 p.m. in May, Sept.). This makes it difficult to see the ★★★ impressively floodlit **Castle of the Counts**, Graslei, etc. unless you overnight in the city.

### St. Bavo's Cathedral                                    ★★

*St. Baafs Plein; April 1–Sept. 30, Mon.–Sat., 9:30 a.m.–noon, 2–6 p.m., Sun. 1–6 p.m.; Oct. 1–Mar. 31, Mon.– Sat., 10:00 a.m.–noon, 2:30–4 p.m., Sun., 2–5 p.m.; admission fee of* BF50 *includes crypt.* Relatively ordinary on the outside, St. Bavo's is anything but inside, with its admirable proportions and rich ornamentation. The Ghent-born future **Emperor Charles V** was christened here on March 7, 1500. Claiming first attention for most visitors to St. Bavo's, whose choir dates from the 13th century, nave and transepts from the 15th, is the world-famous medieval masterpiece by **Jan** and **Hubert van Eyck**, ★★★ *The Adoration of the Mystical Lamb* (1432), a 24-panel polyptych also referred to as *The Ghent Altarpiece.* Recently, it has been restored and relocated within the church (a controversial move, many preferring the naturally lit Donors' Chapel where the altarpiece had been displayed for most of its more than five and a half centuries to the artificial lighting at the new position). An improvement for viewers is that now, unlike in the past, they can walk at their own pace completely around the work, whose side panels are now extended out flat. Perhaps the profit from some of *your* travelers' checks helped American Express pay the bill for cleaning the 24 panels (12 paintings each on the front and back), and framing them under protective glass.

Famed in part because it represents a breakthrough in northern European painting style and technique (see Art under "The Belgian Cultural Legacy") with its Flemish "primitive" realism, and very early use of oil mixed with pigments (which greatly heightened the color and texture possible), the *Altarpiece* generally is thought to have been designed by Hubert, the elder van Eyck brother, in 1420. Hubert died in 1426 before he could contribute much to the execution of the altar retable. His brother Jan, considered the superior painter, completed the 24 panels by 1432. The wealthy childless donors of the work, Joos Vijd and his wife Elizabeth Borluut, appear in rich red robes on a panel beneath the *Annunciation.* Jan van Eyck was honored in his lifetime for this and other paintings, being made both court painter and a member of the *Order of the Golden Fleece* by Duke of Burgundy Philip the Good.

*The Adoration of the Mystical Lamb* is a compilation of Christian, cultural, social, and physical science beliefs about the world at the time of its creation, and it was conceived to assist the faithful by depicting graphically the hidden meaning of the Holy Mass. The center panel shows the slaughtered lamb, on the altar, dripping blood into a cup; the panel above shows Christ enthroned. Other panels show people from all walks of life in the world forming a community of praise and thanksgiving. The van Eycks created over 300 distinct individual faces on the 24 panels, and more than 200 species of flowers, trees, and shrubs are readily identifiable due to their realistic detail. Panels showing music being made recall the centuries-old sentiment that "singing is twice praying, playing is thrice praying."

If an intriguing past adds to a painting's allure, it's little wonder *The Mystical Lamb* is renowned. The 15th-century work had a first brush with destruction in the 1500s, when ultraconservative Calvinists came to St. Bavo's during the **Reformation's** *Iconoclasm* with the mutilation of art works and "graven images" on their mind; the altarpiece survived by being hidden high in the cathedral tower. During the Counter-Reformation, art collector Philip II wanted to acquire the painting for his collection, but in the end it was spared shipment to Spain. Hapsburg Holy Roman Emperor Joseph II, while ruler of the Austrian Netherlands (1765–1790), carried his modesty to the ridiculous degree of ordering the side-panel nude figures of *Adam* and *Eve* replaced with ones in which the parties were clothed in animal skins. (Adam and Eve were "unclothed" again after his death, and Joseph II's versions now hang near the west entrance.) In 1795, French forces shipped all 24 panels to Paris; fortunately, after the 1815 defeat of Napoleon at Waterloo, they were returned to St. Bavo's. The cathedral itself, having made copies, sold the original side panels in 1816 to pay for church restoration. A British antique dealer acquired them, subsequently selling several to **Kaiser Willem I**, who spliced the double-sided panels so they could be displayed along a wall in **Berlin's Imperial Museum**. The nude Adam and Eve panels eventually were purchased in 1861 by **Brussels' Museum of Ancient Art**, which later returned them to St. Bavo's as part of a multinational plan to reconstruct the masterpiece under its home roof. The 1919 *Treaty of Versailles* at the end of World War I ordered the panels that remained in Germany returned to Ghent, and in 1920 the whole work was once again set up in the cathedral.

Perhaps the strangest episode in the legend of the *Lamb* began the night of April 10, 1934, when the *Righteous Judges* and *John the Baptist* panels disappeared. Eventually, a ransom note for BF 1 million arrived, and *John* was recovered from a luggage locker in Brussels' Gare du Nord. But, to this day, the original *Judges* is missing, the only reference to it since being an inaudible whisper from a man on his death bed to his priest. A once wealthy Ghent burgher and former canon at St. Bavo's admitted stealing the panels for ransom, but the priest could not make out the words of his final confession about the fate of the *Judges*. In 1941, the panel was replaced by a copy made by artist **Jef Vanderveken**, who was so good at his job that, not wanting the copy to be mistaken for the original he included the features of the then Belgian king, Leopold III, in the piece.

After Belgium was occupied in 1940 in World War II, Nazi officer **Gehring** came to Ghent specifically to see *The Adoration of the Mystical Lamb*. He showed so much interest in the altarpiece that, after his visit, the bishop hid and then smuggled it out of Belgium to the town of Pau in unoccupied France. However, when the Nazis reached that region of France in 1942, they took possession and shipped it to a castle in German Bavaria. Near the end of the war, Hitler ordered it and other religious art works taken to a salt mine near Salzburg, Austria, on the pretense of protecting them from the approaching "atheistic" Russians who "would have blown them up." American Army soldiers in Austria at the end of the war stumbled across the stolen art. *The Mystic Lamb*, after restoration in Brussels, was joyously welcomed back to St. Bavo's which proclaimed the occasion a feast day.

St. Bavo's has other important pieces, among which are four pillar-shaped *copper candlesticks* (at the tomb of Bishop Allamont, d. 1673) that bear the arms of England's Henry VIII, by whose order and for whose tomb at St. George's Chapel at Windsor they originally were created in 1530. They came into the hands of Oliver Cromwell, who sold them to a Bishop Triest, who presented them to St. Bavo's. In the *Rubens' Chapel* is Pieter Paul's monumental *Conversion of St. Bavo* (the saint's face is said to be a self-portrait of the artist), commissioned directly by the cathedral in 1624. The striking mid-nave white-marble-entwined-with-dark-oak *pulpit* (**Laurent Delvaux**, 1741–1745) is a sculptural testament to Old Man Time, who is being awakened by a trumpet-tooting angel. The *Triptych of the Calvary* (1464) by **Justus van Gent**, in the 12th-century Romanesque crypt, is considered one of the church's finest treasures. St. Bavo's organ sports a sumptuous 1653 baroque-style case. Outside, in a small square behind the cathedral, is a bronze sculpture honoring the brothers van Eyck, shown seated on a bench, their heads wreathed in laurel.

### Gravensteen/Castle of the Counts     ★★★

*Sint-Veerleplein; daily April 1–Sept. 30, 9 a.m.–6:00 p.m., from Oct. –Mar. until 5 p.m. and closed Mon.; ☎ 223.99.77; important elements identified in English; guided tours in English April–Oct. on Sat., Sun. and holidays at 11 a.m. and noon.* This magnificent, almost unrivaled example of a feudal fortress of the counts of Flanders with its massive medieval shape rising from the reflective waters of its moat, was built about 1180 by **Philip of Alsace** and follows the style of crusaders' fortified castles in Syria. The counts' need for a castle was less for the protection of the town and more for control over demanding citizen-workers in Ghent's rapidly expanding cloth industry. Gravensteen was, in fact, stormed by such individuals in 1302 during the period of the *Battle of the Golden Spurs*, and again in 1338 by weavers led by Jacob van Artevelde. In 1349, after occupation by 14 of his fellows, the count of Flanders abandoned the undoubtedly dark and dreary Gravensteen for the airier Gothic **Prinsenhof** (which no longer stands). From that time, the castle ended its military role, though retaining ceremonial functions. In subsequent centuries, it served as Mint and High Court of Justice. Before becoming a cotton-spinning factory from 1797 to 1887, it served as a prison, and its extensive collection of torture instruments, painful even in appearance, date from its prison days and are displayed throughout the rooms. Between 1894 and 1913 the Castle of the Counts was restored, and thereafter opened to the public. Although it's possible to find them closed due to more recent restoration, several rooms in the count's residence tower (*donjon*) usually are open. They include the vaulted *Audience Chamber* where the Council of Flanders sat for 300 years. From the *Upper Hall*, winding stairs lead to the roof, from which there's a fine view across Ghent. The *Great Hall* was the setting for a huge banquet for the seventh chapter meeting of the *Order of the Golden Fleece* given by Philip the Good in 1445. Parts of the 9th-century castle formerly on the site survive and can be seen in the cellars of the keep. When leaving the Gravensteen, go beyond its moat to the corner of Gewad and Burgstraat (across the street from **Hotel Gravensteen**) to see the 1559 Renaissance facade of the ★ **House of the Crowned Heads**, which has portraits of all the Counts of Flanders from Boudewijn to Philip II.

*Ghent's Castle of the Counts (Gravensteen) is an unrivaled example of a feudal fortress.*

### Graslei                                                ★ ★ ★

The Graslei is the site of the old port of Ghent (today, the departure point for cruises of the city's remaining canals). Easily identifiable midway (No. 15) along the row of impressive quayside buildings is **Spijker** or **Koornstapelhuis** (public grain warehouse), the oldest (c. 1200), also the plainest, in Romanesque style, where grain was held as customs duty payment in kind. Also a standout is the 1682 tiny **Tol-huisje** (little customs house). On **Korenlei**, opposite and from which there is a fine view of the Graslei with its buildings reflected in the water the most elegant facade is No. 9, the former 16th-century brewery **De Zwaene** (the swan), on which medallions show swans swimming away from each other.

### Belfroi/Belfry                                              ★

*Sint-Baafsplein; daily mid-March to mid-Nov. 10 a.m.–12:30 p.m., 2–5:30 p.m.; elevator; guided tours including room of carilllonneur at ten minutes past each hour 10 a.m.–5 p.m., except 1 p.m.* Begun in 1313, Ghent's

medieval municipal tower, city symbol of power and autonomy, was finished in 1380 and topped off with a dragon-shaped weathercock. One of the purposes of a belfry was to safeguard town privileges or charters: Ghent's were secured in the *Secret* room under triple lock and key in a solid oak chest. The belfry was named for the bells hung there, which city watchmen would sound in alarm. In 1315, **Roeland** was cast as Ghent's stormbell; weighing 12,000 pounds; it is said to have taken seven strong men to swing Roeland to make it ring. Charles V, displeased with Ghent citizens' rebelliousness, had Roeland removed from the belfry in 1540, though eventually it again took up its position in the tower. In 1659, town fathers melted Roeland down; the vast amount of metal thus produced enabled the famed Hemony brothers to cast a complete 37-bell carillon. (Those bells cast from the original Roeland still form the heart of Ghent's now-expanded carillon, considered one of the best in Belgium.) The largest of the bells cast in 1659, Roeland's heir, rang the hour for Ghent's belfry clock in its G-pitch. Today, it is exhibited on **Emile Braunplein** at the foot of the belfry, having cracked in 1914 when the tower bells were being switched to electric power. The third **Roeland** to hang high in the tower was cast in 1984.

Adjoining the belfry is the ★**Lakenhal/Cloth Hall**. The Cloth Hall, itself a symbol of Ghent's substantial success in the earliest days of Europe's textile industry, was begun in 1425, though with city fortunes changed, not completed until this century. Once serving as a place of assembly for wool and cloth merchants, the restored Gothic ★**underground hall**, divided into three aisles by 20 pillars, today is a restaurant. (See "Where to Eat, Raadskelder.")

### Stadhuis/Town Hall                                            ★

*On the corner of Botermarkt and Hoogpoort; guided visits in English Mon. to Thurs. 3 p.m., meet at tourist information, Stadhuis crypt (☎ 221.24.08).* The Stadhuis facade shows several architectural styles: flamboyant Gothic (by **Waghemakere** and **R. Keldermans**) fronts the Hoogpoort, a sober Renaissance style employed during the Calvinist period faces Botermarkt, with baroque and empire style elements finally finishing the whole in the 17th and 18th centuries. The spread-out construction, from 1321 to 1750, resulted in part from city politics and policies. The interior, viewed only on guided tours, is best noted for the ★★**Pacificatiezaal**, the room in which the *Pacification of Ghent*— meant to restore order after the Reformation outrages between the Catholics and Protestants—was signed on December 8, 1576. The event is noted by a wall plaque; another announces that here for six months in 1814 meetings took place between England and the United States (represented by **John Quincy Adams**) to arrive at the terms for the *Treaty of Ghent* to end the **War of 1812**. A second name for the great wood-beamed, stained glass windowed room is the **Tribunal Hall**, since the **Court of Justice** sat here. The immense floor of 2401 polished light-and-dark-toned stones is laid out in a **maze**. One of the punishments meted out by the court was "humiliation," which meant that in front of the 13 aldermen and other representatives, the guilty person had to make his way on his knees from one end of the room to the other, and retracing his route if he wound up at a "dead-end" in the maze. (The shortest successful route is 500 meters/0.3 mile.) In the **Hall of Honors** hangs an impressive portrait of Vienna's Maria Theresa in a gown made all of lace. The dress, made by orphan girls of Ghent, was a present to the Hapsburg empress, who in turn presented Ghent with this painting of herself wearing the impressive attire. The **Troonzaal** or throne room, a Gothic hall in which the Ghent city council now meets, is hung with huge historic paintings.

## WHERE TO STAY

All the properties included below are located in the center of historic Ghent. Since the *usual* overnight traveler to Ghent is business oriented, inquire about special hotel rates and packages at weekends.

## MODERATE

### Hotel Gravensteen
*Jan Breydelstraat 35, B-9000;* ☎ *225.11.50, FAX 225.18.50.* A friendly welcome awaits at the elegant marble entryway of this well-restored 1865 second empire-style mansion that once belonged to one of Ghent's textile merchants. It's located across from The Castle of the Counts, doors from the Decorative Arts Museum, and a single attractive block from the Graslei. The 17 comfortable, contemporarily furnished rooms all have bath/shower, toilet, TV, telephone, minibar, and individual heat control; buffet breakfast (included) is served in a room facing the back garden. Ask for access to the hotel's top-floor *belvedere* that overlooks the Castle of the Counts, magically illuminated at night. Elevator; parking; major credit cards; year-round weekend rates, discounts during the week—Dec.–Jan. and July–Aug.

## INEXPENSIVE

### St. Jorishof (Cour Saint-Georges)
*Botermarkt 2, B-9000;* ☎ *224.24.24, FAX 224.26.40.* A hostelry from its beginnings in 1228 (making it, some say, Europe's oldest hotel), St. Jorishof today sports a more modern, 16th-century, stepped-gable facade. Used as a guildhall by Ghent's *Crossbows* and by the *States-General of Flanders* for its meetings in the 15th century, here on Feb. 11, 1477, **Mary of Burgundy** was forced to sign Ghent's *Great Privilege*. On this occasion the Lion of Flanders symbol was carved into the monumental mantlepiece of the balconied **Gothic Hall**, today one of Ghent's most popular restaurants (gastronomic fare, decor of stained glass, dark wood). **Emperor Charles V**, born in Ghent in 1500, was a frequent guest at the hotel later in his life, and **Emperor Napoleon** stayed here in 1805. All 36 rooms, most of which are in a modern annex in the hotel's inner courtyard, have pleasant traditional decor, bath and/or shower and toilet, TV, telephone, automatic wake-up, and most have a minibar. Elevator; parking; major credit cards. Hotel closed last 3 weeks of July, 2 weeks beginning Christmas Day.

### Erasmus
*Poel 25;* ☎ *224.21.95, FAX 233.42.41.* This recent addition to Ghent's central city hotel scene is situated in a restored 1593 townhouse. Each of the 11 rooms is individually antique-decorated. There's a back garden for outside breakfasts in summer, and a breakfast room and bar in the cellar. Two stories; no elevator.

## WHERE TO EAT

*Waterzooi*, a chicken or fish soup/stew with vegetables, is Ghent's foremost specialty, with *Gentse hutsepot*, a meat stew, and *stoverij*, steak and kidney flavored with beer, also readily available. *Rabbit* comes young and older: the first with prunes, the later as jugged hare. *Mokken*, a small round cake made of flour and syrup, is a local treat, as is almond-bread and rye bread with currants. A spicy Ghent tradition is *Tierenteyn*, a locally made (for 200 years) dijon-style mustard, that's sold in a shop on Groetenmarkt.

**Jan Breydel** *(Jan Breydelstraat 10;* ☎ *225.62.87; moderate)*, just steps from the *Castle of the Counts*, offers relaxed garden-greenery elegance, showing good taste and a delicate touch in the decor as well as the cuisine. There's a priority on fresh ingredients, seafood, and regional specialties. At **Graaf van Egmond** *(St. Michielsplein 21; open daily;* ☎ *225.07.27; moderate downstairs, inexpensive upstairs)*, if you're lucky and get a table by the window, you'll enjoy a wonderful view of Ghent's famed towers and the *Graslei*. Downstairs in the delightful c. 1200 townhouse with such Flemish dishes as *carbonnade flamande* (beef stew with beer) and, in season, sensational *asparagus à la flamande* are served. The grill upstairs—same view—offers simpler fare. **Het Coornmetershuys** *(Graslei 12; open lunch through evening;* ☎ *223.49.71; moderate; light lunch, inexpensive)*, tucked upstairs behind a 14th-century facade on Ghent's gorgeous *Graslei*, serves Flemish specialties as well as other daily choices to the strains of classical music (music selections are also listed in the menu) in a room whose walls are decorated with musical instruments. In addition to full dinners and light lunches, pancakes, snacks, and pastries are served, so it makes a good refreshment stop even for coffee. With the name **Waterzooi** *(Sint-Veerleplein 2; closed Tues. evening, Wed.;* ☎ *225.05.63; inexpensive)* this could be where you decide to try Ghent's celebrated fish (the original ingredient) or chicken (today, a well-established alternative) stew with vegetables; portions will please your palate and your purse. The **Raadskelder** *(Sint-Baafsplein; open daily 9:30 a.m.–1 a.m.;* ☎ *225.43.34; inexpensive)* is the 15th-century, vaulted cellar of the cloth hall that adjoins the belfry; you can sit in church pews and pause over a cup of coffee or four-course tourist menu. It's large and caters to crowds (you could get caught with a busload of tourists), but the fare is fine, and since you're bound to pass it in your sightseeing at least stick your head in and see the setting.

The **Patershol quarter**, located near the Castle of the Counts, as well as being an interesting district that retains a medieval street pattern. and after long neglect now is being restored, is a neighborhood known for its restaurants. Since many of the buildings in the area were small to begin with, so are the restaurants, and thus reservations are in order. **By den Wyzen en den Zot** *(Hertogstraat 8; noon–2:30 p.m., dinner from 6:30 p.m., closed Sun., Mon.;* ☎ *223.42.30; moderate)* serves up its fish and meat dishes in three beamed rooms in this 17th-century, gabled, brick, corner house. **Valentijn** *(Rode Koningstraat 1; open noon–2:30 p.m., 7–9:30 p.m., closed Sat. lunch, Sun., Mon.;* ☎ *225.04.29; inexpensive, special seasonal monthly menu moderate)* includes traditional dishes (*waterzooi*, eels in green sauce) among its offerings to guests seated in the attractive brick-walled space. **Amadeus** *(Plotersgracht 8; daily 6 p.m.–midnight, Sun. from noon;* ☎ *233.27.74; inexpensive),* which bills itself as a spare-rib restaurant, is darkish and cozy with lots of beveled glass, wood, and old tiles; tables are covered with red and white oilskin, but the napkins are cloth.

Ghent cafes with character include **De Witte Leeuw** *(Graslei 6),* which gives you a chance to step behind one of the Graslei's famous facades. This is one from the 17th century; some 300 beers (8 on tap) are listed as being available. In the c. 1439 setting of **De Dulle Griet** *(Vrijdagmarkt 50; daily noon–1 a.m.;* ☎ *224.24.55; inexpensive)* only 250 sorts of beer are served, but that includes all of Belgium's Trappist-and Abbey-produced brews, in a genuine pub setting: mugs hanging above the bar, kegs for tables. If you decide to dine (reservations suggested), there's a restaurant upstairs with scenes of old Ghent on the walls, dark beams, and a view onto historic *Vrijdagmarkt.* **Het Waterhuis aan de Bierkant** *(Groentenmarkt 9;* ☎ *225.06.80)* is an old cafe specializing in Belgian beers whose terrace is canalside and within sight of several of Ghent's historic buildings.

## THE BELGIAN COAST

Belgium's 40-mile/65-km. North Sea coast, slanting northeast to southwest from Holland to France, lies entirely within the province of West Flanders. In the 12th and 13th centuries, much of it lay under water at high tide; only in the 14th and 15th centuries did the Belgian coast take its current shape. The wide beaches at low tide (up to 2000 ft/600 meters in some spots) attest to the flatness of the land, much of which is polder, kept dry by the extensive use of dikes. Perhaps surprisingly, Belgium's seaside towns are sunnier than those inland, even one as nearby as Bruges. Many Belgians take summer holidays on their own beaches, but Germans, French, and the British join them; the Dutch are less likely to because of their own fine sandy shores in Zeeland just up the coast. Despite its limited length, Belgium's North Sea coast has an unbroken string of resorts with piers, promenades, and seaside recreational opportunities; each with a separate character that tends to pull in a different compatible socio-economic crowd. Most summer visitors do not come to the Belgian coast for culture, but overseas travelers may be interested in the area's isolated and interesting artistic attractions. Then again, if you're suffering from a surfeit of fine art, you can find solace by putting sand between your toes during solitary walks on Belgium's firm beaches or soft dunes, knowing all the while that you're never far from a cool drink or fine meal along any of the shop and restaurant-lined seaside promenades.

# GUIDELINES FOR THE BELGIAN COAST

## SIGHTS

Many area attractions are scenic: sand dunes, broad beaches, nature reserves, sea, all with the hoped-for accompaniment of sun. **De Panne**, whose beach stretches southwest into France to **Dunkirk**, (*Dunkerque*), is renowned for restaurants. Just north at **St. Idesbald** is the former home and present museum with the lifelong works of the late *Belgian surrealist painter* **Paul Delvaux**. Shrimp are big in **Oostduinkerke-aan-Zee**, where the now-only-for-tourists, horseback fishermen work. *Queen of the Coast* **Ostend** retains something of its grande dame air, still welcoming the passenger and car ferries from England that in the 19th century made it the most British beachhead in Belgium. Ostend fishermen maintain a fleet, fish auction, and market that add color to the hotel and restaurant-lined waterfront. Ostend *symbolist artist* **James Ensor** left a studio in his house and artwork in the local museum. Continuing up the coast, **De Haan** has an especially broad and safe swimming beach that's sought out by families with children, while **Blankenberge**, once a small fishing village, has become the liveliest location, (especially popular with holiday makers who enjoy dancing and other night life). **Knokke-Heist**, at the northeast end, is by far the most fashionable resort on Belgium's coast, with its *boutiques*, *galleries*, and *casino*. Gambling is technically against Belgian law, but four casinos flourish on the coast: in addition to Knokke, at Ostend, Blankenberge, and Middelkerke. All have restaurants.

## GETTING AROUND

Knokke-Heist, Blankenberge, Zeebrugge, and Ostend are served by **trains** from Brussels through Bruges; otherwise, a **car** is necessary to explore the coast. Modern **coastal trams** are convenient if you have the time; there's half-hourly service (and, in summer, 15-minute service) from Knokke via Zeebrugge to Ostend, and from Ostend to De Panne (approximately 70 minutes from Ostend to either end of the coast). As at beach resorts everywhere, the coastal road (not always in sight of the sea) can be crowded in summer. **Cycle paths** in dunes and **walking paths** in nature reserves are well signposted. Day tours of **Flanders' battlefields** and other landmarks of the First World War around Ypres depart Bruges on Tues., Thurs., and Sat. (9 a.m.–4:30 p.m.) via Quasimodo Tours *(Poortersstraat 47, 8310 Brugge;* ☎ *(050) 37.04.70, FAX (050) 37.49.60).*

## SHOPPING

**Ostend** is the main town on the Belgian coast, with the largest selection of stores. Upmarket boutiques and art galleries are found in **Knokke**. Shops in both Ostend and Knokke are open year round, also many on Sundays. Elsewhere one finds the usual resort and souvenir shops in season; they're often open seven days a week and closed completely out of season.

## ENTERTAINMENT AND EVENTS

Carrying on tradition for the tourists, the **horseback**, **shrimp fishermen** appear about low tide in the morning (check exact time locally) at **Oostduinkerke-aan-Zee** in July and August, on sturdy Brabant farm horses. (The tradition, it's said, began as early as the late 1400s when farmers, needing to supplement meager earnings, put their horsepower to work dragging nets through the sea.) At the **Knokke casino**, concerts are performed by internationally known entertainers and musical ensembles, and exhibitions are frequent fare. At Easter the **World Press Photo Exhibit** and in summer the **cartoon exhibition**, featuring well-known and new talent, make annual appearances. **Ostend's casino** has varied entertainers and entertainment throughout the year. In 1995 the **Tall Ships** will visit Zeebrugge (August 16–20).

## WHERE TO STAY

The most plentiful choice of better quality hotels is found in Knokke-Heist. Elsewhere along the coast are plenty of three-star properties, a sprinkling of two- and four-star hotels, and a number of *pensions*, many close out of season. In season, especially from late July to early September, when making a reservation be sure to establish whether accommodations are *en pension* (required payment for full board in the hotel restaurant), and whether there's a minimum-length stay.

## WHERE TO EAT

You can choose an eatery with confidence anywhere along the coast. In this resort area for food-loving Belgians, an establishment that didn't deliver much-better-than-decent dishes wouldn't be in business long. Naturally, fresh fish and seafood (especially mussels and the small North Sea "gray" shrimp) are specialties.

## ARRIVING

Passenger/car ferries and the speedier hovercraft sail a number of times daily around the clock and year-round between England's channel port of Ramsgate and Belgium's Ostend and Zeebrugge; other service sails out of Folkestone, Felixstowe and Hull.

## IN THE AREA

Inland from the southwest end of Belgium's coast, from De Panne via Veurne, is **Ypres/Ieper** (pronounced EE'pe), most remembered as the center in World War I of the muddy, bloody Flanders *battle-fields* where poppies blow. Centuries earlier, Ypres (together with Bruges and Ghent) was famous as one of Flanders' fine cloth-making towns; its magnificent flamboyant Gothic **cloth hall** (rebuilt to the original exterior design after being destroyed in the war) serves as a memorable reminder of the period.

## TRAVEL TIPS

Coastal towns are popular with Belgian and European summer holidaymakers, and well-ahead reservations for the better hotel or pension properties in July and August are essential. Tourism information for the whole West Flanders coastal region can be had in Bruges from **Westtoerisme** (*Kasteel Tillegem, 8200 Brugge,* ☎ *(050) 38.02.96).* Otherwise, visit the tourist centers in individual towns.

# WALLONIA

The southern, slightly larger half of Belgium is French-speaking **Wallonia**. Its 5800 square miles comprise the provinces of **Hainaut**, **Namur**, **Liège**, **Luxembourg**, and **Walloon Brabant**. The name Wallonia derives from the *Wala*, romanized early Celtic inhabitants of the northern reaches of Caesar's Gaul, whose development of the French language dates from Roman days. Thus was established the beginnings of Belgium's linguistic/cultural border—to the north of which, in what became Flanders, there arose a Frankish influence, and a Germanic language developed.

The preeminence of French in *both* regions that make up present-day Belgium dates from the 14th century, when the **French Burgundians** fought the **counts of Flanders** and won supremacy in language and law. From that time until late in the 20th century in Belgium—and for many centuries, in the courts of most European rulers, including the English—French was *the* language of politics, law, and culture. The status of the French language conferred what amounted to special treatment for Belgium's Walloons over the Flemish. The government of both populations was conducted solely *en français.* In the law courts it was the same, which meant that Flemings frequently were unable even to understand the charges being brought against them. Perhaps most important of all, schools taught classes only in French, which tended to keep the Flemish uneducated and down on their farms. Only as the *Flemish Movement* gathered strength in the late 19th century and into the 20th did Belgium change from an essentially single-language country to a truly bilingual one.

Wallonia takes a back seat to Flanders in terms of the interests of most overseas travelers to Belgium. However, for visitors with time to see more of the country than its unfailingly fine Flemish cities, Wallonia offers a number of choices. The French-speaking community has many historic, artistically and architecturally significant cities, among them **Tournai**, a Roman-era town and former Frankish capital at the western end of Wallonia, and **Liège**, a once esteemed and influential prince-bishopric, to the east. To a great extent, however, southern Belgium's charms are scenic, clustered in the wooded forests and rushing river gorges of the **Ardennes**.

The *Meuse, Sambre, Ourthe*, and *Semois* river valleys claim picturesque fortress towns: **Namur**, **Dinant**, **Huy**, and **Durbuy**. In the healthy outdoor surroundings, it isn't surprising to find a spa, but Belgium's **Spa** was Europe's prototype. Castles (as old as **Bouillon**, one of whose owners mortgaged it to outfit a company for the *First Crusade* in A.D. 1096, and as elegant as the still-occupied **Beloeil**, seat of the princes of Ligne), abbeys (Orval's earliest ruins date from the 12th century), grand gardens (such as the many-fountained ones at **Annevoie**), and gaping natural caves (as at **Han-sur-Lesse**) punctuate a rural driving route with interesting focal points.

Unlike Flanders's World War I sites around Ypres, Wallonia's battlefields shed light on World War II, especially at **Bastogne** near the Luxembourg border. Bastogne was the center of the once-strategic, now primarily scenic, "bulge" of land in the Ardennes that gave name to Hitler's last desperate, doomed and destructive campaign.

# TOURNAI

## *GUIDELINES FOR TOURNAI*
### SIGHTS

Tournai (*Doornik* in Flemish), with an urban population of 35,000, is dominated by its unique five-towered **cathedral**, a 12th- and 13th-century Romanesque/Gothic masterpiece that's the centerpiece for city orientation. Once Roman and by the 5th century the capital for the Franks, Tournai's numerous historic sights are mostly situated in its southwest quarter, near the **Escaut (Scheldt) River**, and crossed by the picturesque 13th-century **pont des Trous** from which there's a superb view of the city and cathedral towers. Tournai has Belgium's oldest **belfry** (c. 1200) and Europe's oldest **burgher houses** (12th century). Victor Horta's *art nouveau* art museum has paintings by Tournai-born, Flemish "primitive" school founding father **Robert Campin** (*The Master of Flemalle*) and his pupil **Rogier de la Pasture/Rogier van der Weyden**. Other museums show off fine old examples of the city's locally-produced sculpture, tapestries, and porcelain. Skillfully **illuminated**, the cathedral seems to dominate the town center at night even more than during the day.

## GETTING AROUND

Tournai's **rail station** is at the northeast edge of the center city. It's more or less a straight line, and a bit over one mile/two kilometers from the train station up rue Royale and across the river to the cathedral. If you have luggage or prefer to begin walking in the center from which other important sights (**cathedral/belfry/Grand Place**) are accessible by foot, take a taxi from the station. For a 45-minute overview of the city, the tourist office (across from the belfry) can book you a taxi tour with an English commentary cassette tape that keeps in sync with sites.

## SHOPPING

A principal city of the Belgian Walloon province of Hainaut, Tournai is a major shopping center with outlets located principally in the pedestrian precinct around and to the southeast of **place St-Pierre**. Open-air produce and general markets are held Saturdays on the **Grand' Place** and place St-Pierre, 8 a.m.–1 p.m.; at that time there's also a flower market on **place Emile Janson**, which abuts the cathedral. A flea market takes place on place St-Pierre, Sun. 8 a.m.–1 p.m. The **quai du Marché Poisson**, along the river, has assorted antique shops.

## ENTERTAINMENT AND EVENTS

**Carillon concerts** are played at 11:30 a.m. Sats. from June through Aug. in the belfry; there are outside cafes at its base, but because of traffic you might hear the bells better from a bit farther away. Ask at the tourist office about Sunday afternoon **concerts in the cathedral** in July and Aug., and Sunday morning concerts by Conservatory students from Nov.–March. Each second Sunday in June is Tournai's **Day of Four Processions**, which features just that. On the second Sunday in Sept. at 3 p.m. is the historic **Procession of the Plague**, commemorating the deadly epidemic of the year 1090, and during which are displayed some of the cathedral's priceless art treasures.

## WHERE TO STAY

Hotels in the old city with good standards of comfort and service are limited. Plan ahead if you anticipate overlapping with Tournai's major annual trade fairs in April/May and Sept/Oct.

## WHERE TO EAT

Tournai offers a reasonable selection of in-town restaurants serving appetizing food in appealing settings. Cuisine generally is French-influenced, with an emphasis on fresh Belgium ingredients such as endive, Ardennes ham, rabbit, and asparagus. Local sweets include plum tarts and *faluches* (butter and brown sugar cakes).

## ARRIVING

Direct trains from Brussels to Tournai (79 km/48 mi) take about an hour. The city also has direct rail service from Liège and Lille France, (26 km/16 mi). Motorway access is via A 27.

## IN THE AREA

Some 16 mi/27 km southeast of Tournai is **Chateau de Beloeil**, the largest of 30-odd, privately-owned castles in Belgium, which has one of Europe's richest legacies. The residence of the *princes de Ligne* since the 14th century, Beloeil has 15th–19th-century furniture, portraits, tapestries, and objets d'art on view to the public. Its park, one of the finest in Belgium, is attributed to **Le Nôtre**, who designed the gardens at Versailles.

# LIÈGE

## *GUIDELINES FOR LIÈGE*

### SIGHTS

At the heart of Liège are the **Prince-Bishops Palace** on place St-Lambert and **Perron** monument on the adjacent *place du Marché*, both attesting to the city's history of independence. Several restored **mansion-museums**, and the **Museum of Walloon Life** in a former convent, shed light on Liège life. The city's selection of churches with Romanesque foundations includes St. Barthelemy's with its famed 12th-century **baptismal font** by **Renier du Huy**. Readers of works by native son **Georges Simenon** will find that the atmosphere of his books, though often set in Paris, is thickly Liège. Adding flavor to Belgium's Walloon bastion is the river **Meuse** (the *Maas* in nearby

Holland), which flows through the city, separating the old town from the colorful workers' quarter of **Outremeuse**.

## GETTING AROUND

Although Liège is a large city, many of its important sights and museums are located within walking distance of each other, not far from the main **tourist office** (*Feronstree 92*). Staff there can arrange for a guided (English), set-price **city taxi tour**. Taxi ranks are located at *Gare Guillemins, place du Marché, place St-Lambert, place Foch, place de la Cathédrale, place de la Républiqué Française,* and *blvd. d'Avroy.* Liège has a good **bus network**; maps of the system are posted at stops and available at the tourist office. Main terminals are *place Saint-Lambert, place du Theatre, place Cathédrale,* and *place des Guillemins.* There are **boat cruises** on the **Meuse** (schedule at tourist office), though the scenery doesn't justify the full-day river trip to nearby Maastricht in Holland; take a train instead.

## SHOPPING

Liège is famed for its Sunday morning (9 a.m.–2 p.m.) market **la Batte**—a Walloon word that means *embankment*—held along the Meuse between *place Cockerill* and *pont Maghin.* The amazing range of foodstuffs, household items, clothing, small animals, and cosmetic merchandise, combined with thousands of browsers and buyers (many from neighboring Holland and Germany), give this flea market something of the flavor of a medieval fair. Shoppers from near and far also come weekdays to Liège, a major regional market town with one of Europe's largest center-city pedestrian precincts. It has some 5,000 retail outlets, from large department stores and fashion boutiques to antiques shops; prime streets include *rue de la Cathédrale, rue St.-Paul, rue de la Regence, blvd. de la Sauveniere, place du Marché, Feronstree, pont d'Avroy,* and across the river, *rue Jean d'Outre-Meuse.* Antiques shops are clustered around *rue St. Thomas, rue des Mineurs,* and *rue du Palais.*

Liège's **Val Saint Lambert** handcut crystal has been produced since 1826 at a factory south of Liège in Seraing (*Crystalworks Val-Saint-Lambert; rue du Val 245;* ☎ *(041) 37.09.60; FAX (041) 37.67.81; , April–Oct. 31 Tues.–Sun. 10 a.m.–5 p.m., closed Mon.; rest of year Sat., Sun., holidays. only, same hours.; exhibition hall and Val Diffusion shop open year-round Tues.–Sun. 10 a.m.–5 p.m., closed Mon.; guided tours; self-service restaurant; accessible by bus from Jemeppe Gare Routiere in Liège*). There are studio demonstrations of glass-blowing, decoration, and engraving. The exhibition hall has a permanent display of antique and contemporary pieces. The *Val Diffusion* shop sells pieces made by trainees and apprentices.

## ENTERTAINMENT AND EVENTS

Born in Liège, composer **Cesar Franck** (1822–1890) attended the **Conservatoire** *(rue Forgeur 14;* ☎ *22.03.06)*, which still offers concerts of his and other works, as does the **Orchestre Philharmonique** *(rue Forgeur 11;* ☎ *23.67.74)*. The active **Opera Royal de Wallonie** *(place de la Republique Francaise;* ☎ *23.59.10)* occasionally pays honor to Liège-born **Andre Ernest Gretry** (1741–1813), a composer particularly noted for his comic operas. For performance schedules of these, midday and Sunday morning concerts and others, inquire at the tourist office. **Jazz** can be heard in rue Roture in Outremeuse at **Le Lions'Envoile** and **Le Cirque Divers**, and at **Les Caves de Porto** in Feronstree in the old town. Music clubs and cafes also are centered in **le Carré** (Old Town), which is bordered by *blvd. Sauveniere, pont d'Avroy, Vinave d'Ile,* and *rue des Dominicaines.* The 4th weekend in June is observed in the **Commune of Saint-Pholien** with morning concerts, open air mass, festive lights and fireworks, and a meeting of the "giants." August 15 is Liège's **Free Republic of Outremeuse's** feast day, celebrated in the streets with spirited traditional events and a fun fair. **September Nights** is an annual Liège music festival. At the end of September, the **Fêtes de Wallonie** is held in the courtyard of the Prince-Bishops Palace.

## WHERE TO STAY

Comfortable, convenient hotels in Liège are limited, so plan ahead with reservations when possible. The tourist office will assist.

## WHERE TO EAT

Many of Liège's typical dishes are pork specialties (such as *boudin blanc,* a white sausage). City restaurants serve fare from French *haute cuisine* to *potée,* the Walloon word for *stew. Boulets frites* are large firm balls of bread stuffing flavored with meat and doused in gravy. Local street-stand favorites include *bouketes* (thick buckwheat pancakes). The farmstead-studded **Herve** region, to the northeast of Liège, is famous for its odorous cheese; locally, it's served spread on toast and topped with syrup. **Pubs**—Liège's 10,000-strong student population helps support them, and the city's many terrace cafes and taverns—can't legally, but often do, pour *peket,* a powerful local gin.

## ARRIVING

Liège is an international rail crossroads, with direct trains from Brussels and Luxembourg City, and many connections. The principal rail station is **Gare des Guillemins** (with taxis), about 1.5 mi./2 kms. from the *place St-Lambert*. The city also is linked to major European cities by motorway, and to regional cities from its **airport**. If you arrive in Liège by **car**, there's a car park beside the main tourist office *(Feronstreet 90)*, and others at *place Cathédrale, place du Marché, place Saint-Lambert;* center city driving is hampered around place Saint-Lambert because of traffic overload, coupled with construction.

## TRAVEL TIPS

Municipal financial difficulties have interrupted the building of Liège's Metro, leaving an unsightly construction site in front of the **Bishop's Palace** at **place St-Lambert** in the center of the city. The unfortunate fiscal situation also means that museum hours have been reduced because of cutbacks in personnel; confirm the opening hours when you arrive.

# THE MEUSE VALLEY

Upstream and southwest of Liège, the Meuse arches around the western edge of the Ardennes, passing through **Huy**, **Namur**, and **Dinant**, south of which it enters France. Signs of industry and commercial river traffic are few south of Namur, which leaves Dinant favorably situated for the recreational use of the river. Most of the region's other waterways—the **Semois**, **Lesse**, **Sambre**, **Samson**, and **Ourthe**—flow into the **Meuse**, which is Wallonia's water highway of history. From prehistoric days, the Meuse has served as the most convenient means of transportation through the region. It was the route used by Roman legions policing this far northern corner of their Empire, the river road taken by invading Vikings, and a respite river-borne stretch of the long pathway west for medieval central European pilgrims making their way, mostly on foot, from monastery to chapel to Spain's Santiago de Compostela St. James's shrine. The upper valley of the Meuse, which begins south of Namur, has a particular charm, with wooded hillsides, strange rock formations, near-vertical escarpments that plunge to the river, and picturesque villages built in the local blue-gray stone and roofed with local slate.

Today its scenic towns are touted as peaceful sites for tourists, but for many centuries the strategic significance of the Meuse meant that its towns, squeezed onto narrow banks beneath rocky cliffs, were spared few sieges and bombardments. Most Meuse towns are dominated still by their citadels, whose first foundations may have been built more than a thousand years ago.

Although largely vanished as an industry in the upper Meuse valley, the iron ore in its hills, in combination with plentiful timber to feed furnaces, and rushing rivers to power waterwheels, produced a flourishing iron empire in the area early on. Many of today's Mosan titled families can trace their fine castles—some open to the public—and family fortunes back to the forges. The 18th-century gardens that complement the castle at **Annevoie** were funded by ironmaster Charles-Alexis de Montpellier in the 18th century and, at **Jehay Castle**, present resident Count Guy van den Steen carries on the iron tradition as an artist, creating great iron gates and handsome hearthplates for his home.

## *GUIDELINES FOR THE MEUSE VALLEY*

*Dinant's clifftop Citadel dominates the riverside town.*

## SIGHTS

Anchored by the slate-roofed towns of **Huy** and **Dinant** and the city of **Namur** (the administrative capital of Wallonia), the Meuse Valley is dotted with idyllic villages—such as **Celles**, fortified farms, owner-occupied museum **castles** (some with wonderful gardens), and—above all—**citadels** that crown their towns. Many examples of Mosan-style architecture (a mix of Romanesque and Gothic) are to be seen. The Meuse valley offers the opportunity for white-water kayaking and cruising from one town to another to keep up the region's tradition of river travel. Rock climbers can train on sheer cliffs fronting the Meuse.

## GETTING AROUND

You can travel by **train** to Namur and from that major junction to Huy and Dinant, the tracks (and the roads) hugging the river banks in many places. However, the Meuse valley, even with the aid of the **cruise boats** that ply between Namur and Dinant and some of the smaller towns in season, cannot be seen in all its scenic beauty without a **car**.

## SHOPPING

As a provincial capital, **Namur** is the primary urban center for a wide area; its main shopping street is *rue de l'Ange*. **Dinant** has long produced engraved yellow copper (*Dinanderie*) articles for religious or domestic use. Fashioned since well before the 14th century—by which time some 7500 of Dinant's population of 50,000 were employed in dinanderie—copperware in Dinant today has experienced a revival as a cottage industry; hand-beaten items can be found in several shops locally. In **Huy**, which has an ancient tradition of metalworking—12th-century goldsmith **Renier de Huy** created Liège's celebrated baptismal font—craftsmen eventually turned to pewter. Many pewter products can be found in shops.

## ENTERTAINMENT AND EVENTS

Among the many **Wallonia Festival** activities in Namur in September are the historic *stilt-walkers*. Namur and Dinant both have **casinos**, which host many cultural events.

## WHERE TO STAY

Hotels in the region are limited in number and inclined to be very small (the exception being the modern **Novotel**, south of Namur in **Wepion**). Country hotels focus on their kitchens as much as and often more than on guest rooms, which can number as few as a half dozen.

## WHERE TO EAT

The Meuse Valley offers Belgian countryside tourism at its best, so you can feel certain of reaping rewarding meals. In towns, restaurants at hotels always make good, often the best, choices. In the country, restaurants and hotels usually come coupled and will be your best, maybe only, bet for dining. Their kitchens will feature regional specialties such as the fish dish *Escaveche de la Meuse*, as well as river trout and crayfish, and *flamiche*, a bubbling, warm cheese and butter tart. Dinant is well known for its *couque*, hard pastry and honey cookies baked in molds in many forms, sometimes of considerable size. The *fraises* (strawberries) of Wepion are famous.

# THE ARDENNES

The **Ardennes**—possibly the inspiration for Shakespeare's *Forest of Arden* in *As You Like It*—covers nearly one-third of southeast Belgium. The definition of what strictly is and isn't the Ardennes—many non-Belgians hold the inaccurate idea that everything south and east of the Meuse river is a single undifferentiated area—matters most to those who live there. Visitors consulting a map will note the large green forested stretches that indicate the ruralness of the region. The highest reaches of the **Belgian Ardennes**—the Ardennes extend well into the Grand Duchy of Luxembourg—are farthest east in the German-speaking **Cantons de l'Est**, where fine winter skiing exists. The most visited sections of Belgium's Ardennes are more central, sought out for sport by *hunters*—the wild boar is a virtual symbol of the region, and stags and roe deer also are plentiful—and *fishers*, and by almost everyone for the *gastronomic preparation* of the 75 fresh catch in the region's renowned restaurant retreats.

Rivers run through the Ardennes. The **Ourthe** heads roughly south to north, finishing its course by flowing into the Meuse at Liège. The **Semois** cuts the southern Ardennes laterally, snaking east (its headwaters are near Arlon) to west, where it disappears into France under the name *Semoy.* The **Lesse**, rushing through the mid-Ardennes for centuries, has created limestone caverns so vast that the smallest Ardennes village could be set inside the subterranean space. These rivers and their tributaries have sculpted the scenery on exhibit in the Ardennes.

## *GUIDELINES FOR THE ARDENNES*

### SIGHTS

Belgium's forested, river-fed Ardennes region is essentially scenic. The virgin vistas above ground are complemented by an underground landscape of **limestone caves**. (**Han-sur-Lesse's** water-carved caves are an exceptional subterranean sight.) Attractions include **castles** of noble lineage and **monasteries** from the Middle Ages (such as the picturesque ruins of the 9th-century feudal castle—illuminated on summer nights—above **La-Roche**) and small stone-built villages of the Ardennes (like **Redu**, known as the "village du livre" for its many bookshops). **Spa's** natural spring waters and the list of those who have "taken the cure" there since the 16th century have made the town's name synonymous with health resorts since. **Bouillon**, on the viewpoint-stop-studded **Semois** river, is dominated by a castle that its owner *Godfrey* mortgaged to the prince-bishops of Liège for money to raise an army to fight in the **First Crusade** (1096). At **Bastogne**, which put the Ardennes on the map at Christmas of 1944, there's a historical center that brings the Second World War's **Battle of the Bulge** into focus.

## GETTING AROUND

A **car** is essential for visiting the Ardennes. Roads are in reasonable-to-better repair, but don't estimate driving time solely on the kilometers to be covered, since switchbacks in and out of river valleys will slow you down—appropriately. The sights described below are highlights of the region, covered roughly north to south, with no suggested route. The *Belgium Tourist Map* (available from tourist offices) designates the particularly attractive stretches of road in green; you may want to supplement it with a more detailed driving map that shows smaller roads if you plan a real exploration of the Ardennes.

## SHOPPING

Other than regional souvenirs along the way, the Ardennes is not the place for serious shopping, its village stores being, by and large, too small to supply much more than basic needs.

## ENTERTAINMENT AND EVENTS

Hunting season is celebrated the first Sunday of September with an **International Hunting Day** afternoon pageant at **Saint Hubert**. On Nov. 3rd, at the **Feast of St. Hubert** (the patron saint of hunters), the sound of hunting horns reverberates in the Basilica during the *Huntsmen's Mass* and *Blessing of the Animals*. Torchlight visits to **Bouillon Castle** take place on many evenings in July and August. Bouillon and other hilltop castles, ruins, and citadels in the Ardennes are illuminated at night in July and August, and at holiday periods the rest of the year.

## WHERE TO STAY

The most interesting and atmospheric choices in the Ardennes—some of which are renowned—are located in the country or near to but outside of towns, another reason you need a car in the region. Wherever you overnight in the Ardennes, it is expected that you will take dinner there; since most country hotel/restaurants take pride in their kitchen—owners often are chefs—you'll undoubtedly enjoy the experience.

## WHERE TO EAT

The Ardennes plays a leading role in Belgium's reputation as a culinary center. Small family-run hotels may be famed for their restaurant fare, and even casual eateries chanced upon are likely to impress visitors with their food standards. *Jambon d'Ardennes* (ham, thinly sliced) is a specialty offered everywhere, as are other high-quality pork products. Goose appears frequently on menus, and goose pâté is a popular starter. *Wild boar* (sometimes marinated), *marcassin* (young wild boar), and *venison* are served during the fall game season, as is *hare ragout*. *Trout* come fresh from the rivers that rush through the Ardennes, and local *crayfish* may be fried or boiled in hot *bouillon* (named for the region's feudal-age town). Belgian *white* and *blue cattle* produce tasty low-fat beef. If you're not already replete, *tarte au riz* (rice tart) can appropriately end an Ardennes repast.

## ARRIVING

Though not themselves part of it, Namur and Liège are the towns that serve as gateways to the Ardennes. Except for the towns of **Spa** (via Liège) and **Bastogne** (via Namur), Ardennes scenery and finest gastronomic fare are virtually unreachable by rail. A **car** is essential for discovering the delights of the region.

## TRAVEL TIPS

The Ardennes is highly popular with Belgians and other Europeans for weekends; many country inns and hotels feature all-inclusive *gastronomique weekends*. During the fall game season, inns with a reputation for fine food are even more in demand. To enjoy greater schedule flexibility—though by all means book ahead—try to arrange your countryside travel during the week.

## BASTOGNE

**Tourist Information** • *place McAuliffe 24; daily year-round 8:30 a.m.–noon, 1–5:30 p.m., closed Mon.;* ☎ *(061) 21.27.11; pop. 12,000 today, 4,000 in 1944.*

Many people are familiar with the Ardennes because of Bastogne, which held center stage during the **Battle of the Bulge** late in World War II. Since Roman days, the location has been at the intersection of main roads through the Belgian/Luxembourg Ardennes; in 1944 the crossroads became key in the U.S. Army and Allied resistance that made *Bastogne* for **Hitler** comparable to *Waterloo* for Napoleon. In the snowy December of 1944, Bastogne was the gift the Nazis couldn't wrap up for Hitler's Christmas. The ghost of that Christmas past is given substance at the ★ ★**Bastogne Historical Center** and ★ ★**Mardasson Monument**.

Today, Bastogne, once again a modest market town, well-endowed with shops that serve the surrounding Ardennes countryside, is mostly recovered from the shattering results of the Nazi surge of Panzer divisions towards the Meuse that stagnated and "bulged" around the town. Three months to the day before he launched the campaign on **December 16, 1944**, Hitler declared, "I have just made a momentous decision. I shall go over to the counterattack out of the Ardennes with *the objective—Antwerp.*"

Hitler's aim was to trap the British and Canadian armies north of Antwerp, forcing them to surrender, and separating them from the U.S. Army, which he believed would then lack the skill and will to continue fighting alone. Though his own leaders seriously questioned the campaign, Hitler pursued it. **Field Marshal von Rundstedt**, who is unfairly credited with developing it, was quoted as saying, "All, absolutely all, conditions for the possible success of such an offensive are lacking." Nevertheless, Hitler issued handwritten orders stating rigidly "No alterations permitted" in the code-named *WACHT AM RHEIN/Watch on the Rhine.* The code later was changed to *HERBSTNEBEL/Autumn Mist,* though *Winter Snow* would have proved more appropriate, for the battles were fought in what proved to be the coldest winter to date in the 20th century. Hitler's push was to be east to west along a 60-mile north/south front between Monschau (Germany) and Echternach (Luxembourg) by Panzer and infantry divisions, which would quickly reach the *Meuse,* cross it south of Liège and Namur, and then turn northwest for Brussels and Antwerp.

What indications of action the Allied intelligence heard didn't seem to warrant interrupting the planning for upcoming Christmas festivities. Most of the forces were already convinced that the Nazis were too weak to mount a broad attack. And the Ardennes, except for the Nazis' easy breakthrough there in September 1940, was thought to be terrain too troublesome for a ground attack, especially in winter. (As a result of that reasoning, *both* sides regarded the eastern Ardennes as a place for tired troops to rest, and untested ones to get their front line bearings.) **Supreme Commander Eisenhower** expressed concern about the lack of Allied coverage in the area, but allowed **General Omar Bradley** to reassure him.

December 16 dawned gray, making Allied air attack impossible; eight Panzer armored divisions rolled forward from their position on the Germany/Luxembourg border to begin their advance to Antwerp. Within a day they were already well behind in their scheduled crossing of the Meuse. They never would make it. One jeep on Dec. 17 brought the Nazis as close as they would come to crossing the Meuse. Moving ahead of their Panzer divisions—in one of seven confiscated American jeeps (the others were all eventually recaptured) that they hoped would help them seize bridges over the Meuse—were four Nazis, disguised in American overcoats. Their jeep was bound for **Dinant**, whose Meuse bridge was under the guard of a *British Royal Tank Regiment.* Reaching the east side of the Dinant bridge, the four American-cloaked Nazis in the American jeep sped through the British guard—who were thus unable to warn the occupants that the west end of the bridge had been set with antitank mines. The jeep occupants were killed instantly, and the British were relieved to find that under the casualties' American overcoats were Nazi uniforms.

One reason their campaign fell behind schedule so soon is that, from the second day, the Nazis were facing a shortage of fuel, having failed to find the stores of hidden Allied petrol that their plan depended upon. And the **U.S. Army** resistance was more resolute than expected, especially in Luxembourg: **German General Von Manteuffel** said later, "The courageous resistance of the 28th at Clervaux and Wiltz made possible the installation of the (Allied) defence of Bastogne." The "closed in" winter weather, though it hampered Allied air strikes, also made cross-country travel far more difficult. The roads, too few and too small for the Panzer divisions, "bulged" from the traffic. Both sides were confused in their movements, particularly when fog settled over the landscape. Only one fact was clear: all roads in the region ran through one of two points, **Bastogne** or **St. Vith**. Once the latter fell on December 21, the focus was all on the former.

In fact, Bastogne had been surrounded by Nazi Panzer infantry since December 20, but their commanders' freedom to act was frozen by the plan Hitler had foisted on them: *Press on to the Meuse, regardless.* Those inflexible orders, from which even Von Manteuffel would not risk straying for fear of Hitler's wrath, saved Bastogne. Von Manteuffel ordered the 2nd Panzer tanks to head for the Meuse, and left only an infantry division to attack Bastogne, which, though it could surround the town, couldn't break into it.

On December 21, there were few U.S. airborne troops holding on in Bastogne, and they were running low on artillery ammunition and supplies. Fearing Allied reinforcements—said to be on the way from *Patton's Third Army* headquartered then in Luxemburg City—Von Rundstedt had to temper the orders to his outnumbered troops: that they take Bastogne but *only* in such a way as to not hinder the Nazi advance to the Meuse.

On December 22, under siege by the surrounding Nazis, the American perimeter was approached at midday by four Nazis carrying a white flag. The only one who could speak English, and that very limited, requested to see the American commander. He was blindfolded and led to **Brigadier General McAuliffe**, to whom he handed a note from Nazi General Von Luttwitz of the Panzer corps. The message demanded the surrender of the American garrison on honorable terms, stating that otherwise the town and all military and civilians in it would be annihilated. Upon reading it, McAuliffe's immediate reaction was *"Aw, Nuts!"* (Many have suggested that he used a stronger term, but, during one of his many postwar visits back to Bastogne, McAuliffe confirmed the response.) Hard-pressed to find the words for a formal refusal, McAuliffe finally followed the suggestion of a staff member, and simply wrote down his first words—now in the annals of Americana. Handed the note by an American lieutenant, the Nazi spokeman found the slang beyond his comprehension and responded, "I do not understand. Is your commander's reply favorable?" To which the lieutenant replied, "It is certainly not affirmative. In plain English it means the same as 'Go to hell'. You understand that, don't you?" The German saluted, was blindfolded, and driven back to his outpost.

December 23 the skies cleared, and huge Allied C47 transport planes dropped in 144 tons of ammunition and medical and other supplies by parachute. Now the Americans could pick off the Nazis, sitting ducks in their dark uniforms against the snow that had begun to fall. Any natural camouflage in the woods was burned away with napalm.

On Christmas Day, just before dawn, Nazis in 18 tanks broke through into Bastogne. But the Americans met them with such firepower that all 18 soon were put out of operation. Thus, even before the first three Sherman tanks of the *4th Armored* finally arrived on December 26, it was clear that the Nazi effort was lost. Nevertheless, that day Von Manteuffel wrote in his journal, "Despite my advice, Hitler remains stubborn about Bastogne."

On December 30, snow fell thicker. On December 31, the Germans attacked Bastogne 17 times, with heavy losses all around. Of the situation in the ebbing hours of 1944, Von Manteuffel would write, "The ultimate defeat of the *Wehrmacht* was only a question of time, for the men and equipment to carry on the war were lacking." Still, the Nazis mounted further attacks on January 3 and 4, the toll of these last encounters in **the Battle of Bastogne** the heaviest of all. Thereafter, action in the Bulge theater moved away from Bastogne to elsewhere in the Ardennes.

In the **Battle of the Bulge** as a whole, between its opening on December 16, 1944, and closing during the final week of January 1945—by which time the Nazis had been forced back to the approximate line they had held when Hitler began his push to Antwerp—casualties, including wounded, missing in action, and those taken prisoner for both sides amounted to well over 150,000, with more than 21,000 dead.

If you're arriving in Bastogne by car, follow signs to **Mardasson**, 1 mi./2 km. north of the center. There, it's best to begin your visit at the ★★**Bastogne Historical Center** *(Colline du Mardasson; daily, late Feb.-April and Oct.-Nov. 10 a.m.-4 p.m., May, June, and Sept. 9:30 a.m.-5 p.m., July and Aug. 9 a.m.-6 p.m.;* ☎ *(061) 21.14.13, FAX (061) 21.73.73; all displays multilingual, gift/ bookshop with English literature),* which is unique among military museums in that many of the details were authenticated, exhibits created, and commentary scripted with the collaborative help of both **U.S. Army General McAuliffe** and **Nazi General Von Manteuffel**—who worked together here at the center after having fought on opposing sides in the war. The museum has several elements, the first being an illuminated model showing the phases of the Battle of the Bulge around Bastogne, with actual still photographs of the confrontation simultaneously projected onto a circle of screens around the amphitheater. Written and spoken commentary throughout is in English (and other languages). Another of the center's ingredients is its exceptional collection of **authentic uniforms** for both sides (General Baron Von Manteuffel donated the leather greatcoat he wore during the campaign), as well as items brought by returning veterans and those found on the actual battlefield. Several well-done **dioramas** are peopled with wax mannequins of the major players (generals

McAuliffe, Von Manteuffel, Patton, Bradley, and Eisenhower) and display battle gear and lighter equipment of the parachute division, vehicles, and weapons. Finally, the cinema shows **film clips** shot by Americans and Germans during the battle days, beginning with Panzer divisions on the move towards Belgium through Wiltz and Clervaux in Luxembourg. We see not only shelling but also the actual taking of prisoners, troops on both sides walking out with their wounded, and scenes showing the snow-camouflage overcoats and tank covers (made for Allied vehicles from bed sheets donated by Belgians). Also on display is a copy of the Christmas message of McAuliffe to his cold, weary soldiers. Of the 200,000 or so annual visitors to the center, approximately 15 percent are Americans, 50 percent Dutch, and 20 percent Belgian. Allow at *least* an hour for a visit and additional time for the Mardasson Monument near it.

A visit to the Historical Center will give you a deeper appreciation for *The Battle of the Bulge*, whose casualties are commemorated at the close-by ★★**Mardasson Monument/American Memorial** *(free access at all times)*, erected in 1950 under the initiative of the Belgo-American Association. The tall, star-shaped memorial, with the names of the U.S. states inlaid around the upper edges and the sides inscribed with the military companies that participated in the battle, also includes, on ten large stone slabs, a detailed account of the battle written by U.S. military historian S.L.M. Marshall. In the crypt beneath the monument, the 76,890 Americans killed, wounded, or missing at Bastogne and other battles in the Bulge theater are remembered with three chapels (Protestant, Catholic, and Jewish) decorated with mosaic murals by **Fernand Léger**. There's a viewing platform atop the monument; at each of the star's five points is a description of the battle action that took place in that compass direction. Today the land is mostly peaceful rolling pasture.

Elsewhere in the town of Bastogne are monuments of the events of the chilling winter of '44/45. A Sherman tank and a bust of McAuliffe are on the square that bears the brigadier general's name. An **area driving route brochure**, available from the tourist office or historical center, enables you to follow the signposted main stages of the campaign in your car. In summer, a tourist train takes visitors to many of the sites. There are several choices for food on **place McAuliffe**, and just off it is Bastogne's leading plain-but-pleasant 27-room hotel/restaurant **Hotel Lebrun** *(rue de Marché 8; ☎ (061) 21.54.21, FAX (061) 21.54.23; hotel inexpensive, restaurant moderate, menus inexpensive).*

# THE GRAND DUCHY OF LUXEMBOURG

*The castle at Vianden is the Grand Duchy's finest.*

## INTRODUCTION

*"Of all nations on earth, Luxembourg is one of the most stable
and prosperous, where nature is preserved and foreigners—whether residents or tourists—are welcomed. In all, one of the world's
happiest."*

.... Former United Nations Secretary-General

Xavier Perez de Cuellar, 1989

The above statement may not quicken the senses, but it's surely re-assuring about a country many people know little about. Most are surprised to learn what a wealth of treasure and pleasure awaits in this condensed dose of Europe.

## THE LUXEMBOURG LANDSCAPE

The Grand Duchy of Luxembourg, the smallest member state of the European Union (EU), surrounded by Belgium to the north and west, France to the south, and Germany to the east, measures a mere 999 square miles. It is smaller than America's smallest state, Rhode Island, and only 1/16th the size of Switzerland, itself a petite national package. In travel terms, Luxembourg is 50 miles/80 km. north to south, 32 miles/52 km. east to west. You can drive up or down its length in one and a half hours, entirely across it in one.

Geologically, Luxembourg falls into two regions: the hilly slate Ardennes, known as the **Oesling**, in the north and the larger, more populated, fertile river-fed farmland appropriately called **Gutland** (*Good Land*) to the south. The differences in altitude from north to south affect the climate; the high Ardennes have far more rainfall, a cold snowy winter, and a late spring (mid-May), while the south has a milder climate, warmer summer, and longer growing season. More than one third of the Grand Duchy is forest; much of it is preserved by the government or maintained as private hunting reserves—as are the extensive lands owned by Grand Duke Jean.

Geographically, Luxembourg has several distinct regions. Just outside Luxembourg City to the northwest is the **Eisch River Valley**, more memorably known as the *Valley of the Seven Castles*. Most of the famed castles are now picturesque ruins perched above their villages. A short distance directly north, crossing into the Ardennes, is the scenic **Sûre River Valley**. In the forests and towns to the north and south of it, much of Luxembourg's *Battle of the Bulge* action took place in the winter of 1944/45. Midcountry, near the eastern boundary, is the region known as **Little Switzerland**, which is characterized by large, unusual rock formations. Virtually all of Luxembourg's shared eastern border with Germany is created by three rivers, the **Our** in the north, the **Sûre** in the midregion, and the **Moselle** to the south. The Moselle Valley is the vineyard of Luxembourg, and has been since Roman days. The south and southeast sections of the Grand Duchy are the most heavily agricultural.

Luxembourg lies in the heart of industrial Europe, and is itself a highly industrialized nation. Most heavy industry lies in the **terre rouge** in the southwest, where the earth is red from its iron ore con-

GRAND DUCHY OF
LUXEMBOURG

tent. However, despite its reliance on industry (mostly steel), Luxembourg gives the impression of being full of wide-open, unpopulated spaces. And even in the industrial southwest, development is controlled and green space preserved. In the north, the **Sûre River**, which stretches across Luxembourg from the Belgian to the German border, has no industry on it at all, its reaches conscientiously kept clean for their beauty and recreational use. The Grand Duchy has an excellent record of compliance with European Union environmental regulations, ranking second only to Denmark among the 13 member states. According to the World Resources Institute in Washington, D.C., 21.1 percent of Luxembourg's total land area is protected, as compared with 8.6 percent in the United States and 10.6 percent in the United Kingdom.

Tourism, one of the Grand Duchy's five most important revenue sources, is one reason why Luxembourgers work to keep their land pristine. The offer of rambling and hiking in unspoilt countryside is one of its strongest selling points to European travelers; Luxembourg's network of marked walking paths is the densest in the world. But an even more important factor behind the preservation of the Grand Duchy's naturally scenic landscape is that it is an essential element in the quality of life that Luxembourgers seek for themselves.

## THE LUXEMBOURG PEOPLE

*"Of all the countries I have visited, the Grand Duchy of Luxembourg is the smallest, but it is the one that has charmed me most and where hospitality has been most simple and cordial."*

. . . . **Sir Winston Churchill**

One of the wonders of Luxembourg is that, despite being ruled, overrun, occupied, and even incorporated by many mainland European powers over the centuries—up to and including the 20th—its people have maintained a national character entirely their own. Surrounded by Germany, Belgium, and France, Luxembourg is not a composite of the three, but a distinct social and political entity. Despite an inevitable legacy of linguistic, artistic, and social influences from foreign occupiers, the Grand Duchy's own cultural values have the deepest roots.

Lately, there has been a peaceful, productive, "invasion" of foreigners. They now account for 25 percent of the Grand Duchy's total resident population. These foreigners—who account for 40 percent of the jobs in the Grand Duchy's banking industry and include the more than 10,000 individuals who work for one of the European Union institutions based here, plus their families—provide Luxembourg, which has one of the lowest birth rates in the world, with what it can not: a sufficient supply of workers at all skill levels with which to keep its prosperous economy on course.

Luxembourg's commerce is of necessity international. Since its independence in 1839, the country has recognized that it is not large enough to be economically self-supporting. This knowledge creates a cosmopolitan commercial streak in the solid core of traditional family and community values in the Luxembourgers' life. This is illustrated by one humorous self-description: "one Luxembourger, a rose garden; two Luxembourgers, a koffee-klatsch; three Luxembourgers, a band." At heart they are a people who make time for life's basic pleasures.

Amid its international diversity, Luxembourg society retains one element of homogeneity: religion. Some 95 percent of Luxembourgers are Roman Catholic (down from 99.5 percent in 1871, 96.9 percent in 1970). Although they do not hesitate to differentiate themselves as *practicing* or *nonpracticing*, a basic acceptance of the Church and its sacraments is taken for granted. Ever since foreign workers were needed in the country in the last quarter of the 19th century, Luxembourg has drawn mostly Catholic migrants (especially Portuguese, who make up 9 percent of the total population), thus preserving the singular religious character of the country.

Luxembourgers have managed to fashion a very high standard of living for themselves. According to a recent Larousse-published *Euroscopie* (which contains vast collections of statistics on living and working conditions in the EU countries), Luxembourgers, in both material and nonmaterial ways, are the most satisfied with their lot. In addition to having the highest disposable incomes and longest holidays among their European neighbors, they have the greatest number of houses equipped with central heating, washing machines, dishwashers, and electronic gadgets. (Other surveys show that Luxembourgers are the EU's highest domestic consumers of electricity, but with their many rivers they manage to produce it all themselves.) The Grand Duchy also has the most automobiles and hospital beds. Some 60 percent of house dwellers own the lodgings they live in. Luxembourg also has the most telephones per capita in Europe, but is small enough to make do with a single code for the whole country.

A complex history has produced the maxim, "To be a Luxembourger is by necessity to be a European," which one hears expressed in one form or another almost every day in conversations with local people. The lingual pluralism that plays an important part in Luxembourgers' social and professional lives, opening them up to other cultures, begins at an early age. German is taught from the age of six, French from the age of seven, and most students learn English.

One of the founding fathers of the European Union concept, **Robert Schuman** (1886–1963), was born and raised in Luxembourg City. The son of a Luxembourg mother and French father—from Lorraine, which, like Luxembourg, has a multicultural history as a pawn between Germany and France—Robert Schuman lived until the age of 18 in Luxembourg City, in the suburb of **Clausen** in the Alzette Valley. The house in which he grew up, at *rue Jules Wilhelm 4*, is situated just beneath the **Kirchberg Plateau**, where the buildings of the **European Center** rise. In 1990, following restoration, the house opened as the **European Study and Research Centre Robert Schuman**, with the mission of promoting knowledge of the history, and encouraging the further exploration, of European unification.

Raised in Luxembourg, then a student at several German universities, later a French citizen (as a result of the 1919 *Treaty of Versailles* which gave Lorraine back to France) and a member of the French government from 1919 to 1962, Schuman was well prepared and well positioned for his European role. Later in his life, at the pinnacle of his political career, Schuman noted that his early life in Luxembourg had given him "a sense of life I never had to change in the years to follow." He also referred to his formative education in Luxembourg in these words: "There we had the window wide open beyond the political borders, towards East and towards West." Luxembourg is glad to be able to cite Schuman as one of its own; May 9, observed annually as the "birthday" of the European Union, is, in this Catholic country, sometimes referred to as *St. Schuman's Day.*

Luxembourgers have a motto, a line from their national anthem, "*Mir woelle bleiwe wat mir sin,*" which translates, "We want to remain what we are." Among the many things Luxembourgers are is a people who have proven they can cope. (Henry Miller once observed: "In Luxembourg there are no neurotic people and no lunatic asylums.") They have avoided the complexes that could come with trying to feel at home in a world in which their homeland is seemingly insignificant. Luxembourgers display a confidence in and an ease with the times that are enviable.

## *AN HISTORICAL PERSPECTIVE*

Luxembourg's geographic position in Europe has been perceived as central and strategic since its settlement by Romans. Throughout most of its history, Luxembourg has been fortified to protect it from foreign armies. Unfortunately, those very fortifications often invited invaders and, later, European power brokers who felt free to arbitrarily cut Luxembourg down in size and install foreign soldiers in its capital.

Given its diminutive dimensions, the name "The Grand Duchy of Luxembourg" could be considered too much of a mouthful, but at the peak of its political power in the 14th and 15th centuries, during which it provided four rulers who served as Holy Roman Emperors, Luxembourg was much larger physically. However, Luxembourg never has played as important a part on the international stage as it does today. (Its prime minister, **Jacques Santer**, was selected to assume the influential presidency of the European Commission of the EU in January 1995.) Its slight size allows The Grand Duchy to help solve sensitive international situations while eliminating any feeling of competition with larger countries.

The Luxembourg land spent long centuries in international entanglement before it finally achieved the status of independent state. Foreign occupiers since the Middle Ages left their footprints upon the soil, and more ancient antecedents left artifacts beneath it. Evidence of *Neolithic* man (circa 10,000 B.C.) can be seen in the countryside and in the collections of the Musée de l'État in Luxembourg City. In the millennium before Christ the region was occupied by *Celts*. The most significant of those prehistoric tribes in Luxembourg were the *Treveri* (Trier) and *Mediomatrici* (Metz), both of which followed the faith of their priests, the Druids. Remains of Celtic fortified compounds can be seen on the **Titelberg** and around **Mullerthal** ("Little Switzerland").

Caesar's conquest of Gaul (58–51 B.C.) resulted in the incorporation of the Luxembourg area into the Roman Empire. Three major Roman roads connected it to what is now Germany; the most important led to Trier, an administrative center second in importance only to Rome. There followed in the Luxembourg region a rapid process of Latinization, with increased order and security, as well as flourishing trade and agriculture, in particular, *viniculture* along the Moselle. Gallo-Roman villas with baths, mosaic floors, and murals were built both in towns and in the countryside. (Remnants can be viewed in museums in Luxembourg City and Diekirch.) Despite its domination, the Roman influence did not eradicate the region's Celtic culture. The officially forbidden Druidism remained, but Christianity also became established in Luxembourg by the 4th century. As Roman power weakened, Luxembourg faced attacks from the Vandals, Visigoths, and Huns. (Their leader **Attila** is recalled in the local town name **Ettelbruck**, meaning "Attila's bridge.") In A.D. 450, the Franks crossed the Rhine, bringing Roman rule of the region to a close. Thereafter the Franks settled large areas of Luxembourg, especially around the Moselle, and established their Germanic language throughout.

In 496, Frankish **King Clovis** converted to Christianity. As a result, the religion spread among the population. All across Europe monastic orders brought enlightenment to the Dark Ages. In Luxembourg, the era was highlighted in 698, when Anglo-Saxon Benedictine **St. Willibrord** founded the **Echternach Abbey**, which became famous for the **Echternach School of Book Illumination**.

The Frankish Empire, of which Luxembourg remained a part, reached its climax under Emperor **Charlemagne**, who sent some one thousand Saxon families to settle the sparsely populated Ardennes during the 9th century. The Frankish empire faced grave territorial divisions under Charlemagne's weak successors. Under the *Treaty of Verdun* (843), Luxembourg became part of Lorraine, which subsequently was divided between France and Germany by the 870 Treaty of Mersen. This marked the beginning of a conflict that would last over a thousand years, as Luxembourg was perpetually bounced between the powers of France and Germany.

On April 12, 963, **the Abbey of St. Maximin in Trier**, which had been established in the same era as Luxembourg's Echternach Abbey, granted to **Sigefroi, count of Ardennes**, a deed to a rocky promontory on which stood the ruins of a Roman fort known as **Castellum Lucilinburhuc** or "Little Castle." (A copy of the deed can be seen in Luxembourg's *National Library*; the original remains in Trier.) At *Lucilinburhuc*—a name that evolved to *Lutzelburg* and eventually to *Luxembourg*—Sigefroi built a fortified castle. The House of Luxembourg thus born at Sigefroi's fortress remained independent as part of the Frankish Empire for nearly five centuries, though its fortunes rose and fell under the combined influences of family landholdings, adeptness at arms, oaths of loyalty, and well-made marriages.

Knights from Luxembourg accompanied Godfrey de Bouillon on the First Crusade, and served in Asia Minor on subsequent ones.

They had left their Luxembourg castles (**Bourscheid**, **Esch-sur-Sûre**, **Hollenfels**, etc.), whose ruined turrets look so romantic today, though the reality of life within the walls of the feudal fortresses must have been anything but. Some of Luxembourg's absentee landlords fell in battle. Those who returned often were debt ridden, their lands in disarray; some found their castles confiscated by strong arms and swords that had stayed home.

One leader of Luxembourg, **Henry the Blind**, Count of Namur, set in motion events that were to improve the region's situation immeasurably. Late in the 12th century, Henry, having no direct heir, was preparing to bequeath his immense possessions to his nephew Baldwin of Hainault when, at the age of 65, love played a hand; he married Agnes of Gelderland, who gave him a daughter. Baldwin showed his displeasure by pillaging Namur and breaking the power of the aged Henry. But Henry's late-in-life daughter, **Ermesinde** (1196–1247), through resourceful marriages and her own far-reaching ideas of leadership and reform, reestablished Luxembourg's prestige and extended its frontiers from the Moselle to the Meuse. After the death of her second husband, Ermesinde herself took over the reins of rule by bringing together feuding noblemen into a kind of council of state and granting burghers (town citizens) rights, which loosened the hold of feudal lords over them. In 1244, she granted a charter of freedom to the City of Luxembourg. Realizing that education was the key to the continuation of these reforms, Ermesinde also founded schools, convents, monasteries, and cultural institutions. Her legacy to Luxembourg was a secure, well-administered country with long-lasting social institutions. Her heirs continued the family line that would prove one of Europe's most illustrious of the Middle Ages.

In the 14th century, the House of Luxembourg became one of the dominant forces in Europe. In 1308, Ermesinde's great grandson **Henry VII**, Count of Luxembourg, was crowned head of the Holy Roman Empire in Rome. In 1312, **Dante** hailed him as the "Restorer of Justice, Peace, and Liberty." Upon his untimely death in 1313—of malaria in Pisa, where he is buried in the cathedral—Henry's son **John**, who had added Bohemia to the House of Luxembourg by marriage at the age of 14, took over. So popular was John as an ideal of knighthood that he remains Luxembourg's national hero to this day. For the first 30 years of his rule, John set out almost every spring on military campaigns from the North Sea to the Vistula to increase, or keep intact, his landholdings. Despite failing eyesight that gave him the epithet *The Blind*, John answered the appeal of French King Philip VI when England's **Edward II, The Black Prince**, invaded France. All but sightless, John led his army into the *Battle of Crécy* (1346), in which he was slain. In tribute, the victorious Edward said of Luxembourg's John the Blind, "The battle was not worth the death of this man." Edward took the three ostrich feathers from John's helmet, and the motto *Ich dien* ("I serve") in tribute to John's loyalty, and adopted them as the crest and motto for the Prince of Wales; they are still in use by England's current Prince Charles.

**Charles IV**, son of John the Blind, through his own and family marriages and treaties, brought Luxembourg to the size and status his father had sought by the sword. As Holy Roman Emperor, Charles maintained a court at Prague that dazzled all of Europe. When Charles' younger brother **Wenceslas** married **Jeanne, Duchess of Brabant**, thereby acquiring Brabant, Limburg, and much of what is Belgium's Luxembourg province today, he brought the House of Luxembourg to its greatest expanse. Charles honored Wenceslas by making Luxembourg a duchy in 1354. In 1356, Duke Charles and Duchess Jeanne issued one of the most important written municipal charters of merchants' rights, the *Joyeuse Entrée* (Joyous Entry), which was of equivalent significance for Belgium and Luxembourg as the *Magna Carta* was for England. In it, the Duke and Duchess promised that they would impose no restriction on trade, except legal taxes; give subjects the right to revolt if the Duke exceeded his legal powers; and pledged not to declare offensive war "except at the advice, will and consent of our good cities and land."

Nevertheless, **Wenceslas II**, who became Emperor and Duke of Luxembourg in 1383, used his holdings almost exclusively as a source of revenue and troops for armies, and created a series of civil wars between sovereigns that plagued the House of Luxembourg. The last male of the line, Holy Roman Emperor **Sigismund**, who, through marriage, also was the King of Hungary and thus foretold the region's future ties with the Hapsburgs, died in 1437. In 1443, the Duchy of Luxembourg was bought by **Philip the Good of Burgundy** and thereby lost its autonomy and dynasty, becoming a province linked to the Netherlands. Philip established French as Luxembourg's language of government and administration, which it remains today. The Burgundian Netherlands passed to the Hapsburgs in 1477, and among the titles **Charles V** received at his birth in Ghent in 1500 was *Duke of Luxembourg*. From that time, Luxembourg essentially shared the history of the Netherlands.

Staunchly and overwhelmingly Roman Catholic—which it remains today—Luxembourg sided with the Belgians in support of the Catholic Spanish Hapsburg **King Philip II**, rather than with Protestant Holland during the Reformation and subsequent religious upheavals in the 16th century. Luxembourg, often at stake in the battles waged between the European powers, was annexed in 1684 by France's **Louis XIV**, who held the duchy until 1697 when it was returned to Spain. During the French occupation Louis's military architect **Vauban** fortified the site of Luxembourg City so fully that it became known as the "*Gibraltar of the North.*" In 1714, at the end of the war of the Spanish Succession, Luxembourg, along with Belgium, passed to Austria, and remained a part of the Austrian Netherlands until 1795. From that year until the fall of Napoleon in 1814, Luxembourg, together with both Belgium and Holland, was incorporated into revolutionary France.

In 1815, the European powers, meeting at the *Congress of Vienna* to balance the forces on the continent, dared not leave Luxembourg to itself. They felt its strategic position and fortifications made it too strong to ignore, yet its small size left it vulnerable to takeover from others. They "settled" the situation by raising the status of Luxembourg to *Grand Duchy* and giving it as a personal property to the Dutch king. This made the Dutch *House of Nassau's* **Willem I** and his heirs also the hereditary *Grand Dukes of Luxembourg*, a situation which lasted until 1890. But there was more to the arrangement: the Congress of Vienna also called for the territory of Luxembourg lying east of the Moselle and Our rivers to be joined to **Prussia**, and giving, in compensation to the dismembered Grand Duchy, the greater part of the duchy of Bouillon and part of the former prince-bishopric of Liège (territory that conforms today to Belgium's province of Luxembourg). Although linked by the same sovereign, Luxembourg was designated politically independent of Holland and the United Kingdom of the Netherlands. But Europe's ruling powers meddled further with Luxembourg by deciding that the Grand Duchy must be a part of the *Germanic Confederation*, and that Luxembourg City should be a Confederation fortress with a garrison of *Prussians.*

In 1830, the Grand Duchy—with the exception of Luxembourg City, which, with its Prussian garrison, was not allowed to join and thus remained loyal to Holland—united with Belgium in a revolt against the United Kingdom of the Netherlands. When Belgium achieved independence from Holland, the Grand Duchy, again with the exception of Luxembourg City, placed itself under Belgian rule. In 1839, a date of mixed blessings for Luxembourgers—since it

marks both its first true independence and the date of its partition—the *Treaty of London* divided the Grand Duchy in two. The
larger French-speaking western part went to Belgium, becoming
that country's Luxembourg province. The eastern portion remained
with the Dutch, whose King Willem I, persuaded by the logistical
difficulties entailed in maintaining a fiefdom separated from Holland
by a still hostile Belgium, granted Luxembourg a measure of autonomy. Thus, the Grand Duchy assumed her present frontiers and
gained a date from which to mark her independence.

In 1842, at Prussia's insistence, Luxembourg joined the German
*Zollverein* (customs union). That association, in which Luxembourg
remained until the First World War, laid the foundation for the
Grand Duchy's development during the Industrial Revolution. German capital, manpower, and markets were the base upon which Luxembourg created its great steel economy in the last quarter of the
19th century. In 1848, **King Willem II** (1792–1849), by far the preferred of the Grand Duchy's Dutch rulers, gave Luxembourg its
constitution. Willem II is honored in Luxembourg City with an
equestrian statue on **place Guillaume**, named for him. (The statue,
cast in 1884 by sculptor Antonin Mercie, was such a good likeness of
Willem II that the Dutch themselves ordered a copy 40 years later.)
In 1859, with Dutch help, Luxembourg got its first railroad, an
event of such surpassing importance to the Grand Duchy that the
poem *Feierwon*, written to commemorate the occasion, still ranks in
importance with the national anthem *Our Homeland*. In 1867,
upon the dissolution of the Germanic Confederation, the European
powers—nations uneasy about the fortress-capital at the fulcrum of
Europe—met again in London. They certified Luxembourg's freedom, guaranteed the Grand Duchy's neutrality, set up a program for
the dismantling of Luxembourg City's fortresses, and arranged for
the withdrawal of the Prussian garrison. Luxembourgers, not noted
for excess, are said to have danced in the streets as the Prussians departed. Then they went about the business of reaffirming their constitution. In the century since, the Grand Duchy has progressed
from feudal fortress to full-scale modern nation.

In order to maintain its economic independence, Luxembourg was
compelled to call in foreign workers from the time of its steel industrial expansion beginning in the 1870s; from that period, a high percentage of foreigners has remained a characteristic of the country.
Luxembourg's own work force was particularly small because many
residents had emigrated at the end of the 18th and early in the 19th
century, when the country had been impoverished and barely able to

feed its people. (The people of Luxembourg living in the United States today number more than the Grand Duchy's entire population of about 400,000.)

In 1914, despite its neutrality which had been dictated by the European leaders in 1867, Luxembourg was occupied by Germany on August 2. During the First World War, more than 3000 Luxembourgers lost their lives fighting for the Allied cause, a substantial sacrifice for so small a nation. At the end of the war in 1918, **Grand Duchess Marie-Adelaide** was accused of alleged pro-German sympathies. From November 1918 to January 1919, Luxembourgers went through a *Grand Crise* (Great Crisis) that ended with Marie-Adelaide's abdication. Then began a popular process to determine whether Luxembourg should become a republic and elect a president, or place **Charlotte**, sister of Marie-Adelaide, on the throne. In the plebiscite held in the fall of 1919, more than 50 percent of the people chose Charlotte to be Grand Duchess, and her popularity rose much higher in the course of her 45-year reign, during which she enjoyed undiminished affection.

In 1921, to replace the German *Zollverein* trade union, Luxembourg signed a customs and economic treaty with Belgium (*BLEU, the Belgium-Luxembourg Economic Union*), which pegged their currencies to each other. The internationally outlooking Grand Duchy also joined the *League of Nations*. Despite the worldwide depression, Luxembourg's steel industry grew to the point of being ranked seventh in the world in productivity by the end of the 1930s. In 1939, with rumblings of large-scale war again being heard in Europe, Luxembourg reasserted its neutrality. The Grand Duchy also threw a particularly strenuous centenary celebration of its independence, as a message to Hitler to respect its freedom.

But it was to no avail. On May 10, 1940, Hitler's Nazis occupied not only Luxembourg, but Holland and Belgium as well. However, since Luxembourg City had been home to a Prussian (German) garrison in the 19th century, Hitler used that as an excuse to impose an *"absorption" policy* on the Grand Duchy. Unlike Holland, Belgium, and other countries "occupied" by the Fuhrer's forces, Luxembourg was incorporated into the Third Reich, meaning that its citizens were liable for conscription into the *Wehrmacht*.

In 1941, the Nazis undertook a census in the countries they had occupied in the Second World War. On the printed form under the question "What is your nationality?" was the notation that Luxembourgers, as well as Alsatians, should write "German." On the day before it was due, the Nazis recalled the census in the Grand Duchy, having learned that Luxembourgers were planning wholesale defiance on the nationality issue. This resistance was a precurser to a general strike in 1942, staged in response to the call for military service in the *Wehrmacht*. (Women, too, were conscripted, for labor.) Luxembourgers walked out of their factories, after nailing the country's flags to their masts. Extreme reprisals followed. A number of Luxembourgers managed to escape, thereafter enlisting with British, Canadian, U.S., Free French, and Free Belgian forces to fight Hitler. Many who were inducted into the *Wehrmacht*—under threat that otherwise their families would be deported to Prussia—were sent to fight for the Nazis on the Russian front. Between 1943–1945, many Luxembourgers wound up as "irregular" German troops at the Russian POW camp at Tambow. Luxembourgers at Tambow banded together for support and many survived more than two years of incarceration there.

On September 9, 1944, **Pétange**, near the Belgian border in southwest Luxembourg, became the first town in the Grand Duchy to be liberated by soldiers of the First U.S. Army, Fifth Armored Division. It is impossible for us to fully comprehend what liberation meant to Luxembourgers, except to note that these many years later September 9 is still observed annually in Pétange. And every five years since 1944, a large ceremony has been staged at night with a torchlight parade from Pétange's town hall to its town monument. Erected in 1947, its inscription in French reads "In memory of the first American soldier who fell in the liberation of Luxembourg," followed in Letzebuergesch with "Monument to an Unknown Soldier—We Will Never Forget." However, in 1987 the American soldier was identified, thanks to the Luxembourg group CEBA that researches aspects of the war. At the following five-year observance in 1989, family members of the man who had died in the first armored car to cross the border in 1944 were on hand on September 9 for ceremonies that unveiled a plaque to, and renamed the square for, **Hyman Josephson**, 2nd Lieutenant, U.S. Army.

On September 10, 1944, the U.S. Army pushed through to liberate Luxembourg City. Their progress was made so quickly that, fortunately, the rapidly retreating Nazis did not have time to destroy much of the capital. All of the Grand Duchy was quickly freed by the Allies, mostly American, who were joyously welcomed.

Virtually no one on either side of the war believed the Nazis could —or would—mount another large-scale attack. But Hitler conceived and implemented a counter-offensive that, although the port of

Antwerp was its ultimate object, got bogged down and was waged largely in the Luxembourg and Belgian Ardennes. On December 16, with the opening of what became known as the **Battle of the Bulge**, Hitler's soldiers again occupied Luxembourg soil. In the snow and cold of the winter of 1944/45, particularly around **Wiltz** and **Clervaux**, Luxembourg suffered its worst war damage, and the Allies some of their greatest casualties. By the time the last town in Luxembourg was freed for a second time—**Vianden** on February 12, 1945—one-third of Luxembourg's farmland was unusable; 60,000 people were homeless; and half the country's roads, bridges, tunnels, and rail lines had been destroyed. Earlier in the war, many of Luxembourg's steel plants had been burnt out by the Nazis from forced overproduction.

From the late 19th century until the shift away from its industrial base in the latter third of the 20th century, Luxembourg's prosperity rested mainly on steel. The prime company, *Arbed*, at its peak before the widespread steel crisis began in 1975, was Europe's fourth-largest producer, a multinational with 100,000 employees in plants in Europe, America, and Asia. Arbed provided more than steel to Luxembourg's economy since, as was discovered in the 19th century, the waste from the smelting process proved an effective fertilizer for the Grand Duchy's less fertile northern and central farmlands. After the Second World War, Luxembourg put its steel industry back in shape so swiftly that by the mid-1950s, the country had one of the highest GNPs per capita in Europe, but it had learned not to put all its economic aspirations in a single industry. When the steel industry crisis of the 1970s hit, the "Luxembourg Model"—scaling back the number of hours per worker to avoid layoffs—was widely imitated elsewhere. By then, banking had replaced steel as Luxembourg's number one industry.

Post-war economic planning began well before the end came. By September 5, 1944, Antwerp and Brussels had been liberated, and on that day in London, representatives-in-exile of the governments of BElgium, the NEtherlands (Holland), and LUXembourg (which provided the acronym BENELUX) signed a document entitled *Customs Convention*, based roughly on the 1921 BLEU agreement between Belgium and Luxembourg that had proved extremely successful. The intent of the three governments was to form a complete and durable economic union, and restore economic activity by establishing a common tariff of import duties. Not until 1948 did the convention become operational, and not until 1958 was a BENELUX *Treaty of Economic Union* finalized. But, despite rough edges, the treaty survived, primarily because leaders in all three countries never abandoned the conviction that the idea of union was essentially sound. In 1949, Luxembourg became a founding member of the North Atlantic Treaty Organization (NATO), having abandoned its traditional policy of neutrality (it having proved inadequate to guarantee its liberty and independence). The Grand Duchy today has a volunteer army of 450 people.

Even while kinks in the BENELUX treaty were being worked out, Luxembourg was being linked to an expanded European economic union. In 1950 **Jean Monnet**, a far-sighted Frenchman who preferred to remain in the background, proposed a plan to **Robert Schuman**, the Luxembourg-born-and-raised French foreign minister, for the formation of a supranational *European Coal and Steel Community (ECSC)*. Working enthusiastically on the initiative, Schuman suggested that "the pooling of coal and steel production will immediately provide for the establishment of common bases for economic development as a first step in the federation of Europe, and will change the destinies of those regions which have long been devoted to the manufacture of munitions of war, of which they themselves have been the most constant victims." A treaty among the three BENELUX countries, plus Germany, France, and Italy, was signed in 1951, with Luxembourg City established as the seat of High Authority.

The ECSC proved such a success that, in 1955, the foreign ministers of its members solicited suggestions for extended cooperation in economic spheres. The most important message came from the BENELUX, which by then was seeing palpable benefits from its own more complete integration. The BENELUX statement said, "The moment has come to pass into a new state of European integration.... this must be achieved first in the economic field." In 1957, a treaty was signed in Rome between the six ECSC members to form the **European Economic Community** (or *Common Market*). Luxembourg City was designated the headquarters for several of its permanent institutions: the *Secretariat of the European Parliament, the Court of Justice* (which is similar in many ways to the Supreme Court in the United States), the *Court of Auditors*, and, appropriately, the *European Investment Bank*.

Today, with more than 200 banks and a total of close to 1,000 financial institutions that include substantial securities and reinsurance markets, sleek **boulevard Royal** is Luxembourg City's version of *Wall Street*. The Grand Duchy's financial services sector employs about 18,000 people—one in six working Luxembourgers is employed in some facet of the financial business—and accounts for roughly 15 percent of GNP. Private investments in Luxembourg banks are estimated at well over $160 billion.

The Grand Duchy of Luxembourg had its most recent six-month turn in the rotating presidency of the European Community–which officially was renamed the European Union (EU) in 1994–during the first half of 1991. The country holding the presidency can, among other business, put forth ideas of particular interest to it. During its previous presidency in 1985, Luxembourg brought to the signature stage the *Single Europe Act* (referred to as "*1992*"), which was signed onboard the *Marie-Astrid*, the Moselle River cruise ship based at Luxembourg's wine-growing village of **Schengen**. During its 1991 term of presidency, Luxembourg furthered the implementation of numerous European single-market initiatives.

Among the modern buildings of the **European Center** that rise above Luxembourg City from the **Kirchberg Plateau** is the **European School**. It was the first of its kind when conceived in 1953: an educational system for the children of ECSC-employee families that provided, for students speaking totally different mother tongues, an immersion in varied cultural milieus, and stressed the principle of European unity. Today, teachers originating in all the countries of the EU provide lessons for the school's 3percent 000 students, who come from all EU nations and many more. Going from nursery school through high school, the school grants a diploma accepted at any university in the EU. Though now copied by nine others in Europe, Luxembourg's school continues to set the pace, helping the children sitting on its school benches to leave their national mentality behind, providing them with an education that seeks to ensure that the European citizen of tomorrow is open-minded.

## *KEYS TO THE GRAND DUCHY*

### TOURIST OFFICES

National tourist offices for the Grand Duchy of Luxembourg are located in the U.S.A. at 17 Beekman Place, New York, NY 10022, ☎ *(212) 935-8888*, FAX *(212) 935-5896*; and in England at 122 Regent St., London W1R 5FE, ☎ *(071) 434.28.00*, FAX *(071) 734.12.05*. Travel and attraction information within the Grand Duchy are available in Luxembourg City. (See under "Guidelines.")

### WEATHER

Luxembourg has a temperate climate, with no extremes. Although the Ardennes shelter the country from some of the wind and rain that are more constant in Holland and Belgium, an umbrella and raincoat still are suggested. The following chart shows the *average* of the daily high and low temperatures (in Fahrenheit) by month for Luxembourg City, as well as the average number of days each month with no measurable rainfall.

| Average Daily Temperatures in °F In Luxembourg City (Lat. 49 ° 37´—Alt. 1,025´) | | | | | | | | | | | |
|------|------|------|------|-----|------|------|------|-------|------|------|------|
| Jan. | Feb. | Mar. | Apr. | May | June | July | Aug. | Sept. | Oct. | Nov. | Dec. |
| Average Temperature | | | | | | | | | | | |
| 35° | 38° | 42° | 49° | 55° | 61° | 64° | 64° | 60° | 50° | 43° | 38° |
| Days with No Rain | | | | | | | | | | | |
| 16 | 13 | 16 | 14 | 15 | 13 | 15 | 15 | 14 | 14 | 12 | 15 |

## NATIONAL HOLIDAYS

New Year's Day; Easter Monday (date varies); Labor Day (May 1); Ascension Day (date varies); Whit Monday (date varies); National Day (June 23); Assumption (date varies); All Saints' Day (Nov. 1); Christmas Day; St. Etienne (Dec. 26). Days that are not national holidays but on which administrative and public offices, schools, and similar institutions are closed are Carnival (including Shrove Tuesday, date varies); Octave (May/June, date varies); Whit Tuesday (date varies); All Souls' Day (Nov. 2); Christmas Eve; New Year's Eve.

## LANGUAGE

Luxembourg's national official language (since 1984) is **Letzebuergesch**, mostly in oral use. No one else speaks Letzebuergesch: Luxembourgers know that no one learns it unless at his mother's knee. (In fact, the language has been almost entirely an oral tradition over the centuries and only recently was given concrete written form.) Here's a sample to make us appreciate the fact that Luxembourgers have been considerate enough to learn other languages. *Wei geet et lech?* (How are you?), *Kennt Dir mir hellefen?* (Can you help me?) *Vill Gleck!* (Good Luck!).

In practice, Luxembourg is trilingual. Business is conducted in *French* (also the language on street signs). Most newspapers are published in *German* (though ads are in *Letzebuergesch*). Luxembourg City is headquarters for several European Union institutions and many multinational corporations; as in other centers of Europe's Common Market, *English* has long been common ground for communication. English is so widely studied and spoken throughout

Luxembourg that you should have no difficulty getting around and meeting people.

## CURRENCY

Luxembourg francs—written *FLux*—come in 1, 5, 20, and 50 franc coins, and a 50 centime piece (100 centimes = 1 franc). Bank notes exist in 100, 500, 1000 and 5000 values. At press time the U.S. $ was worth approximately 30.8 FLux.

The Luxembourg franc and the Belgian franc, although minted and printed as separate currencies, have the same value and denominations. In Luxembourg, the Belgian franc is accepted everywhere, though the reverse is not the case. When leaving Luxembourg, whether or not you are headed for Belgium, make sure your remaining francs are Belgian, since for currency transactions the Luxembourg franc does not carry the same international recognition as the Belgian franc.

## LUXEMBOURG HOTEL PRICE CATEGORIES

Prices are based on double occupancy, with private toilet and shower and/or bath, and include VAT and service; continental breakfast is usually included. All grades of accommodation in Luxembourg are clean.

| | |
|---|---|
| **Very Expensive** | **FLux 5,000 +** |
| **Expensive** | **4,000–5,000** |
| **Moderate** | **3,000–4,000** |
| **Inexpensive** | **3,000 or less** |

## LUXEMBOURG RESTAURANT PRICE CATEGORIES

Prices are based on a three-course dinner for one, without drinks but *inclusive* of VAT and service.

| | |
|---|---|
| **Very Expensive** | **FLux 3,000 +** |
| **Expensive** | **2,000–3,000** |
| **Moderate** | **1,000–2,000** |
| **Inexpensive** | **1,000 or less** |

## TOURIST SEASON

Officially, the tourist season in Luxembourg runs from Easter to late October. However, some attractions, even in Luxembourg City, and especially so in more rural areas of the Grand Duchy where the focus is on outdoor tourism, close by mid-September. It's wise to confirm opening hours if your travel plans include specific attractions or museums. There are plenty of reasons (scenery, fine dining, walking, little worry about full hotels) to travel out of season, although keep in mind that a number of small rural hotels close entirely then. After September, the weather is more inclined to be gray and windy, though Luxembourg can have an "Indian Summer." In the spring allow trees time to grow new leaves if you want to see this *Green Heart of Europe* at its best.

## TRAVEL DISTANCES

Luxembourg City is centrally located in Europe, posting the following distances to other major cities and transportation hubs:

| City | Miles | Kilometers |
|---|---|---|
| Amsterdam | 223 | 360 |
| Brussels | 127 | 205 |
| Frankfurt | 160 | 258 |
| Ostend | 206 | 332 |
| Paris | 206 | 332 |
| Zurich | 246 | 396 |

## RAIL

While train is an excellent way to get to/from **Luxembourg City**, it is *not* the ideal mode of transportation for touring within the Grand Duchy. The 870-mile Luxembourg National Railways network, although serving the major towns of Ettelbruck, Diekirch, Wiltz, and Clervaux, neglects the best scenery and some of the most special countryside towns. While trains do operate in tandem with the national bus system, and thus afford access— eventually—to practically every location, for travelers with limited time and those desiring to see how exceptionally scenic the Grand Duchy is, they are not recommended. A network ticket is FLux 140 for one day, until 8 a.m. the following day; there's a 50 percent reduction for those over 65.

## DRIVING

If at all possible, explore the remarkably varied and rural regions of the Grand Duchy by car. When working out an itinerary, keep in mind the *scale* of your Luxembourg map. (The tourist office offers a free one of the Grand Duchy that is as detailed a road map as you'll need.) Even allowing for frequent car-stopping scenery and wandering at will in the most interesting towns, you can cover quite a patch of the country on a realistic day's drive. Add an overnight, better two, and you can be a master traveler in this lovely little land.

Although Luxembourg City now faces the same traffic jams at the beginning and end of the business day that have come to plague all

European cities, the situation in the countryside of the Grand Duchy is completely different. Never have I driven on such untrammeled roads, almost all of them unbusy byways. Often when both driving and navigating myself, I have opted to collect a rented car at an airport or other location outside a major city, in order to avoid congestion while I'm becoming familiar with unfamiliar traffic patterns. But there's no need for that in Luxembourg. Ten minutes after departing downtown, you'll be completely in the country and nearly to your first destination, no matter in what direction you're heading. You won't need to know route numbers, only the name of the town where you're headed and an interim village or two. As you'll see from the scenic roads that are highlighted on the map in green, there are so many around the country that you'd be unable to avoid them if you tried. I've even found myself spellbound by stretches not specially marked for scenic appeal.

Throughout Luxembourg road signage is extremely well done, with indicators for upcoming villages and towns appearing at every crossroad that requires one. Many of the well-paved roads are two lanes, and you will occasionally come upon a farm vehicle or truck; be cautious about passing because of the *possibility* of oncoming traffic around a road bend. On any road you may hardly see a car from one quarter hour to another, though you must drive prepared at any time to meet an oncoming car traveling speedily. If one approaches from behind, just pull over when it's safe to let it pass, and go on with your leisurely appreciation of the scenery.

Because Luxembourg's *Value-Added Tax* rate (15 percent) is lower than in many other European countries—an advantage that could eventually disappear as Europe integrates further economically—car-rental rates there are among the least expensive on the continent. Round-trip *Icelandair* transatlantic passengers flying from JFK, New York via Reykjavik, Iceland, to Luxembourg City are entitled to that airline's extremely favorable rental car rates with unlimited mileage (toll-free U.S. inquiries to Icelandair ☎ *(800) 223-5500*).

## THE FLAG

After you've been in Holland, Luxembourg's flag will seem familiar (logically, since until 1890, the hereditary royalty of the Netherlands' *House of Nassau* also were the rulers of Luxembourg). Today, the Grand Duchy's horizontally striped red, white, and blue standard remains the same as Holland's except for a slightly lighter shade of blue, a change made official only in 1981.

## THE GRAND DUCAL FAMILY

The Grand Duchy of Luxembourg is a hereditary constitutional monarchy. Although it finally was granted independence by a conference of European nations in 1867, Luxembourg remained under the rule of then **Dutch King Willem III**, who was Grand Duke of Luxembourg in his own right through the **House of Orange-Nassau** (whose ancestral home is a Grand Duchy landmark, **Vianden Castle**—see "Vianden" under "Tour of the Grand Duchy"). In 1890, Willem III died without a male heir, and the Dutch crown passed to his daughter **Wilhelmina**. However, in Luxembourg, since *Salic Law*, making women ineligible to succeed to the throne, applied at the time, there was a discontinuation of dynastic links with the Orange- Nassaus. Rule passed to **Duke Adolphe of Nassau-Weilburg**, who became founder of Luxembourg's Royal House. When Adolphe's son, **Guillaume I**, who had abolished the Salic Law, died in 1912, his eldest daughter **Marie-Adelaide** became Grand Duchess. When Luxembourg was occupied by the Germans in World War I, Marie-Adelaide remained in the country; afterwards, she was faced with charges of alleged pro-German sympathies, which forced her to abdicate. A referendum put to the people in 1919 confirmed the ruling house and called for her sister Charlotte to assume the throne.

**Grand Duchess Charlotte**, married to **Prince Felix of Bourbon-Parma**, healed Luxembourg's monarchy, becoming a much loved leader. When the Nazis invaded Luxembourg in May 1940, Charlotte escaped the country with her family and ministers and formed a government in exile. Her work—on behalf of Luxembourg and the Allies during the war—in England, Portugal, and Canada (where her son Jean went to university) was a source of pride to her people. On her return to Luxembourg in 1945, Charlotte was greeted by the premier with words of regard from her nation that were often repeated thereafter: "*Madame, we love you.*" (They are inscribed in Letzebuergesch on the sculpture of the former Grand Duchess paid for by public subscription and erected on Luxembourg's **place Clairefontaine** after her death in 1985.) In 1964, after 45 years on the throne, Charlotte abdicated in favor of her son Jean.

Still monarch of Luxembourg today, **Grand Duke Jean**, who was born in 1921 and served as a lieutenant with the *Irish Guards* from 1942 to 1945, married **Princess Josephine-Charlotte** of Belgium, sister of King Albert II. The Ducal Palace in Luxembourg City serves as the royal couple's in-town residence and office; their country castle is north of the capital at Colmar-Berg. Grand Duke Jean, who celebrated the 25th anniversary of his reign in 1989, and Grand Duchess Josephine-Charlotte have five children (and 14 grandchildren). Their eldest son, **H.R.H. Prince Henri**, born in 1955, is heir to the throne. He received his graduate education in France, Switzerland, and England, and holds a masters degree in political science and a Staff College Certificate from the *Royal Military Academy* at Sandhurst, England. The crown prince is highly effective in his job as chairman of the *Board of Economic Development of Luxembourg*. In 1981, he married **Maria Teresa** (now Princess), who was born in Cuba in 1956, her parents moving to New York in 1959 at the time of the revolution. Eventually her family moved to and became citizens of Switzerland, where Maria Teresa met Prince Henri while he was studying at the *University of Geneva*. The popular couple has four children, the eldest a son, **Guillaume**.

# LUXEMBOURG CITY

## GUIDELINES FOR LUXEMBOURG CITY

### SIGHTS

One of the world's most picturesquely situated capitals, Luxembourg City should be enjoyed for its visually engaging setting (with midcity ravine, walled by former fortifications and romantically illuminated at night) as much as for any other specific attractions. From the pedestrian **Promenade de la Corniche** are panoramic vistas that have given it the name "the most beautiful balcony in Europe." The city's *upper town* is set on plateaus above the winding green valley of lower town, the site of several suburbs with cafes, and walking paths with superb views up at the bastions. Centers of activity are in upper town, at the **Place d'Armes** (tourist office), **Marché-aux-Poissons** (the original hub of the ancient city, with the **National Museum** and **Bock casemates**), and **place de la Constitution** (overlooking the *Petrusse Valley*). The **European Center** on Kirchberg Plateau houses the offices of the Luxembourg-based European Union institutions; its modern buildings provide an intriguing contrast to the city's fairy-tale turrets.

### GETTING AROUND

Although the city is not large, Luxembourg's layout is complex, set on several levels and cut by two rivers, the *Alzette* and *Petrusse*, with their rock-walled, wooded valleys. Virtually all sights, shopping, and much of the charm are in the old *upper town*, as distinguished from the modern *European Center* on the Kirchberg Plateau across the dramatic **Grand Duchess Charlotte ("Red") Bridge** (1966), and the

19th-century sections of the city, across the arched **pont Adolphe** (1903) in the direction of the *Gare* (station). Since the views from points in the upper and lower city are so much a part of Luxembourg's beauty, sightseeing on foot will prove the most memorable. The upper city is quite compact, with several sections pedestrianized. The tourist office provides an excellent leaflet (*A Walk through the Green Heart of Europe*) that outlines two 3 mi./5 km. walking tours covering the highlights in both the upper and lower city. Guided city walking tours depart daily from the Tourist Office on the Place d' Armes from April–Oct. at 2:30 and 4:30 p.m.. The elevator (free, operating 6:30 a.m.–2 a.m.) on **place du Saint Espirit** connects the upper town with the lower's **Grund** suburb (cafes and restaurants). Travel by foot can be supplemented as needed by city buses and taxis. Bus terminals and taxi ranks are located at the station, **place Aldringen**, and **place de Paris**; taxis, although tip is included in the fare, are expensive, with surcharges for luggage, travel at night (10 percent), and on Sundays (25 percent). For interesting and easy views from the paved pathways through the Petrusse and Alzette valleys, take **Luxembourg Live**, a tourist train *(April 1–Oct. 31, daily regular departures from 10 a.m.–6 p.m. from the Adolphe Bridge at place de Bruxelles, tickets (220 Flux) from Kiosk Luxembourg Live)*. The 45-minute tours include an English language audio dramatization of the city's turbulent history on headset. Although its audio show is gimmicky, if you're not planning to take independent walks in the center-city valleys, the perspectives of the former fortifications offered during the tour are highly recommended. Because of pedestrian and one- way roads, restricted on-street parking, and the challenge of Luxembourg City's upper and lower city topography, it's preferrable to have a car only when you need one to explore the countryside. **Kemwel** is a reputable, budget-priced, local car rental firm. If you arrive by car, leave it in a center city car park. One and a half-hour motorcoach tours with a drive past major city sights are offered by **Voyages H. Sales** *(26 rue du Cure; 10 a.m. daily Apr.–Oct.;* ☎ *46.18.18; bookings also at tourist office, hotels)*. The company also offers diverse day tours in the Grand Duchy Tuesday–Sunday from June–Sept.

## SHOPPING

Though Luxembourg is not inexpensive, the quality of goods sold is very high, and the range of items for a city its size is surprisingly broad, due to the demands of its cosmopolitan population. Choices range from boutiques along the chic pedestrian **Grand-rue**, to fresh

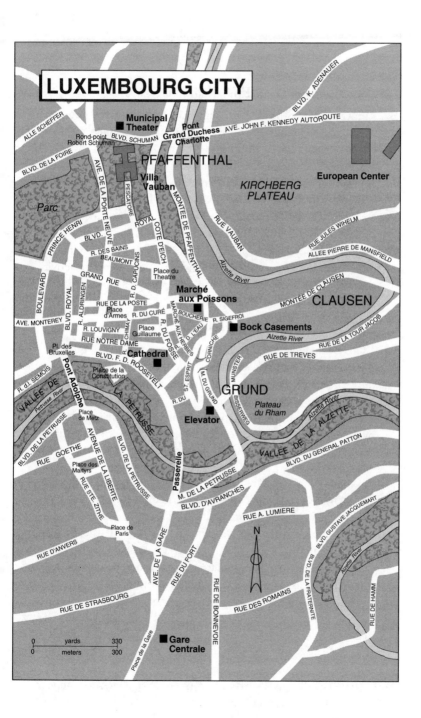

produce and general wares at the Wednesday and Saturday morning open-air markets held on **place Guillaume** in front of the Hôtel de Ville. Luxembourg's own **Villeroy & Boch** provides desirable souvenirs. **Note**: many shops do not open Mondays until 2 p.m.

## ENTERTAINMENT AND EVENTS

In warmer months through September, almost **nightly concerts** on the bandstand entertain *al fresco* diners around **Place d'Armes**. After-dark illumination produces a setting for fairy tales at the former fortifications (year-round in Petrusse Valley). Other city buildings and monuments are floodlighted from late spring through September, and a walk about town to view them is memorable evening entertainment, although the tourist office can provide a listing of concerts and other events. You can also check the "What's On" page in *Luxembourg News Digest*, the country's weekly (Thursday) English-language newspaper. It will give you an idea of the activities of the U.S., British, Canadian, and other English-speaking nationals who live in the Grand Duchy.

## WHERE TO STAY

There's adequate choice for pleasant rooms in Luxembourg City. Because of its relatively small size, the location of a hotel makes less difference here than in larger European capitals. Fall start-up sessions for the European Union Council of Ministers and other congresses/conventions make rooms in the better hotels harder to come by in September and October, and again in April and June; plan ahead if you're travelling in those periods.

## WHERE TO EAT

French/Belgian preparation and German portions is an apt characterization for Luxembourg cuisine. Foods are generally rich, and many regional specialties are similar to those in the Belgian Ardennes: jambon d'Ardennes, paté, charcuterie, venison, hare, sausage, and river fish: pike, trout, and crawfish. The beginning of the *moules* (mussels) season in September (until April) is on the minds of inland Luxembourgers as much as their Benelux cohorts on the coast. Entirely of local origin are the smoked pork and broad bean dish (*Jud mat gardebo'nen*), *Thuringen sausage*, and a strong local cheese *kachkes* (mysteriously described as "cooked in the making" and served on buttered black bread with mustard). In September, *quetsch* (small plums) tarts are a treat. *Filet Américain* appears on many a menu, but you won't be asked how you want it cooked; it's *steak tartare*.

## ARRIVING

Luxembourg's national passenger airline is **Luxair** (☎ *43.61.61*), with one-class service connecting many major European airports with **Findel Airport**, 3.5 miles/6 km. northeast of Luxembourg City. **Public bus #9** runs between the airport and the train station in Luxembourg City; Luxair also operates a full schedule of buses between the airport and the station, and will accept payment in foreign currency. **Icelandair** *(800-223-5500)* has flights to Luxembourg, via Reykjavik, Iceland, from JFK/New York and Baltimore/Washington. **Sabena World Airlines** (*70 Grand-Rue;* ☎ *2.12.12*) has service to/from Brussels.

## IN THE AREA

The **Luxembourg American Cemetery and Memorial at Hamm** (included on most city coach tours), several miles outside Luxembourg City, is the dignified resting place for 5,067 Americans, including **U.S. Army General George (Blood and Guts) Patton Jr.**, who was headquartered in Luxembourg City during the *Battle of the Bulge*, which produced most of the casualties buried here.

## TRAVEL TIPS

Despite their cosmopolitan climate, Luxembourgers maintain a civilized pace of life. Even many professionals hold to the tradition of a two-hour lunch (noon–2 p.m.), which is a standard for most offices, shops, and museums. Many workers go home to have lunch with their families. Even the city's parking meters take a noon–2 p.m. lunch break.

## *LUXEMBOURG CITY IN CONTEXT*

### Luxembourg City Is Europe's Cultural Capital for 1995

*The European Union has designated Luxembourg City as the European Cultural Capital for 1995. Focusing on worthy cities in union-member countries on a rotating basis, the European Cultural Capital spotlight gives selected destinations a special incentive to shine, such as by encouraging a stepped-up schedule for the restoration of historic buildings.*

*Other projects and special events will be a part of Luxembourg City's 1995 celebration as European Cultural Capital.*

Although a small city, its greater population approximately 120,000, Luxembourg is home to a substantial percent of the 400,000 people who live in the Grand Duchy. Atypical of the historic, even romantic, appearance of much of the old capital is **boulevard Royal**, frequently referred to as "Wall Street." But the gleaming glass towers of the modern monetary institutions housed along it do not rise so high that they hide the sky; center city structures cannot surpass in height the *Gella Fra* (gilded woman) atop the **War Memorial** on **Constitution Plaza**. In Luxembourg, buildings are kept in proportion, and business, though prospering, is kept in perspective. Rarely are transactions allowed to encroach on after-work socializing with friends or family over food and drink at one of the cafes on **Place d'Armes** or elsewhere.

Not that business is not held in high regard in Luxembourg City. Luxembourg's annual **Schueberfouer sheep fair**, founded in 1340 by John the Blind, attracted traders of all varieties from all over Europe (on **Grand-Rue** a charming sculptured fountain with sheep and musical instruments commemorates the historic fair) and shows an early commitment to commerce. Today some 85 percent of the country's GNP comes from exports and imports, so there remains a recognition of the country's dependence on foreign trade. Nevertheless, one can hardly argue with Luxembourg's semi-laid-back life-style, since the country has one of the highest standards of living in the world.

From its beginnings, Luxembourg City had a market, **Marché-aux-Poissons** (fish market), situated only a short distance from the castle acquired by Sigefroi in 963. The site may have been one of commercial dealings even earlier, since it was the actual intersection of two important Roman roads: the grand consular road from Paris via Reims and Arlon to Trier, and the one linking Metz via St. Vith and Liège to Aachen. As early as the 4th century, the clifftop site above the Alzette Valley had an observation tower that formed part of the Roman defense system against the Franks, and it probably was useful during invasions led by the dreaded Hungarian, **Attila**, in the first half of the 5th century. By about 450, the Romans gave up on the region. That early fortress, which had became known as **Castellum Lucilinburhuc**, was probably in ruins when **Sigefroi, count of Ardennes**, acquired it on Palm Sunday in 963, in exchange for the Abbey of St. Maximin in Trier. On a neighboring rock, **the Bock**, Sigefroi set about building a new castle (fortress), using his own workmen and employing the farmers and craftsmen who were already living in the valley on the banks of the Alzette, in what today are the suburbs of **Grund** and **Pfaffenthal**. Around the nearby Marché-aux-Poissons market place, Sigefroi's servants and retainers established their homes, thus making it the true center of the rapidly growing village. Between the market and the Bock, Sigefroi began building a court chapel in 987, naming it for **St. Michel**. Expansion was so rapid that by the year 1050 it was necessary to build a second wall to contain the town (which then reached to the present **rue du Fosse**) and meant the addition of a new market on the site of today's **rue du Marché-aux-Herbes**.

The town continued to prosper, receiving its charter from **Countess Ermesinde** in 1244. A third wall became necessary for the upper town and was begun under **John the Blind** in about 1320, taking most of the century to complete. Between 1387 to 1395, the lower town of **Grund** also was surrounded by fortifications, and **Pfaffenthal** was protected by a wall built across the bottom of the Alzette valley and given three gates. Such security measures were considered essential because of the economic and strategic importance of the mills, tanneries, and, above all, the water supplies in the lower town.

Though Luxembourg was elevated to a duchy (from a county) in 1354, and the House of Luxembourg produced rulers of power and prestige in the 14th and 15th centuries, their additional titles, such as Holy Roman Emperor, meant that its leaders often were absentee landlords. And Luxembourg's fortifications alone couldn't fend off the Burgundians, who, under **Philip the Good**, took the town by force one night in 1443, thus confirming the acquisition of the Duchy of Luxembourg by the **House of Burgundy**. From this time, for five hundred years, the strongly fortified town frequently found itself a pawn in the military policies of foreign powers. The Austrians, Spanish, French, Dutch, Prussians and Germans all have laid claim to Luxembourg.

The French under **King Louis XIV** did the most to change the face of the city. Having seiged the town in 1683 and claiming it in 1684, Louis set his great military engineer, **Maréchal de Vauban**, to the task of addressing the changes in defensive fortifications required by more modern weaponry. Luxembourg's high walls and massive towers, built in the Middle Ages, could not stand up to the bombardment by the contemporary artillery, and so Vauban transformed the walls into ramparts and added fortifications beneath the ground. Vauban recruited 3000 laborers and, within the four years from 1684 to 1688, created an impregnable fortress out of the natural advantages of the Luxembourg City setting.

Austrian Hapsburg engineers further strengthened and extended the casemates and forts during their occupation of Luxembourg in the 18th century. By the time they were through, in addition to visible fortified girdles, watchtowers, and bastions, Luxembourg had a virtual underground city in its sandstone rockbed. The **Bock Casemates** alone had a 14 mil./23 km. network of tunnels, and down huge staircases some 120 feet beneath the surface were great galleries to shelter thousands of soldiers as well as their horses, plus barracks, kitchens, bakeries, and slaughterhouses to sustain, and workshops to maintain, the troops.

Again, however, fortifications proved not to be the sole factor for defense. On June 7, 1795, after a seven-month blockade and four-month siege by the *Army of the French Republic*, the fortress city was starved into submission. Reporting the news to the French National Assembly, General Carnot claimed, "This fortress is second only to Gibraltar." After Napoleon's fall in 1814, leaders meeting at the *Congress of Vienna* took over the future course of both the city and the duchy of Luxembourg, though their fates would not, for a while, be the same. Luxembourg City was ordered to accept a Prussian garrison. Dutch **King Willem I** was named hereditary Grand Duke when he was presented with an upgraded Grand Duchy, which he governed as a province in his kingdom. The marking of the boundaries of the Luxembourg City fortress as federal territory took until 1829. (The fortress city, under Prussian insistence, had become a part of the *German Confederation*.) From 1835–1838, Willem undertook extensive repairs and modernization on the fortifications.

Late in the 1850s, the Dutch laid the first railway lines in Luxembourg, and by 1861 the fortress city was connected by train to Trier, and by 1866 to Liège. Ironically, while providing a terrific boost economically, the international rail routes simply enhanced the strategic value of the fortress of Luxembourg, and, as a result, even more extensive work on the fortifications followed. Finally, in 1866, Luxembourg became freed of the need to quarter Prussian troops by the dissolution of the German Confederacy. But it became the object of a complicated conflict between the French Napoleon III and German Bismarck over the use of the famous fortress, leading to a Franco-Prussian crisis that could have degenerated into war. The idea of "neutralizing" Luxembourg, launched by Holland's Prince Henry, took hold with the Dutch King-Grand Duke. In 1867, the **Treaty of London** was signed by Great Britain, Russia, France, Prussia, the Netherlands, Austria, Belgium, Italy and Luxembourg, guaranteeing perpetual neutrality of the Grand Duchy, and the evacuation and eventual razing of the city's fortress. On September 9, the last Prussian soldier left.

On that day in 1867, before dismantling began, the fortifications of Luxembourg City covered nearly 445 acres/180 hectares, the town itself being only 296 acres/120 hectares in area. The dismantling took 16 years, costing over 1-1/2 million gold-currency francs, a staggering sum for the time. The land freed from fortifications was put to good use—picturesque promenades, fine parks, and new residential and business districts. From 1933, the casemates of the Petrusse, with their monumental staircase and five-story height, were restored, and in 1936 work began on the Bock casemates. In 1938, all the old fortifications were converted to civil defense shelters for thousands.

The Nazis, having incorporated the Grand Duchy into the Third Reich, felt free to change the street signs after they invaded Luxembourg in May 1940. The prominent street that today is *avenue de la Liberté* bore the name *Adolphe Hitler Strasse* from 1940 to 1944. From 1940 until September 10, 1944, the headquarters of the Gestapo was located in a villa at 57 blvd. de la Petrusse. (Today, it's the Ministry of Public Health.) Worse, the Nazis tore down the **War Monument** on place de la Constitution that had been built to honor the dead from the First World War. On September 10, 1944, the Nazis were chased out of Luxembourg City for good by the Allies, primarily by U.S. Army forces. General Omar Bradley immediately set up headquarters for the 12th Army Group at 2 place de Metz, and, across that square, in the turreted State Savings Bank, was General H.S. Vandenberg of the 9th US Air Force. From December 21, 1944 (during the *Battle of the Bulge*) until March 27, 1945, **General George Patton** established his H.Q. for the 3rd Army in the Pescatore Foundation (today a senior citizens' home). It was in the chapel of the Foundation on December 23rd that Patton delivered the prayer for fair weather for his troops and air forces, that began: *"Sir, this is Patton talking. The last fourteen days have been straight hell. Rain, snow, more rain, more snow—and I'm beginning to wonder what's going on in Your headquarters. Whose side are You on, anyway?"*

Emerging from the war, Luxembourg soon became a center for activities meant to design a Europe that would not again put itself through such armed conflagrations. In 1952, Luxembourg was chosen as headquarters for the High Authority of the supranational **European Coal and Steel Community** (ECSC), brought into existence with the essential support of Robert Schuman, who had been born and educated in the city. The ECSC led directly to the creation of the **European Community** (EC)–now officially the European Union (EU)–which also chose Luxembourg as the site for several of its permanent institutions. Luxembourg City's prosperous and peaceful present, its development now under the direction of its own people, is a situation in sharp contrast to its heavily fortified past, perpetuated for centuries by fearful foreigners. Today, disarmed and delightful, Luxembourg is setting an example for the world.

## *GUIDEPOSTS*

**Country-wide telephone code 352**

**City Tourist Office** • *Syndicat d'Initiatives et de Tourisme*, place d'Armes ☎ *22.28.09*, FAX *47.48.19*; June 15–Sept. 15 Mon.–Fri. 9 a.m.– 7 p.m., Sat. 9 a.m.–1 p.m., 2–7 p.m., Sun. 10 a.m.–noon, 2–6 p.m.; remainder of year Mon.–Fri. 9 a.m.–1 p.m., 2–6 p.m., closed Sat., Sun. Also City and Grand Duchy information offices at Air Terminus at rail station (place de la Gare ☎ *48.11.99*) daily 9 a.m.–noon, 2–6:30 p.m., closed Sun. Dec.– March; and Findel Airport; ☎ *40.08.08*, Mon.–Fri. 10 a.m.–2:30 p.m. and 4–7 p.m., Sat. 10 a.m.–1:45 p.m., Sun. 10 a.m.–2:30 p.m., and 3:30–6:30 p.m.

**Auto. Assoc.** • *Automobile Club de Luxembourg*, 13 rue de Longwy, Bertrange, open Mon.–Fri. 8:30 a.m.-noon, 1:30–6 p.m.; reciprocal service with other auto clubs, and 24-hour breakdown service, ☎ *45.00.45*.

**Emergencies** • Medical, police, fire: ☎ *012*.

**Post Offices** • 25 rue Aldringen, Mon.–Sat. 7 a.m.–8:30 p.m., also FAX services, ☎ *4.76.51*; daily at place de la Gare, 6 a.m.–10 p.m., and Findel Airport daily 7 a.m.–10 p.m. available.

**Telephone** • 38 place de la Gare; ☎ *4.99.11*.

**Trains** • Chemins de Fer Luxembourgeois, Gare Centrale, information, reservations: 5:30 a.m.–8:30 p.m., ☎ *49.24.24 or 49.90.572*

**Embassies** • U.S.A.: 22 blvd. Emmanuel Servais, ☎ *46.01.23*; United Kingdom: 28 blvd. Royal, ☎ *2.98.64*.

## *WHAT TO SEE AND DO*

The city's weathered sandstone walls, great viaducts, plateaus set with steeples and turrets, and river valleys filled with suburban towns and terraced gardens provide scenes of exceptional interest. The views are equally outstanding whether seen from above, along the **Promenade de la Corniche**, or from below, from paths in the green parks in the center of the valley floor, looking up at the solid stone bastions built into the walls. Its  setting is what makes Luxembourg delightfully unique, so experience that above all else during your stay. Luxembourg is blessed with many parks, built on the land circling the inner city that became available after the fortifications were dismantled. Other squares, many with statues and monuments, add interest to walks around town. Sights are described below in two groupings, the first radiating out from the **Marché-aux-Poissons**, followed by those near the **place de la Constitution**.

### Musée de l'État/National Museum                    ★ ★

*Marché-aux-Poissons (Fish Market), entrance from rue Wiltheim; Tues.–
Fri. 10 a.m.–4:45 p.m., Sat. 2–5:45 p.m., Sun. 10–11:45 a.m. & 2–5:45
p.m., closed Mon.* ☎ *47.93.30.* The museum, located in a former governor's house, has an extensive collection of art and artifacts from all
periods of Luxembourg's history. The archaeological department has
fine prehistoric, Gallo-Roman, and Frankish items, the Gallo-Roman
material being outstanding. Something of the history of the city is
depicted through maps, weapons, and a bronze model of the fortress
before it was dismantled. The art department includes a collection of
works by modern Luxembourg artists, in particular **Joseph Kutter** and
**Dominique Lang**.

The **★ ★ Industrial and Popular Arts** section of the National Museum
*(rue Wiltheim; open Tues.–Fri. from 1–5 p.m., Sat. & Sun. 2–6 p.m.,
closed Mon.; no English documentation but well worth a visit)* is located
across the road in two restored 17th- and 18th-century burghers'
houses. Worth a visit for themselves, the handsome houses, which
retain their original interior design, have high beamed ceilings, old
wooden floors, and stone casement windows (out of which are seen
wonderful views of the Alzette Valley). The decorations, from the
mid-15th to the end of the 18th century, include tapestries, porcelain,
paintings, and freestanding and built-in (wall cupboards) furniture.
The museum seems to get more wonderful as you wander, especially
on the lower floors, which have fully furnished rooms with leather wall
coverings, painted panels, and tiled fireplaces. Down in the vaulted
cellars, which made me wonder if I had somehow stumbled into the
underground network of casemates at the nearby Bock (see below),
was an unusual and fascinating display of dozens of 16th-19th-century
intricately designed cast-iron fireplace pieces and ornamental stoves.

From the museum, walk a few doors down *rue Wiltheim* to **★ "Zum
Welle Mann"** tavern (*closed Mon.*), a part of the museum. Only light
snacks and beverages are served, but the atmosphere and views out the
rear windows over the Alzette valley are superb. At the foot of rue
Wiltheim are the 11th-century **Trois Towers**, from which you can connect with other roads down to the **Pfaffenthal** suburb.

The National Museum is on the site that became the market and hub
of the early town which grew around Sigefroi's castle on the nearby
Bock. In this oldest part of the city is Luxembourg's oldest house **Um
Bock**, on rue Loge, now a restaurant. Across the road is **★ St. Michel's
Church** *(rue Sigefroi).* Originally founded by Sigefroi as his castle
chapel in 987, St. Michel's was extended in the mid-14th century, but
was damaged and rebuilt several times until taking its present appearance in 1688. The Renaissance doorway dates from 1689, a gift from
Louis XIV, hence the French *fleur de lis.* The facade contains the
remains of Roman window vents, while the interior is a typical example of late Gothic vault style.

### Bock Casemates                                                    ★ ★

*entrance at Bock/Promenade de la Corniche; March-September, daily 10 a.m.–5 p.m.; self-guided tour; brochure in English; wear flat shoes for several flights of steep narrow stone stairs with handrails, uneven ground.* During the dismantling of the fortifications beginning in 1867 (the process took 16 years), most of the city's fortifications were blown up. But it was impossible to destroy the underground casemates without damaging the city above them. The main connections and entrances were closed, but about 11 miles/17 km. remain, on several levels connected by staircases. The garrison of the Bock casemate was 1200 men, and the main gallery held 50 cannon in loopholes which were enlarged during the dismantling and now afford remarkable views over the city. During this century's wars, the casemates, which have space for 35,000 people, were used as bomb shelters. **Note:** The Bock casemates should be your first choice if you're not planning to visit both of the city's casemate attractions; they give a far better idea of Luxembourg's former underground fortifications and allow you to explore at your own pace.

In 1963, just opposite the Bock, important remains of Sigefroi's ancient 963 **Luxembourg Castle** (*open at all times*) were discovered. They are preserved as the **Monument of the Millennium** of the city. Beyond the castle, on the **Montée de Clausen** road that leads across the Alzette valley and down into the suburb of **Clausen**, is the "**Hollow Tooth**," a watchtower built by Vauban that got that name from its appearance after being blown up during the dismantlement of Luxembourg's fortifications.

### Promenade de la Corniche                                          ★ ★

Sure-footed, properly shod visitors with stamina for steep stone stairs will find the casemates fascinating from the inside, but if for any reason that excursion isn't possible, a stroll along the pedestrian promenade de la Corniche, which runs downhill from the Bock will give you a good sense of the city's former fortifications and scenic setting. Bridges, here the high arched railway viaduct and the low-lying one across the reflective waters of the Alzette, frame many of Luxembourg's views. From the Corniche you see the 22-story tower (tallest in the Grand Duchy) that indicates the **European Center** on the **Kirchberg Plateau**. It plays a significant part in contemporary Luxembourg life but, unless you have a special interest, there's no real reason for tourists to go there. Walk the Corniche as far as the **place du St-Espirit**, if you want to remain in the upper town, or continue heading steeply down **Montée du Grund** to the bridge at the bottom across the Alzette in the suburb of ★ ★ **Grund** (cafes, restaurants). The free **public elevator** (lift) built into the valley wall will whisk you back up to place du St-Espirit. From there walk to **blvd. Franklin Roosevelt** and past the Cathédrale to place de la Constitution.

## Place de la Constitution ★★

A major orientation point in Luxembourg, this square spreads out in odd patterns due to its topography. Crowning the **Bastion Beck**, built to this amazing level above the Petrusse Valley in the course of the fortification of Luxembourg, place de la Constitution is instantly recognizable by the **War Memorial** obelisk. It was erected in 1923 to commemorate Luxembourgers who gave their lives in the First World War. (Although the Grand Duchy had to comply with its **Statute of Unarmed Neutrality**, a number of its citizens volunteered to serve with the Allied armies, particularly the French.) Atop the slim obelisk was placed the ★ golden statue of a woman (a Victory figure), who soon gained the name *Gelle Fra* (gilded woman), which became commonly used for the whole Constitution Square area. Not appreciating the sentiments it instilled in Luxembourgers, the Nazis pulled the monument down on October 21, six months after their invasion of the Grand Duchy in May 1940. Most of the pieces were recovered and hidden by Luxembourgers, but the action came to symbolize Nazi oppression, and, when the war was over, it became important to re-erect the monument. But it could not be completed because the golden statue remained missing. Finally, it was found in the early 1980s, restored, and, on Luxembourg's National Day, June 23, in 1985, the monument was officially reinaugurated in the presence of His Royal Highness Grand Duke Jean.

If you are facing the Petrusse Valley, to the far left of the square is a long stairway that leads down to ★ paths beneath the walls of the upper town. Other stairs lead to the ★★ green valley floor itself, where you'll find yourself amid some pretty surprising midcity scenery. Wonderful ★★ floodlighting at night.

## Petrusse or Constitution Casemates ★

*place de la Constitution; Easter & Whitsun weekends, July & Aug., approx. 11 a.m.–4 p.m., but hours posted at entrance; guided tours only, 40 mins.* The Petrusse casemates date from the first half of the 17th century, the Spanish era of modernization of the fortifications, although the French Vauban and, in the 19th century, the Austrians also implemented their ideas. The Spanish added many bastions, including the formidable **Bastion Beck**, named for the Spanish governor under whose rule it was begun. Its "platform," after the work was finished by Vauban, reached the level of the present place de la Constitution. The casemate tour, which covers lots of stairways, includes a visit to one of the outside terraces that overlooks the Petrusse Valley.

## Place Guillaume ★

Located upstairs opposite the cathedral on rue Notre Dame, place Guillaume is the setting for the **Hôtel de Ville** *(town hall, not open for tours)*, which was built during the 1830s to replace the former one, now the Ducal Palace. *The European Coal and Steel Community Agreement* was signed in the main council hall in 1952. General markets are held in the square on Wenesday and Saturday, their activity then taking center stage instead of the equestrian statue of Dutch King/Grand Duke of Luxembourg **Willem II** (for whom the square is named), which usually dominates. Willem faces down the short rue de la Reine to the Grand Ducal Palace.

### Grand Ducal Palace

*Corner rue de Marché aux Herbes & rue de la Reine; usually open to the public most days from mid-July to end Aug., during the Grand Duke's vacation.* Several years of extensive renovation have kept the palace closed in recent years, but at press time it was thought that it would be open for the summer of 1995. The palace, whose attractive 1572 facade in Renaissance style has an interesting Spanish-Moorish strapwork decoration—at the time it was built, the Spanish ruled—was originally the town hall, built to replace the previous one on the site, destroyed in 1554 in a gunpowder blast that caused extensive damage in the town. (This site very likely has been the setting for Luxembourg's various town halls since the city received its charter in 1244.) The civil guard met here where, while it served as a town hall, it also housed a prison and the municipal weighing scales. The balustrade, originally in stone, was replaced with one in wrought iron in 1741, when the building was enlarged. From the time Luxembourg was taken by the French in 1795, the palace has served as a building for national government, and, since 1890, it has been the residential palace of the Grand-Ducal family. Various fine buildings that house other government offices are located between the palace and the nearby cathedral.

### Place d'Armes

Taking its name from the days when it served as a parade ground for the French stationed in the city in 1685, the place d'Armes today is the social center of the city, The congenial Luxembourgers' favorite **cafe congregating spot**, has a bandstand that keeps a busy schedule in summer. At one end of the square is a statue of **Michel Lentz**, author of the national anthem, with its famous line "We want to remain what we are." At the other, with the **Tourist Office** tucked into offices there, is the 1906 **Cercle** municipal cultural building, whose pediment is decorated with a frieze depicting the granting of the town charter to Luxembourg by Countess Ermesinde in 1244.

### Maquette/Model ★★

*Rathskeller of the Cercle Theater, entrance on rue de la Cure; daily except Sun. 10 a.m.–12:20 p.m., 2–6 p.m. from Easter–Oct. 14; rest of year apply around the corner at City Tourist Office, place d'Armes; 50–min. Audiovisual show and commentary at the Model is presented in English several times daily, at last check at 11 a.m., 3 and 5 p.m., but confirm times at tourist office.* The Model, located around the corner from place d'Armes, a copy of that made under French King Louis XIV (the original is in the Hotel des Invalides in Paris), shows the full development of the **Lux-**

embourg City fortress, as envisioned by Vauban near the end of the 17th century. The **audiovisual presentation** takes you through the high points of the city's history. A careful study of the Model helps you appreciate what nine centuries of evolution as a fortress meant to the layout of Luxembourg in terms of walls, gates, towers, turrets, bastions, and barriers built on the site.

### Pescatore Museum ★★

*Municipal Park; ave. E. Reuter.* Built on municipal parkland on the site of razed Vauban fortifications, the mansion houses a fine art collection that normally is open to the public during July and August. (Due to its use as an office for the Grand Duke while the Grand Ducal Palace has been under renovation, it has been closed in recent years, but may reopen in the summer of 1995.) Included are works by **Jan Steen**, **Pieter Breughel the Younger**, **Jan Breughel the Younger**, **Teniers the Younger**, **Dou**, **Canaletto**, and **Courbet**.

Located on an adjoining portion of the Municipal Park, where once Fort Louvigny stood, is Radio-Tele Luxembourg, a powerful component of the Grand Duchy's important telecommunications industry. To the north, at the edge of the Municipal park, is **Rond-Point Robert Schuman**. This founding father of the European Union is honored by a monument located near the modern **Municipal Theater**, the city's main performance center. The focal point of the Schuman Monument is several steel girders, signifying Schuman's role in the establishment of the European Coal and Steel Community, which was a precursor to the Common Market. From the monument, *blvd. Robert Schuman* leads across the vivid red **★Grand Duchess Charlotte Bridge** to the **European Center**, practically passing over the house in which he grew up, which sits in the Alzette valley suburb of Clausen.

## *SHOPPING*

Luxembourg's 15 percent VAT (Value-Added Tax) is lower than most in Europe. Although that situation could change as a result of Europe's economic union, at present it means savings for shoppers on the high-quality international items for sale on and near the pedestrian **Grand-Rue**. (Purchases in a single store of FLux 3000 or more qualify for a VAT refund; inquire at the time of purchase.) Luxembourg's shops are small and personalized; there are no department stores in the city. Though many of the fine **Villeroy & Boch** (*2 rue de Fosse*) products are made in factories in Germany, the company maintains its Luxembourg roots (there's a large tableware factory in **Septfontaines** in the Eisch River Valley) that go back to the 18th century. Several of its china patterns are produced in Luxembourg—the 1989 **Mon Jardin** design, **Petite Fleur**, **Naif** (Naive), and Botanic. These lines are somewhat less expensive in the Luxembourg store than they would be elsewhere. A number of private **art galleries** featuring the works of Luxembourgers have opened in the city. If you enjoyed the cast-iron fireback pieces at the Industrial Arts section of the National Museum, look for the miniature items, called "Tak," made in the shape of castles and other subjects by Luxembourg's **Fonderie de Mersch**. There's a flea market on the 2nd and 4th Saturdays each month.

## WHERE TO STAY

Most of the hotels in Luxembourg City itself are independent properties, many family run, some multigenerational. Several international chain hotels, particularly popular with business travelers, are located just outside the city. Near Findel Airport is the **Aerogolf-Sheraton**, and in a wooded suburb several kilometers from the city center is the **Inter-Continental**, popular as a quiet conference site. The **Sofitel** is the only hotel at the European Center on Kirchberg plateau. Most hotels included here have their own restaurants, of a more than acceptable standard. The tradition of hotel-restaurants is strong in this region, and you'll rarely go wrong by dining "in house," since a hotel's restaurant also must satisfy discriminating local customers in order to survive outside of the tourist season. All prices are inclusive of taxes and service.

## VERY EXPENSIVE

**Grand Hotel Cravat**

*29 blvd. F.D. Roosevelt;* ☎ *22.19.75, FAX 22.67.11.* Facing the place de la Constitution, overlooking the Petrusse Valley, the Grand Hotel Cravat sits at the very core of the city's sightseeing, shopping, and business. A fourth-generation family hotel of a superior standard, it offers a traditional European atmosphere and personal Luxembourg service to its international clientele. The renovated rooms on the front facing the Petrusse Valley have the finest hotel room views in the city. The traditional but welcoming marble-floored lobby has a bar that is a popular community convening place, as is the **Taverne**, which serves local informal fare. The 60 guest rooms (most recently renovated) on six floors have bath with bidet, hair dryers, makeup mirrors, good lighting, turn-down services, French-slatted shades for complete darkness, TV, and telephone. Continental breakfast, served in the **Cravat** formal restaurant, is included. Although the Cravat family is more than able to serve diplomats, it can still employ cozy touches such as changing the carpets in the elevator to tell you what day of the week it is. Parking lot.

## EXPENSIVE

**Hotel Central Molitor**

*28 avenue de la Liberté;* ☎ *48.99.11, FAX 48.33.82.* This 1913 3rd-generation refurbished family-run hotel, located midway between the station and place de la Constitution, has a traditional atmosphere in its public rooms, which include a respected restaurant and bar. Behind the stately old facade, the 36 rooms of the four-story hotel all have modern furniture, private bath, telephone, TV, light and doorlock control panel at bedside, wall safe, and sound-proofed doors and windows, and many have minifridges. Underground parking nearby; multiple bus lines just outside hotel.

## MODERATE

**Hotel Français** ★★★

*14 place d'Armes;* ☎ *47.45.34, FAX 46.42.74.* Situated right in the heart of Luxembourg, on the lively *place d'Armes*, this 20-room (plus 6 suites), 5-story hotel has attractive hallways decorated with art works and sitting areas. All the modern rooms have TV, telephone, private bath; twins are larger than doubles. Front rooms face the square, where the hotel has a popular terrace cafe and brasserie. Major credit cards; breakfast included; elevator; car parks nearby; guests allowed to drive to hotel (in pedestrian area) to unload luggage.

## INEXPENSIVE

**Auberge Du Coin** ★★★★

*2 blvd. de la Petrusse;* ☎ *40.21.01, FAX 40.36.66.* This recently renovated, turn-of-the-century home is located in a quiet residential area near the Petrusse Valley, three blocks from ave. de la Liberté. All 35 rooms have lightwood furniture, private bath, TV and telephone. There's a pleasant lobby and an elegant restaurant and a brasserie where breakfast, included, is served.

## *WHERE TO EAT*

The fact that Luxembourg cuisine can be described as substantial and nourishing doesn't mean it's not refined. French influence is featured at many restaurants, although, with a large number of resident nonnationals, many foreign cuisines are represented, Italian and Chinese being particularly popular. Though Eurocrats on expense accounts cause the best restaurants to be pricey, Luxembourgers' own love of good food encourages value for money in all price ranges. Menu prices generally include both VAT and service charges, though it's still customary locally to tip (about 10%) if service is good. Because it is a diplomatic and international business center, Luxembourg City tends toward the more formal in dress, especially outside the summer tourist season; at the best restaurants, men will be most comfortable in suits, women in appropriate dresses. Menus, always posted, in the larger restaurants generally give an English translation of the French. Except for the most casual places, it's a good idea to inquire about reservations, essential at the top spots.

Considered one of the finest restaurants in the city is **Clairefontaine** *(9 place de Clairefountaine; closed Sat. lunch, Sun., holidays, and three weeks from mid-July;* ☎ *46.22.11, FAX 47.08.21; expensive),* located on the expansive square surrounded by elegant old buildings that now house government departments; its French cuisine was described by one Luxembourger as simply *"extraordinary."* **Saint-Michel** *(32 rue de l'Eau; closed Sat., Sun.;* ☎ *22.32.15, FAX 46.25.93; expensive/very expensive),* also serving classic French cuisine, has an elegant setting and service in Luxembourg's oldest and quaintest quarter. For seasonal and French gourmet fare at a more reasonable price, Luxembourgers take themselves to **Speltz** *(8 rue Chimay;*

*closed Sat., Sun.;* ☎ *47.49.50; moderate/expensive),* in a cozy, candlelit 17th-century house.

On at least one night you'll want to dine on the **Place d'Armes** to savor its special local atmosphere. It will be evident that the many Luxembourgers there, who love nothing more than getting together with friends over food and drinks, are among those most enjoying the music coming from the bandstand, the evening air and atmosphere. Cafes rim the square; all have menus posted, so take your pick.

On many local lists the best places for a bottomless bowl of steamed mussels (*moules*) is **Ems** *(30 place de la Gare; daily 11 a.m.–1 a.m.;* ☎ *48.77.99; inexpensive).* Across from the station, it's a friendly brasserie that often gets full, in which case you could find yourself in a great conversation with Luxembourgers sharing your booth. The menu includes a number of regional dishes and local beer and wine. For a complete change of scene and cuisine, but not price, if you've a taste for Italian, a good bet is **Bacchus** *(32 rue du Marché-aux-Herbes; noon–2:30 p.m., 6 p.m.–midnight, closed Mon;* ☎ *47.13.97; inexpensive/moderate).* There's an upmarket atmosphere: peach-colored rattan furniture, lovely Villeroy & Boch pink-marbled ware, and international music piped in for the largely local crowd. The pasta is exceptional (served in starter or main course portions), and there's pizza and calzone.

Fashionable atmospheres are becoming common in the lower town suburb of **Grund**, a delightful excursion via the elevator from place du St. Espirit from the upper town. **Scott's Restaurant** *(4 Bisserweg; noon–2 p.m., 7 p.m.–10:15 p.m., closed Mon.;* ☎ *47.53.52; inexpensive/moderate; reservations taken, ask for table with view of upper city)* was the first eatery to open in the Grund, in 1986, in a restored 1790 building by the Alzette river. Particularly popular with the English, Irish, and Americans living in Luxembourg, the well-presented meals range from fish and meat to salads; decor is fashionable yet fanciful. The pub downstairs is open daily from noon to 1 a.m., serving bar snacks and 25 kinds of beer, inside and on the riverside terrace. Across the way is **Cafe Am/Haeffchen** *(9 Bisserwee; 5 p.m.–1 a.m. daily, closed Mon.; inexpensive),* with delightful outdoor garden seating amid lime trees, or indoors in a living room/library setting that's cozy contemporary (the works of Luxembourg artists hang on the walls) and can be crowded. Drinks, sandwiches, and tempting toasties.

The pastries of Luxembourg are renowned. Two shops traditionally compete as the source of the city's best pastries: **Namur** *(rue des Capucins, more than 125 years in business)* and **Oberweis** *(Grand Rue, over 25 years old).* Better try them both. The popularity of cake and coffee is a holdover tradition from the Austrian era here. Luxembourgers' love for coffee is shown by the fact that there is no word in Letzebuergesch for breakfast: the word "coffee" stands in for it. For superior picnic supplies, plus pastries, pay a visit to **Kaempf-Kohler** on *rue du Cure.*

## ENTERTAINMENT AND EVENTS

Luxembourg's **Schueberfouer** (late August through early September), a large itinerant fair held on the vast Glacis Square near Rond-Point Robert Schuman, is a direct continuation of the annual trade fair founded in 1340 by **John the Blind**. Luxembourg's **National Day** is June 23, but the festivities begin the night before with fireworks and a torchlight parade through town to the Ducal Palace. In December, the place d'Armes hosts the **Christmas Market**, with its decorated stalls and large central Christmas tree, and food stands selling warm mulled wine. On Easter Monday, Luxembourgers gather on Marché-aux-Poissons for a traditional celebration of **Emais'chen**, often attended by the Grand-Ducal Family, that includes the buying of small whistling porcelain birds, sold only on that day. This Catholic country's main religious ceremony is the **Octave** or Pilgrimage of Our Lady of Luxembourg, the city's patron saint, with processions through the streets, decorated with altars of flowers, between the 3rd and 5th Sundays after Easter. Luxembourgers love music and stage a full and varied program of guest performances in symphony, opera, and ballet by Europe's finest companies at the modernistic **Municipal Theater** (near Rond-Point Robert Schuman); the prime season is fall through spring. Annually in spring, Luxembourg hosts **Printemps Musical**, a festival of international artists catering to all musical tastes. Inquire at the tourist office about possible concerts in the National Library.

## IN THE AREA

### Luxembourg American Cemetery and Memorial ★★

*in suburb of Hamm, 3 mi./5 km. west of Luxembourg City, signposted*
At the end of the World War II, 83 temporary U.S. military cemeteries existed in North Africa, the Middle East, Italy, Great Britain, and Western Europe, and a decision was taken after study to consolidate them into 13 permanent U.S. cemeteries in Europe, of which the Luxembourg American Cemetery is one. The people of Luxembourg, in gratitude for the liberation by the *First U.S. Army*, particularly the *Fifth Armored Division*, of their country in September 1944 and again in the Battle of the Bulge in February 1945 by the *U.S. Third Army* commanded by *General George S. Patton Jr.*, purchased this 50 acre/20 hectare site for perpetual use by the American government, the agreement being ratified in 1951.

Most of those buried in the cemetery at Hamm died in the Battle of the Bulge, which opened on December 16, 1944 with a lightning counterattack under **Field Marchal von Rundstedt**, which swept across the northern half of Luxembourg and into Belgium. Northern Luxembourg suffered twice in the Battle of the Bulge, first during the advancing attack by the Nazis, and again during their retreat, forced foot by foot back across the **Siegfried Line** in Germany by the Allies, mostly Americans of the U.S. Third Army. During the heavy fighting in the winter of 1945, the American Burial Service recovered the bodies of victims, burying them in a provisional cemetery at Hamm, which was opened on December 29, 1944. At the end of the war there were 8,411 graves. The cemetery was closed from March 1948 to December 1949, during which time the remains of the dead were either returned to the U.S. or permanently interred in Luxembourg, according to the wishes of the next of kin. When the cemetery opened on December 16, 1949, on the 5th anniversary of the beginning of the battle, 5076 service people lay buried by name beneath white stone Roman crosses or Stars of David, buried without distinction to rank, race, or religion, an exception being made for the 22 pairs of brothers who are buried side by side. The headstones of the 101 graves of unknown soldiers or airmen read "Here lies in honored glory a comrade in arms known but to God." The grave of General Patton, who wished to be buried with his men, is set slightly aside because of the great numbers of people who visit his grave.

Each of America's war cemeteries in Europe was designed individually by an American architect or firm to complement the specific setting, though all have the common elements of a nondenominational chapel, a permanent inscription of the names of those missing in action, and display of the military campaign in the region where the memorial is located. At Luxembourg, the chapel at the woods-encircled cemetery has inscribed above the Blue Belge (Belgian) marble altar the words: "I give unto them eternal life and they shall never perish." The West Pylon on the cemetery terrace that overlooks the field of markers bears a map that shows the military operations in northwest Europe, from the landing in Normandy until the end of the war; the East Pylon has a map illustrating movements of the Battle of the Bulge.

# TOUR OF THE GRAND DUCHY

Luxembourg can claim, with justification, that its historic capital city is also its most picturesque town. This means that visitors whose only time in the Grand Duchy will be spent in Luxembourg City can rest assured that they're seeing sights that are the country's highlights. If you can linger longer, however, you'll be well rewarded for further exploration in the Grand Duchy. As in Luxembourg City, the picturesque and the spectacular combine in the countryside. Though small in scale, the Grand Duchy offers sights and scenery that are remarkable for their variety.

## *GUIDELINES FOR THE GRAND DUCHY*
### SIGHTS

Specific attractions include **Celtic earth forts** at Aleburg near Larochette;**Roman mosaics** and a **Battle of the Bulge** museum in Diekirch; Luxembourg-born photographer Edward Steichen's just-restored **The Family of Man** exhibit in Clervaux Castle, which also houses a collection of **models of the finest castles** in the Grand

Duchy; the attractive historic Abbey town of **Echternach**; and **Vianden Castle**, Luxembourg's finest and best restored feudal fortification (the ancestral home of the House of Orange-Nassau, a heritage shared by the Dutch Royal Family and the Grand-Ducal family). Even without these, the Grand Duchy is memorable for its splendid scenery, which varies from **lush vineyards** that run down sunny slopes to the Moselle, to fantastic **rock formations** in "Little Switzerland," to river-carved valleys and **high plateaus** with far-reaching vistas of fertile farming fields.

## GETTING AROUND

Car is by far the best way to get the full impact of the Grand Duchy's appeal. Second best is to take one of the several sightseeing **day motorcoach tours** offered by **Voyages H. Sales** *(26 rue du Cure; June–Sept. Tues.–Sundays, depending upon the itinerary; departures from Luxembourg City, station and place de la Constitution; information and reservations ☎ 50.10.50).* Among the places visited in different tours are Vianden, Echternach, Clervaux, Little Switzerland, Larochette, and the Moselle Valley, each tour giving a fairly good cross section of Duchy scenery. Luxembourg's **train/bus transportation network** covers the country, but with too time-consuming connections for most visitors. Those who want to give it a try should purchase a bargain one-day *Network Ticket* (FLux 140, valid until 8 a.m. the following day), good for all trains and buses in the Grand Duchy and on municipal buses in Luxembourg City; 50 percent reduction for those over 65. **Bicycles**, if you can take the hilly terrain, can be rented in Luxembourg City, Diekirch, and Vianden (details at local tourist offices).

## SHOPPING

For serious shopping, even Luxembourgers go to the capital, the only city in the Grand Duchy. For basic items and souvenirs, the towns with the largest selection of shops are Diekirch, Wiltz, and Echternach.

## ENTERTAINMENT AND EVENTS

The summer season is filled with special concerts and activities, staged for and enjoyed both by tourists and Luxembourgers during July and August. Among the annual events is **Echternach's Dancing Procession** (Whitsun Tuesday at 9 a.m.), and in June, Echternach hosts the **International Music Festival**. **Remembrance Day** (1st weekend in July) is held annually in Ettelbruck in honor of U.S. Army General **George S. Patton**, commander in Luxembourg during the Battle of the Bulge. **Grevenmacher** on the Moselle River holds the largest **Wine and Grape Festival** with procession (2nd weekend each September) of the several celebrations of the gathering of the grapes from the vineyards.

## WHERE TO STAY

While hotel choices are limited in number in the Grand Duchy (a greater selection exists in the tourism centers of Vianden and Echternach), very pleasant properties are scattered throughout the countryside. All are spotless, run with pleasant personal attention, almost invariably have restaurants, and offer value-for-FLux. In July and August (the high summer tourist season in the countryside), although many Europeans come on camping holidays, reservations at hotels should be made as far ahead as possible. In June and September you should be able to "drop in" and find rooms available, but later than that you may begin to run into hotels in the tourist areas that have closed for the season. Local tourist offices can provide help with accommodations, and are the best source if you are seeking bed-and-breakfast or pension-style accommodations.

## WHERE TO EAT

As has been pointed out before, country hotels, whether rural or in towns, are always a solid choice for a meal.

## TRAVEL TIPS

Remember, when driving on the remarkably traffic-free roads in the Grand Duchy, you must keep in mind the *possibility* of vehicles coming at a good clip around every corner—not always easy to do when, with the possible exception of July and August, you'll often have the roads largely to yourself for miles on end.

## *THE ROUTE*

Because the country's so small, it's possible to take a spontaneous sort of trip in Luxembourg, if that's the type of travel you prefer—keeping in mind the importance of finding a bed for the night in the busy tourist months of July and August. Below is a description of some of the most worthwhile places and sites to consider seeing in the course of your Grand Duchy tour. The route begins with **Clervaux** in the north, then drops southeast to **Vianden**. If you intend to see but one country town in the Grand Duchy, this should be the one. South of Vianden is **Diekirch**, to the southeast of which are **Mullerthal/Little Switzerland** and **Echternach**. South from there the road follows along the **Moselle River**, which forms Luxembourg's border with Germany, past vineyards from which it's a short dash back to Luxembourg City.

## *ON THE ROAD*

### ★CLERVAUX

**Tourist office** • *Castle, April–June, Mon.–Sat. 2–5 p.m.; July–Sept., Mon.–Sat. 9:45–11:45 a.m. & 2–6 p.m; also on Sun. in July & Aug., in Oct. 9:45 –11:45 a.m., and 1–5 p.m.;* ☎ *9.20.72; pop. 1,000.*

The first sight as you approach Clervaux is of the neo-Romanesque (1910) **Benedictine Abbey of St. Maurice**, whose extensive red roof rises in pleasing contrast above the green forest that surrounds it. But once you've wound your way over curving Ardennes roads into the steep town, it's ★ **Clervaux Castle**, rising on a rocky spur, that takes your attention. Its origins go back to the 12th century, but since that time the stolid feudal fortress has undergone numerous additions and alterations, particularly while serving as the seat of the powerful counts who were overlords of extended territories. In 1762, then-owner **Count Adrian-John-Baptist of Lannoy** had the splendid **Loreto Chapel** built in the park of the castle; the castle and chapel were spared destruction by the French Revolutionary Army in the 1790s because the people of Clervaux declared them to be the property of a "Citizen Lannoy." Following inheritance quarrels in the 19th century, the legal victor in 1887 had the administrative buildings in the first court-yard demolished, using the stones to build a luxurious villa (today the **Hotel Parc**, see "Where To Stay") in the adjacent park. Clervaux experienced devastating destruction during the *Battle of the Bulge*, including the castle which, defended by the soldiers of the 110th Regiment of the 28th Infantry Division, fell in flames when the town was taken on December 17, 1944 by the 2nd German Armored Division. Clervaux finally was retaken by the 26th U.S. Infantry on January 26, 1945. Clervaux without its castle was unthinkable, so shortly after the Second World War ended, restoration was begun. Today, the castle is the heart not only of the town's history, but of its present life. The town hall (*Mairie*) and the tourist office are located within its walls. The castle also houses several exhibits.

From the summer of 1994, **Clervaux Castle** *(open daily, in June, 1–5 p.m.; July–Sept. 15, 10 a.m.–5 p.m.; rest of year Sun. & holidays. 1–5 p.m.; closed Jan.& Feb.)* will display the complete set of photographic images (503, assembled from 68 countries) from the original attendance-breaking ★ ★ ★ **The Family of Man** show conceived by Luxembourg-born **Edward Steichen** (1879–1973) when he was director of photography of New York's *Museum of Modern Art* (MOMA). Working on the exhibit for which his vision was to show a time span that included birth, the world at work, family life, friendship, leisure, disease, war, and death, Steichen, at the age of 73, scanned some 2 million photographs and then a short list of 10,000, eventually narrowing the number to 503. It ranged from the works of the world's most famous photographers (though Steichen modestly selected only two of his own images) to simple family snapshots. The Family of Man opened at MOMA in New York in 1955, eventually travelled to 69 countries, and was viewed by over 9 million people. Having kept close ties with Luxembourg all his life, even though he had left the country as a two-year-old, in 1966 Steichen arranged for the most complete version of The Family of Man, minus only a dozen images from the original, to be donated to the Luxembourg government. Steichen himself came to Luxembourg in 1966 to help settle the question of where such a large show could be permanently displayed, since many of the pictures are mounted on large boards. The castle at Clervaux was settled upon. But for many years since, only a limited number of the pictures was displayed; the others, in storage, became moldy and yellow. Fortunately, provisions were made in time for them all to be fully restored and displayed. The problem of space, which is why some of the images were in storage in the first place, has been addressed by the renovation of space within Clervaux Castle.

Elsewhere in Clervaux Castle is an extremely interesting permanent display of *models* of the Grand Duchy's most important ★ **castles** (notes on the history of each castle in English). Since so many of the castles are now in ruins, the models furnish us with a better idea of the originals and how the fortifications were placed on each site. The largest of the more than a dozen models is for Vianden Castle, and, in this one case, is a model of the whole town.

Across the courtyard, still in Clervaux Castle, is a museum of memorabilia from the **Battle of the Bulge**.

On Maria Theresa Square in the pedestrianized center of Clervaux stands the **Monument to the GI 1944–45**, a statue of a typical soldier to honor the sacrifice of the common GI for the liberation of Luxembourg. Don't miss the charming other memorial, "*To our Liberators*," a modern frieze mounted on the wall of the bank building facing the standing monument that depicts a heartwarming scene of citizens greeting the GI.

## *WHERE TO STAY AND EAT IN CLERVAUX*

### Hotel du Parc                                        ★★★

*2 rue du Parc;*  *and FAX 9.10.68; inexpensive.* This 110-year-old elegant mansion, surrounded by century-old trees, sits on a rise across from and at eye level with Clervaux Castle, some of whose stones went into its construction. The 8 attractive guest rooms all have private bath, telephone, and radio. The public rooms have an old-world charm, with plaster work, wood paneling, and monumental fireplaces (with fires laid when the weather warrants) in the dining room and lounge. The kitchen is well regarded, and the place is particularly popular on weekends. Parking; sauna and solarium in cellar.

## ★★★VIANDEN

**Tourist office** • *Victor Hugo House, Grand Rue; open daily April–Oct. 9:30 a.m.–noon and 2–6 p.m., closed Wednsdays rest of year;* ☎ *8.42.57, FAX 84.90.81; inquire about special summer concerts, events; pop. 1,600.*

For many, Vianden is the favorite destination in the Grand Duchy. A medieval town, spreading down a single steep stone street from its craggy heights with fine views to the river **Our** at the bottom, Vianden is defined mostly by its **castle**, which dominates the entire area. A **chair lift** (rue du Sanatorium; daily Easter–Sept., 11 a.m.–6 p.m., both earlier and later hours in July and Aug., ☎ 8.43.23) provides a silent sweep up and over trees to a height (1,444 feet/440 meters) from which one actually looks down at Vianden Castle. At the top there's a terrace cafe, of course, from which to enjoy the surpassing view of the river, town, and grandeur of the forests and grassy plateaus.

### Vianden Castle                    ★ ★ ★

*Daily in March 10 a.m.–5 p.m.; April–Sept. 10a.m.–6 p.m.; in Oct. 10 a.m.–5 p.m.; Nov–Feb.10 a.m.–4 p.m.; English brochure and floor plan for self-guided tour; castle majestically illuminated at night April–Sept.* The Grand Duchy's most historic, best restored, and most frequently photographed castle, Vianden is the ancestral home of *Orange-Nassau, Holland's Royal House,* which has ties to Luxembourg's Grand Ducal family through another Nassau branch. One of the largest feudal fortresses in the area, and certainly the one in the best shape today, the spectacularly situated castle was begun in the 12th century and enlarged in the 13th century, Vianden's peak of power, so that its ★ ★**Count's Hall** could accommodate 500 knights-at-arms. By late in the 13th century, the counts of the *House of Vianden* controlled lands that included 211 villages, hamlets, and mills, and produced **Count Henry II**, who became bishop of Utrecht. That was Vianden's apex. Its nadir came after then-owner King Willem I of Holland/Grand Duke of Luxembourg put the castle up for public auction in 1820. The buyer sold the castle's roof and other parts as building materials, and in 1827 once-proud Vianden was declared a ruin. Ownership eventually evolved back to the Nassaus and the Grand Ducal family, and, in 1978, Grand Duke Jean ceded the castle, then but a shell of its former self, to the state. Since then, Vianden Castle has been painstakingly restored, the process only recently completed. You'll have a great sense of discovery exploring the castle. The "upper" chapel, 13th century, is a jewel, elegant and light, modelled after Charlemagne's palace chapels at Aachen and Nijmegan. It was used by the lords and ladies of Vianden's court, while the "lower" chapel was for the lower classes and servants, who could hear but not see the services in which the upper classes participated. The main section of the castle, built about 1210, has two huge halls. The Count's Hall, lined with wardrobes and wall cabinets, and hung with a 16th-century Flemish tapestry *The Trojan War* and 17th-century tapestries from Amiens and Brussels, is now sometimes the site of **concerts**. The *Banqueting Hall*, where recorded classical music plays faintly, is also finely furnished and has portraits, a 17th-century. Aubusson tapestry *The Wedding at Cana*, and an impressive fireplace. Elsewhere in the castle is an Orange-Nassau genealogy painted on the wall. The counts of Vianden and counts of Nassau first merged in the 14th century, and **René de Chalon**, who died in 1544, was the first count of the Orange-Nassau dynasty. In the same way the castle is a magnificent ★★★ sight from terraces in the town, so are the ★★★ views of the town magnificent from the castle terraces.

Other attractions in Vianden include the **Victor Hugo House**, which shares quarters and opening hours with the ground floor tourist office *(exhibit material in French only)*. French author Victor Hugo lived here in 1871, having been to Vianden before (in 1862, 1863, and 1865). During those visits he produced a series of drawings of the Grand Duchy's castles, and later he published a book of sketches entitled *Les Ardennes*. The house, in which he stayed only from June 6–August 22, 1871, contains photocopies of some of Hugo's drawings, letters, photographs, and other memorabilia. Across the street from the house is a ★ bust of Hugo by **Rodin**, mounted on the corner of the bridge over the Our. The cafe outside the simple **Hotel Victor Hugo** provides great views to accompany a drink.

### The Museum of Rustic Arts                    ★★

*98 Grand-rue; Easter–Sept., daily 10 a.m.– noon, and 2–6 p.m., closed Mon. except in July, Aug. and holidays;* ☎ *8.45.91; no English documentation*. The museum is a former bourgmestre's house with several ground floor rooms of fine furnishings. Almost across the street from the museum is the ancient twin-naved **Trinitarian church**, built in the Gothic style in 1248 and one of the oldest religious buildings in Luxembourg. The restored cloister behind it holds the tombstones of the Counts of Vianden.

## *WHERE TO STAY AND EAT IN VIANDEN*

### Hotel Heintz                    ★★★

*55 Grand-rue;* ☎ *8.41.55, 8.45.59; inexpensive; closed mid-Nov. until Easter*. The Heintz is famous for its hospitable air and congenial family atmosphere that instill a feeling of being well cared for. Guests to Luxembourg from afar invariably find their way here: **Beatrice Patton**, widow of General George; **Margaret Truman**; and **Perla Mesta**, former U.S. Ambassador to Luxembourg, the "Hostess with the Mostest." But the Heintz isn't grand, it's simply gracious. The 30 guest rooms (8 with balconies and view of hills behind hotel) have basic traditional furnishings, all with private bathroom, telephone. The hallways and public rooms in the centuries-old building are appropriately and delightfully decorated in antiques, oil paintings, and orientals, with wonderful wooden chests and clocks. The restaurant is renowned, every detail overseen by owner **Magda Hansen** herself, the fourth generation to provide personalized attention to guests of the homey Heintz. Elevator; parking; private gardens.

## DIEKIRCH

**Tourist office** • *Esplanade; Mon.–Fri. 9 a.m.–noon, 2–5 p.m., from July 1–Aug. 15 9 a.m.–6 p.m. and also on Sat. & Sun. 10 a.m.–noon, & 2–4 p.m.;* ☎ *80.30.23, FAX 80.27.86; pop. 5600.*

### Diekirch Historical/Battle of the Bulge Museum ★★

*10 Bamertal; daily Easter–Oct., 10 a.m.–noon, 2–6 p.m.;* ☎ *80.89.08;*
*guided tours on request; multilingual brochure, exhibit notes.* In large
part, the museum commemorates aspects of the Battle of the Bulge
around Diekirch in the winter of 1944-45 (although the scope of the
museum may be enlarged). The details offered here about what
"*absorption*" into the Third Reich, as opposed to "merely" being
occupied, meant to the lives of Luxembourgers, make us appreciate
their uniquely difficult experience during World War II. Particularly
poignant are the exhibits relating to the compulsory conscription of
young Luxembourg men into the *Wehrmacht* from August 1942. This
act was considered one of the worst of the Nazis war crimes, because
it sent Luxembourgers to the German Front (mostly to Russia) to
wage armed war against the Allied Forces they supported, those Allies
not realizing they were firing on Luxembourgers forced to wear Nazi
uniforms. From 1941, all Luxembourg young men and women were
obliged to provide the Nazis with labor in war industry factories and
to live apart in work camps.

The Diekirch Museum is not political. Its purpose is to show what
happened. The exhibits explain facts such as that by the time of the
*Battle of the Bulge*, most of the German soldiers who were doing the
fighting were not Nazi ideologists but merely 16- or 17-year-olds simply following Hitler's orders. German and American soldiers who
once fought each other have since met here. The museum, which
opened in 1984, was conceived by a young Luxembourg man who had
not been not born when the war ended. **Roland Gaul**, who today is the
public relations staff person for the U.S. Embassy in Luxembourg
City, explains he "just grew up with the **Battle of the Bulge**" and, as
he and his friends out "playing cowboys and Indians" in the woods
would find German helmets or pistols, his interest in a museum developed. The effort to open the museum and run it came from volunteer
efforts. Among the highly interesting exhibits is a model of the Russian prison camp at **Tambow** that claimed so many Luxembourgers.
There are dioramas of the "*white jungle warfare*" in the snow for which
Luxembourg women stitched white clothing together to form camouflage for the U.S. soldiers, to examples of the "propaganda pamphlets" used as psychological warfare from both sides. One such piece,
written by the Germans in correct American slang that was meant to
affect American morale by making them homesick at Christmas, was
dropped over the lines in the Ardennes.

### Municipal Museum ★

*place Guillaume; Easter–Oct., 10 a.m.–12, 2–6 p.m., closed Tues.* Highlights of the local relics from Roman culture on display are two large
4th-century mosaics, which give an idea of the decorative detail to be
found in the villas of the occupiers of the region in that era. One
well-preserved mosaic with a central figure of a lion surrounded by
bright geometrical figures was found in 1926 when excavation works

were proceeding on Diekirch's Esplanade. The other was found in 1950 when a town street was being widened. In it, a stylized flower motif surrounds an intriguing ★ head of a Medusa, which shows a different face when viewed from opposite ends of the mosaic floor.

## ★★ LITTLE SWITZERLAND

Set in the valley of the **Ernz Noire** river, this area of fantastically shaped sandstone rocks and outcrops set in wooded glens and ravines, sometimes is in sight of the road, though often it offers its sights only to those who "walk in" a bit further. The proximity of impressive viewing can be gauged by the number of cars at the several parking sites provided along the road that leads through **Mullerthal** *(pop. 45, altitude 820 ft./250 meters)*. That village, more or less at its center, has given its name to the region, which is full of serious hikers and recreational ramblers in the summer and early fall. The region got its unlikely name "Little Switzerland" (*not* used by Luxembourgers) from the Dutch (who, presumably, were responding overenthusiastically to the area's altitude; they call the only slightly higher spots in Holland's SE Limburg Province the "Dutch Alps"). Under the Dutch King/Grand Duke **Willem II**, Holland first became connected to Luxembourg by **rail**. The exclamations over the scenery around Mullerthal by Dutch soldiers who had served in Luxembourg brought many Dutch here on holiday, particularly once the train could bring them to nearby Diekirch in comfort. Their name for Mullerthal stuck, as did their interest in the area, the Dutch still being the main holiday makers here. The authentic character of the restored village of **Christnach** and the popular tourist center of **Consdorf** are two of the entry points into the Mullerthal. The village of **Waldbillig** (pop. 275), set on a green plateau surrounded by deep forest, was the birthplace in 1827 of **Michel Rodange**, Luxembourg's most famous poet.

## ★ ECHTERNACH

**Tourist office** • *Porte St. Willibrord at Basilica; Mon.–Fri., 9 a.m.– noon, 2–5 p.m., in July and Aug., also on Sat. & Sun.;* ☎ *7.22.30; pop. 4,000.*

Echternach, known as having the most attractive main square in Luxembourg, is also one of Europe's earliest centers of Christianity. **Willibrord**, an Anglo-Saxon missionary from Northumberland, founded a Benedictine Abbey here in 698, which makes Echternach the oldest settlement in the country. Some Roman remains and medieval ramparts add to its historic interest and atmosphere. Echternach's religious, spiritual, and artistic achievements reached their height with the **Echternach School of Book Illumination** in the 10th and 11th centuries. The Kells style (from the *Book of Kells* in Ireland) influenced the monks at Echternach, and it is thought possible that some of the Kells artist-monks may even have come to St. Willibrord's Abbey, since it became one of the best equipped ateliers in Europe for illuminating manuscripts. (There is a museum of illuminations in the abbey.) Although the **Basilica of St. Willibrord**, built around 800, over Willibrord's original abbey, today dates only from after the Second World War, the crypt, c. 800, remains intact. (The *Ardennes offensive* did more damage than centuries of pillaging.) It houses the tomb of St. Willibrord. Echternach's lovely ★★**main square** lacks symmetry, but that is part of its charm. A noticeable part of the irregularity of shape is caused by the ★★ **Denzelt** (the old courtrooms), one reason the Gothic building attracts so much attention. Many of the facades around the square have been restored, which makes it a more pleasant pastime than ever to sit at one of its cafes. The town is known for its unique **Dancing Procession** *(Whitsun Tuesday)*, which takes place on the square, attracting thousands of pilgrims. Dating from the 13th century, the procession may commemorate a perceived healing of epilepsy by St. Willibrord.

## WHERE TO STAY AND EAT IN ECHTERNACH

### Hotel Bel-Air         ★★★★

*1 Route de Berdorf;* ☎ *72.93.83, FAX 72.86.94; moderate.* Located less than a mile/1 km. from the center of Echternach, this modern hotel sits in its own park, offering views from its terraces and glass-walled dining rooms of the Sure Valley. The 33 guest rooms in this well-serviced hotel all have private baths, TV, telephones. Tennis; gourmet restaurant; wooded walks begin just steps from the door.

## ★MOSELLE VALLEY

Leaving Echternach on a scenic route roughly south, in the direction of Trier, you arrive at the Moselle River, with its attractive tree-shaded and path-lined embankments. It's a lovely ride along the river (and *on* the river, too, if you'd like to cruise on the *Princess Marie-Astrid* boat). The colors of the scenery change with the stage of the grapes growing in the vineyards that cover the banks on both the Luxembourg and German sides of the Moselle. As well as being pretty, the vineyards are important business; Luxembourg's Minister of Agriculture also carries the title of Minister of Viniculture.

As you approach **Wormeldange** (from the north), look for signs to **Koeppchen** and follow them up into the vineyards, your destination as you drive through them being the **St. Donat Chapel.** There is a bench from which to survey the ★★**magnificent panorama** that lies before you. Just beyond Wormeldange is ★**Ehnen**, a delightful village of medieval character, with narrow stone streets and the only round church in the Grand Duchy.

# HOLLAND
# BIBLIOGRAPHY:
# RANDOM READINGS

*See also "The Muse," under "The Dutch Cultural Legacy" at front of book*

*The Netherlands in Perspective: The Organizations of Society and Environment,* by William Z. Shetter, Martinus Nijhoff Publishers, Leiden, Holland, 1987, 333 pages. A wide-ranging contemporary picture of Dutch society presented (in English) for anyone with an interest in Holland beneath the surface. Written by a member of the Department of Germanic Studies of Indiana University who has 40 years of personal experience with Holland.

*Europe, a Tapestry of Nations,* by Flora Lewis, Simon and Schuster, 1987. Series of essays on Europe and European countries by a long-time observer of Europe for The New York Times. Includes chapters on The Low Countries: The Bourgeois Monarchies; Netherlands: Dear Father State; Belgium; Divided by Language; and Luxembourg: A Simple Grand Duchy.

*The Europeans,* by Luigi Barzini, Penguin Books, 1983. Essays by a distinguished Italian journalist on various West European countries, including a chapter on The Careful Dutch.

*The Embarrassment of Riches: An Interpretation of Dutch Culture in the Golden Age,* by Simon Schama, Alfred A. Knopf, New York, 1987. A wonderfully readable tome, authoritatively documented and well grounded in art history and appreciation, that brings alive myriad aspects of life as it was in 17th-century Holland.

*Orange & Stuart 1641–1672,* by Pieter Geyl, Charles Scribner's & Sons, New York, 1969. In-depth coverage which communicates the pressures put upon the House of Orange by the more powerful English Stuarts, both when the latter were kings of England and when they were exiled on the continent, in the period prior to the William (Holland's Prince of Orange) and Mary marriage and subsequent reign.

*The First Salute*, by Barbara W. Tuchman, Knopf, 1988. Includes interesting information about the Dutch trade with, early recognition of, and financial support for the American colonies during their War of Independence against England.

*The Hidden Force*, by Louis Couperus, Library of the Indies: University of Massachusetts Press, 1990. Couperus was a member of the class of upper-level East Indies civil servants (for the Dutch colony of Indonesia) in The Hague at the turn of the century. In this book, written in 1900, he shows the mysterious Far East through the uncomprehending eyes of a colonial administrator. A Bridge Too Far, by Cornelius Ryan. The book, originally published in 1974 and from which the film was made, relates the details of the ill-conceived and unsuccessful World War II Market-Garden Operation that hinged upon the taking of the bridge over the Rhine at Arnhem in central Holland in September 1944. Presently out-of-print but available at libraries.

*A Bridge Too Far*, by Cornelius Ryan. The book, originally published in 1974 and from which the film was made, relates the details of the ill-conceived and unsuccessful World War II Market-Garden Operation that hinged upon the taking of the bridge over the Rhine at Arnhem in central Holland in September 1944. Presently out-of-print but available at libraries.

*The Diary of Anne Frank* (originally entitled in Dutch *The Secret Annex*), by Anne Frank. Covering the period from July 9, 1942, when the Frank family had to go into hiding from the Nazis in Amsterdam, less than a month after Anne had received a diary for her 13th birthday. The Diary covers the two-year period during which Anne had to exist in close quarters with her parents, sister, and four strangers, until August 1944, when the family's whereabouts were betrayed to the Nazis by someone seeking the "head money" given as a reward for such information. Anne subsequently died at the Bergen-Belsen concentration camp. From the pages of this diary of difficulties shines the eternal power of human hope: despite her unmarked grave, Anne's wish to "live on after my death" is realized on bookshelves around the world that hold her Diary, and in hearts that share her ideals. (See also Anne Frank House under "Amsterdam, What To See and Do.")

*The Hiding Place*, by Corrie ten Boom, Viking Press, 1971. The story of the Ten Boom family of Haarlem who risked, some losing, their lives to hide and help to safety Dutch resistance workers and others who were hunted by the Nazis during World War II. Their house can be visited. (See also "Ten Boom House" under "Haarlem, What To See and Do.")

*The Assault,* by Harry Mulish, Pantheon, 1986 (translated into English by Claire White). A Dutch writer's account of the Nazi occupation of Holland during World War II.

*Love in Amsterdam,* by Nicolas Freeling, Carroll & Graf. Of the more than 30 literate, introspective novels with contemporary European settings by English-born author Freeling, among the best are a series of crime fiction works set in Holland featuring one Inspector Van Der Valk. The first, Love in Amsterdam, is followed by Because of the Cats, and eight more which impart a fine sense of Dutch place and character. It will be necessary to seek out the titles in libraries and used bookshops.

*Outsider in Amsterdam,* by Janwillem van de Wetering, 1976. This first title in another series of crime fiction set in Amsterdam, this by Dutch author Van de Wetering, is followed by The Corpse on the Dike and several others, the adventures in which unfold through the efforts of police team Grijpstra and deGrier. Libraries and used bookshops also will be needed to track this series down, but the effort worthwhile.

*The Black Tulip,* by Alexandre Dumas (out of print in English). A melodramatic tale which conveys some of the excitement and excess of the Tulipmania era in early 17th-century Holland. (See chapter "The Bulb Field Business.")

*Hans Brinker or The Silver Skates,* by American Mary M. Dodge, many editions still in print; first published in the 1860s. A dated but interesting picture of Dutch life in places such as Broek-in-Waterland, where the story is set, Amsterdam, Haarlem, Leiden, and The Hague. One of the characters in the book relates the fictional tale of a boy who plugged a leaking dike with his pudgy finger and stayed there all night thus saving his village of Spaardam, not far from Haarlem, from inundation. The unlikely deed so captured American tourists' imaginations that the Dutch (who only recently have been raising their children on Hans Brinker) decided to satisfy their visitors' expectations by erecting a statue to the brave Dutch boy. (See also "Spaarden" "In The Area" under "Haarlem.")

# A DUTCH DICTIONARY

While you may never *need* to know Dutch in order to communicate in Holland, it may be *nice* to know some basic words.

## Language Notes

The only difference in the Dutch alphabet from English is the "ij" as a single letter (interchangeable with the letter "y," and pronounced as a "long i.") As an example, the Dutch word "ijs" (meaing *ice* cream) is pronounced as the English "ice." Words beginning with "ij" capitalize both letters, as in *IJsselmeer*, and appear in alphabetized lists under Y. The letter "g" in Dutch has a gutteral sound, much like the "ch" in the Scottish word "loch." An example is the Dutch cheese "*Gouda*," which is correctly pronounced "*HOW' da.*" A basic in the Dutch language is the diminutive "je," which best translates as "little." While employed to indicate small physical size, it also often connotes affection, as when tacked on to people's names or belongings.

| English | Dutch |
| --- | --- |
| **Numbers** | |
| zero | nul |
| one | een |
| two | twee |
| three | drie |
| four | vier |
| five | vijf |
| six | zes |
| seven | zeven |
| eight | acht |
| nine | negen |
| ten | tien |
| eleven | elf |
| twelve | twaalf |
| thirteen | dertien |
| fourteen | veertien |
| fifteen | vijftien |

| English | Dutch |
|---|---|
| sixteen | zestien |
| seventeen | zeventien |
| eighteen | achttien |
| nineteen | negentien |
| twenty | twintig |
| twenty-one | een en twintig |
| fifty | vijftig |
| one hundred | honderd |
| two hundred | tweehonderd |
| one thousand | duizend |
| 1st | eerste |
| 2nd | tweede |
| 3rd | derde |

## Days / Dagen

| Monday | Maandag |
|---|---|
| Tuesday | Dinsdag |
| Wednesday | Woensdag |
| Thursday | Donderdag |
| Friday | Vrijdag |
| Saturday | Zaterdag |
| Sunday | Zondag |

## General

| Please | Alstublieft |
|---|---|
| Thank you, very much | Dank U, zeer |
| Good morning | Dag |
| Good evening | Gouden avond |
| Good night | Goede nacht |
| Good-bye | Tot ziens |
| Mr./sir | Mijnheer |
| Mrs./Ms. | Mevrouw |
| Gentlemen | Heren |
| Ladies | Dames |
| W.C. | De toilet |
| Excuse me | Pardon |
| Yes, no | Ja, neen |
| How much? | Hoeveel? |
| Price | Prijs |

| English | Dutch |
| --- | --- |
| Expensive, cheap | Duur, goedkoop |
| Old, new | Oud, nieuw |
| Where is? | Waar is? |
| To the left | Links |
| To the right | Rechts |
| Entrance, exit | Ingang, uitgang |
| Doctor | Dokter |
| Hospital | Ziekenhuis |
| Post office | Postkantoor |
| Stamp | Postzegel |
| Airmail | Luchtpost |
| Police station | Politiebureau |
| No smoking | Verboden te roken |
| Admission free | Vrije toegang |
| Open, closed | Geopen, gesloten |

## Travel Terms

| English | Dutch |
| --- | --- |
| Travel bureau | Reisbureau |
| The railway station | Het station |
| Return ticket | Retour |
| One-way ticket | Enkele reis |
| Fare | Prijs van het reiskaartje |
| First class | Eerste klas |
| Second class | Tweede klas |
| Fast train | Sneltrein |
| Local train | Stoptrein |
| Dining car | Restaurantiewagen |
| Weekdays only | Alleen op werkdagen |
| Bus/tram stop | Bushalte |
| Room with bath, shower | Kamer met bad, douche |
| Gasoline, petrol | Benzine |
| Oil | Olie |
| Parking place | Parkeerplaats |
| Key | Sleutel |

| English | Dutch |
| --- | --- |
| **Dutch Bill of Fare** | |
| table d'hôte | menu |
| bill of fare, menu | kaart |
| wine list | wijnkaart |
| bill | de rekening |
| Is the tip included? | Service inclusief? |
| fried | gebakken |
| smoked | gerookt |
| rare (almost raw) | bleu |
| medium | half gaar |
| well-done | goed gaar |
| soup | soep |
| bread, white/brown | brood, witte/bruin |
| roll, sandwich | broodje |
| egg | ei |
| cheese | kaas |
| whipped cream | slagroom |

| Meat/Fish | Vlees/Vis |
| --- | --- |
| pork | varkens |
| sausage | bloedworst |
| roast beef | rosbief |
| chicken | kip |
| hare | haas |
| rabbit | konijn |
| venison | ree |
| salmon | zalm |
| trout | forel |
| pike | snoek |
| sole | tong |
| monkfish | lotte |
| herring | haring |
| eel | paling |
| lobster | kreeft |

| English | Dutch |
| --- | --- |
| oysters | oesters |
| shrimp | garnalen |
| mussels | mosselen |
| snails | slakken |

## Vegetables/Fruit — Groeten/Vruchten

| English | Dutch |
| --- | --- |
| asparagus | asperges |
| beans | bonen |
| string beans | snijbonen |
| chicory | witloof |
| cauliflower | bloemkool |
| Brussels sprouts | Brusselse spruitjes |
| cabbage | kool |
| mushrooms | champignons |
| onions | uien |
| peas | erwten |
| potatoes | aardapplen |
| rice | rijs |
| salad | sla, salade |
| apple | appel |
| cherries | kersen |
| lemon | citroen |
| orange | sinaasappel |
| pineapple | ananas |
| strawberries | aardbeien |
| pear | peer |
| peach | perzik |

## Seasonings

| English | Dutch |
| --- | --- |
| sugar | suiker |
| salt | zout |
| pepper | peper |
| mustard | mosterd |
| vinegar | azijn |
| oil | olie |
| honey | honig |

| English | Dutch |
| --- | --- |
| **Beverages** | **Dranken** |
| a bottle of | een fles |
| a glass of, cup of | een glas, kop |
| coffee, tea | koffie, thee |
| milk | melk |
| juice | sap |
| mineral water | mineraalwater |
| beer | bier |
| wine (red, white) | wijn (rode, witte) |

# HOTEL QUICK-REFERENCE TABLES

Prices given below—for a room for two with private bath, *inclusive* of service and VAT—are in Dutch guilders. In cases in which hotels post a range of double room rates, the *lowest* price for *high season* has been used. (**Note**: the number of rooms available at that rate may be limited.) The prices quoted were as accurate as possible at press time, but they may increase during the year-long life of this guide. Always inquire about lower weekend and out-of-season rates when making reservations and, again, for the lowest rate available when checking in.

## HOLLAND

| Hotel | Phone | Price (in guilders) |
|---|---|---|
| **RANDSTAD HOLLAND** | | |
| **Amsterdam (Telephone Code 020)** | | |
| Agora | 6272200 | 125 |
| Ambassade | 6262333 | 275 |
| American | 6245322 | 425 |
| Amstel | 6226060 | 750 |
| Amsterdam Wiechmann | 6263321 | 150 |
| Atlas | 6766336 | 170 |
| Avenue | 6238307 | 190 |
| Borgmann (Villa) | 6735252 | 175 |
| Canal House | 6225182 | 210 |
| Doelen Karena | 6262922 | 345 |
| De l'Europe | 6234836 | 495 |
| Estheréa | 6245146 | 190 |
| Forte Crest Apollo | 6735922 | 435 |
| Golden Tulip Barbizon Palace | 5564564 | 445 |
| Grand Amsterdam | 5553111 | 625 |
| Grand Hotel Krasnapolsky | 5549111 | 485 |
| Ibis Amsterdam Centre | 6389999 | 170 |
| Jan Luyken | 5730730 | 290 |
| Marriott | 6075555 | 425 |
| Owl | 6189484 | 150 |
| Pulitzer | 5235235 | 455 |
| Renaissance Amsterdam | 6212223 | 332 |

| HOLLAND | | |
|---|---|---|
| Hotel | Phone | Price (in guilders) |
| Rho | 6207371 | 125 |
| Rokin | 6267456 | 75 |
| Schiller Karena | 6231660 | 315 |
| Seven Bridges | 6231329 | 110 |
| The Bridge | 6237068 | 150 |
| Toro Hotel | 6737223 | 200 |
| Victoria | 6234255 | 375 |
| Vondel | 6120120 | 170 |
| Washington | 6797453 | 110 |
| **Heemskerk (Telephone Code 02510)** | | |
| Chateau Marquette | 41414 | 200 |
| **Haarlem (Telephone Code 023)** | | |
| Amadeus | 324530 | 110 |
| Carlton Square | 319091 | 260 |
| Golden Tulip Lion D'Or | 321750 | 210 |
| **Leiden (Telephone Code 071)** | | |
| De Doelen | 120527 | 160 |
| Golden Tulip Leiden | 221121 | 275 |
| Mayflower | 142641 | 175 |
| Nieuw Minera | 126358 | 125 |
| **The Hague/Scheveningen (Telephone Code 070)** | | |
| Aquarius | 3543543 | 120 |
| Bel Park | 3505000 | 110 |
| Carlton Beach | 3541414 | 300 |
| City Hotel | 3557966 | 135 |
| Corona | 3637930 | 325 |
| Des Indes | 3632932 | 490 |
| Esquire | 3522341 | 100 |
| ParkHotel | 3624371 | 207 |
| Petit | 3465500 | 155 |
| Seinduin | 3551971 | 135 |
| Steigenberger Kurhaus | 4162636 | 453 |
| **Voorburg (Telephone Code 070)** | | |
| Vreudg & Rust | 3872081 | 225 |
| **Wassenaar (Telephone Code 01751)** | | |
| Auberge de Kievet | 19232 | 275 |
| **Delft (Telephone Code 015)** | | |
| De Ark | 157999 | 175 |
| Leeuwenbrug | 147741 | 155 |
| MuseumHotel | 140930 | 205 |

## HOLLAND

| Hotel | Phone | Price (in guilders) |
|---|---|---|
| **Rotterdam (Telephone Code 010)** | | |
| Atlanta | 4110420 | 240 |
| Bienvenue | 4669394 | 95 |
| Hilton International | 4144044 | 495 |
| Hotel New York | 4862066 | 150 |
| Inntel | 4134139 | 260 |
| Parkhotel | 4363611 | 295 |
| Van Walsum | 4363275 | 135 |
| **Gouda (Telephone Code 01820)** | | |
| Keizerskroon | 28096 | 100 |
| **Utrecht (Telephone Code 030)** | | |
| Malie | 316424 | 170 |
| Scandic Crown | 925200 | 325 |
| Smits | 331232 | 238 |
| ***NORTHERN HOLLAND*** | | |
| **Edam (Telephone Code 02993)** | | |
| De Fortuna | 71671 | 70 |
| **Enkhuizen (Telephone Code 02280)** | | |
| Die Port Van Cleve | 12510 | 135 |
| **Leeuwarden (Telephone Code 058)** | | |
| Oranje | 126241 | 220 |
| **Stavoren (Telephone Code 05149)** | | |
| De Vrouw van Stavoren | 1202 | 90 |
| **Geithoorn (Telephone Code 05216)** | | |
| De Jonge | 1360 | 110 |
| **Blokzijl (Telephone Code 05272)** | | |
| Kaatje Bij de Sluis | 1833 | 250 |
| **Zwolle (Telephone Code 038)** | | |
| Grand Hotel Wientjes | 254254 | 180 |
| **Elburg (Telephone Code 05250)** | | |
| Het Smeede | 3877 | 115 |
| ***CENTRAL HOLLAND*** | | |
| **Apeldoorn (Telephone Code 055)** | | |
| De Keizerskroon | 217744 | 295 |
| **Zeist (Telephone Code 03404)** | | |
| 't Kerchebosch | 14734 | 270 |
| **Baarn (Telephone Code 02154)** | | |
| Kasteel De Hooge | 12541 | 310 |

| HOLLAND | | |
|---|---|---|
| Hotel | Phone | Price (in guilders) |
| **Bosch en Duin (Telephone Code 030)** | | |
| Auberge de Hoefslag | 251051 | 325 |
| **ZEELAND** | | |
| **Middelburg (Telephone Code 01180)** | | |
| Beau Rivage | 38060 | 145 |
| Du Commerce | 36051 | 125 |
| **Veere (Telephone Code 01181)** | | |
| De Campveerse Toren | 1291 | 100 |
| **Zierikzee (Telephone Code 01110)** | | |
| Mondragon | 13051 | 130 |
| **NORTH BRABANT** | | |
| **Den Bosch (Telephone Code 073)** | | |
| Golden Tulip Central | 125151 | 225 |
| **Heusden (Telephone Code 04162)** | | |
| In Den Verdwaalde Koogel | 1933 | 145 |
| **Breda (Telephone Code 076)** | | |
| De Klok | 214082 | 155 |
| **LIMBURG** | | |
| **Maastricht (Telephone Code 043)** | | |
| Beaumont | 254433 | 170 |
| Bergere | 251651 | 156 |
| Du Casque | 214343 | 210 |
| Du Chene | 213523 | 110 |
| Derlon | 216770 | 360 |
| Holiday Inn Crowne Plaza Maas. | 509191 | 345 |
| **Wittem (Telephone Code 04450)** | | |
| Kasteel Wittem | 1208 | 230 |
| **Kerkade (Telephone Code 045)** | | |
| Kasteel Erenstein | 461333 | 190 |

| BELGIUM | | |
|---|---|---|
| Hotel | Phone | Price (in francs) |
| **BRUSSELS** | | |
| **(Telephone Code 02)** | | |
| Amigo | 547.47.47 | 6,750 |
| Atlas | 502.60.06 | 3,800 |
| Chambord | 513.41.19 | 4,295 |
| Dixseptiene | 502.57.44 | 6,600 |
| Ibis Saint-Catherine | 513.76.20 | 3,550 |

| BELGIUM | | |
|---|---|---|
| **Hotel** | **Phone** | **Price (in francs)** |
| Jolly Hotel du Grand Sablon | 512.88.00 | 11,500 |
| Manos | 537.96.82 | 3,500 |
| Metropole | 217.23.00 | 9,400 |
| New Hotel Siru | 217.75.80 | 3,500 |
| Matignon | 513.69.27 | 2,500 |
| Opera | 219.43.43 | 2,200 |
| Royal Windsor | 505.55.55 | 9,750 |
| Stanhope | 506.91.11 | 12,500 |
| Welcome | 219.95.46 | 2,100 |
| **ANTWERP** | | |
| **(Telephone Code 03)** | | |
| Classic Hotel Villa Mozart | 231.30.31 | 5,400 |
| De Rosier | 225.01.40 | 8,500 |
| De Witte Lelie | 226.19.66 | 7,500 |
| Firean | 237.02.60 | 4,400 |
| Rubens | 222.48.48 | 4,950 |
| **BRUGES** | | |
| **(Telephone Code 050)** | | |
| Adornes | 34.13.36 | 2,550 |
| Botaniek | 34.14.24 | 2,200 |
| Bourgoensch Hof | 33.16.45 | 2,350 |
| Die Swaene | 34.27.98 | 4,050 |
| Duc de Bourgogne | 33.20.38 | 3,500 |
| Holiday Inn Crowne Plaza | 34.58.34 | 6,100 |
| Oud Huis Amsterdam | 34.18.10 | 4,600 |
| Romantik Pandhotel | 34.06.66 | 3,600 |
| Ter Brughe | 34.03.24 | 3,200 |
| **GHENT** | | |
| **(Telephone Code 091)** | | |
| Erasmus | 24.21.95 | 2,975 |
| Gravensteen | 25.11.50 | 3,900 |
| St. Jorishof | 24.24.24 | 2,820 |

| LUXEMBOURG | | |
|---|---|---|
| **Hotel** | **Phone** | **Price (in FLux)** |
| **(Telephone code for country 352)** | | |
| **LUXEMBOURG CITY** | | |
| Auberge du Coin | 40.21.01 | 2,800 |
| Central Molitor | 48.99.11 | 4,400 |
| Français | 47.45.34 | 3,900 |
| Grand Hotel Cravat | 22.19.75 | 6,200 |

## LUXEMBOURG

| Hotel | Phone | Price (in FLux) |
|-------|-------|-----------------|
| **THE GRAND DUCHY** | | |
| **Clervaux** | | |
| Du Parc | 9,10,68 | 2,200 |
| **Vianden** | | |
| Hotel Heintz | 8.41.55 | 1,900 |
| **Echternach** | | |
| Bel-Air | 72.93.83 | 3,500 |

# INDEX

# Order Your Fielding Travel Guides Today

| BOOKS | $ EA. |
|---|---|
| Amazon | $16.95 |
| Australia | $12.95 |
| Bahamas | $12.95 |
| Belgium | $16.95 |
| Bermuda | $12.95 |
| Borneo | $16.95 |
| Brazil | $16.95 |
| Britain | $16.95 |
| Budget Europe | $16.95 |
| Caribbean | $18.95 |
| Europe | $16.95 |
| Far East | $19.95 |
| France | $16.95 |
| Hawaii | $15.95 |
| Holland | $15.95 |
| Italy | $16.95 |
| Kenya's Best Hotels, Lodges & Homestays | $16.95 |
| London Agenda | $12.95 |
| Los Angeles Agenda | $12.95 |
| Malaysia and Singapore | $16.95 |
| Mexico | $16.95 |
| New York Agenda | $12.95 |
| New Zealand | $12.95 |
| Paris Agenda | $12.95 |
| Portugal | $16.95 |
| Scandinavia | $16.95 |
| Seychelles | $12.95 |
| Southeast Asia | $16.95 |
| Spain | $16.95 |
| The World's Great Voyages | $16.95 |
| The World's Most Dangerous Places | $19.95 |
| The World's Most Romantic Places | $16.95 |
| Vacation Places Rated | $19.95 |
| Vietnam | $16.95 |
| Worldwide Cruises | $17.95 |

## To order by phone call toll-free 1-800-FW-2-GUIDE
*(VISA, MasterCard and American Express accepted.)*

To order by mail send your check or money order,
including $2.00 per book for shipping and handling (sorry, no COD's) to:
Fielding Worldwide, Inc. 308 S. Catalina Avenue, Redondo Beach, CA 90277 U.S.A.

**Get 10% off your order by saying "Fielding Discount"
or send in this page with your order**

# Favorite People, Places & Experiences

| ADDRESS: | NOTES: |
|---|---|

**Name**

**Address**

**Telephone**

**Name**

**Address**

**Telephone**

**Name**

**Address**

**Telephone**

**Name**

**Address**

**Telephone**

**Name**

**Address**

**Telephone**

**Name**

**Address**

**Telephone**

**Name**

**Address**

**Telephone**

# Favorite People, Places & Experiences

| ADDRESS: | NOTES: |
|---|---|

**Name**

**Address**

**Telephone**

**Name**

**Address**

**Telephone**

**Name**

**Address**

**Telephone**

**Name**

**Address**

**Telephone**

**Name**

**Address**

**Telephone**

**Name**

**Address**

**Telephone**

**Name**

**Address**

**Telephone**

# Favorite People, Places & Experiences

| ADDRESS: | NOTES: |

**Name**

**Address**

**Telephone**

**Name**

**Address**

**Telephone**

**Name**

**Address**

**Telephone**

**Name**

**Address**

**Telephone**

**Name**

**Address**

**Telephone**

**Name**

**Address**

**Telephone**

**Name**

**Address**

**Telephone**

# Favorite People, Places & Experiences

| ADDRESS: | NOTES: |
|---|---|

**Name**

**Address**

**Telephone**

**Name**

**Address**

**Telephone**

**Name**

**Address**

**Telephone**

**Name**

**Address**

**Telephone**

**Name**

**Address**

**Telephone**

**Name**

**Address**

**Telephone**

**Name**

**Address**

**Telephone**

# Favorite People, Places & Experiences

| ADDRESS: | NOTES: |
|---|---|

**Name**

**Address**


**Telephone**

**Name**

**Address**


**Telephone**

**Name**

**Address**


**Telephone**

**Name**

**Address**


**Telephone**

**Name**

**Address**


**Telephone**

**Name**

**Address**


**Telephone**

**Name**

**Address**


**Telephone**

## Favorite People, Places & Experiences

| ADDRESS: | NOTES: |
| --- | --- |

Name

Address

Telephone

Name

Address

Telephone

Name

Address

Telephone

Name

Address

Telephone

Name

Address

Telephone

Name

Address

Telephone

Name

Address

Telephone

# Favorite People, Places & Experiences

| ADDRESS: | NOTES: |
|---|---|

**Name**

**Address**


**Telephone**

**Name**

**Address**


**Telephone**

**Name**

**Address**


**Telephone**

**Name**

**Address**


**Telephone**

**Name**

**Address**


**Telephone**

**Name**

**Address**


**Telephone**

**Name**

**Address**


**Telephone**